D0986927

AM I NOT
A MAN AND A BROTHER

AM I NOT
A MAN AND A BROTHER

The Antislavery Crusade of Revolutionary America
1688-1788

Roger Bruns
Editor

Foreword by Benjamin Quarles

Chelsea House Publishers

1977

Roger Bruns is currently assistant executive director of the National Historical Publications and Records Commission in Washington, D. C., and has been with the commission since completing his graduate work at the University of Arizona in 1967. He has written articles on antislavery in such journals as the *Pennsylvania—Magazine of History and Biography, The Journal of Negro History,* and the *Maryland Historical Magazine.* He is co-editor, with Arthur Schlesinger, jr., of the five volume series, *Congress Investigates: A Documented History, 1792-1974,* published by Chelsea House in association with the R. R. Bowker Company.

Editorial Staff:
Kathryn Hammell, Deborah Weiss, Karyn Browne, Susan Lusk, Laurie Likoff

Printed and Bound in the United States of America.

Library of Congress Cataloging in Publication Data
Main entry under title:

Am I not a man and a brother.

Bibliography: p.
1. Slavery in the United States—Anti-slavery movements—History—Sources. 2. Slavery in the United States—History—Sources. I. Bruns, Roger.
E446.A46 322.4'4'0973 76-6118
ISBN 0-87754-035-7

CHELSEA HOUSE PUBLISHERS

Andrew Norman, President　Harold Steinberg, Chairman and Publisher

A Division of Chelsea House Educational Communications, Inc.
70 West 40th Street, New York, N.Y. 10018

The editor gratefully acknowledges the assistance of associate editors Sara Dunlap Jackson and Mary A. Giunta in the research and preparation of the manuscript for this volume.

Philad. May 15. 1787.

Sir,

I received the Letter you did me the honour of writing to me the 29th of Feby past, with your valuable Present of Cameos, which I am distributing among my Friends, in whose Countenances I have seen such Marks of being affected by contemplating the Figure of the Suppliant, (which is admirably executed) that I am persuaded it may have an Effect equal to that of the best written Pamphlet, in procuring Favour to those oppressed People. Please to accept my hearty Thanks, and believe me to be, with great Esteem,

Sir,

Your most obedient Servant

B Franklin

r. Wedgwood Esqr

Benjamin Franklin to Josiah Wedgwood, May 15, 1787, thanking him for the anti-slavery medallion he designed.

Contents

THE FIRST FUTILE VOICES, 1688-1763

A MOUNTING CRY FOR NATURAL RIGHTS, 1763-1776

THE CRUSADE IN THE WAR YEARS, 1776-1783

THE AFTERMATH OF THE REVOLUTION, 1783-1787

Illustrations

Foreword

The belief that slavery is "a key to the meaning of our national experience," has taken root in recent years. The results have been predictable. Within the last quarter of a century the institution of slavery in the United States has been subject to an unprecedented probing, its investigators providing new insights by making greater use of nontraditional sources and by re-examining those of older acceptance. The institution of slavery cannot be accurately appraised or understood, however, without careful attention to a concomitant development and influence—the crusade against it. The anti-slavery leaders and their organizations tell us much about slavery and, of hardly lesser importance, something about our character as a nation.

Of late the movement against slavery has, like the institution itself, received more attention in academic circles. Relatively speaking, however, the abolitionist impulse in the period before the formation of the new nation has not been accorded its rightful role. AM I NOT A MAN AND A BROTHER is a significant corrective to this imbalance. In this highly revealing documentary history we learn that the crusade against slavery in the United States was launched a century and a half before William Lloyd Garrison spoke out in thunder tones and nearly half a century before the Revolutionary War with its widely proclaimed philosophy of freedom. Noting that the movement was begun in 1688 when a Quaker group at Germantown, Pennsylvania, bluntly condemned "the traffick of men-body," this volume is in essence a case study of the protestations against slavery in colonial and Revolutionary America.

As these vividly-worded documents illustrate, the attack on slavery took many forms. The religiously-toned remonstrances by Quakers were infused with references to natural rights and liberties whereas the protests of the evangelical spokesmen were essentially sermons evoking the prophets Jeremiah and Ezekiel. This oft-sounded note of retributive justice was voiced by slave Caesar Sarter who warned the slaveowners that the day would come "in which you must be accountable for your actions, to, that impartial Judge, who hears the groans of the oppressed and who will sooner or later, avenge them of their oppressors!" The rich variety of protests included mild admonitions, such as Phillis Wheatley's; biting satires, like that of John Trumbull, and slave suits for freedom, like those of Jenny Slew and Elizabeth Freeman. On the purely cerebral level were the thoughtful, carefully reasoned treatises by Anthony Benezet and Benjamin Rush—such spokesmen for the blacks in bondage addressed themselves, point by point, to the pro-slavery arguments advanced in their times.

Richly factual, this collection of source materials furnishes sidelights on a number of important sub-topics, including conditions in the West

African homelands of the transplanted blacks, the transoceanic slave trade, the mental abilities and behavior patterns of the slaves and the fears as to slave uprisings. The usefulness of these documents, some of them practically unknown hitherto, is markedly increased by the well-constructed headnotes by editor Roger Bruns. More than a cataloguing of who said what, when and where, these are essayist in tone, providing background and referring to other contemporary commentators, incidents and developments. Such exemplary introductory remarks make this volume all the more useful for a variety of classroom and research uses. And, finally, it is to be remembered that this book addresses itself to a major theme in our country's history. For it focuses upon a company of men and women many of whom faced social disapproval or worse for making the cause of the slave their own—freedom's precursors in provincial America and its trumpeters in Revolutionary times.

Benjamin Quarles
Professor Emeritus of History
Morgan State University

April 1977

Preface

On May 15, 1787, Benjamin Franklin wrote to Josiah Wedgwood, the influential English potter, "I received the Letter you did me the honour of writing to me the 29th of Feb. past, with your valuable Present of Cameos, which I am distributing among my Friends, on whose Countenances I have seen such Marks of being affected by contemplating the Figure of the Supplicant, (which is admirably executed) that I am persuaded it may have an Effect equal to that of the best written Pamphlet, in procuring Favour to those oppressed Peoples." The "oppressed Peoples" to which Franklin referred were black slaves, reminders to Franklin and other Americans that the Revolution had been something less than inclusive in scope. The existence of slavery in a country demanding rights and liberties and fighting ministerial tyranny encouraged the growth of an antislavery movement involving men of very different religious and political backgrounds. Characterized by a searching intellectual attack against the institution of slavery, as well as vigorous political pressure, the movement produced gradual abolition laws in northern states, the growth of numerous antislavery societies, and a wealth of antislavery literature. Through the presentation of letters, newspaper articles, and pamphlets, this documentary study will examine the literature of the early antislavery crusade from the first futile voice, voices of individual Quakers who protested during the late seventeenth and early eighteenth centuries, to the intensive assault on the institution of slavery during the Revolution.

This series draws upon the works of men such as Benjamin Rush, Thomas Paine, Philip Freneau, and James Otis, men prominent in the political and social controversies of the period. They wrote forcefully about the contradiction between the colonists enslaving the blacks while demanding their own liberty and freedom. From the poet Freneau's description of the slave who "mourns his yet unbroken chains" to Thomas Paine's first published work, an article against slavery published in a Philadelphia newspaper, this series presents antislavery literature varied in approach and remarkable in scope.

While living in a cave outside Philadelphia, Benjamin Lay—the old, vegetarian, hunchbacked dwarf—engaged in a bizarre campaign against the slaveholding Quakers; John Woolman—a Mt. Holly, New Jersey, tailor who wrote and preached antislavery sentiments to Quaker slaveholders—gave the antislavery cause a respectability that zealots such as Benjamin Lay failed to generate; Anthony Benezet—a Quaker schoolmaster who took his antislavery work to the colonial legislators and to the British antislavery activists—wrote some of the most prolific antislavery materials of the Revolutionary era. Many blacks wrote about their feelings for the movement. We have included a letter written by the black poet Phillis

Wheatley stating her intense opposition to slavery and an essay published in *The Essex Journal and Merrimack Packet* by a former slave, Caesar Sarter.

Until recent years, secondary historical studies of the antislavery movement in this country have generally concentrated on the reform efforts immediately before the Civil War. The monographic works, however, of David Brion Davis, Winthrop Jordan, Arthur Zilversmit, and Donald Robinson have recently examined the antislavery movement during the Revolutionary era. While some of the materials in this collection have been published before, there has never been such an extensive document collection showing the antislavery activities of the period. In his two-volume study of early antislavery activities, Davis masterfully demonstrated that the movement was not a peculiarly American phenomenon but instead an interaction of efforts by both Europeans and their American brethren. Although principally an examination of the American reform effort, this presentation reflects material that includes the antislavery activities abroad.

The documentary material presented in this series has been collected from newspapers, manuscript collections, newspapers, contemporary articles and pamphlets, and from private manuscript collectors in the United States and England. The editors have attempted to present transcriptions that reflect the original documents as closely as possible including the irregularities in spelling, punctuation and word usage. Many documents, because of length and repetition of content, have been exerpted.

With all the Bicentennial celebration activities of the past months, a documentary examination of the antislavery movement during the Revolution is especially appropriate. The editors have made a small but sincere effort to combat the effect of Bicentennial full dress battle reenactments, anniversary tea parties, George Washington cherry-tree ice cream, Revolutionary War dolls in contemporary uniforms, birthday cakes laden with two hundred candles, fire hydrants colorfully transformed into miniature figures of Benjamin Franklin and Nathanael Greene, and the buttons, stamps, commemorative ingots, reduced hotel rates, reduced air fares to California, franchised neckties, plaques, songs, flags, contests, full-color T-shirts emblazoned with Washington crossing the Delaware, memorial services, store-wide sales, and one-minute television history lessons, which have bombarded a gasping American public. It is hoped that the presentation of these documents, written many generations ago by individuals passionately opposed to what they felt had constituted the degradation of the black race offers a greater understanding of the question posed by the kneeling supplicant on Josiah Wedgwood's antislavery medallions—"Am I not a Man and a Brother."

Books are engendered by many individuals and organizations and, while it is practically impossible to acknowledge the assistance of all who have contributed to this compilation, we gratefully appreciate the special help of the following: American Philosophical Society; Boston Public Library; Butler Library; Columbia University; Connecticut State Historical Society; Connecticut State Library; Detroit Public Library; Essex Institute; Friends Historical Library of Swarthmore College, Swarthmore, Pa.; Harvard University Library; Haverford College Library; Historical Society of Delaware; Huntington Library; The Library Company of Philadelphia; Library of Congress, particularly the staffs of the Rare Book Room, Manuscript Division, the Microfilm Reading Room, and the Newspaper and Periodical Reading Room; Library of the Boston Athenaeum; Massachusetts Historical Society; New Hampshire Historical Society; New Jersey Historical Society; New-York Historical Society; Newport Rhode Island Bicentennial Commission; New York Public Library; Rhode Island Historical Society; Rutgers University Library; Valentine Museum, Richmond, Va.; Virginia Museum of Fine Arts; University of California at Berkeley; and Yale University.

Also, Miriam Chesley, The Scituate Historical Society, North Scituate, Mass.; Ms. Nancy F. Chudacoff, Rhode Island Historical Society; Hugh Upham Clark, Arlington, Va.; Winifred Collins and M. Freiberg, Massachusetts Historical Society; Susan Danko, Eleutherian Mills Historical Library; Ms. Rosalys H. Hall, board of directors, and Richard Champlin, assistant librarian, Redwood Library and Athenaeum; Dr. James J. Heslin, New-York Historical Society; Ms. Magdalena Houlroyd, special collections librarian, Glassboro State College, N.J.; James Johnson, Moorland-Spingarn Research Center;. Dr. H. G. Jones, Curator, North Carolina Collection, University of North Carolina; Dr. Roy L. Kidman, Rutgers University; John Kok, Newberry Library; E. Richard McKinstry, New Jersey Historical Society; John F. Millar, Newport (Rhode Island) Bicentennial Commission; Robinson Murray III, New Hampshire Historical Society; Martin Petersilia, Washington, D.C.; Ms. Harold C. Pierce, curator, Stockbridge Library Association, Mass.; John E. Powers, Massachusetts Supreme Judicial Court, Boston, Mass.; Dr. George C. Rogers, jr., editor, and Ms. Peggy J. Clark, editorial assistant, Papers of Henry Laurens, University of South Carolina; Dr. Mattie Russell, curator of manuscripts, Duke University Library; M. Thomas, Friends Library, London, Eng.; Wilyna Waite, South Carolina Department of Archives and History; and Dr. Edwin Welch, Library School, University of Ottawa.

Special recognition is graciously given to the following individuals without whose generous assistance and support this volume could not have been completed: Dr. Lloyd E. Hawes, the owner of the Wedgwood Slave Medallion on exhibit at the Smithsonian Institution, who allowed its reproduction for this publication; J. Jefferson Miller, curator, and Sheila Alexander, Division of Ceramics and Glass, and Edith Mayo, Division of Political History, Smithsonian Institution, who patiently answered our queries concerning the Wedgwood Medallion and secured permission to reproduce and use this work of art; Peter Albert, University of Maryland, who gave us numerous references on the movement in Virginia; Earnest Kaiser, Schomberg Collection, New York Public Library, for his advice and assistance in locating materials; Peter Parker and the staff of the Historical Society of Pennsylvania, whose knowledge of the society's collections considerably eased our labor; Julia Ward Stickley, who transcribed documents and gave many leads to other materials; Douglas Penn Stickley, who allowed us to use a copy of his 1973 paper "Freneau and the Americanization of Engligh Poetry"; Doris Cook, manuscript cataloguer, Connecticut Historical Society, who transcribed the manuscript of Levi Hart's "Thoughts on Slavery"; Margaret Cook, curator of manuscripts, Special Collections Division, Earl Gregg, Swem Library, College of William and Mary; Albert Klyberg, director, Rhode Island Historical Society; R. Q. Gurney, T.D., D.L., Bawdeswell Hall, East Dereham, Norfolk, Eng.; R. W. Tucker, Philadelphia, Pa.; Ms. Amy E. Wallis, Darlington, County Durham, Eng.; Jane Rittenhouse, Friends Historical Library of Swarthmore College; and Willman Spawn, American Philosophical Society.

A special thanks is given to Kathy Hammell, Debbie Weiss and Karyn Browne of Chelsea House whose editorial work on the book is greatly appreciated.

Members of the staff of the National Archives and Records Service, including Jane Lange, Clarence Lyons and John P. Butler, extended their able assistance. Typing assistance was provided by Shelley C. Bailey and Sandra Anderson. Moral and research support was given by Richard N. Sheldon and Fred Shelley, National Historical Publications and Records Commission.

Roger Bruns

Washington, D.C.
April 1977

Sara Jackson
Mary Giunta

Introduction

". . . [Y]e pretended votaries for freedom! ye trifling patriots!" declared John Allen in 1774, "continuing this lawless, cruel, inhuman, and abominable practice of enslaving your fellow creatures."[1] "Oh! ye sons of Liberty," Nathaniel Appleton wrote, "pause a moment, give me your ear. Is your conduct consistent? Can you review our . . . struggles for liberty, and think of the slave trade at the same time and not blush?"[2] If a three-penny duty on tea was tyranny, what was an institution which made property of men? As "ye sons of Liberty" proclaimed life, liberty, and the pursuit of happiness, black men, women, and children were being bartered on the auction block.

A colonist wrote in 1774, "I beheld a middle aged African raised and *exposed* on one of the stalls in the shambles of Philadelphia market at Public Sale, as a Slave for life! and this is the capital of Pennsylvania, a land high in the profession of Liberty and Christianity."[3]

In 1775 a Tory writer chided his revolutionary adversaries about their demands for government by the consent of the governed: "Negroe slaves in Boston! It can not be! It is nevertheless very true . . . notwithstanding the immutable laws of nature . . . they actually have in town two thousand Negroe slaves, who never by themselves in person, nor by representatives of their own free election ever gave consent to their present bondage."[4]

The antislavery movement of the American Revolution grew from this paradox. The spectre of slavery bewildered America and its leaders in these years. Patrick Henry described the slave trade as "totally repugnant" to moral dictates, and yet refused to free his slaves because of the "general Inconvenience of living without them."[5] But if, for some, the dilemma was only a nagging guilt, for others it was a call for reform. Samuel Hopkins, for example, who became nauseous at the slave auction in Newport, Rhode Island, delivered a blistering antislavery sermon to an astonished, predominately slavetrading congregation.[6] Hopkins became one of the leading champions of antislavery in America.

At a time when the ideology of natural rights was being so widely debated, individuals such as Samuel Hopkins struggled to end slavery. Hopkins and his fellow reformers also knew that many Americans held powerful religious views that slavery was an unconditional sin against God. This philosophy was increasingly emphasized through the years by the Quakers and shared by many Americans of other religious persuasions. In addition, many colonists were disillusioned by the ever increasing loads of black cargo ships arriving from Africa. The cargos which they contained stimulated visions of a race war and threatened to induce economic havoc.[7]

Since the early 1600s men, women, and children had been herded from their African homes to America in the putrid stench of slaveships. They were inventoried, driven, pilloried, and disgraced. By the eighteenth century slavery was a formidable national institution as prominent northern merchants as well as southern planters realized lucrative profits from the traffic in black labor. Despite the sentiments of such eminent colonial figures as Roger Williams, Cotton Mather, and George Fox that the severity and horrors of slavery should be minimized, no concerted movement against the institution developed in America in those early years.

There were some lonely voices against slavery such as the pious judge of the Massachusetts Superior Court, Samuel Sewall, whose pamphlet, *The Selling of Joseph a Memorial,* raised a spate of criticism from proslavery interests including this poetic composition:

The Negroes Character

Cowardly and Cruel are those Blacks Innate
Prone to Revenge, Imp of inveterate hate.
He that exasperates them, soon espies
Mischief and Murder in their very eyes.
Libidinous, Deceitful, False and Rude,
The spume Issue of Ingratitude.
The Premises consider'd, all may tell,
How near good Joseph they are parallel.[8]

Then there was the old, vegetarian, hunchbacked, cavedwelling dwarf, Benjamin Lay, whose venomous pen was complemented by his bizarre behavior at Quaker meetings. Lay, who had lived in Barbados and had seen slaves groveling for rotten food and garbage in the streets and had seen blacks hideously tortured and murdered, called slavery "[t]he very worst part of the old Whores Merchandize, nasty filthy Whore of Whores, *Babilon's Bastards.*" Attired in full military regalia, at a meeting in Burlington, the obstreperous Lay knifed a bladder of pokeberry juice, showering unsuspecting and startled Quakers with the red "blood" of their slaves. Lay, while attired in sackcloth, on several occasions sprawled in the snow and rain in front of Quaker meetinghouses to dramatize the plight of the Negroes. It is also said that he kidnapped a Quaker's son to give the father an idea of how it felt to have a child stolen.[9]

These men as well as others forcefully challenged many of the prevailing attitudes about Negroes and slavery. They questioned whether: slaves were the Biblical descendants of Ham and were perpetually damned; slavemasters were performing something of a charitable and ministerial function by bringing the poor heathens to civilization and to an acquaintance with the gospel; slaves were lawful captives of war; and the Bible sanctioned the institution of slavery.

It was within the Society of Friends that the religious testimony against slavery first developed in America. Although the Quakers represented only a small proportion of American society in the eighteenth century, the antislavery movement within the sect demonstrated the power of the argument that slavery was a vile contradiction to the Gospel. Robert Barclay wrote, "Christ is in all men as in a seed, yea, and that he never is nor can be separate from that holy pure seed and Light which is in all men."[10] If the Friends accepted this belief that God imparted a measure of His spirit to all men, then chattel slavery, according to a growing number of Quaker writers, had to be a sin. But most slaveholding Quakers did not heed this warning. Although Lay, Ralph Sandiford, John Hepburn, William Southeby, Robert Pyle and George Keith personally assailed the slaveholding practices of the Quakers in the early 1700s as a sin and as a violation of the Quaker testimony of equality, the Scottish traveler Peter Kalm noted in 1748 that the Quakers held as many Negroes as the other colonists.[11] One Quaker, in the middle of the eighteenth century, remarked that he had visited in a single Quarterly Meeting the owners of more than 1,100 slaves.[12] Benjamin Lay, with typical virulence, labelled Quaker slaveholders "a parcel of Hypocrites, and Deceivers" and pictured them wallowing in the "Mire of sin and Iniquity . . . Riding, Snuffing, Chewing Tobacco, & other unclean, foul, indecent & Sinful Practices." Holding slaves, in Lay's eyes, epitomized "foul, indecent & Sinful Practices." Slavery was the very "nature of Hell itself."[13]

Proslavery sentiment in the Society of Friends was represented by wealthy merchant princes in the northern colonies whose profits depended on African markets and West Indian investments and by the slaveholding planters of the tidewater South. Many Quakers who defended slavery were leaders of the Monthly and Yearly Meetings and, therefore, presented a formidable obstacle to reform elements within the Society. That obstacle, nevertheless, eroded with the political crisis in the Quaker community during the French and Indian War.

In the mid-1750s the Quakers comprised a majority in the Pennsylvania Assembly. With the beginning of murderous Indian assaults on the frontier and with the Quaker pacifist principles under unrelenting attack by political enemies who demanded protection for the beleaguered settlers, a number of influential Friends abdicated their powerful positions. The Quakers began to experience a critical period of self-examination. Many Friends, led by men such as Samuel Fothergill, John Churchman, John Woolman, and Anthony Benezet, seriously questioned the Quaker role in American society, including the relationship between church and state, the pacifist ethic, and the haunting question of slavery.

Led by the compassionate New Jersey tailor, John Woolman, who traveled extensively among slaveholding Quakers in the colonies, Friends slowly accepted the position that slavery was a moral and spiritual evil. In 1754 the Philadelphia Yearly Meeting sent a vigorous statement, written by Woolman, to its subordinate meetings calling slavery an "anti-Christian" practice, and in 1776 the Quakers passed a statute of excommunication to all members who continued to hold onto their black property. Not all members of the sect complied with this decree. Many voluntarily dropped out of the Society or were forced out when they refused to bend to the Society's pressures. But, by the 1780s, slavery was a virtually extinct institution among the Quakers of Pennsylvania, that land "high in profession of Liberty and Christianity."[14]

The expression of antislavery sentiments within the Quaker sect produced the most radical reforms. Fundamentally based on religious conviction, the Quaker antislavery campaign expressed the concept that human slavery was a sinful violation against God. But other factors would make slavery an even more vulnerable target for reformers, factors such as the revolutionary climate in America which gave voice to the expressions of natural rights and also the obvious practical disadvantages of having ominous numbers of discontented blacks arriving in the colonies.

The antislavery movement of the American Revolution would become something much more than a struggle within a particular religious sect. The reformers, nevertheless, knew that in the markets of Newport and plantations of the South change would not come easily, especially with prime slaves bringing about fifty pounds sterling a head and the rice and indigo fields of South Carolina and Georgia swallowing huge numbers of fresh imports. With the increasing hostilities between the American colonies and the Mother Country, reformers sought to prick the national conscience. When war erupted the British abolitionist Granville Sharp described slavery as a "dreadful Judgment on the whole *Kingdom*."[15] Benjamin Rush declared that "national crimes require national punishments."[16] As the conflicts of the Revolutionary period generated extensive public debate over such concepts as liberty, equality and the natural rights of man, such a debate could not fail to include the fate of the black slaves.

In 1764 the Bostonian James Otis declared, "The colonists are by the law of nature free born, as indeed all men are, white and black . . . Does it follow that it is right to enslave a man because he is black." Arguing that no logical justification for slavery could be drawn from a "flat nose, a long or short face," Otis called the slave traffic the "most shocking violation of the law of nature."[17] As political orators were extolling freedom and liberty and pamphlets calling for deliverance from British tyranny and oppression poured from the revolutionary presses, abolitionists found they had an incisive philosophical weapon. Even Anthony Benezet emphasized the contradiction between slavery and the arguments for the natural rights of man. Benezet, hardly Enlightenment's child, wrote in 1767, "Indeed, nothing can more clearly and positively militate against the slavery of the Negroes than the several declarations lately published that 'all men are created equal, that they are endowed by their creator with certain unalienable rights.' "[18]

It is ironic that many Enlightenment philosophers, from whom American revolutionary thinkers drew inspiration, had not, as David Brion Davis has pointed out, attacked the institution of slavery. Indeed, many defended slavery on the grounds of tradition, order, "natural" practices of subordination, and private property. The great spokesman for human rights, John Locke, for example, had written that the master shall have "absolute power and authority over his negro slaves."[19] But if Hobbes, Voltaire, and Hume accepted slavery as consistent with rational order, the great exception was Montesquieu. In *L'Esprit des lois* Montesquieu declared, "But as all men are born equal, slavery must be accounted unnatural . . ."[20] It was in this spirit that reformers mounted their attack.

Dedicating a pamphlet to the "Honorable Members of the Continental Congress" in 1776, Samuel Hopkins wrote, ". . . you have acted in the important, noble struggle for LIBERTY, we naturally look to you in behalf of more than half a million persons in these colonies, who are under such a degree of oppression, and tyranny as to be wholly deprived of all civil and personal liberty . . ."[21] Thomas Paine, only a few months before writing *Common Sense*, declared that slavery was "contrary to the light of nature" and that slaves had a "natural, perfect right to freedom."[22] A New Jersey lawyer, Samuel Allinson, asked Americans to consider the torment of the suffering slave ". . . when all inhabitants of North America are groaning under unconstitutional impositions destructive of *their liberty*."[23]

With revolutionists calling for their own freedom, the possibility of having them enact antislavery reforms was enhanced. The subject was discussed at colleges. It was the focus of a pamphlet debate in Philadelphia in the 1770s. Newspapers and sermons throughout the period concentrated on the ideas of freedom and liberty and the semantical relationship between the ideology of the American Revolution and the ideology of antislavery. In a period when abstract philosophical discussions could be heard in the pubs, the question of the black slave arose again and again.

There were factors other than religious or philosophical arguments influencing public attitudes on slavery. The slaveholding planter William Byrd of Virginia had written in 1736, "They import so many Negroes hither, that I fear this Colony will some time or other be confirmed by the Name of New Guinea. I am sensible of many bad consequences of multiplying these Ethiopians amongst us. They blow up the Pride, and ruin the Industry of our White People, who seeing a Rank of poor Creatures below them, detest work for fear it should make them look like slaves. . . ."[24] Byrd spoke of the incessantly increasing numbers of wretched slaves flowing into the southern colonies, of the spirit and temper of the rebellious Negroes which had to be cooled by force and of the gnawing apprehension of a violent, murderous slave rebellion which could tinge southern waters red.

Thirty-four years later, in 1770, alarming accounts of slave terror and vengeance were reported from the West Indian colonies. Colonial officials begged the Crown for more troops. One official lamented, "This considerable disproportion between the white inhabitants and the slaves, the turbulent and savage dispositions of the Negroes ever prone to riots and rebellion, place the peace, security and lives of your Majesty's white subjects in a very precarious and alarming situation."[25] Abolitionists played on this growing fear. If marauding blacks were swarming over the towns of Barbados and the Leeward Islands, what fate awaited Charles Town, South Carolina? If whites' throats were being slit in St. Vincent, what protected them in Georgia? Reformers pointed to the vast disproportion in the southern colonies between blacks and whites, especially in South Carolina where the ratio was reaching an alarming fifteen to one. Dr. Arthur Lee of Virginia warned, ". . . we are like the wretch at the feast; with a drawn sword depending over his head, by a single hair."[26] Benjamin Franklin put it more simply: "Slaves rather weaken than strengthen the

State, and there is therefore some difference between them and sheep; sheep will never make insurrections."[27]

A natural manifestation of the fear of black uprising was an effort by the colonists to curb the increasing influx of slaves. The demands for restrictive duties on importation usually followed periods of slave unrest and were indicative of apprehension that this great mass of blacks pouring into America could portend violence and the horror of an internecine race war. In several colonies efforts to pass laws to prevent the importation of slaves or to raise duties to limit the numbers imported were accompanied by more harsh acts against the slaves themselves. In 1770 a bill before the Rhode Island Assembly to prevent further importation was accompanied by a law providing for the confinement (in cages) and the whipping of slaves found away from their quarters after nine o'clock.[28]

In addition to the fear of slave insurrection and terror, many whites correctly observed that the increasing influx of slaves was lowering the value of the black property they already held and that a glutted market would bring about an economic disaster.

Also, black slave labor was increasingly a threat to white workers. John Adams declared that the impetus for the abolition of slavery in Massachusetts was the "multiplication of labouring white people, who would no longer suffer the rich to employ these sable rivals so much to their injury."[29] When efforts in the colonies to raise duties were thwarted by the British ministry, a ministry that Americans believed had succumbed to the slave lobby in London and to the numerous petitions from the Bristol and Liverpool slave merchants, many colonials were furious. It is not surprising that Thomas Jefferson in a draft of the Declaration of Independence included a philippic against slavery and attacked the British crown for shackling the colonies with an alien institution. Although Jefferson's philippic did not make its way into the final Declaration because of opposition from a deep South still thirsting for slave labor and from northern slave merchants, it nevertheless reflected a widespread desire in the colonies to limit slave importation.

Reformers now had potent weapons—the economic disadvantages to many planters of the increasing slave traffic; the apprehension in the colonies of an increasing population of suspicious Africans threatening revolt; the philosophical relationship of revolutionary ideology with the opposition to African slavery; and the continuing belief of many Americans that human slavery was a tragic and abominable sin. And, unlike the early years when men such as Benjamin Lay had waged quixotic war against the institution, this period witnessed the rise of a genuine movement.

No longer were there men futilely lying in the snow in front of Quaker meetinghouses—now there were men such as Anthony Benezet, gathering information, compiling statistics, writing pamphlets and articles, distributing literature throughout the colonies and to Europe, writing letter after letter to heads of government, religious leaders and politicians, organizing petition campaigns, persuading friends to enlist in the cause. Others engaged in the same work were the Quaker William Dillwyn, who travelled from England to America carrying pamphlets, letters, and messages and writing tracts of his own; the lawyer Samuel Allinson offered his services to the blacks in the courts, and appealed to political leaders for antislavery legislation; the slaveholding merchant of Providence, Moses Brown, became a zealous advocate for black freedom. The New England ministers—Samuel Hopkins, Levi Hart, Benjamin Coleman, Ezra Stiles—all attacked slavery from the pulpits and in pamphlets and newspaper articles as a wretched sin and as a violation of human rights. There were the Methodist emissaries—Thomas Coke and Francis Asbury—spreading John Wesley's views against slavery in Virginia amidst threats and intimidation. There was Wesley himself writing his own *Thoughts on Slavery* in 1774. There were others who were drawn briefly into the slavery controversy and who spoke and wrote against its abuses, men such as Benjamin Rush, Thomas Paine, William Livingston and Benjamin Franklin. Even the "Poet of the Revolution," Philip Freneau, wrote of the oppressed slave in 1776:

> Perhaps in chains he left his native shore
> Perhaps he left a helpless offspring there,
> Perhaps a wife, that he must see no more,
> Perhaps a father, who his love did share.
>
> Curs'd be the ship that brought him o'er the main,
> And curs'd the hands who from his country tore,
> May she be stranded, ne'er to float again,
> May they be shipwrek'd on some hostile shore.[30]

And then there were the blacks themselves. When views of men such as Edward Long are considered, the contributions of the blacks to the antislavery movement are significant. Mr. Long, author of a history of Jamaica, wrote in 1774 that Negroes were a "brutish, ignorant, idle, crafty, treacherous, bloody, thievish, mistrustful, and superstitious people."[31] A member of the Harvard graduating class of 1773 added his conclusion that the Negro was "a conglomerate of child, idiot and madman."[32] These men were only reflecting a widespread acceptance that the black race was an inferior, contemptible, subhuman work force made in the likeness of beasts. In contrast to such notions, Prince Hall, Paul Cuffe and other blacks began to petition colonial legislatures; many others such as Quack Walker and Elizabeth Freeman began suing for freedom in the courts and writing articles. On August 17, 1774, Caesar Sarter, a freeborn black who had been sold into a slavery which for him lasted twenty years, wrote in the *Essex Journal* that America's forefathers risked their lives rather than submit to tyranny. Why then did they saddle thousands of their fellow men with "that CURSE OF CURSES, SLAVERY"? The famous black poetess Phillis Wheatley wrote in the same year, "God grant Deliverances in his own Way and Time, and get him honor upon all those whose Avarice impels them to countenance and help forward the Calamities of their fellow Creatures . . . convince them of the strange Absurdity of their Conduct whose Words and Actions are so diametrically opposite. How will the cry for Liberty, and reverse Disposition for the exercise of oppressive Power over others agree,

I humbly think it does not require the Penetration of a Philosopher to determine."[33]

In 1774 Janet Schaw, a British "lady of quality" visiting Antigua, mistook Negro children for monkeys and later dismissed the brutal treatment of the slaves with the remark that their "natures seem to bear it." She observed, ". . . when one comes to be acquainted with the nature of the Negroes, the horrour of it must wear off."[34] Janet Schaw had not met Phillis Wheatley or Caesar Sarter or Elizabeth Freeman or Quack Walker or Paul Cuffe or Prince Hall or any of hundreds of other black freemen and slaves who joined petition campaigns, wrote articles, and fought against slavery in the courts, who would not allow "the horrour of it" to wear off.

These Americans, both white and black, who comprised the antislavery movement, were often closely tied to Europeans interested in reform. On May 14, 1772, Anthony Benezet began a letter to Granville Sharp in London, "I have long been desirous of having an opportunity to communicate and advise with such well minded Persons in England who have a Prospect of the Iniquity of the Slave Trade and are concerned to prevent its Continuation."[35] This letter inaugurated a twelve-year correspondence that ended only with the Philadelphia Quaker's death in 1784 and signaled a new spirit of cooperation between reformers in Europe and America. Sharp, a junior civil servant in the Ordinance Office turned antislavery barrister, had just learned of his victory in the significant Somerset case when Benezet's letter reached London. Chief Justice Mansfield had ruled that slaveholding had never been sanctioned in English law and the impact of the decision spurred reformers in America.[36] It was through the mutual contacts of Benezet and Sharp, both indefatigable propagandists, and through the strategy and tactics they plotted, that the antislavery movement gained increased momemtum.

Benezet corresponded with David Barclay, the influential British merchant, with Richard Shackleton, a close friend of Edmund Burke, and with Abbe Raynal, whose *Histoire des deux Indes* attacked the institution of slavery. Benezet's magnum opus on slavery, *Some Historical Account of Guinea,* aroused Thomas Clarkson to begin his work against slavery. Sharp corresponded with Benjamin Rush and exchanged views with Benjamin Franklin in London. Pamphlets and extracts of pamphlets, petitions, newspaper articles, and plans for emancipation began to crisscross the Atlantic in astonishing numbers. Philadelphia Quakers, in constant correspondence with their English brethren, sent antislavery tracts to London to be circulated among English schoolchildren. Richard Price, the English moral and political philosopher, sent a tract against slavery to both Henry Laurens and Thomas Jefferson. The American-born William Dillwyn, a pupil of schoolmaster Benezet, formed an antislavery propaganda group in London. Even Josiah Wedgwood, who revolutionized the pottery industry of Staffordshire and who stands alone in the history of English ceramics, struck off numbers of antislavery medallions bearing the image of a kneeling slave in chains and the inscription, "Am I Not a Man and a Brother?" Wedgwood wrote to Benjamin Franklin, "It gives me great pleasure to be embarked on this occasion in the same great and good cause with you, and I ardently hope for the final completion of our wishes. This will be an epoch before unknown to the World, and while relief is given to millions of our fellow Creatures immediately the object of it, the subject of freedom will be more canvassed and better understood in the enlightened nations."[37]

The individuals who represented the vanguard of the American antislavery movement were largely outside the legislative system. It was a diverse group of ministers, lawyers, merchants, planters and schoolteachers who attacked slavery from outside of the political system, filling broadsides, newspaper columns, pamphlets and sermons with their message. They attempted to bring pressure on the colonial legislatures and the Continental Congress by influencing public opinion. It was a veritable network of allies whose principal object was to make the social ills of slavery a political issue and to generate positive legislative action.

But as slavery became an important political question, as the simple paternalistic pleas for kindness to slaves gave way to a demand for national legislation, the reformers faced formidable pressures. There was anxiety among political leaders that action by the Continental Congress repugnant to any of the individual colonies could rupture the tenuous unity between the several states. As one American remarked in 1776, a national law abolishing the slave trade or slavery might "have a tendency to injure the Union which is the basis and foundation of our defence and happiness . . ."[38] An American president more than eighty years later would also anguish over this dilemma. This reluctance by members of the Continental Congress frustrated the reformers, and when leaders in Georgia and South Carolina and northern slave interests demanded that Congress keep the question of slavery out of the Declaration of Independence, Congressional members beat a hasty retreat.

In addition to the fear that an attack on slavery would threaten national unity, most of America's political leaders were genuinely ambivalent about the issue. If Thomas Jefferson proclaimed the slave's natural right to freedom, at the same time he argued that free blacks and whites could not live harmoniously together. George Washington complained to Robert Morris of a "vexatious" lawsuit that a group of Quakers had brought against a Virginia associate. The General wanted it understood that he opposed the institution of slavery generally but ". . . when slaves who are happy and contented with their present masters, are tampered with and seduced to leave them . . . when it happens to fall on a man . . . and he looses his property for want of means to defend it, it is oppression . . ."[39] Richard Henry Lee wrote in 1773, "You know in general I have always thought the Trade bad, but since it will be carried on, I do not see how I could in justice to my family refuse any advantage that might arise from the selling them."[40]

Reformers had not expected the South to yield to antislavery demands;

they realized that only through Congressional legislation could these states be forced to relinquish their black property. Anthony Benezet during the years of the Revolution continually pointed to Georgia and South Carolina, hungering for more black merchandise, drowning their plantations in a mass of discontented slaves, reduced to instigating a system of terror to control the desperate black population. John Laurens—with his father, Henry, one of the few individuals in the deep South to speak out against "the galling abject Slavery of our Negroes"—wrote in 1776, "I have scarcely ever met with a Native of the Southern provinces . . . who did not obstinately recur to the most absurd Arguments in support of Slavery . . . Indeed when driven from every thing else, they generally exclaimed Without Slaves, how is it possible for us to be rich?"[41] William Loundes was a good example of what Laurens was talking about. Loundes would later remark, "Without negroes, this state would degenerate into one of the most contemptible in the Union." General Charles Pinckney would also prove John Laurens an accurate observer. Pinckney referred to slaves as the "wealth" of South Carolina and called the black labor force the state's only natural resource.[42]

But if the antislavery leaders, faced with such obstacles, could not drive the fatal spike into the heart of slavery, they would, nevertheless, make significant progress in the northern states where slavery was less of an economic factor. On April 14, 1775, five days before the battle of Lexington, the first antislavery society in America took the name of "The Society for the Relief of Free Negroes Unlawfully Held in Bondage." The preamble to its constitution called for loosening the "bonds of wickedness . . . at a time when justice, liberty, and the laws of the land are the general topics, among most ranks and stations of men."[43] This society would be followed by others, most notably in New York under the presidency of John Jay. The early limited aims of these and other antislavery societies to promote manumission and to protect free blacks would be broadened to include active political agitation against slavery and the teaching and training of freemen.

In 1780 the Pennsylvania legislature passed the first gradual emancipation act in America. Introduced, by coincidence, on the day Thomas Paine became Clerk of the Assembly, the measure provided that every Negro born in Pennsylvania after passage of the act would become free at the age of twenty-eight. Anthony Benezet is said to have lobbied every member of the Assembly prior to the vote. This act was the most significant of a series of legislative measures directed against slavery in the various northern states. In 1784 Connecticut and Rhode Island passed similar gradual abolition laws. Within a year of the conclusion of the Revolutionary War provision had been made for the abolition of slavery in all of the New England states.[44]

In other states, including some in the South, manumission was facilitated and thousands of slaves were freed under new laws. In addition, Revolutionary War leaders such as Washington now followed their ideals of human rights by freeing slaves in their wills. Although it was an act of questionable moral magnanimity or, as one reformer remarked, "a sacrifice that cost . . . nothing,"[45] many slaves, nevertheless, now achieved freedom on the death of their masters.

In the northern courts slaves sued for freedom and usually won. The Superior Court of Massachusetts in a series of cases upheld the slave's right to freedom under the declaration in the Massachusetts constitution that "all men are born free and equal." When the first federal census was taken in 1790 Massachusetts reported that it had no slaves.[46]

The legislative and legal processes during the period of the Revolution effectively made slavery an institution peculiar to the South. But if slavery was doomed to extinction in the North, where its vulnerability for obvious economic reasons was greater, the reformers had not achieved a legislative victory at the national level. In 1783 a petition to the Congress signed by more than five hundred Quakers was tabled.[47] Other petitions were similiarly dispatched to quiet deaths. And although the Northwest Ordinance of 1787 provided for the abolition of slavery in territories north of the Ohio River, at the same time it made provision for the return of fugitive slaves. The Northwest would not become a sanctuary for runaways.

It was at the Constitutional Convention that the hopes of the reformers for a national victory over slavery were dashed. The vital clause in the final document read: "the importation of such persons as any of the States now existing shall think proper to admit, shall not be prohibited prior to the year one thousand eight hundred and eight." When the slavery issue crowded into the debate at the Convention, it was mostly related to commerce, taxation, and representation. Only a few delegates, principally Gouverneur Morris of New York and Luther Martin of Maryland, spoke of ending slavery, Morris calling it "the curse of heaven."[48] With the "Great Compromise"—that only three-fifths of the slaves would be counted for purposes of both representation and direct taxation—northern fears of southern over-representation were allayed. With the federal sanctioning of the slave trade until 1808, southern fears that the government would disturb what Charles Pinckney had called the "wealth" of South Carolina were mollified. The question of slavery's actual existence never vitally affected the union-making purposes of the delegates. Even Benjamin Franklin, when faced with the hands-off ultimatums from Georgia and South Carolina, fell silent.

James Madison in the Federalist Papers tried to rationalize the decision to allow the slave trade for another twenty years. "It ought to be considered as a great point gained in favor of humanity, that a period of twenty years may terminate for ever within these States, a traffic which has so long and so loudly upbraided the barbarism of modern policy."[49] Madison, like his fellow Virginian Thomas Jefferson, clung to the notion that slavery would self-destruct, would evaporate because of its corrupt nature and its ultimate uselessness. Jefferson looked to the youth that "have sucked in the principles of liberty as it were with their mother's milk, and it is to them I look with anxiety to turn the fate of this question. Be not therefore discouraged."[50]

For the reformers it was a bitter lesson. Granville Sharp considered the

United States Constitution a document fit for the flames, just as William Lloyd Garrison would consider it years later. Sharp attacked the baneful compromising and the hypocrisy: "Remembering the declarations of the American Congress so frequently repeated during the Contention with Britain we could not flatter ourselves that the late Convention would have produced more unequivocal proofs of a regard to consistency of Character from complying with the acknowledged obligations of humanity and justice . . ."[51] Samuel Hopkins lamented, "How does it appear in the sight of Heaven and of all good men . . . that *these States*, who have been fighting for liberty, and consider themselves as the highest and most noble example of zeal for it, cannot agree in any political Constitution, unless it indulge and authorize them to enslave their fellow men . . . Ah! these unclean spirits, like frogs—they, like the Furies of the poets are spreading discord, and exciting men to contention and war . . ."[52]

Samuel Hopkins's vision was accurate, of course. The problem of slavery did not simply go away as Madison and others had hoped. Although the antislavery effort had made genuine progress, America's most anguishing dilemma would have to await its final resolution in another generation, in the days of Robert Barnwell Rhett and John Brown, in the days of the "Furies of the poets . . . spreading discord, and exciting men to contention and war . . ."

NOTES

[1][John Allen], *The Watchman's Alarm to Lord N---h . . .* (Salem, 1774), 27.

[2]Nathaniel Appleton, *Considerations on Slavery in a Letter To a Friend* (Boston, 1767), 19.

[3]*Pennsylvania Packet*, Vol. III, No. 120, February 7, 1774.

[4]George H. Moore, *Notes on the History of Slavery in Massachusetts* (New York, reprinted 1968), 145.

[5]Patrick Henry to Robert Pleasants, January 18, 1773, Library Company, Philadelphia, Pennsylvania.

[6]For the best account of Hopkins's antislavery activities see David S. Lovejoy, "Samuel Hopkins: Religion, Slavery, and the Revolution," *The New England Quarterly*, XL (June, 1967), 227-43.

[7]Appleton, 7.

[8]See "Judge Saffin's Reply to Judge Sewall, 1701," Appendix to Moore, *Notes*, 256.

[9]Thomas Drake, *Quakers and Slavery in America* (New Haven, 1950), 44-46; David Brion Davis, *The Problem of Slavery in Western Culture* (Ithaca, 1966), 291, 320-25.

[10]*An Apology for the True Christian Divinity* (New York, 1827), 143.

[11]*Travels Into North America*, Vol. I (Warrington, 1770), 390.

[12]Arthur Spaid, "Slavery in Pennsylvania," *American Historical Register*, Vol. II (July, 1895), 1186.

[13]*All Slave-Keepers that keep the Innocent in Bondage, Apostates . . .*, (Philadelphia, 1737), 197.

[14]See an excellent discussion of Quakers and slavery in an unpublished thesis, Anne T. Gary Pannell, *The Political and Economic Relations of English and American Quakers (1750-1785)*, submitted for Degree of D. Phil. at St. Hugh's College in 1935; copy at Haverford College Library, Haverford, Pennsylvania.

[15]Granville Sharp to Anthony Benezet, January 7, 1774, copy in possession of Col. A. Lloyd-Baker, Hardwicke Court, Gloucester, England.

[16]*An Address to the Inhabitants of the British Colonies in America Upon Slave-Keeping* (Norwich, 1775), 28.

[17]*The Rights of the British Colonies Asserted and Proved* (Boston, 1764), 29.

[18]*Serious Considerations on Several Important Subjects: On War and its Inconsistency with the Gospel, Observations on Slavery and Remarks on the Nature and bad Effects of Spirituous Liquors* (Philadelphia, 1778), 28.

[19]Davis, 114-20.

[20]Francis W. Kelsy, trans., *De Jure Belli Ac Pacis* (Oxford, 1925), Book I, 38-39.

[21]*A Dialogue Concerning the Slavery of the Africans Showing it to be the Duty and Interest of the American Colonies to Emancipate all the African Slaves: With an Address to the Owners of such Slaves. Dedicated to the Honorable the Continental Congress* (Norwich, 1776), iii.

[22]*Pennsylvania Journal*, March 8, 1775.

[23]Allinson to Patrick Henry, October 17, 1774, Quaker Collection, Haverford College Library.

[24]Elizabeth Donnan, ed., *Documents Illustrative of the History of Slave Trade to America* (Washington, 1931), 131-32.

[25]Gov. Woodley, Leeward Islands, to Lord Hillsborough, November 16, 1770, CO 152/51, Original Correspondence to Secretary of State, Leeward Islands, Public Record Office, London; quoted in George F. Tyson, Jr. and Carolyn Tyson, *Preliminary Report on Manuscript Materials in British Archives Relating to the American Revolution in the West Indian Islands* (St. Thomas, U.S. Virgin Islands, 1973), 24.

[26]Richard K. MacMaster, ed., "Arthur Lee's 'Address on Slavery': An Aspect of Virginia's Struggle to End the Slave Trade, 1765-1774," *The Virginia Magazine of History and Biography*, Vol. 80, No. 2 (April, 1972), 153-57.

[27]W. C. Ford, ed., *Journals of the Continental Congress* (34 vols., Washington, 1904-37), VI, 1080.

[28]William D. Johnston, "Slavery in Rhode Island, 1755-1776," *Publications of the Rhode Island Historical Society*, Vol. II, No. 2 (July, 1894), 130.

[29]Quoted in Arthur Zilversmit, *The First Emancipation: The Abolition of Slavery in the North* (Chicago, 1967), 47.

[30]Quoted in Lorenzo Turner, "Anti-Slavery Sentiment in Literature," *Journal of Negro History*, Vol. XIV (October, 1929), 393.

[31]Quoted in Davis, 461-62.

[32]*A Forensic Dispute on the Legality of enslaving the Africans, Held At the public*

Commencement in Cambridge, New-England, July 21st, 1773 by Candidates For the Bachelor's Degree (Boston, 1773), 26-27.

[33]Phillis Wheatley to Samson Occon, February 1774, *The Connecticut Journal and the New Haven Post-Boy*, April 1, 1774.

[34]Davis, 460-61.

[35]Granville Sharp Letterbook, Library Company.

[36]See numerous letters of Sharp on the Somerset case in Sharp Letterbook, Library Company.

[37]Josiah Wedgwood to Benjamin Franklin, February 29, 1788, Ann Finer and George Savage, eds., *The Selected Letters of Josiah Wedgwood* (New York, 1965), 311.

[38]Massachusetts Historical Society *Proceedings*, 1867-69, 333-34.

[39]George Washington to Robert Morris, April 12, 1786, John C. Fitzpatrick, ed., *The Writings of George Washington from the Original Manuscript Sources, 1745-1799*, Vol. 28, (Washington, 1938), 407.

[40]Richard Henry Lee to "Brother," May 13, 1773, Boston Public Library, Boston, Massachusetts.

[41]John Laurens to Henry Laurens, October 26, 1776, Henry Laurens Papers, South Carolina Historical Society, Columbia, South Carolina.

[42]George Livermore, *An Historical Research Respecting the Opinions of the Founders of the Republic on Negroes as Slaves, as Citizens, and as Soldiers* (Boston, 1862), 167.

[43]Copy in William F. Poole, *Anti-Slavery Opinions Before the Year 1800* (Cincinnati, 1873), 44.

[44]Zilversmit, 109-56.

[45]Pannell, 218.

[46]Zilversmit, 113-16.

[47]Petition is in Record Group 360, Records of the Continental Congress, Item 43, Remonstrances and Addresses to Congress, National Archives; committee report delivered to Congress on January 7, 1784, and, as a short notation on the back of the report indicates, "Question taken and lost." Record Group 360, Item 20, Reports of Committee on State Papers, Vol. II, National Archives.

[48]*Notes of Debates in the Federal Convention of 1787, Reported by James Madison* (Athens, 1966), 411.

[49]E. H. Scott, ed., *The Federalist and Other Contemporary Papers on the Constitution of the United States* (Chicago, Atlanta, New York, 1894), 233-34.

[50]Thomas Jefferson to Richard Price, August 7, 1785, Julian P. Boyd, ed., *The Papers of Thomas Jefferson*, Vol. VIII (Princeton, New Jersey, 1953), 357.

[51]Sharp to New York Society for Manumission of Slaves, May 1, 1788, Columbia University Libraries.

[52]Edwards A. Park, ed., *The Works of Samuel Hopkins* (3 vols., Boston, 1852), Vol. I, 158-59.

Black American sailor in dress of a defeated captain of the British Royal Navy. Anonymous painter captured the scene during the battle.

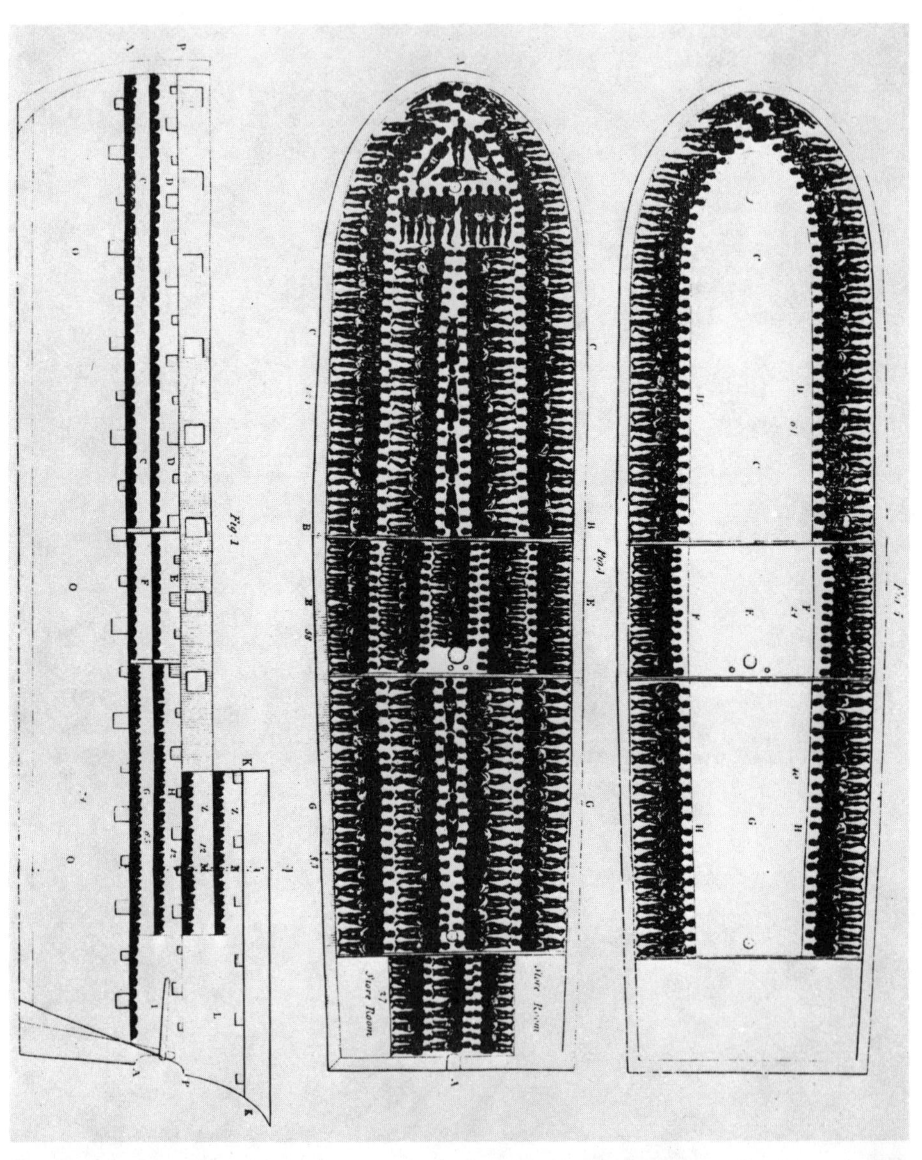

Drawing of a slave ship in British abolitionist Thomas Clarkson's book published in 1808.

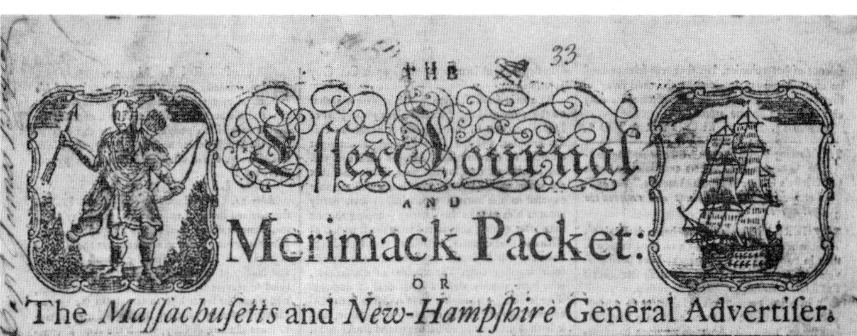

THE Essex Journal AND Merimack Packet: OR The Massachusetts and New-Hampshire General Advertiser.

Vol. I. WEDNESDAY, August 17, 1774. No. 35.

Messrs. PRINTERS,

Please to give the following Address, To those who are Advocates for holding the Africans in Slavery, a place in your next, and you will oblige one, who is a well-wisher to his brethren, who are now in that unhappy state.

AS this is a time of great anxiety and distress among you, on account of the infringement not only of your Charter rights; but of the natural rights and privileges of freeborn men; permit a poor, though freeborn, African, who, in his youth, was trapanned into Slavery, and who has born the galling yoke of bondage for more than twenty years; though at last, by the blessing of God, has shaken it off, to tell you, and that from experience, that as Slavery is the greatest, and consequently most to be dreaded, of all temporal calamities: So its opposite, Liberty, is the greatest temporal good, with which you can be blest! The importance of which, you clearly evince to the world you are sensible of, by your manly and resolute struggles to preserve it. Your fore fathers, as I have been often informed, left their native country, together with many dear friends, and came into this country, then a howling wilderness inhabited, only, by savages, rather choosing, under the protection of their GOD, to risk their lives, among those merciless wretches, than submit to tyranny at home: While, therefore, this conduct gives you their exalted sense of the worth of LIBERTY, at the same time, it shews their utmost abhorrence of that CURSE OF CURSES, SLAVERY.——Your Parliament, to their immortal honor be it mentioned, to whom WE feel that gratitude, which so high a favour naturally produces, in an ingenious mind, have exerted their utmost abilities, to put a final stop, to so iniquitous a business, as the Slave Trade is: That they have not succeeded in their laudable endeavours, was not their fault: But they were defeated by his late Excellency only.——Now, if you are sensible, that slavery is in itself, and in its consequences, a great evil; why will you not pity and relieve the poor, distressed, enslaved Africans?—Who, though they are entitled to the same natural rights of mankind, that you are, are, nevertheless, groaning in bondage! A bondage which will only terminate with life: To them a shocking consideration indeed! Though too little, I fear, thought of by most of you, who enjoy the profits of their labour. As the importation of slaves into this Province is generally laid aside, I shall not pretend a refutation of the arguments, generally brought in support of it; but request you, to let that excellent rule given by our Saviour, to do to others, as you would, that they should do to you, have its due weight with you. Though the thought be shocking—for a few minutes, suppose that you were trepanned away.—The husband from the dear wife of his bosom—the wife from her affectionate husband—children from their fond parents—or parents from their tender and beloved offspring, whom, not an hour before, perhaps, they were fondling in their arms, and in whom they were promising themselves much future happiness: Suppose, I say, that you were thus ravished from such a blissful situation, and plunged into miserable slavery, in a distant quarter of the globe: Or suppose you were accompanied by your wife and children, parents and brethren, manacled by your side—harrowing thought! And that after having suffered the most amazing hardships, your fetters were knocked from your galled limbs, only to expose you to keener anguish!—Exposed to sale, with as little respect to decency, as though you were a brute! And after all this, if you were unwilling to part with all you held dear, even without the privilege of droping a tear over your dear friends, who were clinging round you; equally dreading the cruel seperation, which would probably prove an end of one, you must be plied with that conclusive argument, the cat-o'nine tails, to reduce you to what your inhuman masters would call Reason. Now, are you willing all this should befall you? If you can lay your hand on your breast, and solemnly affirm that you should; Why then go on and prosper! For your treatment of the Africans is an exact compliance with the abovementioned rule: But if, on the other hand, your conscience answers in the negative; Why, in the name of Heaven, will you suffer such a gross violation of that rule by which your conduct must be tried, in that day, in which you must be accountable for all your actions, to, that impartial Judge, who hears the groans of the oppressed, and who will sooner or later, avenge them of their oppressors! I need not tell you, who are acquainted with the scriptures, that this kind of oppression is discountenanced by them. Many passages, to this purpose, might be adduced, but I shall, at present, mention but one, Exod. chap. 20 ver. 16 "And he that stealeth a man, and selleth him, or if he be found in his hand, he shall surely be put to death."

Though we are brought from a land of ignorance, it is as certain, that we are brought from a land of comparative innocence—from a land that flows, as it were, with Milk and Honey—and the greater part of us carried, where we are, not only deprived of every comfort of life: But subjected to all the tortures that a most cruel inquisitor could invent, or a capricious tyrant execute, and where we are likely, from the vicious examples before us, to become ten fold more the children of satan, than we should probably, have been in our native country. Though 'tis true, that some of our wars proceed from petty discords among ourselves, it is as true, that the greater part of them, and those the most bloody, are occasioned, in consequence of the Slave trade.——Though many think we are happier here, than there, and will not allow us the privilege of judging for ourselves, they are certainly in an error. Every man is the best judge of his own happiness, and every heart best knows its own bitterness.——While I feel the loss of my country, and my friends, I can, by sad experience, adopt that expression in Prov. 25th Chap. 20 verse. "As he that taketh away a garment in cold weather, and as vinegar upon nitre, so is he that singeth songs to a heavy heart." Let me, who have now no less than eleven relatives suffering in bondage, beseech you, good people, to attend to the request of a poor African, and consider the evil consequences, and gross heinousness of reducing to, and retaining in slavery a free people. Would you desire the preservation of your own liberty? As the first step let the oppressed Africans be liberated; then, and not till then, may you with confidence and consistency of conduct, look to Heaven for a blessing on your endeavours to knock the shackles with which your task masters are hampering you, from your own feet. On the other hand, if you are still determined to harden your hearts, and turn a deaf ear to our complaints, and the calls of God, in your present Calamities; Only be pleased to recollect the miserable end of Pharaoh, in Consequence of his refusal to set those at Liberty, whom he had unjustly reduced to cruel servitude. Remember the fate of Miriam for despising an Ethiopean woman, Numb. 12 chap. 1st and 10th. verses. I need not point out the absurdity of your exertions for liberty, while you have slaves in your houses, for one minute's reflection is, methinks, sufficient for that purpose.—You who are deterred from liberating your slaves, by the consideration of the ill consequences to yourselves must remember, that we were not the cause of our being brought here. If the compelling us, against our wills, to come here was a sin; to retain us, without our consent, now we are here, is, I think, equally culpable, let ever so great inconvenience, arising therefrom, accrue to you. Not to trespass too much on your patience; would you unite in this generous, this noble purpose of granting us liberty; Your honourable assembly, on our humble petition, would, I doubt not, free you from the trouble of us by making us grants in some back part of the country. If in this attempt to serve my countrymen, I have advanced any thing to the purpose, I pray it may not be the less noticed for coming from an African.

CÆSAR SARTER.

Newbury Port, August 12th, 1774.

A writer in the London Advertiser, who takes the signature of Moderator, concludes an ingenious and spirited essay on American affairs as follows:

SHOULD it happen, and that it may is not beyond the limits of possibility that a coalition of all the provinces of America should be formed into one unanimous alliance to oppose the measures of our government, and join in a determined resolution to cut off all intercourse under dependant circumstances with Great Britain; should the mystic roll of fate bring to pass this, which yet exists but in supposition, how fruitless then would be all our attempts to assert a sovereign right to America, or regain its loss; We might then remain envious spectators of her flourishing situation, and in that situation perceive the visible traces of ill policy and misguided administration. It has been advanced, with a view perhaps to future contingencies, that Great Britain could suffer no loss, but, on the contrary, be a gainer by the independence of her American acquisitions. This assertion, considering the late rapid strides of America toward such a state, is, in the true temporising spirit, exhorting a ready compliance with what is foreseen to be inevitable, for without a revolution in nature, or the supernatural aid of miracles, America may (and the belief is not singular) in future times have the seat of empire within herself, and instead of receiving laws from the island of Great Britain, may enforce a code of her own through her almost boundless continent. This conjecture is far from beyond probability; the present appearance of things carry with them an evident tendency towards its completion; the present perhaps is the important crisis, on which depends the continuance of our possession of the American colonies, or their total independence; they know their strength, and will if incensed, call it forth; our policy, therefore, should be to bind them by ties of affection to the mother country, by gentle, by persuasive measures, but on no account to harbour the most distant idea of adopting compulsatory ones; palliative means may possess them with gratitude, coercive ones will fill them with vindictive rage. Great-Britain may retain the con-

Antislavery essay by Caesar Sarter, an ex-slave, who describes the horror of his former captivity.

RUN away from the subscriber in *Albemarle*, a Mulatto slave called *Sandy*, about 35 years of age, his stature is rather low, inclining to corpulence, and his complexion light; he is a shoemaker by trade, in which he uses his left hand principally, can do coarse carpenters work, and is something of a horse jockey; he is greatly addicted to drink, and when drunk is insolent and disorderly, in his conversation he swears much, and in his behaviour is artful and knavish. He took with him a white horse, much scarred with traces, of which it is expected he will endeavour to dispose; he also carried his shoemakers tools, and will probably endeavour to get employment that way. Whoever conveys the said slave to me, in *Albemarle*, shall have 40 s. reward, if taken up within the county, 4 l. if elsewhere within the colony, and 10 l. if in any other colony, from

THOMAS JEFFERSON.

Advertisement placed by Thomas Jefferson in the Virginia Gazette, *September 14, 1769, for a runaway slave.*

Petition of an African slave, to the legislature of Massachusetts.

To the honourable the senate and house of representatives, in general court assembled:

The petition of Belinda, an African,

Humbly shews,

THAT seventy years have rolled away, since she, on the banks of the Rio de Valta, received her existence. The mountains, covered with spicy forests—vallies, loaded with the richest fruits spontaneously produced—joined to that happy temperature of air, which excludes excess, would have yielded her the most complete felicity, had not her mind received early impressions of the cruelty of men, whose faces were like the moon, and whose bows and arrows were like the thunder and the lightning of the clouds. The idea of these, the most dreadful of all enemies, filled her infant slumbers with horror, and her noon-tide moments with cruel apprehensions! But her affrighted imagination, in its most alarming extension, never represented distresses equal to what she has since really experienced: for before she had twelve years enjoyed the fragrance of her native groves, and ere she had realized that Europeans placed their happiness in the yellow dust, which she carelessly marked with her infant footsteps—even when she, in a sacred grove, with each hand in that of a tender parent, was paying her devotion to the great Orisa, who made all things, an armed band of white men, driving many of her countrymen in chains, rushed into the hallowed shades! Could the tears, the sighs, the supplications, bursting from the tortured parental affection, have blunted the keen edge of avarice, she might have been rescued from agony, which many of her country's children have felt, but which none have ever described. In vain she lifted her supplicating voice to an insulted father, and her guiltless hands to a dishonoured deity! She was ravished from the bosom of her country, from the arms of her friends, while the advanced age of her parents rendering them unfit for servitude, cruelly separated her from them for ever.

Scenes which her imagination had never conceived of, a floating world, the sporting monsters of the deep, and the familiar meeting of billows and clouds, strove, but in vain, to divert her attention from three hundred Africans in chains, suffering the most excruciating torment; and some of them rejoicing that the pangs of death came like a balm to their wounds.

Once more her eyes were blest with a continent: but alas! how unlike the land where she received her being! Here all things appeared unpropitious. She learned to catch the ideas, marked by the sounds of language, only to know that her doom was slavery, from which death alone was to emancipate her. What did it avail her, that the walls of her lord were hung with splendor, and that the dust trodden under foot in her native country, crouded his gates with sordid worshippers! The laws rendered her incapable of receiving property: and though she was a free moral agent, accountable for her own actions, yet never had she a monent at her own disposal! Fifty years her faithful hands have been compelled to ignoble servitude for the benefit of an Isaac Royall, until, as if nations must be agitated, and the world convulsed, for the preservation of that freedom, which the Almighty Father intended for all the human race, the present war commenced. The terrors of men, armed in the cause of freedom, compelled her master to fly, and to breathe away his life in a land, where lawless dominion sits enthroned, pouring blood and vengeance on all who dare to be free.

The face of your petitioner is now marked with the furrows of time, and her frame feebly bending under the oppression of years, while she, by the laws of the land, is denied the enjoyment of one morsel of that immense wealth, a part whereof hath been accumulated by her own industry, and the whole augmented by her servitude.

Wherefore, casting herself at the feet of your honours, as to a body of men, formed for the extirpation of vassalage, for the reward of virtue, and the just returns of honest industry—she prays that such allowance may be made her, out of the estate of colonel Royall, as will prevent her, and her more infirm daughter, from misery in the greatest extreme, and scatter comfort over the short and downward path of their lives: and she will ever pray.

BELINDA.

Boston, February, 1782.

Petition of Belinda, a slave of a Tory sympathizer who fled from America during the War, to the Legislature of Massachusetts for funds from her master's estate to support herself and her daughter, February 4, 1783.

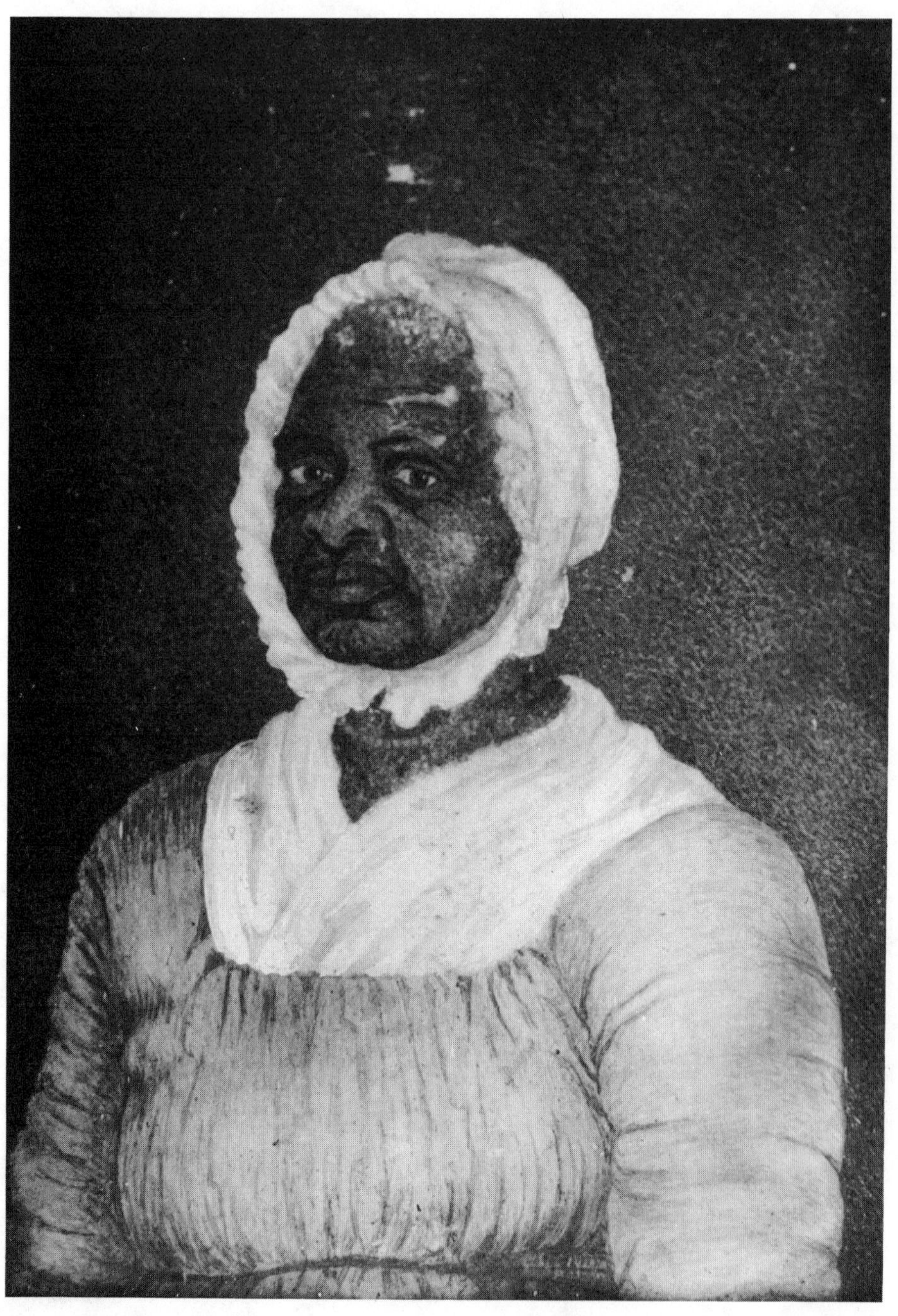

Elizabeth Freeman, a slave who achieved freedom by petitioning a Massachusetts Court in 1781 under the provisions of the Massachusetts Bill of Rights. The case started a precedent for freedom of slaves in that state.

BOSTON, APRIL 20th, 1773.

SIR,

THE efforts made by the legiſlative of this province in their laſt ſeſſions to free themſelves from ſlavery, gave us, who are in that deplorable ſtate, a high degree of ſatisfacton. We expect great things from men who have made ſuch a noble ſtand againſt the deſigns of their *fellow-men* to enſlave them. We cannot but wiſh and hope Sir, that you will have the ſame grand object, we mean civil and religious liberty, in view in your next ſeſſion. The divine ſpirit of *freedom*, ſeems to fire every humane breaſt on this continent, except ſuch as are bribed to aſſiſt in executing the execrable plan.

WE are very ſenſible that it would be highly detrimental to our preſent maſters, if we were allowed to demand all that of *right* belongs to us for paſt ſervices; this we diſclaim. Even the *Spaniards*, who have not thoſe ſublime ideas of freedom that Engliſh men have, are conſcious that they have no right to all the ſervices of their fellow-men, we mean the *Africans*, whom they have purchaſed with their money; therefore they allow them one day in a week to work for themſelve, to enable them to earn money to purchaſe the reſidue of their time, which they have a right to demand in ſuch portions as they are able to pay for (a due appraizment of their ſervices being firſt made, which always ſtands at the purchaſe money.) We do not pretend to dictate to you Sir, or to the honorable Aſſembly, of which you are a member: We acknowledge our obligations to you for what you have already done, but as the people of this province ſeem to be actuated by the principles of equity and juſtice, we cannot but expect your houſe will again take our deplorable caſe into ſerious conſideration, and give us that ample relief which, *as men*, we have a natural right to.

BUT ſince the wiſe and righteous governor of the univerſe, has permitted our fellow men to make us ſlaves, we bow in ſubmiſſion to him, and determine to behave in ſuch a manner, as that we may have reaſon to expect the divine approbation of, and aſſiſtance in, our peaceable and lawful attempts to gain our freedom.

WE are willing to ſubmit to ſuch regulations and laws, as may be made relative to us, until we leave the province, which we determine to do as ſoon as we can from our joynt labours procure money to tranſport ourſelves to ſome part of the coaſt of *Africa*, where we propoſe a ſettlement. We are very deſirous that you ſhould have inſtructions relative to us, from your town, therefore we pray you to communicate this letter to them, and aſk this favor for us.

In behalf of our fellow ſlaves in this province,
And by order of their Committee.

PETER BESTES,
SAMBO FREEMAN,
FELIX HOLBROOK,
CHESTER JOIE.

Circular Letter of the Boston Committee of slaves, an informal group, petitioning each member of the Massachusetts House of Representatives for freedom, April 20, 1773.

to your Honours serious Consideration, whether it is consistent
232c
with the present Claims, of the united States, to hold so many
Thousands, of the Race of Adam, our Common Father, in
perpetual Slavery; Can human Nature endure the Shocking
Idea? can your Honours, any longer Suffer, this great Evil to
prevail under your Government? we entreat your Honours,
let no Considerations of Publick Inconvenience, deter your
Honours, from interposing in Behalf of your Petitioners;
who ask for nothing, but what we are fully persuaded, is ours
to Claim. we beseech your Honours, to weigh this matter,
in the Scale of Justice, and in your great Wisdom and
Goodness, apply such Remedy, as the Evil does require;
and let your Petitioners, rejoice with your Honours, in the
Participation, with your Honours, of that inestimable Blessing,
Freedom and your Humble Petitioners, as in Duty
bound shall Ever pray &c.
dated in Fairfield the 11th Day
of May A D 1779 —

prime a Negro Man
Servant to Mr. Saml. Sturge of Fairfield

his
Prince X a Negro man
mark
Servant of Capt. Stephen Jenings
of Fairfield
in Behalf of themselves and
the other Petitioners

Signed in Presence of
Jonth Sturges.

Excerpt from one of the many slave petitions for freedom to the Joint Assembly of Connecticut, May, 1779.

THE FIRST FUTILE VOICES, 1688-1763

Oh! that all the Libertines, loose Livers, the Magdalens, the Publicans and Harlots, the Smoaking Drunkards, all unclean Persons, Thieves and Covetous, Covetous, the Covetous Earthly minded Idolater, the Superstitious, Formal and Nominal Christians, Preachers and Hearers, the young and old, old, the old Hypocrites too, if possible, I say if possible might be converted, translated, drawn out of that deep, dirty Ditch Hypocrisy. . . .

Benjamin Lay
1737

Germantown Friends' Protest against Slavery, 1688

Printed copy of facsimile made in 1880 by William Kite, Main Vault, Connecticut Historical Society, Hartford, Conn.

The sorrowing exiles from their "Fatherland,"
Leaving their homes in Kriesheim's bowers of vine,

And the blue beauty of their glorious Rhine,
To seek amidst our solemn depths of wood
Freedom from man and holy peace with God:
Who first of all their testimonial gave
Against the oppressor, for the outcast slave . . .

The poet John Greenleaf Whittier's tribute in 1838 was to a small group of Dutch-speaking Mennonites and Friends in Germantown, Pennsylvania, who, one hundred and fifty years before, had attacked human slavery as a sinful abomination. Exiled to America, they perceived slavery as the same kind of horror that their own people had suffered at the hands of the hated Turks. With their European brethren watching the progress of William Penn's "Holy Experiment," the Germantown settlers who signed the following petition saw in black chattel slavery a dreadful embarrassment. How could a community professing religious toleration sanction such a violation of divine law, such a heinous assault on liberty of conscience, they asked. The petition, submitted to a subordinate Friends meeting in April 1688, eventually reached the Yearly Meeting in Burlington, New Jersey, where it was, in effect, tabled. It was nearly seventy years before the Society of Friends took significant steps to end slavery within their sect. But these early petitioners had forcefully asserted that manstealing and slavery were sinful violations of human liberty, divine law, and the Golden Rule. Their sentiments were echoed again and again.

This is to ye Monthly Meeting held at Richard Worrell's.

These are the reasons why we are against the traffick of men-body, as followeth. Is there any that would be done or handled at this manner? viz., to be sold or made a slave for all the time of his life? How fearful and faint-hearted are many on sea, when they see a strange vessel,—being afraid it should be a Turk, and they should be taken, and sold for slaves into Turkey. Now what is this better done, as Turks doe? Yea, rather is it worse for them, which say they are Christians; for we hear that ye most part of such negers are brought hither against their will and consent, and that many of them are stolen. Now, tho they are black, we can not conceive there is more liberty to have them slaves, as it is to have other white ones. There is a saying, that we shall doe to all men like as we will be done ourselves; making no difference of what generation, descent or colour they are. And those who steal or robb men, and those who buy or purchase them, are they not all alike? Here is liberty of conscience, wch is right and reasonable; here ought to be likewise liberty of ye body, except of evil-doers, wch is an other case. But to bring men hither, or to rob and sell them against their will, we stand against. In Europe there are many oppressed for conscience sake; and here there are those oppressed wh are of a black colour. And we who know that men must not comitt adultery,—some do committ adultery, in others, separating wives from their husbands and giving them to others; and some sell the children of these poor creatures to other men. Ah! doe consider well this thing, you who doe it, if you would be done at this manner? and if it is done according to Christianity? You surpass Holland and Germany in this thing. This makes an ill report in all those countries of Europe. where they hear off, that ye Quakers doe here handel men as they handel there ye cattle. And for that reason some have no mind or inclination to come hither. And who shall maintain this your cause, or pleid for it? Truly we can not do so, except you shall inform us better hereof, viz, that Christians have liberty to practise these things. Pray, what thing in the world can be done worse towards us, than if men should rob or steal us away, and sell us for slaves to strange countries; separating housbands from their wives and children. Being now this is not done in the manner we would be done at therefore we contradict and are against this traffic of men-body. And we who profess that it is not lawful to steal, must, likewise, avoid to purchase such things as are stolen, but rather help to stop this robbing and stealing if possible. And such men ought to be delivered out of ye hands of ye robbers, and set free as well as in Europe. Then is Pennsylvania to have a good report, instead it hath now a bad one for this sake in other countries. Especially whereas ye Europeans are desirous to know in what manner ye Quakers doe rule in their province;—and most of them doe look upon us with an envious eye. But if this is done well, what shall we say is done evil?

If once these slaves (wch they say are so wicked and stubbern men) should joint themselves,—fight for their freedom.—and handel their masters and mastrisses as they did handel them before; will these masters and mastrisses take the sword at hand and warr against these poor slaves, licke, we are able to believe, some will not refuse to doe; or have these negers not as much right to fight for their freedom, as you have to keep them slaves?

Now consider well this thing, if it is good or bad? And in case you find it to be good to handel these blacks at that manner, we desire and require you hereby lovingly, that you may inform us herein, which at this time never was done, viz., that Christians have such a liberty to do so. To the end we shall be satisfied in this point, and satisfie likewise our good friends and acquaintances in our natif country, to whose it is a terror, or fairful thing, that men should be handeld so in Pennsylvania.

This is from our meeting at Germantown, held ye 18 of the 2 month, 1688, to be delivered to the Monthly Meeting at Richard Worrel's.

Garret henderich
derick up de graeff
Francis daniell Pastorius
Abraham up Den graef

At our Monthly Meeting at Dublin, ye 30—2 mo., 1688, we having inspected ye matter, above mentioned, and considered of it, we find it so weighty that we think it not expedient for us to meddle with it here, but do rather commit it to ye consideration of ye Quarterly Meeting; ye tenor of it being nearly related to ye Truth.

On behalf of ye Monthly Meeting, Signed,

P. Jo. Hart

This, above mentioned, was read in our Quarterly Meeting at Philadelphia, the 4 of ye 4th mo. '88, and was from thence recommended to the Yearly Meeting, and the above said Derick, and the other two mentioned therein, to present the same to ye above said meeting, it being a thing of too great a weight for this meeting to determine.

Signed by order of ye meeting,

Anthony Morris

Yearly Meeting Minute on the above Protest.

At a Yearly Meeting held at Burlington the 5th day of the 7th month, 1688.

A Paper being here presented by some German Friends Concerning the Lawfulness and Unlawfulness of Buying and keeping Negroes, It was adjudged not to be so proper for this Meeting to give a Positive Judgment in the Case, It having so General a Relation to many other Parts, and therefore at present they forbear It.

George Keith, Pamphlet against Slavery, 1693

George Keith, "An Exhortation and Caution to Friends concerning buying or keeping of Negroes," reprinted in *Pennsylvania Magazine of History and Biography*, 13 (1889):265-70.

In 1789 Benjamin Franklin, reflecting on the progress of the movement to end slavery in America, recalled the early "sowing of the good seed. . . ." Franklin declared, "I find by an old pamphlet in my possession that George Keith, nearly a hundred years since, wrote a paper against the practice . . . wherein a strict charge was given to Friends that they should set their negroes at liberty. . . ." This "strict charge," Franklin noted, was lodged by a zealous, religious agitator who had brazenly admonished the established Quaker membership for pitifully succumbing to worldly influences. Keith was disowned by the Quakers in the midst of his campaign to cleanse and purify the sect, but he formed his own group of "Christian Quakers" to carry on the attack. His literary assault in 1693 on Quaker trafficking in slaves was an extension of his general reform efforts. As did the writers of the Germantown Protest, Keith argued that slavery violated Biblical injuctions. He held up the spectre of Divine vengeance to the "pretended Christians" who practiced this execrable cruelty on innocent blacks. Only by breaking away from the sins of slavery, Keith warned, could Quaker slaveowners and slavetraders avoid "righteous and just judgments." Unlike the Germantown protest, that quietly faded into obscurity, Keith's pamphlet was published, circulated, and widely quoted by later antislavery writers. It is ironic that in later years its author became a missionary for the Society for the Propagating of the Gospel, an organization that steadfastly defended slavery as an institution consistent with Christian principles.

Seing our Lord Jesus Christ hath tasted Death for every Man, and given himself a Ransom for all, to be testified in due time, and that his Gospel of Peace, Liberty and Redemption from Sin, Bondage and all Oppression, is freely to be preached unto all, without Exception, and that *Negroes, Blacks* and *Taunies* are a real part of Mankind, for whom Christ hath shed his precious Blood, and are capable of Salvation, as well as *White Men*; and Christ the Light of the World hath (in measure) enlightened them, and every Man that cometh into the World; and that all such who are sincere *Christians* and true Believers in Christ Jesus, and Followers of him, bear his Image, and are made conformable unto him in Love, Mercy, Goodness and Compassion, who came not to destroy men's Lives, but to save them, nor to bring any part of Mankind into outward Bondage, Slavery or Misery, nor yet to detain them, or hold them therein, but to ease and deliver the Oppressed and Distressed, and bring into Liberty both inward and outward.

Therefore we judge it necessary that all faithful Friends should discover themselves to be true *Christians* by having the Fruits of the Spirit of Christ, which are *Love, Mercy, Goodness, and Compassion* towards all in Misery, and that suffer Oppression and severe Usage, so far as in them is possible to ease and relieve them, and set them free of their hard Bondage, whereby it may be hoped, that many of them will be gained by their beholding these good Works of sincere *Christians*, and prepared thereby, through the Preaching the Gospel of Christ, to imbrace the true Faith of Christ. And for this cause it is, as we judge, that in some places in *Europe* Negroes cannot be bought and sold for Money, or detained to be Slaves, because it suits not with the Mercy, Love & Clemency that is essential to *Christianity*, nor to the Doctrine of Christ, nor to the Liberty the Gospel calleth all men unto, to whom it is preached. And to buy Souls and Bodies of men for Money, to enslave them and their Posterity to the end of the World, we judge is a great hinderance to the spreading of the Gospel, and is occasion of much War, Violence, Cruelty and Oppression, and Theft & Robery of the highest Nature; for commonly the Negroes that are sold to white Men, are either stollen away or robbed from their Kindred, and to buy such is the way to continue these evil Practices of Man-stealing, and transgresseth that Golden Rule and Law, *To do to others what we would have others do to us.*

Therefore, in true *Christian Love*, we earnestly recommend it to all our Friends and Brethren, Not to buy any Negroes, unless it were on purpose to set them free, and that such who have bought any, and have them at present, after some reasonable time of moderate Service they have had of them, or may have of them, that may reasonably answer to the Charge of what they have laid out, especially in keeping Negroes Children born in their House, or taken into their House, when under Age, that after a reasonable time of service to answer that Charge, they may set them at Liberty, and during the time they have them, to teach them to read, and give them a Christian Education.

Some Reasons and Causes of our being against keeping of Negroes for Term of Life.

First, Because it is contrary to the Principles and Practice of the *Christian Quakers* to buy Prize or stollen Goods, which we bore a faithful Testimony against in our Native Country; and therefore it is our Duty to come forth in a Testimony against stollen Slaves, it being accounted a far greater Crime under *Moses's* Law than the stealing of Goods: for such were only to restore four fold, *but he that stealeth a Man and selleth him, if he be found in his hand, he shall surely be put to Death, Exod.* 21. 16. Therefore as we are not to buy stollen Goods, (but if at unawares it should happen through Ignorance, we are to restore them to the Owners, and seek our Remedy of the Thief) no more are we to buy stollen Slaves; neither should such as have them keep them and their Posterity in perpetual Bondage and Slavery, as is usually done, to the great scandal of the *Christian Profession.*

Secondly, Because Christ commanded, saying, *All things whatsoever ye would that men should do unto you, do ye even so to them.* Therefore as we and our Children would not be kept in perpetual Bondage and Slavery against our Consent, neither should we keep them in perpetual Bondage and Slavery against their Consent, it being such intollerable Punishment to their Bodies and Minds, that none but notorious Criminal Offendors deserve the same. But these have done us no harm; therefore how inhumane is it in us so grievously to oppress them and their Children from one Generation to another.

Thirdly, Because the Lord hath commanded, saying, *Thou shalt not deliver unto his Master the Servant that is escaped from his Master unto thee, he shall dwell with thee, even amongst you in that place which he shall chuse in one of thy Gates, where it liketh him best; thou shalt oppress him, Deut.* 23. 15. 16. By which it appeareth, that those which are at Liberty and freed from their Bondage, should not by us be delivered into Bondage again, neither by us should they be oppressed, but being escaped from his Master, should have the liberty to dwell amongst us, where it liketh him best. Therefore, if God extend such Mercy under the legal Ministration and Dispensation to poor Servants, he doth and will extend much more of his Grace and Mercy to them under the clear Gospel Ministration; so that instead of punishing them and their Posterity with cruel Bondage and perpetual Slavery, he will cause the Everlasting Gospel to be preached effectually to all Nations, to them as well as others; *And the Lord will extend Peace to his People like a River, and the Glory of the* Gentiles *like a flowing Stream; And it shall come to pass, saith the Lord, that I will gather all Nations and Tongues, and they shall come and see my Glory, and I will set a sign among them, and I will send those that escape of them unto the Nations, to* Tarshish, Pull *and* Lud *that draw the Bow to* Tuball *and* Javan, *to the* Isles *afar off that have not heard my Fame, neither have seen my Glory, and they shall declare my Glory among the Gentiles, Isa.* 66. 12—18.

Fourthly, Because the Lord hath commanded, saying, *Thou shalt not oppress an hired Servant that is poor and needy, whether he be of thy*

Brethren, or of the Strangers that are in thy Land within thy Gates, least he cry against thee unto the Lord, and it be sin unto thee; Thou shalt neither vex a stranger nor oppress him, for ye were strangers in the Land of AEgypt, Deut. 24. 14, 15. *Exod.* 12. 21. But what greater Oppression can there be inflicted upon our Fellow Creatures, than is inflicted on the poor Negroes! they being brought from their own Country against their Wills, some of them being stollen, others taken for payment of Debt owing by their Parents, and others taken Captive in War, and sold to Merchants, who bring them to the *American* Plantations, and sell them for Bond Slaves to them that will give most for them; the Husband from the Wife, and the Children from the Parents; and many that buy them do exceedingly afflict them and oppress them, not only by continual hard Labour, but by cruel Whippings, and other cruel Punishments, and by short allowance of Food, some Planters in *Barbadoes* and *Jamaica*, 'tis said, keeping one hundred of them, and some more, and some less, and giving them hardly any thing more than they raise on a little piece of Ground appointed them, on which they work for themselves the seventh days of the Week in the after-noon, and on the first days, to raise their own Provisions, to wit, Corn and Potatoes, and other Roots, &c. the remainder of their time being spent in their Masters service; which doubtless is far worse usage than is practised by the *Turks* and *Moors* upon their Slaves. Which tends to the great Reproach of the *Christian Profession*; therefore it would be better for all such as fall short of the Practice of those *Infidels*, to refuse the name of a *Christian*, that those *Heathen* and *Infidels* may not be provoked to blaspheme against the blessed Name of Christ, by reason of the unparallel'd Cruelty of these cruel and hard hearted pretended Christians: Surely the Lord doth behold their Oppressions & Afflictions, and will further visit for the same by his righteous and just Judgments, except they break off their sins by Repentance, and their Iniquity by shewing Mercy to these poor afflicted, tormented miserable Slaves!

Fifthly, Because Slaves and Souls of Men are some of the *Merchandize of Babylon* by which the Merchants of the Earth are made Rich; but those Riches which they have heaped together, through the cruel Oppression of these miserable Creatures, will be a means to draw Gods Judgments upon them; therefore, *Brethren*, let us hearken to the Voice of the Lord, who saith, *Come out of* Babylon, *my People, that ye be not partakers of her Sins, and that ye receive not her Plagues; for her Sins have reached unto Heaven, and God hath remembered her Iniquities; for he that leads into Captivity shall go into Captivity, Rev.* 18. 4, 5. & 13. 10.

Given forth by our Monthly Meeting in Philadelphia, *the* 13*th day of the* 8*th Moneth,* 1693. *and recommended to all our Friends and Brethren, who are one with us in our Testimony for the Lord Jesus Christ, and to all others professing* Christianity.

Robert Piles, "Paper about Negroes," 1698

Robert Piles, "Paper about Negroes," reprinted in *The Friends Intelligencer*, 31 (Apr. 1874):91-92.

Although the early admonitions by the Germantown petitioners and George Keith against slaveholding practices within the Quaker sect produced few substantive changes, other individuals joined their protest. In 1698 Robert Piles, an influential member of the Chester Monthly Meeting, prepared a paper attacking slavery as a violation of religious conviction which could lead to slave terror and uprisings. Piles also confronted the practical questions implicit in abolition efforts—the reimbursement of masters for financial losses sustained upon the release of their slaves and the preparation of slaves for freedom in an alien society. Such questions continued to plague the abolitionist movement throughout the eighteenth century.

Sum time past theyr was sum inclination upon my mind to buy a negro, or negroes, by reason of my English servants being out of theyr times and having a great familie of small children, might bee an help unto mee being for a tearm of life, that I and my children might have ye more liberty, &c.; but theyr arose a question in mee, ye lawfulness theyr of under ye Gospel ministration remembering the command of Christ Jesus, Do unto all men as ye would have all man doe unto you; and wee would not willingly to be slaves tearm of life; also considering yt Christ dieng for all mankind, they being a part, though yet ungathered. I also had heard that they, in theyr own country, did make warr one with another, and sold one another for slaves, and sum being stoln from their country. Now, whether our buying of them do not incurredg rather than discurredg them in that wicked work; I considered, also, that it all friends that are of ability should buy of them that is in this provinc, they being a people not subject to ye truth, nor yet likely so to bee; they might rise in rebellion and doe us much mischief; except we keep a malisha; which is against our principles; and if they should bee permitted to doe us harm, whether our blood will cry inocent whether it will not bee said you might have let them alone. I considered the motion that rose in me to buy off them whether it was not self, knowing hitherto by my moderate and honest indevors I have not wanted food nor raymt, theyrwith bee content, saith ye Apostle; being exercised upon my mind for many dayes considering those things as I was lieng upon my bed as in a sleep I saw myself and a friend going on a road, and by ye roadside I saw a black pott. I took it up, ye friend said give mee part, I said no, I went a little farther and I saw a great ladder standing exact upright, reaching up to heaven up which I must go to heaven with ye pott in my hand intending to carry ye black pot with me, but ye ladder standing so upright, and seeing no man holding of it up, it seemed yt it would fall upon mee; at which I steps down and laid ye pot at ye foot of ye ladder, and said them yt will take it might, for I found work enough for both hands to take hold of this lander, it being so exact upright; at ye foot of this ladder I saw a man that gave those that goeth up this ladder sumthing to refresh them. At this sight I was concerned, and asked the man what this ladder was. Hee said ye light of Christ Jesus, and whoever it bee that his faith bee strong in ye lord, God will uphold that it shall not fall; upon which I awoke and consider this matter, and I found it self must bee left behind, and to lett black negroes or pots alone; but if it bee not lawfull for to buy negroes for term of life in this gospel time, what shall be done with these yt friends have already, whether they ought not to be learned to read english and to put them forward to goe to meetings, and indevors used to convinc them yt ye witness of god might bee reached in them, and whether every quarterly meting should not have full powr to see yt Christian endevors bee used towards them, that if possible they might bee prevailed upon, and if it should please ye lord to open theyr understanding, and bring them mesurably to bee obdient to his hevenly Requiring why should not ye quarterly metings bee proper Judges in setting them free, provided ye maister bee not too much loss and ye servant have not been time enough to Answer his maister then ye quarterly meting may determine ye time wt might bee thought fitt, that no los might be on neyther hand.

Robert Piles

Samuel Sewall, *The Selling of Joseph a Memorial*, 1700

Samuel Sewall, *The Selling of Joseph a Memorial* (Boston, 1700).

Not all controversy surrounding the institution of slavery in these early years was generated within the Society of Friends. In 1700 a Puritan judge of the Massachusetts Superior Court, Samuel Sewall, published a tract entitled "The Selling of Joseph a Memorial." The pamphlet was written during Sewall's legal battle with John Saffin, a wealthy landowner who attempted to keep his black slave in bondage against the terms of a contract providing for the slave's release. After a prolonged and bitter struggle in the courts, the slave was declared free in 1703. The pamphlet, circulated to influential jurists, clergymen, and literary figures during the court battle, refuted numerous proslavery contentions—that blacks were perpetually damned under the posterity of Cham, that the masters were performing a ministerial service in bringing the gospel to the heathen, that slaves were the lawful captives of African wars, and that the institution of slavery was legally sanctioned by the Bible. Antislavery writers waged war against such justifications for over 150 years. As for Sewall, his struggle against slavery had a certain poignancy and redemptive aspect. In 1692 he had been one of the magistrates who sat in judgment of the Salem witches.

Forasmuch *as* Liberty *is in real value next unto* Life: *None ought to part with it themselves, or deprive others of it, but upon most mature consideration.*

The Numerousness of Slaves at this Day in the Province, and the Uneasiness of them under their Slavery, hath put many upon thinking whether the Foundation of it be firmly and well laid; so as to sustain the Vast Weight that is built upon it. It is most certain that all Men, as they are the Sons of *Adam*, are Co-heirs, and have equal Right unto Liberty, and all other outward Comforts of Life. God *hath given the Earth [with all its commodities] unto the Sons of Adam, Psal.*, 115, 16. *And hath made of one Blood all Nations of Men, for to dwell on all the face of the Earth, and hath determined the Times before appointed, and the bounds of their Habitation: That they should seek the Lord. Forasmuch then as we are the Offspring of* God, &c. *Acts* 17. 26, 27, 29. Now, although the Title given by the last Adam doth infinitely better Men's Estates, respecting God and themselves; and grants them a most beneficial and inviolable Lease under the Broad Seal of Heaven, who were before only Tenants at Will; yet through the Indulgence of God to our First Parents after the Fall, the outward Estate of all and every of their Children, remains the same as to one another. So that Originally, and Naturally, there is no such thing as Slavery. *Joseph* was rightfully no more a Slave to his Brethren, than they were to him; and they had no more Authority to *Sell* him, than they had to *Slay* him. And if *they* had nothing to do to sell him; the *Ishmaelites* bargaining with them, and paying down Twenty pieces of Silver, could not make a Title. Neither could *Potiphar* have any better Interest in him than the *Ishmaelities* had. *Gen.* 37, 20, 27, 28. For he that shall in this case plead *Alteration of Property*, seems to have forfeited a great part of his own claim to Humanity. There is no proportion between Twenty Pieces of Silver and Liberty. The Commodity itself is the Claimer. If *Arabian* Gold be imported in any quantities, most are afraid to meddle with it, though they might have it at easy rates; lest it should have been wrongfully taken from the Owners, it should kindle a fire to the Consumption of their whole Estate. 'Tis pity there should be more Caution used in buying a Horse, or a little lifeless dust, than there is in purchasing Men and Women: Whereas they are the Offspring of God, and their Liberty is,

. . . Auro pretiosior Omni.

And seeing God hath said, *He that Stealeth a Man, and Selleth him, or if he be found in his Hand, he shall surely be put to Death.* Exod. 21, 16. This Law being of Everlasting Equity, wherein Man-Stealing is ranked among the most atrocious of Capital Crimes: What louder Cry can there be made of that Celebrated Warning.

Caveat Emptor!

And all things considered, it would conduce more to the Welfare of the Province, to have White Servants for a Term of Years, than to have Slaves for Life. Few can endure to hear of a Negro's being made free; and indeed they can seldom use their Freedom well; yet their continual aspiring after their forbidden Liberty, renders them Unwilling Servants. And there is such a disparity in their Conditions, Colour, and Hair, that they can never embody with us, & grow up in orderly Families, to the Peopling of the Land; but still remain in our Body Politick as a kind of extravasat Blood. As many

Negro Men as there are among us, so many empty Places are there in our Train Bands, and the places taken up of Men that might make Husbands for our Daughters. And the Sons and Daughters of *New England* would become more like *Jacob* and *Rachel*, if this Slavery were thrust quite out of Doors. Moreover it is too well known what Temptations Masters are under, to connive at the Fornication of their Slaves; lest they should be obliged to find them Wives, or pay their Fines. It seems to be practically pleaded that they might be lawless; 'tis thought much of, that the Law should have satisfaction for their Thefts, and other Immoralities; by which means, *Holiness to the Lord* is more rarely engraven upon this sort of Servitude. It is likewise most lamentable to think, how in taking Negroes out of *Africa*, and selling of them here, That which God has joined together, Men do boldly rend asunder; Men from their Country, Husbands from their Wives, Parents from their Children. How horrible is the Uncleanness, Mortality, if not Murder, that the Ships are guilty of that bring great Crouds of these miserable Men and Women. Methinks when we are bemoaning the barbarous Usage of our Friends and Kinsfolk in *Africa*, it might not be unreasonable to enquire whether we are not culpable in forcing the *Africans* to become Slaves amongst ourselves. And it may be a question whether all the Benefit received by *Negro* Slaves will balance the Accompt of Cash laid out upon them; and for the Redemption of our own enslaved Friends out of *Africa*. Besides all the Persons and Estates that have perished there.

Obj. 1. *These Blackamores are of the Posterity of Cham, and therefore are under the Curse of Slavery*. Gen. 9, 25, 26, 27.

Ans. Of all Offices, one would not beg this; viz. Uncall'd for, to be an Executioner of the Vindictive Wrath of God; the extent and duration of which is to us uncertain. If this ever was a Commission; How do we know but that it is long since out of Date? Many have found it to their Cost, that a Prophetical Denunciation of Judgment against a Person or People, would not warrant them to inflict that evil. If it would, *Hazael* might justify himself in all he did against his master, and the *Israelites* from 2 *Kings* 8, 10, 12.

But it is possible that by cursory reading, this Text may have been mistaken. For *Canaan* is the Person Cursed three times over, without the mentioning of *Cham*. Good Expositors suppose the Curse entailed on him, and that this Prophesie was accomplished in the Extirpation of the *Canaanites*, and in the Servitude of the *Gibeonites*. *Vide Pareum*. Whereas the Blackmores are not descended of *Canaan*, but of *Cush*. Psal. 68, 31. *Princes shall come out of Egypt* [Mizraim]. *Ethiopia* [Cush] *shall soon stretch out her hands unto God*. Under which Names, all *Africa* may be comprehended; and their Promised Conversion ought to be prayed for. *Jer.* 13, 23. *Can the Ethiopian change his Skin?* This shows that Black Men are the Posterity of *Cush*. Who time out of mind have been distinguished by their Colour. And for want of the true, *Ovid* assigns a fabulous cause of it.

Sanguine tum credunt in corpora summa vocate
AEthiopum populos nigrum traxisse colorem.
Metamorph. lib. 2.

Obj. 2. *The* Nigers *are brought out of a Pagan Country, into places where the Gospel is preached.*

Ans. Evil must not be done, that good may come of it. The extraordinary and comprehensive Benefit accruing to the Church of God, and to *Joseph* personally, did not rectify his Brethren's Sale of him.

Obj. 3. *The Africans have Wars one with another: Our Ships bring lawful Captives taken in those wars.*

Ans. For aught is known, their Wars are much such as were between *Jacob's* Sons and their Brother *Joseph.* If they be between Town and Town; Provincial or National: Every War is upon one side Unjust. An Unlawful War can't make lawful Captives. And by receiving, we are in danger to promote, and partake in their Barbarous Cruelties. I am sure, if some Gentlemen should go down to the *Brewsters* to take the Air, and Fish: And a stronger Party from *Hull* should surprise them, and sell them for Slaves to a Ship outward bound; they would think themselves unjustly dealt with; both by Sellers and Buyers. And yet 'tis to be feared, we have no other Kind of Title to our *Nigers. Therefore all things whatsoever ye would that men should do to you, do you even so to them: for this is the Law and the Prophets.* Matt. 7, 12.

Obj. 4. Abraham *had Servants bought with his Money and born in his House.*

Ans. Until the Circumstances of *Abraham's* purchase be recorded, no Argument can be drawn from it. In the mean time, Charity obliges us to conclude, that He knew it was lawful and good.

It is Observable that the *Israelites* were strictly forbidden the buying or selling one another for Slaves. *Levit.* 25. 39. 46. *Jer.* 34. 8—22. And God gaged His Blessing in lieu of any loss they might conceit they suffered thereby, *Deut.* 15. 18. And since the partition Wall is broken down, inordinate Self-love should likewise be demolished. God expects that Christians should be of a more Ingenuous and benign frame of Spirit. Christians should carry it to all the World, as the *Israelites* were to carry it one towards another. And for Men obstinately to persist in holding their Neighbours and Brethren under the Rigor of perpetual Bondage, seems to be no proper way of gaining Assurance that God has given them Spiritual Freedom. Our Blessed Saviour has altered the Measures of the ancient Love Song, and set it to a most Excellent New Tune, which all ought to be ambitious of Learning. *Matt.* 5. 43. 44. *John* 13. 34. These *Ethiopians*, as black as they are, seeing they are the Sons and Daughters of the First *Adam*, the Brethren and Sisters of the Last Adam, and the Offspring of God; They ought to be treated with a Respect agreeable.

Servitus perfecta voluntaria, inter Christianum & Christianum, ex parte servi patientis saepe est licita, quia est necessaria; sed ex parte domini agentis, & procurando & exercendo, vix potest esse licita; quia non convenit regulae illi generali: Quaecunque volueritis ut faciant vobis homines, ita & vos facite eis. Matt. 7. 12.

Perfecta servitus paenae, non potest jure locum habere, nisi ex delicto gravi quod ultimum supplicium aliquo modo meretur: quia Libertas ex naturali aestimatione proxime accedit ad vitam ipsam, & eidem a multis praeferri solet.

Ames. Cas. Consc. Lib. 5. Cap. 23. Thes. 2. 3.

Francis Le Jau, Protests against Slavery, 1712

Frank J. Klingberg, ed., *The Carolina Chronicle of Dr. Francis Le Jau, 1706-1717* (Berkeley and Los Angeles, 1956), pp. 107-9; 128-30.

The Society for the Propagation of the Gospel in Foreign Parts (SPG), the missionary arm of the Church of England, nursed a generally conservative view of the slavery question. In fact, many of its ministers were slave holders. Socially dependent on their white parishioners and reluctant to offend their sensibilities, the SPG representatives, although working for the spiritual welfare of the slaves, only rarely attacked the slave system. In 1712, however, Dr. Francis Le Jau, missionary at Goose Greek Parish, *South Carolina, protested vehemently over the torture and horror inflicted upon the slaves. With the number of black inhabitants of South Carolina exceeding whites as early as 1708, it was apparent that the state would be demographically dominated by its black slave population. The ramifications of this racial imbalance would be increased fear and anxiety on the part of the white controlling minority and new steps taken to preserve order and safety. Le Jau's protests against these steps were rebuffed. In 1732 slaves owned by the SPG were identified by the letters S-O-C-I-E-T-Y branded onto their chests.*

[Le Jau to the Secretary, February 20, 1712]

South Carolina Parish of St. James Goose Creek
Feby. 20th 1711/12

. . . I have had of late an opportunity to oppose with all my might the putting of a very unhumane Law and in my Judgmt. very unjust it is in Execution, in Relation to run away Negroes, by a Law Enacted in this Province some years before I came; such an Negroe must be mutilated by amputation of Testicles if it be a man. and of Ears if a Woman. I have openly declared against such punishment grounded upon the Law of God, which setts a slave at liberty if he should loose an Eye or a tooth when he is Corrected. Exod. 21. and some good Planters are of my opinion. I must Informe you of a most Cruel Contrivance a man has Invented to punish small faults in slaves. he puts them in a Coffin where they are crushed almost to death, and he keeps them in that hellish Machine for 24 hours commonly with their feet Chained out, and a Lid pressing upon their stomack, this is a matter of fact universally knowen, when I look upon the ordinary cause that makes those poor Souls run away, and almost dispaire I find it is imoderate labour and want of Victualls and rest. God Alm: inspire the Honourable Society my most Illustrious Patrons to Consider those things so that they may be remedyed for the Encouragemt. of those poor Creatures, . . .

[Le Jau to the Secretary, February 23, 1713]

So Carolina Parish of St. James near
Goose Creek February 23th 1712/13

. . . I will not fail to Acquaint the Society with Some Particular Things wch I think it is my Duty to lay before them And I Submit to their wise Consideration & Judgemt. what Afflicts and Discourages me beyond Expression is to see the pious Designes of the Honrble Society very much Obstructed by the rash Conduct of Some of our Inhabitants. I humbly Apprehend That it is Expected the Missionaries should Endeavor to Promote the knowledge of Christ among the Ignorant Heathens begining with the Poor Negroe & Indian Slaves that live in our families, and Seeking all Opportunities to do good to the free Indians Scattered in the Province till God Gives us meanes to Instruct those Indian Nations that are our Neighbours, Which I firmly hope shall be Accomplished in his own time, But indeed few Masters appear Zealous or even pleased with what the Missionaries try to do for the Good of their Slaves, they are more Cruel Some of them of late Dayes than before, They hamstring main & unlimb those poor Creatures for Small faults, A man within this Month had a very fine Negroe batized, Sensible Carefull & good in all Respects who being wearyed with Labour & fallen asleep had the Mischance to loose a parcell of Rice wch by the Oversetting of a Periogua fell into a River. The man tho Intreated by the Minister of the Parish, who is Brother Maule and some Persons of the best Consideration among us to forgive the Negroe, who had Offended only through Neglect without Malice, thought fit to keep him for several Dayes in Chains, & I am told muffled up that he might not Eat, & Scourge him twice a Day, and at Night to put him into a hellish Machine contrived by him into the Shape of a Coffin where could not Stirr, The punishmt having continued Several Dayes & Nights and there being no Appearance when it should End, the poor Negroe through Despair Ask't one of his Children for a knife & manacled as he was Stabb'd himself with it; I am told this is the 5th Slave that Same man has destroyed by his Cruelty within 2 or 3 Yeares, but he is onely an hired Overseer the Owner of the Slaves lives out of this Province, I own I See everybody almost angry at So much Barbarity, Yet he pretends to go to Church, and they look upon the Man as Guilty of Murder, and So do great many of my Acquaintance who tho not So Barbarous take no Care at all of the Souls of their Slaves, and as little as the[y] can of their bodies I am at a loss when I see them in a praying posture knowing that at the same time they do not love their Neighbour, and what is most Amazeing I cannot make them Comprehend that their Neglect is an habitual state of Sin, I have Seen very Severe Judgemts. . . .

John Hepburn, *The American Defence*, 1715

John Hepburn, *The American Defence of the Christian Golden Rule, or an Essay to Prove the Unlawfulness of Making Slaves of Men. By Him Who Loves the Freedom of the Souls and Bodies of All Men* (n.p., 1715), pp. 1-11; 14-19; 23-36.

In 1715 John Hepburn, a Quaker tailor from New Jersey, published The American Defence of the Christian Golden Rule, *a strident attack on the periwigged, painted-faced, ruffled, laced, powdered, slaveholding class who, with their "twisted Hides and Horse-Whips," robbed blacks of their free will and rights as human beings. Hepburn's remarkable essay catalogued, as no other antislavery piece had done, the evils of slavery: forced labor without pay, violence, cruelty and unlawful punishment, the separation of man and wife, the encouragement of adultery, murder, and war, and its inherent affront to religion. Hepburn included with his essay a section written by an anonymous author entitled, "Arguments against Making Slaves of Men," an exercise which answered numerous proslavery contentions still rampant until the Civil War. Although not a highly educated man, Hepburn had read widely and in his writing used the dialogue form, a literary device especially common in early antislavery literature. His exhortations of the evil effects of slaveholding upon the masters—the idleness, indolence, and corruption of spirit and character—would be preached forcefully but compassionately several decades later by another Quaker tailor from New Jersey—John Woolman.*

The Preface to the Reader

Christian Reader;

It is not singularity or Ostentation that I appear in Print, but my Christian Duty, in Honour to God, and the Salvation and well being of the souls of men, in the Detection of the Anti-christian Practice in *making Slaves* of them who bear the Image of God, *viz.* their fellow, Creature, Man; A Practice so *cruel* and *inhumane*, that the more it is thought upon by judicious men, the more they do abhor it; It being so vile a contradiction to the Gospel of the blessed Messiah.

And if our Negro-Masters were put to it, to bring an Instance that a man denyed the Christian Faith, I think they could not bring a stronger Instance, then that he was found in the Practice of making Slaves of men. And furthermore, I doubt not, but this may be to some a very unwelcome Theam, and they would wonder to find their beloved *Delilah*, the making Slaves of Negros, and others rejected, although the more moderate Christians do full well know, that. I have the Truth on my side. And if these Lines should come to the *Island of Great Britain* (my native Land) I hope the sincere Christians there of all Sects will commend my Christian care, in detecting so gross a corruption as this, crept in by reason of the Fate and Gains it brings to our *American Christians*; And I hope the *learned Christians* there will admonish their *American Brethren*, for putting such an Affront upon the ever blessed *Messiah*, and his glorious Gospel, as this their Practice doth, in making Slaves of Men.

This Practice cannot but be very offensive to sincere and honest hearted Christians, that this Practie should be heard among the Heathen, to harden them in such *heathenish Practices.*

And now, *Reader,* I am going to shew thee a Wonder, and that is, this thirty years that *I* have been in *America,* this Practice has been carried on almost in profound silence, which it is like the Negro-Masters will take it the harder to be opposed now. It is true, *John Tillotson* of *Canterbury* hath two Sermons in print concerning *Restitution,* and he tells them there, that *they cannot have Admittance into Heaven without making Restitution of the wrong done to there fellow Creatures.* And if this be applyed to the wrong done to Negroes, I have Bishop *Tillotson* on my side. This and many other excellent things have dropt from the Pen of that (in many things, no doubt, an) excellent man.

And *Cotton Mather* calls the Inslaving of Negroes, *A crying Sin in the Land.*

And George Fox printed against this Practice, and sent it to the *Barbadoes-Quakers.* Such was the early care of this excellent man above forty years ago; But his Christian Admonition was rejected. It is true, there are some excellent souls among them still, who came out of *Old England,* that have kept their Integrity, namely *John Saltkill, Thomas Chalkley,* and others, who when they see this Abomination acted by their *American Brethren,* they openly bear Testimony in their publick Assemblies, and declare against it (as I am credibly informed) There was another Paper Printed by (I think) *G. Keith* his Party at *Philadelphia;* and half a Sheet was printed against this Practice at *London,* called *the Athenian Oracle,* But the most of all those writings I doubt are destroyed by *Negro-Masters,* that the Reader will find them almost as scarce to be found as the *Phenix* Egg. And last of all, I have appeared against this Practice, although I have lain dormant above this thirty years; for the which I acknowledge my Failure before God and man, and I desire forgiveness of God, and next I desire the forgiveness of man; for the reason that I was silent so long, because I waited for my betters to undertake the work; and if any had appeared in this Work, it is like I had been silent still.

Now whether they will hear or forbear for the future, I hope to be clear of their Blood, and if they will not repent and make Restitution, I cannot help it; for I have faithfully warned them of their Danger; For I earnestly contended for the Truth, and honestly declared against this *Inriching Sin,* in making Slaves of Men. And now I think to end my Preface as I began it, and that is, I chiefly defign the *Honour of God,* and next the *Welfare and Salvation* of Souls. If happily I might be instrumental to deter any one Soul from being catcht with this inriching Sin, or instrumental of the Repentance of Restitution made by one Soul that is and already guilty, then I desire they should give God the Glory, and I make no Question in having my Reward.

And now to find the Longitude,
Many a Man hath gone about,

But the Perpetual Motion,
Our Negro Masters have found out.

New-Jersey,
1st Month, 1714.

John Hepburn

The American Defence Of The Christian Golden Rule

Argument the First.

The more a Man becomes conformable to the Attributes of God, the more just and holy he is, and the more beloved of God, and consequently a more perfect Christian.

First, then, God hath given to man a Free-Will, so that he is Master of his own Choice (whether it be good or evil) and will in no way force and compel the Will of man; yea, not unto that part which is good, far less unto evil, nothwithstanding his Attribute of Omnipotence. And seeing then, it is thus with God and his Creatures, we ought also to do so by our fellow mortals, and therefore we ought not to force and compel our fellow creatures, the Negroes, Nay, not although we judge it for them a better way of living; For when we force their will, this is a manifest Robbery of that noble Gift their bountiful Creator hath given them, and is a right down Contradiction to the aforesaid Attributes of God, and consequently an Anti-Christian Practice And so, those that oppose God and his Attributes, they may expect to incur his Displeasure; So they may find a pregnant Instance in *Pharaoh* and his Egyptian Task-Masters.

2dly. This Practice contradicts Christs command, who commanded us, *To do to all men as we would they should do to us*, or as we would be done by. Now the buying and selling of the *Bodies* and *Souls* of Men, was and is the Merchandize of the Babylonish Merchants spoken of in the *Revelations*. Now the Tyranizing over and making Slaves of our Fellow Creatures, the Negroes, every one knows, or may know, this is not the way they would be done unto.

Now, I have shown you, *first*, That this Practice opposes God and his Attributes, and *2dly*, That it opposes Christ and his Command; And what is this in Effect but to bid Defyance, and to live in Opposition to Christ and his Gospel? and if so, it is a high Degree of an Antichristian Life and Practice.

And now, *my beloved Friends*, who are concerned in this Practice, as you love the Welfare of your immortal Souls, I intreat you (for it is for your sakes I labour) not lightly to look over these considerations, if ye think to receive a *Reward for the Deeds done in the Body*; For how will ye answer when ye are brought before *Gods Tribunal*, and there appear naked and bear before the Son of Man, if ye have lived and dyed in Opposition to his everlasting Gospel, for the Confirmation of which, for our Sakes, cost him his precious Life, and now for a little worldly Interest, got in Opposition to Christ and hs Gospel, by the Bondage and Inslaving of Negroes; the very Reading of which is enough to make all Hearts concerned to tremble. The very thoughts of this makes me declare, for all the Riches and Honours of this world, I would not be found in this Antichristian Life and Practice.

3ly, I have shewed before, That God, who is no respecter of persons, hath given to all men a Freedom of their Wills, to pitch upon their own choice, for both Soul and Body, which are the only parts, next unto the Life, the free donation of our heavenly Father, in this terrestrial world; But it would seem by the Negro-Masters Practice and Arguments, that God did miss the matter, by his Wisdom, when he gave the Negros (his Creatures) the Freedom of their Wills; but our Negro-Masters have found out, by their Inginuity, how to mend this (seeming) Defect, in two respects, to wit, that is to rob them of their Freedom, and make them bond-Slaves and their Posterity forever. And in the next place, they can highly inrich themselves by the Bargain; by the unparallelled and never enough lamented Bondage and Slavery. of those poor Creatures and handy work of God, And can afford to keep themselves with white hands, except at some Times they chance to be besparkled with the Blood of those poor Slaves, when they fall to beating them with their *twisted Hides* and *Horse-whips*, and other *instruments of Cruelty*, too barbarous here to relate, all done in the name of their deservings and correction. And furthermore, they can afford (by their beloved *Diana*, their Slaves) to go with *fine powdered Perriwigs*, and great *bunched Coats*; and likewife keep their Wives idle (*Jezebel-like*) to *paint their Faces*, and *Puff*, and *powder their Hair*, and to bring up their Sons and Daughters in *Idleness* and *Wantonness*, and in all manner of *Pride* and *Prodigality*, in *decking* and *adorning* their Carkasses with poslt and powdered Hair, with *Ruffles* and *Top-knots, Ribbands* and *Lace*, and *gay Cleathing*, and what not; All, and much more, the miserable Effects produced by the Slavery of Negroes; and their Slaves in the *vilest Raggs*, much ado to cover their nakedness, and many of them not a *Shirt* upon their Backs, and some of them not a *Shoe* upon their Foot in *cold Frosts* and *Snow* in the Winter Time, that many of them have their Feet and other members *frozen off*, by reason of their Cruell Usage; and some of them must lie by the *Fire* among the *Ashes*, or be driven out to lie in *Huts* out of Doors among the worst of their *Dogs*, for some of the finest of their Dogs they permit to lie in the bed with themselves.

And they accomodate their Slaves which such Names as these, *Toby, Mando, Mingo, Jack, Hector* and *Hagar*, and such like Names they give their *Dogs* and *Horses*.

And when their Masters see fit they will *hang them up by their Thumbs*, and then command another Negro to beat him so long, as his Master sees fit; this he must not refuse to do, if it were his *own Father*, nay, further, they will force them to be very *Hang-men*, And notwithstanding of all this, some of them must go with a *hung y Belly*, and that which they do get to eat (ye need not doubt but it) is the *worst the House affords*.

Now all that fear God cannot but know that those men who use such Cruelty are not only void of the *Fear of God*, but are even destitute of *humane Civility*, and *Pity* and *Mercy*; Therefore their Example can be no more a Rule for keeping Slaves than it is for using such inhumane Cruelty, which all sober Men abhor; For it cannot be expected that men of such Cruelty have much regard to the lawfulness of what they do, and it is great

Pity that men who are naturally more moderate and merciful should be led to the Practice of an unlawful thing by the Example of the *vilest of men.*

But to return to the Servants of such cruel Masters; By this Description all may see, that they are put under an unavoidable Necessity of having to maintain *Self-Preservation*, an Instinct of Nature belonging to all the Creatures of God; So self-preservation puts them to *steal, rob,* and *lye,* and many other sinfull Actions; nay, some of them when they see themselves surrounded and trappaned with all the Miseries aforesaid, and many more, then they go into Dispair, and miserably *murder themselves*, and som their *Masters*, to get rid of their Tortures and miserable Slavish Life. There was one of them (*I* think) within less then two years ago, shot himself whith a Gun, near his Masters House, within a few miles off the place where I write this lamentable story.

Now for those heinous Sins, as Lying, stealing, Robbing, and Self-Murder; they cannot escape Punishment, by the Justice of God. Now as *I* have said before, they being put under such necessity of sinning, and they themselves being but *Infidels*, I desire the Negro-Masters to inform me, who must answer for all these abominable Sins?

And now, *Reader*, I have given thee a small View of the Usage and Treatment of these poor miserable Slaves; for if I would enlarge upon their Usage, I need write nothing else to swell up a Book to I know not what bigness; The *parting of Man* and *Wife* being such a heinous sin committed by the Negro-Masters, I cannot pass by; The parting the Husband from the Wife, and the Wife from the Husband, and their Children from them both, to make up their Masters Gains, they force them thus to break the seventh Command, and commit Adultery with other strangers, or other mens Wives or Husbands. These and the like Usages, is enough to make them believe, there is no God at all, and harden them in Idolatrous Worship, and make them blaspheme against the holy God, that he takes not immediate Vengeance on such notorious Offenders. And here are the *first three* Commands broken, occasioned by their Masters. And the breaking the *fourth* is evident to all, for some, for want of Food and other necessities, for all their hard weeks Labour to inrich their Master, for to maintain Self-preservation, puts them to work on the First Day of the Week, to supply their pure Necessities, and so break that which their Masters call the Christian Sabbath. And so, here is all the Commands of the first Table broken by them, occasioned by the *Cruelty* of their Masters. And their Children being sold from their Parents, they unavoidably cannot honour them; and here is the breach of the *fifth*. And to get rid of their miserable Tortures, many kill themselves and others; and here is the breach of the *Sixth*. The parting of Man and Wife makes them commit *Adultery* with others; and here is the breach of the *Seventh*. To maintain Self-preservation, they unavoidably must *steal*; and here is the breach of the *Eight*. Then they run away to avoid their Tortures, and when they are catcht their Master will ask them, *Do you not deserve to be hung up and Beat*? and here they must bear False witness against themselves (which is worse than against their Neighbours) and say, *yes, I do, we serve to be hung up and Beat*; and here is the breach of the *ninth*. And when they are in great necessity of Food and Rayment, and have it not of their own, they unavoidably must covet it of their Neighbours, and here is the breach of the *Tenth*.

Now *Reader*, here are all the Ten Commands of God (occasioned by their Masters) broken by them. This is such a Charge, that I doubt it will be too hot or too heavy for the Negro-Masters to answer.

And now that those Christians who *in* their *Baptism* did engage to keep *all Gods holy commands*, should not keep them, but break them themselves and for their own Gains, do lay all manner of unavoidable Necessities upon their Slavs to break them also; This is a poor encouragement for Godfathers indeed.

I may truly say, as *Nestorius* did, who was Arch-Bishop of *Constantinople*, and was banished from them by the prevailing Party in his Time, to the outermost part of the *Roman Empire* among the *Barbarians*, because he said and taught, That *Mary* ought. not to be called the *Mother of God*, but the *Mother of Christ*, and that it could not go down with him to say, that God was a year old, or a Month, or a Day old, &c. As we may read in that great Book Called *Ensebius*, And when he found great Kindness from those Barbarians he wrote a learned and eloquent letter to those Christians that banished him, to this Effect, that *For his Banishment he could undergo it patiently, but his Fear and Lamentation was, that their Actions should go unto the Heathen, that thereby they should be imboldened in* Heathenism, *and give them Advantage to blaspheme against Christ and the Christian Religion*; And so advised them not to be a stop and a Hinderance to that glorious Gospel that had cost so many Lives for the spreading and advancing of it.

Now, I can truly say, that this is my concern as it was the concern of *Nestorius*, that ever the Actions of our *American* Negro-Masters should go unto the *Turks* and other *Heathen* Nations, to harden them in *Mahumetanism* and other *Heathenism*, and to imbolden them to balspheme against Christ and his Gospel, and the purest Christianity.

I with this may come to be the concern of our Negro-Masters, That they be not hinderies, but Advancers of the glorious Gospel, and then I am sure they will be loath to do to any other Man what they would not be done by themselves.

Now, it is not unpossible but that an *American Negro Master* and a *Turk* should meet and discourse this Point betwixt them, And the *Turk* should say,

I am well pleased, Brother that you and we agree so well in this Point, *viz.* in making Slaves of them we can have the Mastery over; And I doubt not but many of us have been at a stand whether it may not be a sin to use our fellow Creatures so cruelly: but now I think it is Time to give over such Doubts, when we see it so mightily practised by the *Christians*, I mean the *American Christians*; I make this Distinction, because it is not practised in *Europe*.

And now, Brother, I would argue a little plainer with you, How comes it to pass, that you find Fault with us for making Slaves of Men, when you yourselves do the same? How can that be an evil and a sin in us, which is a Christian Practice among yourselves? And I hear, that when any of your Slaves turns Christian, and is baptized and receives the Christian Faith, you keep them in perpetual Slavery for all, and so they have no encouragment to turn Christian upon that score, which shews to me, that you have but a small Esteem for your Religion, or at least are very lukewarm for *Proselytes*.

This is worse then *Turks*; for when any of our Slaves turn, and embraces the *Mahometan Faith*, they are no longer Slaves, but presently set free, and many Times preferred to Places of *Trust* and *Dignity*, such zeal have we for Proselytes, and our Religion.

And how comes it that you differ among yourselves in this Practice? for there are some zealous men among you, that both dispute and write against you, and they declare it to be an Antichristian Practice; And the Christians in *Europe* do not practice it. And I have heard that the Gospel was, *Glory to God in the Highest*, and *Peace* and *Good Will to all Men upon Earth*, and that ye should do to all men as ye would they should do to you. And if this be the Gospel of the blessed Messiah, I will tell you plainly, I look upon you to be apostatized in this Point, and I would advise you either to embrace the rest of our *Mahometan* Practices (and then we would receive you) or otherwise to walk more closely to the Rules and Practice of *Christianity*; and not to content yourselves with a Name, and to be a perpetual Scandal to the rest of Christians.

So far *Mahometan*.

And now, *Christians* of after Ages to come, Its not unlikely, but ye may meet with the Force and Assaults of Negro-Masters, as we in this Age have done, (And so, *Christian*, defend thy self as we have done before thee) And so to cloak their Impiety, and to make the best Shew of Pretences they can, they may thus begin.

Negr. Master. Had not Gods People (in all Ages) bond Slaves, bought with their Money?

Christians Answer. So had they their many *Wives* and *Concubines*, and I see no more Reason to plead for Slaves then to plead for many Wives and Concubines. . . .

Negro Master. Hold! I think I have another Proof, which, according to your own Argument, I think will bind you. There is another numerous and famous sect of Christians, called *Quakers*, who by their Practice do show that they have all those aforesaid Marks which thou *hast* nominated, and therefore by consequence of your Argument the only *true* and *real Christians*, and yet there is no People more forward to make Slaves of Negros than they are; And now, if they be infallibly guided in all the other Principles and Practices of *Christianity*, one would think they could not be erroneous in this, *viz*. in making Slaves of Negros. And now, although all my other Arguments should fail, yet this last, one would think, should silence you.

Christians Answer. This, I confess, is the greatest Wonder, to see a People so comformable to the rest of the Principles and Practices of Christianity, induced by the Example of the looser Sorts of Christians, to embrace an enriching Sin, and sacrifice that command of Christ, to do to others what they would not be done by.

And yet I cannot see how they can be a Proof in this, above all other Christians, especially when it is thought by some of the *honest hearted* among them, that about the *eleventh* Year of the eighteenth Century the most of them Sacrificed their primitive Innocence, when they so lovingly agreed and joyned with the other Sects to pay the Souldiers their proportion of Wages to go in the Expedition against their Neighbours of *Canada*; And when they loose their *Innocence*, I know not what they keep that is *lovely* among them.

But here *I* must make a Distinction; There was an honest hearted Remnant among them, that suffered joyfully the spoiling of their Goods in that Day, for the Answer of a good Conscience, and the Defence of the Antient Innocent Principle, in *Denying the use of the Carnal Sword*, Although it was not permitted to be recorded of *suffering for the Truth*, because the most numerous Party of them was guilty; But if the Reader, or any other, should come to question, whether they denyed the Use of the carnal Sword in any sense, for Proof of this, *I* refer such to their *Writings*, Particularly to *Robert Barclay's Apology*, and to the Key wrote by *William Penn*, Where the Reader may see that they deny the Use of the Carnal Sword in any sense, yea, even in *self-preservation*, or so much as in *Self-Defence*, such Innocence was once maintained among them, which made *Robert Barclay* say, that *it was their Innocent Lives* and *Practice that convinced him before he inspected into their Principles*. The Innocent Lives of that People was the motive that convinced this pious learned man. He did not then see them lanching out Money to pay Souldiers to go and kill their fellow Creatures, nor did he see any of them making Slaves of Negroes; These and the like Practices were very remote from that Innocent and harmless People, called *Quakers* in *Robert Barclays* convincing day.

Negro Master. What have we to do with such far-fetch't Proofs? or what was in *Barclay's* Day? I love to keep at home, and the Practice of our *American Christians*; Are there not famous men here among the *Quakers*? and yet they are both Merchants and Masters of Negroes. But I think to argue this Point a little more closely; For before the eleventh year of the eighteenth Century (which is the year thou mentionedst) that they could not be a proof in this Point, more then other Christians, because they joyned with other Sects in the Wars against *Canada*) they had Negro Slaves. But I will bring you to another Instance, *viz*. All the Time preceeding that fore-mentioned Year, particularly *One thousand six hundred ninety two*, when *Andrew Hamilton* was Govenour of the *Jersies*, Did not all the *Quakers* refuse to pay the Souldiers to fight against the French at *Albany*? for the which Refual, great Havock was made of their Goods by Constables. Were not all the *Quakers* at *Amboy* strained, excepting one man that paid to maintain the Wars at *Albany*? And thou sayest, it was no wonder that this man afterward became a Negro-Master; For he was the first of that People that ever I heard of, that sacrificed that Innocent Principle (as thou callest it) and did pay the Rate that was raised to maintain the *Albany* War. Were they not all strained in *Freehold*? And did they not suffer in *Shrewsbury*? was their not a Barrel of Pork rolled out of one of their Cellers in

Shrewsbury, because they refused in any sense to have a hand in the Wars of *Albany*? And yet, all this Time of their Innocence, they did not forget their Interest, but did become Negro-Masters.

I know Practice and Example will go a great way in *Education*, and why should it not go as far in *Argument*? and if it do, *I* have the less to do but make a short Review how *I* have Proved by the Practice and Example of all that diversity of Sects of our *American Christians*, and lastly and mainly by our *American Quakers*.

Now, if what I have said do not amount to a perfect Proof that we may make Slaves of Negros, or any other that we can get the Mastery over, *I* think the *Roman-Catholicks* forever may be silent to bring in the Example and Agreement of the East and West-Orthodox, to be a Proof in that Point of the *Real Presence*.

Christians Answer. There is a good Body of People without the Bounds of your Instance, and that is the *German-Quakers*, who live in *German Town* near *Philadelphia*, Who (to their renowned Praise be it spoken) have above all other Sects in *America*, kept their Hands clean from that *vile Oppression* and *inriching Sin* of making Slaves of their fellow Creatures, the Negros, as I was credibly informed by one of themselves, and so have particular Men of all Sects kept themselves free from this inriching sin.

But now I come to your Instance of *Ninety Two*, that the *Quakers* were all Innocent then, excepting one Man. This amounts to no more then this, that they were an excellent People in that day, far exceeding other Sects of *Christians*, and yet were most shamefully overtaken with this inriching Sin, in breaking Christs Command in making Slaves of Negros, which they would be loath to be done by. Ay, but I have a further Reply to make to you upon that Head (which I think will utterly overturn all that you have said upon it) The *Quakers* had before that Time, embraced *Magistracy*, which cannot be upheld without the *Carnal Sword*, whereby they being apostatized from their primitive Innocency and Purity, and become, in that like the rest of the World, it is no Wonder to see them in a Practice so ageeable to it, in making Slaves of their fellow Creatures for their Gain and Advantage. . . .

Arguments against making Slaves of Men

Argument 1. The *using Mens Labour, and not paying them the Value of it* (*except* the Labourer gives it) is unjust and therefore unlawful.

But the making *Slaves* of Men (whether *Negroes, Indians* or others) is Using their Labour, and not paying them the Value of it.

Therefore the making *Slaves* of *Men* is unlawful.

Arg. 2. Violence is (in ordinary Cases) unlawful, But making *Slaves* of *Men* (against their will) is Violence.

Therefore making *Slaves* of *Men*, is unlawful.

Arg. 3. Punishing Men *without Respect to any Evil they have done*, is unlawful.

But making *Slaves* of *Negros* is punishing *Men* without Respect to any Evil they have done, Therefore the Making *Slaves* of *Negros* is unlawful.

We should think it a sore Punishment to be made *Slaves* ourselves.

Arg. 4. To make men Prisoners, *who have broke no Law*, is (in ordinary Cases) unlawful. But to make Slaves of Negros, is to make men Prisoners, who have broke no Law to deserve it. Therefore to make *Slaves* of *Negros is unlawful.*

Arg. 5. Compelling Men to that which will surely bring them to *Punishment*, is unjust and unlawful.

But making *Slaves* of *Negros*, is compelling men to that which will surely bring them to Punishment. Therefore making *Slaves* of *Negros* is unlawful.

It is a general Observation among the *Negro-Masters*, that *Negros* will not be good without often *Beating*, and that may be (many times) very severe.

Arg. 6. To *banish men their Country*, who have committed no Fault to deserve it, is unlawful.

But to make *Slaves* of *Negros*, is to banish men their Country, who have committed no Fault to deserve it. Therefore, to make *Slaves* of *Negros* is unlawful.

Arg. 7. The necessary laying before Men *Temptations to sin*, is sinful and unlawful.

But making *Slaves* of *Negros*, is a necessary laying before men Temptations to Sin. Therefore the making *Slaves* of *Negros*, is sinful and unlawful.

Experience proves *this*, by the Scores of *Negros* that have murdered themselves, for no other cause but because they were made Slaves and banished their Country.

Arg. 8. Man-stealing (deserves Death by the Law of God, and) is unlawful.

But making *Slaves* of *Negroes* is *Man-stealing*. Therefore making *Slaves* of *Negros* is unlawful.

Arg. 9. Parting Man and *Wife* (procures Gods Curse, and) is unlawful.

But making *Slaves* of *Negros* is (often times) Parting Man and Wife. Therefore making *Slaves* of *Negros* is unlawful; and Those that buy them, partake in the Sin.

Object. They are Heathen, and *make no Scruple of it in their own Country.*

Answer. The more need to avoid doing those things which harden them in their Heathenish Wickedness, and to avoid partaking with them, and making them Worse.

Arg. 10. That which brings People into unnecessary *Danger of their Lives*, is unlawful.

But making *Slaves* of *Negros*, brings People into unnecessary Danger of their Lives. Therefore making *Slaves* of *Negros*, is unlawful.

How many live in *Dangers*, and how many have *lost their Lives* by their own and their Neighbours *Negros*? For they knowing themselves *Slaves*, care little for their Lives, and fear little those Offences for which they must be put to Death.

Arg. 11. That which cannot be done without *Cruelty*, is unlawful.

But making *Slaves* of *Men* for gain, cannot be done without Cruelty. Therefore making *Slaves* of *Men* for Gain, is unlawful.

We should account it the greatest *Cruelty* and *Robbery* to be so dealt by ourselves.

Arg. 12. The using *Men* as if they were *Beasts*, is unlawful.

But making *Slaves* of *Negroes*, is using Men as if they were Beasts.

Therefore making *Slaves* of *Negros*, is unlawful.

Arg. 13. To deface the *Image of God*, is unlawful.

But Robbing Men of their Freedom, is Defacing the Image of God.

Therefore Robbing Men of their Freedom, is unlawful.

Arg. 14. To make *Slaves* of those to whom our Saviour has commanded that his *Gospel should be preached*, is unlawful;

But to make *Slaves* of *Negros*, is to make *Slaves* of those to whom our Saviour has commanded that his Gospel should be preached. Therefore to make *Slaves* of *Negros*, is unlawful.

Arg. 15. To encourage others to make *Slaves* of our *fellow Christians*, is unlawful.

But to make *Slaves* of *Negros*, is to encourage the *Mahometans* to make *Slaves* of Christians. Therefore to make *Slaves* of *Negros*, is unlawful.

Arg. 16. That which is a *Stumbling-block to Unbelievers*, and a hinderance to their Conversion is unlawful, and one of the Worst of Evils. But making *Slaves* of *Negros* (or *Indians*) is a *Stumbling-block* to Unbelievers, and a Hinderance to their Conversion. Therefore making *Slaves* of them, is unlawful, and one of the worst of Evils.

Arg. 17. That which *Weakens the Arguments of Christians against the Heathen*, and has a Tendency to cause some Weak Christians to turn *Mahometan*, is unlawful.

But To make *Slaves* of Negros, does all this. Therefore to make *Slaves* of *Negros* is unlawful.

Christians are inexcusably *required* to make the *Innocence* of their Lives a strong *Argument* to convince such as know not the Truth, *Mat. 5. v. 16.* But by this *Violence* (which was one of the Sins of the *Old World*) and other vices, the Heathen will see no more Excellency in our Religion then in their own.

Arg. 18. The doing by others as we *would not be done by*, is Sinful and unlawful.

But making *Slaves* of *Negros*, is doing by others as we would not be done by.

Therefore the making *Slaves* of *Negros*, is unlawful.

Arg. 19. That which occasions Men to murder one another, is unlawful.

But making *Slaves* of *Negros*, occasions them to murder one another.

Therefore making *Slaves* of *Negros*, is unlawful, and one of the Worst of *Evils*.

The *Negros make War*, and *murder* one another to take Captives to Sell for *Slaves*.

Arg. 20. That which brings a *Reproach upon our holy Religion* is unlawful.

But making *Slaves* of *Negros*, brings a Reproach upon our holy Religion. Therefore the making *Slaves* of *Negros*, is unlawful.

Object. Negroes are more happy when Slaves then free.

Answ. If that were true, so are some *White Men*; but is this a Rule to make them *Slaves*? But for once, we will suppose what some Men say to be true, That *gives a Negro his Freedom* and *give him the Gallows*. It is when they are brought into a Country that does not agree whith their *Constitution* (as might be largely shown) and this shows it the more unlawful to bring them.

Obj. 2. But they Murder one another, and *Tyranize Cruelty over their Captives in their own Country*; and *it is a Merciful Deed to bring them into a Land of Safety, although they be made Slaves by it.*

Answ. 1. That is also too much used among *Christians*, and so the same Argument may be used by the *Turks* to justify their making Slaves of us.

2. If we can help them and prevent such Cruelty, it ought to be by *Teaching them better Examples.*

3. Our Taking of their Captives, does encourage them the more in such Practices.

4. By buying their Captives, we become Partakers with them, and harden them by our Example.

5. Let it be put to the Conscience of such as buy them, whether (ordinarily) any part of their Motive be to help the Miserable? or whether it be purely and only for Gain?

Obj. 3. It is better for a Captive to be made a Slave then to be Murdered.

Ans. 1. I never heard that when a Man saved his Neighbours Life, he was to have him or sell him and his Posterity for Slaves. Suppose he were at cost to do it, a less Reward may compensate that

2. Suppose he had never been a Captive but for the sake of your Buying him, and suppose some others have been killed for the sake of the Price, where is the Kindness then?

Obj. 4. Some Men could not get their Living, if it were not for their Negro-Slaves.

Ans. 1st. Poverty does not make Robbery lawful.

2. Poor Men that cannot get their living without them are not able to buy them.

3. If a man be able to labour, he can so well earn a poor Living (at least) for himself, as his Negro (who cannot labour without Food) can earn a poor Living for *himself*. And if a Man cannot Labour, his Neighbours are indebted to (God that they) help him.

Obj. 5. A Slave that has a good Master has a more comfortable Life than his Master, he being free from care.

Ans. Your way to prove this *Argument* is to give up your self and your Children to be *Slaves* to *good Masters*, and have nothing of your own, and labour as the Negros do, who have good Masters; For if it be not an

Argument for your self, how can you force it to be an *Argument* for another?

Some Negros by being brought into a Christian Country, learn the Christian Faith, and to some of them it becomes the Means of their Salvation, which does Ten Thousand times compensate the Slavery of their whole Life.

Ans. Some Men that are *hanged*, are brought to Repentance by the Expectation of their Speedy Death; Is this a Rule to hang all Persons that take little care for their Salvation because God sometimes (in his mercy) brings good out of evil?

2. We will acknowledge that such Masters as take a diligent care in *this*, do far better then such as use their *Negros* as if they were *Cattle.*

3. I have not heard of one Master in five hundred that do so much as bring their Slaves to the publick worship of God.

4. Grant that you are instrumental of their *Salvation*, Is it not *Simony* in the superlative Degree, when you not only take your Reward of them, and that in this World, and that no less will satisfy you for a little *good Counsel*, &c. than all they have in the World, and their Children after them? And if you will be paid (so excessively) in this world for this good Work, I know not how you can expect your Reward in the Next.

Obj. 7. Canaan was to be a Servant of Servants.

Ans. 1st. A *Prophesy* of what men will do, is neither a *Command* nor *Permission* to do it.

2. It is very unlikely that near one quarter the World [*viz.* all the Negros] should be the Posterity of *Canaan*, who were almost rooted out of the World by *Joshua*; and also that another Quarter of the World, *viz.* the *Indians* of *America*, should be his Posterity too; yea, and the Indians of the *East-Indies* also (for which of them also they make Slaves.)

3. It was not said it should be so to the *End* of the World.

4. The *Canaanites* were Servants to the Children of *Israel* (the seed of *Shem*) in building *Cities* and Raising *Cattle* for them; and so were the *Carthagenians* to the *Romans* (the seed of *Japher*) who soon after received the Gospel.

Obj. 8. The Children of Israel had Lisence from God to make Slaves of the Heathen.

Ans. 1. This was peculiar to the *Jewish Nation*, and no part of the Moral Law; and if any Society of Men can produce the like Lisence to *them*, immediately from God, and prove it, let them keep Slaves also.

2. Then the Church was restrained to that People, but now the Gospel is commanded to be taught unto all People and *Nations everywhere.*

Obj. 9. Perhaps one Sort of People (if they object here as they do in another case) will say, *There is no place in the Bible that has such Words* Thou shalt not make Slaves, &c.

By a Retortion, I would *Answer*, No place has these Words, *Mahomet is a false Prophet*, &c.

Motive 1. Riches gotten by wronging the Labourer, is cursed, see James 5. v. 2, 3, 4, 5. A terrible place to such Men!

Mot. 2. *Killing Men*, must be punished with *Death, because man was created in the Image of God, Gen.* 9. v. 3, 4, 5, 6. And *Man-stealing* must be punished with *Death*; And why? but because *Freedom*, which only makes *Knowledge* useful, is a part of *Gods Image*.

Mot. 3. *If we say, we know him, and keep not his Commandments, we lye, and the Truth is not in us,* 1 *John* 2. v. 4. One of his Commandments is *To do as we would be done by*, Luk. 6. v. 3.

Mot. 4. There are several *Curses* applyed to the *Effect* of making Slaves of Negros, as the *Parting Man* and *Wife*, &c.

Mot. 5. There are several Capital Crimes attending it, as *Murder, Man-stealing*, &c.

Mot. 6. It is a Breach of several Commands at once, As of the *Eight*, in wronging them of their Labour; of the *Ninth*, in the Reproach of Slavery; of the *Sixth*, in Violence and Access to murder; of the *Seventh*, in Access to Adultery, by parting Man and Wife, and so causing them to marry others; of the *First, Second* and *Third*, by bringing a Reproach upon the Name of God in our holy Religion, and so hardening Idolaters; in some, of the *Fourth*, in giving them no Time to play, but on the *Lords Day*.

Mot. 7. We condemn *Robbers* as worthy to dye, because they *Beat-Men*, and sometimes kill them, to take their Money from them. And we *beat* the Negros, and *take them Captives*, and *banish* them from their Country forever, and take their *Wives* and *Children* from them, and sometimes Cause their *Death*, and all to get their Labour from them; which is as much worth as their Money. Can the greatest *Robbers* and *Pyrates* Out-vie us?

Mot. 8. How will our *Religion* look among the *Heathen*! who can judge of it, and of God and of Christ (in whom we believe?) no other way then by our Practice. Is this the way to win them? which we are bound to endeavour; But can we expect it, while we appear to them the *Worst* of Men!

Can we think that God will take this Reproach to his *Name*, and his *Truth*, and not be satisfied in taking Vengeance upon us. And that it may be in the fight of the Heathen.

Mot. 10. What a *Cursed Gain* will this be, if it be the Price of Immortal Souls! Had we instead of Giving them the *Worst of Examples*, endeavoured to learn them *Christ*, from the Time we first knew their Country, what good might have been done!

Mot. 11. Suppose the Case be yet uncertain, in leaving of this Practice, there is no *Danger*; But who would venture so great Injustice upon *Uncertainty*! And stop the Course of the Gospel!

Mot. 12. So long as you do it, not knowing but that it is a sin, so long it is in you a sin; if it were in it self innocent, *Rom.* 14. Ult.

Proposal 1. That *Subscriptions* be taken of all Masters that will set their Negros free, and of the Number of Negros so to be set free, that they may be sent to their own Country.

Prop. 2. That Subscriptions be taken, what each Man (Negro Master, or others) will give to defray the Charge of sending the Negros home.

Prop. 3. That such Negros as had rather serve their Masters, then go home, may be kept still (it being their *Free Act*, and it not being safe to have them free in this Country)

Prop. 4. That the uttermost Pains be taken to instruct them in the Principles of Christian Religion, that (if by the Grace of God they may be *Savingly* converted) they may be instrumental to convert their Country-Men at home; And who knows how much God may bless such *Pious Designs*, and how much this Christian self denying Example may conduce to open the Eyes of those poor Heathen.

And such as are savingly converted, the *Love of Christ will constrain them* to do their utmost to convert their Countrey-Men when they come to them.

Mot. 13. If this Course be instrumental to save *one Soul*, it will a thousand times countervail the Cost.

Mot. 14. The least we part with for the Cause of Christ shall have *an hundred fold* Reward, beside *Eternal Life*, see *Mat.* 10. *ult*, *Mark.* 10. *v.* 30.

Mot. 15. What Pains will men take, and Cross the Ocean for *worldly Gain*! If we will not do something like it for *Spiritual*, it is a sign we have no part therein, *See Mat.* 6. *v.* 21. &c.

Mot. 16. What *Glory* will it be to Eternity, to have been instrumental toward saving one Soul? How much more, toward saving many? *see* Dan. 12. *v.* 3. &c.

Mot. 17. It would be a sad thing in the Day of Judgement to have mens Undoing their whole life, to answer for.

Mot. 18. I know of no other way to make them Restitution for the wrong done them (but the Cost of sending them home to be part, if they desire it) and without Restitution (where it is possible and the Wrong known) we know of no Pardon, *See Levit.* 6. *v.* 4, 5, 6, *&c.*

Mot. 19. We disgrace *our selves*, and our *Religion*, shewing our selves to be *partial* and unreasonable, We condemn the *Turks* for making Slaves of us, and we make Slaves of others. We condemn and *punish* our Negros for seeking by *Running away* to get their Freedom, and yet we should justify ourselves, and one another, in doing the *same*, if we were Slaves to the *Turks*, or any others.

Now, if any one can answer all this, and keep a good Conscience in it, I am content. But if that be done, I have one *Motive* more.

Mot. 20. When the Country grows full of People, and also abounds which Negros, poor People will want Imploy, and must either *beg* or *steal* for their Living, which will be no pleasant thing to *Rich* or *Poor*; and Rich mens Children are sometimes Poor (especially if their Estate be gotten by *Wronging the Labourer*) and (if they Regard not the Honour of God) I believe they would be loath to have their Children hanged for *Thieves*.

But I am amazed to think *Christians* (so called) who keep Negros as if they were Cattle, and had no Soul! Who neither Teach them themselves, nor bring them to Gods Worship, As if they feared the loss of their Money by their Negros Salvation.

These Things I offer to Consideration, desiring wise Men to give their Judgment; for I have no desire to hinder my Country-Men of any Lawful Gain, but cannot believe it lawful to make men Slaves, but I see all these Arguments fully answered, Except they had rather be Slaves, than to go home to their own Country.

Written by a Native of America,
Sept. 14, 1713.

Ralph Sandiford, *A Brief Examination*, 1729

Ralph Sandiford, *A Brief Examination of the Practice of the Times, by the Foregoing and the Present Dispensation: Whereby is manifested how the Devil works in the Mystery, which none can understand and get the Victory over but these that are armed with the Light, that discovers the Temptation and the Author thereof, and gives Victory over him and his Instruments, who are now gone forth, as in the Beginning, from the true Friends of Jesus, having the Form of Godliness in Words, but in Deeds deny the Power thereof; from such we are commanded to turn away* (Philadelphia, 1729), preface; pp. 1-10; 63-74.

George Keith was not the only member to be disowned by the Quakers for his virulent attacks on slavery. Ralph Sandiford later suffered the same fate. Sandiford, a former British trader from Liverpool, once worked for a South Carolina planter and had witnessed the brutal treatment of slaves in the fields. Later, as a merchant in Philadelphia, he saw black merchandise bartered on the auction block. The sight of Quakers trading and profiting from this barbarous practice was, to the sensitive Sandiford, an abomination. When in 1729 his friend Benjamin Franklin agreed to publish the essay, "A Brief Examination of the Practice of the Times," Sandiford became the victim of threats, ostracism, and, finally, disownment. To Sandiford human slavery symbolized moral putrification, a surrender of innocence, a foul spiritual pollution. ". . . The more Men have pretended to Religion," he charged, "the more dark they have been striving to cover their Sin." He called the slaveholding Quakers "False Brethren" who had known the evils of slavery and had succumbed to idleness, greed, and iniquity. For Sandiford, the question of slavery was the supreme test of religious purity; and he maintained that a large number of religious hypocrites failed the test miserably. Broken and ill from the attacks against him, Sandiford abandoned Philadelphia to live in the countryside, where he died in 1733 at the age of forty.

The Preface

My Friendly Reader, Under the Consideration of the Shortness of the Life of Man, and the End for which he was created, engaged my Mind to the Lord that he would make known his Truth unto me, beyond Custom or Tradition in which most content themselves. And though in the Time of Ignorance the Lord winks, and the Sincere in Heart in all Societies and Gatherings are owned by him, yet if he farther manifests himself, who shall withstand him? Tho' in Believing I made not haste, but desired to try all Things, and hold fast by that Universal Love I was then a Witness of, in which I travelled in my Spirit for the Freedom and Redemption of the whole

Body, as being a living Member thereof; Tho' I am sensible it would much more have been recommended to thy Perusal, had it been done by an abler Hand, as many there are under the same Suffering, to the Overthrow of the Faith of some. Yet rejoice not thou over such, but be warned by them, lest thou also fall. Yet to the Glory of the Grace and Power of the Lord, who causes Good to redound from Evil to those that love him (which does not excuse the Evil-Doer) that many have known Deliverance from this Atheistical Practice, and the Offence given by it, being thereby drove into the Sanctuary, where they have seen the Ground and Nature thereof, and the Fruit is brings forth, the End of which is for the Fire; Therefore with a single Eye to the Lord, and as it concerns thy own Eternal Welfare, let it have its due weight with thee before thy Day is determined, and receive it as a Token of Love, and in that Simplicity in which it is committed unto thee, in as few Words as my poor Capacity and the Ease of my Spirit will admit of, without the least Prejudice to any Mortal, much less to the Cause of the Gospel, or the true Ministers thereof, who are for the Gathering of all Nations into the same Love; and they that despise them in that, despise him that sent them; and they that deny him and his Gospel before Men, them will he also deny before his Father and the Holy Angels: Yet we are forewarned by our Lord, to try the Spirits which would go forth to deceive, if possible, the very Elect; and the Apostles saw them gone forth from amongst them, recommending the Believers for their Protection against such, to the Holy Unction in them, in which they discern the Voice of the Lord from the Stranger's, who never since his Fall could bear the Light, much less his Instruments, therefore it is a sure Defence to the Righteous; for if the Trumpet give not a certain Sound, who shall prepare for the Battle? Shall such then, who preach Christ in Words. but in Actions are Antichrist, bring forward the Church, or perfect the Saints Faith, who in this Practice are an Offence to both *Jews* and *Gentiles,* and to the Church of God. And let none think this too uncharitable a Judgement, considering the Nature of this Sin, seeing the Least unrepented of is damnable, yet the greatest Sin against Christ as the Son of Man, with true Repentance (which is always accompanied with Forsaking and Restitution) is pardonable through the great Mercy of our God in his Son, which brings Joy to the very Angels in Heaven, and to his Church and Ministers on Earth, whose Hearts and Souls are open for the Gathering of such unto God.

Our Friend *George Fox*, in a Sermon taken in Shorthand as it was preached at a Monthly-Meeting in *Barbados*, tho' in the Beginning of Time, when many were convinced that had Slaves, he advised them to use them well, and to bring them up in the Fear and Knowledge of God, and after a reasonable Service to set them free, as we may also see in his *Journal*; pag. 354. which was far from encouraging them to buy more after their Convincement: For if they had gone back again into that Trade, what had their Convincement done for them, but bring them into greater Judgment for their Disobedience to the Manifestation? For before Friends were a People, many of them were valiant Men with the Sword, for which they were had in great Esteem amongst Men, because thereby they sought the Nation's Deliverance from the Oppression of Priests, Physicians and Lawyers, the One making a Trade of the Soul, the Other of the Body, and the Other of the Property of the People: And when our Friend *George Fox* was called forth by the Lord to minister, not in the Wisdom of Man, for in that he was unlearned, but in the Openings of Truth, which manifested to him wherein all these were out of the Way, and that by the Universal Grace all might be restored in their Services, both for the Good of Soul and Body; which caused these Worthies to lay down their Swords, as unfit for the Carrying on of so great a Work, which must be done by a higher Power, in which they went forth, having the Sword of the Spirit, which gave them Victory over Principalities & Powers, and Spiritual Wickednesses in High Places: And while Friends stood here, testifying against this Practice, and against every Thing that is high and lifted up, as inconsistent with this glorious Day, then did the Work prosper, that large Meetings were settled herein and flourished. But in Time this dark Trade creeping in amongst us, to the very Ministry, because of the Profit by it, hath spread over others like a Leprosie, to the Grief of the Honest-hearted, that they are constrained to sojourn in Mesech or dwell in the Tents of Kedar, the Habitation of Blood; which the hired Preachers that live by the Law, have testified against, as the highest Immorality which some have gone into when all others have failed them, whereby their Hearers have been convinced by them of the Evil of it. And shall we fall short and lay Waste the Ancient Testimony, which was and is for the Bringing down of all Oppression and Violence, that instead thereof Everlasting Righteousness may be established, and we may have Confidence before God that we have a Conscience void of Offence both towards God and towards all Men, is the fervent Desire of

Thy Friend in the Truth,

R.S.

A Brief Examination of the Practice of the Times

My Friend, Whomsoever Thou art that deals in *Slaves*, or hath had any Fellowship therewith, in the Love of God that desires the Peace and the Restoration of the whole Creation, do I now Salute Thee, that thou mayest consider that Principle and Foundation on which this Practice stands, since for every idle Word we must give an Account, and on all our Actions are established an Eternity, and whomsoever we yield ourselves to Obey, his Servants we are, whether of Sin unto Death, or of Obedience unto Life.

For what comes from God, leads unto God; and what comes from the Devil (who became such by Rebellion) unto Death and Hell, where he is Centred; from whom, all Wrath and Violence proceeded. He was not Created such, nor his Angels, as is observed in the Epistle of *Jude*, that they fell from their first Estate, and from their Habitations God created them in: Which great Fall and Debasement to *Lucifer*, so proud a Spirit that he is termed the Son of the Morning, and being thus defeated in his evil Purpose, raised in him a Principle of Envy against God, and all the Creation, which the Lord made very good, according to his own Nature, and made Man the Top of the Creation, a living Soul, an Image of his own Eternity, who is all Love and Goodness in himself, and his Works are accordingly; and while Man stood in this upright Life, all was perfect Peace and Love, throughout the whole Creation of God, until Evil was introduced by the Insinuations of the Serpent, that envy'd the Happiness thereof, and enticed our first Parents to Eat of the forbidden Fruit, that was good of itself, being created by the Lord, but Evil unto them, in that they disobey'd the Holy Commandment. So that the Lord Created not Death, neither, has he Pleasure in the Destruction of the Living, but thro' Envy of the Devil came Death into the World; and they that do hold on his Side, do find it so, drawing it to them, by Disobedience; as *Eve* immediately and *Adam* Instrumentally, giving Ear to the Temptation, whereby the Mind became captivated to Lust, which being Conceived brought forth Sin, and Sin finished brought forth Death, both to the inward and the outward Man, and a Suffering and Degeneracy, throughout the whole Creation, which groans and travels in Pain to be Delivered, even until now, through the Evil Property and barbarous Disposition of the Natural Man; yet through the Mercy and good Will of God, in the Promised Seed of the Woman, he was not thus left, but put in a Capacity of being restored to his Original Purity and Uprightness, whereby he Governs the Creation, in Love and Tenderness, that they partake of the Benefit of his Redemption.

And these two Births are eminently shewed unto us in *Cain* and *Abel*; *Abel's* Geniture being of the Lord, through the Promised Seed, unto which he was united, gave his Sacrifice Acceptance, which raised Envy in *Cain*, who rejecting this high Birth, as many now do, he became One with the Evil Property that was introduced by his Father the Devil; and his Works of Violence and Oppression (the height of Wickedness in respect to Men) he brought forth, which in Time spread over the whole Earth, for which the Lord destroyed them by the Deluge: And thus *Cain's* Race ended, but his Image and Life remains in all them that Act in the same Principle.

Neither can these Negroes be proved, by any Genealogy, the Seed of *Ham*, whom *Noah* Cursed not, faith *Josephus*, as being too nigh of Blood: But *Noah's* Curse on *Canaan* the youngest Son of *Ham*, is thought a suitable original for the Negro Trade: But the Curse is not so extensive, as you would have it, but is thus expressed, *Cursed be* Canaan, *a Servant of Servants shall he be, unto his Brethren*. So that he was to Serve the meanest of the Offspring of *Shem* and *Japheth*; but the Time came that the *Canaanites* were destroyed with a Mighty Destruction, according to the Promise of the Lord, *Deu*. vii. 23. and *Josephus*, Lib. 4. Chap. 8. and other places. And their Land given unto the Seed of *Abraham*, as the Lord shewed him in a Vision, when he sojourned therin amongst the *Canaanites*, that then had Possession of it, *Genesis* xii. 6, 7. also *Judges* the v. *Deborah* in her Song, rejoyces that the very Stars in their Courses fought against *Sisera*, which is more fully expressed by *Josephus*, Lib. 5. Chap. 1. & 6. that the Lord fought against the *Canaanites*, with Hosts of Judgments, until they were destroyed: So that their Race is ended, as well as that Dispensation; how then can these Negroes or Indians be Slaves to Christians, who are the Lord's Freemen? But if these Negroes are Slaves of Slaves, according to the Curse; Whose Slaves then must their Masters be? . . .

And what greater Unjustice can be Acted, than to Rob a Man of his Liberty, which is more Valuable than Life; and especially after such a manner as this, to take a Man from his Native Country, his Parents and Brethren, and other natural Enjoyments, and that by Stealth, or by way of Purchase from them that have no Right to sell them, whereby thou receivest the Theft, which is as bad. And take them amongst a People of a strange Language, and unnatural Climates, which is hard for them to bear whose Constitutions are tendered by the Heat of their Native Country; for God that made the World, and all Men of one Blood, that dwell upon the Face of the Earth, has appointed them Bounds of their Habitations, *Acts*, 17. 26. Shall we then undertake to remove them, wheresoever Interest shall lead us, to sell them for Slaves, Husband from Wife, and Children from both, like Beasts, with all their Increase, to the vilest of Men, and their Offspring after them, to all Eternity: Oh! hard Lot! Oh! Eternal sinking in Iniquity; without Bottom or Bounds, as to the Will of Man, therefore as *Jacob* said, of *Simeon* and *Levi, Instruments of Cruelty are in their Habitations; O my Soul, come not thou into their Secret, nor be united in their Assembly; for in their Anger they slew a Man,* (but these have slain many) *Cursed be their Anger, for it is fierce, & their Wrath, for it is cruel,* to keep the Creature thus in Bondage, whereby we entail Sin on our Posterity, *ad Infinitum*, tho' our Saviour says, he that dies therein, where he is gone shall never come. Like the *Jews* when they crucified Christ, desired his Blood might remain on them and their Children; and yet so blind were they, as many are now, thro' being accustomed to Sin, that they see not this Trade to be an Evil, tho' it is manifest to a Child in the Light: But if the Light in us becomes Dark, how great is that Darkness, that sees not the Ground and Tendency of this Practice, and the Design of the Enemy against the Church of Christ, in causing the Name of God to be Profaned, and the Truth to be Evil spoken of; as though the Principles thereof led to it; which has Scandalized and hindered the Gospel of Christ among the Heathen, and Burthened the Upright, and offended tender seeking Souls, and caused them to dwell as alone, from all Societies, where this Practice is indulged, and especially in the Ministry, lest they should have Fellowship with that, that contradicts the Gospel of Christ; and yet desires nothing more, than to be One with the Spirits of those that are not defiled with this Iniquity, that now. Works in the Mystery, in this Time of Peace, amongst those that pretend to the Dispensation of the Son of God, and yet have not fulfilled the Law of *Moses*, unto which Negroe Masters would recur for the Justification of their Practice; but let all such be Silent in the Cause of the Gospel, neither let them charge the Law of God foolishly, which expressly forbids either the Stealing of Men, or the receiving them, under the Penalty of Death. Ex. 21. 16. Therefore deceive not thy own Soul, for according to thy Sowing so shall thy Reaping be; if to the Flesh, Corruption, but if to the Spirit, Everlasting Life.

Had Friends, stood clear of this Practice, that it might have been answered to the Traders in Slaves, That there is a People call'd *Quakers* in *Pensilvania*, that will not own this Practice in Word or Deed, then would they have been a burning and a shining Light to these poor Heathen, and a Precedent to the Nations throughout the Universe, which might have brought them to have seen the Evil of it in themselves, and glorifyed the Lord on our Behalf, and like the Queen of the *East* to have admired the Glory and Beauty of the Church of God. But instead thereof, the tender Seed in the Honest-hearted is under Suffering, to see both Elders and Ministers as it were cloathed with it, and their Offspring after them filling up the Measure of their Parents Iniquity; which may be suffered till such Time that Recompence from him that is just to all his Creatures, opens that Eye the God of this World has blinded. Tho' I would not be understood to pervert the Order of the Body, which consists of Servants and Masters, and the Head cannot say to the Foot, *I have no need of thee*; but it is the Converting Men's Liberty to our Wills, who have not, like the *Gibeonites*, offered themselves willingly, or by Consent given their Ear to the Door-post, but are made such by Force, in that Nature that desires to Lord it over their Fellow-Creatures, is what is to be abhorred by all Christians. . . .

But some object, that they may be brought to the Christian Religion thereby, which is the greatest of Charity. Which discovers the great Darkness this Trade brings with it; tho' the Apostle faith of such, that do Evil for Good to come, their Damnation is just; and it is well known that the Ground of this Trade had no such intention; however our Saviour's Rule discovers it, *By the Fruit the Tree is known*, which produces amongst us no such Consequence; for how should you be Instruments to gain them to the Gospel, who have joined, or had Fellowship with their Enemies in Countenancing the Trade, by receiving of the Benefit; but Christ's Church will not be built up by that Power, who is able to take the Kingdom from others, and give it unto them.

And tho' they may be bad in their own Country, yet Vengeance is the Lord's, and he will repay it in his own Time.

And some also offer, that they are under such a Necessity to be supported by the Labour of Bondslaves, that they cannot live without them. So might the Masters of the Gally-Slaves answer; But if it is so, it were better to lose that Life, that we may find a Life in Righteousness; which I am sensible, in the lowest Ebb of Poverty, cannot submit to any unjust Means for a Living, and yet begs not its Bread, but knows its Support from the Providence of God, which causeth the Grass to grow for the Cattle, upon whom the Eyes of all Creatures wait, and he gives them their Food in due Season; who opens his Hand, and satisfies the Desire of every living Thing; and shall we distrust this Providence, who are under the Gospel, unto whom the Promise is, if we seek the Kingdom and the Righteousness thereof, all other Things shall be added; sufficient for the Day is the Evil thereof; and much more the Ministers of the Gospel who are to live by it; for surely, if you overflow in Spirituals, that you are able to minister unto the Church for the Good of Souls, you need not go back to the Heathen for Support in Temporals: Yet if these Things offered are contrary to the Openings of Truth in any Soul, let not such be wanting in tender Love to inform me better; which I have endeavoured in a private Manner, but received not the least Satisfaction of its Consistency with either Nature, Reason, Humanity, or Morality, and much less with Christianity: Therefore, because of the Love that I bear to Truth and Justice, it remained as a Burden to my Life, until I in some Measure, according to my weak Capacity, expressed my self after this Manner, to lay open the Ground and Nature thereof, as a Caution to those that have not considered it, and that I might discharge my Conscience, before I go hence, as a Duty incumbent to my Brethren; that we may all see our Place and Service in the Creation, during our short Abode in Time, that nothing may hinder our Happiness to Eternity; and tho' some should resist the Truth until their Understandings become dark to that Principle, which would have discovered it fully unto them, in the Day of their Visitation, yet the Truth and its Witnesses will be clear of their Blood; tho' their Loss, as *Jerusalem's*, may be lamented, in that they have resisted so many Visitations of the Love of God; whereby they might, as pruned Branches, have shewn forth the Work of the Husbandman, and displayed unto the Heathen throughout the Earth, the Nature of the Vine that bore them; and then Beautiful would they have appeared unto them, being shod with the Preparation of the Gospel of Peace, but terrible as an Army with Banners, against the Whore and all her unrighteous Merchandize. . . . Ah! my Friends! the Consideration of these Things hath been Sorrow of Heart (beyond what may be mentioned) to those that have considered the Worth of Souls. Let such behold and see, if there is any Sorrow to be compared to it; which I would rather have chosen to have bewailed in the Wilderness, were it the Lord's Will, than thus to have appeared against a Crime so much in Request; which promotes Idleness in the Rich, being furnished with Slaves, that it hinders the Poor from Bread; which are Evils in the Commonwealth, and no Doubt had their due Weight with our late Assembly, who in a great Measure have discountenanc'd the Trade, which has given them Honour in the Hearts of the Just, who are refreshed thereby, whose Supplications are to the Lord, that he would prosper the Work in their Hands, and rejoice that there are those that seek the Good of both Church and State.

And in the same Love that desires the Welfare of both, is this freely given, that it may be spread by the Readers amongst such as are concerned in the Trade, or otherwise, as you may see its Service in Righteousness; without striking at any Creature, but at the Evil in all, that the Cause may be removed, and that the Creation may be governed by Love, and this Practice disowned in all Mankind, and especially by all that name the Name of Jesus, that every Creature under the whole Heavens may be delivered from Oppression, as well as

Ralph Sandiford.

To My Select Friends

Dear Friends and Brethren, If any are offended with me, or the foregoing Treatise, because it came not forth with the Concurrence of the Meeting, it is in my Heart to desire your Freedom with me therein, that all Offences may be removed according to the Ability the Lord gives me.

If the Circumstance of the Meeting had been such, it would have been Joy unto me, whereby I should not have known the Baptism I have been baptized with thro' those that were as my Life, being begotten by the same Love, into the Faith which gives Victory over the Spots of the World: and shall we forsake this Hand, to take to the Arm of Flesh, and captivate the Heathen for our bodily Support? The Sense of it hath burdened my Life Night and Day, to behold such go into it, to the corrupting of the World, that they see no Harm in selling them at Vendues like Beasts, in a Christian Country, where we are called forth into that Power thro' which we might have kept it out of both Church and State, which now does more Hurt amongst us than either *Atheists* or *Deists*: And this I offer as a true Witness; that it were better we had never known the Truth, than afterwards to charge Sin on it, as tho' it admitted of such Practices. He that can receive it, let him; if otherwise, I leave it to God the Judge of all, before whom, and the whole Host of Heaven, the Truth thereof will be manifested; and in the Interim I have eased my Spirit in as soft a Stile as I could, to remove that Burden under which I was crushed as under a Mountain, thro' this Earthliness in the esteemed Religious, which so darkned my Understanding, that all seemed lost unto me, being swallowed up in it thro' the Violence of the Tempest, that the Elements which should have been Subjects, prevailed over me, which put Nature out of Course, to the defacing of the whole Body, that I was as a Sign unto you because thereof; and then as tho' the Rod was on my own Back, I suffered with them in the natural Body, in which I would vindicate them in such Language as proceeded from the Exasperation of Oppression; which I am not about to vindicate, but to acknowledge my Infirmities under the Provocation, and the Lord's Mercies in my Deliverance, who knows whereof we are made, and remembers that we are but Dust; that tho' I was as swallowed up in Desperation, yet he caused the Sea to be still, that I might sing of my Deliverances from Ægypt's Bondage and Darkness, and my Preservation thro' the Sea, where I was tossed in Heights and Depths more than on the outward Ocean, that I was given up as fewel for the Fire of Hell; in all which I beheld the Works of the Lord, and his Wonders in the Deep, where he caused his Light to shine again upon me, and mine Eye to see beyond the Iniquity; whereby he restored me to the Land of the Living, where I am known unto you; on which I can subscribe my self unto all Mankind,

Your Friend,

R.S.

Elihu Coleman, *Testimony against Making Slaves of Men*, 1733

Elihu Coleman, "A Testimony against that Anti-Christian Practice of making Slaves of Men, wherein it is shewed to be contrary to the Dispensation of the Law and Time of the Gospel, and very opposite both to Grace and Nature," reprinted in *Friends' Review*, 5 (1851):84-85; 102-4.

Not all Quaker antislavery writers faced the bitterness and antagonism that was directed at George Keith and Ralph Sandiford. In 1733 Elihu Coleman, a Quaker carpenter from Nantucket, Massachusetts, published the first antislavery pamphlet approved by an official body of Friends. As early as 1716 the Nantucket Monthly Meeting determined "that it is not agreeable to truth for Friends to purchase slaves and hold them term of life" and in 1729 members of the Nantucket Meeting addressed the Yearly Meeting at Philadelphia on the question of purchasing slaves. If a majority of Quakers in the American colonies remained indifferent to the issue of slavery, members of some Monthly Meetings, such as that at Nantucket, aggressively assailed the slavetrading and slaveholding practices of their brethren. Elihu Coleman's essay, sanctioned by the Nantucket Meeting, primarily attacked slavery as anti-Christian, but it also asserted that because men were created with a free will slavery violated the right of black men to make critical choices between good and evil. As the antislavery literature in the American Revolutionary period increasingly emphasized the Enlightenment concepts of natural rights, this assertion became more common. But Coleman's essay did not lack impact. Demolishing the proslavery argument that blacks were meant to be slaves because of their wickedness and ignorance, Coleman said, "If that plea would do, I do believe they need not go so far for slaves as now they do."

Such have been the love and goodness of God to men, that in all ages of the world he has had a people, family or church whom he hath called and also chosen, to bear a testimony to his name and truth. Yet it may be observed by them that read the Holy Scriptures, that those people whom he had called, and favoured above all the families of the earth, and had wrought signs and wonders for them, and had exalted them in the sight of their enemies; that those people in times of liberty and ease, grew forgetful of God. This aptness to forget God in the time of ease, the Apostle Paul well knew, after that he had a thorn in the flesh, or the messenger of Satan to buffet him (as he calls it,) for before he was afflicted he went astray, therefore he knew chastisement or affliction to be profitable for him, and could then say, I take pleasure in infirmities, in reproaches, in necessities, in persecutions, in distresses for Christ's sake: For when I am weak, them am I strong. 2 Cor. xii. 10. It may be also observed by them who read the Book of Martyrs or sufferings of the people of God, from the time our Lord was crucified, down to the reign of the bloody Queen Mary, (which history I do believe is believed to be true by most protestants,) that in all that length of time, God had a people whom he had called out of the worship, ways and customs of the world, who were a suffering people, and that in the midst of their greatest sufferings, they were the most immediately upheld by the

Divine power of God; so that they could even rejoice in the flames. But when it pleased God that a good King or Emperor came to rule, so that they were not persecuted or oppressed, that they grew forgetful of God, and some of them became oppressors themselves. Now I do believe that God sometimes afflicteth outwardly, and sometimes inwardly, who best knows the rod that is suitable to chastise them. We may observe also how it hath been with our elder friends, who were a harmless and suffering people, who did not only bear testimony in word, but in practice also, against all outward and carnal weapons; which our friend Robert Barclay observing, said, that it was their innocent lives and conversation that convinced him, before ever he inspected into their principles. He did not see them in this practice of making slaves of their fellow creatures, which practice is upheld by the carnal sword only, but he bore a testimony against the carnal sword, and would not allow of it to be used, although it were in self preservation. Such innocency was in that worthy man, as well as many others in that day, that they would not allow of this practice, having more regard to that command of Christ, (to do to others as we would they should do to us) than to any outward advantage in this world. And after our friend George Fox had travelled in the island of Barbadoes in the West-Indies, where he saw this practice of making slaves, even to that degree, that their houses were black with them, that he bore open testimony against it; when he got home he wrote a little book to them, wherein I find these words,

"And if thy brother, an Hebrew man, or an Hebrew woman, be sold unto thee, and serve thee six years, then in the seventh year thou shalt let him go free from thee, and when thou sendest him out free from thee, thou shalt not let him go away empty: thou shalt furnish him liberally out of thy flock, and out of thy floor, and out of thy wine-press, of that wherewith the Lord thy God hath blessed thee, thou shalt give it to him. And remember that thou wast a bondman in the land of Egypt, and the Lord thy God redeemed thee: therefore I command thee this thing to day." Deut. xv. 12, 13, 14, 15. See here this was to be done by the Jews to such as were of their own people; and indeed this will very well become christians, masters, governors and rulers of families here in this Island and elsewhere, who should outstrip the Jews to deal (as the Lord commanded) with their servants and apprentices, that were of their own nation or people; and to close up all, let me tell you, it will doubtless be very acceptable to the Lord, if so be that masters of families here would deal so with their servants the negroes and blacks whom they have bought with their money, to let them go free after a considerable term of years, if they have served them faithfully: and when they go and are made free, let them not go away empty handed. This I say will be very acceptable to the Lord, whose servants we are, and who rewards us plentifully for our service done him, not suffering us to go away empty. For "who is there even among you," saith the Lord, "that will shut the doors for nought? neither do you kindle a fire on mine altar for nought." Mal. i. 10. So now you, I say, that are Christians, that are redeemed out of the spiritual Egypt; for as the Apostle saith, 1 Cor. vii. 22, "He that is called in the Lord being a servant, is the Lord's free-man," that is, set free from sin, and spiritual bondage. Be ye holy, as your heavenly Father is holy; and be ye merciful, as your heavenly Father is merciful; as is commanded you in Luke vi. 36. And this is the way to have the lost image of God restored and renewed in us; therefore I say, you spiritual Jews, you must exceed the outward Jews in this, who are come to Christ, who is a merciful and faithful High Priest, who is the Saviour of all men, and who tasted death for all men. Heb ii. 17.

And let not your families of white and blacks be like Sodom and Gomorrah, like Zeboim, and the rest of the cities of the plain, or like the Canaanites; lest sudden destruction come upon you, and the Lord root you out as he did them. Let not, I say, your servants under your command, and such as are born in your houses, and bred up in your families, and such as you have bought with money, suffer them not (I say) to take husbands and wives at their pleasure, and then leave them again when they please, and then take others again as fast and as suddenly as they will, and then leave them; this is not well, this may bring the judgments of God upon you; yea, this manifests your families to be unclean and adulterated families.

Now by these words (though but a small part of what he wrote) we may see that he was against making slaves of men. Now I do believe if men were ingenuous to acknowledge to the truth, even as their consciences bear them witness, I need not go any farther for a proof against this practice: but because they did not, I will turn also to the Holy Scriptures, that so they that are in this practice may be condemned by both.

First, we may observe, when God had created man, that he gave him a free will, and would not compel the will of man, no not to that which was good, much less to that which was evil; therefore we ought not to compel our fellow creatures.

Objection.-But had not God's people bond-servants in all ages of the world, bought with their money? To which I answer, that in all the time of the law they had bond-servants bought with their money; but the Apostle saith, "The servant abideth not in the house for ever." Now the word *servant* I understand to be but for a time, but the word *slave* forever. And those that merchandised in slaves we may find were Babylon's merchants, Rev. xviii. 13. And those that had bond-servants under the law, were commanded to let them go free after some time of service, and they were not to let them go empty handed neither, which some of them not observing, the Lord complained by the prophet Jeremiah, that they "have not hearkened unto me, in proclaiming liberty every one to his brother, and every man to his neighbour: behold I proclaim liberty for you, saith the Lord, to the sword, to the pestilence, and to the famine, and I will make you to be removed into all the kingdoms of the earth." Jer. xxxiv. 17.

Objection.—But they were of their own nation that the command was against; now these negroes are not of our own nation, but are mere infidels and strangers. To which objection I'll answer as it is written in Ex. xxii. 21, "Ye shall neither vex a stranger, nor oppress him, for ye were strangers in the land of Egypt." And Exod. xxiii. 9, "Also thou shalt not oppress a stranger, for ye know the heart of a stranger, seeing ye were strangers in the land of Egypt." Now I do not find that it is any more allowable to make a slave of an unbeliever, than a believer, seeing we are commanded, Matt. vii. 12, "Therefore all things whatsoever ye would that men should do to you, do ye even so to them, for this is the law and the prophets." Now we may see that this was not only a command of Christ's, but was the law and the prophets also; and those that come to observe that command, even fulfil both tables at once. Now I have often considered how earnestly some men will search into the etymology or original of some things that may be but small, and in the mean while omit the greater. Now in my judgment every thing ought to be looked upon according to the importance, weight or value of the thing; for to be very zealous in a small thing, and to pass lightly over a greater, that zeal may be more properly called superstition than good zeal, which should be grounded upon knowledge. Now I would have all to consider of this practice of making slaves of negroes, or others that we can get the mastery over, to see upon what foundation it stands, or to see what the original of it was, whether or no pride and idleness were not the first rise of it, that they might go with white hands, and that their wives might (Jezebel like) paint and adorn themselves, and their sons and daughters be brought up in idleness, which may be well termed the mother of all vice; for it is generally the richest sort of people that have them, that could do best without them, for the poor are not so able to get them.

But some may object, as I myself have heard them, that there was a mark set upon Cain, and they do believe that these negroes are the posterity of Cain, because of their hair, and their being so black, differing from all others, and that Canaan was to be a servant of servants to his brethren, whom they take to be of the same lineage. But if we do but observe, and read in the genealogy of Cain, we may find that they were all drowned in the old world, and that Canaan was of the line of Seth. And although it was of the will of God that the world was drowned, because of their great wickedness; yet we may observe also, that there were unclean beasts went into the ark, as well as clean, and that it was the will or permission of God, that there should be a Ham, as well as a Shem and Japhet: by which we may see that God suffers wicked men to live as well as righteous, and we find that the sun shineth on the evil as well as on the good, and that the rain falleth on the unjust as well as the just, and that Christ forbids his followers to meddle with the tares lest they hurt the wheat; therefore, none can have any plea for making them slaves, for their being either ignorant or wicked; for if that plea would do, I do believe they need not go so far for slaves as now they do.

And although Canaan was to be a servant of servants to his brethren, yet the Lord afterwards spake by the prophets, that the son should not bear the iniquity of the father, and the father should not bear the iniquity of the son, but the soul that sinneth should die. Then the posterity of Canaan or of Ham, do not bear their sins. And the apostle Peter saith, "Now I perceive of a truth that God is no respecter of persons, but in every nation he that feareth God and worketh righteousness, is accepted of him." Now, although the negroes might not have the understanding that some other nations have, then I do believe there is the less required, and if they do but as well as they know, I do believe it is well with them. For John the Divine saith, in the Revelations, that he saw them that were "sealed in their foreheads, of the tribes of Israel, of each tribe twelve thousand, which made an hundred and forty and four thousand: And after this I beheld (said he) and lo a great multitude, which no man could number, of all nations, and kindreds, and people, and tongues, stood before the throne, and before the Lamb, clothed with white robes, and palms in their hands, and they cried with a loud voice, saying, salvation to our God, which sitteth upon the throne, and unto the Lamb." Rev. vii. 9, 10. Now, if there were all nations, kindreds, tongues and people, then there were some of the negroes.

Now, although the Turks make slaves of those they can catch, that are not of their religion, yet (as history relates) as soon as any embrace the Mahometan religion, they are no longer kept slaves, but are quickly set free, and for the most part put to some place of preferment; so zealous are they for proselytes and their own religion. Now, if many among those called Christians, would but consider how far they fall short of the Turks in this particular, it would be well; for they tell the negroes that they must believe in Christ, and receive the Christian faith, and that they must receive the Sacrament, and be baptized, and so they do; but still they keep them slaves for all this. Now how partial are those that can judge a negro that should run away from his master, to deserve beating, and if one called a Christian (although it may be no better Christian than the other) should run away from the Turks, they can judge him to be a good fellow, and to have done well. Now I look upon this practice of making slaves to be so great a sin, that even men whose principles will allow of killing men in their own defence, will not allow of making slaves; for they count it better to deprive them of life that rise up against them, than to deprive those of liberty that have done them no harm.

Now, if any one should ask one of the negro's masters, that had a negro child and a child of his own, what harm the one had done, that it should be made a slave more than the other? that they would not I believe be able to answer it; and if they have done us no harm, (as it is evident they have not) then it is very contrary to scripture, and even to nature, to make them suffer. Now if we will but look back into the original of this practice, which ought to be most looked into, and spoken against; for until the cause is removed, I know not how the effect should cease; we shall find that they were stolen in the first place, either by them that fetched them, or they carrying such goods as induced some of their own nation to steal them; and they standing ready to receive them, which is as bad as if they had stolen them themselves.

Now we may find that man-stealing and man-slaying were joined together, and there was the same punishment for the one as for the other. See Exod. xxi. 12, 13, 14, 15, 16. "And he that smiteth a man, so that he die, shall surely be put to death. And he that stealeth a man, and selleth him, or if he be found in his hands, he shall surely be put to death." We may find it also in the New Testament joined with the worst of murderers, as such as were murderers of fathers and murderers of mothers, and man-stealers. 1 Tim. i. 9, 10. The prohibition is general, he that stealeth away man, a brother or a stranger, or heathen, or any man, the punishment is capital; for he that killeth was to be put to death, because it was the image of God. Gen. ix. 6. So he that robbeth a man of his freedom, which only maketh knowledge useful, seems to deface the image of God, and therefore is punished with death.

Objection.—But how can this practice of making slaves be so great a sin, when it is so generally practised among all the societies of people? For let them differ about what they will else, they pretty generally agree about this. To which objection I answer, That if they did but as well agree about all other points as they do about this, they might almost, if not altogether, be termed one community; yet I cannot find this to be a proof: for I take it for a maxim, that, in a general way, the negroes are cruelly used; and therefore I do not find, that their agreement in making slaves can be an example for us, any more than their using them cruelly. Therefore, if we would but consider the thing rightly, we should not find that to be a proof, because it is so general a practice. For we may observe how it was when our Lord was crucified, that there were divers sects of people, and of very differing minds, yet in putting him to death they could generally agree; and though they were so much at variance, that, as the proverb is, they were at daggers' drawing, yet the text has it, "that the same day Pilot and Herod were made friends." Yet some that have annotated thereon, have not scrupled to call that a cursed friendship, that was contracted by putting to death our Lord, that came in love to their souls. But I have a further reply to make to what I have said before, of the general agreement of making slaves: namely, that there are some of all persuasions, I do believe, that cannot allow of this practice: for they seeing it to be contrary to Christ's command, and even to nature; for I have made this observation myself, (though but young in years) that those that dwell nearest the truth, and contend most for it, cannot allow of this practice, for they see it to be oppression and cruelty. But, it may be objected, that there have some spoken against this practice, and they have come to nothing, or have not prospered in it. To which I answer, that a good cause may be badly managed, and by sad experience we often see it is so. Now I do believe, by what has already been said, that all that have not concluded beforehand that they would not see, may see this practice of making slaves to be anti-christian; for it cannot be of Christ, because contrary to his command; therefore of antichrist.

Now I have heard some men say, that they believed they did wrong in getting negroes, but that they did not know what to do with them now they had got them; for if they let them go free after some time, if any mishap befel them, their estates were obliged to maintain them. And though they seem to acknowledge the wrong done to them, yet they seem to be very much afraid lest they should be forced to help them a little, and so seem to rest contented.

Now, suppose that to give the negroes their times, or let them go free here in this country, were wrong, which I do not believe would be wrong, after they had served them some time; but if it were wrong to let them go free, whether or no those that see they did wrong in getting them, ought not to bear a testimony against it? For their keeping them and being silent, encourages others to get them. For instance, the Apostle Paul's advice to the believers, not to join themselves in marriage, a believer with an unbeliever, for he counted it wrong, even so do I; but if a believer had got a wife that was an unbeliever, I do not think that he should put her away, yet, notwithstanding, the practice was wrong, and ought to be spoken against. Now I can truly say, that this practice of making slaves of men, appears to be so great an evil to me, that for all the riches and glory of this world, I would not be guilty of so great a sin as this seems to be. And I do believe many would see it so, were they not blinded by self-interest. Now, as I said in the beginning, how apt men were to forget God in a time of liberty, as we now seem to have, which, if rightly considered, we ought the more to remember him, and to prize his favour therein. For I do not believe if persecution was on foot again, and people were haled to prison as they have been in times past, that many would have more regard to their old practices than now they have. For this practice of making slaves tends to many evils, as parting man and wife; and children from them both. And all this is done by violence, which is forbidden in the scriptures; for there we are commanded to do violence to no man. And lastly, it is a hinderance to the spreading of the Gospel among these poor creatures, for whom (as well as others) our Lord came and laid down his life, and also hath said, that his Gospel should be preached unto all nations. But some may object, as I have heard them, that by this means they come to hear the Gospel preached, and they believed this was the way our Lord intended that nation should have the Gospel preached to them, viz. to be brought slaves here. To which I'll say, the reader may quickly suppose what people these are, for it must be them that buy the Gospel pretty dear themselves; or else they would not think that the negroes should be bond-slaves, and their children after them, for the knowledge of the Gospel. But I do not find that the Gospel was either bought or sold for money; neither do we find that God compelled any to receive it, but only entreated them or advised them to choose life and live. Now by this practice they hate the name of a Christian; for all of us they can get (say they) they make slaves of, and even nature itself tells them that it is wrong.

Now I would have all seriously to consider, that love their own souls, and do believe that they must give an account for the deeds done in the body, to look into their own practices; to see upon what foundation they stand; for God will not forgive what is in our power to help.

Now I have shown by the Scripture the unlawfulness of this practice, as it is now in use, both in the Old Testament and in the New. And now, I would have all to turn their minds inward, to that divine monitor or counsellor, placed in the heart of man, which is as agreeable to the holy Scriptures (I do believe) as any internal thing can be to an external one; to which I'll leave my reader, even to that ever blessed Spirit, One with the Father.

Benjamin Lay, *All Slave-keepers . . . Apostates,* 1737

Benjamin Lay, *All Slave-keepers That keep the Innocents in Bondage, Apostates Pretending to lay Claim to the Pure & Holy Christian Religion; of what Congregation so ever; but especially in their Ministers, by whose example the filthy Leprosy and Apostacy is spread far and near; it is a notorious Sin, which many of the true Friends of Christ, and his pure Truth, called Quakers, has been for many Years, and still are concerned to write and bear Testimony against; as a Practice so gross and hurtful to Religion and destructive to Government, beyond what Words can set forth, or can be declared of by Men or Angels, and yet lived in by Ministers and Magistrates in America* (Philadelphia, 1737), preface; pp. 10-14; 18-23; 29-30; 32-37; 63-64; 74-85, 91-94; 194-98; 201-7; 231-35.

In Ralph Sandiford's last days, his friend Benjamin Lay often visited him. A hunchbacked eccentric, this Quaker abolitionist blamed Sandiford's death on the hounding he had received from slaveholders. A farmer, storekeeper, and bookkeeper, Lay had visited the Holy Land, had had a personal interview with George II, and had held slaves in Barbados. Sickened by what slavery had done to him, Lay went on a bizarre personal campaign to end this institution. He kidnapped a slaveholder's son to show the father how Negroes must feel. He appeared at a Quaker meeting wearing a military coat and sword under his Quaker clothes and concealing a bladder of pokeberry juice in a hollowed-out book. He rose during the meeting and, throwing off his Quaker clothes, thrust the sword through the book, spilling the liquid over astonished Friends. He cried, "It would be as justifiable in the sight of the Almighty if you should thrust a sword through their (slaves') hearts as I do through this book."

Disillusioned with Quakers who held slaves, Lay moved out of Philadelphia to live in a cave six miles away, where he raised vegetables for food and flax for clothing. It was there that he wrote a scathing denunciation of Quakers and ministers who held slaves. He called them "a Parcel of Hypocrites, and Deceivers . . . under the greatest appearance and Pretension to Religion and Sanctity that ever was in the World." His 278-page-book was called All Slave-Keepers that keep the Innocent in Bondage, Apostates. *Benjamin Franklin, who published the rambling, vicious attack, remembered that its author had given him hundreds of pages of manuscript with the instruction to publish them in any order he chose. At the Yearly Meeting of 1738, Lay, the wierd little hermit, was publicly disowned. But 20 years later, the 1758 Yearly Meeting decided to exclude slaveholders from positions of responsibility within the sect.*

The Preface

Impartial Reader, These Things following are so far from offending or grieving my very dear true and tender Friends, called *Quakers*, who love the Truth more then all, that it is by their request and desire that they are made publick; for I can say in the Truth before the Lord, that I love them in & for the Truths sake, and covet their sweet Unity, and pure Fellowship in the Gospel, more than my natural Life, and all things in the World, without it or them, my record is in Heaven.

I say for the Truth, and Friends sake, these things are exposed, and I my self likewise, although not without some fear and trembling, for fear I

W Williams Pinx.
HD. Fecit.
BENJAMIN LAY.
Lived to the Age of 80, in the Latter Part of Which, he Observ'd extreem Temperance, in his Eating, and Drinking,
his Fondness for a Particularity, in Dress and Customs at times Subjected him, to the Redicule of the Ignorant, but his
who were Intimate with Him, thought Him an Honest Religious

Benjamin Lay—vegetarian, hunchbackd, abolitionist dwarf, outside his cave in Philadelphia in the 1730's.

should hurt Truth's cause, which is God's cause, I being and seeing myself so very unfit almost every way, as a Man, yet I can truly say as a Christian, I believ'd it my Duty, but made not haste, for the Lord my good God, the Truth knows, that I have prayed unto him earnestly, many Days and Nights, with great concern of mind, that he would be pleased to raise up and concern some worthy Friend or other, of more repute and Esteem amongst Men; for I know my self to be so very mean and contemptible in the sight of Men, almost in every respect, so that I might and do much question the Event, but shall leave that to the Lord, to whom faithfulness and obedience is required; and no true Peace without it. For I have found long ago, the saying of Truth veryfied, *He that loves any thing more than me, is not worthy of me*: I have often thought of *Moses's* Prayer, and *Gideon's* request, when the Lord was about to send them to deliver his People from Captivity, and many other worthy Men, ay, and Women too, which are mentioned in Holy writ, and many Thousands more no doubt, which we have no Account of there, for it is believ'd, we have but a very small part of what have been written, and yet full enough, if we will but be faithful; my dear, tender and wellbeloved Friends, I beg, I pray, and beseech us, let us be more faithful I intreat, in bowels of Love, let us be faithful, let us be faithful, let us be faithful to God in all things; and then I know blessed be his pure Name, which is the Truth, that when the Scourge shall come, he will secure us in Life or in Death; and that will be enough for us, so be it, saith my Soul, and is in humble request.

Benjamin Lay.

Abington, Philadelphia *County, in* Pennsylvania, *the 17th, 9th Mo.* 1736.

. . . No greater nor no better Law, say I, than to love God above all, and all our Fellow-Creatures as ourselves; these two contain Law, Prophets and Gospel, do to all as we would be done by. No greater Sin Hell can invent, than to prophane and blaspheme the pure and Holy Truth, which is God all in all, and remove God's Creatures made after his own Image, from all the Comforts of Life, and their Country and procure for them, and bring them into all the miseries that Dragons, Serpents, Devils, and Hypocrites, can procure and think of; these things are carried on by Christians, so called, and Ministers too, in the very greatest appearance of Demurity and Sanctity in the whole World, that ever I read or heard of; God which is the Truth, saith we shall not eat this cursed Fruit; our Ministers say we may eat, and lawfully too; which shall we believe?

We pretend not to love fighting with carnal Weapons, nor to carry Swords by our sides, but carry a worse thing in the Heart, as will I believe appear by and by; what, I pray and beseech you, dear Friends, by the tender Mercies of our God, to consider, can be greater Hypocrisy, and plainer contradiction, than for us as a People, to refuse to bear Arms, or to pay them that do, and yet purchase the Plunder, the Captives, for Slaves at a very great Price, thereby justifying their selling of them, and the War, by which they were or are obtained; nor doth this satisfy, but their Children also are kept in Slavery, *ad infinitum*; is not this plainly and substantially trampling the most Blessed and Glorious Testimony that ever was or ever will be in the World, under our Feet, and committing of Iniquity with, both Hands earnestly? Is this the way to convince the poor Slaves, or our Children, or Neighbours, or the World? Is it not the way rather to encourage and strengthen them in their Infidelity, and Atheism, and their Hellish Practice of Fighting, Murthering, killing and Robbing one another, to the end of the World.

My dear Friends, I beg, I would intreat, in all Humility, with all earnestness of mind, on the bended Knees of my Body and Soul; willingly and with all readiness, sincerely, if that would do, that you would turn to the Lord, the Blessed Truth, in your Hearts, for Direction, for Counsel and Advice; that you may quit your selves like Men, honourably, of this so Hellish a Practice. Especially, you that have the Word of Reconciliation to preach to the Children of Men; and if you have any true tenderness of the Love of God in you, as I right well know, blessed be the Name of the Lord, all true Ministers have, you my dear Friends, consider waightily of these important concerns, and quit yourselves of yourselves and Slaves; for a good example in you might do a great deal of good, as a bad one will do, and has done a very great deal of mischief to the Truth; for the Eyes of the People are upon you, some for good, and some for Evil.

And my Friends, you that have Saves, and do minister to others in our Meetings, consider I intreat and beseech you concerning this thing in particular. What Burthens and Afflictions, Bondage, and sore Captivity you bring upon your dear and tender Friends, and keep them in, which cannot touch with this vile and Hellish Practice, but are constrained to bear Testimony against it, as one the greatest Sins in the World, all things considered: And against you too in some sort, as being in the practice yourselves, of that which is directly opposite to your own Pretensions, and a very great stumbling Block in the way of honest, godly Inquirers, which want Peace to their Souls.

What a great Strait these tender hearted mourning Souls must needs be in, think ye, betwixt Love and Duty; they love you dearly for the Truth sake, and yet think it their Duty absolutely in the Fear and Love of God, to testifie against the Sin, and you for continuing in it.

Dear Friends, what Peace can you have, in thus afflicting your Fellow Members; even the same Testimony they have with you in Meetings, where is the Blessed Unity and Fellowship, you have been preaching so many Years, as being sensible of one anothers exercises, Bearers of one another's Burthens, having a deep sence and feeling of others infirmities, or afflictions, or troubles.

What is become of this blessed experience, my Friends? is it all lost as to you, if so I must give my judgment, that you? have not your constant dwelling in him, that was touched with a feeling of our infirmities, tempted in all cases like unto us, yet without Sin; and so are his Saints, for they are all of one, and they live with him Night and Day, in his blessed Kingdom, which is within; and they love him dearly, they cannot avoid it, for he first loved them or us, and we cannot keep back our love from him any more than we can hinder, or stop the Rivers and Streams from running into the *Ocean*: For we having received all from him, of course all return or run to him again; it is the nature of his essence or divine being.

What from Heaven is, to Heaven tends,
That which descended, the same again ascends.
What from the Earth is, to Earth returns again.
That which from Heaven is, the Earth cannot contain.

. . .

Many worthy Men have borne Testimony against this foul Sin, Slave-keeping, by Word and Writing; some of which I have noted elsewhere; but especially *Ralph Sandiford*, amongst many others, has writ excellently well, against that filthy Sin; far beyond what I can or do pretend to, being a Man of so very mean a capacity, and little Learning; but as I firmly believing it to be my duty, in the sight of God; I endeavour to do what I can and leave the Event to the Lord.

And as for any Slave-keepers, who are not impartial in the case; to say that *R.S.* writ in a Spirit of Bitterness, or that he did not end his Life well. As to the first I have read his Book carefully, with Attention; and I do not remember a Word in it contrary to Truth, or any such sharp invectives, as may easily be found in Holy Scripture, both Old and New Testament; altho' I have, it's true, because, I believe in my very Soul the cause does require it, for the nature of those Beasts, is in those Men, which do trade in Slaves; and much worse.

As to the second objection, that he *R.S.* did not end well; let such be intreated to remember the Man of God, that was sent by the Lord, from *Judah*, to declare against the Altar; or that of *Bethel*, and the Miracles wrought by him, the King's Hand withering, and restored by his Prayer; the Altar spliting, and since that his Prophesy fulfilled; of Men's Bones, being offered or Burnt thereon.

And yet this Man of God, never came to the Supulchers of his Fathers, by reason an old lying Prophet leading him out of the way. So was slain by a Lyon.

Judah's Prophet, had but one Hypocritical lying old Prophet, that we read of, to lead him out of the way. But *R.S.* had, and we now have, abundance of Old and Young pretended Prophet's, Prophets to lead us, poor Creatures, out of the way.

And so they will many, unwary Souls; except the Lord our God be pleased to open our Eyes, to see the Hellish Cheat, and devilish Delusion; by which many of our poor Friends have been seduced, and lead aside in the Hellish Darkness or Smoak, of the Bottomless Pit; for whom my very Soul is grieved. *God Almighty is my Witness.*

The *8th Mo. 1736. Benjamin Lay.*

R.S. above-mentioned, was in great Perplexity of mind; and having oppression, which makes a wise man Mad, by which he was brought very low, with many Bodily Infirmities, long before he died; his Book largely set out, read it without partiality or prejudice, which is always blind, or very short-sighted; and you may excellent weighy matters find in it; he was a very tender hearted Man before he came amongst Friends, as well as after, as I have heard from many honest Friends, that had much dealing, and intimate Conversation with him, for many Years, which are now living. But before he died, by reason of his sore Affliction of mind, concerning Slave-keeping, as in his Book largely appear, and Infirmity of Body, he fell into a sort of Delirium: However I do believe if he had lived he would have overcame it; for I went to see him several times, a little before he died; I am not ashamed, nor afraid, to write it, altho' I be censured for it, as I have been with some others, for going to see him, altho' in Affliction, the only time for Visiting, as I humbly conceive, if we go in a right mind.

But O! Say the Slave-keepers, and must confess in their Hearts that Book, *The Mystery of Iniquity*, as it is call'd, and titled; it tells Tales to the World, sets forth to the World's People, what a Parcel of Hypocrites, and Deceivers we are, under the greatest appearance and Pretentions to Religion and Sanctity that ever was in the World; we'll censure him, and his Book too, into the Bottomless Pit, if we can, tho' we can't disprove a Word in it, for it's undeniable Truth, and so unanswerable; for we never understood, that any one ever attempted it, or so much as spake of it; but what of that, Brethren, if it be sinful we are in the Iniquity, in the practice of Slave-keeping; and our Children by our means, incouragement, and appointment, not only so, but our Fathers before us, worthy Men, in their generating Work; and some of them Ministers and Elders, with all Men of renown. They found the sweetness of it, and so do we, and we will continue in it; let who will or dare say nay; we'll condemn *R.* in his Grave, and his Book and all that favour it, or promote its being spread abroad, or being read, that exposes us, and we'll expose that, or especially him that writ it, by Callumnies and Slanders, and Surmises, and by insinuating all that ever we can hear or think of against him, now he is in his Grave; especially we did it before, but now more safely, for he can't contradict or oppose us now; so that if we can but render him odious in his Character, his Book will be invalidated in course with us that hate it, altho' we cannot disprove a tittle of it, especially with our Brethren in strict Unity, in this Iniquity, and foulest of Sins, the Negroe Trade.

If this practice can be proved to be the greatest of Sins (as may easily be done) considering it's Root and Branch, and all the sad Fruit it brings forth; yet we read Christ died for Sinners, and he can forgive the greatest, as well as the least. . . .

Now, dear Friends, behold a Mystery! These Ministers that be Slave-keepers, and are in such very great Repute, such eminent Preachers, given to Hospitality, charitable to the Poor, loving to their Neighbours, just in their Dealings, temperate in their Lives, visiting of the Sick, sympathising with the Afflicted in Body or Mind, very religious seemingly, and extraordinary devout and demure, and in short strictly exact in all their

Decorums, except Slave-keeping, these, these be the Men, and the Women too, for the Devil's purpose, and are the choicest Treasure the Devil can or has to bring out of his Lazaretto, to establish Slave-keeping. By these Satan works Wonders many ways. These are the very Men, or People of both Sexes, that come the nearest the Scribes & Pharisees of any People in the whole World, if not sincere: For the Scribes were exact and demure seemingly in their Appearance before Men, according to Christ's Account of them, and yet the worst Enemies the dear Lamb had, or that the Devil could procure for or against him. And I do surely believe that one such as these, now in this our Day, in this very Country, does more Service for the Devil, and Hurt in the Church, in Slave-keeping, than twenty Publicans and Harlots: For by their extraordinary Conduct, in Hypocrisy, smooth and plausible appearance, they draw into the Snare almost insensibly, and so beguile unstable Souls before they are aware, which is sorrowful to consider as well as write, their Example being much more powerful than others. . . .

I say my own Experience when I lived in *Barbadoes* about 18 Years ago, where we had much Business in Trading, and the poor Blacks would come to our Shop and Store, hunger-starv'd, almost ready to perish with Hunger and Sickness, great Numbers of them would come to trade with us, for they seemed to love and admire us, we being pretty much alike in Stature and otherways; and my dear Wife would often be giving them something for the Mouth, which was very engaging you that read this may be sure, in their deplorable Condition. Oh! my Soul mourns in contemplating their miserable, forlorn, wretched State and Condition that mine Eyes beheld them in then, and it is the same now, and will remain except the great almighty Being, either immediately or instrumentally shall be pleased to put a Stop to it; for they are yearly by Shiploads poured in upon, and received by the People, many Thousands in one Year, Year after Year, as is thought, up and down *America*, besides what vast Numbers are encreased by Generation daily. O Lord God Almighty, where will this Practice lead us that are called thy People, Dearest God, and make so great a Profession of being lead and guided by thy eternal Spirit, which is the glorious Truth unchangeable and precious, and without End. But I trust, dearest One, thou wilt be pleased to stop and end this Practice, that is more like Hell than Heaven, to be sure.

I having made a little Digression, may resume the Matter relating to my dear Wife, and the *Negroes*. She was a tender-hearted Woman, and, as I said, would be very often giving them something or other; stinking Biscuits which sometimes we had in abundance, bitten by the Cockroaches; or rotten Cheese, stinking Meat, decayed Fish which we had plenty of in that hot Country; so my dear sweet *Sarah*, she would hand it to them, here and there to those that she thought wanted it most, tho' all wanted enough, God Almighty knows, except here and there a favourite Slave, one of an hundred or thousand, may be, kept for their Glory and Pride to wait on them, amongst their proud, lazy, dainty, tyrannical, gluttonous, drunken, debauched Visitors, the Scum of the infernal Pit, a little worse than the same that comes off their Sugar when it is boiling, which is composed of Grease, Dirt, Dung, and other Filthiness, as, it may be Limbs, Bowels and Excrements of the poor Slaves, and Beasts, and other Masters, but this I say serves exceeding well to make Rum of, and Molosses, for that is the Use it is put to, with other Ingredients pretty much like it; and these People in the Islands may laugh at us for being ridiculously infatuated, to send away our excellent good Provisions, and other good Things, to purchase such filthy Stuff, which tends to the Corruption of Mankind, and may be send us some of the worst of their Slaves, when they cannot rule them themselves, along with their Rum, to compleat the Tragedy, that is to say, to destroy the People in *Pennsylvania*, and ruin the Country. Dear Friends, or any of my Fellow-Creatures, I must confess I am apt to digress, but when such dangerous Filthiness comes in my Way, I think it my Duty to make it appear if possible to others; for it is so to me, exceeding sinful above Measure, I will assure you, more than what I can speak or write abundantly; if it should be so to you, I hope you will endeavour to avoid it, and pray for Heavens Assistance, without which all is nothing. As to what was touched on before, when my dear *Sarah* had given to them what she thought fit within-doors, we have taken some more of the same sort and thrown it into the Street, stinking as to be sure it was, yet the poor Creatures would come running, and tearing, and rending one another, to get a part in the scramble of that which I am sure some Dogs would not touch, much less eat of, their poor Bellies were so empty, and so ravenous were they, that I never saw a parcel of Hounds more eager about a dead Carcase, than they always were. This Scramble was commonly on the First Day, before we went to Meeting, which was their Market-day, as well as their Hallowing-Day, when they are exempted from their Labour, they come down to Town, many Hundreds of them, they that could get or steal any Thing, a little Sugar, or Cotton, Ginger, Aloes, Rum, Cocoa-Nuts, Pine-Apples, Oranges, Lemmons, Citrons, old Iron, Wood for Firing, steal any Thing out of Houses, Yards, or any where, or any Thing that was not too hot or too heavy, and bring it to Market on a Sunday, as they call it, to get a penny, or something for the Mouth, and they that could not get any thing to bring to Market, they would come to Town if possibly they could hold out and keep from falling down and fainting by the Way, being perished with Hunger and hard Labour the Week before; I say these very miserable Objects that could get no Truck in the Country to bring to Market, yet they would if possible come to Town, and see what they could beg or steal there. (Who can blame them if it was ten times worse, they being under such unmerciful Tyrants.) These Wretches being in Town in this miserable Condition, with not a Crum of good or bad to put into their Mouths, ready to drop as they walked or crawled along the Streets, they many of them hearing of us, for we were very much known amongst them, they would come to our Door, if they came before we were gone to Meeting, and there they would stand as thick as Bees, but much more like *Pharaoh*'s lean Kine, and I may say their

Appearance was dismal enough to move a very hard Heart; so we used to give them a little of something at Times, as we found some Freedom, considering our Circumstances; But if we gave to some, and did not to all, as to be sure we could not, oh how the poor Creatures would look. I say many Hundreds would come and flock about us; and them that receiv'd, O how thankful, with bended Knees; but them that did not, what Words can set forth the dejected sinking Looks that appeared in their Countenances. Shall I ever forget them? . . .

When I have mildly reasoned with some Friends concerning their Hostility, in carrying a Person or Friend, if I may call him so, out of Meetings so often, and keeping of him out by Constable and other ways; as at *Philadelphia, Burlington* and *Concord, Etc.* without so much as pretending they have used any Gospel Order with him, in any Monthly or Quarterly Meeting, as a disorderly Person.

O But say some, he is a very troublesome Person, and has been so for many Years; and is too censorious about Trading in Slaves, or against Traders in, and Keepers of Slavers; And positively affirms, that no Man or Woman, Lad or Lass ought to be suffered, to pretend to Preach Truth in our Meetings, while they live in that Practice; which is all a Lie.

And further, he boldly affirms, that no Person whatsoever has any Right, or ought according to Truths Discipline, to be suffered to have the Rule and Government, or any Part of it, in the Church of God, which is the Kingdom of God, while he himself is in League with the Devil, and is managing the Affairs of his Kingdom, which Slave Trading is, as has been proved.

But some that have not, and will not keep Negroe Slaves of their own, may say, we must not be too censorious, for we are often at their Houses, and Eat and Drink bravely, and have their Negroes to wait on us, our Horses, Wives and Children.

Beside all these Things, we buy, sell, Trade, get Gain by and with them, we must be careful how we offend our Benefactors, and Dear Friends. But here is yet a stronger Bond than the other, Pleasure and Profit, we love to Sleep with their Off-spring, so they be but Rich; for many of us have joyned Affinity with these *Ahabs* (O that hard Word) and *Jezabels* for Gains, by marrying with their rich Children, and if we become Prophets, and can prophesy such things as they like, we shall be highly favoured, and fed at *Jezabel's* Tables, though we should be twice 4500 of us. . . .

My Dear and Well-beloved Friends; my Joy and the Crown of all my sweet Delights in this World, I can truly say, is the true Unity with my true Brethren, which are the true Church in God the Father, and he in them, ever reigning in his own Blessed Kingdom, Body, House, Tabernacle, *New-Jerusalem*, or a Tent, synonimous Terms; while *Israel* abode here, no Divination could prevail, or inchantments against 'em; but when *Israel*, our Dear Friends, went out of their Tent to look at, and long after the Pleasures, Pride, Profit and Friendship of this World, then they came to be snared with this cursed Sin, Negroe-Trading, as well as some other gross Sins, of which this is Chief, considering the Hellish Train of Filthiness, which has, does, and ever will attend it, and is inseparable from it; for it is granted by all sober wise Men that truly fear God, and dearly love the Truth in Sincerity, and are well acquainted with this soul Trade from the beginning, and in all its progressions to this Day; I say such as have had a true Account, do know that those that are employed in this Trade, are some of the worst of Men, and withal some of the worst of Thieves, Pyrates and Murtherers, from whence our lesser Pyrates have proceeded. And many of these lesser Pyrates have been punished with Death, and some other ways; but the much greater Villains by far, not only go free but are encouraged, and have been near 50 Years, if not more, by us as a People, by buying of their cursed Hellish-gotten Ware, at a very great Price. And all this Time pretending to the most holy pure Religion in the whole World, to do unto all, as we would they should do unto us, and as *James* writes, *to Visit the Fatherless, and Widow, in their Afflictions, and keep ourselves unspotted from the World*; but I know no worse Engine the Devil has to make Widows and Fatherless Children, and to bring into Affliction and Bondage, and fore Captivity indeed, than this Hellish practice in *Pennsylvania*, Negroe-Keeping.

But these Hellish Miscreants, these Men-Stealers, pretend they fetch away these poor Creatures, that they may not kill one the other, when they are the Murtherers which sets 'em to the Work, (a cursed work it is) for as I have had an Account, near 35 Years ago, when 10 or 12 Sail of Vessels come on the Coast of *Guinea*, and they cannot catch Negroes enough to Freight their Vessels by the Sea side, and in Rivers where they send their Boats in Search and Pursuit of them, where they are acquainted; for they being us'd to the Business know where to go; and to find out some old Negroes that they have been used to trade with, which will bring off in Canoes, their Wives or Children, or their Neighbours Wives, and Children if they can catch 'em in Woods, or any where else, so bring 'em and sell them to our brave Christians, which come there with Ships for that purpose.——O brave! give 30s. for a Negroe and sell him for 30*l*. or 40, 50, or 60, 70, 80, 90, 100*l*. or more: Who would but be a Trader in Slaves and Souls of Men, altho' he goes to Hell for it, and in the mean time intail an Iniquity on his own, and his Neighbour's Posterity to their Destruction and the Ruin of the whole Country beside.

Above 30 Years ago, when I was a common Sailor, I had this Account, and likewise by some Sailors on Board Capt. *Reeves*, coming this Voyage to *Philadelphia*, who had been at *Guinea*, and I suppose had been Pyrates, they did acknowledge they had been taken by them.

These vile Fellows on Board Capt. *Reeves*, in their Drink used to tell what cursed Work their former Captain and Salors made with the poor Negroes in their Passage, for their Lusts; the Captain 6 or 10 of 'em in the Cabbin, and the Sailors as many as they pleased; with much more too foul for me to mention, or for chaste Ears to hear.

But I pray, I beg, and beseech you my Friends, in the pure Love and Fear of God; consider what part have true Believers with such Infidels, or Christ with such *Belials*, or our Holy pure God with such unholy impure Devils, until we can join these together; now we can never reconcile Slave-Keeping with our Principles; we may as well say as *Solomon* of an Harlot, *their Steps go down to Death and their Feet take hold on Hell.*

Now my dear Friends, let us consider the matter a little further, concerning these Men-Stealers, and weigh it in the Ballance of the Sanctuary, which is Equity and Justice. Consider I say, the different circumstances of times and things; it may be these wicked Creatures have been unhappily brought up to the Black Art, most of their Life time; my Soul pities them on that Account; had they had that good Education, Conversation, Books and Mutual Love, in Holy Illuminations, sweet Communion together in our solemn Meetings and Gatherings together, and the Heavenly Showers which many times, yea very often and frequent to my sure and certain Knowledge, and to the great mutual sweet and heavenly Comfort of my poor Soul, with many more of my dear Friends; I say the many Heavenly Showers that have dropped as the Dew, and distilled as the small Rain, in our tender Souls immediately, many times, yea innumerable, and instrumentally, by the Blessed Messengers of Peace and Salvation, which were sent by the high and lofty one, that inhabiteth eternity and dwelleth in Light, who had a tender regard Blessed by his Holy Name, to those Poor Men and Women too, that were Poor indeed, and truly contrited, and sat trembling before his Divine and Glorious Majesty, ready to receive him that was and is the Word that made all Things; and when they had received him, they or we, We were made to rejoice with Joy unspeakable, being filled with him that was, and is, and ever will be the Glory and true rejoicing of his People, and dear Children, all the World over; that can appeal to him that knows all Things, that they love him more then all things here below, yea than their natural Lives.

Shall we I say as People who have been Blessed with so great Priviledges, and high Favours, forsake the Holy Commandment of Loving God the Truth above all, and turn to worship for covetous ends, the worst Idol that ever the Devil set up in the World.

Sure those wicked Men above-mentioned will rise up in Judgment against us; for had they been so highly favoured in all respects, as Friends as a People have been, who knows but they might have been as great Saints as any in the Church of Christ at this Day; for had Friends stood faithful in their Testimony against this Practice from the beginning they might have convinced many, and stopt 'em in their career; but now they may say, and that truly too, we have been a means to encourage and strengthen them in their wicked ways; for when they brought in a Cargo of Blacks, who more ready to purchase them, and at a great Price, than the Saints, or them that seem so, and would be thought such. Well my dear and tender Friends, although I touch thus close to ease my afflicted mind, which has been tossed as with a Tempest at times, above 17 Years, on this sad Account Slave-Keeping, yet I write not this of all by no means, I know and believe there is many Friends, that dare not touch with it, for any Profit whatsoever. I do hope there is some Thousands will not bow the Knee to this *Baal*, nor kiss his Lips for an Ease or Gain. It has been said, that all do not see it so great a Sin as I and some others make it; and for that reason with others I think it my duty to write and speak the more about it where I come, that Friends and others may be better informed. Some have insinuated, as if the Primitive Saints kept Captive Slaves; this is hellish Censure indeed, to accuse the greatest of Saints with the greatest of Sins; whose Damnation is just, and their reward shall be according to their Works; for they were without Spot, then free from the greatest Spot; holy, as he is holy; perfect, as he is perfect; He that Sanctifieth, and they that are Sanctified, are one. Blessing and Honour, Salvation and Glory to our God, for evermore, *Amen*, faith my Soul.

Cursing and Dishonour, and Damnation is to the Devil and Satan, and his Instruments, that Preach such Doctrines; for they that are Born of God Sin not, neither can they, for his Seed remaineth in them; they cannot Sin, because they are Born of God.

And now my dear Friends and others, you that came in Servants to this Country, and Slaves, although for a short time by your own Consent too, for you to plead for Negroe-Keeping, is almost intolerable.

I say, you that came here poor, vile, miserable wretches, destitute and folorn, and here you were kept to hard Labour, which was good for you, and brought you to a sense of your filthy, abominable, undone, and woful cursed condition which you, many of ye had been in, then O then many of you came to consider of your ways, and were wise in turning to the Lord, into your own Hearts by the moving and rising of his own blessed Light, Life, Grace and pure Love there in your own Souls, which was as a Light shining in a Dark Place, your Hearts dark indeed, by reason of Sin, and that filthy Life which you have lived; you came to be burthened with it, and seek relief in turning to the Lord in your Hearts, where he was and is to be found, blessed be his pure Name which is his Essence or divine Nature, manifest within Men; so when you came to this good experience, you came to love the Society and follow the good example of our worthy Elders, very commendable in you to do, which first settled in this Country; you came to live sober lives, and by your industry, the Almighty favouring, some attained to very large possessions here, being a large Country and few People, but now more numerous, so no occasion for Negro-Slaves; for had this Land been covered with 'em as it is now in some Places, and too much here already, how would you have come to this greatness; you might have perished for want of Business to purchase necessaries. Let it never be forgotten by you, I beseech and pray ye for the Lord's sake, and for your own and your Childrens sake, that are coming up in vast Numbers, as well as them that are, or may become Servants hereafter, with many, yea very many of your own Children, which is very likely by the wicked foul courses many of our Youth take, they may be brought to the same Misery and extremity as you were, by their foolish Lusts and vanities; my Soul mourns in contemplating of it, and is in sore distress and misery, with many of my dear and inwardly beloved Friends, Male and Female, on this sad Account, as well as other gross Sins, many dear tender Souls in our Society, reproachfully called *Quakers* have writ and bore Testimony against this Sin at times, near 50 Years, but were reproached for that likewise; but some are gone to their Graves in Peace; many yet living; as in *Pennsylvania, Jersey, Long-Island, Nantucket, Old-England*, which I have been with at their Houses, and their Writings are extant at this time to my certain knowledge, although many poor seeking Souls, that are bewildered by this wicked Hellish Sin in our Ministers, Slave-Keeping, will not believe or cannot believe it, but rather believe we approve of it as a People with one consent unanimously. When some Friends have been reasoning with some Sober People of other professions in my hearing, concerning the Pride and Covetousness of their hireling Preachers, and concerning Truth's Principles, they have had nothing to say for the one, or against the other; but whether shall we go, say they, we do not approve or like keeping Slaves, it is not doing as we would be done by ourselves; and your People are as greedy as any Body in keeping Negroes for their Gain, (it is too true) but not all said I, no say they again, who shall we believe, we are sure and do know, that your Preachers and Elders, Chief Leaders have 'em; answer was made, not all, for some have testified against it, as a very henious Sin, for many Years, Year after Year; and are gone to their silent Graves in Peace, and many yet living amongst us, as above is mentioned. Why then, say they, do you not separate. Here it is thus written, *Wherefore come out from amongst them, and be ye separate, saith the Lord, and touch not the unclean thing; and I will receive you.* 2 *Cor.* 6, 13, 14 *to* 17. read the next verse with attention, in the fear of the Lord.

I know no worse or greater stumbling Blocks the Devil has to lay in the way of honest Inquirers, than our Ministers and Elders keeping Slaves; and by straining and perverting Holy Scriptures, Preach more to Hell, than ever they will bring to Heaven, by their feigned Humility and Hypocrisy. . . .

Now Friends, you that are Slave-Keepers, I pray and beseech ye, examine your own Hearts, and see and feel too, if you have not the same answer from Truth now within; while you Preach and exhort others to Equity, and to do Justice and love Mercy, and to walk humbly before the Lord and his People, and you yourselves live and act quite contrary, behave proudly, do unjustly and unmercifully, and live in and encourage the grossest Iniquity in the whole World. For I say, you are got beyond Gospel, Law, *Abraham*, Prophets, Patriarchs, to *Cain* the Murtherer, and beyond him too, to the Devil himself, beyond *Cain*, for he Murthered but one, that we know of, but you have many Thousands, or caused 'em to be so, and for ought I know many Hundreds of Thousands, within 50 Years. What do you think of these Things, you brave Gospel Ministers? that keep poor Slaves to Work for you to maintain you and yours in Pride, Pride and much Idleness or Laziness, and Fulness of Bread, the Sins of *Sodom*: How do these Things become your plain Dress, Demure Appearance, feigned Humility, all but Hypocrisy, which according to Truth's Testimony, must have the hottest

Place in Hell; to keep those miserable Creatures at hard Labour continually, unto their old Age, in Bondage and sore Captivity, working out their Blood and Sweat, and Bowels, youthful strength and vigour, then you drop into your Graves, go to your Places ordained or appointed for you; so leave these poor unhappy Creatures in their worn-out old Age, to your proud, Dainty, Lazy, Scornful, Tyrannical, and often beggerly Children, for them to Domineer and Tyrannize over, cursing them and you in your Graves, for working out their youthful Blood and strength for you, and then leave 'em to be a Plague to us; and then of the abuses, miseries and Cruelties these miserable old worn out Slaves go through, no Tongue can express, starved with Hunger, perish with Cold, rot as they go, for want of every thing that is necessary for an Humane Creature; so that Dogs and Cats are much better taken care for, and yet some have had the Confidence, or rather Impudence, to say their Slaves or Negroes live as well as themselves. I could almost wish such hardened, unthinking Sinful devilish Lyars were put into their Places, at least for a time, in a very hard Service, that they might feel a little in themselves, of what they make so light of in other People; and it would be but just upon 'em, and indeed why should they be against it, if the Negroes live as well and better than they; but such notorious Lies will never go down well, with any Sober right tender-hearted People truly fearing God, and that love the Truth above all; for such I believe firmly, when they come to see, and rightly consider the vileness of this practice in all its parts, and the cursed Fruit it brings forth, they will never enter into it; and if they are in, will endeavour to get out as soon as they can; for I do believe if all the Wickedness Tyrany, oppressions and abominable Barbarities were written concerning this Hellish Trade, it would fill a large Volume in Folio.

Many has said, they do not see it so great an Evil or Sin, that is, Negroe-Keeping; who so Blind as them that will not see; but them that are willing to see, I think it my duty to inform them what I can by Word and Writing, and then leave it to the Lord. . . .

I heartily wish we might be brought to see this Sin, as great and as dangerous as it really is, both in Church and State, in Ministers and Hearers, that we might with one accord by Fasting and Prayer, in Spirit and in Truth, Night and Day, in Publick and Private, seek to and beseech the Almighty Lord of Heaven and Earth, that he would be pleased to assist us with Strength and Courage to make War with, and engage against so Capital an Enemy that is so dishonourable to God, and all true Religion, destructive to Government and Mankind in general; for I do believe here is in this Land of *America*, as selfish, sordid, greedy, Covetous, Earthly minded People of almost all Names, as any in the World. Oh! that some Couragious Valiant little *Davids* might be raised up and furnished with their Slings, and Smooth Stones taken out of the Brook of the Lord, the River of Life, that runs through or in the *Paradise* of God, which is Heaven, and sent forth against this great *Goliah*, that defies the very Armies of the living God, and bring him down, cut off his Head, and give his Carcass, with all the uncircumcised Armies, in all Nations and Countries, to the

Beasts of the Field; the Field is the World, Satan is the Beast of the Field, his Fowls are airy, and to the Fowls of the Air, where Satan the Prince of Darkness Rules, there let 'em go together where they belong, Birds of a Feather let 'em go together; if they love to live in Hell, in Sin let 'em take it, and the Reward of it, Torment. Kites amongst Chickens, and Wolves with Lambs, come but to devour, it is their Nature.

The People in these Countries of *America*, have been Blessed with a great deal of Plenty and quiet living for many Years; it is to be feared many, yea the greatest Number by far are grown lukewarm, as to Religion especially, and are become careless, forgetful and negligent to make suitable returns to the Almighty for his innumerable favours which he hath been pleased to shower down upon us continually in such abundance, both Spiritually and Temporally for Body and Soul. I believe there was a time when many tender Souls (I hope there is some yet left) lived in a Divine Sense of these great Blessings, and sincerely endeavoured to make suitable returns or acknowledgments to the Lord, the Giver, for the same; by walking and living an Holy, Pious, Temperate, Righteous, Just and a Strict self-denying Life, and and so manifested their Sincerity and Love to the ever Blessed Truth, in the sight of God and Man.

By avoiding every thing that might seem to be Sin, these were without Sin, not omitting any thing, they in the Light of Truth see to be their Duty. But Oh! Oh! Oh! if such as these Chieftains turn their Backs in the Day of Battle (against Sin and Satan.) What will become of the rest of the Army, if these turn with, or like, the Dog to lick up his Filthiness which he had cast out, and with the Swine that washed to wallowing again in the Mire of Sin and Iniquity of every and any Sort. What will become of us; for old Men, may be some middle Age too, are centred in the Earth, Greedily Grasping and Gaping after the World.

Mamon, Mamon, Mamon, as though Satan ruled in them; for he is God of this World, and Satan is self, self, self unmortified; no worse Devil can be found either in under or above the Ground.

The young ones they are got into the airy Region, where the Prince of Darkness rules in the disobedient Hearts.

Riding, Drinking and Galloping about from House to House, Smoaking, Snufing, Chawing Tobacco, and other unclean. fulsom, foul, indecent and Sinful Practices; spending their precious time in their Master (Satan's) Service, and some wasting the Substance and Estates, which they never wrought for, live and die miserable, and leave their poor Children Forlorn and helpless for others to maintain, when they are gone stinking to their Graves, and have left a bad Savour behind them, by their great Intemperance, Idleness, Carelessness and Slothfulness or altogether, and when they have so consumed their Substance, ride up and down to borrow of others, but take little care to pay it again.

Oh! that the poor tender young Creatures, and old too, that are still remaining, might consider in time and turn to the Lord by unfeigned Repentance and Amendment of Life that so those Evils and Misery, which otherwise will come upon them, might be avoided, is the hearty desire of my mind, and that is the end or intent of my Writing. . . .

And all things considered, it would conduce more to the Welfare of the Province, to have White Servants for a Term of Years, than to have Slaves for Life. Few can endure to hear of a Negro's being made free; and indeed they can seldom use their Freedom well; yet their continual aspiring after their forbidden Liberty, renders them Unwilling Servants. And there is such a disparity in their Conditions, Colour and Hair, that they can never embody with us, & grow up in orderly Families, to the Peopling of the Land: but still remain in our Body Politick as a kind of extra-vasat Blood. As many Negro Men as there are among us, so many empty Places there are in our Train Bands, and the places taken up of Men that might make Husbands for our Daughters. And the Sons and Daughters of *New-England* would become more like *Jacob* and *Rachel*, if this Slavery were thrust quite out of Doors. Moreover it is too well known what Temptations Masters are under, to connive at the Fornication of their Slaves; lest they should be obliged to find them Wives, or pay their Fines. It seems to be practically pleaded that they might be Lawless; 'tis thought much of, that the Law should have Satisfaction for their Thefts, and other Immoralities; by which means, *Holiness to the Lord*, is more rarely engraven upon this sort of Servitude. It is likewise most lamentable to think, how in taking Negroes out of *Africa*, and Selling of them here, That which God has joined together, Men do boldly rend asunder; Men from their Country, Husbands from their Wives, Parents from their Children. How horrible is the Uncleanness, Mortality, if not Murder, that the Ships are guilty of that bring great Crouds of these miserable Men and Women. Methinks, when we are bemoaning the barbarous Usage of our Friends and Kinsfolk in *Africa*, it might not be unseasonable to enquire whether we are not culpable in forcing the *Africans* to become Slaves amongst ourselves. And it may be a question whether all the Benefit received by Negro Slaves, will balance the Accompt of Cash laid out upon them; and for the Redemption of our own enslaved Friends out of *Africa*. Besides all the Persons and Estates that have perished there.

Obj. 1. *These Blackamores are of the Posterity of* Cham, *and therefore are under the Curse of Slavery*. Gen. 9. 25, 26, 27.

Ans. Of all Offices, one would not beg this; *viz.* Uncall'd for, to be an Executioner of the Vindictive Wrath of God; the extent and duration of which is to us uncertain. If this ever was a Commission; How do we know but that it is long since out of Date? Many have found it to their Cost, that a Prophetical Denunciation of Judgment against a Person or People, would not warrant them to inflict that evil. If it would, *Hazael* might justify himself in all he did against his Master, and the *Israelites*, from 2 Kings 8. 10, 12.

But it is possible that by cursory reading, this Text may have been mistaken. For *Canaan* is the Person Cursed three times over, without the mentioning of *Cham*. Good Expositors suppose the Curse entailed on him, and that this Prophesie was accomplished in the Extirpation of the *Canaanites*, and in the Servitude of the *Gibeonites. Vide Pareum.* Whereas the Blackmores are not descended of *Canaan*, but of *Cush.* Psal. 68. 31. *Princes shall come out of Egypt* [Mizraim] *Ethiopia* [Cush] *shall soon stretch out her Hands unto God.* Under which Names, all *Africa* may be comprehended; and their Promised Conversion ought to be prayed for. *Jer.* 13. 23. *Can the Ethiopian change his Skin?* This shews that Black Men are the Posterity of *Cush:* Who time out of mind have been distinguished by their Colour. And for want of the true, *Ovid* assigns a fabulous cause of it.

> *Sanguine tum credunt in corpora summa vocato*
> *Æthiopum populos nigrum traxisse colorem.*
> Metamorph. lib. 2.

Obj. 2. *The* Nigers *are brought out of a Pagan Country, into places where the Gospel is Preached.*

Ans. Evil must not be done, that good may come of it. The extraordinary and comprehensive Benefit accruing to the Church of God, and to *Joseph* personally, did not rectify his Brethrens Sale of him.

Obj. 3. *The* Africans *have Wars one with another: Our Ships bring lawful Captives taken in those Wars.*

Ans. For aught is known, their Wars are much such as were between *Jacob*'s Sons and their Brother *Joseph.* If they be between Town and Town; Provincial or National: Every War is upon one side Unjust. An Unlawful War can't make lawful Captives. And by Receiving, we are in danger to promote, and partake in their Barbarous Cruelties. I am sure, if some Gentlemen should go down to the *Brewsters* to take the Air, and Fish: And a stronger Party from *Hull* should surprise them, and sell them for Slaves to a Ship outward bound: they would think themselves unjustly dealt with; both by Sellers and Buyers. And yet 'tis to be feared, we have no other kind of Title to our *Nigers. Therefore all things whatsoever ye would that Men should do to you, do ye even so to them: for this is the Law and the Prophets.* Matt. 7. 12.

Obj. 4. Abraham *had Servants bought with his Money, and born in his House.*

Ans. Until the Circumstances of *Abraham*'s purchase be recorded, no Argument can be drawn from it. In the mean time, Charity obliges us to conclude, that He knew it was lawful and good.

It is Observable that the *Israelites* were strictly forbidden the buying, or selling one another for Slaves. *Levit.* 25, 39, 46. *Jer.* 34. 8.———22. And God gaged His Blessing in lieu of any loss they might conceit they suffered thereby. *Deut.* 15. 18. And since the partition Wall is broken down, inordinate Self-love should likewise be demolished. God expects that Christians should be of a more Ingenious and benign frame of Spirit. Christians should carry it to all the World, as the *Israelites* were to carry it one towards another. And for Men obstinately to persist in holding their Neighbours and Brethren under the Rigor of perpetual Bondage, seems to be no proper way of gaining Assurance that God has given them Spiritual

Freedom. Our Blessed Saviour has altered the Measures of the ancient Love-Song, and set it to a most Excellent New-Tune, which all ought to be ambitious of Learning. *Matt.* 5. 43, 44. *John* 13: 34. These *Ethiopians*, as black as they are; seeing they are the Sons and Daughters of the First *Adam*, the Brethren and Sisters of the Last Adam, and the Offspring of God; They ought to be treated with a Respect agreeable. . . .

Oh! that all the Libertines, loose Livers, the Magdalens, the Publicans and Harlots, the Smoaking Drunkards, all unclean Persons, Thieves and Covetous, Covetous, the Covetous Earthly minded Idolater, the Superstitious, Formal and Nominal Christians, Preachers and Hearers, the young and old, old, the old Hypocrites too, if possible, I say if possible might be converted, translated, drawn out of that deep, dirty Ditch Hypocrisy.

And all the blind Zealots, and Superstitious Bigots, of all Names, their Nature and Spirit is the same, when invested with a little imaginary Power, how they will rage and persecute furiously them that oppose 'em, reprove 'em, and will not submit to their Rules, Orders and Laws, though never so unjust, and thus it happened to many of our dear Friends called *Quakers*, in *Old* as well as *New-England*, and elsewhere, when they went into their Synagogues, Mass-Houses, or Idol Temples to reprove 'em, for their Hypocrisy and Wickedness, in pretending to Worship him that laid down his Life for his Enemies, and at same time preparing Laws to take away the Lives of his Servants, that came in his Name, to do his Will, as he the Holy one required it at their Hands. I would tenderly advise, and earnestly intreat all my dear Friends to be very careful not to taste nor touch that Dust and Dirt, Persecution, which is the Serpents Meat, and *Cain*'s Mark, and it is Satan's Food, and his Childrens Meat and Drink, and Life, to do the will of their Hellish Father, and Father in Hell, that sends them and sets 'em about that, & all other unrighteousness and Iniquity, and it is as essential to them in that State and Nature, as it was and is to Christ's Brethren and Sisters, and all his true Friends and faithful Followers, to do the will of their Heavenly Father, & Father which is in Heaven, in his Holy Church, his Body, comprised of Sanctified Members, purified Hearts and Souls, washed and cleansed from all Sin; and such as those did of old, and now doth perfectly know a new Birth, a being Born again of him, and in him that is True and is the very Truth itself the very pure Verity of Verities, the Eternal Essence in him only, not in any Book or Books, a Thousand Ship-loads of the very best of Books will do us no good, nor the best of Professions, Ordinances, and Humane Preachers (much less the worst) will do us no good, except Man (Male and Female) be Born again he cannot see the Kingdom or Government of Truth, or of God, which is one; this was and is and ever will be declared of by the Eternal Truth, to all that had, have and shall have Eyes, Ears and Hearts truly prepared to receive it.

And that all, for the Call is gone forth to all, might come to know this new Birth, this being Born again of the incorruptible Seed, and the Word of Truth Eternal, and be washed from all the filthiness of Flesh, as well as

Spirit, from all unrighteousness, and all self righteousness too, that very dangerous Enemy to Man's Happiness, and that all might be redeemed and Translated out of the Kingdom of Sin and Satan, which is Death and Darkness, Hell and Torment, into the Kingdom of the dear Son and Power of Truth, which is pure righteousness, Peace and Joy, in the Holy Ghost, in the pure Hearts and clean Bodies of his Children and Servants he dwells, they are his Body, his Temple and Kingdom, he Rules, Reigns and Governs, and takes delight in pure Hearts, and the pure in Heart see him and know him, and dwell in him, the Truth in him, and he in them, and his Banner over them, and Standard in them, is Faith and pure Love, and these sits and abides under his Divine Shade with great delight, and his Heavenly Fruit is sweet to their taste, and they are ravished with his Beauty, and overcome with his Love at times, and their Cups do overflow, and the Song of the Heavenly Host is known, and here the Bright and Morning Star is seen and doth remain where the Babe Immortal is Born the Proclamation is heard great Joy to all People, Peace on Earth & good will toward all Men, and here the sweet lovely Babe Immortal is formed in the Heavenly Womb, and doth leap for Joy at the sound of the Heavenly Salutation, and when the fulness of time is come the Babe above-mentioned will be Born in the Soul, and his Heavenly Government will be on his Shoulders within, the Divine Essence within, in the Soul that is made perfect through Sufferings, as Christ was; he that can receive it let him. Oh! that this might be the Blessed experience of all Mankind, that the Earth might become a *Paradise* again, to all People, as it is to some; is the sincere and hearty desire of my Soul and Spirit, much more than for all the Wealth in the World abundantly; the Kingdom of Heaven faith Truth, is within you, not known without by any Man, I can truely say.

Darien Protest, January 3, 1739

Allen D. Chandler, ed., *The Colonial Records of the State of Georgia* (Atlanta, 1905), 3:427-28.

"The Want of the Use of Negroes with proper Limitations which if granted, would both induce great Numbers of White People to come here, and also render us capable to subsist ourselves by raising Provisions upon our Lands. . . ." This appeal in 1738 by certain inhabitants of Savannah, Georgia, reflected their increasing demands that the laws excluding slavery from Georgia, the asylum for orphans and debtors, be repealed. Since 1735 slavery had been legally prohibited in the colony, principally for fear that the neighboring Spanish inhabitants might incite slaves to revolt and that a large black population would discourage white immigration to the colony. But soon a large percentage of the colonists sought to secure "black property," and they circulated the Savannah petition requesting that privilege.

On January 3, 1739, a counter-petition, addressed to Governor-General James Oglethorpe, was signed by 18 Scots from Darien. Although certain practical arguments against black importation were not unusual or unsuspected in the document, the last paragraph contained radical antislavery phrases—"shocking to human Nature; Scourge; Scene of Horror; bloody." On June 20, 1739, the Trustees of Georgia refused to permit the importation of the "baneful Commodity" which had brought neighboring colonies, especially South Carolina, to the "Brink of Ruin."

But the 1735 law was not vigorously enforced in the years that followed. Planters brought slaves from South Carolina with impunity, thus establishing human slavery in the colony. In 1749 the Trustees, recognizing the existing situation, repealed the exclusion law. During the American Revolution Georgia politicians were ardent defenders of the institution. As for the Darien Scots, their petition of 1739 was echoed by Darien citizens a generation later. In 1775 a committee from Darien proclaimed, ". . . we hereby declare our disapprobation and abhorrence of the unnatural practice of Slavery in America (however the uncultivated state of our country, or other specious arguments may plead for it), a practice founded in injustice and cruelty, and highly dangerous to our liberties (as well as lives), debasing part of our fellow-creatures below men, and corrupting the virtue and morals of the rest. . . ."

We are informed, that our Neighbors of Savannah have petitioned your Excellency for the Liberty of having Slaves. We hope, and earnestly entreat, that before such Proposals are hearkened unto, your Excellency will consider our Situation, and of what dangerous and bad Consequence such Liberty would be of to us, for many Reasons;

I. The Nearness of the Spaniard, who have proclaimed Freedom to all Slaves who run away from their Masters, makes it impossible for us to keep them without more Labour in guarding them, that what we would be at to do their Work.

II. We are laborious, and know that a White Man may be by the Year more usefully employed than a Negro.

III. We are not rich, and becoming Debtors for Slaves, in case of their running away or dying, would inevitably ruin the poor Master, and he become a greater Slave to the Negro Merchant, than the Slave he bought could be to him.

IV. It would oblige us to keep a Guard-duty at least as severe as when we expected a daily Invasion; and if that was the Case, how miserable would it be to us, and our Wives and Families, to have an Enemy without, and more dangerous ones in our Bosom!

V. It's shocking to human Nature, that any Race of Mankind, and their Posterity, should be sentenced to perpetual Slavery; nor in Justice can we think otherwise of it, than they are thrown amongst us to be our Scourge one Day or another for our Sins; and as Freedom to them must be as dear as to us, what a Scene of Horror must it bring about! And the longer it is unexecuted, the bloody Scene must be the greater. We therefore, for our own sakes, our Wives and Children, and our Posterity, beg your Consideration, and intreat, that instead of introducing Slaves, you'll put us in the way to get us some of our Countrymen, who with their Labour in time of Peace, and our Vigilance, if we are invaded, with the Help of those, will render it a difficult thing to hurt us, or that Part of the Province we possess. We will for ever pray for your Excellency, and are, with all Submission,

New Inverness, 3d
January 1738-9.

Your Excellency's most obliged
humble Servants,

John Mackintosh Moore
John Mackintosh Lynvilge
Ranald M'Donald
H M Hugh Morrison's Mark
John Mc Donald
John Macklean
John Mackintosh Son to L
John Mc Intosh Bain
James Mc Kay

Daniel Clark, First
Alexander Clarke, Son to the above
Donald Clark, Third, his Mark
Jos. B I Burges his Mark
Donald Clark, Second
Archibald A M B M'Bain his Mark
Alexander Monro
William Monro
John Cuthbert.

To his Excellency General
Oglethorpe.

Hugh Bryan, Public Retraction of Antislavery Statements, 1742

South Carolina Commons House of Assembly, *Commons House Journal*, March 1742, no. 17, pt. 2:285-87, South Carolina Department of Archives and History, Columbia, S.C.

By 1741 some antislavery agitators, most notably Hugh Bryan, found themselves the targets of legal action. On March 17, the Grand Jury of Charles Town, South Carolina, charged that Bryan, known by some as "the Grand Prophet," had written a journal foretelling the imminent uprising of South Carolina slaves and the destruction of Charles Town by a black liberation army. Captured by Indians at the age of 16, Hugh Bryan was held as a slave by a half-breed until he was later freed by a sympathetic chief. His harrowing experiences as a white slave initiated a fanatical religious conversion. In the early 1740s, steeped in the fervency of awakening revivalism, Bryan befriended the renowned preacher, George Whitefield. When Whitefield suggested that Bryan might serve a religious mission by teaching Negroes, Bryan accepted the challenge. But when rumors of ominous gatherings of blacks and secret shipments of firearms stirred the Charles Town populace, Hugh Bryan became the subject of an investigation. The Grand Jury alleged that Bryan and others illegally gathered slaves together in the wilderness, under the pretense of religious worship, to foment a revolution. The Grand Jury recommended that "effectual and speedy Measures" be taken against Bryan and his agents of doom. Before such measures were applied, however, Bryan underwent a dramatic change of heart. Suddenly the realization came to Bryan that his prophecies had been inspired, not by the Spirit of God, but by Satan himself. The frightened and intimidated Prophet hastily fired off a letter to the South Carolina Commons House of Assembly explaining that, upon bitter reflection, he had beheld the error of his ways. ". . . As all Men are failable," Bryan lamented, "I hope your Honours will the more easily pardon me in this thing." The antislavery ventures of Hugh Bryan were at an end.

Mr. Speaker presented to the House a Letter from Col. Hugh Bryan, And the same was received.
Ordered,

That the said letter be read, and the same was read accordingly and is in the words following. (that is to say)

To the honble William Bull jun. Esq. Speaker, And To the rest of the honble the Members of the Commons House of Assembly, met at Col. Miles Brewton's in Charles Town this day of March 1741-42.

May it please your Honours, It is with shame, intermixed with joy, that I write you this. I find that I have presumed in my zeal for God's glory beyond his will, and that he has suffered me to fall into a delusion of Satan. Particularly in adhering to the impressions on my mind, though not to my knowledge in my reflections and other occurrences of my journal. This delusion I did not discover till three days past, when after many days intimate converse with an invisible spirit, whose precepts seemed to be wise, and tending to the advancement of religion in general, and of my own spiritual welfare in particular, I found my teacher to be a Lier, and the father of lies; which brought me into a sense of my error; and has much abased my soul with bitter reflections on the dishonor I have done to God, as well as the disquiet which I may have occasioned to my country. Satan till then appeared to me as an Angel of light, in his spiritual conversation! But since I have discovered his wiles, he's appeared a devil indeed; shewing his rage. But God, who is rich in mercy, hath prevented him, and strengthned me. My zeal for God excited Satans malace; and my pride required abasement: therefore it was just with God to desert me. Thus St. Peter was abased for his presumptuous confidence; and holy David, when he presumed that his mountain stood strong, soon found himself weak. My misfortune may caution others, who think they stand, to take heed, lest they fall also. My sincere regard for my country's welfare, and my zeal for my God, put me on sending to you my journal, at the risque of suffering for it; and now my sense of the error, and the ill that may attend it, obliges me (in duty) to send you this, to prevent the uneasiness which my Journal may create to the government. In both I have acted with a conscientious regard to discharge my trust truly to God & my country, and trust truly to God and my country, and therefore, as all men are fallible, I hope your Honors will the more easily pardon me in this thing. I am suprized to hear that I am suspected of secret designs, contrary to the peace and tranquility of the government; and that it is reported that I have furnished spare arms for such design from Charles Town: I so declare that I have procured neither arms nor ammunition of any sort; which if I had, it might easily be known from the merchants who sell those things in Charles Town: and from them your Honors may soon be informed of the certainty. My whole life has been spent among you; and my manner of life and conversation, and former zeal for my countrys welfare, is known to you: and my inclinations with respect to my love and zeal for my countrys good are still the same as formerly. I beg leave only to add that Gods favor is our country's safety; and our sincere obedience to his commands is our wisest method to obtain it. Which wisdom may God of his infinite mercy grant to each member of our community; and especially to your Honors, and all in authority (the feet do naturally travel whither soever the head leads) is the prayer of

Your Honors,
most humble and dutiful servant in Jesus Christ

Hugh Bryan

P.S. May we all keep close to the Law, and to the testimony of our God, and kearken to no other revelation for Divine truth, and work & pray that we enter not into temptation is a further prayer of

Your most unworthy servant

Hugh Bryan

John Woolman, *Some Considerations on the Keeping of Negroes*, 1754

John Woolman, *Some Considerations on the Keeping of Negroes: Recommended to the Professors of Christianity of every Denomination* (Philadelphia, 1754), introduction; pp. 1-24.

John Woolman, the pious Mt. Holly, New Jersey, tailor, is often described as the foremost exemplar of the Quaker ideal, and his Journal remains a significant chronicle of the Quaker personality. Influential at Quaker meetings and a gifted writer, the pacific Woolman gave to the antislavery movement a respectability which was vital. His first published work against slavery, Some Considerations on the Keeping of Negroes, *followed a tour through several slaveholding colonies where he became extraordinarily disheartened by the sight of human misery and degradation so blithely accepted. He appealed to "true heavenly Principle," to the gentleness and compassion implicit in the Quaker faith, and began to travel with missionary zeal through slave colonies such as Maryland, Virginia, and North Carolina, trying to reason with Quaker slaveowners to release their black property.*

Together with the intense disruption occasioned by the French and Indian War and the spirit of benevolence and charity aroused in the Quaker sect, Woolman's efforts helped promote a genuine reassessment (by the Society) of the slavery question. The 1758 Yearly Meeting, at which Woolman made an impassioned plea, issued the following minute, which was accepted by the Society as a rule of discipline: "This meeting very earnestly and affectionately entreates [sic.] Friends . . . if after the sense and judgment of this meeting, now given against every branch of this practice, any professing with us should persist to vindicate it, and be concerned in importing, selling or purchasing slaves, the respective monthly meetings to which they belong, should manifest their disunion with such persons by refusing to permit them to sit in meeting for discipline, or to be employed in the affairs of Truth, or to receive from them any contribution towards the relief of the poor, or other services of the meeting."

In 1762 Woolman published the second part of his Considerations *and for the next ten years continued his extensive travels among the Quakers. On a mission to York, England, in 1772 he died of smallpox. Before his death, Woolman had been a great catalyst for change within the Quaker sect. Perhaps more than any other reformer, he imbued others with some of his own profound sympathy for the black slave. He once wrote of the aged slaves, " . . . When they feel pains, and stiffness in their joints and limbs, weakness of appetite, and that a little labour is wearisome, and still behold themselves in the neglected uncomfortable condition of a slave, . . . For men to be thus treated from one generation to another, who, besides their own distresses, think of the slavery entailed on their posterity, and are grieved. . . ."*

Introduction

Customs generally approved, and Opinions received by Youth from their Superiors, become like the natural Produce of a Soil, especially when they are suited to favourite Inclinations: But as the Judgments of God are

John Woolman and the slave

"John Woolman and the Slave," a drawing showing the Quaker John Woolman pleading for the release of a slave in the 1740's.

without Partiality, by which the State of the Soul must be tried, it would be the highest Wisdom to forego Customs and popular Opinions, and try the Treasures of the Soul by the infallible Standard Truth.

Natural Affection *needs a careful Examination: Operating upon us in a soft Manner, it kindles Desires of Love and Tenderness, and there is Danger of taking it for something higher. To me it appears an Instinct like that which inferior Creatures have; each of them, we see, by the Ties of Nature, love* Self *but; that which is a Part of Self* they love by the same Tie or Instinct. In them it by some Measure does the Offices of Reason, by which, among other Things, they watchfully keep, and orderly feed their helpless Offspring. Thus Natural Affection *appears to be a Branch of* Self-love, *good in the Animal Race, in us likewise, with proper Limitations; but otherwise is productive of Evil, by exciting Desires to promote* some *by Means prejudicial* to others.

Our *Blessed Saviour seems to give a Check to this irregular Fondness in Nature, and, at the same Time, a President for us.* Who is my Mother, and who are my Brethren? *Thereby intimating, that the earthly Ties of Relationship, are, comparatively, inconsiderable to such who, thro' a steady Course of Obedience, have come to the happy Experience of the Spirit of God bearing witness with their Spirits that they are his Children:*——— And he stretched forth his Hands towards his Disciples, and said, Behold my Mother and my Brethren: For whosoever shall do the Will of my Father which is in Heaven *(arrives at the more noble Part of true Relationship)* the same is my Brother, and Sister, and Mother, *Mat.* xii, 48.

This *Doctrine agrees well with a State truly compleat, where* Love *necessarily operates according to the Agreeableness of Things on Principles unalterable and in themselves perfect.*

If *endeavouring to have my Children eminent amongst Men after my Death, be that which no Reasons grounded on those Principles can be brought to support; then to be temperate in my Pursuit after Gain, and to keep always within the Bounds of those Principles, is an indispensable Duty, and to depart from it, a dark unfruitful Toil.*

In *our present Condition, to* love our Children *is needful; but except* this Love *proceeds from the true heavenly Principle which sees beyond earthly Treasures, it will rather be injurious than of any real Advantage to them: Where the Fountain is corrupt, the Streams must necessarily be impure.*

That *important Injunction of our Saviour,* Mat. vi. 33. *with the Promise annexed, contains a short but comprehensive View of our Duty and Happiness:———If then the Business of Mankind in this Life, is, to first seek another; if this cannot be done, but by attending to the Means; if a Summary of the Means is,* Not to do that to another which, in like Circumstances, we would not have done unto us, *then these are Points of Moment, and worthy of our most serious Consideration.*

What *I write on this subject is with Reluctance, and the Hints given are in as general Terms as my Concern would allow: I know it is a Point about which in all its Branches Men that appear to aim well are not generally agreed, and for that Reason I chose to avoid being very particular:———If I may happily have let drop any Thing that may excite such as are concerned in the Practice to a close Thinking on the Subject treated of, the Candid amongst them may easily do the Subject such further Justice, as, on an impartial Enquiry, it may appear to deserve; and such an Enquiry I would earnestly recommend.*

Some Considerations On the Keeping of Negroes.

As Many Times there are different Motives to the same Actions; and one does that from a generous Heart, which another does for selfish Ends:———The like may be said in this Case.

There are various Circumstances amongst them that keep Negroes, and different Ways by which they fall under their Care; and, I doubt not, there are many well disposed Persons amongst them who desire rather to manage wisely and justly in this difficult Matter, than to make Gain of it.

But the general Disadvantage which these poor *Africans* lie under in an enlight'ned Christian Country, having often fill'd me with real Sadness, and been like undigested Matter on my Mind, I now think it my Duty, through Divine Aid, to offer some Thoughts thereon to the Consideration of others.

When we remember that all Nations are of one Blood, *Gen.* iii. 20. that in this World we are but Sojourners, that we are subject to the like Afflictions and Infirmities of Body, the like Disorders and Frailties in Mind, the like Temptations, the same Death, and the same Judgment, and, that the Alwise Being is Judge and Lord over us all, it seems to raise an Idea of a general Brotherhood, and a Disposition easy to be touched with a Feeling of each others Afflictions: But when we forget those Things, and look chiefly at our outward Circumstances, in this and some Ages past, constantly retaining in our Minds the Distinction betwixt us and them, with respect to our Knowledge and Improvement in Things divine, natural and artificial, our Breasts being apt to be filled with fond Notions of Superiority; there is Danger or erring in our Conduct toward them.

We allow them to be of the same Species with ourselves, the Odds is, we are in a higher Station, and enjoy greater Favours than they: And when it is thus, that our heavenly Father endoweth some of his Children with distinguished Gifts, they are intended for good Ends; but if those thus gifted are thereby lifted up above their Brethren, not considering themselves as Debtors to the Weak, nor behaving themselves as faithful Stewards, none who judge impartially can suppose them free from Ingratitude.

When a People dwell under the liberal Distribution of Favours from Heaven, it behoves them carefully to inspect their Ways, and consider the Purposes for which those Favours were bestowed, lest, through Forgetfulness of God, and Misusing his Gifts, they incur his heavy Displeasure, whose Judgments are just and equal, who exalteth and humbleth to the Dust as he seeth meet.

It appears by Holy Record that Men under high Favours have been apt to err in their Opinions concerning others. Thus *Israel*, according to the Description of the Prophet, *Isai*. lxv. 5. when exceedingly corrupted and degenerated, yet remembered they were the chosen People of God, and could say, *Stand by thyself, come not near me, for I am holier than thou.* That this was no chance Language, but their common Opinion of other People, more fully appears by considering the Circumstances which attended when God was beginning to fulfil his precious Promises concerning the Gathering of the *Gentiles*.

The Most High, in a Vision, undeceived Peter, first prepared his Heart to believe; and, at the House of *Cornelius* shewed him of a Certainty that God was no Respector of Persons.

The effusion of the Holy Ghost upon a People with whom they, the *Jewish* Christians, would not so much as eat, was strange to them: All they of the Circumcision were astonished to see it; and the Apostles and Brethren of *Judea* contended with *Peter* about it, till he, having rehearsed the whole Matter, and fully shewn that the Father's Love was unlimited, they are there at struck with Admiration, and cry out; *Then hath God also to the Gentiles granted Repentance unto Life!*

The Opinion of peculiar Favours being confined to them, was deeply rooted, or else the above Instance had been less strange to them, for these Reasons: *First*, They were generally acquainted with the Writings of the Prophets, by whom this Time was repeatedly spoken of, and pointed at. *Secondly*, Our Blessed Lord shortly before expresly said, *I have other Sheep, not of this Fold, them also must I bring*, &c. *Lastly*, His Words to them after his Resurrection, at the very Time of his Ascention, *Ye shall be Witnesses to me, not only in* Jerusalem, Judea, *and* Samaria, *but to the uttermost Parts of the Earth.*

Those concuring Circumstances, one would think, might have raised a strong Expectation of seeing such a time; yet, when it came, it proved Matter of Offence and Astonishment.

To consider Mankind otherwise than Brethren, to think Favours are peculiar to one Nation, and exclude others, plainly supposes a Darkness in the Understanding: For as God's Love is universal, so where the Mind is sufficiently influenced by it, it begets a Likeness of itself, and the Heart is enlarged towards all Men. Again, to conclude a People forward, perverse, and worse by Nature than others (who ungratefully receive Favours, and apply them to bad Ends) this will excite a Behaviour toward them unbecoming the Excellence of true Religion.

To prevent such Error, let us calmly consider their Circumstance; and, the better to do it, make their Case ours. Suppose, then, that our Ancestors and we had been exposed to constant Servitude in the more servile and inferior Employments of Life; that we had been destitute of the Help of Reading and good Company; that amongst ourselves we had had few wise and pious Instructors; that the Religious amongst our Superiors seldom took Notice of us; that while others, in Ease, have plentifully heap'd up the

Fruit of our Labour, we had receiv'd barely enough to relieve Nature, and being wholly at the Command of others, had generally been treated as a contemptible, ignorant Part of Mankind; Should we, in that Case, be less abject than they now are? Again, If Oppression be so hard to bear, that a wise Man is made mad by it, *Eccl.* vii. 7. then a Series of those Things altering the Behaviour and Manners of a People, is what may reasonably be expected.

When our Property is taken contrary to our Mind, by means appearing to us unjust, it is only through divine Influence, and the Enlargement of Heart from thence proceeding, that we can love our reputed Oppressors: If the *Negroes* fall short in this, an uneasy, if not a disconsolate Disposition, will be awak'ned, and remain like Seeds in their Minds, producing Sloth and many other Habits appearing odious to us, with which being free Men, they, perhaps, had not been chargeable. These, and other Circumstances, rightly considered, will lessen that too great Disparity, which some make between us and them.

Integrity of Heart hath appeared in some of them; so that if we continue in the Word of Christ (previous to Discipleship, *John* viii. 31.) and our Conduct towards them be seasoned with his Love, we may hope to see the good Effect of it: The which, in a good Degree, is the Case with some into whose Hands they have fallen: But that too many treat them otherwise, not seeming concious of any Neglect, is, alas! too evident.

When *Self-love* presides in our Minds, our Opinions are bias'd in our own Favour; in this Condition, being concerned with a People so situated, that they have no Voice to plead their own Cause, there's Danger of using ourselves to an undisturbed Partiality, till, by long Custom, the Mind becomes reconciled with it, and the Judgment itself infected.

To humbly apply to God for Wisdom, that we may thereby be enabled to see Things as they are, and ought to be, is very needful; hereby the hidden Things of Darkness may be brought to light, and the Judgment made clear. We shall, then consider Mankind as Brethren: Though different Degrees and, a Variety of Qualifications and Abilities, one dependant on another, be admitted, yet high Thoughts will be laid aside, and all Men treated as becometh the Sons of one Father, agreeable to the Doctrine of Christ Jesus.

> He hath laid down the best Criterion, by which Mankind ought to judge of their own Conduct, and others judge for them of theirs, one towards another, *viz. Whatsoever ye would that Men should do unto you, do ye even so to them.* I take it, that all Men by Nature, are equally entituled to the Equity of this Rule, and under the indispensable Obligations of it. One Man ought not to look upon another Man, or Society of Men, as so far beneath him, but that he should put himself in their Place, in all his Actions towards them, and bring all to this Test, *viz.* How should I approve of this Conduct, were I in their Circumstance and they in mine?

This Doctrine being of a moral unchangeable Nature, hath been likewise inculcated in the former Dispensation; *If a Stranger sojourn with thee in your Land, ye shall not vex him; but the Stranger that dwelleth with you, shall be as One born amongst you, and thou shalt love him as thyself, Lev.* xix. 33, 34. Had these People come voluntarily and dwelt amongst us, to have called them Strangers would be proper; and their being brought by Force, with Regret, and a languishing Mind, may well raise Compassion in a Heart rightly disposed: But there is Nothing in such Treatment, which upon a wise and judicious Consideration, will any Ways lessen their Right of being treated as Strangers. If the Treatment which many of them meet with, be rightly examined and compared with those Precepts, *Thou shalt not vex him nor oppress him; he shall be as one born amongst you, and thou shalt love him as thyself*, Lev. xix. 33. Deut. xxvii. 19. there will appear an important Difference betwixt them.

It may be objected there is Cost of Purchase, and Risque of their Lives to them who possess 'em, and therefore needful that they make the best Use of their Time: In a Practice just and reasonable, such Objections may have Weight; but if the Work be wrong from the Beginning, there's little or no Force in them. If I purchase a Man who hath never forfeited his Liberty, the natural Right of Freedom is in him; and shall I keep him and his Posterity in Servitude and Ignorance? "How should I approve of this Conduct, were I in his Circumstances, and he in mind?" It may be thought, that to treat them as we would willingly be treated, our Gain by them would be inconsiderable: And it were, in divers Respects, better that there were none in our Country.

We may further consider, that they are now amongst us, and those of our Nation the Cause of their being here; that whatsoever Difficulty accrues thereon, we are justly chargeable with, and to bear all Inconveniencies attending it, with a serious and weighty Concern of Mind to do our Duty by them, is the best we can do. To seek a Remedy by continuing the Oppression, because we have Power to do it, and see others do it, will, I apprehend, not be doing as we would be done by.

How deeply soever Men are involved in the most exquisite Difficulties, Sincerity of Heart, and upright Walking before God, freely submitting to his Providence, is the most sure Remedy: He only is able to relieve, not only Persons, but Nations, in their greatest Calamities.

David, in a great Strait, when the Sense of his past Error, and the full Expectation of an impending Calamity, as the Reward of it, were united to the agravating his Distress, after some Deliberation, faith, *Let me fall now into the Hands of the Lord, for very great are his Mercies; let me not fall into the Hand of Man*, I Chron. xxi. 13.

To act continually with Integrity of Heart, above all narrow or selfish Motives, is a sure Token of our being Partakers of that Salvation which *God hath appointed for Walls and Bulwarks*, Isa. v. 26. Rom. xv. 8. and is, beyond all Contradiction, a more happy Situation than can ever be promised by the utmost Reach of Art and Power united, nor proceeding from heavenly Wisdom.

A Supply to Nature's lawful Wants, joined with a peaceful, humble Mind, is the truest Happiness in this Life; and if here we arrive to this, and remain to walk in the Path of the Just, our Case will be truly happy: And though herein we may part with, or miss of some glaring Shews of Riches, and leave our Children little else but wise Instructions, a good Example, and the Knowledge of some honest Employment, these, with the Blessing of

Providence, are sufficient for their Happiness, and are more likely to prove so, than laying up Treasures for them, which are often rather a Snare, than any real Benefit; especially to them, who, instead of being exampled to Temperance, are in all Things taught to prefer the getting of Riches, and to eye the temporal Distinctions they give, as the principal Business of this Life. These readily overlook the true Happiness of Man, as it results from the Enjoyment of all Things in the Fear of God, and, miserably substituting an inferior Good, dangerous in the Acquiring, and uncertain in the Fruition, they are subject to many Disappointments, and every Sweet carries its Sting.

It is the Conclusion of our blessed Lord and his Apostles, as appears by their Lives and Doctrines, that the highest Delights of Sense, or most pleasing Objects visible, ought ever to be accounted infinitely inferior to that real intellectual Happiness suited to Man in his primitive Innocence, and now to be found in true Renovation of Mind; and that the Comforts of our present Life, the Things most grateful to us, ought always to be receiv'd with Temperance, and never made the chief Objects of our Desire, Hope, or Love: But that our whole Heart and Affections be principally looking to that *City, which hath Foundations, whose Maker and Builder is God.* Did we so improve the Gifts bestowed on us, that our Children might have an Education suited to these Doctrines, and our Example to confirm it, we might rejoice in Hopes of their being Heirs of an Inheritance incorruptible.

This Inheritance, as Christians, we esteem the most valuable; and how then can we fail to desire it for our Children? O that we were consistent with ourselves, in pursuing Means necessary to obtain it!

It appears, by Experience, that where Children are educated in Fulness, Ease and Idleness, evil Habits are more prevalent, than in common amongst such who are prudently employed in the necessary Affairs of Life: And if Children are not only educated in the Way of so great Temptation, but have also the Opportunity of lording it over their Fellow Creatures, and being Masters of Men in their Childhood, how can we hope otherwise than that their tender Minds will be possessed with Thoughts too high for them? Which, by Continuance, gaining Strength, will prove, like a slow Current, gradually separating them from (or keeping from Acquaintance with) that Humility and Meekness in which alone lasting Happiness can be enjoyed.

Man is born to labour, and Experience abundantly sheweth, that it is for our Good: But where the Powerful lay the Burthen on the Inferior, without affording a Christian Education, and suitable Opportunity of improving the Mind, and a Treatment which we, in their Case, should approve, that themselves may live at Ease, and fare sumptuously, and lay up Riches for their Posterity, this seems to contradict the Design of Providence, and, I doubt, is sometimes the Effect of a perverted Mind: For while the Life of one is made grievous by the Rigour of another, it entails Misery on both.

Amongst the manifold Works of Providence, displayed in the different Ages of the World, these which follow (with many others) may afford Instruction.

Abraham was called of God to leave his Country and Kindred, to sojourn amongst Strangers: Through Famine, and Danger of Death, he was forced to flee from one Kingdom to another: He, at length, not only had Assurance of being the Father of many Nations, but became a mighty Prince, *Gen.* xxiii. 6.

Remarkable was the Dealings of God with *Jacob* in a low Estate, the just Sense he retained of them after his Advancement, appears by his Words; *I am not worthy of the Least of all thy Mercies*, Gen. xxxii. 10 xlviii. 15.

The numerous Afflictions of *Joseph*, are very singular; the particular Providence of God therein, no less manifest: He, at length, became Governor of *Egypt*, and famous for Wisdom and Virtue.

The Series of Troubles *David* passed through, few amongst us are ignorant of, and yet he afterwards became as one of the great Men of the Earth.

Some Evidences of the Divine Wisdom appears in those Things, in that such who are intended for high Stations, have first been very low and dejected, that Truth might be sealed on their Hearts, and that the Characters there imprinted by Bitterness and Adversity, might in after Years remain, suggesting compassionate Ideas, and, in their Prosperity, quicken their Regard to those in the like Condition: Which yet further appears in the Case of *Israel*: They were well acquainted with grievous Sufferings, a long and rigorous Servitude, then, through many notable Events, were made Chief amongst the Nations: To them we find a Repetition of Precepts to the Purpose abovesaid: Though, for Ends agreeable to infinite Wisdom, they were chose as a peculiar People for a Time; yet the Most High acquaints them, that his Love is not confined, but extends to the Stranger; and, to excite their Compassion, reminds them of Times past, *Ye were Strangers in the Land of Egypt*, Deut. x. 19. Again, *Thou shalt not oppress a Stranger, for ye know the Heart of a Stranger, seeing ye were Strangers in the Land of* Egypt, Exod. xxiii. 9.

If we call to Mind our Beginning, some of us may find a Time, wherein our Fathers were under Afflictions, Reproaches, and manifold Sufferings.

Respecting our Progress in this Land, the Time is short since our Beginning was small and Number few, compared with the native Inhabitants. He that sleeps not by Day nor Night, hath watched over us, and kept us as the Apple of his Eye. His Almighty Arm hath been round about us, and saved us from Dangers.

The Wilderness and solitary Desarts in which our Fathers passed the Days of their Pilgrimage, are now turned into pleasant Fields; the Natives are gone from before us, and we established peaceably in the Possession of the Land, enjoying our civil and religious Liberties; and, while many Parts of the World have groaned under the heavy Calamities of War, our Habitation remains quiet, and our Land fruitful.

When we trace back the Steps we have trodden, and see how the Lord hath opened a Way in the Wilderness for us, to the Wise it will easily appear, that all this was not done to be buried in Oblivion; but to prepare a People for more fruitful Returns, and the Remembrance thereof, ought to humble us in Prosperity, and excite in us a Christian Benevolence towards our Inferiors.

If we do not consider these Things aright, but, through a stupid Indolence, conceive Views of Interest, separate from the general Good of the great Brotherhood, and, in Pursuance thereof, treat our Inferiors with Rigour, to increase our Wealth, and gain Riches for our Children, what then shall we do, when God riseth up, and when he visiteth, what shall we Answer him? Did not he that made Us, make Them, and *Did not one Fashion us in the Womb*? Job. xxxi. 14.

To our great Master we stand or fall, to judge or condemn is most suitable to his Wisdom and Authority; my Inclination is to persuade, and intreat, and simply give Hints of my Way of Thinking.

If the Christian Religion be considered, both respecting its Doctrines, and the happy Influence which it hath on the Minds and Manners of all real Christians, it looks reasonable to think, that the miraculous Manifestation thereof to the World, is a Kindness beyond Expression.

Are we the People thus favoured? Are we they whose Minds are opened, influenced, and govern'd by the Spirit of Christ, and thereby made Sons of God? Is it not a fair Conclusion, that we, like our heavenly Father, ought, in our Degree, to be active in the same great Cause, of the Eternal Happiness of, at least, our whole Families, and more, if thereto capacitated?

If we, by the Operation of the Spirit of Christ, become Heirs with him in the Kingdom of his Father, and are redeemed from the alluring counterfeit Joys of this World, and the Joy of Christ remain in us, to suppose that One remaining in this happy Condition, can for the Sake of earthly Riches, not only deprive his Fellow Creatures of the Sweetness of Freedom (which, rightly used, is one of the greatest temporal Blessings) but therewith neglect using proper Means, for their Acquaintance with the Holy Scriptures, and the Advantage of true Religion, seems at least, a Contradiction to Reason.

Whoever rightly advocates the Cause of some, thereby promotes the Good of all. The State of Mankind was harmonious in the Beginning, and tho' Sin hath introduced Discord, yet, through the wonderful Love of God, in Christ Jesus our Lord, the Way is open for our Redemption, and Means appointed to restore us to primitive Harmony. That if one suffer, by the Unfaithfulness of another, the Mind, the most noble Part of him that occasions the Discord, is thereby alienated from its true and real Happiness.

Our Duty and Interest is inseparably united, and when we neglect or misuse our Talents, we necessarily depart from the heavenly Fellowship, and are in the Way to the greatest of Evils.

Therefore, to examine and prove ourselves, to find what Harmony the Power presiding in us beats with the Divine Nature, is a Duty not more incumbent and necessary, than it would be beneficial.

In Holy Writ the Divine Being saith of himself, *I am the Lord, which exercise Loving Kindness, Judgment and Righteousness in the Earth; for in these Things I delight, saith the Lord,* Jer. ix. 24. Again, speaking in the Way of Man, to shew his Compassion to *Israel,* whose Wickedness had occasioned a Calamity, and then being humbled under it, it is said, *His Soul was grieved for their Miseries,* Judg. x. 16. If we consider the Life of our Blessed Saviour when on Earth, as it is recorded by his Followers, we shall find, that one uniform Desire for the eternal, and temporal Good of Mankind, discovered itself in all his Actions.

If we observe Men, both Apostles and others, in many different Ages, who have really come to the Unity of the Spirit, and the Fellowship of the Saints, there still appears the like Disposition, and in them the Desire of the real Happiness of Mankind, has out-ballanced the Desire of Ease, Liberty, and, many times, Life itself.

If upon a true Search, we find that our Natures are so far renewed, that to exercise Righteousness and Loving Kindness (according to our Ability) towards all Men, without Respect of Persons, is easy to us, or is our Delight; if our Love be so orderly, and regular, that he who doth the Will of our Father, who is in Heaven, appears in our View, to be our nearest Relation, our Brother, and Sister, and Mother; if this be our Case, there is a good Foundation to hope, that the Blessing of God will sweeten our Treasures during our Stay in this Life, and our Memory be savory, when we are entred into Rest.

To conclude, 'Tis a Truth most certain, that a Life guided by Wisdom from above, agreeable with Justice, Equity, and Mercy, is throughout consistent and amiable, and truly beneficial to Society; the Serenity and Calmness of Mind in it, affords an unparallel'd Comfort in this Life, and the End of it is blessed.

And, no less true, that they, who in the Midst of high Favours, remain ungrateful, and under all the Advantages that a Christian can desire, are selfish, earthly, and sensual, do miss the true Foundation of Happiness, and wander in a Maze of dark Anxiety, where all their Treasures are insufficient to quiet their Minds: Hence, from an insatiable Craving, they neglect doing Good with what they have acquired, and too often add Oppression to Vanity, that they may compass more.

O that they were wise, that they understood this, that they would consider their latter End! Deut. xxxii. 29.

Anthony Benezet, Pamphlet on Negroes in Africa, 1762

Anthony Benezet, *A Short Account of that Part of Africa Inhabited by the Negroes, With Respect to the Fertility of the Country; the good Disposition of many of the Natives, and the Manner by which the Slave Trade is carried on. Extracted from divers Authors, in order to shew the Iniquity of that Trade, and the falsity of the Arguments usually advanced in its Vindication* ... (Philadelphia, 1762), pp. 1-25; 63-80.

In the eighteenth century, the philosopher David Hume and the Scottish jurist Lord Kames were writing of the natural inferiority of the black race; scientists such as Buffon, Pierre de Maupertius, and Linnaeus were describing the development of man as a "Chain of Being" and relegating the black race to the lower rung of the evolutionary ladder; and Edward Long, author of The History of Jamaica, *was referring to blacks as "brutish, ignorant, idle, crafty, treacherous, bloody, thievish, mistrustful, and superstitious." At the same time, the Quaker schoolmaster Anthony Benezet was writing, "Negroes are generally a sensible humane and sociable People, . . their Capacity is as good, and as capable of Improvement as that of the Whites." Benezet's 1762 pamphlet,* A Short Account of that Part of Africa Inhabited by the Negroes, *was a major effort to bring together writings of philosophers, jurists, and English, French, and Dutch factors who had worked in Africa to prove that blacks were "different from the stupified and malicious People some would have them thought to be." This unique pamphlet, marshalling evidence from a wide variety of sources, was followed by many other Benezet compilations.*

The work of the gentle Quaker would establish him as the most prolific and influential propagandist against slavery in the eighteenth century. Working through Quaker meetings and committees, Benezet zealously wrote letter after letter to heads of government, religious leaders, politicans, and others interested in reform. He lobbied during legislative sessions, preached to Quaker slaveowners and exchanged books and pamphlets with a wide-ranging group of individuals in America and Europe. Benezet strongly influenced others such as Thomas Clarkson, John Wesley, and Benjamin Rush to begin their work against slavery. In 1767 Granville Sharp, who later became one of the most influential figures in the international abolition movement, was browsing in a London bookstore when he noticed Benezet's A Short Account. *The work so stirred Sharp that he had it reprinted. It was through such publications, through such an exchange of information, that the movement significantly grew to end what Benezet called "Oppression and Injustice . . . scarcely to be parallelled by any Example in the present or former Ages."*

It is a Truth, as sorrowful as obvious, that Mankind too generally are actuated by false Motives, and substitute an imaginary Interest in the Room of that which is real and permanent: And it must be acknowledged by every Man, who is sincerely desirous of becoming acquainted with himself, and impartially inspects his own Heart, that Weakness and inbred Corruption attend human Nature; which cannot be restored to its original Purity, but through the Efficacy of the Blood of Jesus Christ, our blessed Saviour. So that notwithstanding the imagined moral Rectitude pleaded for, and the boasted Pretences of the present Age, to refined Conceptions of

Things beyond our Forefathers, till this Divine Help is embraced, the Heart of Man will remain corrupt, and its Power of distinguishing between Good and Evil will still be obscured by Prejudice, Passion and Interest. Covetousness and Pride have introduced many iniquitous Practices into civil Society, which tho' odious in themselves, and most pernicious in their Consequences, yet being calculated to gratify our favorite Passions, have been adopted thro' Custom, and enforced so strongly by Example, as to become familiar to us; so that by Degrees we silence the Dictates of Conscience, and reconcile ourselves to such Things as would, when first proposed to our unprejudiced Minds have struck us with Amazement and Horror.

A lamentable and shocking Instance of the Influence which the Love of Gain has upon the Minds of those who yield to its Allurements, even when contrary to the Dictates of Reason, and the common Feelings of Humanity, appears in the Prosecution of the *Negroe Trade*, in which the *English* Nation has long been deeply concerned, and some in this Province have lately engaged. An Evil of so deep a Dye, and attended with such dreadful Consequences, that no well-disposed Person (anxious for the Welfare of himself, his Country, or Posterity) who knows the Tyranny, Oppression and Cruelty with which this iniquitous Trade is carried on, can be a silent and innocent Spectator. How many Thousands of our harmless Fellow Creatures have, for a long Course of Years, fallen a Sacrifice to that selfish Avarice, which gives Life to this complicated Wickedness. The Iniquity of being engaged in a Trade, by which so great a Number of innocent People are yearly destroyed, in an untimely and miserable Manner, is greatly aggravated from the Consideration that we, as a People, have been peculiarly favoured with the Light of the Gospel; that Revelation of Divine Love, which the Angels introduced to the World, by a Declaration *of Peace on Earth, and Good Will to Men . . . of every Nation, Kindred, Tongue and People*. How miserable must be our Condition, if, for filthy Lucre, we should continue to act so contrary to the Nature of this Divine Call, the Purpose of which is to introduce an universal and affectionate Brotherhood in the whole human Species; by removing from the Heart of every Individual, who submits to its Operation, the Darkness and Corruption of Nature, and transforming the selfish, wrathful, proud Spirit, into Meekness, Purity and Love: For this End the Son of God became Man, suffered, and died; and the whole Tenor of the Gospel declares, that for those who refuse, or neglect the Offers of this great Salvation, the Son of God has suffered in vain.

The End proposed by this Essay, is to lay before the candid Reader the Depth of Evil attending this iniquitous Practice, in the Prosecution of which, our Duty of God, the common Father of the Family of the whole Earth, and our Duty of Love to our Fellow Creatures, is totally disregarded; all social Connection and tender Ties of Nature being broken, Desolation and Bloodshed continually fomented in those unhappy People's Country. It is also intended to invalidate the false Arguments, which are frequently advanced, for the Palliation of this Trade, in Hopes it may be some Inducement to those who are not defiled therewith to keep themselves clear; and to lay before such as have unwarily engaged in it, their Danger of totally losing that tender Sensibility to the Sufferings of their Fellow Creatures, the Want whereof sets Men beneath the Brute Creation: A Trade by which many Thousands of innocent People are brought under the greatest Anxiety and Suffering, by being violently rent from their Native Country, in the most cruel Manner, and brought to our Colonies, to be employed in hard Labour, in Climates, unsuited to their Nature, or in a State of the most abject and barbarous Slavery, subject to the Humours and inhuman Lash of some of the most hard hearted and inconsiderate of Mankind, without any Hopes of ever returning to their Native Land, or seeing an End to their Misery: Nor must we omit, in this dismal Account, the Weight of Blood which lies on the Promoters of this Trade, from the great Numbers that are yearly butchered in the Incursions and Battles which happen between the *Negroes*, in order to procure the Number delivered to the *Europeans*; and the many of these poor Creatures whose Hearts are broken, and they perish through Misery and Grief, on the Passage. May the Almighty preserve the Inhabitants of *Pennsylvania* from being further defiled by a Trade, which is entered upon from such sensual Motives, and carried on by such devilish Means.

Persons whose Minds are engrossed by the Pleasures and Profits of this Life, are generally so taken up with present Objects, that they are but little affected with the distant Sufferings of their Fellow Creatures, especially when their Wealth is thereby increased. Nevertheless every one who is in any respect concerned in this wicked Trafique, if not so hardned by the Love of Wealth, as to be void of Feeling, must upon a serious Recollection, be impressed with Surprize and Terror, from a Sense that there is a righteous God, and a State of Retribution which will last for ever. It is frequently alledged, in excuse for this Trade, that the *Negroes* sold in our Plantations, are mostly Persons who have been taken Prisoners in those Wars which arise amongst themselves, from their mutual Animosities; and that these Prisoners would be sacrificed to the Resentment of those who have taken them Captive, if they were not purchased and brought away by the *Europeans*. It is also represented, that the *Negroes* are generally a stupid, savage People, whose Situation in their own Country is necessitous and unhappy, which has induced many to believe, that the bringing them from their Native Land is rather a Kindness than an Injury.

To confute these false Representations, the following Extracts are proposed to the candid Reader's Consideration; they are taken from the Writings of the principal Officers, not only in the *English*, but in the *French* and *Dutch* Factories, or Settlements in *Guiney*, some of whom have lived many Years in those Countries, and have been Eye-witnesses to the Transactions they relate. By which it will appear, that the *Negroes* are generally a sensible humane and sociable People, and that their Capacity is as good, and as capable of Improvement as that of the Whites. That their Country, though unfriendly to the *Europeans*, yet appears peculiarly agreeable, and well adapted to the Nature of the *Blacks*, and so fruitful as to furnish its Inhabitants plentifully with the Necessaries of Life, with much less Labour than in our more northern Climates.

And as to the common Arguments alledged in Defence of the Trade. *viz.* That the *Slaves* sold to the *Europeans* are Captives taken in War, who would be destroyed by their Conquerors if not thus purchased; it is without Foundation: For altho' there were doubtless Wars amongst the *Negroes* before the *Europeans* began to trade with them, yet certain it is, that since that Time, those Calamities have prodigiously encreased, which is principally owing to the Solicitations of the white People, who have instigated the poor *Africans* by every Method, even the most iniquitous and cruel, to procure Slaves to load their Vessels, which they freely and gladly purchase without any Regard to the Precepts of the Gospel; the Feelings of Humanity, or the common Dictates of Reason and Equity.

This plainly appears from the Account given by *Andrew Brue*, General Director of the *French* Factory at *Senagal*, who travelled much on and about the two great Rivers of *Senagal*, and *Gambia*. In *Astley's* Collection of Voyages, he is spoken of as a Person of Judgment, and one who had had sufficient Opportunities by his long Residence there, of gaining a thorough Knowledge of the Manners, Customs and Dispositions of the People inhabiting the Country, for about four hundred Miles along the Coast, extending on each Side the before mentioned Rivers. Speaking of the Papel *Negroes* (amongst whom he was then endeavouring to erect a Factory) he says

They are at continual Wars with their Neighbours, whom they invade as often as they think it for their Advantage. . . . These Wars of theirs are never long, generally speaking, they are Incursions or Expeditions of five or six Days. He adds.

The Europeans *are far from desiring to act as Peace-Makers amongst them*, i.e. (*the* Negroes) *which would be contrary to their Interest, since the greater the Wars are, the more* Slaves.

William Bosman, Factor for the *Dutch*, at *Delmina*, where he resided sixteen Years, relates

That one of the former Commanders hired an Army of the *Negroes*, of *Jafferia* and *Cabesteria*, for a large Sum of Money, to fight the *Negroes* of *Commany*, which occasioned a Battle, which was more bloody than the Wars of the *Negroes* usually are: And that another Commander gave, at one Time, *Five Hundred Pounds*, and at another Time *Eight Hundred Pounds*, to two other *Negroe* Nations, to induce them to take up Arms against their Country People.

This is confirmed by *Barbot*, Agent General of the *French African* Company, who says;

The *Hollanders*, a People very zealous for their Commerce at the Coast, were very studious to have the War carried on amongst the *Blacks*, to distract, as long as possible, the Trade of the other *Europeans*; and to that Effect were very ready to assist upon all Occasions, the *Blacks*, their Allies, that they might beat their Enemies, and so the Commerce fall into their Hands.

But nothing shews more plainly, that the *Europeans* are the chief Instruments in inciting the *Negroes* to the Perpetration of those unnatural Wars, by which they are kept in continual Alarms, their Country laid waste, and such great Numbers carried into Captivity, than the Account given by *William Smith*, who was sent by the *African* Company to visit their Settlements, in the Year 1726, from the Information he received of one of the Factors, who had resided ten Years in that Country, *viz.*

That the discerning Natives account it their greatest Unhappiness that they were ever visited by the *Europeans*:——That we Christians introduced the Traffick of Slaves, and that before our coming they lived in Peace; but, say they, it is observable, that wherever Christianity comes, there comes with it a Sword, a Gun, Power and Ball.

This is farther confirmed by two Occurrences related by *Andrew Brue*, the Director at *Senegal*, before mentioned: The first at *Page 30. viz.* That having acquainted the King he was ready to trade with him, if he had a sufficient quantity of *Slaves*; the King procured three Hundred *Slaves*, but wanting Goods to double the Value of what the Company would allow for those *Slaves*, and they refusing to trust him, as he was already in their Debt; the Director proposed having a Licence for seizing upon so many of his People as would pay for what more Goods he wanted, but this the King refused to consent to, saying it might occasion a Disturbance amongst his Subjects; and so was forced, says the *Author*, to want the Goods he desired for that Time; which disappointment put the King greatly out of Humour. The second Occurrence is mentioned at *Page 150, viz.* The Director received Complaints of the continual Insults the Company's Servants suffered at Fort St. *Joseph*, from one *Babel* the King's Alkair, by forbidding the Trade, in order to oblige the Factor to pay the King as high Duties as those paid to the neighbouring King, or to force the *French* to quit the Country. Upon this Complaint, the general Director *Brue*, sent Orders to the Commander of the Fort, to provide the Place with proper Necessaries for its Defence, and then to punish *Bable* rigorously, not only by burning his Village, but also by seizing himself, Wives and Children, if he found Opportunity.

Thus the Matter remained for some Time, when the *Author* says, the *Negroes* recommenced their Ill-usage to the *French*, which went so far, that a Factor was murdered: Upon which, the Commander having assembled all his Forces, attacked the Village, which he plundered and burnt; killed near sixty of the *Negroes*, who had taken up Arms, wounded double the Number, carried off all the Cattle, and made four Hundred *Slaves*. The *Author* adds, "So severe and seasonable a Punishment, threw a Terror on all the Country, and obliged the King and his Bakerris to sue for Mercy."

The Commander suffered himself to be long intreated before he would grant them Peace, and in the mean Time sent down his Slaves and Booty by the Barks to Fort St. *Louis*. Little need be said to shew the unjust and barbarous Conduct of the *French* Officers in these Transactions, the Truth of which cannot be questioned, as they are taken from the Relation given by *Brue* himself. In the first Instance, the Head of a Christian Factory endeavours to persuade a Heathen King to break thro' every sacred and human Tie; which shews, that so he could but procure *Slaves*, he was quite indifferent as to the Means, be they ever so criminal. And in the second, this Christian Factor himself shews the greatest Disregard to the Right of Mankind, and the Feelings of Humanity, on so slight a Pretence as the Demand of Duties, by his own Confession, no greater than they paid elsewhere; gives to his Officers the most cruel and unreasonable Orders, which on the Death of a Factor (which might be occasioned by his own Rashness or Imprudence) are executed with the utmost Severity. And what makes it look likely, that procuring a Number of *Slaves* was his chief Motive, is, that after this Treatment the Officer gives no Ear to their Intreaties for Peace, till he has sent off the Booty of four Hundred *Slaves* he had made in the Encounter. But supposing the *Negroe* Officer to have been to blame, what had the common People done to be thus cruelly butchered and dragged into Captivity. What an Example was this to be given from Christians to Heathens. Could any Thing be more likely to confirm the *Negroes* in the detestable Practice of enslaving their unhappy Countrymen.

As to the Account of the natural Disposition of many of the *Negroes*, and of the Fruitfulness of their Country, the forementioned Authors, as well as many others, have wrote largely upon it. *M. Adanson*, in his Account of the Country and Natives of *Goree*, where he was so lately as the Year 1754, after giving an Account of the delightful Aspect of the Country, says;

> The Simplicity of the Natives, their Dress and Manners, revived in my Mind the Idea of our first Parents; and I seemed to contemplate the World in its primitive State;——they (the *Negroes*) are generally speaking, very good natured, sociable and obliging. I was not a little pleased (says he) with this my first Reception;——it convinced me, that there ought to be a considerable Abatement made in the Accounts I have read and heard every where of the savage Character of the *Africans*.——I observed, both in *Negroes* and *Moors*, great Humanity and Sociableness, which gave me strong Hopes that I should be very safe amongst them, and meet with the Success I desired in my Enquiries after the Curiosities of the Country.

Bosman, speaking of the *Negroes* of that Part of *Guiney* where he then was, says;

> They are generally a good Sort of People, honest in their Dealings; others he describes as being generally friendly to Strangers, of a mild Conversation, courteous, affable, and easy to be overcome with Reason; in Conversation they discover a great Quickness of Parts and Understanding.

He adds, . . . That some *Negroes*, who have had an agreeable Education, have manifested a Brightness of Understanding equal to any of us.

William Smith's Account of the Natives is, That

> he found them a civil good natured People, industrious to the last Degree, and their Country exceeding fertile.——It is easy (says he) to perceive what happy Memoirs they are blessed with, and how great Progress they would make in the Sciences, in Case their Genius was cultivated with Study: They explain themselves in choice Terms, their Expressions noble, and Manners polite; . . . this (he adds) is to be understood of the People of Distinction, as Officers, Merchantmen, and the like; for Peasants, Workmen and Shepherds, are as ignorant in these Parts as elsewhere.

Barbot says,

The Inhabitants of *Oedo* are, for the Generality, very civil, good natured People, easy to be dealt with, condescending to what the *Europeans* require of them, in a civil Way; but if treated with Haughtiness and rudely, they are stiff and high, and will not yield on any Account.

A. Brue, speaking of the People of *Benin*, says,

They are generally good natured and civil, and may be brought to any Thing by fair and soft Means. If you make them Presents, they will recompense them double. If you want any Thing of them, and ask it, they seldom deny it, even tho' they had Occasion for it themselves: But to treat them harshly, or think to gain any Thing of them by Force, is to dispute with the Moon.

Artus, speaking of the same People, says,

They are a sincere inoffensive People, and do no Unjustice either to one another or Strangers. He adds, that it is a capital Crime there to injure a Foreigner, which is severely punished.

In the Collection of Voyages, we are told,

That some Writers have represented the Natives of *Cape Mesurado*, as faithless and cruel; but it is very likely this Representation of their Dispositions was occasioned by the Resentment they had shewn for the Ill-usage received from the *Europeans*; for Capt. *Philips* declared them to be civil and courteous.

And *Snock* says,

He found them a civil good natured People; but that the late Injury they had received from the *English*, who had carried off some of their People, had so exasperated them, that it was to be feared some *English* they had in their Power, would fall a Sacrifice to their Resentment.

Altho' the extream Heat in many Parts of *Guinea*, is such, as is neither agreeable nor healthy to the *Europeans*, yet it is well suited to the Constitution of the *Negroes:* And it is to those Heats that they are indebted for the Fertility of their Land, which in most Places is so great, that with little Labour Grain and Fruit will grow in the greatest Plenty.

Andrew Brue, speaking of the great River *Senagal*, which runs many Hundred Miles within Land, says,

The farther you go from the Sea, the Country on the River seems more fruitful, and well improved. It abounds in *Indian* Corn, which is a never failing Commodity here. . . . The Island of *Bifesha*, which is formed by an Arm of that River, abounds in *Indian* and *Guinea* Corn, Rice, Pulse, Tobacco and Indigo. Wheat thrives well after the second Crop. Cotton-trees in plenty. . . . Here are vast Meadows, which feed large Herds of great and small Cattle. . . . Poultry are numerous, as well as wild Fowl.

Yet it sometimes happen that there is great scarcity in particular Places, arising from the unprovident Disposition of some of the *Negroes*, who have little thought of making any Provision but from one Harvest to another, so that they are liable to suffer when that fails, or when the Locust devour the Produce; these Insects sometimes come in such Swarms as to darken the Air, and destroy every green Thing that lays in their Way.

The same *Author*, in his Travels to the South of the River *Gambia*, expresses his Surprise to see

The Land so well cultivated, as he observed it to be; scarce a Spot lay unimproved, the low Ground divided by small Canals, were all sowed with Rice; the higher Ground planted with *Indian* Corn and Millet, and Pease of different Sorts. Beef and Mutton very cheap, as well as all other Necessaries of Life.

Bosman says,

The *Indian* and *Guinea* Corn is here sown and reaped twice every Year; the first Harvest is in *August*, and the other the latter End of the Year, though but small; Corn grows with little Trouble, very speedily taking Root. *Indian* Corn grows in the upper Lands, in prodigious Quantities, and where Corn won't grow, there Rice increases in Abundance, and Yamms and Potatoes are in the greatest Plenty.

Speaking of the Kingdom of *Fida*, he says,

The Country was very populous, many large Villages, besides innumerable small Ones, through the whole Country, plentifully provided with Corn, Potatoes and Fruit, which grew close to each other; in some Places a Foot-path is the only Ground that is not covered with them, the *Negroes* leaving no Place, which is thought fertile, uncultivated, even within the Hedges which inclose their Villages: And the very next Day after they have reaped they are sure to sow again.

This fine Country is now very much depopulated, which, it is likely, was owing to the Incursions made upon them by their Neighbours, in order to get Slaves to sell to the *Europeans*. For the same *Bosman*, speaking of the neighbouring Nation of *Pope*, says; "They depend on Plunder and the *Slave-Trade*, in which they exceed some of their Neighbours."

Other Parts of the Country he describes, as

being full of Towns and Villages; the Soil very rich, and so well cultivated, as to look like an entire Garden, abounding in Rice, Corn, Oxen, Goats and Poultry; and the *Negroes* to be laborious.

W. Smith gives much the same Account of the Country of *Delmina*, and *Cape Corse*, &c. for Beauty and Goodness; and adds, "The more you come downward towards that Part called the *Slave-Coast*, the more delightful and rich the Soil appears."

Barbot says,

The Inland People employ themselves in Tillage and Trade, and supply the Markets with Corn, Fruit and Palm Wine; the Country producing such vast Plenty of *Indian* Wheat, that Abundance is daily exported, as well by *Europeans* as *Blacks*, resorting theither from other Parts. He adds, That the Country of *Delmina*, (which was formerly very powerful and populous, though now so much drained of its Inhabitants, by the intestine Wars fomented amongst the *Negroes* by the *Dutch*, that there does not remain enough Inhabitants to till the Country;) abounded with fine well-built and populous Towns, enriched with vast Fields of Corn, Cattle, Palm Wine and Oil. The Inhabitants all applying themselves, without Distinction, to Agriculture, sowing Corn, pressing Oil, and drawing Wine from Palm Trees, with both of which it is plentifully stored; others to fishing, and boiling Salt, and other Trades, on their own Account, or as Brokers for the Inland *Blacks*.

Many more Accounts could be given of the good Disposition of the Generality of the *Negroes*, and of the Plenty their Country affords; but the Foregoing are sufficient to shew them to be entirely different from the stupified and malicious People, some would have them thought to be. They have Judgment and Industry sufficient to cultivate their Country, which in most Parts abounds in the Necessaries of Life, and are so far from being uncapable of Society, that they are generally a kind and well disposed People. Neither are they to be dispised, with respect to the Manner in which Justice is administred, in several of the *Negro* Governments, which from the Accounts given by divers Authors, appears to be done with so much Equity and Dispatch, as might well be worthy the Imitation of some more civilized People.

Collec. *Page 259* [*sic*], *Le Maire*, speaking of the Government of the *Jalofs* (whose Country is of a large extent) says,

The King has under him several Ministers of State, who assist him in the Government and Exercise of Justice. The grand *Jerafo* is the chief Justice thro' all the King's Dominion, and goes his Circuit from Time to Time to hear Complaints and determine Controversies. The King's Treasurer exercises the same Employ, but with a more limited Power, and has under him Alkairs, who are Governors of Towns or Villages.—

Barbot confirms the above Account, and adds, "That the chief Justice inspects the Behaviour of the Alkairs of the several Districts."

Vasconselas, quoted by *Barbot*, says,

That the *Negroes* on this Coast, much excell the *Senegas* in their civil Government, as much better observing distributive and communative Justice, and proceeding with much Prudence and Secrecy in the Affairs which concern the Preservation or aggrandizing of their State, being very impartial in distributing Rewards, and inflicting Punishment. The Antientest are preferred to be the Prince's Counsellors, who keep always about his Person; and the Men of Most Judgment and Experience are the Judges, fitting every where in Oyer and Terminer. They order Justice to be done on the Spot.

A. Brue, speaking of the *Fuli*, whose Country joins to the *Jalofs*, says,

That being curious to see the Method by which they administer Justice, he was carried to a Place where he could observe what passed incognito. The King was surrounded by ten of his oldest Officers, who heard the Parties separately, and after causing them to retire, consulted his Officers, as to the Decision; after which the Parties were called in, and the Sentence pronounced, and put immediately in Execution. He saw none here who acted either as Counsel or Attorney, each pleaded his own Cause in very proper Terms.

The same Author, at *Page* 110 [*sic*], speaking of the Country of *Cabo*, situate on a Branch of the *Gambia*, says,

The King was much regretted at his Death, equally by his Subjects and Strangers. He had settled so good a Policy thro' all his Dominions, that the Merchants might have left their Goods on the High-way, without being stolen. Whenever a White Man visited him, as soon as he reached the Frontiers of the Kingdom his Charges were defrayed; nor durst the People exact any Thing of Strangers, under Pain of being sold for Slaves.

Peter Holben, who was sent from the Court of *Prussia* to make astronomical Observations at the *Cape Good-hope*, which is situate on the southmost Part of *Africa*, speaking of the Government and Disposition of the *Negroe* Inhabitants of that Country, commonly called *Hottentots*, says,

Every Village or Kraal has a Court of Justice, for civil and criminal Affairs, composed of the Captain and all the Men of the Kraal, who meet for this Purpose in the open Field, sitting in a Circle. Justice among the *Hottentots* never suffer as in *Europe*, either by Corruption or which is as bad, Delay. They have no Lawyer, thank Heaven: The Plaintiff and Defendant plead their own Cause. The Court hears them, and by a Majority of Votes decrees Possession or Damage, in case of Assault or Battery, or other Trespass, without Appeal or Obstacle. In criminal Matters, as Murders, Adulteries and Robberies; the Guilty find no Protection or Favour, either from his Wealth or Rank. When a Difference happens between two Villages of the same Nation, it is referred to the Judgment of a national Court, who when they form their Revolutions, execute them with as much Steadiness and Vigour as a *Roman* Senate. The *Author* adds: The *Europeans* may boast of their Learning, Arts and Politeness; but where among them can they shew so wise, so happy a Government as that of the *Hottentots;* owing entirely to this, that it has for its Basis the most perfect Liberty of the People.

They are the only *Negro* Nation that we know of, that are not engaged in making and selling *Slaves*; this wicked Practice appears to be unknown amongst these People.

From what has been said, it may be concluded that the *Negroes* might have been happy, if the *Europeans* had not bore the Name only, but had, indeed, acted the Part of Christians, in using their Endeavours, by Example as well as Precept, to make them acquainted with the glad Tidings of the Gospel, and with that change of Heart, and Redemption from Sin, which Christianity proposes; this, if attended to, would have necessarily been productive of the peaceable Fruits of Righteousness; Innocence and Love, would have reigned in the Room of Animosities and Bloodshed, thus the Christians instead of provoking the Vengeance of a Jealous God, would have been the happy Instruments of compleating these poor *Africans* Happiness. But the Reverse has happened; the *Europeans*, forgetful of their Profession and Duty, as Men and Christians, have conducted in such a Manner; as must necessarily raise in the Minds of the Thoughtful and well-disposed *Negroes*, the utmost Scorn and Detestation of the Christian Name. They have made all other Considerations give way to an insatiable Desire of Gain, and are become the principal and moving Cause of the most abominable and dreadful Scene, that was, perhaps, ever acted upon this Globe: Every Thing, even the Power of the *Negro* Kings have been made subservient to answer this wicked Purpose; instead of being Protectors of their People, these Rulers, allured by the tempting Baits laid before them by the Factors, &c. have invaded the Liberties of their unhappy Subjects, and become their Oppressors; as is fully evidenced by the following Account, viz.

Francis Moore, Factor to the *African* Company, in 1730, tells his Readers,

That when the King of *Barsalli* wants Goods or Brandy, he sends a Messenger to the *English* Governor at *James's* Fort, to desire he would send up a Sloop with a Cargo of Goods, which, says the *Author*, the Governor never fails to do: Against the Time the Vessel arrives, the King plunder some of his Enemies Towns, selling the People for such Goods as he wants, which commonly is Brandy or Rum, Gunpowder, Ball,

Fire-arms, Pistols and Cutlasses for his Soldiers, &c. and Coral and Silver for his Wives and Mistresses. . . . If he is at War with no neighbouring King, he falls upon one of his own Towns, and makes bold to sell his own miserable Subjects. He often goes with some of his Troops by a Town in the Day-time, and returns in the Night, and sets Fire to three Parts of it, placing Guards at the Fourth, to seize the People that run out of the Fire, then ties their Arms behind them, and marches them to *Joar* or *Robone*, where he sells them.

Brue, the *French*, Factor, says,

That having received Goods, he wrote to the King, that if he had a sufficient Number of Slaves, he was ready to trade with him; this Prince, says that Author, as well as the other *Negroe* Monarchs, have always a sure Way of supplying his Deficiencies, by selling their own Subjects, for which they seldom want Pretensions of some Kind or other, to justify their Rapine.

These *Negroe* Kings, thus seeking Pretences to cover their Crimes, shew they are not quite void of Shame, nor insensible that Covetousness induces them to act a Part so inconsistent with their Duty; but here they may plead the Example and Solicitation of the more knowing *Europeans*.

The King had Recourse to this Method, by seizing three Hundred of his own People, and sent Word to *Brue*, that he had the Slaves ready to deliver for the Goods. The same Author further adds, That some of the Natives are, on all Occasions, endeavouring to surprize and carry off their Country People: They land (says he) without Noise, and if they find any lone Cottage, without Defence, they surround it, and carry off all the People and Effects to their Boat. . . . The Slaves are sold to the *Europeans*, unless they be Persons of some Rank, whose Friends can redeem them by paying two Slaves, or five or six Oxen.

John Barbot says,

The Slaves sold by the *Negroes* are for the most Part Prisoners of War, or taken in the Incursions they make into their Enemies Territories; others are stolen away by their own Countrymen. Abundance of little *Blacks*, of both Sexes, are stolen away by their Neighbours, when found abroad, on the Roads or in the Woods, or else in the Corn Fields, at the Time of the Year when their Parents keep them there all Day, to scare away the devouring small Birds. . . .

And now Reader, if from the Example of others, and without a sufficient Knowledge of the deplorable Consequences attendant on this Trade, thou hast inadvertently engaged therein, let me beseech thee, by the Mercies of Christ Jesus our Lord (those Mercies which, perhaps, e'er long, thou and I shall desire to fly to as our only Refuge) that thou wouldst refrain a Practice so inconsistent with thy Duty, both as a Christian and a Man. Remember, the first and chief Commandment is, *Thou shalt love the Lord thy God with all thy Heart*. And that the Second like unto it is, *Thou shalt love thy Neighbour as thyself*. That our blessed Redeemer has enjoined us to *do unto others as we would they should do unto us*; and that it will be those who have been *righteous* and *merciful* to their Fellow-Creatures, that will be intitled to the Mercy of the Great Judge of Heaven and Earth, before whom we must all appear, to give an Account of the Deeds done in the Body.

And as for those who confess themselves now, convinced of the Iniquity, and Injustice of buying and selling their Fellow-Creatures, and yet continue to keep those *Negroes* they are possessed of in Bondage, for the Sake of the Profit arising from their Labour, it behoves them seriously to consider their Motives for such a Conduct; whether the Distinction they make between buying a *Negroe* and keeping the same *Negroe*, or his Offspring, in perpetual Bondage, is not a Plea founded more in Words than supported by Truth; for it must be obvious to every Person, who is not blinded by the Desire of Gain, that the Right by which these Men hold the *Negroes* in Bondage, is no other than what is derived from those who stole them, who having no other Title, but that which Robbers have over their Prey, could not convey any better to the Purchaser; and that therefore to continue to hold them in Bondage, for worldly Advantage, by no other Right than that which those guilty Men give them, is consenting to, and partaking of their Guilt. Instances may fall out, where Men of Candour may be concerned in the Purchase of *Negroes*, purely from a Principle of Charity; and there are also many of the *Blacks*, amongst us, whose Dispositions, Infirmities or Age, makes it necessary they should be under Care; but in the Case beforementioned, where Persons declare themselves convinced of the Injustice and Iniquity of this Trade, and are possessed of *Negroes* who are capable of managing for themselves, and have sufficiently paid, by their Labour, for their Purchase or bringing up, besides the Profit some Families have reaped, during a long Course of Years, from the Labour of their Progenitors; it is the undoubted Duty of their Possessors to restore them their Liberty; and also to use all reasonable Endeavours, to enable them to procure a comfortable Living, not only as an Act of Justice to the Individuals, but as a Debt due, on Account of the Oppression and Injustice perpetrated on them, or their Ancestors; and as the best Means to avert the Judgments of God, which it is to be feared will fall on Families and Countries, in Proportion as they have, more or less, defiled themselves with this iniquitous Traffick.

Doubts may arise in the Minds of some, whether the foregoing Accounts, relating to the natural Capacity and good Disposition of many of the Inhabitants of *Guinea*, and of the violent Manner in which they appear to be torn from their native Land, is sufficiently founded on Truth, as the *Negroes* who are brought to us are seldom heard to complain, and do not manifest that Docility and Quickness of Parts which might be expected from this Account; Persons who may make such Objections, are desired impartially to consider whether this is not owing to the many Discouragements these poor *Africans* labour under, though in an enlightened Christian Country, and the little Opportunity they have of exerting and improving their natural Talents. They are constantly employed in servile Labour, and the abject Condition in which we see them, from our Childhood, has a natural Tendency to create in us an Idea of a Superiority and induces many to look upon them as an ignorant and contemptible Part of Mankind; add to this, that they have but little Opportunity of freely conversing with such of the Whites as might impart Instruction to them, the endeavouring of which would, indeed, by most, be accounted Folly, if not Presumption. A Fondness for Wealth, or for gaining Esteem and Honour, is what prompts most Men to the Desire of excelling others, but these Motives for the Exertion and Improvement of their Faculties can have but little or no Influence upon the Minds of the *Negroes*, few of them having Hopes of attaining to any Condition beyond that of Slavery; so that tho' the natural Capacity of many of them be ever so good, yet they have no Inducement or Opportunity of exerting it to any Advantage, which naturally tends to depress their Minds, and sink their Spirits into Habits of Idleness and Sloth, which they would, in all Likelihood, have been free from, had they stood upon an equal Footing with the white People: Nevertheless it may, with Truth, be said, that amongst those who have obtained their Freedom, as well as those who remain in Servitude, some have manifested as much Sagacity and Uprightness of Heart as could have been expected from the Whites, under the like Circumstances; and if all the free *Negroes* have not done the same, is it a Matter of Surprize? Have we not Reason to make Complaint with Respect to many of our white Servants, when from under our Care, tho' most of them have had much greater Advantages than the Blacks; who, even when free, still labour under the Difficulties before-mentioned, having but little Access to, and Intercourse with, the white People; they yet remained confined within the former Limits of Conversation with those of their own Colour, and consequently have but little more Opportunity of Knowledge and Improvement than when in Slavery.

And if they seldom complain of the unjust and cruel Usage they have received, in being forced from their native Country, &c. it is not to be wondered at; as it is a considerable Time after their Arrival amongst us before they can speak our Language, and, by the Time they are able to express themselves, they cannot but observe, from the Behaviour of the Whites, that little or no Notice would be taken of their Complaints; yet let any Person enquire of those who had attained the Age of Reason, before they were brought from their native Land, and he shall hear such Relations as, if not lost to the common Feelings of Humanity, will sensibly affect his Heart. The Case of a poor *Negroe*, not long since brought from *Guinea*, is a recent Instance of this Kind. From his first Arrival he appeared thoughtful and dejected, the Cause of which was not known till he was able to speak *English*, when the Account he gave of himself was, that he had a Wife and Children in his own Country, that some of them being sick and thirsty, he went, in the Night-time, to fetch Water at a Spring, where he was violently seized, and carried away by some Persons who lay in Wait to catch Men, whence he was transported to *America*; the Remembrance of his Family, Friends, and other Connections left behind, which he never expected to see any more, were the principal Causes of his Dejection and Grief. Can any compassionate Heart hear this Relation without being affected with Sympathy and Sorrow? And doubtless the Case of many of these unhappy People would, upon Enquiry, appear attended with Circumstances equally tragical and aggravating. Now, that you have studied the Book of

Conscience, and those that are learned in the Law, what will you say to this deplorable Case? When, and how, has this Man forfeited his Liberty? Does not Justice loudly call for its being restored to him? Has he not the same Right to demand it as any of us should have, if we had been violently snatched by Pyrates from our native Land? Where Instances of this Kind frequently occur, and are neither enquired into, nor redressed by those whose Duty it is *to seek Judgment, and relieve the Oppressed,* what can be expected, but that the Groans and Cries of these Sufferers will reach Heaven; and *what shall ye do when* God *riseth up, and when he visiteth, what shall ye answer him? Did not he that made them make us, and did not one fashion us in the Womb?*

It is scarce to be doubted but that the foregoing Accounts will beget in the Heart of every considerate Reader an earnest Desire to see a Stop put to this complicated Evil; but the Objection with many is, what shall be done with those Negroes already imported and born in our Families? Must they be sent to *Africa?* That would be to expose them in a strange Land, to greater Difficulties than many of them labour under at present. To set them suddenly free here would be perhaps attended with no less Difficulty, for undisciplined as they are in Religion and Virtue, they might give a loose to those evil Habits, which the fear of a Master would have restrained. These are Objections which weigh with many well-disposed People; and indeed it must be granted there are Difficulties in the Way; nor can any general Change be made, or Reformation effected without some: But the Difficulties are not so great but that they may be surmounted. If the Government was so sensible of the Iniquity and Danger attendant on this Practice, as to be willing to seek a Remedy, doubtless the Almighty would bless this good Intention, and such Methods would be thought of as would not only put an End to the unjust Oppression of the Negroes, but might bring them under such Regulations, as would enable them to become profitable Members of Society. For the furtherance of which, the following Proposals are offered to Consideration; to be improved by those in whose Power it is to remedy this mighty Evil. In the first Place, that all farther Importation be absolutely prohibited. And as to those already purchased, or born among us, after serving so long as shall be adequate to the Money paid, or the Charge of bringing them up (which may be decided by Courts of Justice) let them by Law be declared free: Nevertheless let the same Court of Justice have Power to lengthen the Time of any Slave's Servitude, upon legal proof, being made, of that Slave's having wilfully neglected his Duty. Let every Slave thus set free be enrolled in the County Court, and obliged to be a Resident during a certain Number of Years within the said County, under the Inspection of the Overseers of the Poor. Thus being in some Sort still under the Directions of Governors, and Notice of those who were formerly acquainted with them, they would be obliged to act circumspectly, and to make a proper Use of their Liberty; and their Children have an Opportunity of such Instruction as might be provided for them, under the Tuition of proper Instructors; thus both Parents and Children might grow up to be useful Members of the Community. And further, where the Nature of the Country would permit, as certainly the uncultivated Condition of our Southern Colonies easily would; suppose a small Tract of Land, for Instance, five and twenty Acres were assigned to every Negro Family, and they obliged to live upon and improve it (when not hired out to work for the Whites) this would encourage them to exert their Abilities, and become industrious Subjects: Thus both Planters and Tradesmen would be plentifully supplied with chearful and willing-minded Labourers; much vacant Land would be cultivated; the Produce of the Country greatly encreased; Arts and Manufactures advanced; the Taxes for the Support of Government lessened to Individuals, by the encrease of Taxables. And the Negroes instead of giving just Cause of fearful Apprehensions, and weakning the internal Strength of the Government where they reside, as they certainly must in their present Condition. Would become interested in its Security and Welfare.

The mistaken Opinion, which most People have entertained, that the Negroes in *Africa*, live in the same wild unsettled Manner as the *American Indians* do, has led many to think it impossible to bring them into that civilized Order which is requisite for their becoming good Members of Society, but, it is hoped, what has already been said on that Head, will convince the candid Reader, that this Opinion is founded on mistaken Apprehensions; and to put this Matter in a yet clearer Light, it may not be amiss to add, that altho' amongst the many Nations living on that Part of *Africa*, inhabited by the Negroes, which extend many Thousand Miles, there is doubtless some People of a more savage Disposition than others, yet certain it is, that the natural Disposition of the Generality of the Negroes is widely different from the roving Dispositions of our Indians; they generally settle together, and employ themselves in Agriculture and Commerce. Some large Nations are represented as industrious and careful in the Cultivation of their Lands; breeding Cattle, and carrying on a Trade to distant Parts. An Instance of this appears from the Account we have of the principal Nations, settled back of the Factories of *Goree* and *Senegal*, Places of great Trade, in the Latitude of 15 to 20 Degrees North, lately taken by the *English* from the *French*, from whence great Numbers of Slaves have for a long Time been Yearly exported to the Plantations. In the 2d Vol. of the Collection, we are told that this Country, which is situate between the River *Senegal* and *Gambia*, and extends many Hundreds of Miles, is chiefly inhabited by three Negroe Nations, *viz.* The *Mandigos*, the *Fullys*, and the *Jalofs: Andrew Brue*, the general Director, often beforementioned, says, the *Mandigos* are dispersed all over the Country, they are the most rigid *Mahometans* among the Negroes, they drink no Wine or Brandy, and are politer than the other Negroes; the chief Trade of the Country goes thro' their Hands; they are laborious and industrious, keeping their Grounds well cultivated, and breeding a good Stock of Cattle. . . . Some of these People who are settled up the River *Senegal*, carry on a Trade to all the neighbouring Kingdoms; and by these Means amass Riches, and propagate the *Mahometan* Religion wheresoever they go. . . . The Author agrees they are a good Sort of People, honest, industrious, and very ready to learn Arts and Sciences.

The *Fully*'s are settled on both Sides of the River *Senegal*; their Country, which is very fruitful and populous, extends near four Hundred Miles from East to West. They are ordinarily of a deep tawny Complexion, appearing to bear some Affinity with the *Moors*, to whose Country they join on the North. They are a well made People, and tho' they seem tender, yet they will labour stoutly at hard Work, are good Farmers, and make great Harvests of Corn, Cotton, Tobacco, Pease, &c. and breed a great Number of Cattle of all Kinds. . . . *Brue* says the Company gets the best Hides from them. And *Labat* in his Account of the *West-Indies*, speaking of the different Nations of Negroes sold for Slaves at *Martinico*, mentions these *Fully* as a People more suitable than most other Negroes to take care of Cattle, *&c.* Some of these *Fully* Blacks, who dwell on both Sides the River *Gambia* are in Subjection to the *Mandigos*, amongst whom they have settled from Time to Time; having been, probably, driven out of their own Country by War or Famine. They have Chiefs of their own, who rule with much Moderation. They live in Clans, build Towns, and are not subject to any Kings of the Country, though they live in their Territories; for if they are ill-treated by one Nation, they break up their Town and remove to another. They are also strict *Mahometans*, few amongst them will drink Brandy, or any Thing stronger than Water and Sugar: Their Form of Government goes on easy, because the People are of a good quiet Disposition, and so well instructed in what is just and right, that a Man who does ill is the Abomination of all, and none will support him against the Chiefs. In these Countries the Natives are not covetous of Land, desiring no more than what they use, and as they do not plough with Horses and Cattle, they can use but very little, therefore the Kings, are willing to give the *Fully*'s leave to live in their Countries, and cultivate Lands. They plant Tobacco near their Houses, and Cotton all round their Towns, which they fence in together; beyond that they sow *Indian* and *Guinea* Corn and Rice: As they are industrious and frugal, they have more Corn and Cotton than they consume, which they sell at reasonable Rates: Their Clothing is of white Cotton of their own Manufacture: They are a clean People, especially the Women. As they are hospitable and kind to all, it is reckoned a Blessing to have a *Fully* Town in the Neighbourhood: They never suffer any of their own Nation to want, but support the Old, the Blind, and the Lame; and as far as their Abilities goes supply the Necessities of the *Mandigos*, great Numbers of whom they have maintained in Famines. They are rarely angry, and the Author could never hear them abuse one another.

In the Collection, we have also a favorable Account of the Conduct and Disposition of a Number of free Negroes settled on the *Cape Verd* Islands. The Account is principally taken from the Writings of *George Roberts*, who was Shipwreck'd on one of those Islands; they are ten in Number, the largest called *St. Jago*, is settled by the *Portuguese*; the rest are mostly inhabited by Negroes or Mulattoes, which our Author says happened in the following Manner, *viz.*

The *Portuguese* settled on the two largest Islands, provided themselves with Negroe-Slaves from *Guinea* to do their Work; and as it was usual with them to atone for their Sins on their Death-bed, by giving one or more Slaves their Freedom, these Free-Blacks, being in a Climate natural to them, increased fast; many became Tenants to the Whites, others not brooking their lordly and oppressive Deportment, went over to the lesser Islands. These lesser Islands having been bestowed by the King to some of his Nobles: They appoint deputy Governors, who are generally Negroes.

Their Priests are also Negroes, who (Roberts says)

make better and soberer Clergymen than the Whites, these being mostly of loose and vicious Lives, which caused the Bishop, who was a Man of a meek and mild Disposition, to prefer the Blacks, with no more Education than what they could have at *St. Jago.* This (adds the Author) was a commendable Practice of the Bishop; who met with a great deal of Trouble on that Account, from the Fryars, who made a Practice of ridiculing the Ignorance of these Negroe-Priests.

The *Portuguese* Inhabitants of those Islands are said (in the Collection) to bear but a poor Character, being generally represented as a proud, lazy, ignorant People; but on the Contrary, the Free-Negroes, who are much the greatest Number, are said to be mostly an innocent good tempered People. *Roberts* speaks particularly well of the Black Governor of *Bonavista*, and of Captain *Domingo*, a sensible Black on that Island, who was a fair Dealer, and could read *French* and *English*. The Governor, Priest and People of the Island of *Mayo*, were all Negroes, tho' being subject to the *Portuguese*, they had their Religion and Language. . . . Captain *Dampier*, who was on this Island many Years before *Roberts*, says,

The Governor had his Patent from the Governor of *St. Jago*; that the Negro who held that Office in the Year 1699 was a very civil, sensible Man, and, adds, that the Inhabitants were generally a good Sort of People, that they looked well, being fat and fleshy, tho' the Island appears so barren to a Stranger, as scarce to have Food for its Inhabitants.

The Island upon which *Roberts* was Shipwreck'd was called *St. John*; it was wholly inhabited by Blacks, he says, that tho' very ignorant and superstitious, yet they were the most innocent and harmless of all those Islanders. He speaks highly of their moral Virtue, especially their Charity, Humility and Hospitality: He particularly commends their Veneration for Age. While he lay sick he was lodged by one of the chief Inhabitants, and supplied with all kind of Necessaries: Every Day some or other would come to see how he did, and scarce ever without a Fowl, or some Fruit for him: They shewed him great Kindness in every other Respect, and freely assisted him in building a small Vessel to carry him off the Island, when he talked of making them a Return for these Favours, they said, they were glad they had been of any Service to him, and thought it their Duty to serve Strangers in Distress.

Upon the Whole, of what has been said, it must appear to every honest unprejudiced Reader, that the Negroes are equally intituled to the common

Priviledges of Mankind with the Whites, that they have the same rational Powers; the same natural Affections, and are as susceptible of Pain and Grief as they, that therefore the bringing and keeping them in Bondage, is an Instance of Oppression and Injustice of the most grieous Nature, such as is scarcely to be parallelled by any Example in the present or former Ages. Many of its woful Effects have already been expressed, but those which more particularly calls for the Notice and Redress of the Government, arises from its inconsistancy with every Thing that is just and humane, whence the worst Effects naturally flow to the Religion and Morals of the People where it prevails. Its destructive Consequences to labouring People, and Tradesmen is no less worthy the Attention of those who have Inclination and Power to serve their Country. This Rank of People, as they are the chief Strength and Support of a Community; so their Situation and Welfare calls for the particular Care of every prudent Government; but where Slave-keeping prevails, their Places and Services being supplied by the Negroes, they find themselves slighted, disregarded, and robbed of the natural Oppertunities of Labour common in other Countries, whereby they are much discouraged and their Families often reduced to Want: To which may be added the Discouragement also given by this Trade to many poor People, that can scarce get Bread in our Mother Country, who, if not prevented, on Account of the great Number of Negroes, would be likely to come over into the Colonies where they might, with Ease, procure to themselves a more comfortable Living than at Home. Another direful Effect arises from the fearful Apprehensions and Terrors which often seize the Minds of the People, for the Suppression of which the most cruel Methods are pursued, such as are indeed a Reproach to Christianity, and will by Degrees harden the Hearts of those who are active therein, so as totally to exclude them from that Tenderness and Sympathy for the Sufferings of their Fellow Creatures, which constitutes the Happiness of Society, and is the Glory of intelligent Beings. As for the Possessors of the Negroes themselves, though the Sumptuousness and Ease in which they live, and the Attendance and Obsequiousness of their Slaves, may raise in their Minds an imagined Apprehension of their being Persons more happy, and of greater Importance than other People, who do live in the like Affluence and State; yet happy would it be if they were sensible how great is their Mistake and could be persuaded seriously to consider and apply the Parable of the rich Man and poor *Lazarus*, mentioned by our Saviour, whereby they might plainly perceive that they have no Cause to exult, because of their Power and Plenty, but have rather Occasion to mourn over themselves, their Children, and their Country; the natural Effect of their Situation being such as has been repeatedly observed.

To fill Men with Haughtiness, Tyranny, Luxury and Barbarity; corrupting the Minds, and debasing the Morals of their Children, to the unspeakable Prejudice of Religion and Virtue, and the Exclusion of that holy Spirit of universal Love, Meekness and Charity, which is the unchangeable Nature and Glory of true Christianity.

Anthony Benezet to Joseph Phipps, May 28, 1763

Spriggs MSS, Ms. vol. 156/56, Friends House Library, London, Eng.

Anthony Benzet's propaganda effort is illustrated in this letter to Joseph Phipps in London, an individual known to the Philadelphia Quaker only through friends. Benezet addressed numerous such appeals for support for over 20 years, asking that pamphlets be reprinted and distributed, petitions be prepared, politicians be approached, and information be transmitted. Benezet remarks in this letter that he feared the black masses would rise up against their masters in the South if they became aware of their own numbers. Repeating this fear in numerous other letters, he was careful not to include in his writings inflammatory language which might incite literate blacks to rebellion. The peaceful Quaker detested slavery but was also haunted by the spectre of a racial war.

Philadia ye 28th 5th mo 1763

Respected Friend Joseph Phipps From the encouragement I have received from our Friend Willm Logan & a confidence in the sincerity of thy Desires for the suppression of every Thing which might impede the Progress of Truth & righteousness in the Earth, I make bold, tho personally unknown, affectionately to salute thee, and request a little of the attention, on a subject which has long been a matter of deep concern to many well minded People in these Parts, of the World, which if ever it receives a proper Check must come from amongst you. I mean the Negro Trade, the purchasing & bringing the poor Negroes from their native Land, and subjecting them to a State of perpetual Bondage, and that often the most cruel & oppressive, in which the English Nation is so deeply engaged, & which, with additional sorrow, we observe to be greatly encreasing in these Northern Colonies, and likely still more to encrease, by the New Acquisitions the English have lately made of the Factories on the great River Senegal. I herewith send thee some Treatizes lately published here, wherein is truly sett forth the great Wickedness with which this Trade is carried on; whereby so many Thousands of our Fellow Creatures, equally with us the Objects of Christ's redeeming Grace, & as free as we by Nature, are yearly brought to a miserable & untimely End. I beg thou wouldst be pleased seriously to read it thro', which I doubt not, but thou will perceive it to be a matter which calls for the most deep Consideration, of all who are most concerned for the civil, as well as religious welfare of their Country, and desirous to avert those judgments which evils of so deep a dye must necessarily sooner or later bring upon every People who are deffiled thereby. How an evil of so deep a dye; has so long not only passed unnoticed, but has even had the Countenances of the Government, and been supported by Law, is surprizing, and must in a great measure have arisen, from that, our late & present gracious Kings, & many worthy men in Government, in whose power it would have been to have put a Stop to the

Trade, have been unacquainted with the corrupt Motives which gives life to it; and the Groans, the numberless dying groans, which daily ascend to God, the common Father of Mankind, from the broken Hearts of those our deeply oppressed Fellow-Men, in this worse than Egyptian Bondage; or we should not, I think I may venture to say would not, have so long continued in a practice so inconsistant with the british apprehension of what we owe to the rights & Liberties of Mankind; so dishonorable to humanity, and which as Wm Foster expressed it at Page 37 "Bids that God, who is the God & Father of the Gentiles, unconverted to Christianity, most daring & bold Defiance, and spurns at all the Principles, both of natural and revealed Religion. Thou may'st depend upon the Truth of what is attested in the Treatise, concerning the Nature of the Trade and the barbarous usage the poor Africans receive from their invaders and cruel Taskmasters as we have purposely aimed at being below rather than above the Truth in the Account.

Much more might have been said in the Treatise of the Civil and temporal Evil which attends this wicked Practice, more especially with respect to the Danger our Southern Colonies are exposed to from the vast disproportion there is, between the Number of the Negroes, and the whites, but it was too tender a point to expose to ye view of such of the blacks, as can read. In the Treatise, the Proportion in South Carolina is said to be fifteen Blacks to a white, but by their own account, the difference is rather twenty to one. In Georgia & Carolina the Negroes are not hemmed in by the Sea, as they are in the Islands, but have a back Country uninhabited for some hundreds of miles, where the Negroes might not only retire, but who expect to be supported & assisted by the Indians. The new acquisition the English have made of Land to the westward as far as the Mississippi will provide the Government an advantageous opportunity of beneficial employment for the Negroes, should the British nation attend to justice . . . which, certainly, require that a prohibition be put to the Trade and a Provision be made for . . . freedom of these now amongst us, after a reasonable time of service.

Should ye Almighty suffer the Negroes to become sensible of their State so as to rise upon their Masters, who can express the horror & distress the white inhabitants would be reduced to and indeed that this has not yet been the case; is certainly an unmerited Miracle of divine Kindness and Mercy to the Inhabitants of those Colonies, which there is no reason to expect the continuation of without repentence and amendment. By account lately received from a pious man, who is returned from a religious visit to Barbie, a Dutch Settlemt near Surinam, we understand that a great number of Negroes, at least eighty thousand have at different times fled from those Settlement & have taken refuge, at first about 30 miles & now about an Hundred Miles back of the Settlement, from whence they sometimes make incursions upon the Inhabitants, who notwithstanding their endeavours & the assistance they have received from Holland are not able to suppress them but will, in all probability be obliged to come to terms with them.

Whether anything can be done which will prove a Remedy is uncertain. but certain it is the Duty, and will be the concern, of every Lover of God & Man to endeavour for it.

If the Treatize was reprinted amongst you, with such amendments as might be thought necessary, & dispersed amongst those in whose power it is to put a restraint upon the Trade &c particularly of our gracious King, his Councelors, and each member of both Houses of Parliament had one put in their Hands, might it not with divine Assistance, answer some good end; surely they are not so void of feeling, but that if the impression many have received from the false & falacious Arguments generally advanced in defence of the Trade were removed, some would endeavor the suppression of this enormous Evil. I shall take it very kind if thou would if by a few Lines let me know thy sentiments thereon.

With affectionate regard I remain thy Friend

Anthony Benezet

A MOUNTING CRY FOR NATURAL RIGHTS, 1763-1776

At a time when the general rights and liberties of mankind . . . [have] become so much the subjects of universal consideration; can it be an inquiry indifferent to any, how many of those who distinguish themselves as the Advocates of Liberty, remain insensible and inattentive to the treatment of thousands and tens of thousands of our fellow men. . . .

Anthony Benezet,
1767

James Otis, *Rights of the British Colonies*, 1764

James Otis, *The Rights of the British Colonies Asserted and Proved* (Boston, 1764), pp. 438-41.

"The colonists are by the law of nature free born, as indeed all men are, white and black. . . ." Thus did James Otis in 1764 link natural rights with black chattel slavery. John Adams later remarked, "Young as I was, and ignorant as I was, I shuddered at the doctrine he taught; and I have all my life shuddered, and still shudder, at the consequences that may be drawn from such premises. . . ."

Otis, a Harvard-educated lawyer, had resigned his post as advocate general of the Vice-Admiralty Court to attack the British government's decision to enforce the Navigation Acts. Otis's participation in a series of court cases, including the famous Writs of Assistance case in 1761, established him as a leader of the popular opposition in Massachusetts. His pamphlet, Rights of the British Colonies Asserted and Proved, *printed shortly after the passage of the Sugar Act in April 1764, was a bold effort to assert the limits of Parliament's control over the colonies. And in pleading the case of the colonists against arbitrary power, Otis pointed to the plight of the black slaves. It is ironic that the satiric wit of Montesquieu, to which Otis made reference, was later used by proslavery advocates to bolster their own position. When Montesquieu declared that it was impossible to pity black-skinned, squashed-nosed creatures, or when he scoffed that it was impossible for beings who preferred glass necklaces to gold ones to be considered men, his words were seized upon to prove Negro inferiority. But James Otis better understood his searing humor. Arguing with Montesquieu that slavery violated natural rights and human liberty, Otis lent his voice to the burgeoning antislavery movement.*

. . . In order to form an idea of the natural rights of the colonists, I presume it will be granted that they are men, the common children of the same Creator with their brethren of Great Britain. Nature has placed all such in a state of equality and perfect freedom to act within the bounds of the laws of nature and reason without consulting the will or regarding the humor, the passions, or whims of any other man, unless they are formed into a society or body politic. This it must be confessed is rather an abstract way of considering men than agreeable to the real and general course of nature. The truth is, as has been shown, men come into the world and into society at the same instant. But this hinders not but that the natural and original rights of each individual may be illustrated and explained in this way better than in any other. We see here, by the way, a probability that this abstract consideration of men, which has its use in reasoning on the principles of government, has insensibly led some of the greatest men to imagine some real general state of nature agreeable to this abstract conception, antecedent to and independent of society. This is certainly not the case in general, for most men become members of society from their birth, though separate independent states are really in the condition of perfect freedom and equality with regard to each other, and so are any number of individuals who separate themselves from a society of which they have formerly been members, for ill treatment or other good cause, with express design to found another. If in such case there is a real interval between the separation and the new conjunction, during such interval the individuals are as much detached and under the law of nature only as would be two men who should chance to meet on a desolate island.

The colonists are by the law of nature freeborn, as indeed all men are, white or black. No better reasons can be given for enslaving those of any color than such as Baron Montesquieu has humorously given as the foundation of that cruel slavery exercised over the poor Ethiopians, which threatens one day to reduce both Europe and America to the ignorance and barbarity of the darkest ages. Does it follow that 'tis right to enslave a man because he is black? Will short curled hair like wool instead of Christian hair, as 'tis called by those whose hearts are as hard as the nether millstone, help the argument? Can any logical inference in favor of slavery be drawn from a flat nose, a long or a short face? Nothing better can be said in favor of a trade that is the most shocking violation of the law of nature, has a direct tendency to diminish the idea of the inestimable value of liberty, and makes every dealer in it a tyrant, from the director of an African company to the petty chapman in needles and pins on the unhappy coast. It is a clear truth that those who every day barter away other men's liberty will soon care little for their own. To this cause must be imputed that ferocity, cruelty, and brutal barbarity that has long marked the general character of the sugar islanders. They can in general form no idea of government but that which in person or by an overseer, the joint and several proper representative of a creole and of the d——l, is exercised over ten thousand of their fellow men, born with the same right to freedom and the sweet enjoyments of liberty and life as their unrelenting taskmasters, the overseers and planters.

It is to be wondered at if when people of the stamp of a creolean planter get into power they will not stick for a little present gain at making their own posterity, white as well as black, worse slaves if possible than those already mentioned?

There is nothing more evident, says Mr. Locke, than "that creatures of the same species and rank, promiscuously born to all the same advantages of nature and the use of the same faculties, should also be equal one among another without subordination and subjection, unless the master of them all should by any manifest declaration of his will set one above another and confer on him by an evident and clear appointment an undoubted right to dominion and sovereignty." "The natural liberty of man is to be free from any superior power on earth, and not to be under the will or legislative authority of man, but only to have the law of nature for his rule." This is the liberty of independent states; this is the liberty of every man out of society and who has a mind to live so; which liberty is only abridged in certain instances, not lost to those who are born in or voluntarily enter into society; this gift of God cannot be annihilated.

The colonists, being men, have a right to be considered as equally entitled to all the rights of nature with the Europeans, and they are not to be restrained in the exercise of any of these rights but for the evident good of the whole community.

By being or becoming members of society they have not renounced their natural liberty in any greater degree than other good citizens, and if 'tis taken from them without their consent they are so far enslaved.

They have an undoubted right to expect that their best good will ever be consulted by their rulers, supreme and subordinate, without any partial views confined to the particular interest of one island or another. Neither the riches of Jamaica nor the luxury of a metropolis should ever have weight enough to break the balance of truth and justice. Truth and faith belong to men as men from men, and if they are disappointed in their just expectations of them in one society they will at least wish for them in another. If the love of truth and justice, the only spring of sound policy in any state, is not strong enough to prevent certain causes from taking place, the arts of fraud and force will not prevent the most fatal effects.

In the long run, those who fall on arbitrary measures will meet with their deserved fate. The law of nature was not of man's making, nor is it in his power to mend it or alter its course. He can only perform and keep or disobey and break it. The last is never done with impunity, even in this life, if it is any punishment for a man to feel himself depraved, to find himself degraded by his own folly and wickedness from the rank of a virtuous and good *man* to that of a brute, or to be transformed from the friend, perhaps father, of his country to a devouring lion or tiger.

The unhappy revolutions which for ages have distressed the human race have been all owing to the want of a little wisdom, common sense, and integrity in the administration of those whom, by their stations, God had in kindness to the world rendered able to do a great deal for the benefit of mankind with the exertion of a small portion of private and public virtue.

Slew v. *Whipple*, 1766

Records of the Inferior Court of the Court of Common Pleas, Commonwealth of Massachusetts, vol.—,(Sept. 1760-July 1776), p. 520. Records of the Superior Court of Judicature, Commonwealth of Massachusetts, vol. 1766-7. p. 175, as reprinted in George H. Moore, *Notes on the History of Slavery in Massachusetts* (New York, 1866, 1968), pp. 113-14.

The young lawyer, John Adams, who "shuddered" at James Otis's pronouncements of the slaves' natural right to freedom witnessed and participated in several "freedom suits" in Massachusetts during the period of the American Revolution. In many of these cases, when slaves brought suit against their masters, the ideas of natural rights and human liberty were given practical application. Adams, who in some instances acted as counsel for the defendants, wrote in 1795, "The Arguments were much the same as have been urged since in Pamphlets and Newspapers, in Debates in Parliament &c arising from the Rights of Mankind. . . ."

On March 5, 1762, Jenny Slew of Ipswich, Massachusetts, sued her master, John Whipple, charging that he had illegally held her in bondage. Slew's claim to freedom was based on the fact that her mother had been white; Whipple's defense rested on the plaintiff's previous marriages to blacks and the claim that Slew, born a slave, could never prove her right to liberty. In 1766 the Essex Superior Court of Judicature in Salem, overturning a lower court decision, ruled in favor of Slew and awarded her damages and costs. Although the Slew v. Whipple *decision was technically based on Slew's white ancestry, this case, as well as others that followed, was a forum for ideological appeals. Adams, who witnessed the case, recorded the words of one of the judges: "This is a Contest between Liberty and Property—both of great Consequence, but Liberty of most importance of the two."*

Jenny Slew of Ipswich in the County of Essex, spinster, Pltff., agst. John Whipple, Jun., of said Ipswich Gentleman, Deft., in a Plea of Trespass for that the said John on the 29th day of January, A.D. 1762, at Ipswich aforesaid with force and arms took her the said Jenny, held and kept her in servitude as a slave in his service, and has restrained her of her liberty from that time to the fifth of March last without any lawfull right & authority so to do and did her other injuries against the peace & to the damage of said Jenny Slew as she saith the sum of twenty-five pounds. This action was first brought at last March Court at Ipswich when & where the parties appeared & the case was continued by order of Court to the then next term when & where the Pltff appeared & the said John Whipple Jun, came by Edmund Trowbridge, Esq. his attorney & defended when he said that there is no such person in nature as Jenny Slew of Ipswich aforesaid, Spinster, & this the said John was ready to verify wherefore the writ should be abated & he prayed judgment accordingly which plea was overruled by the Court and afterwards the said John by the said Edmund made a motion to the Court & praying that another person might endorse the writ & be subject to cost if any should finally be for the Court but the Court rejected the motion and then the Deft. saving his plea in abatement aforesaid said that he is not guilty as the plaintiff contends, & thereof put himself on the Country, & then the cause was continued to this term, and now the Pltff. reserving to herself the liberty of joining issue on the Deft's plea aforesaid in the appeal says that the defendant's plea aforesaid is an insufficient answer to the Plaintiff's declaration aforesaid and by law she is not held to reply thereto & she is ready to verify wherefore for want of a sufficient answer to the Plaintiff's declaration aforesaid she prays judgment for her damages & costs & the defendant consenting to the waving of the demurrer on the appeal said his plea aforesaid is good & because the Pltff refuses to reply thereto He prays judgment for his cost. It is considered by the Court that the defendant's plea in chief aforesaid is good & that the said John Whipple recover of the said Jenny Slew costs tax at   the Pltff appealed to the next Superior Court of Judicature to be holden for this County & entered into recognizance with sureties as the law directs for prosecuting her appeal to effect.

Jenny Slew of Ipswich, in the County of Essex, Spinster, Appellant, versus John Whipple, Jr. of said Ipswich, Gentleman Appellee from the judgment of an Inferior Court of Common Pleas held at Newburyport within and for the County of Essex on the last Tuesday of September 1765 when and where the appellant was plaint., and the appellee was defendant in a plea of trespass, for that the said John upon the 29th day of January, A.D. 1762, at Ipswich aforesaid with force and arms took her the said Jenny held & kept her in servitude as a slave in his service & has restrained her of her liberty from that time to the fifth of March 1765 without any lawful right or authority so to do & did other injuries against the Peace & to the damage of the said Jenny Slew, as she saith, the sum of twenty-five pounds, at which Inferior Court, judgment was rendered upon the demurrer then that the said John Whipple recover against the said Jenny Slew costs. This appeal was brought forward at the Superior Court of Judicature &c., holden at Salem, within & for the County of Essex on the first Tuesday of last November, from whence it was continued to the last term of this Court for this County by consent & so from thence unto this Court, and now both parties appeared & the demurrer aforesaid being waived by consent & issue joined upon the plea tendered at said Inferior Court & on file. The case after full hearing was committed to a jury sworn according to law to try the same who returned their verdict therein upon oath, that is to say, they find for appellant reversion of the former judgment four pounds money damage & costs. It's therefore considered by the Court, that the former judgment be reversed & that the said Slew recover against the said Whipple the sum of four pounds lawful money of this Province damage & costs taxed 9*l*. 9*s*. 6*d*.

Arthur Lee, "Address on Slavery," March 19, 1767

Slavery Collection, Earl Gregg Swem Library, College of William and Mary, Williamsburg, Va.

In 1767 a man who once characterized Africans as brutes with a "savage appetite for blood" and referred to the Negro race as "the most detestable and vile that ever the earth produced" wrote one of the most significant antislavery articles of the eighteenth century. While a medical student at the University of Edinburgh in 1764, Arthur Lee published an essay in which he described the native of Guinea as fit for slavery. But Lee's racist notions did not lead him to a defense of slavery. He saw the institution as abominable, retarding the growth of commerce and learning, violating justice, and exposing the community to a looming horror of black insurrection. In 1767 Lee was back in Virginia and his repulsion at the ever-increasing black labor forced had not abated. His major essay on slavery, addressed to members of the Virginia House of Burgesses, was published in William Rind's Virginia Gazette *on March 19, 1767. The essay was intended to be a two-installment discussion of the "Abolition of Slavery and the Retrieval of Specie in the Colony," but, following a storm of protest raised by the publication of the section on slavery, Rind judiciously refused to publish the sequel.*

Arthur Lee, appealing to both religious sanctions and natural law, threatened Virginia slaveholders with divine vengeance, "deluges of blood," and inexorable general corruption of society. It is not surprising that readers of Rind's sheet reacted with anger and furor. It is significant, however, that one month after Lee's essay appeared in print, a bill was passed by the Virginia Assembly laying a higher duty on imported slaves. Although the bill was later rejected by the Crown, its passage reflected Virginia's increasing awareness of the possible nefarious effects of slavery on the colony. Arthur Lee continued to oppose slavery. He wrote to Granville Sharp in 1773, "In whatever Light we view Slavery, it is inadmissable. . . . In a political Light, it is pernicious—in a legal Light, unjust—in a moral Light, inhuman—in a religious Light, impious. . . ." This was Lee's only contribution to the growing body of antislavery literature. But, this essay was abridged and reprinted by Anthony Benezet to be distributed throughout America and Europe.

To Mr. Rind,

Sir— Permit me, in your paper, to address the members of our Assembly, on two points, in which the publick interest is very dearly concern'd.

The abolition of Slavery & the Retrieval of Specie, in this Colony, are the Subjects, on which I would bespeak their Attention. They are both to be accomplish'd by the same means.

Chosen as you are, Gentlemen, to watch over & provide for the publick weal and Welfare, whatever is offer'd, as tending to those desirable purposes, will I hope, meet from you a favourable ear. And, be the fate of my Sentiments as it will, I flatter myself that your pardon at least will be Indulged to the Writer.

Long and serious Reflection upon the nature & Consequences of Slavery, has Convinced me, that it is a Violation both of Justice and Religion; that it is dangerous to the safety of the Community in which it prevails; that it is destructive to the growth of arts & Sciences; and lastly, that it produces a numerous & very fatal train of Vices, both in the Slave, and in his Master. To prove these assertions, shall be the purpose of the following essay.

That Slavery, then, is a violation of Justice, will plainly appear when we consider what Justice is. It is simply & truly defin'd, as by Justinian, constans et perpetua voluntas jus suum cuique tribuendi, a constant Endeavour to give every man his right.

Now, as freedom is unquestionably the birth-right of all mankind, of Africans as well as Europeans, to keep the former in a State of slavery is a constant violation of that right, and therefore of Justice.

The ground on which the civillians, who favour Slavery, admit it to be just, Namely, Consent, force, and birth, is totally disputable. For surely a Man's own will or Consent, cannot be allow'd to introduce so important an innovation into society as that of Slavery, or to make himself an out-law, which is really the State of a Slave, since neither Consenting to nor aiding the Laws of ye Society, in which he lives, he is neither bound to obey them, nor entitled to their protection. To found any right in force, is to frustrate all right, and involve every thing in confusion, violence and rapine. With these two the last must fall, since if the Parent cannot be justly made a Slave, neither can the Child be born in Slavery. Le droit des gens, a voulu que les prisoniers, &c.

"The law of nations, says Baron Montesquieu, has doom'd prisoners to Slavery, to prevent their being Slain. The Roman civil law, permitted debtors whom their Creditors might treat ill, to Sell themselves. And the Law of nature requires that children, whom their parents, being Slaves, cannot maintain, should be slaves like them. These reasons of the Civillians are not just; it is not true that a Captive may be slain, unless in case of absolute necessity; but if he hath been reduced to slavery it is plain that no such necessity existed, since he was not slain.

It is not true that a freeman can sell himself. For sale supposes a price, but in this act the Slave & his property becomes immediately that of his Master, the slave therefore can receive no price, nor the Master pay &c. And if a man cannot sell himself, nor a prisoner of war be reduced to Slavery, much less can his Child." Such are the Sentiments of this illustrious civillian; his reasonings, which I have been oblidged to contract, the reader, interested in this subject, will do well to consult at large.

Yet even these rights of impossition very questionable, nay, refutable as they are, we have not to authorize the Bondage of the Africans. For neither do they consent to be our Slaves, nor do we purchase them of their Conquerors. The British Merchants obtain them from Africa by violence, artifice & treachery, with a few trinkets to prompt those unfortunate & destestable people to enslave one another by force or Strategem. Purchase them indeed they may, under the authority of an act of British Parliment. An act entailing upon the Africans, with whom we were not at war, and over whom a British Parliment could not of right assume even a shadow of authority, the dreadfull curse of perpetual slavery upon them and their children forever. There cannot be in nature, there is not in all history, an instance in which every right of men is more flagrantly violated. The laws of the Antients never authorized the making slaves but of those nations whom they had conquer'd; yet they were Heathens and we are Christians. They were misled by a false and monstrous religion, divested of humanity, by a horrible & Barbarous worship; we are directed by the unering preceps of the revealed religion we possess, enlightened by its wisdom, and humanized by its benevolence. Before them were gods deformed with passions, and horrible for every cruelty & Vice; before us is that incomparable pattern of Meekness, Charity, love, and justice to mankind, which so transcendently distinguished the founder of Christianity and his ever amiable doctrines. Reader—remember that the corner stone of your religion is to do unto others as you wou'd they shou'd do unto you; ask then your own Heart, whether it would not abhor anyone, as the most outrageous violator of this & every other principle of right, Justice & humanity, who should make a slave of you and your Posterity forever. Remember that God knoweth the heart. Lay not this flattering unction to your Soul, that it is the custom of the Country, that you found it so, that not your will, but your Necessity consents; Ah think, how little such an excuse will avail you in that awfull day, when your Saviour shall pronounce judgment upon you for breaking a law too plain to be misunderstood, too sacred to be violated. If we say that we are Christians, yet act more inhumanly and unjustly than Heathens, with what dreadfull justice must this Sentance of our blessed Saviours fall upon us: Not every one that sayeth unto me, Lord, Lord, shall enter into the Kingdom of Heaven; but he that doeth the will of my Father which is in heaven. Think a moment how much your temporal, your eternal wellfare, depends upon the abolition of a practice, which deforms the Image of your God; tramples on his reveal'd will, infringes the most Sacred rights, and violates humanity.

Enough I hope has been said to prove that slavery is in violation of justice and religion. That it is dangerous to the safety of the State in which it prevails, may be as safely asserted.

What one's own experience hath not taught, that of others must decide. From hence does history derive its utility. For being, when truly written, a faithfull record of the transactions of mankind, and the consequences that flow'd from them; we are thence furnished with the means of judging what will be the probable effect of transactions similar amoung ourselves. We learn then from history, that slavery, wherever encouraged, has sooner or later been productive of very dangerous commotions. I will not trouble my reader here with quotations in support of this assertion, but content myself with referring those, who may be dubious of its truth, to the histories of Athens, Lacedaemon, Rome, and Spain. And that this observation may bear its full weight, let me beg that it be remember'd these states were remarkable for being the most warlike in the world; the bravest and best trained to discipline and arms.

That we are not such is but too obvious. Yet it does not appear that the slaves in those Communitys, were so numerous as they are in ours. Demothenes during his orphanage, had been defrauded of a large fortune; and in his oration for retrieving it enumerates 52 Slaves. Tacitus, in mentioning a roman Nobleman, who was assassinated by one of his Slaves; records the whole number amounting to 400, to have suffered Death for that crime. From these facts we may conclude, that the proportion of slaves among the antients was not so great as with us; and as, notwithstanding this, the freemen, tho' infinitely better armed and disciplined than we are, were yet brought to the very brink of ruin by the insurrections of their Slaves; what powerfull reasons have not we, to fear even more fatal consequences from the greater prevalence of Slavery among us. How long how bloody and destructive, was the contest between the Moorish slaves and the native Spaniards, and after almost deluges of blood had been shed, the Spaniards obtain'd nothing more, than driving them into the mountains; from whence they remain themselves subjected to their perpetual inroads. Less bloody indeed, though not less alarming, have been the insurrections in Jamaica; and to imagine that we shall be forever exempted from this Calamity, which experience teaches us to be inseperable from slavery, so encouraged, is an infatuation as astonishing, as it will be surely fatal. On us, or on our posterity, the inevitable blow, must, one day, fall; and probably with the most irresistable vengeance the longer it is protracted. Since time, as it adds strength and experience to the slaves, will sink us into perfect security and indolence, which debillitating our minds, and enervating our bodies, will render us an easy conquest to the feeblest foe. Unarm'd already and undisciplined, with our Militia laws contemned, neglected or perverted, we are like the wretch at the feast; with a drawn sword depending over his head by a Single hair; yet we flatter ourselves, in opposition to the force of reason and conviction of experience, that the danger is not imminent.

To prosecute this Subject farther, at present, would I perceive Mr. Rind, engross too much of your paper, and most likely disgust the reader, I must therefore take leave to defer what remains to the next week. Happy shall I be if my poor attempts should prompt more able Heads to think and write upon a Subject, of such lasting import to the welfare of the Community. Strongly, I confess, am I attached to the positions here laid down, because they are formed upon long and serious deliberation; Yet I am open to that conviction, which truth ever operates on minds unseduced by Interest, and uninflamed by passion.

I am, Sir,
Your humble Servant

Philanthropos

Anthony Benezet, *A Caution and Warning*, 1767

Anthony Benezet, A Caution and Warning to Great Britain and Her Colonies in a Short Representation of the Calamitous State of the Enslaved Negroes in the British Dominions: Collected from various Authors, and submitted to the Serious Consideration of All, more especially of Those in Power (Philadelphia, 1767), pp. 1-48.

With the publication of A Caution and Warning . . . *in 1766, the depth and intensity of Anthony Benezet's research into the problem of Negro slavery becomes obvious. In this pamphlet the Quaker abolitionist marshaled an incredible variety of sources. Although Benezet's simple method of listing quotation after quotation lacked literary style, he presented an effective case. In discussing the blacks in their African homeland, Benezet cited British, Dutch, and French observers, the author of an account of Gorée and Senegal, and an official of the African Company. He painted an idyllic portrait of an uncorrupted people of simple genius and good disposition living in an Eden-like paradise abundant with food, temperate in climate, and rich in soil. Describing the nature of the slave trade and slavery, Benezet quoted Francis Moor and N. Brue, writers on the West Indies such as Thomas Jeffery, a surgeon aboard a slave ship, and even George Whitefield. He wrote of the countless deaths in the putrid holds of slave ships, the whippings, beatings, mutilations, and the final and complete degradation of blacks on the plantations.*

In appealing to natural law, he quoted from the writings of Montesquieu, George Wallis's System of the Laws of Scotland, *Francis Hutchinson's* System of Moral Philosophy, *and James Foster's* Discourses on Natural Religion and Social Virtue. *He further buttressed his pamphlet with references to a Roman missionary, Richard Baxter, George Fox, an Irish historian, a Liverpool memorandum book, Mosaic law, Common law, and the Bible. Benezet's reputation as the most detailed chronicler of information on the evils of slavery was now established. His pamphlet was reprinted in England and translated into French; by 1783 it had been distributed to approximately 800 members of Parliament and officers of the Crown. Its influence in the antislavery movement, both in America and Europe, was vital.*

At a Time when the general Rights and Liberties of Mankind, and the Preservation of those valuable Privileges, transmitted to us from our Ancestors, are become so much the Subjects of universal Consideration; can it be an Enquiry indifferent to any, how many of those who distinguish themselves as the Advocates of Liberty, remain insensible and inattentive to the Treatment of Thousands and Tens of Thousands of our Fellow-Men, who, from Motives of Avarice, and the inexorable Decree of Tyrant Custom, are at this very Time kept in the most deplorable State of Slavery, in many Parts of the *British* Dominions?

The Intent of publishing the following Sheets, is more fully to make known the aggravated Iniquity attending the Practice of the Slave-trade; whereby many Thousands of our Fellow-Creatures, as free as ourselves by Nature, and equally with us the Subjects of Christ's redeeming Grace, are yearly brought into inextricable and barbarous Bondage; and many, very many, to miserable and untimely Ends.

The Truth of this lamentable Complaint is so obvious to Persons of Candour, under whose Notice it hath fallen, that several have lately published their Sentiments thereon, as a Matter which calls for the most serious Consideration of all who are concerned for the civil or religious Welfare of their Country. How an Evil, of so deep a Dye, hath so long not only passed uninterrupted by Those in Power, but hath even had their Countenance, is indeed surprising, and, Charity would suppose, must, in a great Measure, have arisen from this, that many Persons in Government, both of the Clergy and Laity, in whose Power it hath been to put a Stop to the Trade, have been unacquainted with the corrupt Motives which give Life to it; and the Groans, the dying Groans, which daily ascend to God, the common Father of Mankind, from the broken Hearts of those his deeply oppressed Creatures; otherwise the Powers of the Earth would not, I think I may venture to say, could not, have so long authorised a Practice so inconsistent with every Idea of Liberty and Justice, which, as the learned *James Foster* says, *Bids that God, which is the God and Father of the Gentiles, unconverted to Christianity, most daring and bold Defiance; and spurns at all the Principles both of natural and revealed Religion.*

Much might justly be said of the temporal Evils which attend this Practice, as it is destructive of the Welfare of human Society, and of the Peace and Prosperity of every Country, in Proportion as it prevails. It might be also shewn, that it destroys the Bonds of natural Affection and Interest, whereby Mankind in general are united; that it introduces Idleness, discourages Marriage, corrupts the Youth, ruins and debauches Morals, excites continual Apprehensions of Dangers, and frequent Alarms; to which the Whites are necessarily exposed from so great an Encrease of a People, that, by their Bondage and Oppressions, become natural Enemies, yet, at the same time, are filling the Places, and eating the Bread of those who would be the Support and Security of the Country. But as these, and many more Reflections of the same Kind, may occur to a considerate Mind, I shall only endeavour to shew, from the Nature of the Trade, the Plenty which *Guiney* affords its Inhabitants, the barbarous Treatment of the *Negroes*, and the Observations made thereon by Authors of Note, that it is inconsistent with the plainest Precepts of the Gospel, the Dictates of Reason, and every common Sentiment of Humanity.

In an Account of the *European* Settlements in *America*, printed in *London*, 1757, the Author, speaking on this Subject, says,

The *Negroes* in our Colonies endure a Slavery more compleat, and attended with far worse Circumstances, than what any People in their Condition suffer in any other Part of the World, or have suffered in any other Period of Time: Proofs of this are not wanting. The prodigious Waste which we experience in this unhappy Part of our Species, is a full and melancholy Evidence of this Truth. The Island of *Barbados* (the *Negroes* upon which do not amount to Eighty Thousand) notwithstanding all the Means which they use to encrease them by Propagation, and that the Climate is in every Respect (except that of being more wholesome) exactly resembling the Climate from whence they come; notwithstanding all this, *Barbados* lies under a Necessity of an annual Recruit of Five Thousand Slaves, to keep up the Stock at the Number I have mentioned. This prodigious Failure, which is at least in the same Proportion in all our Islands, shews demonstratively that some uncommon and unsupportable Hardship lies upon the *Negroes*, which wears them down in such a suprising Manner; and this, I imagine, is principally the excessive Labour which they undergo.

In an Account of Part of *North-America*, published by *Thomas Jeffery*, printed 1761, speaking of the Usage the *Negroes* receive in the *West-India* Islands, thus expresses himself:

It is impossible for a human Heart to reflect upon the Servitude of these Dregs of Mankind, without in some Measure feeling for their Misery, which ends but with their Lives. . . . Nothing can be more wretched than the Condition of this People. One would imagine, they were framed to be the Disgrace of the human Species, banished from their Country, and deprived of that Blessing Liberty, on which all other Nations set the greatest Value; they are in a Manner reduced to the Condition of Beasts of Burden: In general a few Roots, Potatoes especially, are their Food, and two Rags, which neither screen them from the Heat of the Day, nor the extraordinary Coolness of the Night, all their Covering; their Sleep very short; their Labour almost continual; they receive no Wages, but have Twenty Lashes for the smallest Fault.

A considerate young Person, who was late in one of our *West-India* Islands, where he observed the miserable Situation of the *Negroes*, makes the following Remarks:

I meet with daily Exercise, to see the Treatment which these miserable Wretches meet with from their Masters, with but few Exceptions. They whip them most unmercifully, on small Occasions. They beat them with thick Clubs, and you will see their Bodies all whaled and scarred; in short, they seem to set no other Value on their Lives, than as they cost them so much Money; and are not restrained from killing them, when angry, by a worthier Consideration, than that they lose so much. They act as though they did not look upon them as a Race of human Creatures, who have Reason, and Remembrance of Misfortunes, but as Beasts, like Oxen, who are stubborn, hardy and senseless; fit for Burdens, and designed to bear them. They won't allow them to have any Claim to human Privileges, or scarce, indeed, to be regarded as the Work of God. Though it was consistent with the Justice of our Maker to pronounce the Sentence on our common Parent, and through him on all succeeding Generations, *That he and they should eat their Bread by the Sweat of their Brows;* yet does it not stand recorded, by the same eternal Truth, *That the Labourer is worthy of his Hire?* It cannot be allowed, in natural Justice, that there should be a Servitude without Condition; a cruel endless Servitude. It cannot be reconcileable to natural Justice, that whole Nations, nay, whole Continents of Men, should be devoted to do the Drudgery of Life for others, be dragged away from their Attachments of Relations and Societies, and made to serve the Appetites and Pleasures of a Race of Men, whose Superiority has been obtained by an illegal Force.

A particular Account of the Treatment these unhappy *Africans* receive in the *West-Indies*, was lately published, which, even by those who, blinded by Interest, seek excuses for the Trade, and endeavour to palliate the Cruelty exercised upon them, is allowed to be a true, though rather too favourable, Representation of the Usage they receive, which is as follows, *viz.*

The Iniquity of the Slave-trade is greatly aggravated by the Inhumanity with which the *Negroes* are treated in the Plantations, as well with Respect to Food and Cloathing, as from the unreasonable Labour which is commonly exacted from them. To which may be added the cruel Chastisements they frequently suffer, without any other Bounds, than the Will and Wrath of their hard Task-masters. In *Barbados*, and some other of the Islands, six Pints of *Indian* Corn, and three Herrings, are reckoned a full Week's Allowance for a working Slave; and in the System of Geography it is said, *That in* Jamaica *the Owners of the* Negroe *Slaves, set aside for each a Parcel of Ground, and allow them* Sundays *to manure it, the Produce of which,* with sometimes a few Herrings, or other salt Fish, *is all that is allowed for their Support.* Their Allowance for Cloathing in the Islands is seldom more than six Yards of Ozenbrigs each Year: And in the more Northern Colonies, where the piercing westerly Winds are long and sensibly felt, these poor *Africans* suffer much for Want of sufficient Cloathing, indeed some have none till they are able to pay for it by their Labour. The Time that the *Negroes* work in the *West-Indies*, is from Day-break till Noon; then again from Two o'Clock till Dusk (during which Time they are attended by Overseers, who severely scourge those who appear to them dilatory) and before they are suffered to go to their Quarters, they have still something to do, as collecting of Herbage for the Horses, gathering Fuel for the Boilers, *&c.* so that it is often Half past Twelve before they can get Home, when they have scarce Time to grind and boil their *Indian* Corn; whereby it often happens that they are called again to Labour before they can satisfy their Hunger: And here no Delay or Excuse will avail, for if they are not in the Field immediately upon the usual Notice, they must expect to feel the Overseer's lash. In Crop-time (which lasts many Months) they are obliged (by Turns) to work most of the Night in the Boiling-house. Thus their Owners, from a Desire of making the greatest Gain by the Labour of their Slaves lay heavy Burdens on them, and yet feed and cloath them very sparingly, and some scarce feed or cloath them at all; so that the poor Creatures are obliged to shift for their Living in the best Manner they can, which occasions their being often killed in the neighbouring Lands, stealing Potatoes, or other Food, to satisfy their Hunger. And if they take any Thing from the Plantation they belong to, though under such pressing Want, their Owners will correct them severely, for taking a little of what they have so hardily laboured for, whilst they themselves riot in the greatest Luxury and Excess.—It is a Matter of Astonishment, how a People who, as a Nation, are looked upon as generous and humane, and so much value themselves for their uncommon Sense of the Benefit of Liberty, can live in the Practice of such extreme Oppression and Inhumanity, without seeing the Inconsistency of such Conduct, and without feeling great Remorse: Nor is it less amazing to hear these Men calmly making Calculations about the Strength and Lives of their Fellow-Men; in *Jamaica*, if six in ten, of the new imported *Negroes*, survive the Seasoning, it is looked upon as a gaining Purchase: And in most of the other Plantations, if the *Negroes* live eight or nine Years, their Labour is reckoned a sufficient Compensation for their Cost. . . . If Calculations of this Sort were made upon the Strength and Labour of Beasts of Burden, it would not appear so strange, but even then a merciful Man would certainly use his Beast with more Mercy than is usually shewn to the poor *Negroes*.—Will not the Groans of this deeply afflicted and oppressed People reach Heaven, and, when the Cup of Iniquity is full, must not the inevitable Consequence be pouring forth of the Judgments of God upon their Oppressors? But, alas! is it not too manifest that this Oppression has already long been the Object of the Divine Displeasure? For what heavier Judgment, what greater Calamity can befal any People, than to become a Prey to that Hardness of Heart, that Forgetfulness of God, and Insensibility to every religious Impression; as well as that general Depravation of Manners, which so much prevails in the Colonies, in Proportion as they have more or less enriched themselves, at the Expence of the Blood and Bondage of the *Negroes*?

The Situation of the *Negroes* in our Southern Provinces on the Continent, is also feelingly set forth by *George Whitefield*, in a Letter from *Georgia*, to the Inhabitants of *Maryland, Virginia, North* and *South-Carolina*, printed in the Year 1739, of which the following is an Extract.

As I lately passed through your Provinces, in my Way hither, I was sensibly touched with a Fellow-feeling of the Miseries of the poor *Negroes*, Whether it be lawful for Christians to buy Slaves, and thereby encourage the Nations from whom they are bought, to be at perpetual War with each other, I shall not take upon me to determine; sure I am, it is sinful, when bought, to use them as bad, nay worse, than as though they were Brutes; and whatever particular Exception there may be (as I would charitably hope there are some) I fear the Generality of you, that own *Negroes*, are liable to such a Charge; for your Slaves, I believe, work as hard, if not harder, than the Horses whereon you ride. These, after they have done their Work, are fed and taken proper Care of; but many *Negroes*, when wearied with Labour, in your Plantations, have been obliged to grind their own Corn, after they return home; your Dogs are caressed and fondled at your Tables; but your Slaves, who are frequently stiled Dogs or Beasts, have not an equal Privilege; they are scarce permitted to pick up the Crumbs which fall from their Master's Table.—Not to mention what Numbers have been given up to the inhuman Usage of cruel Task-masters, who, by their unrelenting Scourges, have ploughed their Backs, and made long Furrows, and at length brought them even to Death. When passing along, I have viewed your Plantations cleared and cultivated, many spacious Houses built, and the Owners of them faring sumptuously every Day, my Blood has frequently almost run cold within me, to consider how many of your Slaves had neither convenient Food to eat, or proper Raiment to put on, notwithstanding most of the Comforts you enjoy were solely owing to their indefatigable Labours, . . . The Scripture says, Thou shalt not muzzel the Ox that treadeth out the Corn. Does God take Care for Oxen; and will he not take Care of the *Negroes* also? Undoubtedly he will.—Go to now ye rich Men, weep and howl for your Miseries that shall come upon you: Behold the Provision of the poor *Negroes*, who have reaped down your Fields, which is by you denied them, crieth; and the Cries of them which reaped; are entered into the Ears of the Lord of Sabaoth. We have a remarkable Instance of God's taking Cognizance of, and avenging, the Quarrel of poor Slaves, 2 *Sam*. xxi. 1. There was a famine in the Days of *David*, three Years, Year after Year; and *David* enquired of the Lord: And the Lord answered, It is for *Saul*, and his bloody House, because he slew the *Gibeonites*. Two Things are here very remarkable: *First*, These *Gibeonites* were only Hewers of Wood, and Drawers of Water; or, in other Words, Slaves like yours.

Secondly, That this Plague was sent by God many Years after the Injury, the Cause of the Plague, was committed. And for what End were this and such like Examples recorded in holy Scriptures? without Doubt, for our Learning.—For God is the same To-day,as he was Yesterday, and will continue the same for ever. He does not reject the Prayer of the Poor and Destitute; nor disregard the Cry of the meanest *Negroe*. The Blood of them spilt for these many Years, in your respective Provinces, will ascend up to Heaven against you.

Some who have only seen *Negroes* in an abject State of Slavery, broken-spirited and dejected, knowing nothing of their Situation in their native Country, may apprehend, that they are naturally insensible of the Benefits of Liberty, being destitute and miserable in every Respect, and that our suffering them to live amongst us (as the *Gibeonites* of old were permitted to live with the *Israelites*) though even on more oppressive Terms, is to them a Favour; but these are certainly erroneous Opinions, with Respect to far the greatest Part of them: Although it is highly probable, that in a Country which is more than Three Thousand Miles in Extent from North to South, and much from East to West, there will be barren Parts, and many Inhabitants more uncivilized and barbarous than others; as is the Case in all other Countries: Yet, from the most authentic Accounts, the Inhabitants of *Guiney* appear, generally speaking, to be an industrious, humane, sociable People, whose Capacities are naturally as enlarged, and as open to Improvement, as those of the *Europeans*; and that their Country is fruitful, and in many Places well improved, abounding in Cattle, Grain and Fruits: And as the Earth yields all the Year round a fresh Supply of Food, and but little Cloathing is requisite, by Reason of the continual Warmth of the Climate; the Necessaries of Life are much easier procured in most Parts of *Africa*, than in our more Northern Climes. This is confirmed by many Authors of Note, who have resided there; among others M. *Adanson*, in his Account of *Gorée* and *Senegal*, in the Year 1754, says,

Which Way soever I turned my Eyes on this pleasant Spot, I beheld a perfect Image of pure Nature; an agreeable Solitude, bounded on every Side by charming Landscapes, the rural Situation of Cottages in the Midst of Trees; the Ease and Indolence of the *Negroes*, reclined under the Shade of their spreading Foliage; the Simplicity of their Dress and Manners; the whole revived in my Mind the Idea of our first Parents, and I seemed to contemplate the World in its primitive State: They are, generally speaking, very good-natured, sociable and obliging. I was not a little pleased with this my first Reception; it convinced me, that there ought to be a considerable Abatement made in the Accounts I had read and heard every where of the savage Character of the *Africans*. I observed, both in *Negroes*, and *Moors*, great Humanity and Sociableness, which gave me strong Hopes that I should be very safe amongst them, and meet with the Success I desired, in my Enquiries after the Curiosities of the Country.

William Bosman, a principal Factor for the *Dutch*, who resided Sixteen Years in *Guiney*, speaking of the Natives of that Part where he then was, says, "They are generally a good Sort of People, honest in their Dealings;" others he describes as

being generally friendly to Strangers, of a mild Conversation, affable, and easy to be overcome with Reason. He adds, That some *Negroes*, who have had an agreeable Education, have manifested a Brightness of Understanding equal to any of us.

Speaking of the Fruitfulness of the Country, he says,

It was very populous, plentifully provided with Corn, Potatoes and Fruit, which grew close to each other; in some Places a Foot-Path is the only Ground that is not covered with them, the *Negroes* leaving no Place, which is thought fertile, uncultivated; and immediately after they have reaped, they are sure to sow again. Other Parts he describes as being full of Towns and Villages, the Soil very rich, and so well cultivated as to look like an entire Garden, abounding in Rice, Corn, Oxen and Poultry, and the Inhabitants laborious.

William Smith, who was sent by the *African* Company to visit their Settlements on the Coast of *Guiney*, in the Year 1726, gives much the same Account of the Country of *Delmina* and *Cape-Corse*, &c. for Beauty and Goodness, and adds,

The more you come downward towards that Part called *Slave-Coast*, the more delightful and rich the Soil appears.

Speaking of their Disposition, he says,

They were a civil, good-natured People, industrious to the last Degree. It is easy to perceive what happy Memories they are blessed with, and how great Progress they would make in the Sciences, in case their Genius was cultivated with Study.

He adds, from the Information he received of one of the Factors, who had resided ten Years in that Country,

That the discerning Natives account it their greatest Unhappiness, that they were ever visited by the *Europeans*—That the Christians introduced the Traffic of Slaves, and that before our coming they lived in Peace.

Andrew Brue, a principal Man in the *French* Factory, in the Account he gives of the great River *Senegal*, which runs many Hundred Miles up the Country, tells his Readers,

The farther you go from the Sea, the Country on the River seems more fruitful and well improved. It abounds in *Guiney* and *Indian* Corn, Rice, Pulse, Tobacco, and Indico. Here are vast Meadows, which feed large Herds of great and small Cattle; Poultry are numerous, as well as wild Fowl.

The same Author, in his Travels to the South of the River *Gambia*, expresses his Surprize, to

see the Land so well cultivated; scarce a Spot lay unimproved; the low Grounds, divided by small Canals, were all sowed with Rice; the higher Ground planted with *Indian* Corn, Millet, and Peas of different Sorts; Beef and Mutton very cheap, as well as all other Necessaries of Life.

The Account this Author gives of the Disposition of the Natives, is, "That they are generally good-natured and civil, and may be brought to any Thing by fair and soft Means." *Artus*, speaking of the same People, says, "They are a sincere, inoffensive People, and do no Injustice either to one another or Strangers."

From these Accounts, both of the good Disposition of the Natives, and the Fruitfulness of most Parts of *Guiney*, which are confirmed by many other Authors, it may well be concluded, that their Acquaintance with the *Europeans* would have been a Happiness to them, had those last not only bore the Name, but indeed been influenced by the Spirit of Christianity. But, alas! how hath the Conduct of the Whites contradicted the Precepts and Example of Christ? Instead of promoting the End of his coming, by preaching the Gospel of Peace and good Will to Man, they have, by their Practices, contributed to inflame every noxious Passion of corrupt Nature in the *Negroes*; they have incited them to make War one upon another, and for this Purpose have furnished them with prodigious Quantities of Ammunition and Arms, whereby they have been hurried into Confusion, Bloodshed, and all the Extremities of temporal Misery, which must necessarily beget in their Minds such a general Detestation and Scorn of the Christian Name, as may deeply affect, if not wholly preclude, their Belief of the great Truths of our holy Religion. Thus an insatiable Desire of Gain hath become the principal and moving Cause of the most abominable and dreadful Scene, that was perhaps ever acted upon the Face of the Earth; even the Power of their Kings hath been made subservient to answer this wicked Purpose; instead of being Protectors of their People, these Rulers, allured by the tempting Bait laid before them by the *European* Factors, &c. have invaded the Liberties of their unhappy Subjects, and are become their Oppressors.

Divers Accounts have already appeared in Print declarative of the shocking Wickedness with which this Trade is carried on; these may not have fallen into the Hands of some of my Readers, I shall, therefore, for their Information, select a few of the most remarkable Instances that I have met with, shewing the Method by which the Trade is commonly managed all along the *African* Coast.

Francis Moor, Factor to the *African* Company on the River *Gambia*, relates, That when the King of *Barsalli* wants Goods, &c. he sends a Messenger to the *English* Governor, at *James'* Fort, to desire he would send up a Sloop with a Cargo of Goods; which (says the Author) the Governor never fails to do: Against the Time the Vessel arrives, the King plunders some of his Enemies Towns, selling the People for such Goods as he wants.—If he is not at War with any neighbouring King, he falls upon one of his own Towns, and makes bold to sell his own miserable Subjects.

N. Brue, in his Account of the Trade, &c. writes,

> That having received a Quantity of Goods, he wrote to the King of the Country, That if he had a sufficient Number of Slaves, he was ready to trade with him. This Prince (says that Author) as well as other *Negroe* Monarchs, has always a sure Way of supplying his Deficiencies, by selling his own Subjects.—The King had Recourse to this Method, by seizing Three Hundred of his own People, and sent Word to *Brue*, that he had the Slaves ready to deliver for the Goods.

The Misery and Bloodshed, consequent of the Slave-Trade, is amply set forth by the following Extracts of two Voyages to the Coast of *Guiney*, for Slaves. The first in a Vessel from *Liverpool*, taken *verbatim* from the original Manuscript of the Surgeon's Journal, *viz.*

Sestro, December the 29th, 1724. No Trade To-day, though many Traders come on board; they inform us, that the People are gone to War within Land, and will bring Prisoners enough in two or three Days; in Hopes of which we stay.

The 30th. No Trade yet, but our Traders came on board To-day, and informed us, the People had burnt four Towns of their Enemies, so that To-morrow we expect Slaves off. Another large Ship is come in. Yesterday came in a large *Londoner.*

The 31st. Fair Weather, but no Trade yet; we see each Night Towns burning; but we hear the *Sestro* Men are many of them killed by the Inland *Negroes*, so that we fear this War will be unsuccessful.

The 2d *January.* Last Night we saw a prodigious Fire break out about Eleven o'Clock; and this Morning see the Town of *Sestro* burnt down to the Ground (it contained some Hundred of Houses) so that we find their Enemies are too hard for them at present, and, consequently, our Trade spoiled here; so that about Seven o'Clock we weighed Anchor, as did likewise the three other Vessels, to proceed lower down.

The second Relation, also taken from the original Manuscript Journal of a Person of Credit, who sent Surgeon, on the same Account, in a Vessel from *New-York* to the Coast of *Guiney*, about eighteen Years past, is as follows, *viz.*

Being on the Coast, at a Place called *Basalia*, the Commander of the Vessel, according to Custom, sent a Person on Shore with a Present to the King, acquainting him with his Arrival, and letting him know, they wanted a Cargo of Slaves. The Kind promised to furnish them with Slaves; and, in order to do it, set out to go to War against his Enemies; designing also to surprise some Town, and take all the People Prisoners: Some Time after, the King sent them Word, he had not yet met with the desired Success, having been twice repulsed, in attempting to break up two Towns; but that he still hoped to procure a Number of Slaves for them; and in this Design he persisted till he met his Enemies in the Field, where a Battle was fought, which lasted three Days, during which Time the Engagement was bloody, that four Thousand five Hundred Men were slain on the Spot.

The Person that wrote the Account beheld the Bodies, as they lay on the Field of Battle.

Think (says he in his Journal) what a pitiable Sight it was, to see the Widows weeping over their lost Husbands, Orphans deploring the Loss of their Fathers, *&c. &c.*

Those, who are acquainted with the Trade, agree, that many *Negroes* on the Sea Coast, who have been corrupted by their Intercourse and Converse with the *European* Factors, have learnt to stick at no Act of Cruelty for Gain. These make it a Practice to steal Abundance of little Blacks of both Sexes, when found on the Roads, or in the Fields, where their Parents keep them all Day to watch the Corn, *&c.* Some Authors say, the *Negroe* Factors go six or seven Hundred Miles up the Country with Goods, bought from the *Europeans*, where Markets of Men are kept in the same Manner as those of Beasts with us; when the poor Slaves, whether brought from far or near, come to the Sea-shore, they are stripped naked, and strictly examined by the *European* Surgeons, both Men and Women, without the least Distinction or Modesty; those which are approved as good, are marked with a red hot Iron, with the Ship's Mark, after which they are put on board the Vessels, the Men being shackled with Irons, two and two together. Reader, bring the Matter Home, and consider whether any Situation in Life can be more completely miserable than that of those distressed Captives. When we reflect, that each Individual of this Number had some tender Attachment, which was broken by this cruel Separation; some Parent or Wife, who had not an Opportunity of mingling Tears into parting Embrace; perhaps some Infant, or aged Parent, whom his Labour was to feed, and Vigilance protect; themselves under the dreadful Apprehension of an unknown perpetual Slavery; pent up within the narrow Confines of a Vessel, sometimes six or seven Hundred together, where they lie as close as possible. Under these complicated Distresses they are often reduced to a State of Desperation, wherein many have leaped into the Sea, and have kept themselves under Water, till they were drowned; other have starved themselves to Death, for the Prevention whereof some Masters of Vessels have cut off the Legs and Arms of a Number of those poor desperate Creatures, to terrify the rest. Great Numbers have also frequently been killed, and some deliberately put to Death, under the greatest Torture, when they have attempted to rise, in order to free themselves from their present Misery, and the Slavery designed them. An Instance of the last Kind appears particularly in an Account given by the Master of a Vessel, who brought a Cargo of Slaves to *Barbados*; indeed it appears so irreconcileable to the common Dictates of Humanity, that one would doubt the Truth of it, had it not been related by a serious Person, of undoubted Credit, who had it from the Captain's own Mouth. Upon an Enquiry, What had been the Success of his Voyage? he answered,

> That he had found it a difficult Matter to set the *Negroes* a fighting with each other, in order to procure the Number he wanted; but that when he had obtained this End, and had got his Vessel filled with Slaves, a new Difficulty arose from their Refusal to take Food; those desperate Creatures chusing rather to die with Hunger, than to be carried from their native Country.

Upon a farther Enquiry, by what Means he had prevailed upon them to forego this desperate Resolution, he answered,

> That he obliged all the *Negroes* to come upon Deck, where they persisting in their Resolution of not taking Food, he caused his Sailors to lay Hold upon one of the most obstinate, and chopt the poor Creature into small Pieces, forcing some of the others to eat a Part of the mangled Body; withal swearing to the Survivors, that he would use them all. one after the other, in the same Manner, if they did not consent to eat.

This horrid Execution he applauded as a good Act, it having had the desired Effect, in bringing them to take Food.

A similar Case is mentioned in *Astley's* Collection of Voyages, by *John Atkins*, Surgeon on board Admiral *Ogle's* Squadron,

> of one *Harding*, Master of a Vessel, in which several of the Men Slaves, and a

Woman Slave, had attempted to rise, in order to recover their Liberty; some of whom the Master, of his own Authority, sentenced to cruel Death, making them first eat the Heart and Liver of one of those he killed. The Woman he hoisted by the Thumbs, whipped and slashed with Knives before the other Slaves, till she died.

As detestable and shocking as this may appear to such, whose Hearts are not yet hardened by the Practice of that Cruelty, which the Love of Wealth, by Degrees, introduceth into the human Mind; it will not be strange to those who have been concerned or employed in the Trade. Now here arises a necessary Query to those who hold the Ballance and Sword of Justice, and who must account to God for the Use they have made of it. Since *our* English *Law is so truly valuable for its Justice,* how can they overlook these barbarous Deaths of the unhappy *Africans* without Trial, or due Proof of their being guilty of Crimes adequate to their Punishment? Why are those Masters of Vessels (who are often not the most tender and considerate of Men) thus suffered to be the sovereign Arbiters of the Lives of the miserable *Negroes;* and allowed, with Impunity thus to destroy, may I not say murder, their Fellow-Creatures, and that by Means so cruel, as cannot be even related but with Shame and Horror.

When the Vessels arrive at their destined Port in the Colonies, the poor *Negroes* are to be disposed of to the Planters, and here they are again exposed naked, without any Distinction of Sexes, to the brutal Examination of their Purchasers; and this, it may well be judged, is to many of them another Occasion of deep Distress, especially to the Females: Add to this, that near Connections must now again be separated, to go with their several Purchasers. In this melancholy Scene, Mothers are seen hanging over their Daughters, bedewing their naked Breasts with Tears, and Daughters clinging to their Parents, not knowing what new Stage of Distress must follow their Separation, or if ever they shall meet again; and here what Sympathy, what Commiseration are they to expect? why, indeed, if they will not separate as readily as their Owners think proper, the Whipper is called for, and the Lash exercised upon their naked Bodies, till obliged to part.

Can any human Heart, that retains a Fellow-feeling for the Sufferings of Mankind, be unconcerned at Relations of such grievous Affliction, to which this oppressed Part of our Species are subjected! God gave to Man Dominion over the Fish of the Sea, and over the Fowls of the Air, and over the Cattle, *&c.* but imposed no involuntary Subjection of one Man to another.

The Truth of this Position has of late been clearly set forth, by Persons of Reputation and Ability, particularly *George Wallis,* in his System of the Laws of *Scotland,* whose Sentiments are so worthy the Notice of all considerate Persons, that I shall here repeat a Part of what he has not long since published, concerning the *African* Trade, *viz.*

If this Trade admits of a moral or a rational Justification, every Crime, even the most atrocious, may be justified: Government was instituted for the Good of Mankind. Kings, Princes, Governors, are not Proprietors of those who are subjected to their Authority; they have not a Right to make them miserable. On the contrary, their Authority is vested in them, that they may, by the just Exercise of it, promote the Happiness of their People: Of Course, they have not a Right to dispose of their Liberty, and to sell them for Slaves: Besides, no Man has a Right to acquire or to purchase them: Men and their Liberty are not either saleable or purchasable, one therefore has Nobody but himself to blame, in case he shall find himself deprived of a Man, whom he thought he had, by buying for a Price, made his own; for he dealt in a Trade which was illicit, and was prohibited by the most obvious Dictates of Humanity. For these Reasons, every one of those unfortunate Men, who are pretended to be Slaves, has a Right to be declared to be free, for he never lost his Liberty; he could not lose it; his Prince has no Power to dispose of him: of Course the Sale was void. This Right he carries about with him, and is intitled every where to get it declared. As soon, therefore, as he comes into a Country, in which the Judges are not forgetful of their own Humanity, it is their Duty to remember that he is a Man, and to declare him to be free.—This is the Law of Nature, which is obligatory on all Men, at all Times, and in all Places.—Would not any of us, who should be snatched by Pirates from his native Land, think himself cruelly abused, and at all Times intitled to be free? Have not these unfortunate *Africans*, who meet with the same cruel Fate, the same Right? Are not they Men as well as we, and have they not the same Sensibility? Let us not, therefore, defend or support a Usage, which is contrary to all the Laws of Humanity.

Francis Hutchinson also, in his System of Moral Philpsophy, speaking on the Subject of Slavery, says,

He who detains another by Force in Slavery, is always bound to prove his Title. The Slave sold or carried away into a distant Country, must not be obliged to prove a Negative, That he never forfeited his Liberty. The violent Possessor must, in all Cases, shew his Title, especially where the old Proprietor is well known. In this Case each Man is the original Proprietor of his own Liberty: The Proof of his losing it must be incumbent on those, who deprived him of it by Force. Strange (says the same Author) that in any Nation, where a Sense of Liberty prevails, where the Christian Religion is professed, Custom, and high Prospect of Gain, can so stupify the Consciences of Men, and all Sense of natural Justice, that they can hear such Computation made about the Value of their Fellow-Men, and their Liberty, without Abhorrence and Indignation.

The noted Baron *Montesquieu* gives it, as his Opinion, in his *Spirit of Law*, Page 348,

That nothing more assimilates a Man to a Beast than living amongst Freemen, himself a Slave; such People as these are the natural Enemies of Society, and their Number must always be dangerous.

The Author of a Pamphlet, lately printed in *London*, intituled, *An Essay in Vindication of the Continental Colonies of* America, writes,

That the Bondage we have imposed on the *Africans*, is absolutely repugnant to Justice. That it is highly inconsistent with civil Policy: *First*, as it tends to suppress all Improvements in Arts and Sciences, without which it is morally impossible that any Nation should be happy or powerful. *Secondly*, as it may deprave the Minds of the Freemen; steeling their Hearts against the laudable Feelings of Virtue and Humanity. And, *lastly*, as it endangers the Community, by the destructive Effects of civil Commotions; need I add to these (says that Author) what every Heart, which is not callous to all tender Feelings, will readily suggest; that is is shocking to Humanity, violative of every generous Sentiment, abhorrent utterly from the

Christian Religion; for as *Montesquieu* very justly observes, *We must suppose them not to be Men, or a Suspicion would follow that we ourselves are not Christians.*— There cannot be a more dangerous Maxim, than that Necessity is a Plea for Injustice. For who shall fix the Degree of this Necessity? What Villain so atrocious, who may not urge this Excuse; or, as *Milton* has happily expressed it,

———And with Necessity,
The Tyrant's Plea, excuse his dev'lish Deed?

That our Colonies want People, is a very weak Argument for so inhuman a Violation of Justice.—Shall a civilized, a Christian Nation encourage Slavery, because the barbarous, savage, lawless *African*, hath done it? Monstrous Thought! To what End do we profess a Religion whose Dictates we so flagrantly violate? Wherefore have we that Pattern of Goodness and Humanity, if we refuse to follow it? How long shall we continue a Practice, which Policy rejects, Justice condemns, and Piety dissuades? Shall the *Americans* persist in a Conduct, which cannot be justified; or persevere in Oppression, from which their Hearts must recoil? If the barbarous *Africans* shall continue to enslave each other, let the Daemon Slavery remain among them, that their Crime may include its own Punishment. Let not Christians, by administring to their Wickedness, confess their Religion to be a useless Refinement, their Profession vain, and themselves as inhuman as the Savages they detest.

James Foster, in his *Discourses on Natural Religion and Social Virtue*, also shews his just Indignation at this wicked Practice, which he declares to be *a criminal and outrageous Violation of the natural Right of Mankind.* At Page 156, 2d Vol. he says,

Should we have read concerning the *Greeks* or *Romans* of old, that they traded, with View to make Slaves of their own Species, whom they certainly knew that this would involve in Schemes of Blood and Murder, of destroying or enslaving each other, that they even fomented Wars, and engaged whole Nations and Tribes in open Hostilities, for their own private Advantage; that they had no Detestation of the Violence and Cruelty; but only feared the ill Success of their inhuman Enterprizes; that they carried Men like themselves, their Brethren, and the Offspring of the same common Parent, to be sold like Beasts of Prey, or Beasts of Burden; and put them to the same reproachful Trial of their Soundness, Strength and Capacity for greater bodily Service; that quite forgetting and renouncing the original Dignity of human Nature, communicated to all, they treated them with more Severity and ruder Discipline, than even the Ox or the Ass; who are void of Understanding;—should we not, if this had been the Case, have naturally been led to despise all their *pretended Refinements of Morality*; and to have concluded, that as they were not Nations destitute of Politeness, they must have been *intire Strangers to Virtue and Benevolence.*

But, notwithstanding this, we ourselves (who profess to be Christians, and boast of the peculiar Advantage we enjoy, by means of an express Revelation of our Duty from Heaven) are, in Effect, these very untaught and rude Heathen Countries. With all our superior Light, we instil into those, whom we call savage and barbarous, the most despicable Opinion of human Nature. We, to the utmost of our Power, weaken and dissolve the universal Tie, that binds and unites Mankind. We practise what we should exclaim against, as the utmost Excess of Cruelty and Tyranny, if Nations of the World, differing in Colour, and Form of Government from ourselves, were so possessed of Empire, as to be able to reduce us to a State of unmerited and brutish Servitude. Of Consequences, we sacrifice our Reason, our Humanity, our Christianity, to an unnatural sordid Gain. We teach other Nations to despise, and trample under Foot, all the Obligations of social Virtue. We take the most effectual Method to prevent the Propagation of the Gospel, by representing it as a Scheme of Power and barbarous Oppression, and an Enemy to the natural Privileges and Rights of Men.

Perhaps, all that I have now offered, may be of very little Weight to restrain this Enormity, this aggravated Iniquity. However, I shall still have the Satisfaction, of having entered my private Protest against a Practice, which, in my Opinion, bids that God, who is the God and Father of the Gentiles, unconverted to Christianity, most daring and bold Defiance, and spurns at all the Principles, both of natural and revealed Religion.

How the *British* Nation first came to be concerned in a Practice, by which the Rights and Liberties of Mankind are so violently infringed, and which is so opposite to the Apprehensions *Englishmen* have always had of what natural Justice requires, is indeed surprising. It was about the Year 1563, in the Reign of Queen *Elizabeth*, that the *English* first engaged in the *Guiney* Trade; when it appears, from an Account in *Hill's Naval History*, Page 293, That when Captain *Hawkins* returned from his First Voyage to *Africa*, that generous spirited Princess, attentive to the Interest of her Subjects, sent for the Commander, to whom she expressed her Concern, lest any of the *African Negroes* should be carried off without their free Consent, *declaring it would be detestable, and call down the Vengeance of Heaven upon the Undertakers.* Captain *Hawkins* promised to comply with the Queen's Injunction: Nevertheless, we find in the Account, given in the same History, of *Hawkin's* Second Voyage, the Author using these remarkable Words, *Here began the horrid Practice of forcing the* Africans *into Slavery.*

Labut, a *Roman* Missionary, in his Account of the Isles of *America*, at Page 114, of the 4th Vol. mentions, that *Lewis* the 13th, Father to the present *French* King's Grandfather, was extremely uneasy at a Law, by which all the *Negroes* of his Colonies were to be made Slaves; but it being strongly urged to him, as the readiest Means for their Conversion to Christianity, he acquiesced therewith.

And although we have not many Accounts of the Impressions which this piratical Invasion of the Rights of Mankind gave to serious minded People, when first engaged in, yet it did not escape the Notice of some, who might be esteemed in a peculiar Manner as Watchmen, in their Day, to the different Societies of Christians, whereunto they belonged. *Richard Baxter*, an eminent Preacher amongst the Nonconformists, in the last Century, well known, and particularly esteemed by most of the serious Presbyterians and Independents, in his Christian Directory, mostly wrote about an Hundred Years ago, fully shews his detestation of this Practice, in the following Words,

Do you not mark how God hath followed you with Plagues, and, may not Conscience tell you, that it is for, your Inhumanity to the Souls and Bodies of Men?—To go as Pirates, and catch up poor *Negroes*, or People of another Land, that never forfeited Life or Liberty, and to make them Slaves, and sell them is one of the worst Kinds of Thievery in the World, and such Persons are to be taken for the common Enemies of Mankind; and they that buy them, and use them as Beasts, for their meer Commodity, and betray; or destroy, or neglect their Souls, are fitter to be called Devils than Christians. It is an heinous Sin to buy them, unless it be in Charity to deliver them.—Undoubtedly they are presently bound to deliver them; because, by Right, the Man is his own; therefore no Man else can have a just Title to him.

We also find *George Fox*, a Man of exemplary Piety, who was the principal Instrument in gathering the religious Society of People, called Quakers, expressing his Concern and Fellow-feeling for the Bondage of, the *Negroes*: In a Discourse taken from his Mouth, in *Barbadoes*, in the Year-1671, he says,

> Consider with yourselves, if you were in the same Condition as the Blacks are,—who came Strangers to you, and were sold to you as Slaves; I say, if this should be the Condition of you or yours, you would think it hard Measure: Yea, and very great Bondage and Cruelty. And, therefore, consider seriously of this, and do you for and to them, as you would willingly have them, or any other, to do unto you, were you in the like slavish Condition, and bring them to know the Lord Christ.

And in his Journal, Page 431, speaking of the Advice he gave his Friends at *Barbados*, he says,

> I desired also, that they would cause their Overseers to deal mildly and gently with their *Negroes*, and not to use Cruelty towards them, as the Manner of some had been, and that after certain Years of Servitude they should make them free.

In a Book printed in *Liverpool*, called *The Liverpool Memorandum Book*, which contains, among other Things, an Account of the Trade of that Port, there is an exact List of the Vessels employed in the *Guiney* Trade, and of the Number of Slaves imported in each Vessel, by which it appears, that in the Year 1753, the Number imported to *America*, by Vessels belonging to that Port, amounted to upwards of Thirty Thousand; and, from the Number of Vessels employed by the *African* Company, in *London* and *Bristol*, we may, with some Degree of Certainty, conclude there are, at least, One Hundred Thousand *Negroes* purchased and brought on board our Ships yearly from the Coast of *Africa*, on their Account. This is confirmed in *Anderson's* History of Trade and Commerce, printed the Year before last, where it is said, at Page 68 of the Appendix "*That* England *supplies her* American *Colonies with Negroe-slaves, amounting in Number to above One Hundred Thousand every Year.*" When the Vessels are full freighted with Slaves, they set out for our Plantations in *America*, and may be Two or Three Months on the Voyage, during which Time, from the Filth and Stench that is among them, Distempers frequently break out, which carry off a great many, a Fifth, a Fourth, yea sometimes a Third of them; so that taking all the Slaves together, that are brought on board our Ships yearly, one may reasonably suppose, that at least Ten Thousand of them die on the Voyage. And in a printed Account of the State of the *Negroes* in our Plantations, it is supposed that a Fourth Part, more or less, die at the different Islands, in what is called the Seasoning. Hence it may be presumed, that, at a moderate Computation of the Slaves, who are purchased by our *African* Merchants in a Year, near Thirty Thousand die upon the Voyage, and in the Seasoning. Add to this, the prodigious Number who are killed in the Incursions and intestine Wars, by which the *Negroes* procure the Number of Slaves wanted to load the Vessels: How dreadful then is the Slave-Trade, whereby so many Thousands of our Fellow-Creatures, free by Nature, endued with the same rational Faculties, and called to be Heirs of the same Salvation with us, lose their Lives, and are truly, and properly speaking, murdered every Year. For it is not necessary, in order to convict a Man of Murder, to make it appear, that he had an Intention to commit Murder. Whoever does, by unjust Force or Violence, deprive another of his Liberty, and, while he has him in his Power, reduces him, by cruel Treatment, to such a Condition as evidently endangers his Life, and the Event occasions his Death is actually guilty of Murder. It is no less shocking to read the Accounts given by Sir *Hans Sloan*, and others, of the inhuman and unmerciful Treatment those Blacks meet with who survive the Seasoning in the Islands, often for Transgressions, to which the Punishment they receive bears no Proportion.

And the horrid Executions, which are frequently made there upon Discovery of the Plots laid by the Blacks, for the Recovery of their Liberty; of some they break the Bones, whilst alive, on a Wheel; others they burn, or rather roast to Death; others they starve to Death, with a Loaf hanging before their Mouths.

Thus they are brought to expire, with frightful Agonies, in the most horrid Tortures. For Negligence only they are unmercifully whipped, till their Backs are raw, and then Pepper and Salt are scattered on the Wounds to heighten the Pain, and prevent Mortification. Is it not a Cause of much Sorrow and Lamentation, that so many poor Creatures should be thus racked with excruciating Tortures, for Crimes which often their Tormentors have occasioned. Must not even the common Feelings of human Nature have suffered some grievous Change in those Men, to be capable of such horrid Cruelty towards their Fellow-Men? If they deserve Death, ought not their Judges, in the Death decreed them, always to remember that these their hapless Fellow-Creatures are Men, and themselves professing Christians. The *Mosaic* law teaches us our Duty in these Cases, in the merciful Provision it made in the Punishment of Transgressors, *Deuter.* xxv. 2. *And it shall be, if the wicked Man be worthy to be beaten, that the Judge shall cause him to lie down, and to be beaten before his Face, according to his Fault, by a certain Number, Forty Stripes he may give him, and not exceed.* And the Reason rendered is out of Respect to human Nature, *viz. Lest if he should exceed, and beat him above these, with many Stripes, then thy Brother should seem vile unto thee. Britons* boast themselves to be a generous, humane People, who have a true Sense of the Importance of Liberty; but is this a true Character, whilst that barbarous, savage Slave-trade, with all its attendant Horrors, receives Countenance and Protection from the Legislature, whereby so many Thousand Lives are yearly sacrificed? Do we indeed believe the Truths declared in the Gospel? Are we persuaded that the Threatnings, as well as the Promises therein contained, will have their Accomplishment? If indeed we do, must we not tremble to think what a Load of Guilt lies upon our Nation generally and individually, so far as we in any Degree abet or countenance this aggravated Iniquity?

We have a memorable Instance in History, which may be fruitful of Instruction, if timely and properly applied; it is a Quotation made by Sir *John Temple*, in his History of the *Irish* Rebellion, being an Observation out of *Giraldus Cambrensis*, a noted Author, who lived about Six Hundred

Years ago, concerning the Causes of the Prosperity of the *English* Undertakings in *Ireland*, when they conquered that Island; he saith,

That a Synod, or Council of the Clergy, being then assembled at *Armagh*, and that Point fully debated, it was unanimously agreed, that the Sins of the People were the Occasion of that heavy Judgment then fallen upon their Nation; and that especially buying of *Englishmen* from Merchants and Pirates, and detaining them under a most miserable hard Bondage, had caused the Lord, by Way of just Retaliation, to leave them to be reduced, by the *English*, to the same State of Slavery. Whereupon they made a public Act in that Council, that all the *English*, held in Captivity throughout the whole Land, should be presently restored to their former Liberty.

I shall now conclude with an Extract from an Address of a late Author to the Merchants, and others who are concerned in carrying on the *Guiney* Trade: Which also, in a great Measure is applicable to others, who, for the Love of Gain, are in any Way concerned in promoting or maintaining the Captivity of the *Negroes*.

As the Business, you are publicly carrying on before the World, has a bad Aspect, and you are sensible most Men make Objections against it, you ought to justify it to the World, upon Principles of Reason, Equity and Humanity; to make it appear, that it is not unjust Invasion of the Persons, or Encroachments on the Rights of Men; or for ever to lay it aside.—But laying aside the Resentment of Men, which is but of little or no Moment, in Comparison with that of the Almighty, think of a future Reckoning; consider how you shall come off in the great and awful Day of Accompt: You now heap up Riches, and live in Pleasure; but, oh! what will you do in the End thereof? and that is not far off. What if Death should seize upon you, and hurry you out of this World, under all that Load of Blood-guiltiness, that now lies upon your Souls? The Gospel expressly declares, that Thieves and Murderers shall not inherit the Kingdom of God. Consider, that at the same time, and by the same Means, you now treasure up worldly Riches, you are treasuring up to yourselves Wrath, against the Day of Wrath, and Vengeance, that shall come upon the Workers of Iniquity, unless prevented by a timely Repentance.

And what greater Iniquity, what Crime that is more heinous, that carries in it more complicated Guilt, can you name than that, in the habitual, deliberate Practice of which you now live? How can you lift up your guilty Eyes to Heaven? How can you pray for Mercy to him that made you, or hope for any Favour from him that formed you, while you go on thus grosly and openly to dishonour him, in debasing and destroying the noblest Workmanship of his Hands in this lower World? He is the Father of Men; and do you think he will not resent such Treatment of his Offspring, whom he hath so loved, as to give his only begotten Son, that whosoever believeth in him might not perish, but have everlasting Life? This Love of God to Man, revealed in the Gospel, is a great Aggravation of your Guilt; for if God so loved us, we ought also to love one another. You remember the Fate of the Servant, who took hold of his Fellow-Servant, who was in his Debt, by the Throat, and cast him into Prison: Think then, and tremble to think, what will be your Fate, who take your Fellow Servants by the Throat, that owe you not a Penny, and make them Prisoners for Life.

Give yourselves Leave to reflect impartially upon, and consider the Nature of, this *Man-Trade*, which, if you do, your Hearts must needs relent, if you have not lost all Sense of Humanity, all Pity and Compassion towards those of your own Kind, to think what Calamities, what Havock and Destruction among them, you have been the Authors of, for filthy Lucre's Sake. God grant you may be sensible of your Guilt, and repent in Time.

Nathaniel Appleton, *Considerations on Slavery*, 1767

Nathaniel Appleton, *Considerations on Slavery in a Letter to a Friend* (Boston, 1767), pp. 3-20.

"Oh! ye sons of liberty, pause a moment, give me your ear. Is your conduct consistent? can you review our late struggles for liberty, and think of the slave-trade at the same time, and not blush?" These lines were written anonymously in 1767 by Nathaniel Appleton, a merchant, a 1749 Harvard graduate, and later a member of the Committee of Correspondence. The writer reminded his countrymen of the "late struggles for liberty"—of the Stamp Act crisis and the inflamed speeches and tracts calling for justice and liberty from British oppression and tyranny. Drawing upon the growth of the movement for American colonial autonomy with its claims of natural rights, writers such as Appleton turned arguments for American freedoms to the advantage of the slave. Throughout the period these writers emphasized the inconsistency inherent in slaveholding colonists calling for liberty. Although Appleton repeated the religious arguments against slavery, the heinous stories of the slave trade and the middle passage, and attempted to explain the roots of racial prejudice in the youth, his main object was to shame slaveholding patriots into reform.

The Publisher To The Printers

It is some years since I received the first of these letters from a friend: since which I have been frequently solliciting him to consent to their being made publick, and have very lately by his second letter prevailed with him.

The Subject is so interesting to mankind in General, that the candid reader I trust will excuse any Apology for my offering them to his impartial consideration. It is very surprizing says a late ingenious French Author,

that the Greeks and Romans, with so much knowledge and humanity had slaves like the Barbarians, instead of Domestics; it is still more surprising, perhaps, that christian nations with the Gospel before their Eyes, should condemn their brethren in the colonies to all the horrors of slavery, because they are *black*. The first man, who said to another, *you shall be my slave, for I am stronger than you*; must have had the heart of a Tyger. But the first man, who said to another, *I see you are poor, if you will receive your subsistance from me, you shall be my domestic*, made a contract useful for both.

Considerations, &c.

Sir, I understand you have thoughts of being concerned in the African slave-trade. My regard to the welfare of all mankind, and particular affection for you, leads me at this time to write you my sentiments upon Slavery, and the *slave-trade*.—And I doubt not but you will excuse my thus meddling in your business, when you consider I have no private ends to answer. If what I shall offer upon the subject, should be thought of no weight, it will only interrupt you a few minutes; but if I should be so happy as to convince you, that however profitable the trade may be to some adventurers, yet that it is contrary to humanity, christianity, the interest of the province, and of private families, I shall not only be sure of your desisting from so vile a trade, but have great hopes, that your example and influence in this place, will, in time, produce an act of government to prevent the further importation of slaves among us; and I can flatter myself, that the example of this province may influence others; but if not, we can be gloriously single.

Great-Britain, the envy of the world, does not permit a slave on her happy island; but gives to every one freedom, which stamps him image of his God.

Before I enter upon the arguments for and against the trade, permit me to contrast a Briton and a negro slave in America, neither chargeable with any crime cognizable by the public—A Briton has the free disposal of his time, to employ it in that way he likes best; all he gains by his industry, he hath sole right to; none of it can be taken from him, but by his consent; he may marry, no man can separate him from the object of his affections; his house is his castle; none (unless he has made himself obnoxious to the public) may intrude upon him. Happy Briton! The slave has neither command of his time, nor choice of his employ; must labour incessantly during his master's pleasure; can make no claim to the produce of his own industry; a bare subsistance is all he receives; and tho' he has labour'd 20 years, and earn'd his master an estate, yet even then he is liable to be sold, and often is, for want of employ, or for fear that in his old age he should be a burthen upon the wealthy heirs. He can't marry, because marriage is founded on *promise,* and slaves can promise nothing. They are indeed; sometimes, to please them, indulged a sham-marriage, which is dissolved again at the master's will, without consulting the slaves' inclination. He is sold out of the country, and so shifted from hand to hand (if he lives to be old) 'till he is a burthen, and wished out of life to save expence. Shocking contrast! Whatever ends a wise God may have in permitting such various fortunes to the children of men, yet surely no man can be justified in being instrumental of such hard fate to any of his *fellow creatures.*

Humanity makes us feel for the evils we know any of our species labour under; and unless hardened by education or custom, we naturally resent the pain or hardships of others; especially, when we see them imposed on *innocence* by the hand of oppression, which is certainly the case of all those poor children, who are dragg'd from their mother's arms, and never taste the sweets of liberty.

I should have thought none but the harden'd wretch could have entertained a thought of planning a voyage to Africa with design to bring off its inhabitants, and *curse* them with perpetual slavery; even supposing they were in some sort our enemies; but how is it aggravated when we know that the Africans are an harmless people, having never gone beyond their own bounds, to trouble mankind; and but for the interruption from white people might enjoy all the sweets of a rural life, being bless'd with a fine fruitful soil, which yields with small labour all the necessaries of life. This is the people who by some strange fatality are pitched upon by the Europeans for slaves; and how are they made such? not by giving an open challenge to fight them that the captivated on either side may expect to be enslaved; this would have the appearance of heroism. No! but the basest means are used to accomplish the basest end. It is well known we have been above a century past crouding our luxuries upon the Africans; and when the gold dust of their land could not satisfy us, they were tempted to sell their brethren, to purchase our intoxicating liquors and childish toys; thus we imposed upon their weakness, and encouraged their barbarity by appearing ready purchasers of their people for perpetual slaves: This trade for the lives of men being once established, has set all Africa by the ears; all honest industry among them is laid aside for the more profitable business of trapaning one another; all common confidence is destroyed; and indeed their natural affections are very much weaken'd by their immoderate fondess for our luxuries—Pray Sir, is not this inhumane in us?—But further, I find by the accounts of that trade, that when a powerful black Prince has collected by force or artifice a number of his colour, they are offer'd to the whites for sale; then an inspector, perhaps a physician, is employ'd by the purchasers to view the slaves, who are stripped of every rag which modesty had procured, and male and female handled in a manner not to be related, to select the sound in wind and limb: in their choice they pay no regard to former connections, husband and wife are parted, parents and children are seperated, the weakly wife will not be taken to accompany the healthy husband. Oh! methinks I hear their screeches, rending the very Heavens, when these horrid scenes take place! the *unhappy healthy* are immediately hand-tied, and then two and two are yoked by their necks like horses for shipping, and drove in herds by their masters to the sea-coast, and stow'd in the hold of a vessel: Owners are so greedy of a large freight that they croud the negroes in such numbers and under such close confinement least they should rise, as renders their passage almost intolerable. Upon a moderate computation it is reckon'd that 10, or 12,000 die yearly on their passage, and, in seasoning, either in the sickly islands or in the cold climates, those that survive are fix'd for life to their destined slavery—It is well known that the greatest number by far of these miserable creatures, are fix'd on the West India islands, where their fate in general is so extremely hard as to shock a humane tongue to relate or a humane ear to hear.—Tho' they spend 6 days in 7, in unremitted labour for their masters, constantly over-looked, by cruel drivers, yet the master does not think himself obliged to provide food for his slaves; indeed he allows them Sundays to till a small piece of land for themselves, and carry the produce to market, by which they subsist—If one day's labour in a week is sufficient to support a man and his children, how excessive hard is it to be obliged to work the other six, for those whom they must hate? I need not relate any particulars of the unbounded whippings which they are exposed to, and commonly experience upon every slight offence. The least opposition discover'd in them, or attempt to free themselves from their miserable state is sure and certain death, and that with all the aggravation that cruelty can invent, such as starving to death in the midst of plenty, in which state I have heard Gentlemen say, they live in a cage from 7 to 9 days. Oh! horrid! Pray Sir consider, is it for any moral evil that this part of our fellow men are thus extremely tormented? Can the stale and flimsy pretence that Africans used to kill their captives before we appear'd to buy 'em, justify the hellish practice of the present day? even tho' it should be granted that that was the fate of some; for without all doubt a much greater number are now yearly destroyed in the extra-wars occasioned by the demand for slaves.

The shocking noisome passages, as mentioned above, besides the self-murthers they are drove to by despair, such as starving, or strangling themselves, beating their brains against the ship, or jumping over-board; the sickly climates to which they are carry'd; the excessive labor to which the greatest part are drove, which we may well think vastly shorten their days: for a slave of 40 years is scarce worth owning When you take all these circumstances into consideration, I doubt not, Sir, but you'll be convinced that there are more lives lost now among the Africans yearly, than before the present practice of slavery commenced; and that the Balance of misery is vastly increased against them; and all this by us christians.

Nor do I think that the scandalous vindication which some have had the effrontery to offer, will satisfy a lover of truth and justice, viz. that but for the slave-trade, the West-India islands could not be cultivated to such amazing profit, *let them sink then*—Others have said, that if the slave trade was prohibited, many gentlemen of immense fortunes must be ruin'd, *let them, and beg.* 'Tis more honourable to seek a support by begging than by theft, as every man does who lives by the forced labour and privation of the liberty of any of his fellow-creatures; and tho' many a palliative have been compounded by some, even of the right reverend clergy for the consciences of those who have been troubled, in a serious hour; yet I believe they have been too modest to think them sufficient cures for such malignant wounds. This leads me Sir, to address you as a christian, for such you appear to be: and pray how can this practice be reconciled with the great law of charity, so much applauded by all, viz. *Do to others, as ye would that they should do to you.* I never found a man but was staggered at that short sentence, when apply'd to the present subject. I know indeed the great advantages 'tis pretended slaves receive, by being brought from a land of heathenish darkness and idolatry, to a land highly favoured with the light of the glorious gospel; and so bless'd with the means of salvation. But let those that appease their consciences with this specious argument, consider first, that we are not to do evil that good may come of it: and further, what a very small proportion of these poor transported slaves have the least chance of being benefited by christianity. For I take it, and doubt not you join me, that it is no breach of charity to say, that all those Africans, which are carry'd to our West-India islands, are carried from a land of ignorance and innocence to a land of glaring wickedness, where they have constant examples of every vice, and where they are likely to become seven-fold more the children of satan, than when in their native country.

And as to those few who are called happy in being brought into these Northern Colonies, very little can be said of the advantages which they receive, or the improvement they make of it, for from the best observations that I have been able to make (and I have long thought on the subject) I don't believe there is one in Ten of those that have had the best opportunity that know any more of the christian religion, except the name, than their brethren now in Guinea; and of those that do know something more than the heathen, how few have we reason to think are influenced by the motives and principles of our holy religion.

I shall next point you to a few passages of that Book, the injunctions of which we confess to be universally binding upon all that know them.

The jews were strictly forbid *man-stealing,* as in Exod. 21.16. He that stealeth a man and selleth him, or if he be found in his hands, he shall be surely be put to *death*—I know that the Jews in their traditions confined this prohibition to their nation; because in Deuteronomy 24, & 7. it is said, If any man be found stealing any of *his brethren,* &c. then that thief shall die—but even according to their explanation, they held that the thief was obliged to restore the person stolen, tho' a stranger, to his liberty again.

But whatever distinctions the Jews made between themselves and other nations, we know that the wall of partition has long since been taken down, and we are taught in the Gospel to esteem all men, our brethren especially, those who have not injured us in any respect, either as a nation or private person: of this we can not have the least doubt, when we hear our Lord saying on the Mount, "Love your enemies, bless them that curse you, do good to them that hate you, &c. that ye may be the children of your Father which is in Heaven"—If this be scripture, or the word of God to mankind, and the enslaving a poor innocent People, in the method now practiced, be consistent therewith, I acknowledge all my ideas of the words are confounded, and the scriptures are wrote in an unknown language to me.

But if there still remains any doubt in your mind whether the writers of the new testament had any respect to the practice I am now condemning, please to read St. Paul's first epistle to Timothy I Chap. 9th, and 10th Verses, in which *men stealing* is placed in the midst of a very black catalogue of vices, viz. "Profane, murtherers of parents, whoremongers, *men stealers,* lyers and perjured persons, &c. all which are contrary to found doctrine according to the glorious Gospel of the blessed God."—How trifling must be the excuse, which some, who hold slaves, have made, viz. That they are not men stealers, having bought them with their money: that they would not be concerned in the trade upon any account, but seeing they are brought here, and will be sold to somebody, they may as well buy as others, they will treat 'em as well or better. Oh! ye fools or knaves, for in one of these classes I think you must be ranked, Is reason to be blinded with such a thin veil? Is the most valuable blessing in life, *liberty,* to be thus trifled with?—It is most certain that were there no purchasers, there would be no sellers—the prospect of a market here and elsewhere, to those who employ slaves, is the sole cause and constant support, of that ungenerous and wicked trade. I don't conceive a whit odds between the man who goes personally and steals a negro lad from his parents hut, in Guinea, and brings him here, and enslaves him for life, and the man who purchases one, that others have brought here: except in the first case, some degree of courage is requisite, which is valuable in it self,—in the latter case there is baseness, infinite meanness without the shadow of a virtue—Were we exposed to the same curse, should not we think that the abettors of our misery, were the children of the devil, suffered by the wrath of God to dwell on the Earth, to encrease the heavy load of human woes? Can any who are concerned in this black hellish business, pretend to the character of christians? I can't conclude this part, without making the following application to any one that ever purchased a slave. Can you lay your hand on your breast, and declare in the presence of almighty God, that you verily think, after the most mature consideration, that in purchasing one of the human race as innocent as yourself, and making him subsurvient to your sovereign will, all his days, without a chance of freedom, that you in no respect deviate from that *rule* laid down by Christ, *whatsoever ye would that men should do to you, do ye even so to them*—if you can say thus, and think you shall be able to say so, when closing the scene of this life, and have no compunctions of conscience in your last moments, for having so far promoted and encouraged the slave trade, as to be a purchaser; if this is your sober thoughts, go on, buy more, dip largely in the trade, for it is profitable, and blacken these fair northern climates, as the West-Indies are *black*.

What I next propose, Sir, is, to show that the slave trade is inconsistent with the interest of the Province; and I doubt not but that alone would be a sufficient reason with you to desist.

By the importation of black slaves, we prevent the importation of white servants; and it is well known that there are thousands in Europe, who would gladly come among us, and might be brought here for a quarter the cost of a black man: these white people would do all the labour for us, that we have any right to receive from others; those that cannot pay a passage, must doubtless sell part of their time for it; after that is expired, they can let themselves as servants at as low a rate as a negro can be maintained, reckoning his cost, the risque of his life, &c. (perhaps I may in my next give you an account of the particulars of the annual cost of a slave) These white people when they have served some years in the lowest capacities, turn out upon our waste lands, marry and in a few years we see a Town well settled; and in less than fifty years, there will be four fold increase: by this means our country will fill up, we become respectable, and secure from an enemy, and furnished with every conveniency of life: Tho' it has been plead, that prohibiting the importation of slaves, would cut off a large branch of trade, yet it must be remembered that upon the whole, it is an unprofitable one for the community, because real riches (if rum may be called so) are sent from this place for an article which we either might have from among ourselves, or we might import with little or no exportation; and tho' individuals may make a good advance upon their stock, yet the riches are wholly got from ourselves, a trade which you well know Sir, is always esteem'd disadvantageous to a community. I take it to be the policy of a state to consult measures to have the greatest number of laborers, and those so interested in the welfare of the community, as to be always desirous and ready to support and defend it: But how contrary to all this is the policy of suffering the importation of a sett of people, which at best puts a gain into the pockets of but a few men, and indulges the vanity and haughty tempers of a few more; instead of being a defence and support of the common wealth, are often its terror, and sometimes its destruction: For it must be constantly expected that a slave will improve every opportunity to throw off his burthen, and imposition: New-York, & most of the Southern colonies, and West-Indies, have experienced something of that, which is enough to make all those that set a just value upon domestic security, to tremble: it has been objected that their numbers are at present so inconsiderable, that nothing of that can be feared. I grant it for the present, but what security have we that this will be the case long. I will remind you of another great evil to the community, consequent upon our having black slaves which doubtless you have observed, and that is, the great inconvenience our poorer sort of People are put to by this means, who would gladly serve us for a support, but then they must be upon a level with negro slaves; they being born free, can't think of such a disgrace as they esteem it, and so often spend their youth in idleness, and for want of proper employ and government then, become ever after poor vagrants; and as to the female part of our poor youth, its too well known that courses they often take, and rather than work in the low employments, chose to trust their faces for a living, This is big with evils, that I shall not pretend to enlarge upon——.

I shall now consider, as I promised in the beginning, how this trade affects private families; and evils that begin there seldom end 'till the public feel them. When a slave is introduced into a family, at once commences an amazing distinction: they are indeed among us allowed to be of the human species; yet so very inferior, as scarcely to be intitled to any of its priviledges: Nay, when I think of it, I don't know of one priviledge they have above the brutes; for as to eating, drinking and sleeping, they are allowed them for the same reason that the beasts are, to support life and vigour, to do our labour; but as to *choice* or *property,* it is certain they can have none: Notwithstanding, I say, they are allowed by us to be of our species, yet so very low, that the first idea which children have of slaves, is, that they are not intitled to the same tenderness, nor even justice, that whites are. This produces an haughty and imperious conduct toward them, and often cruelty; this spirit indulged towards the servants of the family, naturally influences their behaviour to all they esteem their inferiors in any sort, and ten to one this temper grows up with them, and they ever after be despised by the wise and humane, and hated by all.—All writers upon the education of youth, have held it a sacred point to keep the minds of children as susceptible as possible, of kindness and compassion, for their fellow creatures. I think the great Mr. Lock, would not have them familiar to hurting any of the domestic animals, least that heavenly spark, *compassion,* should be extinguished, or prevented growing into that flame, which is the light and glory of the human species.—But I fear your patience is exhausted, and so conclude,

Sir, your Friend, and humble Servant,

A.B.

P.S. I here inclose a few Lines, which I think must please you. They are taken from a Poem wrote by *James Grainger*, M.D. at *St. Christopher's*, one of the English West-India Islands.

Yet, Planter, let humanity prevail.—
Perhaps thy Negro, in his native land,
Possest large fertile plains, and slaves, and herds;
Perhaps when'er he deign'd to walk abroad,
The richest si ks, from where the Indus rolls,
His limbs invested in their gorgeous pleats:

Perhaps he wails his Wife, his children, left
To struggle with adversity: perhaps
Fortune, in battle for his country fought,
Gave him a captive to his deadliest foe:
Perhaps incautious, in his native Fields,
(On pleasurable scenes his mind intent)
All as he wandered; from the neighbouring grove
Fell ambush dragg'd him to the hated main.—

Were they even sold for crimes; ye polish'd say!
Ye, to whom learning opes her amplest page!
Ye, whom the knowledge of a living God
Should lead to virtue! Are ye free from crimes?
Ah pity, then these uninstructed swains;
And still let mercy soften the decrees
Of rigid justice, with her lenient hand.

Oh, did the tender muse possess the power
Which Monarchs have, and Monarchs oft abuse:
'Twould be the fond ambition of her soul
To quell tyrannic sway; knock off the chains
Of heart-debasing slavery; give to Man
Of every colour, and of every clime,
Freedom, which stamps him image of his God.
Then laws, Oppression's scourge, fair virtue's prop,
Offspring of wisdom! should impartial reign,
To knit the whole in well-accorded strife:
Servants, not slaves; of choice, and not compell'd;
The Blacks should cultivate the Cane-land Isles.

A Second Letter To a Friend.

Sir, This brings you my consent to publish the Letter I wrote you some years ago, upon the African slave trade: My objection arose from a hope that some abler hand would undertake a subject, in my apprehension, worthy the best head and best heart: But as yet nothing has appeared, tho' the very enlarged sentiments of Liberty which have lately prevailed among all ranks of people, one would think, naturally tended to raise up many writers against that cruel practice of enslaving the *Blacks*.

It has always appeared very strange to me, how people can be so sensibly affected with what has but a remote tendency to deprive them of their smallest right or priviledge, and yet remain so insensible of the deplorable state of so many of our species that live among us; and further, can actually plan and execute the most sordid views of gain, at the expense of the property, and every priviledge (*held dear by all mankind*) of those poor Africans, whom the white people have strangely fix'd upon as the objects of their rapine.

With what consistency can an American-Captain, trading upon the Guinea Coast for slaves, open his mouth and plead for liberty, and his natural rights? Perhaps the ignorance and poverty of some of that sett of men may be offer'd, as an extenuation of their guilt; especially as they'll immediately ask, why do the learned and rich, and even professed christians engage in the same traffic, and yet talk loudly of liberty, civil and religious, and tell us that without liberty, and the free disposal of a man's time & property, life itself is not worth having? When an Englishman would paint the greatest curse that can befall him, it is to be no better off than an African slave; and yet he will deliberately plan a scheme to increase the number of these wretches, with no greater temptation perhaps than to add a few more pounds to his crowded bags. Oh miserable slaves to wealth! did you never once consider your baseness as men, thus to plot and design the ruin of so many of your harmless fellow creatures? Can you consider yourselves, as enjoying the blessings of the British constitution, whose first principle is the security of your liberty and property; and feel no pity or compassion for those unhappy people, whose lot has fallen under the severe rod of tyranny and oppression? Can you devise to rob them of those few remains of liberty, which they enjoy, and not only break up their tenderest connections, but drag them into every part of the American world, and put them into the power of even the greatest villian, if he has money to purchase? Is this the effect of your progress in all the noble arts and sciences? is this the effect of your christian knowledge? Shameful fruit! Oh! ye sons of liberty, pause a moment, give me your ear, Is your conduct consistent? can you review our late struggles for liberty, and think of the slave-trade at the same time, and not blush? Methinks were you an African, I could see you blush. How should we have been confounded and struck dumb, had Great Britain thrown this inconsistency in our faces? how justly might they, and all mankind have laughed at our pretensions to any just sentiments of Liberty, or even humanity? We claim our descent from the ancient Britons, who have resolved from time to time, that no inhabitant of their island shall be a slave; and shall we, whose Fathers fled to America for greater Liberty than they enjoyed in Britain; shall we, I say, suffer Slavery to be so much as once named among us?—The years 1765 & 1766, will be ever memorable for the glorious stand which America has made for her Liberties; how much glory will it add to us, if at the time we are establishing Liberty for ourselves and children, we show the same regard to all mankind that come among us? that while we are preventing the chains being put upon us, we are knocking them off from those who already have them on?—This will shew all the world, that we are true sons of Liberty, and will be expressive of such noble, disinterested and generous sentiments, as will give us the highest esteem among mankind, and will for ever prevent any bad ministry harbouring a thought of making the least infringement upon our privileges; for the people that will forego so lucrative a trade, on such principles, must be a noble, must be an unconquerable people.

I can't but hope this subject will appear of importance to most people: If so, no doubt the honorable house of Representatives, and the other branches of Government, will take it into their most serious consideration, and rejoice to have the opportunity, and be the means of fixing such lasting honor upon the people they represent and govern. Oh! what heart-felt joy must possess the breast of every one, while he is tasting the sweets of Liberty, while he is setting under his own fig-tree, and under his own vine, while he is delighting himself with his sweet companion, and his smilling offspring around him, and none to make him afraid; if at the same time he is conscious that he has done his utmost that all his fellow-men might enjoy the same happiness?—It is not for me to point out to my superiours what particular laws are necessary to be made, to effect so noble and christian a design. Without all doubt, it will be thought necessary immediately to prohibit any future importation of slaves, which, as Dr. Franklin says, has already blackened half America.—As we are one of the greatest colonies, and have in more instances than one, given the lead in affairs of high importance; let us not wait for the example of any other of our sister-colonies: It is praise-worthy to follow good examples: but much more so to set them.

I am, Sir, a well-wisher to all Mankind, and especially your Friend, and humble Servant,

A.B.

Massachusetts-Bay, December 1766.

Anthony Benezet to The Society for the Propagation of the Gospel, April 26, 1767; The Society's Reply, February 3, 1768

MS Box 5/22 (1), Friends House Library, London, Eng.

When the Society for the Propagation of the Gospel in Foreign Parts began its work in North America in the early 1700s, parish priests and special catechists labored for the salvation of the heathen slaves, establishing classes to teach the catechism and to prepare blacks for baptism. Against the suspicions and often open hostility of slaveholding communities, dedicated and courageous missionaries such as Francis Le Jau taught slave children and adults to read and recite scripture. The official purpose behind such missionary endeavors, however, angered antislavery reformers. The Society, which owned large plantations in Barbados stocked with hundreds of slaves, continually assured slaveholders that it was not in the business of promoting temporal freedom for blacks. Its work was meant to produce Christian slaves who, with an understanding of the gospel and a hope of salvation, would be faithful and obedient to their masters. In 1767 Anthony Benezet caustically asked the Society whether ending the slave trade was not a worthy goal for an organization designed to propagate the gospel. The Society admonished the Quaker and suggested that he cease his meddling. (After all, the institution of slavery was Biblically sanctioned.)

To the Society for the Propagating the Gospel

Gentlemen, I make bold hereby, respectfully to salute you, and let you know that I have, with much satisfaction, observed, by the last years printed acct. of the Transactions of your Society, that the unjust Captivity, and Grievous Sufferings of the Negroes, in the British Plantations are become the objects of your Consideration. I herewith transmitt to your Society a Number of Treatise publish'd here, viz. A caution to Great Britain and her Colonies, with respect to the Negro Trade, which contains a particular acct. of the corrupt motives & wicked means by which that infamous Trafick of our fellow Creatures, (free by Nature & as well as we the Objects of redeeming Grace) are annually brought to a miserable & untimely End; if possible to raise the attention & inform the Judgment of those, whose Business & Duty it is to put a stop to a Trade, which is, by much, the greatest impediment to the promulgation of the Gospel of Jesus Christ, in every part where it prevails. I earnestly request you would please to read it, when I doubt not but you will yet farther be convinced that it is a Matter which calls for the most deep consideration of all those who are concerned for the welfare of their Country, & desirous to avert those Judgments, which evils of so deep a dye must necessarily bring upon every people who are defiled therewith; And permit me, Gentlemen, respectfully, & yet earnestly, to request that you would seriously consider whether the necessity of at least endeavouring to put a Stop to this infamous Traffick, is not an Object peculiarly worthy the attention & labour of a Society appointed for the Propagation of the Gospel—Whether by your appointment, & station, you are not more particularly those from whom it's expected an effectual alarm will be sounded on such an occasion, where-in the Cause of Christianity, & the Welfare of the Nation are so deeply concern'd.

I need not trouble you here with the particulars of this complicated iniquity, as you will find the principal of them set forth in the Pamphlets, yet I may say much might have been added with respect to the Evil whch attends this Practice where it prevails, from that opposition, which it raises both in young & old, to the very Nature of the Gospel, by the haughtiness & cruelty to which, from their Youth, they are inured, to the exclusion of that Spirit of universal Love and Charity which is the unchangeable Nature of Christianity.

The answer from the Society

Sir Your Letter to the Society for propagating the Gospel in foreign parts, of the 26th of April last, hath been considered by them with all due attention, & I am directed to assure you, that they have a great esteem for you, on account of the tenderness & humanity which you express for the Negro Slaves, & are extremely desirous that they should be treated with the utmost care & kindness, both with regard to Temporals and Spirituals; That their labour should be made easy to them in all respects; that they should be provided with proper conveniences, & accomodations to render their situations comfortable; and especially that they should be regularly instructed in the principles of the Christian Religion. The Society have, for many years past, uniformly given directions to their Agent in Barbadoes, agreeable to these sentiments, which they believe have been observed in a good degree; However they have lately sent to make more particular enquiries into this matter, with full purpose of transmitting in the strongest terms such further orders as may be found necessary, and of watching over the execution of them, with all possible attention, hoping that the good effects of their Example will have a proper, & by degrees, a general influence on other owners of Slaves in America; But they cannot condemn the practice of keeping Slaves as unlawful, finding the contrary very plainly implied in the precepts, given by the Apostles, both to Masters & Servants; which last were for the most part Slaves; And if the doctrine of the unlawfulness of Slavery should be taught in our Colonies, the Society apprehend that Masters, instead of being convinced of it, will grow more suspicious and cruel, and much more unwilling to let their Slaves learn Christianity; and that the poor Creatures themselves if they come to look on this doctrine, will be so strongly tempted by it to rebel against their Masters, that the most dreadful consequences to both will be likely to follow; And therefore, tho' the Society is fully satisfied that your intention in this matter is perfectly good, Yet they most earnestly beg you not to go further in publishing your Notions, but rather to retract them, if you shall see cause, which they hope you may, on further consideration.

I am, with great regard, & esteem Your affectionate humble servt

D Burton

Abington Street
Westminister
Febry 3' 1768

Anthony Benezet to David Barclay, April 29, 1767

Ms. in possession of R. Q. Gurney, Bawdeswell Hall, East Dereham, Norfolk, Eng.

Anthony Benezet's propaganda campaign had a special effect on members of London's Quaker leadership. Benezet deluged the London Meeting for Sufferings with a seemingly inexhaustible stream of tracts, pamphlets, and letters detailing the evils of slavery and appealing for English Friends to arouse public opinion against the institution. In 1767 Benezet solicited support from David Barclay, a member of an influential Quaker slavetrading merchant family with close ties to the Royal African Company. Benezet's charge to Barclay, as it was to numerous other prominent English Quakers, was to proselytize, to inform, to "stir up . . . attention." In 1773 the London Meeting for Sufferings, then practically devoid of slaveowners, appointed a special committee on slavery propaganda to influence "Persons in Power" in the British government. One of the leading figures on the committee was David Barclay.

Philad. ye 29th 4th Month 1767

Respected Friend Having an Oppertunity, by my old Pupil Samuel Fisher, who is now embarking for London, I make use of it respectfully & affectionately to salute thee, more especially, as I have to remember thy kindness, formerly, manifested to my dear Father; of which he always retained a grateful Sense. I herewith send thee some Treatises on the Slave-

Trade; the purchasing & bringing the poor Africans from their native Country & subjecting them to a State of perpetual Bondage, & that often the most cruel, in which we as a Nation are so deeply engaged; and which is still likely to encrease, from the new Acquisition made on the great River Senegal. I request thou wilt be pleased to read the Treatise, when I am persuaded thou wilt perceive it to be a Matter which calls for the most deep Consideration, of all who are concerned for the civil, as well as religious Welfare of their Country. The principal intent in the publishing this Piece is, that it may be put in the Hands of Persons of Interest & Power on your side of the Water, if possible, to stir up their attention, & inform their Judgment from an apprehension that many are unacquainted with the corrupt Motives, & most wicked Methods by which so many thousands, yea tens of thousands of our Fellow Creatures, as free as ourselves by nature, & equally with us the Objects of redeeming Grace, are yearly brought to a miserable & untimely end. Whether we can do any thing, effectual, in stirring up those in whose Power it is to apply a Remedy, or at least prevent the encrease of this mighty evil, is uncertain; however it is the Duty & will, I trust, become the concern of every lover of God & Man to endeavour for it. Much might have been said of the continual Danger the southern Colonies are exposed to, from the vast disproportion between the Negroes & the whites, but this was thought to be a Subject of too tender a nature to be exposed to view, in places where it might fall into the Hands of the Negroes. Nevertheless the thoughtful Inhabitants cannot but be under the most painful Apprehensions, when they reflect upon the Distress and Horror they would be reduced to, if the Almighty should suffer the Negroes to become sensible of their Strength and rise upon their Masters. And, indeed; that this has not already been the Case is an unmeritted favour of Providence.

I perceive by this Week's News Paper, that the Dutch Colony of Surinam is, thought, to be in imminent Danger, indeed its what I have long expected. From the Accts I received abt. 4 years ago of a sober Man, upon whom I could depend, who had resided some time in that country, as a Missionary amongst the Indians, there was then eighty or an Hundred Thousand Negroes, who at different times had revolted from the several Settlements who were in a Body, at about One Hundred Miles from the Capital; another less Body was at about thirty Miles back, with these last the Governmt of Surinam had come to terms, on condition that they should admitt no more Run-away Negroes amongst them: The fear of the Home-Negroes revolting & the Terror least either or both those Bodies of Run-aways should join them, filled the Person who gave me the Relation which such fears, that he was extreemly anxious to come away. Hence thou may'st judge in what Danger some of our Colonies are in, where the disproportion is said to be from 10 to 15 Blacks to a White; having in some parts a vast Country back, thinly inhabited by Indians, most of whom are but unfavourably disposed to the English. Our Friend John Hunt, who approves of my writing to thee on this Head, desires to be affectionately remembered to thee; he is in good Health & intends to morrow to set out for Virginia, if possible, to collect the Money which remains due to him there

With sincere love I remain thy respectful Friend

Anthony Benezet

Endorsed, For David Barclay in London

Thomas Nicholson, Open Letter to the Quakers, June 1, 1767

Miscellaneous Collection, Negroes, The Historical Society of Pennsylvania, Philadelphia, Pa.

Antislavery sentiment among Quakers of North Carolina can principally be traced to the indefatigable exertions of one man—Thomas Nicholson of Perquimans County. Nicholson, author of several religious tracts, maintained a close correspondence with Quakers in Pennsylvania, distributing pamphlets that rolled off northern presses and discussing strategies and tactics with others interested in reform. In the case of the North Carolina Quakers, such strategy was of vital concern. Voluntary manumission was severely restricted in North Carolina, as in other southern colonies. With colonial leaders fearing the growth of a large, uneducated, destitute, free black population, manumissions were limited to cases of special meritorious service and, in addition, required licenses from the county courts—licenses that were difficult to obtain. Even though Thomas Nicholson's reform work, such as his 1767 open letter to the Friends, inspired North Carolina Quakers to renounce slavery, the practical difficulties of freeing black property were overwhelming. If Quaker slaveowners released individual slaves without a license, these slaves could be jailed and sold at public auction. With this bewildering moral dilemma, most Quakers held onto their slaves, at least officially, and began to pay wages to them and to grant them special privileges. Nicholson and others continued to approach the North Carolina Assembly for redress, but their work to produce a relaxed manumission policy was futile. In 1780 North Carolina Quakers were still drawing up petitions to the Assembly. A group of Quakers wrote, ". . . This obstruction should not discourage them from prosecuting their clear religious duty of restoring to liberty such of these afflicted people who are still detained in bondage by any of their members, and to do every thing in their power to procure justice for them, and preserve them from the future oppression of avaricious men."

6 mo. 1st: 1767

To any judicious and enquiring Friend I have for many Years been much distressed in my mind on account of Negroes remaining Slaves in our Society for several Reasons,

First, being convinced in my Gudgment that the Slave Trade is a very wicked and abominable Practice, contrary to the natural Rights and Privileges of all mankind, . and against the Golden Rule of doing to others as we would be done unto.—

Secondly, fully believing that they prove a Snare to Friends' Children, by being made use of as Nurseries to pride, Idleness and a Lording Spirit over our Fellow Creatures, and oftentimes by their contrary Behaviour prove Provocations to Masters and Mistresses to anger Passion and unsavory Expressions to the wounding of their Spirits.—

Thirdly, it appears to me to be a Contradiction to our peaceable

Principles and Testimony against War and Fighting, under a Gospel Dispensation to keep Captives taken by the Sword against their own free will and Consent, and that if our own negroes should ever be concerned in rising to endeavour to recover their Freedom it would be ungrateful in us towards our Fellow Subjects to refuse our Assistance to subdue them.

Fourthly, where true Endeavours have been used to inculcate Principles of true Religion Piety and Virtue within for the good of their Souls, it hath appeared to me to have had but a small effect and looks to me that it will remain to be the case with all such in whom the Seeds of Discontent and uneasiness remain under a Sense of their State of Bondage and Slavery.—

Now let any thoughtful person seriously consider whether it is not reasonable to Suppose that any person convinced in their Judgment of the above Evils and Difficulties, and at the same Time in possession (mostly by inheritance and breeding in their Families) of eighteen or twenty of them aggravated by the Laws of the province to sell them at public Sale to the highest Bidder, and the Mony to be put to the use of the Parish, if freed by their Master or Mistress, excepting for meritorious Causes to be allowed of by the County Court, and I think they must Sympathize with me in my Distress of mind.

Upon the whole I think I can honestly say that on the Terms of any Expedient being fallen upon to let them have their Freedom on reasonable and lawful Terms I am willing to give up mine, and until such a Method can be fallen upon there is nothing that appears to me to be more safe and expedient in the present Distress than for those that have them (that are willing to live with them and behave themselves well) to keep them and use them well, and after a reasonable number of Years of Servitude to defray the Cost or Charges of raising them, to make them free under proper Guardians and Restrictions to keep them from becoming a public Charge or Offense to Government, and such as behave badly, and are not content to live with their present Master or Mistress to be sold to other Masters or Mistresses, in which all reasonable Regard ought to be paid to the Choice of the said Slaves with their new master or mistress.

And as it is evident that the burnt Child dreads the Fire, and none knows so well where the Shoe pinches as those that wear it, I should think it expedient for Friends to discourage the practise as much as possible, by advising those who have their Hands clear of them, to keep them so, and by no means to involve themselves in a Difficulty that they will find hard work to extricate themselves from if ever they come rightly to weigh the matter in a true Ballance.

Thomas Nicholson

John Trumbull, Satire on Slavery, July 6, 1770

The Connecticut Journal, and New-Haven Post-Boy, July 6, 1770

Although John Trumbull, at the age of seven years, successfully passed the entrance examinations for Yale College, he waited until he reached the mature age of thirteen to enter that institution. As a student, Trumbull, disillusioned with a Yale curriculum he considered deficient in English composition and literary interpretation, began to write satirical poetry. It was then that Trumbull produced his first notable work, "Epithalamium," a burlesque written in 1769. In 1770 the young poet, writing under the pen name "The Correspondent," published the first of a series of thirty-eight essays in The Connecticut Journal and New-Haven Post-Boy. *In his eighth essay, published on July 6, Trumbull launched an impassioned satirical defense of slaveholding—the right of superior beings to trample over the rights and privileges of their inferiors. Defending the slavery of the Africans as a charitable service that delivered thousands of heathens into the light of Christianity, Trumbull suggested that other peoples such as the Chinese, the Tartars, the Laplanders, even the Turks and Papists, could benefit from such missionary instruction in the Christian faith. Trumbull's essay, reminiscent of Jonathan Swift's "A Modest Proposal," was one of the most devastating pieces of antislavery satire of the Revolutionary years.*

It is strange that any persons should be so infatuated, as to deny the right of enslaving the black inhabitants of Africa. I cannot look on silently and see this inestimable privilege, which hath been handed down inviolable from our ancestors, wrenched out of our hands, by a few men of squeamish consciences, that will not allow them, or others peaceably to enjoy it. I therefore engage in the dispute and make no doubt of proving to every unprejudiced mind, that we have a natural, moral, and divine right of enslaving the Africans.

I shall pass over the arguments drawn from the gradation of things throughout the universe, and the privilege every creature naturally enjoys, of trampling upon those, who stand below him in the scale of being. For I must confess, however oddly it may sound, that after a long course of observations upon the conduct of mankind, many nice calculations upon the magnitude and density of human nature in different latitudes, I am much in doubt, whether there be any thing in our boasted original superiority.

It is positively foretold in the scriptures, that the children of Ham, should be servants of servants to their brethren. Now if our adversaries will but allow these two points, that a prophecy concerning anything that shall be done, may be construed into a permission for the doing of it, and that the Africans are the children of Ham, which is plain from their being servants of servants to their brethren; the controversy is brought to a point, and there needs nothing further to be said upon the subject.

Besides, was not the slave trade carried on exactly in the same manner, by Abraham and several other good patriarchs, whom we read of in ancient history? Those Gentlemen will doubtless be allowed to have been perfect patterns and examples. (N.B. I am not now speaking concerning the cases of divorce and polygamy.)

The whole world is the property of the righteous; consequently the Africans, being infidels and heretics, may rightly be considered as lawful plunder.

I come now to the most weighty part of the argument; and that it may be conducted with due decorum, I desire my readers to lay their hands on their hearts, and answer me to this serious question, Is not the enslaving of these people the most charitable act in the world? With no other end in view than to bring those poor creatures to Christian ground, and within hearing of the gospel, we spare no expence of time or money, we send many thousand miles across the dangerous seas, and think all our toil and pains well rewarded. We endure the greatest fatigues of body, and much unavoidable trouble of conscience, in carrying on this pious design; we deprive them of their liberty, we force them from their friends, their country and every thing dear to them in the world; despising the laws of nature, and infringing upon the rules of morality. So much are we filled with disintered benevolence! so far are we carried away with the noble ardor, the generous enthusiasm of christianizing the heathen! And are they not bound by all the ties of gratitude, to devout their whole lives to our service, as the only reward that can be adequate to our superabundant charity?

I am sensible that some persons may doubt whether so much pains be taken in teaching them the principles of Christianity; but we are able to prove it not only by our constant assertions, that this is our sole motive, but by many instances of learned pious negroes. I myself have heard of no less than three, who know half the letters of the alphabet, and have made considerable advances in the Lord's prayer and catechism. In general, I confess they are scarcely so learned; which deficiency we do not charge to the fault of any one, but have the good nature to attribute it merely to their natural stupidity; and dulness of intellect.

But with regard to morality, I believe we may defy any people in the world to come into competition with them: There is among them no such thing as luxury, idleness, gaming, prodigality, and a thousand such like vices, which are wholly monopolized by their masters. No people are more flagrant examples of patience, forbearance, justice and a forgiving temper of mind, &c. And none are so liberally endowed with that extensive charity, which the scriptures tell us, endureth all things.

I would just observe that there are many other nations in the world, whom we have equal right to enslave, and who stand in as much need of Christianity, as these poor Africans. Not to mention the Chinese, the Tartars, or the Laplanders, with many others, who would scarcely pay the trouble of christianizing, I would observe that the Turks and the Papists, are very numerous in the world, and that it would go a great way towards the millennium, if we should transform them to Christians.

I propose at first, and by way of trial, in this laudable scheme, that two vessels be sent, one to Rome, and the other to Constantinople, to fetch off the Pope and the Grand Signior; I make no doubt but the public, convinced of the legality of the thing, and filled to the brim, with the charitable design of enslaving infidels, will readily engage in such an enterprise. For my part, would my circumstances permit, I would be ready to lead in the adventure and should promise myself certain success, with the assistance of a select company, of seamen concerned in the African trade. But at present, I can only shew my zeal, by promising when the affair is concluded, and the captives brought ashore, to set apart several hours in every day, when their masters can spare them, for instructing the Pope in his creed, and teaching the Grand Signior, to say his catechism.

Anthony Benezet, An Account of Guinea, 1771

Anthony Benezet, *Some Historical Account of Guinea, its Situation, Produce, and the general Disposition of its Inhabitants, An Inquiry into The Rise and Progress of the Slave Trade, Its Nature, and lamentable Effects. . .* (Philadelphia, 1771), pp. i-iv; 1-23; 25; 29-42; 44-48; 52-76; 81-144.

In 1771 Anthony Benezet composed one of the most significant antislavery works of the eighteenth century. The British abolitionist Thomas Clarkson later wrote of Some Historical Account of Guinea, *"In this precious book I found almost all I wanted. I obtained by means of it a knowledge of, and gained access to the great authorities of Adanson, Moor, Barbot, Smith, Bosman, and others."*

Something of a scientific treatise, the pamphlet, with its long, plodding compilation of facts and quotations from merchants, travelers, factors, and other authorities on Africa, was the most exhaustive effort yet undertaken to describe the West African setting and culture which, Benezet asserted, was being raped and despoiled by the horrors of the slave trade. He drew an idyllic portrait of an African Eden of plentiful food and temperate climate, enjoyed by innocent natives. He pictured the Africans as simple, humane, industrious, and although somewhat superstitious and idolatrous, sober and intelligent. Once taken from their Eden, however, they were broken by demeaning, rigorous labor, denied education, and suffered punishment and the loss of relatives. Humiliated by a caste system that destroyed initiative, self-esteem and honor, slaves sank to a pitiful physical and emotional state characterized by fear, docility, depression, and idleness. Such traits were not innate, Benezet argued; he accused white slaveholders of forcing a heinous subjugation upon the black race and then using the fruits of their misery to prove the race inferior. "Let us diligently compare and impartially weigh the situation of those ignorant Negroes and these enlightened Christians; then lift up the scale & say which of the two are the greater savages."

Introduction

The slavery of the Negroes having, of late, drawn the attention of many serious minded people; several tracts have been published setting forth its inconsistency with every christian and moral virtue, which it is hoped will have weight with the judicious; especially at a time when the liberties of mankind are become so much the subject of general attention. For the satisfaction of the serious enquirer who may not have the opportunity of seeing those tracts, and such others who are sincerely desirous that the iniquity of this practice may become effectually apparent, to those in whose power it may be to put a stop to any farther progress therein; it is proposed, hereby, to republish the most material parts of said tracts: and in order to enable the reader to form a true judgment of this matter, which, tho' so very important, is generally disregarded, or so artfully misrepresented by those whose interest leads them to vindicate it, as to bias the opinions of people otherwise upright; some account will be here given of the different parts of Africa, from which the Negroes are brought to America; with an impartial relation from what motives the Europeans were first induced to undertake, and have since continued this iniquitous traffic. And here it will not be improper to premise, that tho' wars, arising from the common depravity of human nature, have happened, as well among the Negroes as other nations, and the weak sometimes been made captives to the strong; yet nothing appears, in the various relations of the intercourse and trade for a long time carried on by the Europeans on that coast, which would induce us to believe, that there is any real foundation for that argument, so commonly advanced in vindication of that trade, viz.

That the slavery of the Negroes took its rise from a desire, in the purchasers, to save the lives of such of them as were taken captives in war, who would otherwise have been sacrificed to the implacable revenge of their conquerors.

A plea which when compared with the history of those times, will appear to be destitute of Truth; and to have been advanced, and urged, principally by such as were concerned in reaping the gain of this infamous traffic, as a palliation of that, against which their own reason and conscience must have raised fearful objections.

Chap. I

Guinea affords an easy living to its inhabitants, with but little toil. The climate agrees well with the natives, but extremely unhealthful to the Europeans. Produces provisions in the greatest plenty. Simplicity of their housholdry. The coast of Guinea described from the river Senegal to the kingdom of Angola. The fruitfulness of that part lying on and between the two great rivers Senegal and Gambia. Account of the different nations settled there. Order of government amongst the Jalofs. Good account of some of the Fulis. The Mandingos; their management, government, &c. Their worship. M. Adanson's account of those countries. Surprizing vegetation. Pleasant appearance of the country. He found the natives very sociable and obliging.

When the Negroes are considered barely in their present abject state of slavery, broken-spirited and dejected; and too easy credit is given to the accounts we frequently hear or read of their barbarous and savage way of living in their own country; we shall be naturally induced to look upon them as incapable of improvement, destitute, miserable, and insensible of the benefits of life; and that our permitting them to live amongst us, even on the most oppressive terms, is to them a favour. But, on impartial enquiry, the case will appear to be far otherwise; we shall find that there is scarce a country in the whole world, that is better calculated for affording the necessary comforts of life to its inhabitants, with less solicitude and toil, than Guinea. And that notwithstanding the long converse of many of its inhabitants with (often) the worst of the Europeans, they still retain a great deal of innocent simplicity; and, when not stirred up to revenge from the frequent abuses they have received from the Europeans in general, manifest themselves to be a humane, sociable people, whose faculties are as capable of improvement as those of other Men; and that their oeconomy and government is, in many respects, commendable. Hence it appears they might have lived happy, if not disturbed by the Europeans, more especially, if these last had used such endeavours as their christian profession requires, to communicate to the ignorant Africans that superior knowledge which Providence had favoured them with. In order to set this matter in its true light, and for the information of those well-minded people who are desirous of being fully acquainted with the merits of a cause, which is of the utmost consequence; as therein the lives and happiness of thousands, and hundreds of thousands, of our fellow *Men* have fallen, and are daily falling, a sacrifice to selfish avarice and usurped power, I will here give some account of the several divisions of those parts of Africa from whence the Negroes are brought, with a summary of their produce; the disposition of their respective inhabitants; their improvements, &c. &c. extracted from authors of credit; mostly such as have been principal officers in the English, French and Dutch factories, and who resided many years in those countries. But first it is necessary to premise; as a remark generally applicable to the whole coast of Guinea, "*That the Almighty, who has determined and appointed the bounds of the habitation of men on the face of the earth,*" in the manner that is most conducive to the well-being of their different natures and dispositions, has so ordered it, that altho' Guinea is extremely unhealthy to the Europeans, of whom many thousands have met there with a miserable and untimely end, yet it is not so with the Negroes, who enjoy a good state of health, and are able to procure to themselves a comfortable subsistence, with much less care and toil than is necessary in our more northern climate; which last advantage arises not only from the warmth of the climate, but also from the overflowing of the rivers, whereby the land is regularly moistened and rendered extremely fertile; and being in many places improved by culture, abounds with grain and fruits, cattle, poultry, &c. The earth yields all the year a fresh supply of food: Few clothes are requisite, and little art necessary in making them, or in the construction of their houses, which are very simple, principally calculated to defend them from the tempestuous seasons and wild beasts; a few dry reeds covered with matts serve for their beds. The other furniture, except what belongs to cookery, gives the women but little trouble; the moveables of the greatest among them amounting only to a few earthen pots, some wooden utensils, and gourds or calabashes; from these last, which grow almost naturally over their huts, to which they afford an agreeable shade, they are abundantly stocked with good clean vessels for most houshold uses, being of different sizes, from half a pint to several gallons.

That part of Africa from which the Negroes are sold to be carried into slavery, commonly known by the name of Guinea, extends along the coast three or four thousand miles. Beginning at the river Senegal, situate about the 17th degree of North latitude, being the nearest part of Guinea, as well to Europe as to North America; from thence to the river Gambia, and in a southerly course to Cape Sierra Leona, comprehends a coast of about seven hundred miles; being the same tract for which Queen Elizabeth granted charters to the first traders to that coast: From Sierra Leona, the land of Guinea takes a turn to the eastward, extending that course about fifteen hundred miles, including those several divisions known by the name of *the Grain Coast, the Ivory Coast, the Gold Coast, and the Slave Coast, with the large kingdom of Benin*. From thence the land runs southward along the coast about twelve hundred miles, which contains the *kingdoms of Congo and Angola*; there the trade for slaves ends. From which to the southermost Cape of Africa, called the Cape of Good Hope, the country is settled by Caffres and Hottentots, who have never been concerned in the making or selling slaves.

Of the parts which are above described, the first which presents itself to view, is that situate on the great river Senegal, which is said to be navigable more than a thousand miles, and is by travellers described to be very agreeable and fruitful. Andrew Brue, principal factor for the French African company, who lived sixteen years in that country, after describing its fruitfulness and plenty, near the sea, adds,

> The farther you go from the sea, the country on the river seems the more fruitful and well improved; abounding with Indian corn, pulse, fruit, &c. Here are vast meadows, which feed large herds of great and small cattle, and poultry numerous: The villages that lie thick on the river, shew the country is well peopled.

The same author, in the account of a voyage he made up the river Gambia, the mouth of which lies about three hundred miles South of the Senegal, and is navigable about six hundred miles up the country, says,

> That he was surprized to see the land so well cultivated; scarce a spot lay unimproved; the low lands, divided by small canals, were all sowed with rice, &c. the higher ground planted with millet, Indian corn, and pease of different sorts; their beef excellent; poultry plenty, and very cheap, as well as all other necessaries of life.

Francis Moor, who was sent from England about the year 1735, in the service of the African company, and resided at James Fort, on the river Gambia, or in other factories on that river, about five years, confirms the above account of the fruitfulness of the country. William Smith, who was sent in the year 1726, by the African company, to survey their settlements throughout the whole coast of Guinea, says, "The country about the Gambia is pleasant and fruitful; provisions of all kinds being plenty and exceeding cheap." The country on and between the two above-mentioned rivers is large and extensive, inhabited principally by those three Negro nations known by the name of Jalofs, Fulis, and Mandingos. The Jalofs possess the middle of the country. The Fulis principal settlement is on both sides of the Senegal; great numbers of these people are also mixed with the Mandingos; which last are mostly settled on both sides the Gambia. The government of the Jalofs is represented as under a better regulation than can be expected from the common opinion we entertain of the Negroes. We are told in the Collection, That the King has under him several ministers of state, who assist him in the exercise of justice. *The grand Jerafo* is the chief justice thro' all the King's dominions, and goes in circuit from time to time to hear complaints, and determine controversies. *The King's treasurer* exercises the same employment, and has under him Alkairs, who are governors of towns or villages. That the *Kondi*, or *Viceroy*, goes the circuit with the chief justice, both to hear causes, and inspect into the behaviour of the *Alkadi*, or chief magistrate of every village in their several districts.

Vasconcelas, an author mentioned in the collection, says, The ancientest are preferred to be the *Prince's counsellors*, who keep always about his person; and the men of most judgment and experience are the judges.

The Fulis are settled on both sides of the river *Senegal*: Their country, which is very fruitful and populous, extends near four hundred miles from East to West. They are generally of a deep tawny complexion, appearing to bear some affinity with the Moors, whose country they join on the North: They are good farmers, and make great harvest of corn, cotton, tobacco, &c. and breed great numbers of cattle of all kinds. *Bartholomew Stibbs*, (mentioned by *Fr. Moor*) in his account of that country says, "*They were a cleanly, decent, industrious people, and very affable.*" But the most particular account we have of these people, is from *Francis Moor* himself, who says,

Some of these Fuli blacks who dwell on both sides the river Gambia, are in subjection to the Mandingos, amongst whom they dwell, having been probably driven out of their country by war or famine. They have chiefs of their own, who rule with much moderation. Few of them will drink brandy, or any thing stronger than water and sugar, being strict Mahometans. Their form of government goes on easy, because the people are of a good quiet disposition, and so well instructed in what is right, that a man who does ill, is the abomination of all, and none will support him against the chief. In these countries, the natives are not covetous of land, desiring no more than what they use; and as they do not plough with horses and cattle, they can use but very little, therefore the Kings are willing to give the Fulis leave to live in their country, and cultivate their lands. If any of their people are known to be made slaves, all the Fulis will join to redeem them; they also support the old, the blind, and lame, amongst themselves; and as far as their abilities go, they supply the necessities of the Mandingos, great numbers of whom they have maintained in famine.

The author, from his own observations, says, "They were rarely angry, and that he never heard them abuse one another."

The Mandingos are said by *A. Brue* before mentioned,

To be the most numerous nation on the Gambia, besides which, numbers of them are dispersed over all these countries; being the most rigid Mahometans amongst the Negroes, they drink neither wine nor brandy, and are politer than the other Negroes. The chief of the trade goes through their hands. Many are industrious and laborious, keeping their ground well cultivated, and breeding a good stock of cattle. Every town has an *Alkadi*, or *Governor*, who has great power; for most of them having two common fields of clear ground, one for corn, and the other for rice, *the Alkadi* appoints the labour of all the people. The men work the corn ground, and the women and girls the rice ground; and as they equally labour, so he equally divides the corn amongst them; and in case they are in want, the others supply them. This Alkadi decides all quarrels, and has the first voice in all conferences in town affairs.

Some of these Mandingos who are settled at Galem, far up the river

Senegal, can read and write Arabic tolerably, and are a good hospitable people, who carry on a trade with the inland nations.

They are extremely populous in those parts, their women being fruitful, and they not suffering any person amongst them, but such as are guilty of crimes, to be made slaves.

We are told from Jobson,

That the Mahometan Negroes say their prayers thrice a day. Each village has a priest who calls them to their duty. It is surprizing (says the author) as well as commendable, to see the modesty, attention, and reverence they observe during their worship. He asked some of their priests the purport of their prayers and ceremonies; their answer always was, *That they adored God by prostrating themselves before him; that by humbling themselves, they acknowledged their own insignificancy, and farther intreated him to forgive their faults, and to grant them all good and necessary things, as well as deliverance from evil.*

Jobson takes notice of several good qualities in these Negroe priests, particularly their great sobriety. They gain their livelihood by keeping school for the education of the children. The boys are taught to read and write. They not only teach school, but rove about the country, teaching and instructing, for which the whole country is open to them; and they have a free course through all places, though the Kings may be at war with one another.

The three fore-mentioned nations practise several trades, as smiths, potters, sadlers, and weavers. Their smiths particularly work neatly in gold and silver, and make knives, hatchets, reaping hooks, spades and shares to cut iron, &c, &c. Their potters make neat tobacco pipes, and pots to boil their food. Some authors say that weaving is their principal trade; this is done by the women and girls, who spin and weave very fine cotton cloth, which they dye blue or black. F. Moor says, the Jalofs particularly make great quantities of the cotton cloth; their pieces are generally twenty-seven yards long, and about nine inches broad, their looms being very narrow; these they sew neatly together, so as to supply the use of broad cloth.

It was in these parts of Guinea, that M. Adanson, correspondent of the Royal Academy of Sciences at Paris, mentioned in some former publications, was employed from the year 1749, to the year 1753, wholly in making *natural* and *philosophical* observations on the country about the rivers Senegal and Gambia. Speaking of the great heats in Senegal, he says,

It is to them that they are partly indebted for the fertility of their lands; which is so great, that, with little labour and care, there is no fruit nor grain but grow in great plenty.

Of the soil on the Gambia, he says,

It is rich and deep, and amazingly fertile; it produces spontaneously, and almost without cultivation, all the necessaries of life, grain, fruit, herbs, and roots. Every thing matures to perfection, and is excellent in its kind.

One thing which always surprized him, was the prodigious rapidity with which the sap of trees repairs any loss they may happen to sustain in that country: "And I was never," says he, "more astonished, than when landing four days after the locusts had devoured all the fruits and leaves, and even the buds of the trees, to find the trees covered with new leaves, and they did not seem to me to have suffered much." "It was then," says the same author, "the fish season; you might see them in shoals approaching towards land. Some of those shoals were fifty fathom square, and the fish crowded together in such a manner, as to roll upon one another, without being able to swim. As soon as the Negroes perceive them coming towards land, they jump into the water with a basket in one hand, and swim with the other. They need only to plunge and to lift up their basket, and they are sure to return loaded with fish."

Speaking of the appearance of the country, and of the disposition of the people, he says,

Which way soever I turned mine eyes on this pleasant spot, I beheld a perfect image of pure nature; an agreeable solitude, bounded on every side by charming landscapes; the rural situation of cottages in the midst of trees; the ease and indolence of the Negroes, reclined under the shade of their spreading foliage; the simplicity of their dress and manners; the whole revived in my mind the idea of our first parents, and I seemed to contemplate the world in its primitive state. They are, generally speaking, very good-natured, sociable, and obliging. I was not a little pleased with this my first reception; it convinced me, that there ought to be a considerable abatement made in the accounts I had read and heard every where of the savage character of the Africans. I observed both in Negroes and Moors, great humanity and sociableness, which gave me strong hopes that I should be very safe amongst them, and meet with the success I desired in my enquiries after the curiosities of the country.

He was agreeably amused with the conversation of the Negroes, their *fables, dialogues*, and *witty stories* with which they entertain each other alternately, according to their custom. Speaking of the remarks which the natives made to him, with relation to the *stars* and *planets*, he says,

It is amazing, that such a rude and illiterate people, should reason so pertinently in regard to those heavenly bodies; there is no manner of doubt, but that with proper instruments, and a good will, they would become *excellent astronomers*.

Chap. II.

The Ivory Coast; its soil and produce. The character of the *natives* misrepresented by some authors. These misrepresentations occasioned by *the Europeans* having treacherously carried off many of their people. *John Smith, surveyor to the African company*, his observations thereon. *John Snock*'s remarks. *The Gold Coast, and Slave Coast, these have the most European factories*, and furnish the greatest number of slaves to *the Europeans*. Exceeding fertile. The country of *Axim*, and of *Ante*. Good account of the *inland people*. Great fishery. Extraordinary trade for slaves. *The Slave Coast. The kingdom of Whidah*. Fruitful and pleasant. The natives kind and obliging. Very populous. Keep regular markets and fairs. Good order therein. Murder, adultery, and theft severely punished. The King's revenues. The principal people have an idea of the true God. Commendable care of the poor. Several small governments depend on *plunder* and the *slave* trade.

That part of Guinea known by the name of the *Grain*, and *Ivory Coast*, comes next in course. This coast extends about five hundred miles. The soil appears by account, to be in general fertile, producing abundance of rice and roots; indigo and cotton thrive without cultivation, and tobacco would be excellent, if carefully manufactured; they have fish in plenty; their flocks greatly increase, and their trees are loaded with fruit. They make a cotton cloth, which sells well on the Coast. In a word, the country is rich, and the commerce advantageous, and might be greatly augmented by such as would cultivate the friendship of the natives. These are represented by some writers as rude, *treacherous people,* whilst several other *authors* of credit give them a very different character, representing them as *sensible, courteous, and the fairest traders on the coast of Guinea.* In the Collection, they are said to be averse to drinking to excess, and such as do, are severely punished by the King's order: On enquiry why there is such a disagreement in the character given of these people, it appears, that though they are naturally inclined to be *kind to strangers,* with whom they are *fond of trading,* yet the *frequent injuries* done them by Europeans, have occasioned their being *suspicious and shy:* The same cause has been the occasion of the ill treatment they have sometimes given to innocent strangers, who have attempted to trade with them. As the Europeans have no settlement on this part of Guinea, the trade is carried on by signals from the ships, on the appearance of which the natives usually come on board in their canoes, bringing their gold-dust, ivory, &c. which has given opportunity to some villainous Europeans to carry them off with their effects, or retain them on board till a ransom is paid. It is noted by some, that since the European voyagers have carried away several of these people, their mistrust is so great, that it is very difficult to prevail on them to come on board. *William Smith* remarks,

> As we past along this coast, we very often lay before a town, and fired a gun for the natives to come off, but no soul came near us; at length we learnt by some ships that were trading down the coast, that the natives came seldom on board an English ship, for fear of being detained or carried off; yet at last some ventured on board; but if these chanced to spy any arms, they would all immediately take to their canoes, and make the best of their way home. They had then in their possession one *Benjamin Cross,* the mate of an English vessel, who was detained by them to make reprisals for some of their men, who had formerly been carried away by some English vessel.

In the Collection we are told, *This villainous custom is too often practised, chiefly by the Bristol and Liverpool ships, and is a great detriment to the slave trade on the windward coast. John Snock, mentioned in Bosman,* when on that coast, wrote,

> We cast anchor, but not one Negro coming on board, I went on shore, and after having staid a while on the strand, some Negroes came to me; and being desirous to be informed why they did not come on board, I was answered, that about two months before, the English had been there with two large vessels, and had ravaged the country, destroyed all their canoes, plundered their houses, and carried off some of their people, upon which the remainder fled to the inland country, where most of them were at that time; so that there being not much to be done by us, we were obliged to return on board. When I enquired after their wars with other countries, they told me they were not often troubled with them; but if any difference happened, they chose rather to end the dispute amicably, than to come to arms.

He found the inhabitants civil and good-natured. Speaking of the *King of Rio Sestro,* lower down the coast, he says,

> He was a very agreeable, obliging man, and that all his subjects are civil, as well as very laborious in agriculture, and the pursuits of trade. *Marchaise* says, That

though the country is very populous, yet none of the natives (except criminals) are sold for slaves.

Vaillant never heard of any settlement being made by the Europeans on this part of *Guinea*; and *Smith* remarks,

That these coasts, which are divided into several little kingdoms, and have seldom any wars, is the reason the slave trade is not so good here as on *the Gold and Slave Coast*, where the Europeans have several forts and factories.

A plain evidence this, that it is the intercourse with the Europeans, and their settlements on the coast, which gives life to the slave trade.

Next adjoining to the *Ivory Coast*, are those called the *Gold Coast*, and the *Slave Coast*; authors are not agreed about their bounds, but their extent together along the coast may be about five hundred miles. And as the policy, produce, and oeconomy of these two kingdoms of Guinea are much the same, I shall describe them together.

Here the Europeans have the greatest number of forts and factories, from whence, by means of the Negro factors, a trade is carried on above seven hundred miles back in the inland country; whereby great numbers of slaves are procured, as well by means of the wars which arise amongst the Negroes, or are fomented by the Europeans, as those brought from the back country. Here we find the natives *more reconciled to the European manners and trade*; but, at the same time, *much more inured to war*, and ready to assist the European traders in procuring loadings for the great number of vessels which come yearly on those coasts for slaves. This part of Guinea is agreed by historians to be, in general, *extraordinary fruitful and agreeable*; producing (according to the difference of the soil) vast quantities of rice and other grain; plenty of fruit and roots; palm wine and oil, and fish in great abundance, with much tame and wild cattle. Bosman, principal factor for the Dutch at D'Elmina, speaking of the country of Axim, which is situate towards the beginning of the Gold Coast, says,

The Negro inhabitants are generally very rich, driving a great trade with the Europeans for gold: That they are industriously employed either in trade, fishing, or agriculture; but chiefly in the culture of rice, which grows here in an incredible abundance, and is transported hence all over the Gold Coast. The inhabitants, in lieu, returning full fraught with millet, jamms, potatoes, and palm oil. . . .

J. Barbot also remarks, with respect to the countries of Ante and Adom,

That the soil is very good and fruitful in corn and other produce, which it affords in such plenty, that besides what serves for their own use, they always export great quantities for sale; they have a competent number of cattle, both tame and wild, and the rivers abundantly stored with fish, so that nothing is wanting for the support of life, and to make it easy.

In the Collection [Astley's] it is said,

That the inland people on that part of the coast, employ themselves in tillage and trade, and supply the market with corn, fruit, and palm wine; the country producing such vast plenty of Indian corn, that abundance is daily exported, as well by Europeans as Blacks resorting thither from other parts. These inland people are said to live in great union and friendship, being generally well tempered, civil, and tractable; not apt to shed human blood, except when much provoked, and ready to assist one another. . . .

Bosman speaks in commendation of the civility, kindness, and great industry of the natives of Whidah; this is confirmed by Smith who says,

The natives here seem to be the most gentleman-like Negroes in Guinea, abounding with good manners and ceremony to each other. The inferior pay the utmost deference and respect to the superior, as do wives to their husbands, and children to their parents. All here are naturally industrious, and find constant employment; the men in agriculture, and the women in spinning and weaving cotton. The men, whose chief talent lies in husbandry, are unacquainted with arms; otherwise, being a numerous people, they could have made a better defence against the King of Dahome, who subdued them without much trouble. Throughout the Gold Coast, there are regular markets in all villages, furnished with provisions and merchandize, held every day in the week, except Tuesday, whence they supply not only the inhabitants, but the European ships. The *Negro Women* are very expert in buying and selling, and extremely industrious; for they will repair daily to market from a considerable distance, loaded like packhorses, with a child, perhaps, at their back, and a heavy burden on their heads. After selling their wares, they buy fish and other necessaries, and return home loaded as they came. . . .

With respect to government, William Smith says,

That the Gold Coast and Slave Coast are divided into different districts, some of which are governed by their Chiefs, or Kings; the others, being more of the nature of a commonwealth, are governed by some of the principal men, called Caboceros, who, Bosman says, are properly denominated civil fathers, whose province is to take care of the welfare of the city or village, and to appease tumults.

But this order of government has been much broken since the coming of the Europeans. Both Bosman and Barbot mention *murder and adultery to be severely punished on the Coast, frequently by death; and robbery by a fine proportionable to the goods stolen.*

The income of some of the Kings is large. Bosman says,

That the King of Whidah's revenues and duties on things bought and sold are considerable; he having the tithe of all things sold in the market, or imported in the country.

Both the above-mentioned authors say, *The tax on slaves shipped off in this King's dominions, in some years, amounts to near twenty thousand pounds.*

Bosman tells us,

The Whidah Negroes have a faint idea of a true God, ascribing to him the attributes of almighty power and omnipresence; but God, they say, is too high to condescend to think of mankind; wherefore he commits the government of the world to those inferior deities which they worship.

Some authors say, the wisest of these Negroes are sensible of their mistake in this opinion, but dare not forsake their own religion, for fear of the populace rising and killing them. This is confirmed by William Smith, who says,

That all the natives of this coast believe there is one true God, the author of them and all things; that they have some apprehension of a future state; and that almost every village has a grove, or public place of worship, to which the principal inhabitants, on a set day, resort to make their offerings.

In the Collection it is remarked as an excellency in the Guinea government,

That however poor they may be in general, yet there are no beggars to be found amongst them; which is owing to the care of their chief men, whose province it is to take care of the welfare of the city or village; it being part of their office, to see that such people may earn their bread by their labour; some are set to blow the smith's bellows, others to press palm oil, or grind colours for their matts, and sell provision in the markets. The young men are listed to serve as soldiers, so that they suffer no common beggar.

Bosman ascribes a further reason for this good order, viz.

That when a Negroe finds he cannot subsist, he binds himself for a certain sum of money, and the master to whom he is bound is obliged to find him necessaries; that the master sets him a sort of task, which is not in the least slavish, being chiefly to defend his master on occasions; or in sowing time to work as much as he himself pleases.

Adjoining to the kingdom of Whidah, are several small governments, as Coto, great and small Popo, Ardrah, &c. all situate on the Slave Coast, where the chief trade for slaves is carried on. These are governed by their respective Kings, and follow much the same customs with those of Whidah, except that their principal living is on plunder, and the slave trade.

Chap. III

The kingdom of Benin; its extent. Esteemed the most potent in Guinea. Fruitfulness of the soil. Good disposition of the people. Order of government, Punishment of crimes. Large extent of the town of Great Benin. Order maintained. The natives honest and charitable. Their religion. The kingdoms of Kongo and Angola. Many of the natives profess christianity. The country fruitful. Disposition of the people. The administration of justice. The town of Leango. Slave trade carried on by the Portugueze. Here the slave trade ends.

Next adjoining to the Slave Coast, is the kingdom of Benin, which, though it extends but about 170 miles on the sea, yet, spreads so far inland, as to be esteemed the most potent kingdom in Guinea. By accounts, the soil and produce appear to be in a great measure like those before described, and the natives are represented as a reasonable good-natured people. Artus says, "They are a sincere, inoffensive people, and do no injustice either to one another, or to strangers." William Smith confirms this account, and says,

That the inhabitants are generally very good-natured, and exceeding courteous and civil. When the Europeans make them presents, which in their coming thither to trade they always do, they endeavour to return them doubly.

Bosman tells us, "That his countrymen the Dutch, who were often obliged to trust them till they returned the next year, were sure to be honestly paid their whole debts."

There is in Benin a considerable order in government. Theft, murther, and adultery, being severely punished. Barbot says, "If a man and a woman of any quality be surprized in adultery, they are both put to death, and their bodies are thrown on a dunghill, and left there a prey to wild beasts." He adds, "The severity of the laws in Benin against adultery, amongst all orders of people, deters them from venturing, so that it is but very seldom any persons are punished for that crime." Smith says,

Their towns are governed by officers appointed by the King, who have power to decide in civil cases, and to raise the public taxes; but in criminal cases, they must send to the King's court, which is held at the town of Oedo, or Great Benin. This town, which covers a large extent of ground, is about sixty miles from the sea."

Barbot tells us,

That it contains thirty streets, twenty fathom wide, and almost two miles long, commonly extending in a straight line from one gate to another; that the gates are guarded by soldiers; that in these streets markets are held every day, for cattle, ivory, cotton, and many sorts of European goods. This large town is divided into several wards, or districts, each governed by its respective King of a street, as they call them, to administer justice, and to keep good order. The inhabitants are very civil and good natured, condescending to what the Europeans require of them in a civil way.

The same author confirms what has been said by others of their justice in the payment of their debts; and adds, "That they, above all other Guineans, are very honest and just in their dealings; and they have such an aversion for theft, that by the law of the country it is punished with death." We are told by the same author, "That the King of Benin is able upon occasion to maintain an army of a hundred thousand men; but that, for the most part, he does not keep thirty thousand." William Smith says, "The natives are all free men; none but foreigners can be bought and sold there. They are very charitable, the King as well as his subjects." Bosman confirms this, and says, "The King and great Lords subsist several poor at their place of residence on charity, employing those who are fit for any work, and the rest they keep for God's sake; so that here are no beggars."

As to religion, these people believe there is a God, the efficient cause of all things; but, like the rest of the Guineans, they are superstitiously and idolatrously inclined.

The last division of Guinea from which slaves are imported, are the kingdoms of Kongo and Angola: these lie to the South of Benin, extending with the intermediate land about twelve hundred miles on the coast. Great numbers of the natives of both these kingdoms profess the christian religion, which was long since introduced by the Portugueze, who made early settlements in that country.

In the Collection it is said, that both in Kongo and Angola, the soil is in general fruitful, producing great plenty of grain, Indian corn, and such quantities of rice, that it hardly bears any price, with fruits, roots, and palm oil in plenty.

The natives are generally a quiet people, who discover a good understanding, and behave in a friendly manner to strangers, being of a mild conversation, affable, and easily overcome with reason.

In the government of Kongo, the King appoints a judge in every particular division, to hear and determine disputes and civil causes; the judges imprison and release, or impose fines, according to the rule of custom; but in weighty matters, every one may appeal to the King, before whom all criminal causes are brought, in which he giveth sentence; but seldom condemneth to death.

The town of Leango stands in the midst of four Lordships, which abound in corn, fruit, &c. Here they make great quantities of cloth of divers kinds, very fine and curious; the inhabitants are seldom idle; they even make needle-work caps as they walk in the streets.

The slave trade is here principally managed by the Portugueze, who carry it far up into the inland countries. They are said to send off from these parts fifteen thousand slaves each year.

At Angola, about the 10th degree of South latitude, ends the trade for slaves.

Chap. IV

The antientest accounts of the Negroes is from the Nubian Geography, and the writings of Leo the African. Some account of those authors. The Arabians pass into Guinea. The innocency and simplicity of the natives. They are subdued by the Moors. Heli Ischia shakes off the Moorish yoke. The Portuguese make the first descent in Guinea, from whence they carry off some of the natives: More incursions of the like kind. The Portugueze erect the first fort at D'Elmina: They begin the slave trade. Cada Mosto's testimony. Anderson's account to the same purport. De La Caza's concern for the relief of the oppressed Indians. Goes over into Spain to plead their cause. His speech before Charles the Fifth.

The most antient account we have of the country of the Negroes, particularly that part situate on and between the two great rivers of Senegal and Gambia, is from the writings of two antient authors, one an Arabian, and the other a Moor. The first wrote in Arabic, about the twelfth century. His works, printed in that language at Rome, were afterwards translated into Latin, and printed at Paris, under the patronage of the famous Thuanus, chancellor of France, with the title of *Geographica Nubiensis*, containing an account of all the nations lying on the Senegal and Gambia. The other wrote by John Leo, a Moor, born at Granada, in Spain, before the Moors were totally expelled from that kingdom. He resided in Africa; but being on a voyage from Tripoli to Tunis, was taken by some Italian Corsairs, who finding him possessed of several Arabian books, besides his own manuscripts, apprehended him to be a man of learning, and as such presented him to Pope Leo the Tenth. This Pope encouraging him, he embraced the Romish religion, and his description of Africa was published in Italian. From these writings we gather, that after the Mahometan religion had extended to the kingdom of Morocco, some of the promoters of it crossing the sandy desarts of Numidia, which separate that country from Guinea, found it inhabited by men, who, though under no regular government, and destitute of that knowledge the Arabians were favoured with, lived in content and peace. . . .

. . . Since Leo's time, the Europeans have had very little knowledge of those parts of Africa, nor do they know what became of his great empire. It is highly probable that it broke into pieces, and that the natives again resumed many of their antient customs; for in the account published by William Moor, in his travels on the river Gambia, we find a mixture of the Moorish and Mahometan customs, joined with the original simplicity of the

Negroes. It appears by accounts of antient voyages, collected by Hackluit, Purchas, and others, that it was about fifty years before the discovery of America, that the Portugueze attempted to sail round Cape Bojador, which lies between their country and Guinea; this, after divers repulses occasioned by the violent currents, they effected; when landing on the western coasts of Africa, they soon began to make incursions into the country, and to seize and carry off the native inhabitants. As early as the year 1434, Alonzo Gonzales, the first who is recorded to have met with the natives, being on that coast, pursued and attacked a number of them, when some were wounded, as was also one of the Portugueze; which the author records as the first blood spilt by christians in those parts. Six years after, the same Gonzales again attacked the natives, and took twelve prisoners, with whom he returned to his vessels; he afterwards put a woman on shore, in order to induce the natives to redeem the prisoners; but the next day 150 of the inhabitants appeared on horses and camels, provoking the Portugueze to land; which they not daring to venture, the natives discharged a volley of stones at them, and went off. After this, the Portugueze still continued to send vessels on the coast of Africa; particularly we read of their falling on a village, whence the inhabitants fled, and, being pursued, twenty-five were taken. . . .

. . . It is undoubted, that the practice of making slaves of the Negroes, owes its origin to the early incursions of the Portugueze on the coast of Africa, solely from an inordinate desire of gain. This is clearly evidenced from their own historians, particularly *Cada Mosto*, about the year 1455, who writes, "That before the trade was settled for purchasing slaves from the Moors at Arguin, sometimes four, and sometimes more Portugueze vessels, were used to come to that gulph, well armed; and landing by night, would surprize some fishermen's villages, that they even entered into the country, and carried off Arabs of both sexes, whom they sold in Portugal." And also, "That the Portugueze and Spaniards, settled on four of the Canary islands, would go to the other island by night, and seize some of the natives of both sexes, whom they sent to be sold in Spain."

After the settlement of America, those devastations, and the captivating the miserable Africans, greatly increased.

Anderson, in his history of trade and commerce, at page 336, speaking of what passed in the year 1508, writes,

> That the Spaniards had by this time found that the miserable Indian natives, whom they had made to work in their mines and fields, were not so robust and proper for those purposes as Negroes brought from Africa; wherefore they, about that time, began to import Negroes for that end into Hispaniola, from the Portugueze settlements on the Guinea coasts; and also afterwards for their sugar works.

This oppression of the Indians had, even before this time, rouzed the zeal, as well as it did the compassion, of some of the truly pious of that day; particularly that of Bartholomew De las Casas, bishop of Chapia; whom a desire of being instrumental towards the conversion of the Indians, had invited into America. It is generally agreed by the writers of that age, that he was a man of perfect disinterestedness, and ardent charity; being affected with this sad spectacle, he returned to the court of Spain, and there made a true report of the matter; but not without being strongly opposed by those mercenary wretches, who had enslaved the Indians; yet being strong and indefatigable, he went to and fro between Europe and America, firmly determined not to give over his pursuit but with his life. After long solicitation, and innumerable repulses, he obtained leave to lay the matter before the Emperor Charles the Fifth, then King of Spain. As the contents of the speech he made before the King in council, are very applicable to the case of the enslaved Africans, and a lively evidence that the spirit of true piety speaks the same language in the hearts of faithful men in all ages, for the relief of their fellow creatures from oppression of every kind, . . .

Chap. V

First account of the English trading to Guinea. Thomas Windham and several others go to that coast. Some of the Negroes carried off by the English. Queen Elizabeth's charge to Captain Hawkins respecting the natives: Nevertheless he goes on the coast and carries off some of the Negroes. Patents are granted. The King of France objects to the Negroes being kept in slavery: As do the college of Cardinals at Rome. The natives, an inoffensive people; corrupted by the Europeans. The sentiments of the natives concerning the slave-trade, from William Smith: Confirmed by Andrew Brue and James Barbot.

It was about the year 1551, towards the latter end of the reign of King Edward the Sixth, when some London merchants sent out the first English ship, on a trading voyage to the coast of Guinea; this was soon followed by several others to the same parts; but the English not having then any plantations in the West Indies, and consequently no occasion for Negroes, such ships traded only for gold, elephants teeth, and Guinea pepper. This trade was carried on at the hazard of losing their ships and cargoes, if they had fallen into the hands of the Portuguese, who claimed an exclusive right of trade, on account of the several settlements they had made there. In the year 1553, we find captain Thomas Windham trading along the coast with 140 men, in three ships, and sailing as far as Benin, which lies about 3000 miles down the coast, to take in a load of pepper. Next year John Lock traded along the coast of Guinea, as far as D'Elmina, when he brought away considerable quantities of gold and ivory. He speaks well of the natives, and says, "*That whoever will deal with them must behave civilly, for they will not traffic if ill used.*" In 1555, William Towerson traded in a peaceable manner with the natives, who made complaint to him of the Portuguese, who were then settled in their castle at D'Elmina, saying, "*They were bad men, who made them slaves if they could take them, putting irons on their legs.*"

This bad example of the Portuguese was soon followed by some evil disposed Englishmen; for the same captain Towerson relates, "That in the course of his voyage, he perceived the natives; near D'Elmina, unwilling to come to him, and that he was at last attacked by them; which he understood was done in revenge for the wrong done them the year before, by one captain Gainsh, who had taken away the Negro captain's son, and three others, with their gold, &c. This caused them to join the Portuguese, notwithstanding their hatred of them, against the English." The next year captain Towerson brought these men back again; whereupon the Negroes shewed him much kindness. Quickly after this, another instance of the same kind occurred, in the case of captain George Fenner, who being on the coast, with three vessels, was also attacked by the Negroes, who wounded several of his people, and violently carried three of his men to their town. The captain sent a messenger, offering any thing they desired for the ransom of his men: but they refused to deliver them, letting him know, "*That three weeks before, an English ship, which came in the road, had carried of three of their people; and that till they were brought again, they would not restore his men, even tho' they should give their three ships to release them.*" It was probably the evil conduct of these, and some other Englishmen, which was the occasion of what is mentioned in Hill's naval history, viz. "That when captain Hawkins returned from his first voyage to Africa, Queen Elizabeth sent for him, when she expressed her concern, lest any of the African Negroes should be carried off without their free consent; which she declared would be detestable, and would call down the vengeance of heaven upon the undertakers." Hawkins made great promises, which nevertheless he did not perform; for his next voyage to the coast appears to have been principally calculated to procure Negro slaves, in order to sell them to the Spaniards in the West Indies; which occasioned the same author to use these remarkable words: "*Here began the horrid practice of forcing the Africans into slavery: an injustice and barbarity, which, so sure as there is vengeance in heaven for the worst of crimes, will some time be the destruction of all who act or who encourage it.*" This captain Hawkins, afterwards sir John Hawkins, seems to have been the first Englishman who gave public countenance to this wicked traffic. . . . How Queen Elizabeth suffered so grievous an infringement of the rights of mankind to be perpetrated by her subjects, and how she was persuaded, about the 30th year of her reign, to grant patents for carrying on a trade from the North part of the river Senegal, to an hundred leagues beyond Sierra Leona, which gave rise to the present African company, is hard to account for, any otherwise than that it arose from the misrepresentation made to her of the situation of the Negroes, and of the advantages it was pretended they would reap from being made acquainted with the christian religion. This was the case of Lewis the XIIIth, King of France, who, Labat, in his account of the isles of America, tells us, "Was extremely uneasy at a law by which the Negroes of his colonies were to be made slaves; but it being strongly urged to him as the readiest means for their conversion to christianity, he acquiesced therewith." Nevertheless, some of the christian powers did not so easily give way in this matter; for we find,

That cardinal Cibo, one of the Pope's principal ministers of state, wrote a letter on behalf of the college of cardinals, or great council at Rome, to the missionaries in Congo, complaining that the pernicious and abominable abuse of selling slaves was yet continued, requiring them to remedy the same, if possible; but this the missionaries saw little hopes of accomplishing, by reason that the trade of the country lay wholly in slaves and ivory.

From the foregoing accounts, as well as other authentic publications of this kind, it appears that it was the unwarrantable lust of gain, which first stimulated the Portugueze, and afterwards other Europeans, to engage in this horrid traffic. By the most authentic relations of those early times, the natives were an inoffensive people, who, when civilly used, traded amicably with the Europeans. It is recorded of those of Benin, the largest kingdom in Guinea, *That they were a gentle, loving people*; and Reynold says, "*They found more sincere proofs of love and good will from the natives, than they could find from the Spaniards and Portugueze, even tho' they had relieved them from the greatest misery.*" And from the same relations there is no reason to think otherwise, but that they generally lived in peace amongst themselves; for I don't find, in the numerous publications, I have perused on this subject, relating to these early times, of there being wars on that coast, nor of any sale of captives taken in battle, who would have been otherwise sacrificed by the victors: Notwithstanding some modern authors, in their publications relating to the West Indies, desirous of throwing a veil over the iniquity of the slave trade, have been hardy enough, upon meer supposition or report, to assert the contrary.

It was long after the Portugueze had made a practice of violently forcing the natives of Africa into slavery, that we read of the different Negroe nations making war upon each other, and selling their captives. And probably this was not the case, till those bordering on the coast, who had been used to supply the vessels with necessaries, had become corrupted by their intercourse with the Europeans, and were excited by drunkenness and avarice to join them in carrying on those wicked schemes, by which those unnatural wars were perpetrated; the inhabitants kept in continual alarms; the country laid waste; and, as William Moor expresses it, *Infinite numbers sold into slavery*. But that the Europeans are the principal cause of these devastations, is particularly evidenced by one, whose connexion with the trade would rather induce him to represent it in the fairest colours, to wit, William Smith, the person sent in the year 1726 by the African company to survey their settlements, who, from the information he received of one of the factors, who had resided ten years in that country, says, "*That the discerning natives account it their greatest unhappiness, that they were ever visited by the Europeans.*"—"*That we christians introduced the traffick of slaves; and that before our coming they lived in peace.*"

In the accounts relating to the African trade, we find this melancholy truth farther asserted by some of the principal directors in the different factories; particularly A. Brue says, "*That the Europeans were far from desiring to act as peace-makers amongst the Negroes; which would be acting contrary to their interest, since the greater the wars, the more slaves were procured,*" And William Bosman also remarks, "That one of the former *commanders gave large sums of money to the Negroes of one nation, to induce them to attack some of the neighbouring nations, which occasioned a battle which was more bloody then the wars of the Negroes usually are.*" This is confirmed by J. Barbot, who says, "*That the country of D'Elmina, which was formerly very powerful and populous, was in his time so much drained of its inhabitants by the intestine wars fomented amongst the Negroes by the Dutch, that there did not remain inhabitants enough to till the country."*

Chap. VI

The conduct of the Europeans and Africans compared. Slavery more tolerable amongst the antients than in our colonies. As christianity prevailed amongst the barbarous nations, the inconsistency of slavery became more apparent. The charters of manumission, granted in the early times of christianity, founded on an apprehension of duty to God. The antient Britons, and other European nations, in their original state, no less barbarous than the Negroes. Slaves in Guinea used with much greater lenity than the Negroes are in the colonies.—Note. How the slaves are treated in Algiers, as also in Turkey.

Such is the woeful corruption of human nature, that every practice which flatters our pride and covetousness, will find its advocates! This is manifestly the case in the matter before us; the savageness of the Negroes in some of their customs, and particularly their deviating so far from the feelings of humanity, as to join in captivating and selling each other, gives their interested oppressors a pretence for representing them as unworthy of liberty, and the natural rights of mankind. But these sophisters turn the argument full upon themselves, when they instigate the poor creatures to such shocking impiety, by every means that fantastic subtilty can suggest; thereby shewing in their own conduct, a more glaring proof of the same depravity, and, if there was any reason in the argument, a greater unfitness for the same precious enjoyment: for though some of the ignorant Africans may be thus corrupted by their intercourse with the baser of the European natives, and the use of strong liquors, this is no excuse for high-professing christians; bred in a civilized country, with so many advantages unknown to the Africans, and pretending to a superior degree of gospel light. Nor can it justify them in raising up fortunes to themselves from the misery of others, and calmly projecting voyages for the seizure of men naturally as free as themselves; and who, they know, are no otherwise to be procured than by such barbarous means, as none but those hardened wretches, who are lost to every sense of christian compassion, can make use of. Let us diligently compare, and impartially weigh, the situation of those ignorant Negroes, and these enlightened christians; then lift up the scale and say, which of the two are the greater savages.

Slavery has been of a long time in practice in many parts of Asia; it was also in usage among the Romans when that empire flourished; but, except in some particular instances, it was rather a reasonable servitude, no ways comparable to the unreasonable and unnatural service extorted from the Negroes in our colonies. A late learned author, speaking of those times which succeeded the dissolution of that empire, acquaints us, that as christianity prevailed, it very much removed those wrong prejudices and practices, which had taken root in darker times: after the irruption of the Northern nations, and the introduction of the feudal or military government, whereby the most extensive power was lodged in a few members of society, to the depression of the rest, the common people were little better than slaves, and many were indeed such; but as christianity gained ground, the gentle spirit of that religion, together with the doctrines it teaches, concerning the original equality of mankind, as well as the impartial eye with which the Almighty regards men of every condition, and admits them to a participation of his benefits; so far manifested the inconsistency of slavery with christianity, that to set their fellow christians at liberty was deemed an act of piety, highly meritorious and acceptable to God. Accordingly a great part of the charters granted for the manumission or freedom of slaves about that time, are granted *pro amore Dei, for the love of God, pro mercede animae, to obtain mercy to the soul.* Manumission was frequently granted on death-beds, or by latter wills. As the minds of men are at that time awakened to sentiments of humanity and piety, these deeds proceeded from religious motives. The same author remarks, That there are several forms of those manumissions still extant, all of them founded *on religious considerations,* and *in order to procure the favour of God.* Since that time, the practice of keeping men in slavery gradually ceased amongst christians, till it was renewed in the case before us. And as the prevalency of the spirit of christianity caused men to emerge from the darkness they then lay under, in this respect; so it is much to be feared that so great a deviation therefrom, by the encouragement given to the slavery of the Negroes in our colonies, if continued, will, by degrees, reduce those countries which support and encourage it but more immediately those parts of America which are in the practice of it, to the ignorance and barbarity of the darkest ages.

If instead of making slaves of the Negroes, the nations who assume the name and character of christians, would use their endeavours to make the nations of Africa acquainted with the nature of the christian religion, to give them a better sense of the true use of the blessings or life, the more beneficial arts and customs would, by degrees, be introduced amongst them; this care probably would produce the same effect upon them, which it has had on the inhabitants of Europe, formerly as savage and barbarous as the natives of Africa. Those cruel wars amongst the blacks would be likely to cease, and a fair and honorable commerce, in time, take place throughout that vast country. It was by these means that the inhabitants of Europe, though formerly a barbarous people, became civilized. Indeed the account Julius Caesar gives of the ancient Britons in their state of ignorance, is not such as should make us proud of ourselves, or lead us to despise the unpolished nations of the earth; for he informs us, "That they lived in many respects like our Indians, being clad with skins, painting their bodies, &c." He also adds, "That they, brother with brother, and parents with children, had wives in common." A greater barbarity than any heard of amongst the Negroes. Nor doth Tacitus give a more honourable account of the Germans, from whom the Saxons, our immediate ancestors, sprung. The Danes, who succeeded them (who may also be numbered among our progenitors) were full as bad, if not worse.

It is usual for people to advance as a palliation in favour of keeping the Negroes in bondage, that there are slaves in Guinea, and that those amongst us might be so in their own country; but let such consider the inconsistency of our giving any countenance to slavery, because the Africans, whom we esteem a barbarous and savage people, allow of it, and perhaps the more from our example. Had the professors of christianity acted indeed as such, they might have been instrumental to convince the Negroes of their error in this respect; but even this, when inquired into, will be to us an occasion of blushing, if we are not hardened to every sense of shame, rather than a *palliation* of our iniquitous conduct; as it will appear that the slavery endured in Guinea, and other parts of Africa, and in Asia, is by no means so grievous as that in our colonies. William Moor, speaking of the natives living on the river Gambia, says, "That some of the Negroes have many house slaves, which are their greatest glory; that those slaves live so well and easy, that it is sometimes a hard matter to know the slaves from their masters or mistresses. And that though in some parts of Africa they sell their slaves born in the family, yet on the river Gambia they think it a very wicked thing." The author adds, "He never heard of but one that ever sold a family slave, except for such crimes as they would have been sold for if they had been free." And in Astley's collection, speaking of the customs of the Negroes in that large extent of country further down the coast, particularly denominated the coast of Guinea, it is said, "They have not many slaves on the coast; none but the King or nobles are permitted to buy or sell any; so that they are allowed only what are necessary for their families, or tilling the ground." The same author adds, "*That they generally use their slaves well, and seldom correct them.*"

Chap. VII

Montesquieu's sentiments on slavery. Moderation enjoined by the Mosaic law in the punishment of offenders. Morgan Godwyn's account of the contempt and grievous rigour exercised upon the Negroes in his time. Account from Jamaica, relating to the inhuman treatment of them there. Bad effects attendant on slave-keeping, as well to the masters as the slaves. Extracts from several laws relating to Negroes. Richard Baxter's sentiments on slave-keeping.

That celebrated civilian Montesquieu, in his treatise *on the spirit of laws*, on the article of slavery says, "*It is neither useful to the master nor slave; to the slave, because he can do nothing through principle (or virtue); to the master, because he contracts with his slave all sorts of bad habits, insensibly accustoms himself to want all moral virtues; becomes haughty, hasty, hardhearted, passionate, voluptuous, and cruel.*" The lamentable truth of this assertion was quickly verified in the English plantations. When the practice of slave-keeping was introduced, it soon produced its natural effects; it reconciled men, of otherwise good dispositions, to the most hard and cruel measures. It quickly proved, what, under the law of Moses, was apprehended would be the consequence of unmerciful chastisements. Deut. XXV.2. "*And it shall be if the wicked man be worthy to be beaten, that the judge shall cause him to lie down, and to be beaten before his face, according to his fault, by a certain number; forty stripes he may give him, and not exceed.*" And the reason rendered, is out of respect to human nature, viz. "*Lest if he should exceed, and beat him above these with many stripes, then thy brother should seem vile unto thee.*" As this effect soon followed the cause, the cruelest measures were adopted, in order to make the most of the poor *wretches* labour; and in the minds of the masters such an idea was excited of inferiority, in the nature of these their unhappy fellow creatures, that they soon esteemed and treated them as beasts of burden: pretending to doubt, and some of them even presuming to deny, that the efficacy of the death of Christ extended to them. Which is particularly noted in a book, intitled *The Negroes and Indians advocate,* dedicated to the then Archbishop of Canterbury, wrote so long since as in the year 1680, by Morgan Godwyn, thought to be a clergyman of the church of England. *The same* spirit of sympathy and zeal which stirred up the good Bishop of Chapia to plead with so much energy and kindred cause of the Indians of America, an hundred and fifty years before, was equally operating about a century past on the minds of some of the well disposed of that day; amongst others this worthy clergyman, having been an eye witness of the oppression and cruelty exercised upon the Negro and Indian slaves, endeavoured to raise the attention of those, in whose power it might be to procure them relief; . . .

These accounts of the deep depravity of mind attendant on the practice of slavery, verify the truth of Montesquieu's remark of its pernicious effects. And altho' the same degree of opposition to instructing the Negroes may not now appear in the islands as formerly, especially since the Society appointed for propagating the Gospel have possessed a number of Negroes in one of them; nevertheless the situation of these oppressed people is yet dreadful, as well to themselves as in its consequence to their hard task-masters, and their offspring, as must be evident to every impartial person who is acquainted with the treatment they generally receive, or with the laws which from time to time have been made in the colonies, with respect to the Negroes; some of them being absolutely inconsistent with reason, and shocking to humanity. By the 329th act of the assembly of Barbadoes, page 125, it is enacted,

> That if any Negroe or other slave under punishment by his master, or his order, for running away, or any other crime or misdemeanors towards his said master, unfortunately shall suffer in life or member, (which seldom happens) no person whatsoever shall be liable to any fine therefore. But if any man shall, *of wantonness, or only of bloody-mindedness or cruel intention, wilfully kill a Negroe, or other slave of his own, he shall pay into the public treasury, fifteen pounds sterling.*

Now that the life of a man should be so lightly valued, as that fifteen pounds should be judged a sufficient indemnification of the murder of one, even when it is avowedly done *wilfully, wantonly, cruelly, or of bloody-mindedness,* is a tyranny hardly to be paralleled: nevertheless human laws cannot make void the righteous law of God, or prevent the inquisition of that awful judgment day, when, "*at the hand of every man's brother the life of man shall be required.*" By the law of South Carolina, the person that killeth a Negroe is only subject to a fine, or twelve months imprisonment: It is the same in most, if not all the West-Indies. And by an act of the assembly of Virginia, (4 Ann. Ch. 49. sect. 27. p. 227.) after proclamation is issued against slaves, "that run away and lie out, *it is lawful for any person whatsoever to kill and destroy such slaves, by such ways and means as he, she, or they shall think fit, without accusation or impeachment of any crime for the same.*—And lest private interest should incline the planter to mercy, it is provided, "*That every slave so killed, in pursuance of this act, shall be paid for by the public.*"

It was doubtless a like sense of sympathy with that expressed by Morgan Godwyn before mentioned, for the oppressed Negroes, and like zeal for the cause of religion, so manifestly trampled upon in the case of the Negroes, which induced Richard Baxter, an eminent preacher amongst the Dissenters in the last century, in his *christian directory*, to express himself as follows, viz. "Do you mark how God hath followed you with plagues; and may not conscience tell you, that it is for your inhumanity to the souls and bodies of men?"—"To go as pirates, and catch up poor Negroes, or people of another land, that never forfeited life or liberty, and to make them slaves, and sell them, is one of the worst kinds of thievery in the world; and such persons are to be taken for the common enemies of mankind; and they that buy them and use them as beasts for their mere commodity, and betray, or destroy, or neglect their souls, are fitter to be called devils incarnate than christians: It is an heinous sin to buy them, unless it be in charity to deliver them. Undoubtedly they are presently bound to deliver them, because by right the man is his own, therefore no man else can have a just title to him."

Chap. VIII

Griffith Hughes's account of the number of Negroes in Barbadoes. Cannot keep up their usual number without a yearly recruit. Excessive hardships wear the Negroes down in a surprising manner. A servitude without a condition, inconsistent with reason and natural justice. The general usage the Negroes meet with in the West Indies. Inhuman calculations of the strength and lives of the Negroes. Dreadful consequences which may be expected from the cruelty exercised upon this oppressed part of mankind.

We are told by Griffith Hughes, rector of St. Lucy in Barbadoes, in his natural history of that island, printed in the year 1750, "That there were between sixty-five and seventy thousand Negroes, at that time, in the island, tho' formerly they had a greater number: That in order to keep up a necessary number, they were obliged to have a yearly supply from Africa: That the hard labour, and often want of necessaries, which these unhappy creatures are obliged to undergo, destroy a greater number than are bred there." He adds, "That the capacities of their minds in common affairs of life are but little inferior, if at all, to those of the Europeans. If they fail in some arts, he says, it may be owing more to their want of education, and the depression of their spirits by slavery, than to any want of natural abilities." This destruction of the human species, thro' unnatural hardships, and want of necessary supplies, in the case of the Negroes, is farther confirmed in *an account of the European settlements in America*, printed London, 1757, where it is said, par. 6. chap. 11th,

The Negroes in our colonies endure a slavery more compleat, and attended with far worse circumstances, than what any people in their condition suffer in any other part of the world, or have suffered in any other period of time: Proofs of this are not wanting. The prodigious waste which we experience in this unhappy part of our species, is a full and melancholy evidence of this truth. The island of Barbadoes, (the Negroes upon which do not amount to eighty thousand) notwithstanding all the means which they use to increase them by propagation, and that the climate is in every respect (except that of being more wholesome) exactly resembling the climate from whence they come; notwithstanding all this, Barbadoes lies under a necessity of an annual recruit of five thousand slaves, to keep up the stock at the number I have mentioned. This prodigious failure, which is at least in the same proportion in all our islands, shews demonstratively that some uncommon and unsupportable hardship lies upon the Negroes, which wears them down in such a surprising manner.

In an account of part of North America, published by Thomas Jeffery, 1761, the author, speaking of the usage the Negroes receive in the West India islands, says,

It is impossible for a human heart to reflect upon the servitude of these dregs of mankind, without in some measure feeling for their misery, which ends but with their lives.—Nothing can be more wretched than the condition of this people. One would imagine, they were framed to be the disgrace of the human species; banished from their country, and deprived of that blessing, liberty, on which all other nations set the greatest value, they are in a measure reduced to the condition of beasts of burden. In general, a few roots, potatoes especially, are their food, and two rags, which neither screen them from the heat of the day, nor the extraordinary coolness of the night, all their covering; their sleep very short; their labour almost continual: they receive no wages, but have twenty lashes for the smallest fault.

A thoughtful person, who had an opportunity of observing the miserable condition of the Negroes in one of our West India islands, writes thus,

I met with daily exercise to see the treatment which those miserable wretches met with from their masters; but with few exceptions. They whip them most unmercifully on small occasions: you will see their bodies all whealed and scarred; in short, they seem to set no other value on their lives, than as they cost them so much money; and are restrained from killing them, when angry, by no worthier consideration, than that they lose so much. They act as though they did not look upon them as a race of human creatures, who have reason, and remembrance of misfortunes, but as beasts; like oxen, who are stubborn, hardy, and senseless, fit for burdens, and designed to bear them: they won't allow them to have any claim to human privileges, or scarce indeed to be regarded as the work of God. Though it was consistent with the justice of our Maker to pronounce the sentence on our common parent, and through him on all succeeding generations, *That he and they should eat their bread by the sweat of their brows:* yet does it not stand recorded by the same eternal truth, *That the labourer is worthy of his hire?* It cannot be allowed, in natural justice, that there should be a servitude without condition; a cruel, endless servitude. It cannot be reconcileable to natural justice, that whole nations, nay, whole continents of men, should be devoted to do the drudgery of life for others, be dragged away from their attachments of relations and societies, and be made to serve the appetite and pleasure of a race of men, whose superiority has been obtained by illegal force.

Sir Hans Sloane, in the introduction to his natural history of Jamaica, in the account he gives of the treatment the Negroes met with there, speaking of the punishments inflicted on them, says, page 56.

> For rebellion, the punishment is burning them, by nailing them down to the ground with crooked sticks on every limb, and then applying the fire, by degrees, from the feet and hands, burning them gradually up to the head, whereby *their pains are extravagant.* For crimes of a less nature, gelding or chopping off half the foot with an axe.—For negligence, they are usually whipped by the overseers with lance-wood switches.—After they are whipped till they are raw, some put on their skins pepper and salt, to make them smart; at other times, their masters will drop melted wax on their skins, and use several *very exquisite torments.*

In that island, the owners of the Negroe slaves set aside to each a parcel of ground, and allow them half a day at the latter end of the week, which, with the day appointed by the divine injunction to be a day of rest and service to God, and which ought to be kept as such, is the only time allowed them to manure their ground. This, with a few herrings, or other salt fish, is what is given for their support. Their allowance for cloathing in the island, is seldom more than six yards of oznabrigs each year. And in the more northern colonies, where the piercing westerly winds are long and sensibly felt, these poor Africans suffer much for want of sufficient cloathing; indeed some have none till they are able to pay for it by their labour. The time that the Negroes work in the West Indies, is from day-break till noon; then again from two o'clock till dark (during which time, they are attended by overseers, who severely scourge those who appear to them dilatory); and before they are suffered to go to their quarters, they have still something to do, as collecting herbage for the horses, gathering fuel for the boilers, *&c.* so that it is often past twelve before they can get home, when they have scarce time to grind and boil their Indian corn; whereby, if their food was not prepared the evening before, it sometimes happens that they are called again to labour before they can satisfy their hunger. And here no delay or excuse will avail; for if they are not in the field immediately upon the usual notice, they must expect to feel the overseer's lash. In crop time (which lasts many months) they are obliged, by turns, to work most of the night in the boiling house. Thus their owners, from a desire of making the greatest gain by the labour of their slaves, lay heavy burdens on them, and yet feed and cloath them very sparingly, and some scarce feed or cloath them at all; so that the poor creatures are obliged to shift for their living in the best manner they can, which occasions their being often killed in the neighbouring lands, stealing potatoes, or other food, to satisfy their hunger. And if they take any thing from the plantation they belong to, though under such pressing want, their owners will correct them severely for taking a little of what they have so hardly laboured for; whilst many of themselves riot in the greatest luxury and excess. It is a matter of astonishment how a people, who, as a nation, are looked upon as generous and humane, and so much value themselves for their uncommon sense of the benefit of liberty, can live in the practice of such extreme oppression and inhumanity, without seeing the inconsistency of such conduct, and feeling great remorse. Nor is it less amazing to hear these men calmly making calculations about the strength and lives of their fellow men. In Jamaica, if six in ten of the new imported Negroes survive the seasoning, it is looked upon as a gaining purchase. And in most of the other plantations, if the Negroes live eight or nine years, their labour is reckoned a sufficient compensation for their cost. If calculations of this sort were made upon the strength and labour of beasts of burden, it would not appear so strange; but even then, a merciful man would certainly use his beast with more mercy than is usually shewn to the poor Negroes. Will not the groans, the dying groans, of this deeply afflicted and oppressed people reach heaven? and when the cup of iniquity is full, must not the inevitable consequence be, the pouring forth of the judgments of God upon their oppressors? But alas! is it not too manifest that this oppression has already long been the object of the divine displeasure? For what heavier judgment, what greater calamity, can befal any people, than to become subject to that hardness of heart, that forgetfulness of God, and insensibility to every religious impression, as well as that general depravation of manners, which so much prevails in these colonies, in proportion as they have more or less enriched themselves at the expence of the blood and bondage of the Negroes.

It is a dreadful consideration, as a late author remarks, that out of the stock of eighty thousand Negroes in Barbadoes, there die every year five thousand more than are born in that island; which failure is probably in the same proportion in the other islands. *In effect, this people is under a necessity of being entirely renewed every sixteen years.* And what must we think of the management of a people, who, far from increasing greatly, as those who have no loss by war ought to do, must, in so short a time as sixteen years, without foreign recruits, be entirely consumed to a man! Is it not a christian doctrine, *that the labourer is worthy of his hire?* And hath not the Lord, by the mouth of his prophet, pronounced, "*Wo unto that man who buildeth his house by unrighteousness, and his chambers by wrong; who uses his neighbour's service without wages, and giveth him nought for his work?*" And yet the poor Negro slaves are constrained, like the beasts, by beating, to work hard without hire or recompence, and receive nothing from the hand of their unmerciful masters, but such a wretched provision as will scarce support them under their fatigues. The intolerable hardships many of the slaves undergo, are sufficiently proved by the shortness of their lives.—And who are these miserable creatures, that receive such barbarous treatment from the planter? Can we restrain our just indignation, when we consider that they are undoubtedly *his brethren! his neighbours! the children of the same Father, and some of those for whom Christ died, as truly as for the planter himself.* Let the opulent planter, or merchant, prove that his Negro slave is not his brother, or that he is not his neighbour, in the scripture sense of these appellations; and if he is not able so to do, how will he justify the buying and selling of his brethren, as if they were of no more consideration than his cattle? The wearing them out with continual labour, before they have lived out half their days? The severe whipping and torturing them, even to death, if they resist his insupportable tyranny? Let the hardiest slave-holder look forward to that tremendous day, when he must give an account to God of his stewardship; and let him seriously consider, whether, at such a time, he thinks he shall be able to satisfy himself, that any act of buying and selling, or the fate of war, or the birth of children in his house, plantation, or territories, or any other circumstance whatever, can give him such an absolute property in the persons of men, as will justify his retaining them as slaves, and treating them as beasts? Let him diligently consider whether there will not always remain to the slave a *superior* property or right to the fruit of his own labour; and more especially to his own person; that being which was given him by God, and which none but the Giver can justly claim?

Chap. IX

The advantage which would have accrued to the natives of Guinea, if the Europeans had acted towards them agreeable to the dictates of humanity and christianity. *An inordinate* desire of gain in the Europeans, the true occasion of the slave trade. Notice of the misrepresentations of the Negroes by most authors, in order to palliate the iniquity of the slave trade. Those misrepresentations refuted, particularly with respect *to the Hottentot Negroes.*

From the foregoing accounts of the natural disposition of the Negroes, and the fruitfulness of most parts of Guinea, which are confirmed by authors of candour, who have wrote from their own knowledge, it may well be concluded, that the Negroes acquaintance with the Europeans might have been a happiness to them, if these last had not only bore the name, but had also acted the part, of Christians, and used their endeavours by example, as well as precept, to make them acquainted with the glad tidings of the gospel, which breathes peace and good will to man, and with that change of heart, that redemption from sin, which christianity proposeth; innocence and love might then have prevailed, nothing would have been wanting to complete the happiness of the simple Africans: but the reverse has happened; the Europeans, forgetful of their duty as men and christians, have conducted themselves in so iniquitous a manner, as must necessarily raise in the minds of the thoughtful and well-disposed Negroes, the utmost scorn and detestation of the very name of christians. All other considerations have given way to an insatiable desire of gain, which has been the principal and moving cause of the most *iniquitous and dreadful scene* that was, perhaps, ever acted upon the face of the earth; instead of making use of that superior knowledge with which the Almighty, the common Parent of mankind, had favoured them, to strengthen the principle of peace and good will in the breasts of the incautious Negroes, the Europeans have, by their bad example, led them into excess of drunkenness, debauchery, and avarice; whereby every passion of corrupt nature being inflamed, they have been easily prevailed upon to make war, and captivate one another; as well to furnish means for the excesses they had been habituated to, as to satisfy the greedy desire of gain in their profligate employers, who to this intent have furnished them with prodigious quantities of arms and ammunition. Thus they have been hurried into confusion, distress, and all the extremities of temporal misery;

every thing, even the power of their Kings, has been made subservient to this wicked purpose; for instead of being protectors of their subjects, some of those rulers, corrupted by the excessive love of spirituous liquors, and the tempting baits laid before them by the factors, have invaded the liberties of their unhappy subjects, and are become their oppressors.

Here it may be necessary to observe, that the accounts we have of the inhabitants of Guinea, are chiefly given by persons engaged in the trade, who, from self-interested views, have described them in such colours as were least likely to excite compassion and respect, and endeavoured to reconcile so manifest a violation of the rights of mankind to the minds of the purchasers; yet they cannot but allow the Negroes to be possessed of some good qualities, though they contrive as much as possible to cast a shade over them. A particular instance of this appears in Astley's collection, vol. 2. p. 73, where the author, speaking of the Mandingos settled at Galem, which is situated 900 miles up the Senegal, after saying that they carry on a commerce to all the neighbouring kingdoms, and amass riches, adds, "That excepting *the vices peculiar to the Blacks*, they are a good sort of people, honest, hospitable, just to their word, laborious, industrious, and very ready to learn arts and sciences." Here it is difficult to imagine what vices can be peculiarly attendant on a people so well disposed as the author describes these to be. With respect to the charge some authors have brought against them, as being void of all natural affection, it is frequently contradicted by others. In vol. 2. of the Collection, p. 275, and 629, the Negroes of North Guinea, and the Gold Coast, are said *to be fond of their children, whom they love with tenderness*. And Bosman says, p. 340, "Not a few in his country (viz. Holland) fondly imagine, that parents here sell their children, men their wives, and one brother the other: but those who think so deceive themselves; for this never happens on any other account but that of necessity, or some great crime." The same is repeated by J. Barbot, page 326, and also confirmed by Sir Hans Sloane, in the introduction to his natural history of Jamaica; where speaking of the Negroes, he says,

> They are usually thought to be haters of their own children, and therefore it is believed that they sell and dispose of them to strangers for money: but this is not true; for the Negroes of Guinea being divided into several captainships, as well as the Indians of America, have wars; and besides those slain in battle, many prisoners are taken, who are sold as slaves, and brought thither: but the parents here, although their children are slaves for ever, yet have so great love for them, that no master dares sell, or give away, one of their little ones, unless they care not whether their parents hang themselves or no.

J. Barbot, speaking of the occasion of the natives of Guinea being represented as a treacherous people, ascribes it to the Hollanders (and doubtless other Europeans) usurping authority, and fomenting divisions between the Negroes. At page 110, he says,

> It is well known that many of the European nations trading amongst these people, have very unjustly and inhumanly, without any provocation, stolen away, from time to time, abundance of the people, not only on this coast, but almost every where in Guinea, who have come on board their ships in the harmless and confiding manner: these they have in great numbers carried away, and sold in the plantations, with other slaves which they had purchased.

And although some of the Negroes may be justly charged with indolence and supineness, yet many others are frequently mentioned by authors *as a careful, industrious, and even laborious* people. But nothing shews more clearly how unsafe it is to form a judgment of distant people from the accounts given of them by travellers, who have taken but a transient view of things, than the case of the Hottentots, viz. those several nations of Negroes who inhabit the most southern part of Africa: *these people* are represented by several authors, who appear to have very much copied their relations one from the other, as so savage and barbarous as to have little of human, but the shape: but these accounts are strongly contradicted by others, particularly Peter Kolben, who has given a circumstantial relation of the disposition and manners of those people. He was a man of learning, sent from the court of Prussia solely to make astronomical and natural observations there; and having no interest in the slavery of the Negroes, had not the same inducement as most other relators had, to misrepresent the natives of Africa. He resided eight years at and about the Cape of Good Hope, during which time he examined with great care into the customs, manners, and opinions of the Hottentots; whence he sets these people in a quite different light from what they appeared in former authors, whom he corrects, and blames for the falsehoods they have wantonly told of them. At p. 61, he says, "The details we have in several authors, are for the most part made up of inventions and hearsays, which generally prove false." Nevertheless, he allows they are justly to be blamed for their sloth.—*The love of liberty and indolence is their all: compulsion is death to them. While necessity obliges them to work, they are very tractable, obedient, and faithful; but when they have got enough to satisfy the present want, they are deaf to all further intreaty.* He also faults them for their nastiness, the effect of sloth; and for their love of drink, and the practice of some unnatural customs, which long use has established amongst them; which, nevertheless, from the general good disposition of these people, there is great reason to believe they might be persuaded to refrain from, if a truly christian care had been extended towards them. He says, "They are eminently distinguished by many virtues, as their mutual benevolence, friendship, and hospitality; they breathe kindness and good will to one another, and seek all opportunities of obliging. Is a Hottentot's assistance required by one of his countrymen? he runs to give it. Is his advice asked? he gives it with sincerity. Is his countryman in want? he relieves him to the utmost of his power." Their hospitality extends even to European strangers: in travelling thro' the Cape countries, you meet with a chearful and open reception, in whatsoever village you come to. In short, he says, page 339, "The integrity of the Hottentots, their strictness and celerity in the execution of justice, and their charity, are equalled by few nations. *In alliances, their word is sacred; there being hardly any thing they look upon as a fouler crime than breach of engagements. Theft and adultery they punish with death.*" They firmly believe there is a God, the author of all things, whom they call the God of gods; but it does not appear that they have an institution of worship directly regarding this supreme Deity. When pressed on this article, they excuse themselves by a tradition, "*That their first parents so grievously offended this great God, that he cursed them and their posterity with hardness of heart; so that they know little about him, and have less inclination to serve him.*" As has been already remarked, these Hottentots are the only Negroe nations bordering on the sea, we read of, who are not concerned in making or keeping slaves. Those slaves made use of by the Hollanders at the Cape, are brought from other parts of Guinea. Numbers of these people told the author, "That the vices they saw prevail amongst christians; their avarice, their envy and hatred of one another; their restless discontented tempers; their lasciviousness and injustice, were the things that principally kept the Hottentots from hearkening to christianity."

Father Tachard, a French Jesuit, famous for his travels in the East Indies, in his account of these people, says, "The Hottentots have more honesty, love, and liberality for one another, than are almost any where seen amongst christians."

Chap. X

Man-stealing esteemed highly criminal, and punishable by the laws of Guinea: No Negroes allowed to be sold for slaves there, but those deemed prisoners of war, or in punishment for crimes. Some of the Negroe rulers, corrupted by the Europeans, violently infringe the laws of Guinea. The King of Barsailay noted in that respect.

By an inquiry into the laws and customs formerly in use, and still in force amongst the Negroes, particularly on the Gold Coast, it will be found, that provision was made for the general peace, and for the safety of individuals; even in W. Bosman's time, long after the Europeans had established the slave-trade, the natives were not publicly enslaved, any otherwise than in punishment for crimes, when prisoners of war, or by a violent exertion of the power of their corrupted Kings. Where any of the natives were stolen, in order to be sold to the Europeans, it was done secretly, or at least, only connived at by those in power: this appears from Barbot and Bosman's account of the matter, both agreeing that man-stealing was not allowed on the Gold Coast. The first says, "*kidnapping or stealing of human creatures is punished there, and even sometimes with death.*" And W. Bosman, whose long residence on the coast, enabled him to speak with certainty, says, "*That the laws were severe against murder, thievery, and adultery.*" And adds, "*That man-stealing was punished on the Gold Coast with rigid severity and sometimes with death itself.*" Hence it may be concluded, that the sale of the greatest part of the Negroes to the Europeans is supported by violence, in defiance of the laws, through the knavery of their principal men, who, (as is too often the case with those in European countries) under pretence of encouraging trade, and increasing the public revenue, disregard the dictates of justice, and trample upon those liberties which they are appointed to preserve.

Fr. Moor also mentions man-stealing as being discountenanced by the Negroe Governments on the river Gambia, and speaks of the inslaving the peaceable inhabitants, as a violence which only happens under a corrupt administration of justice; he says,

The Kings of that country generally advise with their head men, scarcely doing any thing of consequence, without consulting them first, except the King of Barsailay, who being subject to hard drinking, is very absolute. It is to this King's insatiable thirst for brandy, that his subjects freedoms and families are in so precarious a situation.

Whenever this King wants goods or brandy, he sends a messenger to the English Governor at James Fort, to desire he would send a sloop there with a cargo: *this news, being not at all unwelcome,* the Governor sends accordingly; against the arrival of the sloop, the King goes and ransacks some of his enemies towns, seizing the people, and selling them for such commodities as he is in want of, which commonly are brandy, guns, powder, balls, pistols, and cutlasses, for his attendants and soldiers; and coral and silver for his wives and concubines. In case he is not at war with any neighbouring King, he then falls upon one of his own towns, which are numerous, and uses them in the same manner: He often goes with some of his troops by a town in the day time, and returning in the night, sets fire to three parts of it, and putting guards at the fourth, there seizes the people as they run out from the fire; he ties their arms behind them, and marches them either to Joar or Cohone, where he sells them to the Europeans.

A. Brue, the French director, gives much the same account, and says,

That having received goods, he wrote to the King, that if he had a sufficient number of slaves, he was ready to trade with him. This Prince, as well as the other Negroe monarchs, has always a sure way of supplying his deficiencies, by selling his own subjects, for which they seldom want a pretence. The King had recourse to this method, by seizing three hundred of his own people, and sent word to the director, that he had the slaves ready to deliver for the goods.

It seems, the King wanted double the quantity of goods which the factor would give him for these three hundred slaves; but the factor refusing to trust him, as he was already in the company's debt, and perceiving that this refusal had put the King much out of temper, he proposed that he should give him a licence for taking so many more of his people, as the goods he still wanted were worth; but this the King refused, saying "*It* might occasion a disturbance amongst his subjects." Except in the above instance, and some others, where the power of the Negroe Kings is unlawfully exerted over their subjects, the slave trade is carried on in Guinea with some regard to the laws of the country, which allow of none to be sold, but prisoners taken in their national wars, or people adjudged to slavery in punishment for crimes; but the largeness of the country, the number of kingdoms or commonwealths, and the great encouragement given by the Europeans, afford frequent pretences and opportunities to the bold designing profligates of one kingdom, to surprize and seize upon not only those of a neighbouring government, but also the weak and helpless of their own; and the unhappy people, taken on those occasions, are, with impunity, sold to the Europeans. These practices are doubtless disapproved of by the most considerate amongst the Negroes, for Bosman acquaints us, that even their national wars are not agreeable to such. He says, "If the person who occasioned the beginning of the war be taken, they will not easily admit him to ransom, though his weight in gold should be offered, for fear he should in future form some new design against their repose."

Chap. XI

An account of the shocking inhumanity, used in the carrying on of the slave-trade, as described by factors of different nations, viz. by Francis Moor, on the river Gambia; and by John Barbot, A. Brue, and William Bosman, through the coast of Guinea. *Note*. Of the large revenues arising to the Kings of Guinea from the slave-trade.

First, Francis Moor, factor for the English African Company, on the river Gambia, writes,

That there are a number of Negro traders, called joncoes, or merchants, who follow the slave-trade as a business; their place of residence is so high up in the country as to be six weeks travel from James Fort, which is situate at the mouth of that river. These merchants bring down elephants teeth, and in some years two thousand slaves, most of which, they say, are prisoners taken in war. They buy them from the different Princes who take them; many of them are Bumbrongs and Petcharies; nations, who each of them have different languages, and are brought from a vast way inland. Their way of bringing them is tying them by the neck with leather thongs, at about a yard distant from each other, thirty or forty in a string, having generally a bundle of corn or elephants teeth upon each of their heads. In their way from the mountains, they travel thro' very great woods, where they cannot for some days get water; so they carry in skin bags enough to support them for a time. I cannot (adds Moor) be certain of the number of merchants who follow this trade, but there may, perhaps, be about an hundred, who go up into the inland country, with the goods which they buy from the white men, and with them purchase, in various countries, gold, slaves, and elephants teeth. Besides the slaves, which the merchants bring down, there are many bought along the river: These are either taken in war, as the former are, or men condemned for crimes; *or else people stolen, which is very frequent*.—Since the slave-trade has been used, all punishments are changed into slavery; there being an advantage on such condemnation, *they strain for crimes very hard, in order to get the benefit of selling the criminal.*

John Barbot, the French factor, in his account of the manner by which the slaves are procured, says, "The slaves sold by the Negroes, are for the most part prisoners of war, or taken in the incursions they make in their enemies territories; others are stolen away by their neighbours, when found abroad on the road, or in the woods; or else in the corn fields, at the time of the year when their parents keep them there all the day to scare away the devouring small birds." Speaking of the transactions on that part of Guinea called the Slave Coast, where the Europeans have the most factories, and from whence they bring away much the greatest number of slaves, the same author, and also Bosman says, "The inhabitants of Coto do much mischief, in stealing those slaves they sell to the Europeans, from the upland country.—That the inhabitants of Popo excell the former; being endowed with a much larger share of courage, they rob more successfully, by which means they increase their riches and trade." The author particularly remarks, "*That they are encouraged in this practice by the Europeans*; sometimes it happens, according to the success of their inland excursions, that they are able to furnish two hundred slaves or more, in a few days." And he says, "The blacks of Fida, or Whidah, are so expeditious in trading for slaves, that they can deliver a thousand every month."—"If there happens to be no stock of slaves there, the factor must trust the blacks with his goods, to the value of one hundred and fifty, or two hundred pounds; which goods they carry up into the inland country, to buy slaves at all markets, for above six hundred miles up the country, where they are kept like cattle in Europe; the slaves sold there being generally prisoners of war, taken from their enemies like other booty, and perhaps some few sold by their own countrymen, in extreme want, or upon a famine, as also some as punishment of heinous crimes." So far Barbot's account; that given by William Bosman is as follows:

When the slaves which are brought from the inland countries come to Whidah, they are put in prison together; when we treat concerning buying them, they are all brought out together in a large plain, where, by our surgeons, they are thoroughly examined, and that naked, both men and women, without the least distinction or modesty. Those which are approved as good, are set on one side; in the mean while a burning iron, with the arms or name of the company, lies in the fire, with which ours are marked on the breast. When we have agreed with the owners of the slaves, they are returned to their prisons, where, from that time forward, they are kept at our charge, and cost us two pence a day each slave, which serves to subsist them like criminals on bread and water; so that to save charges, we send them on board our ships the very first opportunity; before which, their masters strip them of all they have on their backs, so that they come on board stark naked, as well women as men. In which condition they are obliged to continue, if the master of the ship is not so charitable (which he commonly is) as to bestow something on them to cover their nakedness. Six or seven hundred are sometimes put on board a vessel, where they lie as close together as it is possible for them to be crowded.

Chap. XII

Extracts of several Journals of Voyages to the coast of Guinea for slaves, whereby the extreme inhumanity of that traffick is described, *Melancholy* account of a ship blown up on that coast, with a great number of Negroes on board. *Instances* of shocking barbarity perpetrated by masters of vessels towards their slaves, *Inquiry* why these scandalous infringements, both of divine and human laws, are overlooked by the government.

The misery and bloodshed attendant on the slave-trade, are set forth by the following extracts of two voyages to the coast of Guinea for slaves. The first in a vessel from Liverpool, taken *verbatim* from the original manuscript of the Surgeon's Journal, *viz.*

"Sestro, December the 29th, 1724, No trade to day, though many traders came on board; they informed us, that the people are gone to war within land, and will bring prisoners enough in two or three days, in hopes of which we stay."

The 30th. "No trade yet, but our traders came on board to day, and informed us the people had burnt four towns of their enemies, so that to-morrow we expect slaves off: another large ship is come in. Yesterday came in a large Londoner."

The 31st. "Fair weather, but no trade yet; we see each night towns burning, but we hear the Sestro men are many of them killed by the inland Negroes, so that we fear this war will be unsuccessful."

The 2nd of January. "Last night we saw a prodigious fire break out about eleven o'clock, and this morning see the town of Sestro burnt down to the ground; (it contained some hundreds of houses) so that we find their enemies are too hard for them at present, and consequently our trade spoiled here; therefore, about seven o'clock, we weighed anchor, as did likewise the three other vessels, to proceed lower down."

The second relation, also taken from the original manuscript Journal of a person of credit, who went surgeon on the same trade, in a vessel from New-York, about twenty years past, is as follows; *viz.*

Being on the coast, the Commander of the vessel, according to custom, sent a person on shore with a present to the King, acquainting him with his arrival, and letting him know, they wanted a cargo of slaves. The King promised to furnish them with the slaves; and, in order to do it, set out to go to war against his enemies; designing to surprise some town, and take all the people prisoners. Some time after, the King sent them word, he had not yet met with the desired success; having been twice repulsed, in attempting to break up two towns, but that he still hoped to procure a number of slaves for them; and in this design he persisted, till he met his enemies in the field, where a battle was fought, which lasted three days, during which time the engagement was so bloody that four thousand five hundred men were slain on the spot.

The person who wrote the account, beheld the bodies, as they lay on the field of battle. "Think (says he in his Journal) what a pitiable sight it was, to see the widows weeping over their lost husbands, orphans deploring the loss of their fathers, *&c. &c.*" In the 6th vol. of Churchill's collection of Voyages, page 219, we have the relation of a voyage performed by Captain Philips, in a ship of 450 tuns, along the coast of Guinea, for elephants teeth, gold, and Negroe slaves, intended for Barbadoes; in which he says, that they took "seven hundred slaves on board, the men being all put in irons two by two, shackled together to prevent their mutinying or swimming ashore. That the Negroes are so loth to leave their own country, that they often leap out of the canoe, boat, or ship, into the sea, and keep under water till they are drowned, to avoid being taken up, and saved by the boats which pursue them."—They had about twelve Negroes who willingly drowned themselves; others starved themselves to death.—Philips was advised to cut off the legs and arms of some to terrify the rest, (as other Captains had done) but this he refused to do. From the time of his taking the Negroes on board, to his arrival at Barbadoes, no less than three hundred and twenty died of various diseases.

Reader, bring the matter home to thy own heart, and consider whether any situation can be more completely miserable than that of these distressed captives. When we reflect that each individual of this number had probably some tender attachment, which was broken by this cruel separation; some parent or wife, who had not an opportunity of mingling tears in a parting embrace; perhaps some infants, or aged parents, whom his labour was to feed, and vigilance protect; themselves under the most dreadful apprehension of an unknown perpetual slavery; confined within the narrow limits of a vessel, where often several hundreds lie as close as possible. Under these aggravated distresses, they are often reduced to a state of despair, in which many have been frequently killed, and some deliberately put to death under the greatest torture, when they have attempted to rise, in order to free themselves from present misery, and the slavery designed them. Many accounts of this nature might be mentioned; indeed from the vast number of vessels employed in the trade, and the repeated relations in the public prints of Negroes rising on board the vessels from Guinea, it is more than probable, that many such instances occur every year. I shall only mention one example of this kind, by which the reader may judge of the rest; it is in Astley's collection, vol. 2. p. 449, related by John Atkins, surgeon on board admiral Ogle's squadron, of one "Harding, master of a vessel in which several of the men-slaves and women-slaves had attempted to rise, in order to recover their liberty; some of whom the master, of his own authority, sentenced to cruel death, making them first eat the heart and liver of one of those he had killed. The woman he hoisted by the thumbs, whipped, and slashed with knives before the other slaves, till she died." As detestable and shocking as this may appear to such whose hearts are not yet hardened by the practice of that cruelty, which the love of wealth by degrees introduceth into the human mind, it will not be strange to those who have been concerned or employed in the trade.

Now here arises a necessary query to those who hold the balance of justice, and who must be accountable to God for the use they have made of it. That as the principles on which the British constitution is founded, are so favourable to the common rights of mankind, how it has happened that the laws which countenance this iniquitous traffic, have obtained the sanction of the legislature? and that the executive part of the government should so long shut their ears to continual reports of the barbarities perpetrated against this unhappy people, and leave the trading subjects at liberty to trample on the most precious rights of others, even without a rebuke? Why are the masters of vessels thus suffered to be the sovereign arbiters of the lives of the miserable Negroes, and allowed with impunity thus to destroy (may I not properly say, *to murder*) their fellow-creatures; and that by means so cruel, as cannot be even related but with shame and horror?

Chap. XIII

Usage of the Negroes, when they arrive in the West Indies. An hundred thousand Negroes brought from Guinea every year to the English colonies. The number of Negroes who die in the passage and seasoning. These are, properly speaking, murdered by the prosecution of this infamous traffic. Remarks on its dreadful *effects and tendency*.

When the vessels arrive at their destined port in the colonies, the poor Negroes are to be disposed of to the planters; and here they are again exposed naked, without any distinction of sexes, to the brutal examination of their purchasers; and this, it may well be judged, is, to many, another occasion of deep distress. Add to this, that near connexions must now again be separated, to go with their several purchasers; this must be deeply affecting to all, but such whose hearts are feared by the love of gain. Mothers are seen hanging over their daughters, bedewing their naked breasts with tears, and daughters clinging to their parents, not knowing what new stage of distress must follow their separation, or whether they shall ever meet again. And here what sympathy, what commiseration, do they meet with? Why, indeed, if they will not separate as readily as their owners think proper, the whipper is called for, and the lash exercised upon their naked bodies, till obliged to part. Can any human heart, which is not become callous by the practice of such cruelties, be unconcerned, even at the relation of such grievous affliction, to which this oppressed part of our species are subjected.

In a book, printed in Liverpool, called *The Liverpool Memorandum*, which contains, amongst other things, an account of the trade of that port, there is an exact list of the vessels employed in the Guinea trade, and of the number of slaves imported in each vessel; by which it appears that in the year 1753, the number imported to America by one hundred and one vessels belonging to that port, amounted to upwards of thirty thousand; and from the number of vessels employed by the African company in London and Bristol we may, with some degree of certainty, conclude, there are one hundred thousand Negroes purchased and brought on board our ships yearly from the coast of Africa. This is confirmed in Anderson's history of Trade and Commerce, lately printed; where it is said, "That England supplies her American colonies with Negroe slaves, amounting in number to above one hundred thousand every year." When the vessels are full freighted with slaves, they sail for our plantations in America, and may be two or three months in the voyage; during which time, from the filth and stench that is among them, distempers frequently break out, which carry off commonly a fifth, a fourth, yea sometimes a third or more of them: so that taking all the slaves together, that are brought on board our ships yearly, one may reasonably suppose, that at least ten thousand of them die on the voyage. And in a printed account of the state of the Negroes in our plantations, it is supposed that a fourth part, more or less, die at the different islands, in what is called the seasoning. Hence it may be presumed, that at a moderate computation of the slaves who are purchased by our African merchants in a year, near thirty thousand die upon the voyage, and in the seasoning. Add to this, the prodigious number who are killed in the incursions and intestine wars, by which the Negroes procure the number of slaves wanted to load the vessels. How dreadful then is this slave-trade, whereby so many thousands of our fellow creatures, free by nature, endued with the same rational faculties, and called to be heirs of the same salvation with us, lose their lives, and are, truly and properly speaking, murdered every year! For it is not necessary, in order to convict a man of murder, to make it appear that he had an *intention* to commit murder; whoever does, by unjust force or violence, deprive another of his liberty, and, while he hath him in his power, continues so to oppress him by cruel treatment, as eventually to occasion his death, is actually guilty of murder. It is enough to make a thoughtful person tremble, to think what a load of guilt lies upon our nation on this account; and that the blood of thousands of poor innocent creatures, murdered every year in the prosecution of this wicked trade, cries aloud to Heaven for vengeance. Were we to hear or read of a nation that destroyed every year, in some other way, as many human creatures as perish in this trade, we should certainly consider them as a very bloody, barbarous people; if it be alledged, that the legislature hath encouraged, and still does encourage this trade. It is answered, that no legislature on earth can alter the nature of things, so as to make that to be right which is contrary to the law of God, (the supreme Legislator and Governor of the world) and opposeth the promulgation of the Gospel of *peace on earth, and good will to man.* Injustice may be methodized and established by law, but still it will be injustice, as much as it was before; though its being so established may render men more insensible of the guilt, and more bold and secure in the perpetration of it.

Chap. XIV

Observations on the disposition and capacity of the Negroes: Why thought inferior to that of the Whites. Affecting instances of the slavery of the Negroes. Reflections thereon.

Doubts may arise in the minds of some, whether the foregoing accounts, relating to the natural capacity and good disposition of the inhabitants of Guinea, and of the violent manner in which they are said to be torn from their native land, are to be depended upon; as those Negroes who are brought to us, are not heard to complain, and do but seldom manifest such a docility and quickness of parts, as is agreeable thereto. But those who make these objections, are desired to note the many discouragements the poor Africans labour under, when brought from their native land. Let them consider, that those afflicted strangers, though in an *enlightened Christian country*, have yet but little opportunity or encouragement to exert and improve their natural talents: They are constantly employed in servile labour; and the abject condition in which we see them, naturally raises an idea of a superiority in ourselves; whence we are apt to look upon them as an ignorant and contemptible part of mankind. Add to this, that they meet with very little encouragement of freely conversing with such of the Whites, as might impart instruction to them. It is a fondness for wealth, for authority, or honour, which prompts most men in their endeavours to excell; but these motives can have little influence upon the minds of the Negroes; few of them have any reasonable prospect of any other than a state of slavery; so that, though their natural capacities were ever so good, they have neither inducement or opportunity to exert them to advantage: This naturally tends to depress their minds, and sink their spirits into habits of idleness and sloth, which they would, in all likelihood, have been free from, had they stood upon an equal footing with the white people. They are suffered, with impunity, to cohabit together, without being married; and to part, when solemnly engaged to one another as man and wife; notwithstanding the moral and religious laws of the land, strictly prohibiting such practices. This naturally tends to beget apprehensions in the most thoughtful of those people, that we look upon them as a lower race, not worthy of the same care, nor liable to the same rewards and punishments as ourselves. Nevertheless it may with truth be said, that both amongst those who have obtained their freedom, and those who remain in servitude, some have manifested a strong sagacity and an exemplary uprightness of heart. If this hath not been generally the case with them, is it a matter of surprize? Have we not reason to make the same complaint of many white servants, when discharged from our service, though many of them have had much greater opportunities of knowledge and improvement than the blacks; who, even when free, labour under the same difficulties as before: having but little access to, and intercourse with, the most reputable white people, they remain confined within their former limits of conversation. And if they seldom complain of the unjust and cruel usage they have received, in being forced from their native country. &c. it is not to be wondered at; it being a considerable time after their arrival amongst us, before they can speak our language; and, by the time they are able to express themselves, they have great reason to believe, that little or no notice would be taken of their complaints: yet let any person enquire of those who were capable of reflection, before they were brought from their native land, and he will hear such affecting relations, as, if not lost to the common feelings of humanity, will sensibly affect his heart. The case of a poor Negroe, not long since brought from Guinea, is a recent instance of this kind. From his first arrival, he appeared thoughtful and dejected, frequently dropping tears when taking notice of his master's children, the cause of which was not known till he was able to speak English, when the account he gave of himself was, "That he had a wife and children in his own country; that some of these being sick and thirsty, he went in the night time, to fetch water at a spring, where he was violently seized and carried away by persons who lay in wait to catch men, from whence he was transported to America. The remembrance of his family, friends, and other connections, left behind, which he never expected to see any more, were the principal cause of his dejection and grief." Many cases, equally affecting, might be here mentioned; but one more instance, which fell under the notice of a person of credit, will suffice. One of these wretched creatures, then about 50 years of age, informed him,

> That being violently torn from a wife and several children in Guinea, he was sold in Jamaica, where never expecting to see his native land or family any more, he joined himself to a Negroe woman, by whom he had two children: after some years, it suiting the interest of his owner to remove him, he was separated from his second wife and children, and brought to South Carolina, where, expecting to spend the remainder of his days, he engaged with a third wife, by whom he had another child; but here the same consequence of one man being subject to the will and pleasure of another man occurring, he was separated from his last wife and child, and brought into this country, where he remained a slave.

Can any, whose mind is not rendered quite obdurate by the love of wealth, hear these relations, without being deeply touched with sympathy and sorrow? And doubtless the case of many, very many of these afflicted people, upon enquiry, would be found to be attended with circumstances equally tragical and aggravating. And if we enquire of those Negroes, who were brought away from their native country when children, we shall find most of them to have been stolen away, when abroad from their parents, on the roads, in the woods, or watching their corn-fields. Now, you that have studied the book of conscience, and you that are learned in the law, what will you say to such deplorable cases? When, and how, have these oppressed people forfeited their liberty? Does not justice loudly call for its being restored to them? Have they not the same right to demand it, as any of us should have, if we had been violently snatched by pirates from our native land? Is it not the duty of every dispenser of justice, who is not forgetful of his own humanity, to remember that these are men, and to declare them free? Where instances of such cruelty frequently occur, and are neither enquired into, nor redressed, by those whose duty it is *to seek judgment, and relieve the oppressed*, Isaiah i. 17. what can be expected, but that the groans and cries of these sufferers will reach Heaven; and what shall we do *when God riseth up? and when he visiteth*, what will ye answer him? *Did not he that made them, make us; and did not one fashion us in the womb?* Job xxxi. 14.

Chap. XIV

The expediency of a general freedom being granted to the Negroes considered. *Reasons* why it might be productive of advantage and *safety to the Colonies*.

It is scarce to be doubted, but that the foregoing accounts will beget in the heart of the considerate readers an earnest desire to see a stop put to this complicated evil; but the objection with many is, What shall be done with those Negroes already imported, and born in our families? Must they be sent to Africa? That would be to expose them, in a strange land, to greater difficulties than many of them labour under at present. To set them suddenly free here, would be perhaps attended with no less difficulty; for, undiciplined as they are in religion and virtue, they might give a loose to those evil habits, which the fear of a master would have restrained. These are objections, which weigh with many well disposed people, and it must be granted, these are difficulties in the way; nor can any general change be made, or reformation effected, without some; but the difficulties are not so great but that they may be surmounted. If the government was so considerate of the iniquity and danger attending on this practice, as to be willing to seek a remedy, doubtless the Almighty would bless this good intention, and such methods would be thought of, as would not only put an end to the unjust oppression of the Negroes, but might bring them under regulations, that would enable them to become profitable members of society; for the furtherance of which, the following proposals are offered to consideration: That all farther importation of slaves be absolutely prohibited; and as to those born among us, after serving so long as may appear to be equitable, let them by law be declared free. Let every one, thus set free, be enrolled in the county courts, and be obliged to be a resident, during a certain number of years, within the said county, under the care of the overseers of the poor. Thus being, in some sort, still under the direction of governors, and the notice of those who were formerly acquainted with them, they would be obliged to act the more circumspectly, and make proper use of their liberty, and their children would have an opportunity of obtaining such instructions, as are necessary to the common occasions of life; and thus both parents and children might gradually become useful members of the community. And further, where the nature of the country would permit, as certainly the uncultivated condition of our southern and most western colonies easily would, suppose a small tract of land were assigned to every Negroe family, and they obliged to live upon and improve it, (when not hired out to work for the white people) this would encourage them to exert their abilities, and become industrious subjects. Hence, both planters and tradesmen would be plentifully supplied with chearful and willing-minded labourers, much vacant land would be cultivated, the produce of the country be justly increased, the taxes for the support of government lessened to individuals, by the increase of taxables, and the Negroes, instead of being an object of terror, as they certainly must be to the governments where their numbers are great, would become interested in their safety and welfare.

Chap. XV

Answer to a mistaken opinion, that the warmth of the climate in the West-Indies, will not permit white people to labour there. No complaint of disability in the whites, in that respect, in the settlement of the islands. Idleness and diseases prevailed, as the use of slaves increased. *The great* advantage which might accrue to the British nation, if the slave trade was entirely laid aside, and a fair and friendly commerce established through the whole coast of Africa.

It is frequently offered as an argument, in vindication of the use of Negroe slaves, that the warmth of the climate in the West Indies will not permit white people to labour in the culture of the land: but upon an acquaintance with the nature of the climate, and its effects upon such labouring white people, as are prudent and moderate in labour, and the use of spirituous liquors, this will be found to be a mistaken opinion. Those islands were, at first, wholly cultivated by white men; the encouragement they then met with, for a long course of years, was such as occasioned a great increase of people. Richard Ligon, in his history of Barbadoes, where he resided from the year 1647 to 1650, about 24 years after his first settlement, writes, "that there were then fifty thousand souls on that island, besides Negroes; and that though the weather was very hot, yet not so scalding but that servants, both christians and slaves, laboured ten hours a day." By other accounts we gather, that the white people have since decreased to less than one half the number which was there at that time; and by relations of the first settlements of the other islands, we do not meet with any complaints of unfitness in the white people for labour there, before slaves were introduced. The island of Hispaniola, which is one of the largest of those islands, was at first planted by the Buccaneers, a set of hardy laborious men, who continued so for a long course of years; till following the example of their neighbours, in the purchase and use of Negroe slaves, idleness and excess prevailing, debility and disease naturally succeeded, and have ever since continued. If, under proper regulations, liberty was proclaimed through the colonies, the Negroes, from dangerous, grudging, half-fed slaves, might become able, willing-minded labourers. And if there was not a sufficient number of these to do the necessary work, a competent number of labouring people might be procured from Europe, which affords numbers of poor distressed objects, who, if not overlooked, with proper usage, might, in several respects, better answer every good purpose in performing the necessary labour in the islands, than the slaves now do.

A farther considerable advantage might accrue to the British nation in general, if the slave trade was laid aside, by the cultivation of a fair, friendly, and humane commerce with the Africans; without which, it is not possible the inland trade of that country should ever be extended to the degree it is capable of; for while the spirit of butchery and making slaves of each other, is promoted by the Europeans amongst the Negroes, no mutual confidence can take place; nor will the Europeans be able to travel with safety into the heart of their country, to form and cement such commercial friendships and alliances, as might be necessary to introduce the arts and sciences amongst them, and engage their attention to instruction in the principles of the christian religion, which is the only sure foundation of every social virtue. Africa has about ten thousand miles of sea coast, and extends in depth near three thousand miles from east to west, and as much from north to south, stored with vast treasures of materials, necessary for the trade and manufactures of Great-Britain; and from its climate, and the fruitfulness of its soil, capable, under proper management, of producing in the greatest plenty, most of the commodities which are imported into Europe from those parts of America subject to the English government; and as, in return, they would take our manufactures, the advantages of this trade would soon become so great, that it is evident this subject merits the regard and attention of the government.

David Cooper, *A Mite Cast into the Treasury*, 1772

David Cooper, *A Mite Cast into the Treasury: or, Observations on Slave-Keeping* (Philadelphia, 1772), pp. iii-iv; 5-22.

In 1772 David Cooper, New Jersey Quaker, wrote that slaveholders were committing acts of violence "against the strongest of laws, the law of nature . . ." and were robbing individuals of their freedom, a "right which was never given by the universal Father to any one of his creatures over one another." Cooper's pamphlet, A Mite Cast into the Treasury, *was essentially a religious attack against slavery which was, as were many antislavery tracts in the period of the American Revolution, infused with allusions to natural rights and natural liberty. Although this period also gave rise to a number of secular political essays on slavery, Cooper's pamphlet illustrates Winthrop Jordan's theme in* White Over Black *that the natural rights theory and the religious affirmation of equality were not incompatible in antislavery literature. Cooper's characterization of men as "free agents" still carried with it the assumption that God remained the Supreme Being, dispensing all judgments. The popularity of Cooper's pamphlet, published anonymously, led to a second printing.*

In later years Cooper corresponded frequently with his son-in-law, Samuel Allinson, another New Jersey Quaker prominent in the antislavery movement. They exchanged views on everything from the doctrine of free will to horseracing and slavery. Their alliance was a strong link in the growing network of antislavery writers and propagandists.

Introduction

The power of prejudice over the minds of mankind is very extraordinary; hardly any extreams too distant, or absurdities too glaring for it to unite or reconcile, if it tends to promote or justify a favourite pursuit. It is thus we are to account for the fallacious reasonings and absurd sentiments used and entertained concerning negroes, and the lawfulness of keeping them slaves. The low contempt with which they are generally treated by the whites, lead children from the first dawn of reason, to consider people with a black skin, on a footing with domestic animals, formed to serve and obey, whom they may kick, beat, and treat as they please, without their having any right to complain; and when they attain the age of maturity, can scarce be brought to believe that creatures they have always looked upon so vastly below themselves, can stand on the same footing in the sight of the Universal Father, or that justice requires the same conduct to them as to whites; and those prejudices having been generally countenanced in time past, are become so riveted, that too few even of the sober and religious, can hear the voice of impartial justice, in favour of that abused people, with a proper degree of patience and attention. I therefore request all such into whose hands this may fall, to divest themselves of every bias arising either from prejudice, or temporal views, and coolly weigh the following hints, and, if any thing is met with, that tends to promote christian rectitude, embrace it; without regarding the hand from whence it comes, ever bearing in mind who it was that declared,—"Such measure as you mete, shall be measured to you again." Mat. vii. 2.

Observations on Slave-keeping

Open thy mouth for the dumb, and all such as are appointed to destruction, and plead the cause of the poor and needy. 2 Prov. xxxi. 8, 9.

My mind having been frequently led to consider the inconsistency of the practice of slave-keeping, and making traffic of our fellow-men, to the precepts and doctrine of our blessed Lord and Lawgiver, which, with regard to duty one to another, is sum'd up in this short command, viz. "Whatsover ye would that men should do to you, do ye even so to them," and wishing to see an end put to this unrighteous practice among christians, felt an inclination to fling a few hints together, several of which to me appeared new on the subject, which may possibly lead some more closely to inspect their own situation, in order to discover how far they stand approved by impartial justice in this business, and as the Jewish law was positive, "That whoever stealeth a man and selleth him, or if he be found in his hand, he shall surely be put to death." Ex. xxi. 16. The following queries may be worthy our serious attention.

Query I. Was this part of the ceremonial law intended only for the Jewish nation, or founded on universal distributive justice, adapted to the nature of things, and equally necessary to the rest of mankind?

II. Is he who encourages the thief to steal and receives the goods, more innocent than the thief?

III. As christians consider it unlawful to make slaves of their fellow-believers, does the precepts of Christ, or nature of things give a christian any stronger title to his native freedom than an African?

IV. If it was a heinous crime to take a fellow-servant by the throat and deprive him of his liberty because he could not pay a just debt, is it not much more so to deprive our fellow-servants of their freedom who owe us nothing, nor ever did us the least injury?

V. Is not the command which prohibits the coveting our neighbour's ox, servant, &c. broke with a much deeper degree of guilt, by coveting his person, and when in our power the making him our slave?

VI. Does not he, who for gain, buys, sells, or keeps in slavery the descendants of those who were unjustly deprived of their freedom, thereby justify the original act, and put himself in the place of the first agressor?

Object. But the negroes brought here are captives taken in war, and, by the custom of the country belong to the victors, who have a right to slay or otherwise dispose of them.

To pass over the Europeans being the occasion of those wars by their demand for slaves, and that many of the negroes brought here, have been stole, &c. let us consider how far a custom allowed of among benighted Africans, is to be countenanced and upheld by enlightened christians, who are commanded to, "Do unto others, as they would have others do unto them," not to a part only, to those of their own religion or colour, but to all men; wherefore no christian can keep a slave or be accessary thereto, without (in some degree) incurring the guilt of breaking his Lord's command, unless he is willing himself and posterity should be slaves; and as to this custom of selling those of their own nation and colour into perpetual slavery, from parents, husbands, wives, children, and all the tender connections of life; who can think of it without the utmost abhorrence. Shall we then, shall christians plead it as an excuse for our conduct, when at the same time we are the moving cause which produce those effects, as certainly as the weights in a clock are the cause of its striking. Remove the weights and the striking ceases. Let all who bear the christian name leave buying slaves, and this-infernal custom of theirs, of selling their brethren will I believe equally cease. A custom that casts the most indelible odium on the whole people, occasioning some from hence to infer that they are a different race, formed by the Creator for brutal services, to drudge for us with their brethren of the stalls.—However extravagant such a supposition may appear, it is the only rational one that can fully justify the practice, and give peace of mind to a slave-keeper; for until he can persuade himself that this is the case, the above precept must continually reproach him with being a hypocrite and no christian who can thus live in a deliberate opposition to Christ's command; and I am fully persuaded there is few to be found who justifies the practice but is more or less tinctured with this opinion. Well then if this people's custom of going to war for no other purpose than to take prisoners; stealing, kidnapping, &c.

their neighbours and children, in order to sell them for slaves, cannot be thought of without raising the utmost detestation, as what the most effectually saps and destroys every social tie, on which all temporal happiness stands—is black with every guilt, and the most truly infernal of any practice that ever obtained among mankind—What excuse, what plea, will our negro masters make at the great day of retribution, for encouraging those execrable crimes by receiving the plunder?—It will be none, I doubt, to say my negro was born in my father's house, or in America, and therefore not obtained in that way; for I consider the person who was brought from his native country against his will and made a slave, to exist in each individual of his posterity, however distant in point of time. And the person in whose hand such posterity is found, so long as the injury is continued, to represent the original stealer or plunderer, whose right hath been conveyed down to him and is that by which he claims property in such posterity, consequently represents him in whom this claim ultimately existed; nor can he wash his hands from this guilt by delivering such pretended property either by sale or gift to another, more than Pilot washed his from the guilt of Christ's death, whom he knew to be innocent, and had it in his power to have set at liberty.

But to return to the source of this evil; if we look upon the first move so odious, so hateful, and find ourselves filled with indignation and abhorrence against the perpetrators, how can we countenance and encourage, and thereby become promoters, abetters, and accessories therein, which every one in a less or greater degree is, who buys, sells, or keeps in slavery one of these people after the age the law of nature gives each human being an equal right to freedom; for can there be a greater absurdity than to say, I detest the plunderer, when I am greedily sharing the spoils, or innocent of the guilt, if I refuse to make restitution to the true owner of his property of which I am in possession, and of which he was unjustly deprived.—This opens a large field for consideration, for it really appears to me impossible for any one of their own seeking and choice, to be concerned in slave-keeping, or partake of the profits, without incurring a degree of the original guilt. For if an innocent free-man, who had no ways forfeited his freedom, was by force taken from his native country and made a slave and begets children, who by virtue of the original injury are kept slaves, and they beget others, and so on for twenty generations, the first wrong, a robbery of freedom, is continued, and exists in each of these, as much as it did in their common ancestors; nor can I defend or justify my title to one of them without defending and justifying the original injury on which my right is founded, and my refusing to restore this stolen property, of which I am possessed, to its right owner shews that I approve the original act, and being a sharer of the spoils, become a sharer of the guilt, as also justly chargable with a repetition of the crime; for every individual of the human species by the law of nature comes into the world equally intitled to freedom at a proper age, altho' their parents may have been unjustly deprived of, or forfeited theirs. Children are not to answer for the sins of their parents; and whoever having the care or possession of a child, and denys him his freedom at an age the laws of his country gives it to others, and without any act or consent of the party to justify it, commits an act of violence against the strongest of laws, the law of nature,—robs that individual of his inherent property, his freedom, a right which was never given by the universal Father to any one of his creatures over one another, without some fault on their part, not even to parents over their children.—A property more sacred, interesting, and essential to us as free agents, and accountable creatures than any other. And whoever partakes of the labour of such, or the profits arising therefrom, become sharers of the spoils of oppression.—Can we then believe the Supreme Being to be an indifferent spectator of this inhuman trade, this assumed authority of one part of his intelligent creatures levelling another part with the brute animals to drudge and toil for their will and pleasure. Buy and sell them like cattle, deprived of every rational enjoyment, with the addition of every species of human misery.—If he really is a God taking cognisance of the actions of men—of one flesh hath created all nations of people—is no respector of persons, but renders to every man according to his works—is particularly attentive to the cries of the poor and needy—will he not assuredly judge for those things? "Rob not the poor, because he is poor, neither oppress the afflicted in the gate. For the Lord will plead their cause, and spoil the soul, of those that spoiled them." Prov. xxii. 22, 23.

The scripture mentions the wicked balance, and bag of deceitful weights, the use of which, I believe was never more apparent than in this dark business, in excusing the keeping slaves, and in raising difficulties against setting them free, it would be endless to attempt a catalogue of the trifling and absurd reasons used on these occasions, nor have I any inclination, my intent being only just to hint at matters; to reason with those who justify slave keeping, after its unlawfulness hath been so plainly and abundantly proved, would appear idle in me. But such who solemnly pretend to condemn the practice, yet shelter themselves under supposed difficulties in setting theirs free, or willing to free them after they have spent the prime of life in their service, or make them pay so much per year to secure their estates, &c. I would beg of such to lay aside the false balance and deceitful weights, and use the true.—Weigh this matter in Christ's scales. "Do unto others, as ye would they should do to you." This will oblige you to set your negroes free at the same age your own children are, without unjustly coveting their labour till they are 25 or 30 years of age, or compelling them to pay you a yearly sum. They have as good a right to their freedom at twenty-one in the eyes of unbiased justice as your own sons, and to deny it to them, is as I said before, a repetition of the crime which brought their ancestors out of their own country, viz. a robbing them of their freedom, which if born and continued there, they would have enjoyed, nor can their being born among christians cancel this invariable law of nature, or make the seizing their freedom by force here, any less injustice than had it been done there; the injury to the individual is the same, and equally incompatible with doing as we would be done unto.—Should one of your sons be kept an apprentice by force, a year longer than his master had a right, satisfaction must be made, or a prosecution commenced and what not, for redress. But the poor Africans having no advocate but his master's conscience, may be kept year after year, and perhaps die at his drudgery like a horse at the plow, or have his freedom restored at a time of life when it is rather a punishment than favour.

Object. But surely thou wilt admit of some distinction between the children of white people born free, and those of our slaves who cost us great sums of money which we have not been repaid, or perhaps bought young and not earned half their cost by the time they are of age, as is my case. I have a woman bought when young, who having had children fast, hath earned very little of her purchase money, and if I should set all these free as they arrive to the age of men and women, shall be a great looser by them; thou wilt hardly say that would be reasonable.

My friend thy reasoning proceeds from the bag of deceitful weights; the true balance discovers justice to be quite another thing than thou seems to think it, here is no respect of persons. Justice to thy negroe weighs as heavy as justice to thyself, a small loss in thy interest put in this scale against the freedom of an innocent fellow-creature, weighs but as a feather against mount Atlas, perhaps the barely claiming no right to them after the age of 18 and 21 may fall greatly short of christian justice in this scale; let us therefore a little investigate this matter.

Query. How came thee possessed of this woman?

Ans. I bought her of an African merchant, who brought her from Guinea when a child.

Query. How came he by her?

Ans. I know not: I suppose he bought her of them who had a right to sell her.

A right to sell her! No one, not even her father could have such a right longer than till she came to the age of a woman, at which time she was pronounced free by the law of nature, the rules of equity and justice, and precepts of Christ, whether in her father's house, or a master's, in her native country, or among strangers; this inherent right she carries with her, and cannot be diseized of but by her own consent.—But it is very likely she was stolen from her parents, and then justice will say the perpetrater had not the least right to her, consequently could convey none, but that he deserved death for the act.—If this is the chain of conveyance on which thy title to these negroes stands, thou sees it is none at all, but that the life of the person thou holds under, was justly forfeited for being the means of putting them into thy power; therefore if thou had been a christian in deed and in truth, that is, been dictated in all thy conduct by the precepts of Christ, which are the perfections of justice, would sooner have cast thy money into the fire, than have made such an unchristian purchase, by doing of which, thou approved of, and made thyself a partner in all the string of crimes committed in procuring, bringing, and selling this child for a slave; but having done it, should then have acted the part of a father by her, been more earnest in giving her a christian education, than to make her earn her purchase-money, and have claimed no right to her after she came to woman's age.—This is as thou would desire a child of thine should be treated in the like circumstances; but as thou did not then discharge a christian duty by her, hath now an additional cumber, and ought to do this by her children; for being under thy care, their own father cannot do it, and by a free act of thy own, thou stands his substitute as to their education, and ought to discharge a father's duty to them in that respect.

Object. I act the part of a father by negroes! be at the cost of raising them, schooling and what not, and when they are able to earn something set them free!—I'll assure thee I'll do no such thing, it would be injustice to myself and family.—Why at that age they'll bring me near 100l. per head.

Do not be warm my friend, I am not about to force thee to obey the laws of God, "To deal justly, and love mercy." I know thou has the laws of men on thy side. I am only endeavouring to shew thee it would be abundantly thy greatest interest so to do; and as thou calls thyself a christian, should expect much rhetorick need not be used to convince thee that to be such it is absolutely necessary to obey Christ's precepts and doctrine; to which there is nothing more diametrically opposite than the slave trade from first to last.—But if, with Dives, thou art preferring this world's treasure to that which ought to be had up in heaven,—I fear thou will share his lot in the conclusion.

Object. I am not preferring this world's treasure in that sort, but think it very just these negroes should serve me till they are 25 or 30 years of age to pay for their bringing up, and then a yearly sum for some time to secure my estate from charge.

Thou art still using the false balance, the true one will decide quite otherwise. It hath been already shewn, that by the law of nature and precepts of christianity, thou had not the least right to the mother's labour after she was of woman's age, and thy keeping her against her will, was robbing her of her freedom, which at that time became her own property, and in consequence of that unlawful act, now claims her children;—but can justly have no other, or greater power over them than that of a father until they are men and women, when having received from thee a christian education to enable them to get a living, and be useful members of society, ought then enjoy their freedom as fully as thy own children. And as to paying a yearly sum to secure thy estate, it is the height of injustice; this incumbrance was not brought on by any fault or act of theirs, but by thyself, and as it was of thy own seeking, ought to bear the burden, and not punish innocent persons for thy faults. Do the best the present circumstances will admit of, "Loose the bands of wickedness, and let the oppressed go free," and thereby atone for what cannot be recalled; for whoever attempts, to satisfy justice by setting their negroes free by halves in that sort, will find themselves, as much mistaken, I believe, as Ananias and his wife, in trying to deceive the apostles with a part of the money their possessions sold for.—It is inflicting a penalty upon them,—and for what?—Justice abhors punishing an innocent person; and if they are innocent why shall they not enjoy their natural rights as fully and absolute as the rest of mankind. Or is it their being born of a different colour from ourselves that gives us this prerogative of dealing with them as we please; making natural justice quite another thing when apply'd to negroes, from what it is when apply'd to those of our own colour. However this simple circumstance may have prejudiced our minds, it may be well for all who are concerned with this people to remember, that they are equally the work of an Almighty hand, with a soul to save or loose, as themselves, and being so, doubtless will avenge their cause, altho' in his mercy he forbears long, the time of retribution will come; justice is as much his attribute as mercy.

Object. Thou says much of doing as we would be done unto, &c. for my part I think it a great happiness for the negroes that they are brought here, whereby they become acquainted with the christian doctrine, which they would have remained ignorant of, had they continued in their own country.

A hopeful argument! fabricated by the same hand as those in favour of the Spanish inquisition, and with about as much sense and reason. Those murderers it is said, will with a very grave face tell an heretick at the time they are torturing him in the most exquisite manner, that they do it out of pure regard for his soul; thus for the good of their souls, destroy hereticks in a more horrible sort than a lion, or tiger, does his prey. And these make use of the most unchristian means to get and keep their fellow-men in their power, and render them the most miserable of human beings, to make them acquainted forsooth and in love with christianity, which it is well known is the least of their concern, and that few take more care to instill into their negroes than into their cattle. But this plea tho' often used, is too absurd and ridiculous to be seriously refuted, shall therefore dismiss the subject after giving another sample of like pious concern for the souls of men, which may bring it more feelingly home to ourselves. The duke of Parma on hearing of Queen Elizabeth's proclaiming a day of thanksgiving for the defeat of the Spanish Armada, exclaimed! "Mistaken woman! Blind Nation! to return thanks for the greatest misfortune that could have befallen them! for had that enterprise succeeded, they would all have been converted to the true catholic faith."—Now had they obtained their ends, butchered thousands, and enslaved the rest, I suppose we should think it the greatest insult on reason, to say it would have been a real kindness to the English, tho' it might be so said with much more propriety and truth, than it can respecting negroes, who are brought from their native land, where they enjoyed freedom and independance in a more extensive degree than we do, and placed here on a footing with the brute creatures, that are generally treated with greater care and tenderness than they. In the other case, the people of England by submitting to the conquerors, would have enjoyed their civil and natural privileges. How far that is from being the case with slaves, concerns their master's awfully to consider.

Petition to King George III from Virginia House of Burgesses, April 1, 1772

John Pendleton Kennedy, ed., *Journals of the House of Burgesses of Virginia, 1770-1772* (Richmond, 1906), pp. 283-84.

During the Revolutionary era Virginians who sought the prohibition of the slave trade, whatever their motives, indirectly supported the aims of abolitionists. A general movement to prohibit or restrict the importation of slaves developed in Virginia during the late 1760s and 1770s. Though their bills were unacceptable to the Crown, the General Assembly sought three times to levy prohibitive duties on the importation of slaves, and in 1772 the Burgesses resolved Nemine contradicente *to petition King George III to "remove all Restraints on his Governors from passing Acts of Assembly, which [were] intended to check this pernicious Commerce. . . ." Finally in 1778, the war having removed the King's restraints, the General Assembly passed legislation prohibiting slave importation. Although there is some evidence that that measure and the 1772 petition were based on philosophical and moral grounds, it was the fear of slave rebellion and the persuasion of economic self-interest that produced that long-sought legislation: the simple law of supply and demand interlaced with concern for personal safety. Yet, few antislavery proponents were not inspired to learn that Virginians considered the importation of slaves a "Trade of great Inhumanity," as the 1772 petition declares.*

. . . *Mr Harrison* reported from the Committee appointed upon *Friday*, the twentieth Day of last Month, to draw up an Address to be presented to his Majesty, that the Committee had drawn up an Address accordingly, which they had directed him to report to the House; and he read the same in his Place, and afterwards delivered it in at the Clerk's Table; where the same was read, and is as followeth, *viz.*

Most Gracious Sovereign, We, your Majesty's dutiful and loyal Subjects, the Burgesses of Virginia, *now met in General Assembly, beg Leave, with all Humility, to approach your Royal Presence.*

The many Instances of your Majesty's benevolent Intentions and most gracious Disposition to promote the Prosperity and Happiness of your Subjects in the Colonies, encourage us to look up to the Throne, and implore your Majesty's paternal Assistance in averting a Calamity of a most alarming Nature.

The Importation of Slaves into the Colonies from the Coast of Africa *hath long been considered as a Trade of great Inhumanity, and, under its present Encouragement, we have too much Reason to fear will endanger the very Existance of your Majesty's* American *Dominions.*

We are sensible that some of your Majesty's Subjects in Great-Britain *may reap Emoluments from this Sort of Traffic, but when we consider that it greatly retards the Settlement of the Colonies, with more useful Inhabitants, and may, in Time, have the most destructive Influence, we presume to hope that the Interest of a few will be disregarded when placed in Competition with the Security and Happiness of such Numbers of your Majesty's dutiful and loyal Subjects.*

Deeply impressed with these Sentiments, we most humbly beseech your Majesty to remove all those Restraints on your Majesty's Governors of this Colony, which inhibit their assenting to such Laws as might check so very pernicious a Commerce.

Your Majesty's antient Colony and Dominion of Virginia *hath, at all Times, and upon every Occasion, been entirely devoted to your Majesty's sacred Person and Government, and we cannot forego this Opportunity of renewing those Assurances of the truest Loyalty, and warmest Affection, which we have so often, with the greatest Sincerity, given to the best of Kings, whose Wisdom and Goodness we esteem the surest Pledges of the Happiness of all his People.*

The said *Address* being read a second Time;

Resolved, Nemine contradicente, That the House doth agree with the Committee in the said Address, to be presented to his Majesty.

Resolved, That an Address be presented to his Excellency the Governor, to desire that he will be pleased to transmit the Address to his Majesty, and to support it in such Manner as he shall think most likely to promote the desirable End proposed.

Ordered, That the said Address be presented to the Governor by the Gentlemen who drew up the Address to his Majesty. . . .

Anthony Benezet to Granville Sharp, May 14, 1772

Granville Sharp Letterbook, The Library Company, Philadelphia, Pa.

In 1765 Granville Sharp, a former linen-draper turned junior civil servant in the Ordnance Office in London, saw a black slave, Jonathan Strong, who had been severely beaten, flogged, and left to die on the street. Sharp, deeply affected by the bloodied sight, was stirred to help Strong to gain his freedom in the courts. For two years, with suits and countersuits surrounding the Strong case, Sharp studied law. In 1769 he published The Injustice and Dangerous Tendency of Tolerating Slavery in England. *Now an ardent abolitionist, he fired off letters to numerous influential politicians and religious leaders, appealing for their support. He warned the Archbishop of Canterbury in May 1769 that British government was answerable for the heinous sins of slavery and "may draw heavy Judgments upon this Kingdom."*

On May 14, 1772, Anthony Benezet wrote the first of a notable series of letters which passed between these two indefatigable antislavery enthusiasts. It is an intriguing coincidence that even before their formal correspondence began, each had reprinted a work of the other—Sharp reprinted Benezet's A Short Account of Guinea *and Benezet reprinted Sharp's 1769 treatise. Sharp had continued his legal crusade in 1772 when he became actively involved in what later became a landmark case in the antislavery movement, the case of James Somerset. Anthony Benezet was not privy to the facts surrounding the Somerset deliberations or to the possible ramifications of the court decision, but in a few months he learned much of the story from its chief spokesman.*

Philadelphia ye 14th May 1772

Esteemed Friend Granville Sharp I have long been desirous of having an opportunity to communicate & advice with such well minded Persons in England who have a Prospect of the Iniquity of the Slave Trade and are concerned to prevent its Continuation. And I should have been well pleased to have wrote to thee thereon had I known how to direct particularly as I had taken the freedom to republish but a part of thy acceptable & I trust serviceable Treatise on that interesting Subject, but now finding by a Letter I received from my respected Friend John Wesley that he is acquainted with thee and having a good opportunity by my Friend Captain Falconer Master of the Britannia I make free affectionately to Salute and send thee some copies of a Treatise lately published here on that iniquitous Traffic, giving the best account of its Origine, Progress &c which we have been able to procure. I doubt not but it may be amended and enlarged by some more able Hand, on your side the Water. I trust thou wilt excuse the freedom we have taken in so much curtailing thy Treatise; we esteem the whole to be very instructive and much to the matter nevertheless it was thought most expedient to abridge it for different reasons, one of which was from the general disposition of the People here whose attention was most likely to be drawn so far as to be willing to read it if limited to that part which immediately concerns us, I trust the generosity of thy heart will excuse the freedom we have taken, even tho' thou should not quite approve of our Reasons for so doing. It is certainly incumbent on every Lover of God & Man to use their best endeavours that a Stop may be put to this unnatural and barbarous Traffic as well on Account of its dreadfull Effect on the poor Negroes in the devastation it occasions in their Country, the destruction & intolerable suffering it entails on those who remain in Bondage & their Offspring, but yet much more so in the Case of their Lordly Oppressors, the People of the West Indies and Southern Colonies, to whom this dreadfull evil will, in its Consequences extend beyond time even in the Regions of Eternity by corrupting their Morals and hard'ning their Hearts to so great a Degree, that they and their offspring become alienated from God, estranged from all good and are hastening to a State of greater far greater and more deeply corrupt Barbarity, than that from whence our Northern Progenitors sprung, before their acquaintance with Christianity. Proof of this is not wanting, it appears even from the wicked Laws, which thou hast quoted in thy Treatise, which bad as they are thro' fear or favour, are seldom put in Execution, and also from the most miserable education of their Youth, who from their Childhood being trained up in willfullness, Pride, Idleness and Tyranny over their Slaves, grow up in Licentiousness and Riot.

My friend John Wesley gives me expectation he will consult with thee, about the expediency of making some weekly publication in the Publick Prints, on the Origine, Nature and dreadfull Effects of the Slave Trade; which appears absolutely necessary, as many well minded People, who may have some Influence are ignorant of the Case; and also, because, way may, thereby, be made for a farther Attempt; towards the removal of this potent Evil, to which we think nothing will so effectually conduce, as a Representation to the King and both Houses of Parliament; this is what we have a right to do and what will, at least, be a Testimony on the behalf of Truth, indeed, we cannot be at the same time *Silent* and *innocent* Spectators of the most horrid Scene, if rightly considered, in itself and in its Consequences that was perhaps ever acted upon the Face of the Earth. I have wrote to several of the principal Persons amongst our Friends, the Quakers, on this head, earnestly requesting they would consider whether as they are better acqtd with the prodigious iniquity and dreadfull Consequences attendant on this Practice, and had so publickly in their general yearly Epistle, to their Churches everywhere declared their abhorence of it, it was not their Duty, either as a people, or by their Principal Members, to endeavour the removal of it, by such a Representation. I have also mentioned the matter and sent some of the last and former Treatises to our Agent Benjamin Franklin who, I know, has a due sense of its iniquity and evil consequences; and would, I am persuaded, use his influence, in endeavouring, that an End should be put to the trade. I published in the Year 1767 a smaller Treatise on this Head entitled A Caution to Great Britain & her Colonies &c: which our Meeting has transmitted to the Meeting in London, requesting they would cause it to be Reprinted and put into the Hands of the several Members of Parliament, which was accordingly done, and an Account transmitted to us that Six Hundred Copies had been actually delivered to, or left at the Lodgings of so many Members of both Houses of Parliament & this was done with a View to forward the design of a National Enquiry, and I have the more hopes of the good effect which may attend an immediate Application to the King, and also the Queen (who bears so amiable a Character) from a paragraph which appeared in Our News Papers of this month, vizt: "*We hear that a Parliamentary Enquiry into the Conduct of the East India Company in Bengal was originally proposed by a great Personage who was much shocked* with the Account he received of the "oppression exercized over the poor Natives." Will anything less than such an Application excuse us to God the Common Father of Mankind, when inquisition is made for the blood of so many Thousands, and tens of thousands, may I not say Hundreds of Thousands of our Fellow Men (I.E. our Neighbours, who weare by the Gospel enjoined to love as ourselves) so unjustly shed and yet shedding daily, by Our Nation under the Sanction of Laws made by our Representatives in Parliament What shall We do when God riseth up and when he visiteth? What shall We answer him? Did not he that made them make us, and did not one fashion us in the Womb. I beg and earnestly entreat by the Mercies of God (that this matter of an Applicatn to the King and Parliament may be weighty with you) by those Mercies that each of us shall ere long and perhaps very soon recur to, when we shall have, with the greatest Joy or Grief, to remember that Mercy is, with the Blessing, promised to the mercifull; and fullness of Heart to those who truly hunger and thirst after Righteousness, who sincerely Breath, that Sin & Iniquity may be suppressed & righteousness cover the Earth, as the Waters cover the Sea. The Mode of such a representation you may better Judge of than we can pretend to point out, I doubt not, but thou wilt upon enquiry, find more well minded people ready to cry you good speed in this weighty Service, than you are aware of; the most solid amongst all Dissenters, particularly the Presbyterians, would be well pleased to see an End put to the Slave-Trade; and many to Slavery itself; the People of New England have made a Law that nearly amounts to a prohibition of the Trade and, I am informed, have proposed to the Governor & Council that all Negroes born in the Country should be free at a certain Age. I know the flood of Impiety & Selfishness which as a Torrent seems to overflow, will be a great Discouragement; but let us remember, that the Lord's power is above the power of Darkness; his hand is not shortened, that he cannot save by few as well as many. The People of Maryland and Virginia are so convinced of the unexpediency, if not all, of the iniquity of any further importation of Negroes, that a prudent Person, who spent some time in those provinces, tells me, he thinks ten or twenty thousand people would freely join in a Petition to the Parliament against any further import. As perhaps the danger of encreasing the Number of Negroes in the Islands and Colonies, may have Influence on the Government to prohibit any further Import, it may not be amiss to observe, that, by a late Computation, there is about Eight Hundred and Fifty Thousand Negroes in the English Colonies and Islands: In Jamaica alone, by the Pole Tax, in that Island, for the year 1768 it appears, there was then 166,914 taxable Negroes, doubtless there was enough more who either eluded the Tax or who where not taxable, to make up two hundred thousand, and by the best Account I can obtain, not many more if any, but fifteen thousand Whites; and the trade for Slaves still carried on with such Vigour, that we have reason to conclude, there is still yearly, at least an hundred thousand violently brought from Africa, by the English alone; these are employ'd to make some new Settlements, as in the Island Tobago, St Vincents &ca; & also to make up Deficiencies and to sell to the Spaniards.

I remain thy Friend

Anthony Benezet

To Granville Sharp
I shall take it kind if thou wilt send me a few lines in answer.

Granville Sharp to Anthony Benezet, August 21, 1772

The Quaker Collection, Haverford College Library, Haverford, Pa.

In 1771 James Somerset, a black slave from America, escaped from his master while in England. Subsequently recaptured, Somerset was placed on board a ship bound for Jamaica to be sold again into slavery. When Granville Sharp, actively engaged in his antislavery campaign, took Somerset's case to the courts, the affair took on absorbing dimensions. Sharp sought a definitive decision on the legality of slavery in England. Writing to a friend shortly before the trial, he remarked, "I have long formed my Opinion upon the subject, and am thoroughly convinced that the State of Slavery, in which a Negro may be before his arrival in England, gives no title whatever to Service here, either on the ground of property, or on the presumption of a Contract."

Lord Chief Justice Mansfield, after twice adjourning the case, recommending settlement out of court, and urging Parliament to legislate in lieu of a court decision, finally concluded the case in June 1772. His reluctant decision was: "The state of Slavery . . . is so odious that nothing can be suffered to support it but positive law. Whatever inconvenience therefore may follow from the decision, I cannot say this case is allowed or approved by the law of England; and therefore the black must be discharged." The justice recognized no positive law sanctioning the sale or seizure of slaves on British soil. To reformers like Sharp and Anthony Benezet, this was a concrete precedent upon which to build. And as Sharp's letter on August 21, 1772, indicates, the two men would plot strategies and devise tactics for their continued antislavery assault.

Dear Sir— I return you many thanks for the books which I reced from Captn Falconer, as also your letter.—Before I receiv'd it I began to draw up some arguments ag:st Slavery, in order to communicate them to my friends, before the next meeting of Parliamt: but thro' continual employment in my business &c I have proceeded very slowly and have not yet finished them, and shall not I fear for some time longer.—My former tracts were built chiefly upon the laws of England, but my present work is, for the most part, founded on Scripture, to obviate the doctrines of some late Writers and disputers who have ventured to Assert, that Slavery is not inconsistent with the Word of God.—You need not have made an Apology for having Abridg'd my book, it is sufficient satisfaction to find thereby that you thought it capable of doing some service in a cause which we have both of us so much at heart &c—

Some copies of your book arrived here very opportunely, just before the famous cause of Jas. Somerset ag:st Cha: Steward Esqr. came to a hearing, in the Court of Kings bench, Doctr Fothergill having made me a present of a copy I desired him to procure as many copies as he could, and he accordingly sent me 5 more, which I immediately disposed of as follows, one to Lord Mansfield, one to Lord North and the other four to the four learned Counsel who had generously undertaken to plead gratis for Jas Somerset.—I have since sent copies to all the Judges, as also copies of a little tract which I printed upon the same Occasion, as an Appendix to my former book, to obviate some false prejudices relating to the doctrines of *Property in Slaves*. I have sent you a copy of the judgmt given by Lord Mansfield in the case of Somerset, this judgmt would have done Ld Mansfield honor had he not all long seemed inclined to the other side of the Question. After the 2d days argument before any Judicial determination was given he advised the West India Merchts to apply to Parliamt while they continued to sit; and Mr Ross Fuller accordingly made a Motion in the house for "*Securing property in negroes and other Slaves* in this kingdom". however he did not succeed, but it is apprehended, that he and the other West India Merchants will use their Utmost endeavors to carry their point next sessions. It is on this account that I have now undertaken to write once more upon the subject, in order to apprize disinterested people of the dangerous tendency of such a measure. I shall endeavor to prepare what few friends I have in Parliamt, for an oppositn to such a destructive proposal in case it should again be renewed. I had thoughts once of addressing myself to the Bishop and Clergy in order to shew them the necessity of uniting their influence & interest on this occasion; but I have since had an opportunity of throwing this business upon the Arch Bishop of York, whose application to his Brethren the Clergy would certainly be effectual if he should approve of my hint, and should think such a Measure likely to be Attended with success. I have the satisfaction however to be inform'd that he is become *a Zealous advocate for freedom* and is desirous of doing every service to the cause that he can.—Your proposal of petitioning Parliamt is certainly very proper, if the subject of the petition be confined to the *African Slave trade* which is protected & encouraged by Parliament; but with respect to the Toleration of Slavery *in the Colonies*, I apprehend the British Parliament has no right to interfere, and that your Petition on this head shou'd be addressed *only to the King, or the King in Council*,—my reason for this Opinion I wrote at large in a letter to a person of Weight in the Ministry; a copy of which I send you inclosed. Because I think our brethren of the Colonies can't be too much upon their Guard with respect to the dignity & independence of their own assemblies.—You mention the informn you have receiv'd from a person who had spent some time in Maryland & Virginia, *that he thinks* 10 or 20 thousand people wou'd freely join in a Petitn to Parlt ag:st the further importation of Negroes, such a Petitn would retrive in some respect the honor of those colonies, and be a glorious proof that they are not destitute of Christian & Social principles, and it wou'd probably lay the foundation for a total prohibition of that most abomin:ble traffic. Yet as I have mentioned above, respect must be had to the rights of the Colonies, and a Petitn from thence if address'd to the Parlt ought to relate to the Slave trade in genl, with its bad effects & dangerous Consequences in general, and not merely to the *importation of Slaves into the Colonies*, because *they have a right themselves to prohibit such importatn*, respectively, in their own assemblies, with the Kings Concurrence; which they will be sure to obtain *in this matter* if it is ask'd by a Majority.—But with respect to the Petitn to Parlt against the iniquity of the Slave trade in general and its bad effects in the Colonies, if you could procure even less than a thousand hands I shou'd think it a very considerable point gain'd as it would aford an excellent argument ag:st the pretended necessity of holdg Slaves in the Colonies, which is always Alleged as the reason of the encouragemt: given by Parlt: to the African trade; a Petitn also to the King from a *small number* if a larger one or a Majority cannot be obtained ag:st the *Toleration of Slavery in the Colonies* might have very good effects, for tho' it wou'd not be likely to succeed in *the whole* yet it might at least Occasion the setting on foot some wholesome regulations by way of restraint in the Masters. I am told of some regulations that have taken place in the Spanish Colonies which do the Spaniards much honor, and are certainly worthy our imitation in case we shou'd not be so happy as to obtain an entire Abolition of Slavery: and probably you would find many American Subjects that would be willing to promote *such regulations*, tho' the same people would tremendously oppose the scheme of a *total Abolition of Slavery*. I have never seen an Acct of the Spanish Regulations in Writing but I understand that they are to the followg effect.—As soon as a Slave is landed his name price &c are registered in a public Register, and the Master is obliged by Law to Allow him one *Working day* in every week, to himself, *besides Sunday*; so that if the Slave chooses to Work for his Master on that day he receives the Wages of a Freeman for it; and whatever he gains by his labor on that day is so secured to him by law that the Master cannot deprive him of it. As soon as the Slave is able to purchase *another Working day* the Master is obliged to sell it to him at a proportionate price Viz:t 1/5 part of his orig.l Cost; and so likewise the Remg 4 days at the same rate as soon as the slave is able to redeem them; after wch he is absolutely free. This is such encouragement to industry, that even the most indolent are tempted to exert themselves.—Men who have thus worked out their freedom are enured to the labor of the Country and are certainly the most useful subjects that a Colony can acquire.—Regulations might be formed upon the same plan, to encourage the industry of Slaves, that are *already imported into the Colonies* which wou'd teach them how to maintain themselves, and be as useful as well as less expensive to the Planter. They would by such means become members of Society, and have an Intst in the Welfare of the Community, which wou'd add greatly to the Strength & security of each Coly. Whereas at present many of the Planters are in continual danger of being cut off by their Slaves, a fate which they but too justly deserve.

Be pleas'd to inform me whether you shall be likely to procure any such Petit:ns or Memorials as are mentioned above, because I would endeavor to prevail on some of the Bishops to present the Mem:ls that are for the King; as also on S:r Geo: Savile, or some other respectable Member of the lower House to present the Petit:n to Parl:t.—I shou'd not mention this did I not apprehend that the Colony Agents in Genl are rather prejudiced in favor of the Slave trade, on acct of their Connections & continual intercourse with Interested people; but yet this matter will require good Considn: because the business is certainly in the Regular Channel, when conducted by your own Agents. Lord Dartmouth, who is lately appointed Secretary for the Colonies is esteemed a humane & religious man, and his Mediation with the King & Council might probably be very efficacious were he applied to from your side the Water by way of Memorial accompanying the Petit:n &c if sign'd by any Respectable number of American Subjects, and then the business wou'd be in a regular tract. I need not assure you how much you have my Good Wishes for Prosperity & success in your benevolent undertakings & that I shall always think myself happy in lending what little assistance may happen to be in my power &c &c

Signed

Granville Sharp.

Old Jewry London Augst 21:st 1772

James Swan, *A Disuasion to Great Britain*, 1772

James Swan, *A Disuasion to Great-Britain and the Colonies from the Slave Trade to Africa. Shewing The Contradiction this Trade Bears, both to Laws divine and provincial; the Disadvantages arising from it, and Advantages from abolishing it, both to Europe and Africa, particularly to Britain and the Plantations. . .* (Boston, 1772), pp. v-xvi; 17-24; 28-36; 41-55; 61-70.

In 1772 James Swan, a British merchant who had recently arrived in Boston, published a lengthy pamphlet, A Disuasion to Great Britain. *Attacking slavery on many grounds—religious, economic, and moral—Swan, in his self-styled "sermon," threatened every "Merchant and Shipmaster who is in this Trade of Man-slavery" with the wrath of God, terrible punishment which could not only affect them but also "their children unto the third and fourth generation. . . ." Although this pamphlet was apparently Swan's only contribution to the growing body of antislavery literature, it had a pronounced effect. In 1773, at the request of several blacks in Boston, Swan revised the piece. He dedicated it to the governor and legislature of Massachusetts and presented them with a copy to submit with the blacks' own petition against slavery.*

The Dedication

To all Friends to LIBERTY.

Fellow Subjects, It is to you I dedicate this Treatise, and beg your protection of the same, hoping it will meet with a kind reception.

The approbation men of character and sense have given the following Work, has made me venture it into your hands: And I hope in the perusal you will keep in view the Author, I am certain you cannot then fail of making great allowances. I am a *North-Briton!* And when you know that, it alone may be judged by some, sufficient to brand me with the hateful name of *Tory*, and thereby condemn this Dissuasion. But let me inform you (for there is no general rule without an exception) that I am a most sincere well-wisher to the common cause of *Liberty*, both *personal* and *constitutional*; then you will, give me a place in the list of your staunch Friends, and accept of this Attempt, as intended to be a mean of abolishing one great part of *Slavery* here.

If there is any merit in endeavouring to set free from *Bondage* our fellow creatures, and in trying to promote the good and welfare of any nation, province, country, or individual, surely I may claim it; for my sincere endeavour is to these purposes: And if I should happen to miss my aim, I shall sit down satisfied with the merit of a good intent.

Readers, I have but one favour to ask of you, which is, to peruse this Performance with an open unbiased mind; overlooking any defects you may observe in these sheets, knowing they are the hasty and undigested thoughts of the Author, put together with more good intent than ability; after this you may either reject or practice, according to your own consciences, and the light of this Treatise, if there is any to be found in it. *Enslaving* your fellow men, and using and massacring them as they do in the *West-Indies* and Southern Provinces, is a matter of too great importance to be only slightly thought of. And as I hope you have the *humanity* of *Britons*, and that *love of Liberty*, with which every true *Englishman* is, or ought to be possessed of, you will not countenance it, but declare yourselves as I do *well-wishers of the British Empire, and consequently enemies to* Slavery.

Accept then, Friends and Brethren in one common cause, this small token of that love and veneration which I bear to freedom, (for no country can be called free where there is one Slave) and give me leave to subscribe myself,

Your Friend and humble Servant,

James Swan.

The Preface

I had not well arrived in *America*, when casting my eyes on so many Black Slaves, I immediately found a warm inclination arise in my breast, to do my endeavours for relieving them by publishing to the world my sentiments upon their state.

Scarce had I time to draw a breath of this air, before I immediately applied myself to enquire into the state of this *Slavery*, and the constitution upon which it is founded, and having met with proper preliminaries by way of foundation for a small Treatise, I set myself to work in forming, and in short finished this Pamphlet.

From the consideration of the smallness of this production, and my inability to treat the subject properly, I was nigh resolving not to prefix my name hereto: But thinking again, some opposite party might take hold of that, I thought it most proper to shew my common signature, knowing the cause I defend is good and well founded.

Some will no doubt be surprised that I have wrote this Dissuasion after the form of a Sermon: It is easily accounted for. A Sermon being *a discourse of instruction pronounced by a Divine for the edification of the people.* I am no Divine nor ever expect to be; but I hope that is no reason why these sheets should not be of publick benefit, as my design was for that end; I chose to write it in this form, as being the truest way to display with perspicuity and plainness the unlawfulness, *&c.* of the Slave Trade, for which purpose I have attempted it in different heads and branches, in some of which are contained many pertinent remarks or observations on this inhuman Commerce; and I thought further, it was the easiest method for myself, and plainest for my Readers; it being intended for the weakest and highest capacities.

It may be objected by some, that the writings on this subject are too numerous already. I answer, that however many there may be extant, (although I could find but very few) yet there are none so full as not to admit of amendments or improvements: If so, and that these may not altogether be of inconsiderable use to mankind, why may not I make them? and why may they not be transmitted to mankind?

A Treatise of this kind may not be unnecessary, notwithstanding many Books, Pamphlets, and Letters have been published on the subject.

But however ineffectual this Treatise may prove hereafter among men, this I comfort myself with, it is as full, considering the largeness, as any upon the subject which I have seen; and there are few arguments that possibly could be advanced, or citations drawn from Scripture concerning man-selling, *&c.* that have escaped, in trying to wean men from this base and inhuman trade. And in fine, if this Work meets with encouragement equal to the Author's care and endeavours to make it the most useful of the kind, by having the desired effect he shall esteem himself sufficiently rewarded.

With regard to the Dissuasion, I leave the Reader to judge, after having read it over cooly and impartially, whether it ought to be approved or disapproved; if the former, it will no doubt meet with his protection in publick. But I have something to ask, which I beg may not be refused, and that is, if you have not a fund of patience laid up in store, before you begin to peruse it, you are requested to lay it aside, until you have.

There is one finall part of it taken from *Postlethwayt's* Dictionary of Commerce. Another part from *A. Benezett's* Caution to *Great-Britain* and her Colonies, both which Authors I am very glad were born before me, they having assisted me so far. And with regard to the remaining part, I can tell where it came from.

As it is necessary in order to bring about a change in any, particularly a publick affair, to touch the minds of the people with a just and true sense of the unlawfulness of the thing wanted to be removed, that to the end they may be unanimous in the abolishment thereof; this Dissuasion I am convinced you will find upon perusal, is calculated for that purpose, and am very sensible, that it alone never can strike the great blow without the legislative force added to it

I will detain you no longer; indeed I have almost run into an Introduction amidst this Preface: But it could not well be otherwise, the connexion between them was so great, and had I separated them, I shonld have incurred your displeasure, by increasing the Prolegomenas to a degree larger than the Dissuasion itself.

J. S.

A Dissuasion, *&c.*

The subject of which these few sheets treat, would have been one of the last I should have ventured upon; had not the delusion of the men who are concerned in enslaving the people called *Negroes* appeared so glaring, and the contradiction that the *Slave Trade* bears to Christianity, prompted me to it.

I Shall be as cool and impartial in treating of this matter, as any British subject or Christian can: But why do I say cool? It is impossible I should speak cooly of such base, unchristan, and inhuman practices, in a land of Liberty and Christianity: However, in case any thing should be mentioned in the sequel that may give unintended offence to any person, I hope the tender feelings for these distressed Captives, with which I am possessed, and the warmth that is in my breast, to have this Trade abolished, will be sufficient excuse.

I propose dividing the following Treatise into these different heads.

I. Shew, that this custom of making Slaves of our fellow-men, is expressly against the revealed laws of God.

II. That it is likewise against the law of nature, and the Charter of this Province.

III. The disadvantages arising from this base Trade.

IV. The advantages arising from abolishing it. And,

V. Conclude with a short admonition to those concerned, and a method to put the Trade of *Africa* on a just and lawful footing.

The first-head was, That the custom of making Slaves of our fellow creatures, is expressly against the revealed laws of God. And in treating of this part, I shall divide it into the following branches. 1st. By the laws of God, *He that stealeth and selleth a man, shall be put to death.* 2d. *He in whose hands he shall be found, shall be put to death*, by the same laws. 3d. *He that buyeth a Servant and serveth him six years, shall set him free the seventh, and furnish him liberally with what he hath.* And 4th. *If thy Brother*, that is, your fellow-creature, *be sold unto thee, thou shall not compel him to serve as a Bond-man; but as an hired Servant.*

The first branch under this head is, *He that stealeth and selleth a man, shall be put to death.* This is one of the most express laws of *Moses*, as you may see in *Exod.* xxi. 16, two first, and last clauses of the verse, there mentioned in the most peremptory words; *And he that stealeth a man, and selleth him, shall surely be put to death.* It certainly can be looked upon in no other light in the Merchants and Ship-masters who are in this Trade to *Africa*, than stealing of men, being accessary to and aiding in inciting them to war one with another, and for this purpose, supplying them with prodigious quantities of arms and ammunition, whereby they are hurried into confusion, bloodshed, and all the extremities of temporal misery, which must consequently beget in their minds such a general detestation and scorn of the Christian name, as may deeply affect, if not wholly preclude, their belief of the great truths of our holy religion. Thus an insatiable desire of gain prevails with their Kings, who, instead of being protectors of their people, for this alluring bait laid before them, by the *European* and *American* Factors, or Ship-masters, invade the Liberties of these unhappy people, and occasion their opression. These Kings, whenever they want goods send to the Ship-masters, acquainting them they have Negroes, and sometimes the Factors and Ship-masters send to acquaint them, that they have a quantity of goods, and want Slaves for the same. These Chiefs, whether they have Slaves then or not, agree, and immediately go to war with their neighbours, and in procuring three or four hundred prisoners, burn five or six towns, . . .

It is a known custom among the Factors who reside in *Africa*, and the Ship-masters who trade there, to corrupt many Negroes on the sea coast, who stop at no act of cruelty for gain. They make it a practice, to steal abundance of little Blacks of both sexes, when found on the roads, or in the fields, where their Parents keep them all day to watch the corn, &c. Can it be denied that the *Africans* are *stolen* after so many proofs of it, and if it is not direct stealth in the Ship-masters, *&c.* yet it is the same in effect; for if they did not go there and entice the Chiefs with money or goods, there would be no wars, as is the case at present; and there would be none stolen if the stealers were not bribed by the Factors or Ship-masters; and not only those that are made Slaves of, there would still be ten thousand others who are killed in the broils, that would be saved, were they to discontinue this base Trade.

Thus far I have shewn that they are stolen. They may say they pay for them. I answer, they give money or goods by way of price to some of the Princes and Negroes, who, for the sake of lucre, take them prisoners by war or stealth, so that what money they give these scoundrels, (forgive me the expression; for, what name can a man expect who would take his Father or Brother and sell them for gain?) who take them in these ways cannot be looked upon as a price paid in lieu, for the Negroes themselves never condescend to be mancipated, as they get none of the money that is pretendedly given for them. They at length arrive at the port, the Ship-master sell them at a most exorbitant profit, and in a few voyages he makes what he calls his fortune; this is all he aimed at and wished for; and what follows, secures his eternal destruction, unless timely repented of: For the truth of this, I could mention very striking instances of men, who I see almost every day; but I do not chuse mentioning names, for fear of seeing them contemned and despised by every well thinking person. . . .

The second branch was, *If he be found in his hands, he surely shall be put to death.* This is the third and fourth clause of the before cited verse in *Exod. If he be found in his hands.* This is to be understood in two senses, either found in the Ship-master's hands who stole him, or bought, as he says, or in the person's hands who purchases him. As to the first of these senses in which this passage may be taken, if the laws of God, yea, even of man, were to be put into execution, he, the stealer, or even the buyer, would be punished with death, for it is clear as to Man-stealing, that it deserves death, by the above passage of Scripture, and it is no less with regard to buying: But why do I say buying? For no money can be equal to the worth of a man: Buying, I admit that word because Ship-masters and others in this Trade, say, for their justification that they purchased the Negroes, but as there are no laws, either of God or man, for the buying and stealing of *Africans,* I am inclined to think it cannot be supposed, but they justly deserve death. And in the second sense, the man who buys the *Africans* or Negroes is still as culpable as the stealer, and liable to the same punishment, for Scripture does not point out particularly either of them, but only just, *If he be found in his hands,* that is, in any man's hands, so that it can be proved he stole or bought him, *he surely shall be put to death.*

The third part was, *He that buyeth a Servant and serveth him six years, shall set him free the seventh, and furnish him liberally with what he hath.* The first part of this branch is proved in three different texts, *viz Exod.* xxi. 2. *Deut.* xv. 12. and *Jer.* xxxiv. 14. In all which parts it is expressly mentioned, *That if an* Hebrew *Servant be sold unto thee,* or if you buy him he *shall serve thee six years, and the seventh, thou shall let him go free from thee*, that is, he shall pay nothing for his Liberty.

Some persons for argument sake may object to this, saying, these people are not *Hebrews*, as mentioned in these texts of Scripture, but *Heathens*. This may be difficult enough to determine. However, admit they are *Heathens*, (although it is well known they are not) it must be owned by those who know them, that the natives of *Africa* have exalted notions of a Deity. It is an odd method these Traders take to civilize and teach them the Christian religion, by importing one hundred thousand of them yearly into *Virginia* and other Southern Provinces, together with the *West-India* Islands, where they are kept in greater darkness than before, as they are not allowed to worship God on the Sabbath; but are employed in worldly business on that day, which is a scandal to the Rulers of the *British* Colonies and Islands where such things are practised. It is subversive of the Christian religion not to allow those ignorant people the benefit of it, who make up more than two thirds of the inhabitants of the beforementioned places. It is expressly against the laws of God; for he gave *Paul* and other Apostles commission to go and preach the gospel to every nation, kindred, and tongue; but instead of that, where the gospel is preached throughout the *British* Colonies, and where these people might expect to receive the light of it; I say, instead of that, they are kept from divine worship on Sundays, and never once in their lifetime admitted to church, but obliged to cultivate their finall piece of ground allowed them by their Masters.

The last part of the verse runs thus, *And shall furnish him liberally with what he hath*. That is, when the Servant hath served thee six years, as expressed in Exod. xxi. 2, and *Deut*. xv. 12. *Then in the seventh year you shall let him go free from you*; and in ver. 13. *Thou shall not let him go away empty*. Ver. 14. *Thou shall furnish him liberally out of thy flock, and out of thy floor, and out of thy wine press; of that wherewith the* Lord *thy* God *hath blessed thee, thou shalt give him. This is in token that thou dost acknowledge the benefit that thou hast received by his labours*. Marg. Bible.

It is still further required to set your Servants or Bond-men free at the above appointed time, by the 15th verse of the same chap. *And thou shalt remember that thou wast a Bond-man in the land of* Egypt, *and the* Lord *thy* God *redeemed thee, therefore I command thee this thing to day. I command thee*. You are ordered, yea, commanded to do *this thing*. What thing? To set free your Bond-Servants after six years service. You are commanded to do it *to day, viz*. At the expiration of six years, for, says God, by the voice of his Servant, *I command thee this thing to day*.

There is a blessing promised to those who do this thing in ver. 18 of the above chap. After enjoining that it may not seem hard unto you in sending away this Servant, as he hath been worth a double hired one, in serving thee six years, he says, *and the* Lord *thy* God *shall bless thee in all that thou doest*. Sweet encouragement for poor sinful souls! To be blessed in every thing that they do. What man will forfeit this great blessing for the sake of the service of one, two, or more Servants for life? Will he allow himself to be cursed by God in every thing that he doeth for the small gain he can make by their services? This charming promise of a blessing in all that thou doest, and the dreadful events that may take place in contradicting the command of God, I hope will make such impressions upon the minds of men, that they will not bind Servant to serve above six years; but will set him at liberty in the seventh year, and give him liberally of what the Lord hath blessed them with, as required in the above cited text. If you think you have not enough of this, pass along to

The fourth and last section on this head, *if thy Brother be sold unto thee, thou shall not compel him to serve as a Bond-man; but as an hired Servant.* This is proved by *Lev.* xxv. 39, 40. where it is said, *If thy Brother that dwelleth by thee be waxen poor, and be sold unto thee, thou shalt not compel him to serve as a Bond-servant.* This is expressly against making Slaves of any of our poor Brethren, or compeling them to serve as Bond-servants. *If thy Brother that dwelleth by thee be waxen poor,* are the words of the verse; the poor *Africans* who fall into the hands of the Men-wolves that prowl on their coasts, are obliged to serve their lifetime, and their children after them: This is being Bond-men with a witness, and as we have great reason to believe they are poor enough when they steal them, they are kept so forever after, not having means to make a penny themselves. The *Africans* will be understood, if not primarily intended, to be the people mentioned in this text! It is said, *Thy Brother who dwelleth by thee*: When they are in *Africa* it is certain they are at a great distance; but when they come to *America* or the *West-Indies* they then dwell by us; therefore I think, from the above citations, no person can buy these people, and oblige them and their children to serve as Slaves, without incuring the displeasure of God and his punishments for disobeying his just commands.

It may be added, as in v. 42d of the same chap. *For they are my servants, which I brought forth out of* Eygpt; *they shall not be sold as Bond-men.* The last part of this verse is expressly against *selling* them as Bond-men. Should it be objected, that the *Africans* were not *brought forth out of the land of* Egypt, it would not affect the controversy. I would sincerely advise every man who is in this abominable Trade not to persist in it, seeing the many threats and commands against him in God's laws, and the blessings that are promised if he does not.

The IId General Head proposed, is, That this practise of making Slaves of our Brethren is likewise against the law of nature, and the Charter of this Province. The first part of this head, may be easily proved by the following texts of Scripture; *Matt.* vii. 12. *Therefore all things whatsoever ye would that men should do to you, do ye even so to them. Luke* vi. 31. *And as you would that men should do to you, do ye so to them likewise.* Who is that proud one that will not receive these instructions? And who is that man that will do unto any person, either white or black, Christian or Savage, contrary to what he would that he should do to him? This would be acting contrary to reason and common sense. Would any person consent to have himself torn from his friends and native country, and be made a Slave for life, and to have his dear, dear little children continue in the same condition from one generation to another? No; surely no person would agree to that. Well then, it certainly must be contrary to the laws of nature, christianity, and subversive of the texts just quoted, which were wrote for our direction and guidance in this world. It is likewise certain, that those who carry on this Trade, do not unto men as they would men should do to them; for if these poor people which they, the Ship-masters take from their own Country and then sell for Slaves, were doing to them as they are done to, they would (were it in their power, which seldom is the case, the owners being conscious of the wrong they are doing, and dreading what naturally would follow) revenge the injury they receive in being made Slaves, and resume that Liberty again, which was wrongful-taken from them; I say, they would often revenge the injury offered them by killing the Captain of the ship who had taken them to be mancipated for life, and would serve in the same manner the Owners of the vessel if they could get them, who are no better than the Masters, in putting them into such employ. Who could find fault with them? No person. They were only retrieving the most common blessing we enjoy, Liberty, and instead of being punished, the law would protect them in so noble an action. But,

Readers, before I leave this, let me beg you to "bring the matter home to yourselves, and think whether any condition in life can be more completely miserable than that of those distressed Captives. On reflecting, that each of them had some tender attachments which were broke by the cruel separation! Some Parent or Wife who had not an opportunity of mingling tears in a parting embrace! Perhaps some infant or aged Parent whom his labour was to feed, and vigilance protect! and himself under the dreadful apprehensions of perpetual Slavery." . . .

I think it is time to leave this part and go to the last, *viz.* That this base custom is likewise against the Charter of this Province; as is clearly and most simply demonstrated by a clause in said Charter, granted by King *William* and Queen *Mary*, dated at *Westminster*, the 7th of *October*, in the third year of their reign, wherein, *inter alia*, it is established and ordained, *That all and every of the Subjects of Us, our Heirs, and Successors, which shall go to and inhabit within our said Province and territory, and every of their Children which shall happen to be born there, or on the seas in going thither, or returning from thence, shall have and enjoy all* Liberties *and immunities of* Free *and natural Subjects within the dominions of Us, Our Heirs, and Successors, to all intents, constructions, and purposes whatsoever, as if they and every of them were born within our realm of* England. I need say but little as to this branch of the head further than to observe, that the clause of the Charter just cited, proves clearly, and which cannot be further disputed, *that all and every of the Subjects, the Inhabitants of* New-England, *which shall come to and inhabit within the Province and territory of the same, and every of their Children which shall happen to be born there, shall have and enjoy all the* Liberties, &c. *of* Free *and natural Subjects of the realm of* England. Indeed I am sorry to mention that this Charter should have been so long subverted and remained unobserved by the Publick in so interesting a point, when by timely observance it might have saved many thousands from slavery that are now dead and mouldered into dust. I hope this easy found light will not be too late discovered to direct and save the present Slaves from their Bondage, which many! too many! groan under: So that I expect the inhabitants of the *American* Provinces will not give any person an opportunity of charging them with that infamous character of making or keeping any man or woman Slaves, when they are complaining daily that their Liberties are wrested from them, and little think how they deprive these poor Black People of their Freedom, when there is as little reason for it as there is for making Slaves of *British* Subjects. The above cited clause in the Charter, says, *Those born in or shall come to and dwell within the Province of the* Massachusetts-Bay are Free; from which I am led to think, and which every person must see, will extend to Black as well as White. But, Reader, excuse me, whoever you are, that may take offence at my construing this clause of the Charter in the manner I have done, it is only my opinion, and every one is at liberty to enjoy his own sentiments upon it as well as I; therefore I flatter myself of hearing soon, that means will be taken by the Legislature of most, if not all the Provinces of *North-America*, and the *West-India* Islands, totally prohibiting the importation of Negroes into the *British* Plantations; and setting at Liberty with universal consent, every Negro throughout the whole, at least in *North-America*, which will be an honour to human nature, to say that this great and this only remaining hinderance to the absolute freedom as well as legality of the *English* trade is now happily and gloriously abolished; and then we may all cry with shouts of joy! which few more countries in the four quarters of the globe can, *That complete* Freedom *both in people and trade is allowed throughout the British Islands and Plantations in* America *and* the West-Indies?

The IIId General Head proposed was, To shew the disadvantages arising from this base Trade. This head I propose to consider separately, and shall 1st. Shew the disadvantages to *Africa* in taking so many of its natives away yearly. 2d. Treat of the hurt and prejudice of this Trade with *Europe*. 3d. Shew the disadvantages to the *British* Plantations in *America*, particularly to the *West-Indies*, in carrying Black People thither.

The first part of this head is, To shew the disadvantages to *Africa* in taking so many of its natives yearly. Before I enter upon this branch it may not be improper to mention a few observations which Mr. *Postlethwayt* makes upon the great qualities which this country abound with. "Its situation for commerce is certainly beyond any of the other quarters of the world, for it stands in the center between the other three, and has thereby a much nearer communication with *Europe*, *Asia*, and *America*, than any other quarter, has with the rest. It is wonderfully accommodated for commerce by the interposion of islands, and more particularly by the assistance of the trade winds, which render the navigation safe, easy, and constant. It is furnished with the greatest and most convenient navigable rivers, and perhaps with as many of them as any other of the chief parts of the world: Such are the *Nile, Nubia, Niger, Natal,* which are rivers of the first magnitude; besides these there are innumerable others, though not equal to the former, are yet very excellent streams, situated for navigation and commerce, and which by their noble courses penetrate far inland; if the *Europeans, &c.* would cultivate a human and Christian like commerce with the *Africans,* they might through these rivers become the medium of an endless beneficial commerce, The country is populous beyond credibility, the soil fruitful, the season for the greatest part mild and clement, and the air salubrious." I must stop in the midst of this agreeable description, being afraid of leading myself into an undue length in this narrative of the beautious perfection of that rich and fruitful part of the world.

I shall now consider the disadvantages to *Africa* in taking so many of its natives away yearly. But it is needless to speak much on this head, as most of my Readers will perceive the prejudices to *Africa* in thus draining it of the inhabitants yearly in the manner *Britain* and the Plantations do. I shall mention a few of them. 1st. There can be no loss to any country (particularly to one like *Africa* that is yet mostly to cultivate) equal to that of depopulating it. 2d. It prevents the inland country, where the incessant broils are carried on, from defending themselves against the attacks and encroachments made on their properties by the Kings and Chiefs, whereby many thousands of their subjects being taken prisoners, are sold to the Coasters, they being nourished and caressed by the *Europeans,* particularly by *Britain* and the Colonies, in doing so, for the sake of the Slave Trade to *America,* and the *West-Indies*; and further, in consequence of this depriving them of defending themselves against these base assaults, it prevents them entirely from cultivating and manuring that fruitful and rich country, to the degree it is capable of. 3d. It ever obstructs the civilizing of those people, and consequently of propagating amongst them the Christian religion, and extending the Trade into the bowels of *Africa,* which by contrary means might be easily practicable. 4th. That whilst the slaving Trade of those people, continue to be the great object of the powers that trade there it is to be feared it will ever, as it does at present spirit up wars and hostilities amongst the Negro Princes and Chiefs, for the sake of making captives of each other for sale. And 5th. The greatest disadvantage to *Africa,* by thus draining it of the inhabitants is, that it prevents them from cultivating and peopling that great fertile country, of introducing *European* arts and sciences amongst them, and of carrying on a friendly, civil, and christian Commerce with them into the heart of their region.

The second branch alluding to the third head was, to treat of the prejudice to *Africa,* and its trade with *Europe.* It is an absolute fact, that these people are incessently at war with their neighbouring Princes so that they cannot get their business looked into or followed, and consequently a great hinderance to the manufacturing such quantities of their country's produce of every kind, to send to *Europe* and *America, &c.* as they might do, were this Slave Trade abolished, and the Rulers in amity, friendship, and concord, one with another.

It is further a hurt to the *African* trade with *Europe,* for the Slave Trade has so gained upon the minds of those men that traffick to *Africa*, that they never once think of the other commodities, at least in such quantities as *Europe* might consume were the attention necessary paid to it by making this the only object of the traders notice, I believe it would turn out much more profitable to keep wholly to the produce of this country, *viz.* gums, ivory, gold and silver dust, *&c.* and to resign that base unchristian Trade of Man-selling.

Lastly, on this head, To shew the disadvantages to the *British* Plantations in *America, &c.* in bringing Black people into them. This will be made very easily appear when you consider, that these numerous Black People, which are yearly brought into the southern-most parts of *North America* and the *West-Indies* were very poor at that time, not having a penny to command, and never so much as once in their lifetime had it in their power to make one half that sum for themselves, so that the different Provinces in the Continent, and the Islands in the *West-Indies* are filled with these necessitous Black People, and must be put upon the townships to which they belong, in case this enslaving them be ever abolished, which I flatter myself, and I hope not vainly, will be done in time, and that with effect. Further, why do they fill their Plantations with Black People, so unnatural to the Whites, the Proprietors of the different Colonies, when it seems no way difficult to obtain White People to serve free in their stead? *Europe* in general affords numbers of poor and distressed objects for that purpose, and if these were not overworked, as the Negroes generally are, they would make as good Servants for the *American* and *West-India* Plantations as the Blacks do. And if the *Europeans* were upon a level with regard to the price of labour, in their Colonies, I cannot but think they would reap great advantage in laying aside the Slave Trade, and cultivate a friendly and civilized Commerce with the *Africans*. Until this is done it does not seem possible that the inland trade of that country should ever be extended to the degree it is capable of; for while the spirit of *Butchery* and making Slaves of each other, is promoted by the *Europeans, Americans, &c.* amongst those people, they will never be able to travel with safety into the heart of the country, or to cement such commercial friendship and alliance with them, as will actually introduce our arts and manufactures.

The IVth General Head was, To shew the advantages arising from abolishing this base custom. This Head I propose dividing into two parts, 1st. The advantages to *Africa*, and 2d. The advantages to *Europe* particularly to *Britain* and the Plantations in *America* and the *West-Indies*.

First to *Africa*. The advantages that would arise to it, in abolishing this base and unchristian-like Commerce are numerous, some of which may be comprehended under the following. 1st. The abolishing this Trade may be a means of peopling this country, and of cultivating it in the same manner with any other country in *Europe* or *Asia*, so as to render it capable of bearing in as great abundance as the *East-Indies*, spices of equal quality to those of *Banda, Ternate,* and *Amboyna*; I say, the like spices might be produced on the rich and fruitful shores of *Melinda* on the east side, or of the slave coast on the west side of *Africa*, and that as easy and to as great advantage, as where they are now raised; the latitude being the same, and soil not unlike; and, in short, cinnamon and all others, the production of *East* and *West-Indies*, by proper management might be raised here as well as in those parts. 2d. It would introduce the Christian religion among them, which is a shame to these nations who pretend to hold fast the principles of Christianity, to keep so long hid, and of consequence, be a means of bringing among them the more civilized arts and sciences. 3d. It will recommend the *European* dress, and introduce their customs among the natives, and of course civilize them like other Christian nations. Lastly. It will be a means of bringing this country to as great perfection in trade, riches, and grandeur, as any in *Europe*, it being a much more fertile and plentious soil for many valuable productions.

Much more could I say upon the numerous advantages arising to this excellent country: But let what has been said suffice, I leave the rest to the Reader's own feeling, if he has any, for this poor distressed *Africa* which groans under a heavy load of oppression.

The next thing in course is, the advantages that would arise to *Europe* in thus carrying on a Christian-like Commerce with *Africa*. This trade even in its present state, excluding that of the Slaves, is as advantageous as any that is now followed; and what will it be when a friendly traffick is carried on? It is as it were all profit, the first cost being some things of *European*, particularly of *British* manufactures, and others generally purchased with them; for which there is in return, gold, elephant's-teeth, wax, gums, cotton-wool, divers dying-woods, and Slaves: But this last piece of Commerce, *viz.* Man-slaving, I am far from making a part of the *British* trade, and I dare say every humane person will be likeminded. These are articles which the country abound in, and would be still cheaper to an immense degree, were the inland parts settled with their own people; but instead of that, a hundred thousand are yearly carried away. *Britain* pays but little for the commodities it exports to *Africa*, being mostly, as observed before, its own produce, such as worsted and conton cloths of all kinds, brass, iron, and copper work of every sort, particularly large quantities of all kinds of defensive arms, with powder and shot in proportion; *East-India* goods, every kind of *British* manufactures, and a good deal of *American* and *West-India* rum, &c. It is not easy to say what vast quantities of the above *British* and *American* productions would be exhausted yearly among so great a people, and in so very extensive a country, were the Slave Trade stopped. It is the interest of every Merchant in *Britain* and the Plantations who are now concerned in traffick to *Africa*, to cultivate the inland commerce in its utmost extent, as having no manner of concern with the Slave Trade, there being the greatest reason to believe, that where they now export twenty shillings worth of commodities thither, they would then export an hundred pound; and I am inclined to think when the trade comes to be extended to the degree it will admit of, notwithstanding those goods that are imported from *Africa*, there will still be discovered an infinite variety of trafficable articles, with which the present Traders are totally unacquainted, and this Trade become the most beneficial to *Britain*,

America, and the *West-Indies*, of any that is at present on foot, as it is common to every individual, and of which the government has taken much notice, by granting an annual sum of ten thousand pounds sterling for the maintaining and upholding the forts and castles in the *British* Settlements in *Africa*, so that they are entirely defended against the attacks of any enemy, and their Trade and Colonies secured by irresistible strength of forts and castles.

A Great deal more could be mentioned on the thousands of advantages that may arise to the interest of *Britain* and the Plantations in abolishing this wicked Trade: However, I shall detain my Readers no longer on this head, but as proposed,

Conclude the whole with some short admonitions to those concerned, and a method to put this Trade to *Africa* upon a just and lawful footing. I advise every Merchant and Shipmaster who is in this Trade of Man-slaving to renounce and give it up. What arguments or reason, pray, can be advanced for his justification, when he sees such threats and curses against him, particularly mentioned in the first head? Why should any person incur the penalties of God's Law so daringly for the sake of gain? Should they think themselves on a death-bed, what agonies and troubles of mind must they undergo in the thoughts of enslaving so many miserable creatures, of murdering so many thousands of innocent people in the wars they occasion, treacherously taking them out of their own country, using them barbarously, massacring numbers of them in all the cruel ways imaginable on the passage, selling them for life, and depriving them even of a comfortable living, notwithstanding they serve for nothing else; surely the judgment of God must come upon such men who will thus use their own Brethren who were born to inherit the same salvation with us, and if his judgment does not come upon them, it will pursue their children unto the third and fourth generation, until the riches that have been thus scandalously amassed be squandered away, and they become as poor as these Negroes themselves, by selling of whom such unjust gain was made. But this is only one way out of thousands that God chuses to afflict his enemies in this world. . . .

I would add one necessary query more, to those who hold the sword of justice, and who must account to God for the use they make of it. Since the *English* Law is so truly valuable for its justice, how can they overlook the barbarous deaths and wrongful Slavery of the unhappy *Africans*, without trial or proof of being guilty of crimes adequate to their punishments? Why are those Masters of vessels (who are not the most considerate of men) suffered to be sovereign arbiters of the lives of these miserable Negroes in their passage, and allowed with impunity to destroy, may I not say murder their fellow creatures in a manner so cruel as can never be related but with shame and horror? Answer me this, ye pretended Judges and Governors in the different Colonies where such practices are used, and not be shocked at the negligence you have sleeped in. Since you are put in remembrance of it now, I hope and sincerely wish, I, or any other person may not have occasion to remind you of the same again, but that you will punish with equity all those who import Negroes; there being hundreds of poor

Europeans that would be glad to come and serve in any of the *British* Plantations, and those that could not pay a passage doubtless would sell part of their time for it; and this I make no doubt, considering they have not the charge of their funeral and death-bed expences and sundry other things to pay, will come nigh if not full as cheap as buying and keeping Negroes; and it will be attended with this advantage, that these White people when they have served some years in the lowest capacities turn out upon the waste land, marry, and in a few years we see a town well settled, and in less than fifty years there will be an increase of fourfold; by this means the country will fill up and we become respectable and secure from an enemy, and furnished with every conveniency of life. And you Governors, *&c.* who have the legislative power in your hands will still further make Laws and put them in execution, stopping any further importation of Slaves into the Provinces or Islands where you are the Representative head, so that in that time they may furnish themselves with sufficient numbers, and by proper usage keep up that quantity which so much decrease by improper management. Now give me leave to proceed.

In a method to put this Trade to *Africa* on a just and lawful footing. First, in order to this, it is my humble opinion, if I may be allowed to give it, that there be a number of men who may chuse to venture in this Trade, both in *Britain* and the Colonies, that shall be incorporated into separate bodies by the name of *English*, or *British; American*, or *New England African* companies, or by the denomination of other Provinces in *America*, or Plantations in the *West-Indies*; and these companies shall equip and rig out as many vessels as they think proper, loading them with *British America*, *East* and *West-India* goods, and bring back in return, the rich and plentiful produce of *Africa*. But before I go any further into this point it must be observed, there is one real hinderance in the way which must be removed, or else no man or company need ever think of penetrating into the heart of this country, but just content themselves with taking the skim of this Trade, leting the body stand, and that is, the Slave Trade; this must be entirely renounced and given up by the *Europeans*, particularly by *Britain* and the Colonies; then we may with a good face and conscience travel into the heart of *Africa*, and meet with a friendly and hearty reception from the natives, who will trade with us, and give in exchange their valuable productions for our goods which are generally exported thither.

When that great, that only chief obstacle, the Slave Trade is removed, then *Britain* and the Colonies will flourish by so great and profitable a Commerce. Think what a great addition it will make to their traffick, the furnishing a hundred thousand people annually, more than are at present with cloathing, powder, shot, and warlike arms, and many more things needless here to enumerate out of England; rum, and sundry other articles out of *America* and the *West-Indies*. It is supposed that the above extraordinary number of Blacks are taken out of *Africa* yearly, and either murdered or made Slaves of, by the ships that go there out of *Boston, &c.* and what advantages may arise to the inhabitants in peopling, and consequently of cultivating and manuring their ground, and of bringing their rich trade to the perfection it is capable of, with *Britain, &c.* is hard to say, when the innermost parts of that great and fruitful country is settled, and a free and happy trade carried into the heart of it: But thus far I will venture to say, as I have done already, that where twenty shillings worth of commodities is at present exported an hundred pound will be, when a friendly Commerce is carried on with the natives.

These companies may say, that if once this trade is set on foot, other *European* powers, who have Settlements in *Africa* will invade them whenever they begin to thrive by not having sufficient funds for the keeping in good defence the forts, &c. on the Settlements. As to this I answer, that those companies have a sum of ten thousand pounds sterling annually, from the Crown of *Britain*, for maintaining and upholding the forts and castles that are built upon the *British* Colonies, which with the duties arising from the Trade will be sufficient to maintain, uphold, and defend them with strength superior to the strongest enemy.

Thus far I hope I have removed your fears of inability in supporting and continuing this Trade, and likewise have moved ways and means to put the same on a just and lawful footing. Now let me, patient Reader, conclude with a short Exhortation to the Ship-masters and Merchants concerned in this Trade, in part of which I have had recourse again to my good old Friend Mr. *Benezet*.

I Beg you all would fly from the oppression and Bondage to which the poor *Africans* are subjected, loose the bonds from off their necks, and thereby extricate yourselves from a custom which is pernicious to your welfare here and hereafter; and as you are sensible most men have objections to this base, unlawful Trade, you ought to vindicate yourselves to the world, upon principles of reason, honesty, and humanity, and then you will not attack the persons, or invade the rights of these people. I believe those who are concerned in this Trade will be at a loss to make this justification but upon motives so weak and unreasonable, that I do not think any of them which have been advanced for their defence worthy of notice; and if they are undeserving of that, they certainly are below regard; therefore I think *you should forever lay it aside.* This is the best and shortest way; for *there should be no trade carried on,* it being a national and provincial concern, *but such as is justifiable both to* God *and man,* and this is in direct opposition to both. But laying man's resentment aside, which is of little moment in comparison with that of the Almighty's, I counsel you once more to think of a future reckoning, consider what reasons you will be able to produce at the great and last day. You now accumulate riches and live in pleasure; but what will you do in the end, and that will be but short? What if you should be called hence and hurried out of this world under the vast load of blood guiltiness that is now lying on your souls? How many thousands have you been the instruments to, and primary cause of being killed in the wars and broils with the *African* Chiefs, wanting to obtain your number to enslave; and how many have you killed in the passage, when these poor Creatures were trying to retrieve their Liberty which they had in their own country, and which you unjustly take from them, or rather chusing to die than take food to nourish and preserve themselves for being mancipated with their children after them?

It is declared in the most express terms in Scripture, that thieves and murderers shall not inherit the kingdom of God. You who are in this Trade take warning by that, and if you have any thoughts or Christian feeling you must certainly renounce it; for that you are thieves and murderers (I hope after what has been said) will not be disputed; and you should think that at the same time and by the same means you are treasuring up worldly riches, you are treasuring up fountains of wrath against the day of anger and vengeance that shall come upon the workers of iniquity, unless timely repented of.

What injustice is greater? What offence more heinous? Is there any carries in it more consummate guilt than that in which you now live? How can you lift your culpable eyes to Heaven? How can you pray for mercy, or hope for favour from him that made and formed you, while you go on thus boldly and publickly dishonouring him, in degrading and destroying the noblest workmanship of his hands in this sublunary world? Can you think that God will hear your prayers, receive your supplications, or grant your desires, while you act thus grossly and openly against his divine revealed will and pleasure? And do you suppose that he who is the Parent of all nations, the Protector of all people, and the Father of all men, will not revenge the male-treatment of his offspring whom he once so loved as to give his only begotten Son, *that whosoever believed in him should not perish, but have everlasting life*? This love of God to man, which is disclosed in Scripture, adds double provocation to your crimes; for if God regards us with so much affection, we ought also to esteem one another.

Permit yourselves for a moment to reflect equitably and deliberately upon the nature of this horrid, detestable, vile, and abominable Man-Trade, and your hearts must certainly relent, if you have not lost all sense of benevolence, all sympathy and compassion towards those of your Brethren who have the same capacities, understandings and souls, and who were born to inherit the same salvation with you; I say, if you are not callous to every Christian, humane, and manly sensibility, you certainly must feel compassion for those extremely oppressed people, when you think what miseries, what devastations and massacres among them you have been the author of, and all for filthy lucre's sake. The thoughts of this accursed Trade touches my very heart, and finding if I continue any longer I shall get out of the bounds of decency, must therefore conclude. And if all you have read should have no weight upon your hardned hearts, this remains for my consolation that I have done my duty; and I pray! Fervently pray! That God would have mercy on your sinful souls; and that he of his infinite goodness would grant that you may be made sensible of your guilt and repent of these your execrable and really detestable deeds.

The Author makes no doubt but the Publick, after reading this Pamphlet, will readily agree with him, that the words in the Dedication are verified, "That it was put together with more good intent than ability," which he is very sensible of: But at the same time thinks all criticism and scrutinizing should be laid aside, when they reflect, that the will to do good is next in order to the action itself.

Anthony Benezet, Unpublished Notes on Thomas Thompson's Proslavery Pamphlet, 1772

Thomas Thompson, *The African Trade for Negro Slaves, Shewn to Be Consistent with Principles of Humanity, and with the Laws of Revealed Religion* (Canterbury, n.d.), Anthony Benezet's copy in Rutgers University Library, New Brunswick, N.J., pp. title; 11; 15; 23.

In 1772 the Reverend Thomas Thompson, a proslavery Anglican missionary who had traveled extensively in Africa and the West Indies in the 1740s and 1750s, published The African Trade for Negro Slaves, Shewn to Be Consistent with Principles of Humanity, and with the Laws of Revealed Religion. *Thompson contended that slavery, sanctioned institutionally by the ancient Jewish constitutions, was consistent with God's immutable laws and the laws of nature. Thompson's 31-page essay, infused with Biblical citations, was a formidable challenge to the arguments of antislavery writers such as Anthony Benezet who condemned slavery as a heinous sin. In Benezet's own copy of the pamphlet, he jotted down in the margins appropriate rejoinders. At one point in his argument Thompson had written that if a national institution such as slavery, supported by Parliament, were a violation of religious precept, it would have to be considered a national sin. Benezet had no doubts. "Certainly a national Sin!" he noted, "so that we have great reason to dread the consequences."*

THE

AFRICAN TRADE

FOR

NEGRO SLAVES,

SHEWN TO BE

CONSISTENT WITH PRINCIPLES

OF

HUMANITY,

AND WITH THE LAWS OF

REVEALED RELIGION.

By THO. THOMPSON, M. A.

SOMETIME FELLOW OF C. C. C.

CANTERBURY:

PRINTED AND SOLD BY SIMMONS AND KIRKBY.
SOLD ALSO BY ROBERT BALDWIN, BOOKSELLER
IN PATER-NOSTER ROW, LONDON.

[11]

they have ſuffered in their own country! Fair as this ſeems in theory, it would exhauſt the treaſure of any kingdom to reduce it into practice. We muſt endeavour then to make the beſt of what we have: and it may be ſufficient, if a lawful trade can be proved, where we cannot ſhew a boaſted virtue.'

This ſubject will grow more ſerious upon our hands, when we conſider the buying and ſelling negroes, not as a clandeſtine or piratical buſineſs, but as an open, public trade; encouraged and promoted by acts of parliament. For ſo, if being contrary to religion, it muſt be deemed a national ſin; and as ſuch may have a conſequence, that would

B 2

certainly a national Sin! so that we have great reason to dread the consequency. The Author does not seem to consider the weight of this part of his own argument— which cannot be ballanced by all his subsequent sophistry

[15]

the release of bond-servants, in case of their turning, and becoming proselytes to the law.

From these premises this conclusion may be drawn, that the buying and selling of slaves is not contrary to the law of nature. For the Jewish constitutions were strictly therewith consistent in all points: and these are, in certain cases, the rule by which is determined by learned lawyers and casuists, what is, or is not, contrary to nature.

That there were bond-servants or slaves in christian families, even in the apostolic age, appears clearly from St. *Paul's* 1st epis. to the *Corinth.* chap. 7, ver. 20, &c. "Let

every

This is a false foun=dation! for the Jewish Constitutions were not strictly consistent there=with & if else why did our Lord in=struct the Jews concerning the giving a Bill of Divorce (allowed by Moses) & marrying another, & that saying "From the beginning it was not so? plainly intim=ating that it was contrary to the original Law of Nature.

but not with St. Pauls Will which appears as clearly by the latter part of the same quotation. X page 16

[23]

are often treated : theſe miſeries ariſe not from the nature of their caſe, conſidered merely as ſlaves, but from the injuſtice and cruelty of their owners. The proper work of ſlaves is nothing above their ſtrength; and every real hardſhip that is impoſed on them is an abuſe of power.

No pretended necessity of Commerce can ballance these avowed evils.

Therefore no man should be allowed such power

By the law of nature, all perſons are free. But abſolute freedom is incompatible with civil eſtabliſhments. Every man's liberty is reſtricted by national laws, and natural priviledge does rightly yield to legal conſtitutions; which are deſigned and enacted for the public weal.

Absolute Freedom is not incompatible with civil establishments: because absolute freedom can only consist in restraining Evil Doers by just & equitable Laws, that the Weak & Poor may be as free as the Rich & Strong, for all men ought to be absolutely free to do good according to their abilities, & if they are not free to do evil, it is not to be accounted a restraint upon liberty; but a restraint only upon Tyranny; so that the author —has manifestly confounded the one term for the other.

The

Patrick Henry to Robert Pleasants, January 18, 1773

Granville Sharp Letterbook, The Library Company, Philadelphia, Pa.

During the American Revolutionary years Robert Pleasants, a wealthy Quaker planter from Henrico County, Virginia, became one of the most vigorous antislavery advocates in the southern colonies. He corresponded with Quakers in England and America, distributed pamphlets and articles, and solicited support from Virginia legislators. Pleasants was a vital link in the burgeoning antislavery propaganda movement. It is not surprising that he broached the subject of slavery with one of the influential colonial leaders in his state, Patrick Henry. Henry, the solemn orator with, in Lawrence Henry Gipson's words, "deep-set, piercing eyes, aquiline nose, heavy eyebrows, hollow cheeks, and a mouth that never really wreathed a smile," had since the early 1760s bitterly defied what he regarded as Parliamentary oppression. In 1763, as a young lawyer arguing a case in the Hanover County court, Henry assailed "the bondage of the people who were denied the privilege of enacting their own laws." In 1765 in the Virginia House of Burgesses he introduced a number of radical resolutions against the Stamp Act. By 1773, when Pleasant's appealed for Henry's support in achieving manumission and in attacking the slave trade and slavery in general, Henry wielded considerable power in colonial Virginia. His response to Pleasants was disappointing. Although Henry recognized the repugnance of the "abominable Practice" and was a respected spokesman for natural rights, he was "drawn along by the general inconvenience of living without them."

In the following years antislavery leaders heard many such comments from a variety of individuals. Indeed, a few months earlier, John Knox Gordon, an influential South Carolina jurist, wrote to Anthony Benezet, "I found my self under an absolute necessity of falling in with the Customs of the place. . . . I most heartily wish I could do without them, but tho I cannot reconcile myself to the measure, yet I flatter myself, their Servitude is easier with me. . . ."

Hanover Jan 18. 1773

I take this oppertunity to acknowledge the receipt of Anthony Benezet's Book against the Slave Trade, I thank you for it. It is not a little surprising, that Christianity, whose chief excellence consists in softning the human heart, in cherishing and improving the finer feelings, should encourage a practice so repugnant to the first impression of right and wrong; what adds to the wonder is, that this abominable practice, has been introduced in the most enlightened Ages, Times that seem to have pretensions to boast of high improvement, in the Arts, Sciencies and refined morality have brought into general use, and guarded by many laws, a species of violence and Tyranny which our more rude and more barbarous, but more honest Ancestors detested.

Is it not amazing, that at a time, when the rights of Humanity are defined, and understood with precision, in a Country above all others fond of Liberty, That in such an Age; and such a Country we find men professing a Religion, the most humane, mild, meek gentle, and generous, adopting a principle as repugnant to humanity, as it is inconsistant with the Bible, and destructive to liberty; every thinking, honest Man rejects it in speculation;

How few in practice, from conscientous motives, the world in general, has denyed your people a share of its honours. but the wise will ascribe to you a just tribute of virtuous praise for the practice of a train of Virtues, amongst which your disagreement to Slavery, will be principally ranked. I cannot but wish well to a people, whose System imitates the example of him whose life was perfect. And believe me, I shall ever honour the Quakers for their noble effort to abolish Slavery. It is equally calculated to promote moral, and political good.

Would any one believe that I am master of Slave, of my own purchase: I am drawn along by the general inconveniency of living without them, I will not, I cannot justify it; however culpable my conduct, I will so far pay my duty as to own the excellency and rectitude of her precepts, and to lament my want of conformity to them.

I believe a time will come, when an opportunity will be afforded, to abolish this lamentable evil; every thing we can do is to improve it, if it happens in our day, if not let us transmit to our descendants, together with our Slaves, a pity for their unhappy lot, and abhorence for Slavery. If we cannot reduce this Reformation to practice, let us treat the unhappy victims with lenity; it is the furthest advance towards Justice. It is a debt we owe to the purity of Religion to shew that it is at variance with that Saw which warrants Slavery. It is an instance that silent meetings the Scoff of Reverend Doctors have done, that which learned and elaborate preaching could not effect; so much preferable, are the genuine dictates of conscience and a steady attention to its feelings, above the teachings of those men who pretend to have found a better guide. I exhort you to persevere in so worthy a resolution. Some of your people disagree or at best are lukewarm in the abolition of Slavery, many treat the resolution of your meetings with ridicule, and among those who throw contempt on it, are Clergymen, whose surest guard against ridicule and contempt, is a certain act of Assembly. I know not where to stop, I could say many things on this subject, a serious review of which give a gloomy perspective to future times. Excuse this scrowl and believe me with esteem, &c.

Josiah Quincy, Journal Entries on Slavery, March 1773

Josiah Quincy, "Journal of Josiah Quincy, Junior, 1773," *Massachusetts Historical Society Proceedings*, 49 (October 1915-June 1916), pp. 456-57.

In 1770 Josiah Quincy, the young, brilliant Massachusetts lawyer, surprised and angered many of his associates when he, along with John Adams, appeared in court to defend the British soldiers involved in the "Boston Massacre." Later Quincy's gesture was applauded by many of these same individuals as a selfless act of duty and devotion to the law. Within two years of the trial Quincy was a strong leader of the patriot cause, writing essays in Massachusetts newspapers and exchanging views with various colonial leaders. When he was almost thirty-years-old Quincy contracted tuberculosis—a disease which took his life two years later, a week after the battle of Lexington. On February 8, 1773, Quincy sailed for the southern states, seeking to regain his health in the warmer climate. After traveling through South Carolina, dining with leaders of the state, and interviewing politicians and planters, Quincy stopped to write in his journal. His few private reflections, entitled "General Remarks and Observations on South Carolina," are a graphic testament to much of what John Woolman preached to Quaker slaveholders about slavery's vile effects on the master classes and their children. Woolman wrote, "seed sown with the Tears of a confined oppressed People, Harvest cut down by an overborne discontented Reaper, makes Bread less sweet to the taste of an Honest Man."

. . . Slavery may truly be said to be the peculiar curse of this land: Strange infatuation! it is generally thought and called by the people its blessing. Applicable indeed to this people and their slaves are the words of our Milton:

> So perfect in their misery,
> Not one perceive their foul disfigurement.

A few years ago, it is allowed, that the blacks exceeded the whites as seventeen to one. There are those who now tell you, that the slaves are not more than three to one, some pretend not so many. But they who talk thus are afraid that the slaves should by some means discover their superiority. Many people express great fears of an insurrection, others treat the idea as chimerical. I took great pains (finding much contrariety of opinion) to find out the true proportion. The best information I could obtain fixes it at about seven to one, my own observation leads me to think it much greater.

The brutality used towards the slaves has a very bad tendency with reference to the manners of the people, but a much worse with regard to the youth. They will plead in their excuse "this severity is necessary." But whence did or does this necessity arise? From *the necessity* of having vast multitudes sunk in barbarism, ignorance and the basest and most servile employ! By reason of this slavery, the children are early impressed with infamous and destructive ideas, and become extremely vitiated in their manners, they contract a negroish kind of accent, pronunciation and dialect, as well as ridiculous kind of behaviour: even many of the grown people, and especially the women, are vastly infected with the same disorder. Parents instead of talking to their very young children in the unmeaning way with us, converse to them as though they were speak[ing] to a new imported African.

From the same cause have their Legislators enacted laws touching negroes, mulattoes and masters which savor more of the policy of Pandemonium than the English constitution:—laws which will stand eternal records of the depravity and contradiction of the human character: laws which would disgrace the tribunal of Scythian, Arab, Hottentot and Barbarian are appealed to in decisions upon life limb and liberty by those who assume the name of Englishmen, freemen and Christians: the place of trial no doubt is called a Court of Justice and equity—but the Judges have forgot a maxim of English law—*Jura naturalia sunt immutabilia*—and they would do well to remember that no laws of the (little) creature supersede the laws of the (great) creator. Can the institutions of man make void the decree of God?

These are but a small part of the mischiefs of slavery, new ones are every day arising, futurity will produce more and greater.

Mr. Lynch told me that he knew several negroes who had refused to implore a forgiveness when under sentence of death, though a pardon was insured on this easy term. Preferring death to their deplorable state, they died with a temper deserving a better fate. There is much among this people of what the world call hospitality and politeness, it may be questioned what proportion there is of true humanity, Christian charity and love. . . .

Benjamin Rush, Address on Slavery, 1773

Benjamin Rush, *An Address to the Inhabitants of the British Settlements in America upon Slave-Keeping* (Philadelphia, 1773), pp. 1-30.

"Slavery is so foreign to the human mind, that the moral faculties, as well as those of understanding are debased, and rendered torpid by it." Thus did the erudite Philadelphia physician, Benjamin Rush, enter the ranks of antislavery pamphleteers in 1773. With a bill dealing with slavery before the Pennsylvania Assembly and with the necessary Quaker support lined up, Anthony Benezet, the incessant lobbyist, asked the Presbyterian Rush to write a pamphlet attacking slavery. Rush, who for several years had expressed strong antislavery views to friends in Europe and America, obliged Benezet with, An Address to the Inhabitants of the British Settlements in America, Upon Slave-Keeping. *He called the African Company an "incorporated band of robbers" and vigorously asserted the innate equality of the blacks, declaring that their abject condition as slaves had created among whites "an idea of superiority over them, which induces most people to look upon them as an ignorant and contemptible part of mankind."*

Shortly after the publication of the tract the assembly increased the duty on imported Negroes but refused to grapple with the institution of slavery itself. Rush, himself, made many instant enemies and became the target of, as he later remembered, "the most virulent attack that was ever made upon me." The most serious proslavery volley came from Richard Nisbet, a West Indian planter living in Philadelphia who published Slavery not Forbidden by Scripture, *an offering which asserted that the Negro race was inferior "in every respect." With that publication and the continuing criticism of his entrance into the antislavery vanguard, Rush became deeply emeshed in the antislavery debate.*

An Address, &c.

So much hath been said upon the subject of Slave-keeping, that an apology may be required for this address. The only one I shall offer is, that the evil still continues. This may in part be owing to the great attachment we have to our own interest, and in part to the subject not being fully exhausted. The design of the following address is to sum up the leading arguments against it, several of which have not been urged by any of those authors who have written upon it.

Without entering into the history of the facts which relate to the slave trade, I shall proceed immediately to combat the principal arguments which are used to support it.

And here I need hardly say any thing in favor of the Intellects of the Negroes, or of their capacities for virtue and happiness, although these have been supposed by some to be inferior to those of the inhabitants of Europe. The accounts which travellers give us of their ingenuity, humanity, and strong attachment to their parents, relations, friends and country, show us that they are equal to the Europeans, when we allow for the diversity of temper and genius which is occasioned by climate. We have many well-attested anecdotes of as sublime and disinterested virtue among them as ever adorned a Roman or a Christian character. But we are to distinguish between an African in his own country, and an African in a state of slavery in America. Slavery is so foreign to the human mind, that the moral faculties, as well as those of the understanding are debased, and rendered torpid by it. All the vices which are charged upon the Negroes in the southern colonies and the West-Indies, such as Idleness, Treachery, Theft, and the like, are the genuine offspring of slavery, and serve as an argument to prove that they were not intended, by Providence for it.

Nor let it be said, in the present Age, that their black color (as it is commonly called) either subjects them to, or qualifies them for slavery. The vulgar notion of their being descended from Cain, who was supposed to have been marked with this color, is too absurd to need a refutation.—Without enquiring into the Cause of this blackness, I shall only add upon this subject, that so far from being a curse, it subjects the Negroes to no inconveniences, but on the contrary qualifies them for that part of the Globe in which providence has placed them. The ravages of heat, diseases and time, appear less in their faces than in a white one; and when we exclude variety of color from our ideas of Beauty, they may be said to possess every thing necessary to constitute it in common with the white people.

It has been urged by the inhabitants of the Sugar Islands and South Carolina, that it would be impossible to carry on the manufactories of Sugar, Rice, and Indigo, without negro slaves. No manufactory can ever be of consequence enough to society, to admit the least violation of the Laws of justice or humanity. But I am far from thinking the arguments used in favor of employing Negroes for the cultivation of these articles, should have any Weight.—M Le Poivre, late envoy from the king of France, to the king of Cochin-China, and now intendant of the isles of Bourbon and Mauritius, in his observations upon the manners and arts of the various nations in Africa and Asia, speaking of the culture of sugar in Cochin-China, has the following remarks—"It is worthy observation too, that the sugar cane is there cultivated by freemen, and all the process of preparation and refining, the work of free hands. Compare then the price of the Cochin-Chinese production with the same commodity which is cultivated and prepared by the wretched slaves of our European colonies, and judge if, to procure sugar from our colonies, it was necessary to authorize by law the slavery of the unhappy Africans transported to America. From what I have observed at Cochin-China, I cannot entertain a doubt, but that our West-India colonies, had they been distributed without reservation amongst a free people, would have produced double the quantity that is now procured from the labour of the unfortunate negroes.

What advantage, then, has accrued to Europe, civilized as it is, and thoroughly versed in the laws of nature, and the rights of mankind, by legally authorizing in our colonies, the daily outrages against human nature, permitting them to debase man almost below the level of the beasts of the field? These slavish laws have proved as opposite to its interest, as they are to its honour, and to the laws of humanity. This remark I have often made.

Liberty and property form the basis of abundance, and good agriculture: I never observed is to flourish where those rights of mankind were not firmly established. The earth, which multiplies her productions with a kind of profusion, under the hands of the free-born labourer, seems to shrink into barrenness under the sweat of the slave. Such is the will of the great Author of our Nature, who has created man free, and assigned to him the earth; that he might cultivate his possession with the sweat of his brow; but still should enjoy his Liberty."

Now if the plantations in the islands and the southern colonies were more limited, and freemen only employed in working them, the general product would be greater, although the profits to individuals would be less,—a circumstance this, which by diminishing opulence in a few, would suppress Luxury and Vice, and promote that equal distribution of property, which appears best calculated to promote the welfare of Society.—I know it has been said by some, that none but the natives of warm climates could undergo the excessive heat and labor of the West-India islands. But this argument is founded upon an error; for the reverse of this is true. I have been informed by good authority, that one European who escapes the first or second year, will do twice the work, and live twice the number of years that an ordinary Negro man will do: nor need we be surpriz'd at this, when we hear that such is the natural fertility of soil, and so numerous the spontaneous fruits of the earth in the interior parts of Africa, that the natives live in plenty at the expence of little or no labor, which, in warm climates, has ever been found to be incompatible with long life and happiness. Future ages, therefore, when they read the accounts of the Slave Trade (—if they do not regard them as fabulous)—will be at a loss which to condemn most, our folly, or our Guilt, in abetting this direct violation of the Laws of nature and Religion.

But there are some who have gone so far as to say that Slavery is not repugnant to the Genius of Christianity, and that it is not forbidden in any part of the Scriptures. Natural and Revealed Religion always speak the same things, although the latter delivers its precepts with a louder, and more distinct voice than the former. If it could be proved that no testimony was to be found in the Bible against a practice so pregnant with evils of the most destructive tendency to society, it would be sufficient to overthrow its divine Original. We read it is true of Abraham's having slaves born in his house; and we have reason to believe, that part of the riches of the patriarchs consisted in them; but we can no more infer the lawfulness of the practice, from the short account which the Jewish historian gives us of these facts, than we can vindicate telling a lie, because Rahab is not condemned for it in the account which is given of her deceiving the king of Jericho. We read that some of the same men indulged themselves in a plurality of wives, without any strictures being made upon their conduct for it; and yet no one will pretend to say, that this is not forbidden in many parts of the Old Testament. But we are told the Jews kept the Heathens in perpetual bondage. The Design of providence in permitting this evil, was probably to prevent the Jews from marrying among strangers, to which their intercourse with them upon any other footing than that of slaves, would naturally have inclined them. Had this taken place—their National Religion would have been corrupted—they would have contracted all their vices, and the intention of providence in keeping them a distinct people, in order to accomplish the promise made to Abraham, that "in his Seed all the Nations of the earth should be blessed," would have been defeated; so that the descent of the Messiah from Abraham, could not have been traced, and the divine commission of the Son of God, would have wanted one of its most powerful arguments to support it. But with regard to their own countrymen, it is plain, perpetual slavery was not tolerated. Hence, at the end of seven years or in the year of the jubilee, all the Hebrew slaves were set at liberty, and it was held unlawful to detain them in servitude longer than that time, except by their own Consent. But if, in the partial Revelation which God made, of his will to the Jews, we find such testimonies against slavery, what may we not expect from the Gospel, the Design of which was to abolish all distinctions of name and country. While the Jews thought they complied with the precepts of the law; in confining the love of their neighbour "to the children of their own people," Christ commands us to look upon all mankind even our Enemies as our neighbours and brethren, and "in all things, to do unto them whatever we would with they should do unto us." He tells us further that his "Kingdom is not of this World," and therefore constantly avoids saying any thing that might interfere directly with the Roman or Jewish Governments: so that altho' he does not call upon masters to emancipate their slaves, or upon slaves to assert that Liberty wherewith God and Nature had made them free, yet there is scarcely a Parable or a Sermon in the whole history of his life, but what contains the strongest arguments against Slavery. Every prohibition of Covetousness—Intemperance—Pride—Uncleanness—Theft—and Murder, which he delivered,—every lesson of meekness, humility, forbearance, Charity, Self-denial, and brotherly-love, which he taught, are levelled against this evil;—for Slavery, while it includes all the former Vices, necessarily excludes the practice of all the latter Virtues, both from the Master and the Slave.—Let such, therefore, who vindicate the traffic of buying and selling Souls, seek some modern System of Religion of support it, and not presume to sanctify their crimes by attempting to reconcile it to the sublime and perfect Religion of the Great Author of Christianity.

There are some amongst us who cannot help allowing the force of our last argument, but plead as a motive for importing and keeping slaves, that they become acquainted with the principles of the religion of our country.—This is like justifying a highway robbery because part of the money acquired in this manner was appropriated to some religious use.—Christianity will never be propagated by any other methods than those employed by Christ and his Apostles. Slavery is an engine as little fitted for that purpose as Fire or the Sword. A Christian Slave is a contradiction in terms. But if we enquire into the methods employed for converting the Negroes to Christianity, we shall find the means suited to the end proposed. In many places Sunday is appropriated to work for themselves. Reading and writing are discouraged among them. A belief is even inculcated among some, that they have no Souls. In a word,—Every attempt to instruct or convert them, has been constantly opposed by their masters. Nor has the example of their christian masters any tendency to prejudice them in favor of our religion. How often do they betray, in their sudden transports of anger and resentment (against which there is no restraint provided towards their Negroes) the most violent degrees of passion and fury!—What luxury—what ingratitude to the supreme being—what impiety in their ordinary conversation do some of them discover in the presence of their slaves! I say nothing of the dissolution of marriage vows, or the entire abolition of matrimony, which the frequent sale of them introduces, and which are directly contrary to the law of nature and the principles of christianity. Would to Heaven I could here conceal the shocking violations of chastity, which some of them are obliged to undergo without daring to complain. Husbands have been forced to prostitute their wives, and mothers their daughters, to gratify the brutal lust of a master. This—all—this is practised—Blush—ye impure and hardened monsters, while I repeat it—by men who call themselves christians!

But further—It has been said that we do a kindness to the Negroes by bringing them to America, as we thereby save their lives, which had been forfeited by their being conquered in war. Let such as prefer or inflict slavery rather than Death, disown their being descended from or connected with our mother countries.—But it will be found, upon enquiry, that many are stolen or seduced from their friends, who have never been conquered; and it is plain, from the testimony of historians and travellers, that wars were uncommon among them, until the christians who began the slave trade, stirred up the different nations to fight against each other. Sooner let them imbrue their hands in each others blood, or condemn one another to perpetual slavery, than the name of one christian, or one American be stained by the perpetration of such enormous crimes. Nor let it be urged that by treating slaves well, we render their situation happier in this Country than it was in their own.—Slavery and Vice are connected together, and the latter is always a source of misery. Besides, by the greatest humanity we can show them, we only lessen, but do not remove the crime, for the injustice of it continues the same. The laws of Retribution are so strongly inculcated by the moral governor of the world, that even the ox is entitled to his reward for "treading the Corn." How great then must be the amount of that injustice which deprives so many of our fellow creatures of the *just* reward of their labour!

But it will be asked here, What steps shall we take to remedy this Evil, and what shall we do with those Slaves we have already in this Country? This is indeed a most difficult question. But let every man contrive to answer it for himself. If you possessed an estate which was bequeathed to you by your ancestors, and were afterwards convinced that it was the just property of another man, would you think it right to continue in the possession of it? would you not give it up immediately to the lawful owner? The voice of all mankind would mark him for a villain who would refuse to comply with this demand of justice. And is not keeping a slave after you are convinced of the unlawfulness of it—a crime of the same nature? All the money you save, or acquire by their labor is stolen from them; and however plausible the excuse may be that you form to reconcile it to your consciences, yet be assured that your crime stands registered in the court of Heaven as a breach of the eighth commandment.

The first step to be taken to put a stop to slavery in this country, is to leave of importing slaves. For this purpose let our assemblies unite in petitioning the king and parliament to dissolve the African company. It is by this incorporated band of robbers that the trade has been chiefly carried on to America. We have the more reason to expect relief from an application at this juncture, as, by a late decision in favor of a Virginia slave, at Westminister-Hall, the Clamors of the whole nation are raised against them. Let such of our countrymen as engage in the slave trade, be shunned as the greatest enemies to our country, and let the vessels which bring the slaves to us, be avoided as if they bore in them the Seeds of that forbidden fruit, whose baneful taste destroyed both the natural and moral world.—As for the Negroes among us, who, from having acquired all the low vices of slavery, or who, from age or infirmities are unfit to be set at liberty, I would propose, for the good of society, that they should continue the property of those with whom they grew old, or from whom they contracted those vices and infirmities. But let the young Negroes be educated in the principles of virtue and religion—let them be taught to read, and write—and afterwards instructed in some business, whereby they may be able to maintain themselves. Let laws be made to limit the time of their servitude, and to entitle them to all the privileges of free-born British subjects. At any rate let Retribution be done to God and to Society.

And now my countrymen, What shall I add more to rouse up your Indignation against Slave-keeping. Consider the many complicated crimes it involves in it. Think of the bloody Wars which are fomented by it, among the African nations, or if these are too common to affect you, think of the pangs which attend the dissolution of the ties of nature in those who are stolen from their relations. Think of the many thousands who perish by sickness, melancholy and suicide, in their voyages to America. Pursue the poor devoted victims to one of the West India islands, and see them exposed there to public sale. Hear their cries, and see their looks of tenderness at each other upon being seperated.—Mothers are torn from their Daughters, and Brothers from Brothers, without the liberty of a parting embrace. Their master's name is now marked upon their breasts with a red hot iron. But let us pursue them into a Sugar Field, and behold a scene still more affecting than this—See! the poor wretches with what reluctance they take their Instruments of Labor into their hands.—Some of them, overcome with heat and sickness, seek to refresh themselves by a little rest.—But, behold an Overseer approaches them.—In vain they sue for pity.—He lifts up his Whip, while streams of Blood follow every stroke. Neither age nor sex are spared.—Me-thinks one of them is a woman far advanced in her pregnancy.—At a little distance from these behold a man, who from his countenance and deportment appears as if he was descended from illustrious ancestors.—Yes.—He is the son of a Prince, and was torn, by a stratagem, from an amiable wife and two young children—Mark his sullen looks!—now he bids defiance to the tyranny of his Master, and in an instant plunges a Knife into his Heart—But, let us return from this Scene, and see the various modes of arbitrary punishments inflicted upon them by their masters. Behold one covered with stripes, into which melted wax is poured—another tied down to a block or a stake—a third suspended in the air by his thumbs—a fourth obliged to set or stand upon red hot iron—a fifth,—I cannot relate it.—Where now is Law or justice?—Let us fly to them to step in for their relief.—Alas!—The one is silent, and the other denounces more terrible punishments upon them. Let us attend the place appointed for inflicting the penalties of the law. See here one without a limb, whose only crime was an attempt to regain his Liberty—another led to a Gallows for eating a morsel of Bread, to which his labor gave him a better title than his master—a third famishing on a gibbit—a fourth, in a flame of Fire!—his shrieks pierce the very heavens.—O! God! Where is thy Vengeance!—O! Humanity—Justice—Liberty—Religion!—Where,—where are ye fled.——

This is no exaggerated Picture. It is taken from real Life.—Before I conclude I shall take the liberty of addressing several Classes of my countrymen in behalf of our Brethren (for by that name may we now call them) who are in a state of Slavery among us.

In the first place let Magistrates both supreme and inferior, exert the authority they are invested with, in suppressing this evil. Let them discountenance it by their example, and show a readiness to concur in every measure proposed to remedy it.

Let Legislators, reflect upon the Trust reposed in them. Let their laws be made after the Spirit of Religion—Liberty—and our most excellent English Constitution. You cannot show your attachment to your King or your love to your country better than by suppressing an evil which endangers the dominions of the former, and will in Time destroy the liberty of the latter. Population, and the accession of strangers, in which the Riches of all countries consist, can only flourish in proportion as slavery is discouraged. Extend the privileges we enjoy, to every human creature born among us, and let not the Journals of our Assemblies be disgraced with the records of laws, which allow exclusive privileges to men of one color in preference to another.

Ye men of Sense and Virtue—Ye Advocates for American Liberty, rouse up and espouse the cause of Humanity and general Liberty. Bear a testimony against a vice which degrades human nature, and dissolves that universal tie of benevolence which should connect all the children of men together in one great Family.—The plant of liberty is of so tender a Nature, that it cannot thrive long in the neighbourhood of slavery. Remember the eyes of all Europe are fixed upon you, to preserve an assylum for freedom in this country, after the last pillars of it are fallen in every other quarter of the Globe.

But chiefly—ye Ministers of the Gospel, whose Dominion over the principles and actions of men is so universally acknowledged and felt,—Ye who estimate the worth of your fellow creatures by their Immortality, and therefore must look upon all Mankind as equal;—let your zeal keep pace with your Opportunities to put a stop to Slavery. While you enforce the duties of "tithe and cummin," neglect not the weightier laws of justice and humanity. Slavery is an Hydra sin, and includes in it every violation of the precepts of the Law and the Gospel. In vain will you command your flocks to offer up the incence of Faith and Charity, while they continue to mingle the Sweat and Blood of Negro slaves with their sacrifices.—If the Blood of Able cried aloud for vengeance;—If, under the Jewish dispensation, Cities of refuge could not screen the deliberate murderer—if even manslaughter required sacrifices to expiate it,—and if a single murder so seldom escapes with impunity in any civilized country, what may you not say against that trade, or those manufactures—or Laws which destroy the lives of so many thousands of our fellow creatures every year?—If in the Old Testament "God Swears by his holiness, and by the excellency of Jacob, that the Earth shall tremble, and every one mourn that dwelleth therein for the iniquity of those who oppress the poor and crush the needy," "who buy the poor with silver, and the needy with a pair of shoes," In what judgments may you not denounce upon those who continue to perpetrate these crimes, after the more full discovery which God has made of the law of Equity in the new Testament. Put them in mind of the Rod which was held over them a few years ago in the Stamp and Revenue Acts. Remember that national crimes require national punishments, and without declaring what punishment awaits this evil, you may venture to assure them, that it cannot pass with impunity, unless God shall cease to be just or merciful.

Benjamin Rush, Answer to Richard Nisbet, 1773

Benjamin Rush, *A Vindication of the Address To the Inhabitants of the British Settlements, on the Slavery of the Negroes in America, in Answer to a Pamphlet entitled, "Slavery not Forbidden by Scripture; Or a Defence of the West-India Planters from the Aspersians thrown out against them by the Author of the Address"* (Philadelphia, 1773), pp. 1-54.

When Richard Nisbet, a West Indian planter, responded to Benjamin Rush's Address with a ringing defense of slavery, he based much of his argument on the woeful savagery and innate inferiority of the black race. Nisbet, in Slavery Not Forbidden by Scripture, *wrote that Africans were "utterly unacquainted with the arts, letters, manufactures, and everything which constitutes civilized life." He discounted Phillis Wheatly as something akin to a parrot, characterizing her work as "a few silly poems." Dr. Rush's answer,* A Vindication of the Address, *blamed manifestations of African barbarism upon environment: ". . . All the differences we perceive in respect to virtue and vice, knowledge and ignorance, may be accounted for from climate, country, degrees of civilization, forms of government, or accidental causes."*

Rush hoped to demonstrate that blacks were not languishing at the bottom of some evolutionary ladder. Rush developed his environmentalist thesis, declaring finally, "You have attempted to sink Creatures, formed like yourself, in the Image of God, and equally capable of Happiness both here and hereafter, below the rank of 'Monsters and Barbarians,' or even Brutes themselves."

Richard Nisbet had provoked the good doctor to compose a highly influential antislavery pamphlet, which was circulated widely throughout the colonies and in England in the following years.

There is no Subject so sacred that has not sometimes been exposed to Obloquy. The immortality of the Soul, the Obligations of Morality, and even the Existence of a Supreme Being, have all in their Turns been treated as unworthy of Belief. On the other Hand, there is no Subject so subversive of the Happiness of Mankind, but what has had in Advocates.—Adultery—Perjury,—and even Suicide, have all been defended as lawful. Posterity will hardly believe that human Ingenuity could rise higher, and that a Man had lived, who had undertaken to defend Slavery, Should they seek his Name or Country, how will they be surprized to hear that he was descended from a Briton;—that he lived under the Protection of British Laws:—And that he was still connected with Great Britain. The Person I mean is the Author of a Pamphlet, entitled "Slavery not forbidden by Scripture, "or a Defence of the West-India Planters," &c. and who calls himself a West-Indian.

The Author of this Defence begins, by pleading in behalf of the Slavery of the Negroes in the West Indies, "the imperfections of all "human Institutions." This must be acknowledged by every Body, but is by no means an Apology for our not doing every thing that lies in our Power to Remedy them. Shall Judges descend from their Benches, and cease to distribute Justice, because Fraud and Violence still prevail in Society? Shall Physicians cease to relieve the Pains of the Sick, because the Body must at last pay the Tribute to Mortality? Shall the Clergy cease to inculcate the Duties of Religion, because they cannot put an entire stop to the progress of Vice and Infidelity?—

Improvements of all kinds in Society are progressive. It is impossible to review the Constitution and Laws of Great Britain, without admiring the gradual Improvements which have been made in both: Many of which at their first Proposal were no Doubt treated as visionary and impracticable. The abolition of domestic Slavery is not an Utopian Scheme. It was abolished by Constantine the first Christian Emperor throughout the Roman Empire. It ceased in many parts of Europe after the Reformation. It is unknown in Britain. It's Foundations are now shaking in Spain and Portugal. It begins to loose Ground in America. The Assembly of Virginia have petitioned for a Law to prevent the future importation of Negroes amongst them. The Assembly of Pennsylvania have imposed a Duty of twenty Pounds Currency upon every Negro, imported into the Province. The inhabitants of the Province of Massachusetts Bay have instructed their Representatives to enact Laws to restrain it. Reason and Humanity with respect to Negro Slavery, have at last awakened in the West-Indies, and many respectable Planters now wish to extricate themselves from it. With such Success, and Prospects, I venture once more to take up my Pen in behalf of the poor Africans. Great Events have often been brought about by slender Means. Permanent changes in Government are seldom produced suddenly. It shall be our Business to collect Materials:—The next Generation we hope, will behold and admire the finished Temple of African Liberty in America.

The Author of the Defence in the next place attempts to prove that Slavery is not forbidden by Moses, the Jewish Lawgiver; without repeating the Reason mentioned in the Address, for the distinction which was made between Hebrew and Heathen Slaves; and which is not overthrown by our Author's Appeal to the Power of the Supreme Being, I shall remark here, that Providence never employs extraordinary Means to accomplish an End, when ordinary ones will do. Where there is no *Legal* Impediment, we find that differences of Nation—Religion, or even Color, cannot prevent People from marrying amongst each other. That the Jews should continue a distinct People at this Time, under so many Circumstances unfavourable to it, cannot be equalled by any similar Case in History; and therefore has always been looked upon as a standing Miracle.—But again, we are not to set up a few detached Texts of Scripture against the whole Tenor of the Jewish Law. It is not thus we interpret our English Laws, or Acts of Parliament. Can it be supposed that the Supreme Being could deliver a System of Laws that should contradict each other, or favour Injustice and Violence? This would be to degrade him below a Lycurgus, or a Justinian, or even Mahomet himself. I shall only add further, upon this Head, that although the chief Design of rendering the Slavery of the Heathens perpetual, was to prevent the Jews from intermarrying with them, yet this Evil like the Divorces spoken of by our Saviour, was permitted amongst them, upon the Account of the "Hardness of their Hearts." "From the beginning it was not so."—That is, the same Law of Nature, which in the Beginning of the World forbid Divorces, upon trifling Occasions, likewise forbid Slavery. But The depravity of the Jews, and in particular their proneness to mix with, and adopt the Customs of other Nations, rendered a Dispensation from the Rigor of the Moral Law necessary, not only with respect to the keeping of Slaves, but to other things, equally repugnant to its Perfection, and Purity. But the same Plea cannot be made under the Christian Dispensation. Every seeming imperfection which was accommodated to the State of Knowledge, and Society amongst the Jews, was abolished by Christianity; instead of "an Eye for an Eye, or a Tooth for a Tooth," we are commanded "not to resist Evil, but to him that smiteth on the right cheek, to turn the other also." Can it be believed that this divine Lawgiver, who inculcated such Patience of Injuries, could approve of an Evil, which involved in it every thing that was destructive to the Happiness of Individuals and Society? Although he reproved Vice in all its shapes, yet (I repeat it again) he maintained a regard to the Roman and Jewish Governments. This appears plain from his ordering Tribute to be paid to Caesar. It appears likewise from his Behaviour to the Woman caught in Adultery. Had he condemned her, he would have offended against the Roman, and had he acquitted her, he would have abrogated that Part of the Jewish Law which related to that Crime. He only commands her to "go and sin no more."

The Author of the Defence employs several Pages to shew the Loss that would arise to the Planters, and to Great-Britain, from the Manumission of the Negroes in the West-Indies. I am far from recommending such a Step to the Planters—It would be as prejudicial to the Slaves as to their Masters. Men used to Slavery, such as prevails in the Southern Colonies and West-Indies, are ever afterwards unfit for Liberty. The first Thing proposed was to leave of importing them. The Evil after this would in some Measure remedy itself. As to the loss Britain would sustain, it should not be mentioned. It hath been proved by Mons. Le Poivre, that she would derive not only Reputation, but immense Riches from it. Many Families in Algiers would perhaps suffer a few temporary Inconveniences, and the Revenues of that State be lessened, by their calling home their piratical Ships.—But will any Man pretend, upon this Account, to vindicate their flagrant Violations of the Laws of Nature and Nations?—If political Advantages can justify the Infringement of the Laws of Justice and Humanity, then let us cease to look with Horror upon the Massacre of the Protestants in France and Ireland—of the English at Amboyna—and of the Jews in Spain. It cannot be repeated too often, that the Obligations of Morality are alike binding upon Communities and Individuals; and History as well as daily Observation shew us, that they both promote their true Interest in Proportion as they comply with them. . . .

Our Author attempts to palliate the Account given of the Severity of the Punishments inflicted upon the Negroes. To such as know the Weakness, and Depravity of Human Nature, no Accounts of the Cruelty of these Punishments will appear exaggerated. Invest the proud—passionate—ambitious, and covetous Creature Man, with an absolute Dominion (such as is held in the West-Indies) over the Lordly independant Creature Man, and we may venture from what we know of Human Nature, to tell what will be the Consequence. It is true, as our Author remarks, most of the Natives of the West Indies are educated in Britain, in the Principles of Liberty and Humanity; but why are they sent from Home to be educated?—Why do Parents give up the most sacred Charge Heaven can deposit in their Hands, the Formation of the Minds of their Children, to Strangers? Why is the Love of their native Country (so necessary in Human Societies) to be weakned, or destroyed by a foreign Education? It is because it is so difficult for them to improve in Learning or Virtue at Home, where they are exposed to Vice from every Quarter, and where they breathe nothing but the polluted Atmosphere of Slavery. But have all the Planters in the West Indies been educated in the Principles of Liberty and Humanity? Or do those who have had a British Education always reside at their Estates, or look after their Negroes? Perhaps they may in some Cases disapprove of their Punishments, these being inflicted by Overseers or their Dependants; yet they are generally too far removed from them to prevent, or regulate them.

It is to no Purpose to urge here that Self Interest leads the Planters to treat their Slaves well. There are many things which appear true in Speculation, which are false in Practice. The Head is as apt to mistake its real Interest, as the Heart its real Happiness. It would be the Interest of every Man to live agreeable to the Rules of Reason and Morality; but, how few in this Respect pursue their true Interest? It would be the Interest of Great Britain to give over attempting to tax her Colonies: It would be her Interest likewise to abolish Slavery in every Part of her Dominions; but how has she sacrificed her Interest in these Respects, to the Party or private Considerations of a few weak, or bad Men.

I shall not leave the Account I have given of the cruel Treatment of the Slaves in the West-Indies to rest upon my own Authority.

The Rev. Mr. Godwyn a Clergyman of the Church of England, in relating the Difficulties he met with, in endeavouring to instruct the Negroes in Barbadoes, in the principles of Christianity, informs us, that "they treat their Negroes with far less Humanity, than they do their Cattle, for they do not Starve their Horses, nor pinch the Cow by whose Milk they are sustained. The more innocent and laborious are worked to Death. They are tormented and whipped almost, and sometimes quite to Death, even for slight miscariages."

Sir Hans Sloan (who resided many years in Jamaica) in his Introduction to the Natural History of that Island, gives the following account of the Punishments inflicted on the Negroes. "For Rebellion, the Punishment is burning them, by nailing them down on the Ground, with crooked Sticks on every Limb, and then applying the Fire by Degrees from the Feet and Hands, burning them gradually upon the Head, whereby their Pains are extravagant. For Crimes of a Less Nature Castration or chopping off half the Foot with an Axe. For Negligence they are usually Whipped by the Overseers with Lance-wood Switches. After they are whipped 'till they are raw, some put on their Skins Pepper and Salt to make them smart; at other Times their Masters will drop Melted Wax on their Skins, and use several very exquisite Torments."—I could here add the Testimonies of many Gentlemen of Character who have witnessed Tortures (if possible) more cruel than these, in several of the Islands, and who are ready if required to give in their Names. But for the Honour of Human Nature I shall suppress them. Let not our Author after this, be offended at the harshest Epithets that can be given to those who inflict these Punishments. If he is, let him defend the West-India Planters from the Aspersions of Dr. Campbell, who speaking of the Negroes in the West Indies, says, "They endure a Slavery more complete, and attended with far worse Circumstances, than what any People in their Condition suffer, in any other Part of the World; or have suffered, in any other Period of Time." Let him defend them from the Aspersions of Huberus, who in his Defence of the necessity of a mild Slavery in some Countries adds, "I speak only of that kind of Slavery which was in Use amongst civilized Nations—not of that which prevails amongst Barbarians, or which the Africans endure in America." Let him defend them from the Aspersions of Dr. Adam Smith, who speaking of the Contempt of Death and Torture which prevails amongst Savage Nations, has the following Passage, "There is not a Negro from the Coast of Africa, who does not in this Respect possess a Degree of Magnanimity, which the Soul of his sordid Master is too often scarce capable of conceiving. Fortune never exerted more cruelly her Empire over Mankind, than when she subjected those Nations of Heroes, to the Refuse of the Jails of Europe, to Wretches who possess the Virtues neither of the Countries which they come from, nor of those they go to, and whose Levity, Brutality, and Baseness, so justly expose them to the Contempt of the Vanquished." Here I must turn Advocate for the first Inhabitants of the West-India Islands. Many of them fled from religious and civil Persecution. Most of them were descended from the first Families in Great Britain. The first Settlers in Barbadoes in a particular manner, who fled from the Tyranny of Cromwell, carried with them some of the purest Blood in the Nation. But what a Change has Negro-slavery made in some of their Posterity!—to be mistaken by a most ingenious Writer, from their "Levity, Brutality, and Baseness"—for "The Refuse of the Jails of Europe"— In a Word, if our Author means to defend the Slave Trade, or the West-India Planters to any purpose, let him defend them from the Aspersions of Montesquieu, Franklin, Wallis, Hutchinson, Sharp, Hargrave, Warburton, and Forster, who have all employed their Talents against them. The flashes of their Eloquence have long been seen at a Distance. I shall think myself Happy if I have served as an Instrument of *conducting* them to those Piles of Iniquity, which Slavery has raised in the British Settlements in America.

The Author of the Defence endeavours to palliate the Severity of the *penal* Laws which relate to Slaves in the West-Indies by saying, that they may appear "harsh at first Sight". We shall mention a few of them, extracted from the laws of Jamaica, and see whether they do not appear harsh upon a closer Examination. "If a Slave strike a White-Man, two Justices with three Freeholders, may punish him with Death, provided such Offence was not committed by his Master's Order, or in a legal Defence of *his* Goods." What a Door is here opened for Injuries of all kinds against the Slaves!—Even Self Preservation, the first Law of Nature, which often shews itself in Instinct, anticedent to the slower Operations of Reason, is here suspended by the Law of the Land. "Killing a Slave found stealing, or running away in the Night, shall be no Damage." "Runaway Slaves may have a Foot cut off by order of two Justices and three Freeholdes." "Persons wilfully killing Slaves shall for the first time be guilty of Felony, and the second Murder". Where are the Laws in any other civilized Country which make a distinction between a *first* and *second* Murder?—The difficulty of proving this Crime (so much complained of in other Countries) is encreased, by a Negro not being suffered to be a Witness in their Courts.

The small number of White People here, renders it extremely difficult to prove this or any other Crime by their Evidence.

I Hope it will not be thought that I am about to desert the Cause of Humanity, when I maintain with the Author of the Defence, that these severe Laws, and arbitrary Punishments are "absolutely necessary to the Safety and good Government of the Islands." Despotic Governments always require severe Laws. It is the same in Domestic Slavery: The natural Love of Liberty which is common to all Men, and the Love of Ease which is peculiar to the Inhabitants of Warm Climates, can only be overcome by severe Laws and Punishments. While Slaves are employed in a Climate and Labor, and treated with an Inhumanity, unknown to former Ages—While every Nerve must be kept stretched, and every Pore *constantly* open—While the Ideas of Liberty are kept up in the Minds of any of them, by the yearly Importation of Cargoes from Africa—While they are denied so many of the Necessaries and Comforts of Life, and lastly while their Proportion is so much greater than that of the white People, nothing but the Whip, melted Wax, Brine, the Gallows, the Stake, and the Gibbet, will long prevent Insurrections among them. Even these are often ineffectual for that Purpose. In spite of them all, Human Nature is now aiming to regain her Dignity, amongst the Slaves, in the Brasils, Surinam, and Chili, who have at last asserted their Liberty. Are not these Insurrections the beginnings of universal Retribution and Vengance upon European Tyranny, in America? and is it not high time for Britain to change her Conduct, and to adopt some safe and equitable means of abolishing Slavery in her Colonies.

The Author of the Defence endeavours to strengthen his Cause by degrading the Genius and Manners of the Africans, below the ordinary rank of human Creatures. Few Travellers possess Abilities, Introductions, or Languages, proper to acquire a complete knowledge of National Characters. Nations often differ widely in the compass of a few Years, and even the same Nation is different, in different parts of the same Kingdom. How widely do the Manners of the Chinese differ according to Du Haldt, and the Author of Lord Anson's Voyage round the World. The one describes the interior parts of the Country, the other, a Sea-port town. Human Nature is the same in all Ages and Countries; and all the difference we perceive in its Characters in respect to Virtue and Vice, Knowledge and Ignorance, may be accounted for from Climate, Country, Degrees of Civilization, form of Government, or other accidental causes, "Mankind (says that Citizen of the World Mr. Baretti) are of one great Family, and he is not a Friend to that Family, who contributes his Mite towards keeping it in Discord, by partial and false Representations. It is the Devil's Business to spread such erronious Notions, that Men may not consider themselves as Brothers, but contemn and hate each other."

Without availing myself of the Authorities of Smith, Adanson, Astley, Bosman, and others who speak in high Terms of the Africans, I shall allow that many of them are inferior in Virtue, Knowledge, and the love of Liberty to the Inhabitants of other parts of the World: but this may be explained from *Physical* causes. The different Nations of Africa are divided from each other by vast tracts of uninhabited Lands. This is the reason why this quarter of the Globe has never been the seat of a wide extended Empire; and hence the Natives continue chiefly in a Savage or Barbarous State, for Arms (on which extensive Empire has always been founded) and the Arts of Civilization have generally travelled together. Moreover the Heat of the Climate in Africa, by bringing on Indolence of Mind, and Body, exposes them at all Times to Slavery, while the Fertility of the Soil renders the Want of Liberty a less Evil to them, than it is to the Inhabitants of Northern, or less Warm and fruitful Countries. These last Causes, have likewise fixed Slavery in Asia: but from the undivided Nature of this Country, it has not been confined as in Africa to petty Monarchies, but extended through large Empires: Hence the Asiatics are a civilized People.

Could it be proved, that the Negroes are the only People in the World, who are ignorant of a Supreme Being, or that Worship Idols, it might add Weight to our Author's Argument derived from these Facts, to shew that they are an inferior Race of Men. Human Inventions in all Ages have corrupted Natural, as well as Revealed Religion. The Natives of Peru so famous in History, were discovered in a State of the most blind Idolatry; Examples of the same Kind are to be found without Number, in the Accounts of Travellers, of every Age and Country. In the Polite City of Athens, there were many who worshipped an "unknown God," and in Ephesus others, who lived altogether "without God in the World."

The best Definition that can be given of Man is, that he is a Creature capable of Religion. Who has not heard of the Christian Church in Africa? If Christianity has made less Progress, and been more corrupted in this Country than in many others, it must be ascribed among other Causes to its opposing Polygamy, a vice to which the Heat of the Climate, the early Maturity, and speedy Decay of the Women, and the peculiar fertility of the Soil, strongly disposes them. It is owing to the less severe Restraints which Mahomet laid upon this Vice, that his Religion continues to prevail throughout the greatest Part of this Country.

Our Author's last Charge against the Genius and Manners of the Africans, is founded upon their being "unacquainted with Friendship and Gratitude," and upon their being "separated from their nearest Relations without looking after them, or bidding them farewell." Friendship and Gratitude are founded upon the Wants and Weaknesses of Man in a State of Society. If any of the Negroes appear to be Strangers to these Virtues, it must be ascribed to their independent Mode of Life, as Savages, which exempts them from most of those Weaknesses, and artificial Wants, which are introduced by civilized Life. The Savage is indebted entirely to his Bow and Fishing Rod, for his Support. The Woods and Brooks, by satisfying chief of his Desires, raise him above the Obligations of Friendship and Gratitude. They likewise, by precluding all comparative Ideas, render him a Stranger to Envy and Ambition. The seeming Indifference with which some of the Negroes part from their Relations, must be ascribed in like Manner to their Character as Savages; it being esteemed amongst them the highest Mark of Heroism to bear the utmost Degrees of Pain and Misery without complaining. But this Insensibility to the Ties of Nature, Friendship, and Gratitude, is far from being general amongst the Negroes, The Natives of Congo, I have been informed by a Gentleman who has witnessed the Sale of many Cargoes of Slaves in the West-Indies, always show Signs of Grief upon being parted from their Friends, and Relations. The Cormanties are always prone to Insurrections. The Natives of Angola generally seek to destroy themselves. The Degrees of Natural Affection, Love of Liberty, and Resentment, discovered by the Negroes, are always proportioned to the Progress they had made in political, and domestic Happiness, in their own Country.

The Amusements, Songs &c. of the Negroes, are urged as signs of their Happiness, or Contentment in Slavery. Every one knows how often the Mind flies to these, to relieve itself from Melancholy. Although some of their Songs, like those of *civilized* Nations, are Obscene and Warlike, yet I have been informed that many of them, as well as their Tunes, are of a most plantive Nature, and very expressive of their Misery.

To a Mind divested of those Prejudices with which Custom leads us to view objects, the same Follies and Vices will appear under different forms in every state of Society, not only in the Individuals of the different Ranks and Characters of Mankind, but amongst different Nations likewise.

Where is the difference between an African Prince, with his face daubed with Grease, and his Head adorned with a Feather; and a modern Macaroni with his artificial Club of Hair daubed with Powder and Pomatum? Where is the difference between the British Senator who attempts to enslave his fellow subjects in America, by imposing Taxes upon them contrary to Law and Justice; and the American Patriot who reduces his African Brethren to Slavery, contrary to Justice and Humanity? Where is the difference between the sceptical Philosopher who will not allow those Men to be his equals in Genius or Manners, who differ from him in a few trifling Customs; and the bigotted Christian who will not allow those Christians to partake of the merits of his Saviour who mix with their worship a few trifling Ceremonies? Where is the difference between the Mahometan Negro who maintains three or four Wives agreeable to the Religion of his Country; and the European Christian who keeps three or four Mistresses contrary to the Religion of his Country? Where is the difference between the Pagan Negro who worships an evil Spirit, and uses a few ceremonies at a Funeral; and the superstitious Christian who worships God from a fear of the Devil, and connects his future Happiness with a Sacrament before, and a Funeral right after, his Death? Where is the difference between the African Savage, whose scanty wants are supplied by Nature and the European Nobleman, whose numerous wants are supplied by Art? They are both alike free from the Obligations of Friendship and Gratitude. It would lead us too far from our subject to shew in how many other Instances, the same rural sports, the same violent and lasting Resentments, the same Arts of Address and Dissimulation, and the same want of Affection in the Union of the sexes, Mark a Resemblance between the extremes of civilized, and the savage Life.—Lastly; where is the difference between that civilized Nation that yearly destroys 50,000 souls by her Trade under the sanction of Laws; and that barbarous Nation which destroys the same number with the Sword, without the sanction of Laws? The proportion of Vice is the same in both Nations. In the latter it appears like certain Diseases in strong Constitutions upon the Extremities and surface of the Body, whereas in the former it is thrown upon the Vitals. Still however, like the dreaded Worm of Africa it spreads its malignant Influence to every part of the Body, and unless it be wholly extracted, will at last end in its entire Dissolution. But supposing our Author had proved the Africans to be inferior in every thing to the Inhabitants of the other quarters of the Globe will his Cause derive any strength from it? Would it avail a man to plead in a Court of Justice that he defrauded his Neighbour, because he was inferior to him in Genius or Knowledge?

Was I an arbitary Prince in a Country whose Laws punished the lowest degree of Inferiority of Genius or Manners with perpetual Slavery, and should a Man claim a fellow subject for a Slave upon the best proofs of his being deficient in both,—I would suffer the unfortunate Criminal to go free, and inflict upon the Prosecutor the whole penalty of the Law. This Man's Genius and Manners above all others, would render him fit for nothing but Slavery.

I come now to enquire into the causes which have prevented the encrease of the Negroes in the West-Indies. These must be fought for, not in their "carelessness in preserving their Health" as our Author supposes, but in their peculiar situation and manner of Life as Slaves. The Africans multiply in their own Country with a Rapidity that is hardly credible, and from their Color and certain Customs which Experience has taught them, they are exempted from those Diseases which prove so fatal to the Europeans that come amongst them.

Three Causes concur to check Population in a Country, namely, Luxury, Debauchery, and Slavery. The first of these by encreasing our wants, encreases the difficulties of supporting a Family; the second renders the Sexes unfit, while the last abates the Appetite, for propagating the Species. All these produce their Effects according to their Degree, or according to their being more or less combined. Slavery operates differently, whether it be of a political, or domestic Nature. Political Slavery in some Countries has but little influence upon Population, such as in some parts of Asia, and Africa. In others it operates against it, as in Russia, and most of the states of Italy. Domestic Slavery in like manner sometimes exists under such alleviations as to have little influence upon Population. This was the case in Egypt. The Israelites multiplied in a rapid manner during their Captivity. That they were treated with Lenity we learn from the history of Joseph. Had Masters possessed a right over the Lives of their Slaves, Potiphar would have avenged the dishonour Joseph was accused of attempting to bring on his Bed, and not have consigned him over to be tried, condemned and punished by the municipal Law of the Country. Slaves encreased nearly in the same proportion as Freemen in the virtuous

Ages of the Roman Empire. We read of some who owned 10,000, and others 20,000 of them. That the Romans treated their Slaves with Lenity, we learn from the testimony of Seneca. It is true the Romans imported many Slaves from the Barbarous Countries they subdued, but this was in the declension of their Empire. It was not 'till this time that we read of the Ergastula, or House of Correction for Slaves. They partook of the dissolute manners of their Masters, and therefore foreign supplies were necessary to repair the waste which Debauchery had introduced amongst them. It is true also, the right of Life was held over Slaves, and Tortures were inflicted upon them in criminal Cases: But the same right was held by the Romans over their own Children, and Tortures were inflicted in like cases upon Freemen. They were seldom put in Execution upon either, in the early Ages of the Empire. Slaves multiplied among the antient Germans, by whom they were treated with the Familiarity of Children, according to the Testimony of Tacitus. Slaves have multiplied moreover in the Northern and Middle colonies of America. But in the West-Indies they have never encreased by ordinary Population. We shall first prove this Fact, and then assign the reasons of it.

Ligon in his Account of Barbadoes tells us that in the year 1646 there were 20,000 Whites on that Island, besides, to use his own Words "a far greater number of Blacks." In the year 1676 the Negroes in Barbadoes amounted to above one hundred thousand. Upon a Parliamentary enquiry into the state of the African Trade in the year 1728 it appeared that in three years only the number of Negroes imported into Barbadoes, Jamaica, and Antigua amounted to 42,000, besides what were carried to St. Kitts, Nevis, and Monserrat. From this it appears, that the Island of Jamaica, allowing it only an equal proportion with Barbadoes and Antigua, imported 14,000 Negroes in three years. When we consider the great increase of the demand for Sugar, and the other Produce of that Island, since the year 1728, we cannot admit of less than 5,000 Negroes being imported there every year since. Let us now enquire what is the present number of the Negroes in these Islands. In Barbadoes they do not exceed 100,000, and in Jaimaica they do not amount to 200,000. If in the latter they have encreased by a few thousands within these forty years it is not owing to ordinary Population, but to the many new Estates which have lately been settled on that Island. When we look back and estimate the numbers which have been sacrificed by this Trade, and when we look forward, and estimate the encreasing proportion which it must destroy, if it continues upon its present footing, we would wish to forget the obligations we owe to Justice, Humanity, Religion, and to the British name. What War, or Pestilence ever made such Havock with the human species? Spaniards blush at the Recital of the Massacre of the Indians in South America, and wish to blot it out of their Histories. But Britons, once famed thro' every quarter of the Globe for their love of Justice, Humanity and Liberty,—nay more, British Americans, the descendants of those illustrious Men of whom Britain at one period of her History was not worthy,—British Americas, who a few years ago risked their all in opposing the claims of the British Parliament; these very Americans, have fallen into a trade more destructive to their fellow

Creatures than Spanish tortures, they have pursued it upwards of an hundred years, and what is more—they defend it as lawful.

Having proved that the Negroes in the West-Indies do not encrease by ordinary population, I come now to enquire into the Reasons of it.

Of the three Causes we mentioned which concur to check population, the two last, namely, Debauchery, and Slavery, act chiefly upon the Negroes. Dr. Bancroft ascribes their Decerase entirely to Debauchery, but we shall find that Slavery (under its peculiar aggravations in the West-Indies) has a great share in destroying them. The Appetite for propagating the Species amongst the Blacks, bears no relation to the heat of the Climate, or to the degrees of the same Appetite in the White People. A greater proportion of Infants than in other Countries, perish in their Birth. Their Children besides being subject to all the numerous Diseases of Children in warm Countries, have one that is peculiar to them, and which arises from their peculiar Circumstances as Slaves, which proves fatal to Numbers. The Want of Confidence in Fathers in the Fidelity of their Wives, and the Wretchedness of Mothers, have always been found to lessen that care which is the Offspring of Natural Affection in Parents for their Children. This disregard in Parents for their Posterity, is encreased among the Slaves in the West-Indies by the Reflection of the Misery they have entailed upon them;—here then we discover another Source of Accidents and Mortality among the Negro Children.

I must not omit taking Notice of a Disease called the *Seasoning*, which destroys many of the Negroes. It arises partly from their unwholesome Diet on Shipboard, and partly from the Hippocondriac Disorder, which their new and wretched Manner of Life brings on them. Now when we add to all these, the hard Labor which the Negroes undergo in a Climate not intended for it—their spare Diet—and their intemperance in drinking the most pernicious Liquors; we may account for the immense Waste of them in the West-Indies. They all stand charged upon Slavery.

I know it has been said by some, that the Climate of the West-Indies destroys many of the Negroes. But Experience convinces us that this is not the Case. They are even exempted from the most fatal epidemic Diseases to which the White People are subject. Nor should the Mortality among the Whites be attributed entirely to the Climate. The most populous Nations, and the longest lived People, have always been found in warm Countries. The Mortality of the Europeans arises from their carrying with them to the West-Indies their European Diet, and Manners. These, together with that Luxury which is founded on the Labor of the Negroes, have prevented the Increase of White People in the Islands. The Assembly of Jamaica have in vain attempted, by Laws made for that Purpose, to encourage Artificers and Labourers (who constitute the greatest Body of the People in all Countries) to settle amongst them. They can never reconcile themselves to working with Slaves. It is owing to these Causes, that the Number of White People in Jamaica has not exceded 30,000 at one time, in the Course of Ninety Years. Compare this, with the Province of Pennsylvania, whose inhabitants in the same Space of Time, from ordinary Population and the

Accession of Strangers, have amounted to near 400,000 Souls. In these consist the true Riches and Glory of Britain. "In the Multitude of People is the King's Honor, but in the Want of People is the Destruction of a Prince."

Thus we see that the Slave Trade is not only repugnant to Religion, and the true Interests of our Mother Country, but that it offers Violence to the oeconomy of Nature. The Air—the Sea—Heaven and Earth—all the Elements, conspire against it.

The Author of the Defence endeavours to shelter the West-India Planters under the Practices of some of the "Firmest Supporters of Religion in England, both of the Clergy and Laity." The greatest Sanctity of Office, and the highest attainments in Wisdom, will not always preserve Men from Vice and Error. The Clergy of every Church are as apt to confound the Attributes of the Deity, with a few detached Passages in the Scriptures, as Lawyers are, to confound Natural Equity with Acts of Parliament, or as Physicians are, to mistake the Operations of Nature for those of Medicine. A Planter in one of the West-India Islands who felt some uneasiness in his Mind from keeping Negro Slaves, wrote lately to a learned Divine in London, to know whether it was unlawful. The Divine wrote for answer, that the Jews had Slaves—that it was not forbidden in the New Testament—that domestic Slavery had existed in every Age and Corner of the World—and that by treating his Slaves well, he committed no Crime in keeping them. Had this Planter listened a little longer to the Voice of Heaven, speaking in his Heart, or consulted the whole Tenor of his Bible, he would have received a very different Answer to his Question. I beg leave to add here, that the same Arguments derived from Scripture and Precedents, which establish domestic, likewise establish political Slavery. The Jews, God's peculiar People, were under Bondage to the Egyptians, and unless we oppose the whole Spirit of Christianity, to a few single Precepts, St. Paul's advice to the Romans is a much stronger Proof of the Lawfulness of political Slavery, than any yet adduced from the Old or New Testament, in Favor of the Lawfulness of domestic Slavery. If domestic Slavery is agreeable to the Will and Laws of God, political Slavery is much more so.—Then it follows, that our British Constitution was obtained unjustly—King Charles the First did no wrong—Passive Obedience was due to Oliver Cromwell—King James the Second was the Lord's Anointed—The Revolution was a Rebellion—King William was a Tyrant—The illustrious House of Hanover are Usurpers—and the Right of the British Parliament to tax the American Colonies, is unlimited and indisputable.—Ancient and modern Precedents should have no Weight in this Dispute; for political as well as domestic Slavery, has existed amongst civilized Nations in every Age, and Corner of the World. But has its Iron Sceptre been softened, by the few despotic Kings who have been wise and just, and the few Nations which have lived happily and flourished in that State? In a Word, if we reason from Example, where shall we stop? For where is the Error, or Vice, that has not been admitted as true, or practised as lawful, in some Age or Country? "There is a Way which seemeth right unto a Man; but the end thereof are the Ways of Death."

The Reader will here pardon my saying a Word or two of myself. I am called upon by the Author of the Defence to answer a Question.—Should I become "an Owner of a West-India Estate by the Death of a Relation, or some other unexpected Means," he desires to know "whether I could lay my Hand on my Heart, and say, with a safe Conscience, that I would instantly free all my Slaves, and destroy my Sugar Works." Suppose I should refuse to do this, the Subject remains where it did,—I should then commit a Crime for which I should *justly* "loose the Esteem of Men of Sense, and of a rational Way of thinking."

And now my West-India Friend, give me leave in my turn to ask you a few Questions. Lay your Hand upon *your* heart, and tell me; would you like to be sold, for no fault, or torn against your will from your Sisters and Brothers, and carried into a foreign Country, to be subjected to the absolute dominion of a Master; to be obliged to labor without intermission, to cease to make any further improvements in Virtue or Knowledge; to be fed and cloathed scantily; to be tempted by your situation to all the low Vices of Slavery, to be punished in the most cruel manner if you attempted to regain your Liberty; Would you like to be told, if you should complain of your hard fate, that the "Imperfection of Human Society required that you should be a Slave; that Moses the Jewish Law-giver commanded it, that the Gospel did not proclaim a jubilee to Slaves; that you had "no Genius" that Mr. Hume had said, from your Ignorance of the Religion, and your backwardness in acquiring the Language, and Learning of the Country you were in, you belonged to an inferior race of Men, that you wanted feeling, because Resentment, and the prospect of greater Misery absorbed the Grief you would otherwise have shewed upon parting with your Family; that your Master was "educated in a Country of Liberty and Humanity," and that it was his "interest to treat you well"; that the Tortures inflicted upon you for attempting to regain your Liberty, "were inferior to those inflicted upon Damien, and the Conspirators against the Life of the present King of Portugal"; that "all Happiness was comparative"; that you were "much happier than the Peasants of Scotland, Ireland, and Poland;" that upon the whole your situation was more to be envied than pitied, "and that you might quit the World with the certainty that your Children would be treated with the same care you had experienced yourself"?—I anticipate your Answer to these Questions. You would not. Then Sir pause a few Minutes, and reflect upon what you have done. You have called in question the Justice and goodness of the Supreme Being. You have charged the Father of Mankind with being the Author of the greatest Evils to his Children. You have aimed to establish Principles, which justify the most extensive and cruel Depradations which have been made by Conquerors and Tyrants, upon the Liberties and Lives of Mankind, and which at the same time condemn those glorious Events, and illustrious Men, that Britain and her Colonies, are indebted to for their Liberty and Prosperity. You have misrepresented the true Interests of our Mother Country. You have attempted to palliate Crimes which are founded on a Pride and Depravity of Soul, unavoidable in Masters and Slaves in the West-Indies. You have thrown a Veil over the true Causes which destroy so many Thousands of your fellow Creatures every year. You have (to use your own Words) "unworthily traduced" not "many of my valuable Friends" but the *whole* of your *own* Brethren—the poor Africans. You have attempted to sink Creatures, formed like yourself, in the Image of God, and equally capable of Happiness both here and hereafter, *below* the rank of "Monsters and Barbarians", or even Brutes themselves. You have—but I forbear to add to the Reproaches to which you have exposed yourself.—"As a Person cannot err so grosly as not to be able to make Atonement" I hope you will not fail immediately to ask forgiveness of your Maker, and your Country, for the Attack you have made upon the Rights of Mankind.

Perhaps some of my West-India Readers are waiting to see an Apology, for the Account I have given in the Address of the Punishments inflicted upon the Negroes in the West-Indies. If they are, they will certainly be mistaken. Although the Address "was written hastily," yet the most ingenious Tortures that ever were inflicted upon a West-India Slave, should not prevail upon me to acknowledge, that is was written "without sufficient Proofs of what I advanced," The Authorities upon which I have rested all my Facts, cannot be contradicted. But I am far from applying the Account that is given of the inhuman Practices of *some* Masters, to all the Planters in the West-Indies. If it is unfair to reason against the Practice of any Thing in itself lawful, from its Abuse; it is not so, to reason against Practices, in themselves unlawful, from their Abuse. The rankest Weeds, and the most delicious Fruits, often grow in the same Soil. I honour the West-Indians for their Hospitality, Generosity, and Public Spirit. I have had the Pleasure of knowing many of them, who were distinguished for their Humanity, and every other Virtue that could adorn human Nature. There are some Metals so pure that they receive no Rust from being exposed to the moistest Atmosphere; so there are some Dispositions naturally so good, that they cannot contract the least soile of Vice—even from Slavery.

I have avoided as much as possible every Thing through the whole of this Vindication, that could draw me from my Subject to the Author of the Defence. I shall not even give him the Pain of repeating here the many unkind Insinuations and Reflections he has thrown out against me. He was perhaps warm when he wrote them—When he cools, I am persuaded he will be "sorry for his ungenerous abuse of a man who never injured him," or any other *Individual* born in the West-Indies.

Personal Slavery Established, 1773

Anonymous, *Personal Slavery Established by the Suffrages of Custom and Right Reason Being a Full Answer to the Gloomy and Visionary Reveries, of all the fanatical and enthusiastical Writers on that Subject* (Philadelphia, 1773), pp. 3-26.

The pamphlet warfare in Philadelphia between Benjamin Rush and Richard Nisbet spawned several articles and tracts on both sides of the slavery issue. One intriguing publication, carrying a dedication "To the Worshipful Committee-Men of the Royal African Company," attacked writers such as Rush who had dared assail the institution of slavery. This anonymous pamphlet was, however, not an attack on antislavery writers but one of the most clever, adroit antislavery satires of the eighteenth century. Written as a parody on Nisbet's Slavery Not Forbidden by Scripture, *the pamphleteer showered unbridled praise upon the philanthropic good works of slave dealers, those altruistic "worthy sirs" who rescued ignorant heathens from their African savagry. The essay, placing the Negro race on an evolutionary ladder next to the Ourang Outang, (sic), asserted that no kingdoms of any importance had risen in Africa, none, that is, except "Bildulgerid, Ethiopia, Nubia, Abissinia, Morocco, and many others that are rather large."*

The pamphleteer dismissed John Woolman as a "visionary enthusiast," attacked Anthony Benezet as a theorist who could have no legitimate opinions on slavery because he owned no slaves, and charged Rush with blasphemy for suggesting that slavery, although not expressly forbidden by the scriptures, was repugnant to Christianity. And, as Jonathan Swift had done in "A Modest Proposal" nearly 50 years before, the pamphleteer on the last page suggested a ghastly remedy to food shortage problems.

The Dedication

To the Worshipful Committee-Men of the Royal African Company

May it please your Worships, The intention of the publication before you, being to vindicate a cause which has been a principal object of your attention, has a consequent claim to your patronage, I shall therefore make no apology for inscribing it to you. Notwithstanding the endeavours of ignorant bigots, to represent the Slave trade in an odious light, I hope this humble attempt to expose them, will meet your approbation; and convince the world that the lustre of your characters is by no means impaired, but that like pure metal, the more they are rubbed by those enthusiastic advocates for liberty, the brighter they will shine. I am under no personal obligations to you—the gratitude I feel arises from a nobler source—it is a just tribute to that generous disinterested exertion of benevolence and philanthropy, which has been the principal means of heaping wealth and honours on Europeans and Americans, and rescuing many millions of wretched Africans, as *brands from the fire*, and even compelling them to the enjoyment of a more refined state of happiness, than the partiality of fate had assigned them in their native state. Go on, worthy sirs! in the glorious work; and continue to merit from every liberal mind, that gratitude and admiration, which warmly impress that of, honoured gentlemen,

Your most obedient, and very humble servant,

The Author

The Preface

It is well observed by some author I have read, that the best human institutions partake of imperfection; and the most excellent constitution has its defects.—The liberty of the press has doubtless some advantages; but it may be questioned whether these outweigh its inconveniencies. We may certainly reckon among the latter, the opportunities with which it furnishes *weak* men of venting the idle dreams of a distempered brain; or designing ones of carrying on their dark purposes, by misrepresentation, slander, or other mischievous means. Had it not been for this unrestrained liberty of the press, the task I have undertaken would have been probably needless; and I had been spared the distress which attends me, in being obliged to expose my poor abilities to the publick view. Confiding however in its candour, I will not increase my claim on its patience by a long preface. I will only say, that in gratitude to the author of "*Slavery not forbidden by scripture*, &c." I have endeavoured to adopt this plan so fully, that the following pages may answer the purpose of a second edition of that celebrated work, with some corrections, transpositions, and emendations.

New-Castle County, Nov. 26th, 1773

Personal Slavery Established, &c.

Having attentively perused several of the late publications on the subject of personal Slavery, I think it may not be amiss if I state, in a summary way, the arguments adduced in them for and against the practice; and draw such conclusions, as may be warrantable from the premises. The first on the subject, which I shall notice, is a pamphlet intitled,

Considerations on keeping Negroes, &c. by John Woolman. As his arguments against the practice are all drawn from the Old and New Testament, and their authority has been long since rejected by some of our most prevailing systems of politicks, I think it is unnecessary to say more, than it appears to be the dull productions of a visionary enthusiast.—The next work in my catalogue, is

A short account of that part of Africa inhabited by the Negroes, &c. The author or compiler of this work has taken great pains to convince us, that he concurs with a number of other authors in condemnation of the Slave-trade, as unjust, cruel, and impolitic; and to support their opinions, relates a number of what he would suppose are facts. Now as those supposed facts constitute the foundation of most of his arguments, if they are removed little need be said to prove his opinions to be idle and nugatory. Those facts are generally the relations of men, who are, or have been concerned or employed in the trade to Africa for Slaves, unsupported by a single affidavit, or any other *legal* proof of their authority; and moreover men speaking in a cause in which they are parties; and therefore cannot be supposed to tell the *whole* truth, even could we suppose what they have told is truth. I could produce numberless authorities from our law books, to prove that no evidence can be admitted but what is well established *on oath*, and that all offered by parties to the matter in dispute, must be rejected. Such is the law, and the law being allowed to be the perfection of reason, it follows that the arguments of our author on the subject of slavery, are not only unreasonable, but also illegal, and therefore inadmissable.—Proceed we therefore to consider,

A caution and warning to Great-Britain and her colonies, &c. by Ant. Benezet. I will promise that on a particular enquiry, I have found that this gentleman has no Negroes, and no concern in trade. We can therefore be at no difficulty in accounting for a certain contraction of sentiment, evident in his abstract ideas of right and wrong. They are merely theoretick, and a little acquaintance with men and things would convince him, are better calculated for the amusement of recluse bigots, than the attention of men endued with a more liberal turn of thinking, and enlarged ideas. The general arguments he has made use of, are so similar to those of the last mentioned piece, that the objections I have advanced in considering *that*, are also applicable to this. The extract of a sermon preached by the Bishop of Gloucester, which he has presumptuously tacked to the end of his pamphlet, is such an absurd rhapsody, as in less corrupt times would have deprived the Bishop of his See. Perhaps it has been tenderly winked at, as owing to that intense application, which at the time that it opened the treasure of knowledge to his view, obscured his faculties in using them.

The next piece on the subject, which I have met with, is *an address to the inhabitants of the British Settlements in America, upon Slave-keeping, &c.* As this piece is particularly animadverted on in a judicious and very candid defence of the practice in general, and particularly of the West-India planters from the calumnies it contains, I shall state the sum of the arguments from each, together. This last tract is entitled,

Slavery not forbidden by Scripture; or, a Defence of the West-India planters from the aspersions, &c. by a West-Indian. As the author's place of residence was such, as must afford him the best opportunities of being well acquainted with his subject; and it does not appear from the title page, that he had any concern in the slave trade, nor had reaped any advantage from the labour of slaves, we cannot hesitate in giving his sentiments their due weight, in opposition to all that has been advanced against Slavery, by men who have not had his opportunities. From the observations I have already made, I have left but little room to doubt which side of the question I espouse; and it will appear further evident from those I may make, as in expressing my sentiments of the address I shall be apt, very frequently to use the words of the Defence, in adopting this method, I hope I shall not incur the charge of plagiarism, as I believe the essence of that crime consists in borrowing from an author without confessing the debt. These things being premised, I shall proceed to consider the Address not only as it relates to Slavery, but also as a most scandalous and audacious libel on *every* individual inhabitant of *every* island in the West-Indies.

The author of the Address, pretending to aim at the reformation of mankind, points out the practice of personal Slavery, as one particular that *he* thinks requires it, and recommends the adoption of a plan that he opines would be likely to abolish it, never giving himself time to consider our natural frailties—the impossibility of absolute perfection—that there are faults in every human institution, and that till self-interest ceases to have influence over the actions of men, proposals that strike at the very root of their temporal interests—their ease—their convenience and grandeur, will never be listened to. He might as well have poured forth his eloquence against the lawless ambition of Kings in sacrificing millions of their fellow creatures—the knavery of Statesmen—the avarice of Bishops, Lawyers, Physicians and Merchants—the endless endeavours of men universally to overreach one another, and the continued scene of bloodshed and cruelty exhibited by most of our favourite sports; all which it is evident, from his not mentioning them, he secretly approves; I say, he might as well have poured forth his eloquence on all or any of these, as exercise his declamatory powers on Slavery. A man of a liberal and benevolent way of thinking, would have seen that they are all but the necessary consequences of the imperfection of our nature; and that his leisure hours might have been better employed, than in railing at slavery, which at the worst cannot be said to sacrifice millions for so trifling a pittance as a small spot of land.

The Addresser absurdly endeavours to prove from scripture, that the Slavery tolerated by the Mosaic law, was essentially different from that now imposed on the Africans; and gives some reasons (as specious as he can make them) to convince us they might have particular reasons for the kind of slavery they did tolerate. He might as well have inferred that if the advocates for Slavery, justify the practice under that law; the other parts of it, in every particular, are still obligatory; and although subjecting us to some inconvenient ceremonies, would give us a title to many valuable priviledges, as turning off a wife we might be tired of, &c. &c. But as I observed at setting out, the authority of scripture is now generally rejected by men of a liberal way of thinking. I shall therefore be more brief on any arguments drawn from it on either side, and confine myself to such, as in my own opinion, are reasonable and in point. Is it not highly probable that the Africans we enslave, are descendants of the very same Heathen that were *round about* the Israelites, who we all know lived a long time in Africa? If so, as they still remain unconverted, are they not yet in the same predicament with their ancestors? And as, without much arrogance we may esteem ourselves as Israelites, or at least descended from them, will it be denied that we are entitled to the liberty of enslaving the Africans and the Heathen *round about* us also? This last is a trade we might drive on with very little shipping, and may be worthy of consideration.

Our author, in attempting to prove the inconsistency of Slavery under the Christian dispensation, is quite blasphemous. He would infer that although there is no *express* precept against the Slave-trade to Africa or keeping Slaves, they are both absolutely repugnant to the very genius and spirit of Christianity. Just as if we were to imagine any evil was intended to be removed that was not expressly forbidden in the New-Testament. This would be to suppose that the lawless ambition of Kings sacrificing millions of their fellow creatures, and the little catalogue of other necessary consequences of the imperfection of our nature, before mentioned, are inconsistent with the Christian religion. How absurd is such reasoning? How impious its author! 'Tis well he is not within the reach of a Popish inquisition; he certainly would have made a principle character in an *Auto de fe*.

Notwithstanding his absurdities, and his being totally unacquainted with the subject, I admit his arguments have some weight in these northern colonies. Truth and justice should have very distinct ideas annexed to them at the pole, from what they convey under the equinoctial. There is a certain *political necessity* by which those ideas should be regulated; and as this necessity may be very different in different latitudes, a practice may be meritorious in the West-Indies, which in Canada is far otherwise. Had our author and his associates confined their slander to their own countrymen, and *expressly* excepted the West-Indians from any share in them, I should have had no objection to the display of their abilities. He certainly never considered that the inhabitants of the British islands in the West-Indies, hold to the value of £22,000,000 in live stock, exclusive of quadrupeds and other chattels; and that were his pernicious doctrines, (which thus impiously exclude the idea of political necessity) to prevail, they might soon be twenty-two millions of money poorer than they now esteen themselves to be.—Rum, Sugar, Rice and Indigo are indispensible necessaries of life, and if we exclude Negroes, we must introduce white men in their cultivation, which would never answer; for they could not sustain the labour as well as blacks, as this author himself is pleased, with unusual candour, to allow; and perhaps it might be rather difficult (especially if they were Britons) to persuade them to submit, to what their masters might think a proper correction in compelling them to it. The obstinacy of their tempers might occasion an exertion of spirit in the masters, that would sometimes bring the lives of the latter as well as the former into some danger, as without doubt it would happen now and then, that a surviving fellow servant might be hardy enough to inform, and claim the vengeance of the laws, which in the case of white men, may not be suffered to remain as they now are. Besides this, there would be a danger that industrious servants would frequently become masters; and if this ever happened in the sugar colonies, and they were not able to make fifty hogsheads of sugar each; by joining in the expence, they might obviate the difficulties arising from the great expence of sugar-works; for it appears it is no more worth while to erect proper works for the manufacture of any less quantity, than it would be in a wheat country, for every petty farmer to build a mill for the grinding his own grain. By such means in time the great estates of the West-Indians would be divided, and many families, who by honest Industry have risen to affluence, could rise no *higher*. This would probably discourage that profusion of expence, for which the West-Indians have been always remarkable, and which has been so advantageous to the Mother Country, a consideration highly worthy of attention; even if by such a division of estates, the revenues of government were not lessened, which would certainly be the case if the number of *whites* was increased, who would undoubtedly consume more among themselves. Now the quantity of West-India produce does not only benefit Britain in respect to the revenue, but the Sugar, &c. sent home, by giving employment to the refiners of Sugar, sailors, ship-builders, &c. also *creates* an increase of its inhabitants; whether by any prolific, or what other quality in the Sugar, &c. I cannot tell; but such is the fact, as I am informed by the *Defence*.

Was government sufficiently stupid to listen to the complaint of the author of the *Address* and his associates, or any such visionary enthusiasts, and proclaim liberty to *four hundred* thousand Negroes, who are said to be in the British islands only, it is most probable that near *four* thousand gentlemen Christians, and among them some of the richest

British subjects, would be immediately reduced to a most calamitous situation—would be obliged to content themselves with what they have already so equitably acquired by their labour; and one hundred times that number of poor stupid Negroes would be turned adrift, and forever after deprived of *their* kind care and protection. What an unchristian conduct would this be? I am really quite tired of this writers absurdities; nor less shocked at his want of humanity.

Had he and his associates confined themselves to the supposed propriety of prohibiting the African trade in general terms, I should not have felt the least desire of combatting their opinions. But he has represented the West-India Planters as a set of hardened monsters; or at least that many cruel punishments are inflicted on their Slaves by *some* of them. He little thinks I can trace most of his malicious hints to the identical persons he aims at. Does he idly imagine that there is any difficulty in seeing that the syringe of his venom is principally levelled against the Hon. Mr.——of Bar—s, John——, Esq; of Ant—a, Mr.——of St. K—s,—a certain Honourable and worthy gentleman of Jam—ca, who commonly wears blue cloaths, &c. &c. I could point out several others who are evidently the particular objects of his slander, were I so disposed; but these are sufficient to satisfy the public, that his reflections are altogether *personal*, and that his *Address* is written solely with a design to spread them. As to his particular instances of barbarity, he does not mention one that is well supported by proof, and we cannot admit the possibility of the facts, as the author of the *Defence* assures us *he* never was an eye-witness of one single instance as particularized in the *Address*, &c. and yet with a candour that is ever the companion of truth, he does allow a *few* instances of the kind mentioned, had happened. One or two more of these fanatic writers adduce authorities for some of their assertions of this sort. I would not offer to impeach the credit of Sir Hans Sloan, but he was certainly a milky tempered man, whose mind was not properly impressed with the idea of the *political necessity* of such a conduct to keep slaves in *proper* awe; and I must say, I think as he had received civilities from many gentlemen in Jamaica, and considerable additions were there made to his collection of natural curiosities, his character as a *gentleman* would have shone quite as conspicuously, had he suppressed some of his reflections on their behaviour to their slaves.—The deserving part of the Negroes will maintain their good behaviour, and the worthless from motives of fear take care *never to merit* punishment; so that the little severity commonly used among them is *unmerited* and merely *in Terrorem*. But when they are faulty, and you omit correction, they will surely *laugh* heartily at your folly. If you are foolish enough to be indulgent and easy with them, they will not only exercise their risible faculties, but become compleat villains; and the chances are ten to one that your particular favourites are the ringleaders in every insurrection. Notwithstanding all this, such is their clemency and forbearance, that the most severe penalties are inflicted on any one who chastises a Negroe without acquainting the proprietor, or if he should unluckily be in England, why then rather than you should be *laughed* at (which we all know is very provoking) a formal complaint to his Manager, who is always or *generally* a gentleman by birth or education, will answer the purpose. The whip with which the driver always follow the Negroes while at their work, is only carried as a badge of authority, and so little used, that like Edward the Confessor's sceptre, it may be handed down to succeeding generations.

Another objection of our sagacious *Addressor* is pointed at the severity of the laws in the southern colonies and islands, respecting Negroes. His ignorance accompanies him in every line; and yet I admit that at first sight, many of them do really *appear* harsh, and give an idea *rather* unfavourable of the clemency of their legislatures; but on examination, the harshness of this first *appearance* will entirely vanish; they will appear excuseable and absolutely necessary to the *good* government, and safety of the white people. Thus the *looming* of the fogs of ignorance, when dispelled by the winds of *political necessity*, will no more deceive us.—The disproportion of whites and blacks is there very great; and self-preservation, that first and ruling principle of human nature, has made them jealous and *perhaps* severe in their laws, but they are but mere *threats* as it were, and only held up, as the drivers whip, to intimidate delinquents. They are found to be essential in the very *being* of those colonies. Is it not strange that those thunder headed scribblers cannot view them through the medium of this political necessity on which I have so clearly insisted?—Slaves are never *capitally* punished but for the most flagrant crimes, nor condemned without the clearest proof; nay, such is their tenderness on this head, that I have known a humane gentleman frequently to conceal the most attrocious crime, rather than suffer the unhappy perpetrator to be punished with *death*. To suppose that masters would choose to forfeit their service forever, which is the undeniable consequence of a *capital* punishment, would be to prove them destitute of common sense as well as compassion. In some cases we allow slaves have been burnt or gibited alive, but neither of these modes of punishment, nor any other *ever* used among them, can come under the idea of severity, if we reflect on what Ravailac, Damien, and others have suffered for murdering, or attempting to murder Kings, or even that *cruel* Israelitish practice of boreing the ear of a Slave with an awl, and obliging him to do all his work *fastened* in that shocking manner to a door post, which 'tis probable he was obliged to drag after him, when he had occasion to move.

The charge of starving their Slaves is as groundless, and may as easily be refuted. Would you, wise Sir! esteem it good policy to starve a yoke of oxen, and especially in seed time and harvest, on the labour of which you depended for bread? It is certainly true that they do not invite negroes to their turtle feasts, nor feed them with the nicest dainties; but they have a proper allowance of corn in all places; in some they are allowed a part of Sunday, and in others even all that day, to raise their own provisions. Nay, it is not very uncommon for very good masters, to give them their daily allowance, and all Sunday besides to themselves. Hence it sometimes happens that provident cunning fellows (for such there are even among these brutes) have been known to sell *considerable* quantities of produce, and indulge themselves with a variety of *luxuries*.

It is very evident that notwithstanding the accounts of fabulous voyagers, the Negroes on the western coasts of Africa, are the most stupid, beastly race of animals in human shape, of any in the whole world. The brutality, nastiness, indolence and other *criminal* propensities of the Hottentots, are a convincing proof of the truth of my assertion; and though I admit they are not destitute of hospitality to strangers (of which Aesop gives us many instances, even in four footed beasts) yet I am far from thinking this can counterbalance their execrable fondness for raw flesh.—The author of the *Defence* asserts that there are four or five different species of men,—with submission, I will limit them to four, viz. 1st, Europeans, 2d, Assiaticks, 3d, Americans, and 4th, Africans, and retracting the word *species*, substitute *genus*, which is more expressive of my idea as being a general term, by which I would distinguish the last as only a *species* of that *genus*, though utterly devoid of reason. Carrying this idea a little further, I would yet subdivide the Africans into five *classes*, arranging them in the order as they approach nearest to reason, as 1st, Negroes, 2d, Ourang Outangs, 3d, Apes, 4th, Baboons, and 5th, Monkeys. The opinion of their irrationality is so well supported by *facts*, that to those acquainted with them, I need advance very little on the subject; but to remove every scruple from the sceptic, a little undeniable evidence may not be improper.—There never was a civilized nation of any other complexion than *white*; nor ever any individual eminent either in action or speculation that was not rather inclining to the *fair*. Africa, except a small part of it, inhabited by those of our own colour, is totally overrun with Barbarism—nay such is the contaminating influence of black, that I fear I need not except *even* the *whites* among *them*. Perhaps this observation may assist us in accounting for the few appearances of Barbarism we now and then discover among the *whites* in our southern colonies and islands, where *blacks* bear so large a proportion to their number. But to proceed from this short digression, Africa has no kingdoms of any eminence, but chiefly consists of petty monarchies, excepting Bildulgerid, Ethiopia, Nubia, Abissinia, Morocco, and many other that are rather large. That they are *all* perpetually at war with each other, we are well assured, for it is certainly the case with all the petty nations, that are not very distant from our European factories on their western coasts, from the river Senegal to the Cape of Good Hope; the Hottentots, Ferlys and some few others, only excepted. The stupidity of the natives cannot be attributed to climate; for that rule would also effect the Chinese and the West-Indians themselves; and besides, the Moors (who are situated at no great distance from the Slave coasts) have always made a figure in history, and the Egyptians were once eminent for the progress of the arts. But these are rather instances of the powers of sagacious instinct than a proof of my opinion, respecting the irrationality of *all* Africans, being erroneous. Let not any in answer to what I have said relating to their governments and wars, object the similarity of description given by Tacitus and other historians, of many European nations in early ages. Such an objection can have no weight, when we consider the Europeans are blessed with reason, and therefore capable of improvement. Besides the descriptions of this kind are made by Roman authors, who generally gave an exaggerated picture of the manners of any people with whom they were at war, and especially if they had any particular designs on them, or to enslave them or any thing else for which they could pretend no just authority, for such representations might afford them some excuse for their lawless ambition. This furnishes us too, with another strong reason for discrediting abundance of idle tales, on which the arguments of these gloomy oppugners of Slavery are founded, as I have before observed.

I could never perceive the Africans have the most distant notions of a supreme being, which had they any rational powers, they would certainly have either by intuition, or the benefit of the connection which those near our factories especially must have with abundance of *pious* white people, whose lawful concerns carrying them into Africa, we may suppose spare no opportunities of benefitting them in any sense. In the conversation of these, the Negroes would frequently hear imprecations, that would communicate the *notion* of the whites on this subject. They have, however, a confused notion of an evil spirit called *Jumbee*, who is able to do them mischief, and it is a custom among them to hang a broken bottle, a bit of rag, or any thing else by way of charm near their ground, which they call *Oby*, and is I suppose their good spirit. When their property is thus guarded, few Negroes will have the boldness to steal any part of it. How such irrationals came by even so much religion is hard to find, except we may be allowed a conjecture that they have a faint notion of image worship; borrowed probably from Roman itinerant Missionaries, as I think Baretti tells us that among the Catholicks, when any indecency is intended in the presence of a picture Saint or Madona, a cloth is carefully placed before the picture to conceal such indecency from their view. They also make some little shew of religion at their funerals, but this too may be well attributed to imitation; and we may assign the same cause, if we discover any think like sentiments of friendship, gratitude, or other social ties among them.—In arts and sciences, they have never made the least progress, which is another strong proof of their brutality. In their music, although there seems to be a kind of discordant harmony, I have never been able to discover their having any notion of the *gamut*; neither have they adopted our best system of astonomy. When did we ever hear of a Caractacus or a Newton, a Boadicea or a Confucius existing in Africa. It is true history informs us that it once had a Hannibal, a Ptolemy and a Hipparchus, but then there is no positive proof of their being *natives* of it.—The author of the address has attempted to prove they have some *genius*. I will be candid enough to allow there have been surprizing instances of *docility* in Negroes. Such for instance was that of a Negroe fellow in Jamaica, who seemed to have some parts and learning, and could talk in a manner, that had his colour been concealed, and he had stuck a piece of wax on his nose to make it a little more prominent, might have been mistaken for a rational creature possessing a tolerable knowledge in the law. I have myself seen several Negroes, who by dint of great labour and attention in their owners, have become very good mechanicks, as jewellers, watch-makers, &c. Nay I have known more than one of them who were capable of keeping a set of books in the Italian method in a neat correct manner. But we are not to suppose a few such instances, or that a mere *Lusus Naturae* can add any strength to the supposition of their being endued with reason. We all know that extraordinary instances of docility in brutes have naturally excited great admiration in all ages. Pliny and many others have given us surprizing relations of this kind, and I have been told when a boy, of an elephant in Africa following the occupation of a tinker with some reputation. The ingenuity of mechanicks have also furnished us with occasions of wonder in imitations of divers kinds; for instance, the inanimate flying eagle at Vienna—the crowing cock at Strasburg—the speaking clock in Ireland, and abundance more, which sufficiently prove the ingenuity of Europeans, but do by no means convince us that the said eagle, cock and clock were rational beings. Indeed what we are told of ingenuity in Negroes, has sometimes a little staggered my hypothesis; and would induce a suspicion of their mother's fidelity, was not the whole race of them so extremely forbidding in their persons; and the antipathy of all the *whites* to them and their descendants so unconquerable, as entirely to satisfy me on that head. The probability of the falsity of such relations, or of their being much exaggerated to gratify a natural fondness for the marvellous and wonderful, is much more in its favour.

The *Addresser* endeavours to convince us that Negroes pine and degenerate in the islands. It is evidently otherwise; for when an estate there is sold, much higher prices are given for their two footed stock born in the West-Indies, than for those imported from Africa.—Would this wise-acre himself give as much for a horse which had not been broke to the shafts or saddle, as for one that had those advantages? Surely not.

He then goes on with his objections to the method of carrying on the Slave-trade. The reasons I suggested in my observations on the pamphlets I first took notice of, preclude the necessity of my enlarging on this particular point. It is very plain that Slaves are bought in a *fair* course of trade; and even could he prove that it is not in the course of a *fair* trade, it would be nothing to the purpose—if a commodity, a cow for instance, is brought to me for sale, is it my business to enter with a critical nicety, into an enquiry by what means the seller procured her? I am sure if I did, I should forfeit all pretensions to the character of a gentlemen; and I am as confident, that *whatever* the means are, by which slaves are brought among us, or whether their servitude in the West-Indies is voluntary or not; or even if I should admit all the accounts of the villainies and cruelties practised in the trade were short of the truth, I should yet be justified in the purchase of them, as it is a most certain introduction to health and happiness in a situation, where they have fewer cares, and less anxiety about to-morrow, than any people in the whole world. They have (in a general way however) their usual allowance of provisions, and are entirely exempted from all the distresses attendant on war. The Negroe it is true, cannot easily change his master, but to make amends for this slight inconvenience, he enjoys a singular advantage over his brother in freedom of being *carefully* attended in sickness, and of having the same provision in old age as in youth. Instead of being oppressed to feed a large family, like the free comfortless labourers in Europe, the more children he has, the richer he becomes; for the moment a child is born, the happy parents receive as much additional provision, as with their own allowance, will amount to *more* than they can eat; and in case of their own death, (if by living among *whites*, they should chance to have attained any thing like reflection) they will quit the world with the comfortable certainty of their children being brought up with the *same* kind care, they formerly experienced themselves. What Philosopher, Epicurean or Stoick, could wish for more? In these islands and colonies only, do the highly favoured Africans realize the fabulous history of the golden age. Was their happy state but known in Great-Britain and Ireland—what emigrations there would be in search of this terrestrial elysium? Acts of Parliament would then be really necessary—not indeed to comply with the visionary schemes of gloomy enthusiasts—but to prevent the entire depopulation of those kingdoms.

The cause I plead is so well supported by the Suffrages of Custom and Right Reason, that I fear I have made an apology to the public necessary for detaining it's attention so long on arguments drawn from self-evident principles. I have heard of a certain Philosopher who wrote a large folio volume to prove that light came from the Sun. I flatter myself I am more excuseable, as I write for the reformation of gloomy fanaticks, who to mulish obstinacy join a most illiberal and malevolent turn of thinking; and I have no less in view than to convince them of errors far more mischievous in their consequences, than any that could arise from its remaining undetermined, what may be the true source of light.

That the *Address* is a scandalous libel, in which some of the West-Indians are unworthily traduced, I have already proved; and am sure that the least the public can do, to testify a decent detestation of it's most malevolent slanders, is to have it formally committed to the flames by the hands of the common hangman. The inhabitants should consider that the West-Indies form a considerable branch of their commerce, and that therefore it ill becomes them to suffer *any* practice to be opprobriously stigmatized as unjust or impolitic, in which the West-Indians happen to be concerned. They should also remember, that a genteel sum of money was lately received from that quarter, for the use of their College, for which they have been highly commended by its Provost. Every one must suppose that in delivering his commendations, he spoke the sentiments of the other Professors, and surely those Gentlemen, equally remarkable for their piety and learning, would not have bestowed praises on a people, whose conduct in *any* respect was exceptionable. It is therefore evident that all the Professors are Advocates for Slavery, and being learned and pious, it naturally follows that the Slave-trade in itself and in its consequences, is not at all inconsistent with religion or sound policy.

What will not this same *Addresser* and *his associates* deserve, if in resentment for their infamous usage of them, the West-Indians should determine to decline their commerce with the northern colonies of America? Resentment working in men of honour, may carry them a great way. They may find resources to supply themselves with flour and pork, or with succedaneums that will do as well. The white people of fortune in the West-Indies are comparatively but few in number, and might be supplied nearly with all *they* use of these articles from the Carolinas. It would then only remain to supply the lower class of whites, and the demands of the Negroes.—It is supposed that one hundred thousand Slaves are yearly shipped in the African ports for the British West-India islands. Of these perhaps twenty thousand die on the passage. Now when their death is not occasioned by any bad disorder, if there was a proper quantity of salt on board, the bodies might be cured in pickle or smoak; and the same method pursued with those that die on land, or are past labour. A considerable quantity of provision might be thus procured that would furnish a tolerable succedaneum for *pork* and hams. I have never heard that this kind of meat is deemed unwholesome, but on the contrary, that the Cannibals are a hardy robust race of people.—The scheme is new, and might not be very eligible—I only mention it as a *dernier resort*, and which a very high degree of resentment only could ever incline them to have recourse to.

John Allen, *On the Beauties of Liberty*, 1773

John Allen, *An Oration on the Beauties of Liberty, or the Essential Rights of the Americans. Delivered at the Second Baptist Church in Boston Upon the last Thanksgiving, Dec. 3d, 1772*, 4th ed. (Boston, 1773), pp. v-vi; xviii-xx; xxvi-xxix; 60-62; 73-80.

Following the burning of the British revenue vessel, the Gaspee, *in the waters of Naragansett Bay by citizens of Providence, Rhode Island, on June 9, 1772, a royal commission was convened to investigate the affair. So well were the patriot arsonists shielded by sympathetic friends that no substantive evidence was unearthed by the commission. But the inquisitorial proceedings did lay bare the bitter hostility between the Rhode Island colonists and the British authorities.*

On December 3, 1772, an obscure minister, recently arrived from London, delivered a stinging, denunciatory oration to the congregation of the Second Baptist Church in Boston. Using the Gaspee *commission as a basis upon which to launch his tirade against British policy, John Allen declared, "I . . . love my King; but I revere the Rights of an Englishman before any king on earth. I would greatly distinguish between a righteous King and a reigning Despot. . . ." Allen, a discontented and frustrated Baptist pastor and agitator who was once arrested in England for forgery, later published the address. "An Oration on the Beauties of Liberty" proved to be one of the most popular, widely circulated, pamphlets in the Revolutionary period. In its fourth printing, in 1773, Allen's polemic against British tyranny was supplemented with strictures on the slavery of the Africans. "This unlawful, inhuman practice is a sure way for mankind to ruin America," Allen warned. As the semantical link between political subjugation and human slavery was being sounded in New England pulpits, John Allen was one of the few Baptists to join the chorus.*

To the Right Honorable the Earl of Darthmouth.

My Lord, When I view the original right, power, and *Charter* confirmed, sealed, and ratified to the province, or inhabitants of *Rhode-Island*, and its standing in full force, and unrepealed for more than an hundred years; surely your Lordship will not blame them, if they stand fast in the Liberty wherein they were made free: The words of their Charter are,

> Be it enacted, that no freeman, shall be taken, or imprisoned, or deprived of his freehold, or liberty, or free custom, or be out-lawed, or exiled, or otherwise destroyed; nor shall be oppressed, judged, or condemned, but by the laws of this colony.—And that no man, of what state or condition soever, shall be put out of his land; or tenements, nor taken, nor imprisoned, nor disinherited, nor Banished (observe this my Lord) nor any way destroyed, or molested, without being, for it, brought to answer, by a due course of law of this Colony.

As a fly, or a worm, by the law of nature, have as great a right to Liberty and Freedom, (according to their little sphere in life) as the most potent monarch upon earth: And as there can be no essential difference between your Lordship and myself in the kingdom of Liberty, but what is political, I therefore, without any further apology, take leave to ask your Lordship, Whether any one that fears God and loves his neighbor as himself, (which is the true scripture-mark of a Christian) will Oppress his fellow-creatures? If he does, where are the beauties of christianity? Not to be seen in this life, however they may be in the next. . . .

. . . Liberty, my Lord, is the native right of the *Americans*; it is the blood-bought treasure of their Forefathers; and they have the same essential right to their *native laws* as they have to the air they breath in, or to the light of the morning when the sun rises: And therefore they who oppress the *Americans* must he as great enemies to the law of nature, as they who would be, if it were in their power, vail the light of the sun from the universe. My Lord, the *Americans* have a privilege of boast of above all the world: They never were in bondage to any man, therefore it is more for them to give up their Rights, than it would be for all *Europe* to give up their Liberties into the hands of the *Turks*. Consider what *English* tyranny their Forefathers fled from; what seas of distress they met with; what savages they fought with; what blood-bought treasures, as the dear inheritance of their lives, they have left to their children, and without any aid from the King of *England*; and yet after this, these free-born people must be counted Rebels, if they will not loose every right to Liberty, which their venerable Ancestors purchased at so great expence as to lose their lives in accomplishing; and shall not their descendants be strenuous to maintain inviolate those sacred Rights, which God and Nature have given them, to the latest posterity. O *America! America* let it never be said that you have deserted the Grand Cause, and submitted to *English* ministerial *tyranny*. . . .

. . . But it may be meet to let your Lordship know, that if the *Americans* unite (as there seems a good prospect) to stand, as a *band of brethren* for their Liberties. They have a right, by the law of God, of nature, and of nations, to reluct at, and even to resist any military or marine force. But surely the exile troops in their Castle, and the marine force in their harbour must be intended in readiness for the *French*, not for *Americans*; for can it ever enter into the heart of a mother to murder her children? of a King to kill his subjects? of an agent to destroy the rights of the *Colonies* he represents? But suppose, my Lord, that it should be the bloody intent of the Ministry, to make *Americans* subject to their *Slavery*; what can the Ministry expect but *blood* for *blood, life* for *life*, and *death* for *death* to decide the contention. This bloody scene is infinitely far from being desired, nor can it ever be executed but at the expence of the destruction of *England*. And you will find, my Lord, that the *Americans* will not submit to be Slaves: They know the use of the gun, and the millitary art as well as any of his Majesty's troops at St. *James's*: And where his Majesty has one soldier, *America* can produce fifty free men, and all volunteers; and raise a more potent army of men in three weeks, than *England* can in three years. But God forbid that I should be thought to aim at rouzing the *Americans* to arms, without their rights, liberties, and oppression call for it. For they are unwilling to beat to arms: As loyal subjects they love their King: They love their Mother-Country: They call it their Home, and wish nothing more than the prosperity of *Britain*, and the glory of their King. But they will not give up their rights, nor be slaves to any power upon earth. Therefore, my Lord, as a peace-maker; as their agent; as their friend, lay their grievance before their King. Let the *Americans* enjoy their birthright blessings, and *Britain* her prosperity. May there be a mutual union between the mother and her children, in all the blessings of life, trade, and happiness: Then, my Lord both *Britons* and *Americans*, will call you blessed. . . .

The Parliament of *England* cannot justly make any laws to tax the *Americans*; for they are not the Representatives of *America*; and therefore they are no legislative power of *America*. The House of Lords cannot do it, for they are Peers of *England*, not of *America*; and if neither King, Lords, nor Commons have any right to oppress or destroy the Liberties of the *Americans*, why is it then that the *Americans* do not stand upon their own strength, and shew their power and importance, when the life of life, and every Liberty that is dear to them is in danger?

Therefore, let me advise you with all the power of affection, with all the pathos of soul, (as one who esteems the full possession of Rights of the *Americans*, as the highest blessing of this life) to stand alarmed. See your danger—death is near—destruction is at the door.—Need I speak? Are not your harbours blockaded from you? Your castle secured by captives—your lives destroyed—revenues imposed upon you—taxation laid—military power oppressing—your Charter *violated*—your Governor pensioned—your constitution declining—your Liberties departing, and not content with this, they now attack the *life*, the soul and *capitol* of all your Liberties, to create your Judges, and make them independent upon you for office or support, and erect new Courts of Admiralty, to take away by violence, the husband from his family, his wife, his home, his friends. Such cruelty and tyranny ought ever to be held in the most hateful contempt, the same as you would *a banditti of slave-makers on the coast of* Africa.

Has not the voice of your Father's blood cried yet loud enough in your ears, "Ye Sons of *America* scorn to be Slaves?" Have you not heard the voice of blood in your streets, louder than that which reached Heaven, that cried for vengeance. That was, faith the Lord to *Cain*, the voice of thy brother's blood, but this is of many brethren. Therefore, if there be any vein, any nerve, any soul, any life, or spirit of Liberty in the Sons of *America*, shew your love for it; guard your freedom, prevent your chains; stand up as one man for your Liberty; for none but those, who set a just value upon this blessing are worthy to enjoy it. . . .

Remarks on the Rights and Liberties of the Africans

[Personal Liberty]

Here let me claim your attention. Every tie of nature, every sensation of humanity, every bowel of pity, every compassion as a Christian, engages me to speak for the Personal Liberty and Freedom of those, who are the most distressed of all human beings, the natives of *Africa*. Were they thus distressed by *Indians*, *Mahometans*, or *Turks* with respect to their Liberty, they would have a right to be redressed and set free; but for mankind to be distressed and kept in Slavery by Christians, by those who love the Gospel of Christ; for such to buy their Brethren (for *of one blood he has made all nations*) and bind them to be Slaves to them and their heirs for life. Be astonished, ye Christians, at this! And what is more shocking even to the tenderness of nature, is to *export them*, for filthy lucre into the hands of Men-tyrants. But what is more alarming yet, and exceeds all bounds, is, for one Christian, and Member of a Church, to export another, and banish her to be a Slave, when in full communion in the Church. Was ever such a thing heard of in the house of God before! Tell it not in *Gath!* Publish it not in the streets of *Boston*! Shall no plea be heard? Shall no argument prevail to *let these oppressed ones* Go Free. Have Christians lost all the tenderness of nature, the feelings of humanity, or the more refined sensations of christianity? Or have the Ministers in silence forgot to shew their people this iniquity? O could they bear to see—to see did I say? nay to feel their children rent from their arms, and see them bound in irons and banished to be *Slaves*! O killing thought! But for Christians to encourage this bloody and inhuman Trade of *Man-stealing*, or *Slave-making*, O how shocking it is! while it may be, their nearer kindred want employment, if not bread to eat. This unlawful, inhuman practice is a sure way for mankind to ruin *America*, and for Christians to bring their children, and their children's children to a morsel of bread. Much has been wrote, and well wrote to dissuade the *Americans* from the practice of so great an Evil; many begin to listen to the laws of humanity and the force of the argument: But surely what the Prophet *Isaiah* says will be sufficient with every true Minister of the Gospel, and with every Christian and Son of Liberty in *America; Isa.* lviii. 6. *Loose the bands of wickedness, undo the heavy burdens, let the oppressed go free, that ye break every yoke.*

What follows is desired to be published with the Oration, having been offered to one of the Publishers of a News-Paper, but was refused a place;

but as the Printer is determined, even at the hazard of his life, to maintain inviolable, that inestimable Priviledge of mankind, Liberty *of the* Press, which can never be wanted more than at this time, when near one sixth part of the inhabitants of *America* are held in real *Slavery*, under the different pretences of interest and religion, however well grouuded the former may be, sure I am the latter must be very vague, as the conduct of the Buyers of these People serve daily to confirm every thinking person in this opinion: For reasons above, shall comply with the request of an Advocate for a multitude of these distressed People, who are unjustly held in *Bondage* by those who profess to act on principles of Liberty and Religion, by inserting the following Piece, with the Circular Letter which was sent with the same.

Christian Brethren, Should I attempt to delineate the dire effects which the iniquitous and cruel Trade of *Slave-making* has occasioned, both in *Africa* and *America*, I should paint out such scenes of distress, havock, and detestation, as must not only serve to shock human nature, but would swell my piece to a volume much larger than ever was published in the universe. Let it suffice, kind Reader, (and may I be permitted to address myself in particular to you, my Reverend Fathers and Brethren, who are employed in preaching the *glorious Gospel of Liberty*, and who must shortly give an account of your Stewardship) to lead you to the distant clime of *Africa*. Look ye into the native country of the distressed *Africans!* Who would not shudder at viewing the tender parent weeping for the loss of a favorite son! A daughter whose plighted vows, perhaps, have been given in the conubial state! Dutiful children, with the filial piety bewailing their irretrievable misfortune by losing an affectionate, tender, and loving father, brother, sister, neighbour, or companion! These being torn from the bosoms of each other must certainly break the strongest bonds of nature and friendship. Think! O think of this! if not totally lost to all sense of feeling, you whose hearts are adamant! I mean the Buyers and Sellers of *Africans*, however you may gloss your practice with the *pretence of christianizing* these People. I need not mention the recent proofs we have of the ill consequences arising by peopling our Islands with these *Africans*, as their frequent revolts so often occasion streams of blood to be shed, as well on the side of the Whites as Blacks. But may it not with truth be said, these revolutions are occasioned by the cruel treatment they meet with from their Masters? But allowing they were used in the kindest manner, is it reasonable to think they can be satisfied with their condition, as their minds must ever be imbittered with the melancholly reflection, that let their behaviour be what it may, they and their children are to be held in *Bondage* so long as they live! Nature trembles at such a thought, much more to experience it! What Christian, in this practice, who would not shudder at viewing our Saviour's eternal rule of righteousness!

The following Circular Letter, accompanied with Mr. *Swan*'s Piece, entitled a Dissuasive to *Great Britain* and her Colonies from the *Slave-Trade*, were lately presented to the Gentlemen who are chosen *Representatives* for this Province.

Boston, April 20, 1773.

Sir, The efforts made by the Legislative of this province in their last sessions to free themselves from *Slavery*, gave us, who are in that deplorable state, a high degree of satisfaction. We expect great things from men who have made such a noble stand against the designs of their *fellow-men* to enslave them. We cannot but wish and hope, Sir, that you will have the same grand object, we mean civil and religious *Liberty*, in view in your next session. The divine spirit of *Freedom* seems on every humane breast on this Continent, except such as are bribed to assist in executing the execrable plan.

We are very sensible that it would be highly detrimental to our present Masters, if we are allowed to demand all that of *right* belongs to us for past services; this we disclaim. Even the *Spaniards*, who have not those sublime ideas of *Freedom* that *English* men have, are conscious that they have no right to all the services of their fellow-men, we mean the *Africans*, whom they have purchased with their money; therefore they allow them one day in a week to work for themselves, to enable them to earn money to purchase the residue of their time, which they have a right to demand in such portions as they are able to pay for, (a due appraizment of their services being first made, which always stand at the purchase money.) We do not pretend to dictate to you, Sir, or to the honorable Assembly, of which you are a member: We acknowledge our obligations to you for what you have already done, but as the people of this province seem to be actuated by the principles of equity and justice, we cannot but expect your House will again take our deplorable case into serious consideration, and give us that ample relief which, *as men*, we have a natural right to. . . .

We are willing to submit to such regulations and laws, as may be made relative to us, until we leave the province, which we determine to do as soon as we can from our joynt labours procure money to transport ourselves to some part of the coast of *Africa*, where we propose a settlement. We are very desirous that you should have instructions relative to us, from your town, therefore we pray you to communicate this letter to them, and ask this favor for us.

In behalf of our fellow Slaves in this Province, and by order of their Committee,

Peter Bestes,
Sambo Freeman,
Felix Holbrook,
Chester Joie.

Anthony Benezet to Granville Sharp, March 29, 1773

Granville Sharp Letterbook, The Library Company, Philadelphia, Pa.

As the friction between the American colonies and the British government intensified, the effect upon the British West Indies was disastrous. West Indian survival was dependent upon British military and naval power. At the same time, the West Indian economy depended on American sugar and slave trade, a trade that was significantly curtailed during the Revolutionary War. A profound disruption of West Indian society resulted—inflated prices, a decline in shipping, an alarming decrease in essential raw materials, and, in some instances, starvation. With this general malaise came cataclysmic disturbances from the immense slave population.

Throughout the war years, Anthony Benezet, as he did in his letter to Granville Sharp on March 23, 1773, wrote of slave uprisings all over the world and relayed them to his antislavery compatriots. But most of his tales of horror came from the West Indies—Jamaica, Honduras, St. Kitts, and numerous other areas. There were tales of massive numbers of starving runaways and numerous riots and rebellions. If Benezet needed ammunition to warn the American South of the dangers resulting from the disproportion of white planters to large masses of discontented blacks held in servitude by force, he needed only to look to the West Indies. And if American colonial assemblies were reluctant to take positive steps to legislate against the slave trade itself, as Benezet lamented, the country might very well find itself "as tho' seared with an hot Iron."

Philadia ye. 29th-March 1773
Rec. 25 May

Respected Friend Granville Sharp I wrote thee, at large, in answer to the first letter thou wert so kind as to write to me by Captain Sutton, who I understand is arrived with you; by him I also sent some books, all which I hope soon to hear came to thy hand; Since which my friend Samuel Emlen telling me, thou hadst wrote to him expressive of thy desire I should speedily send thee an answer, with respect to what Petitions or Memorials might be expected from the Colonies. I immediately wrote again, by a Vessel bound to Dublin, giving thee the best account I was capable of the situation of things, in those respects amongst us, since that time, upon the Petition laid before our Assembly, Signed by the Clergy and weighty persons of every religious denomination, of which I sent thee a Copy, expressive of our desire, that under a consideration of the iniquity and evil effect of the Slave Trade, they would Petition the King and Parliament, that an end might be put to that most iniquitous commerce; the Assembly immediately took our Petition into consideration, agreeing to the expediency of its contents; but upon entering into the merits of the cause, they did not judge the matter was yet ripe for them to put in a Petition to the King or Parliament; but thought best, for the present, to lay a farther duty on all Slaves, to be imported, into this Province which is now made perpetual at twenty pounds per Head: which duty it is thought will amount to a tacit prohibition of the trade, and have made the Law perpetual which was to be in force but a number of Years; they apprehended that the passing or refusal of this Law, by the King and Council, will better enable them to judge what farther step to take, with respect to making head with the King and Parliament, that the Slave Trade may be put an end to, which all orders of People here desire may be done. It is the same in New York, where in consequence of our having procured Copies of our Petition, to the Assembly and other Papers, which had been printed here Viz. an Extract of thy Letter to me; the Address from Virginia and also a Pamphlet which was printed on this occasion, to be given to the members of the Assembly, the Clergy and other weighty members of Society all of which, I think were reprinted there; their Assembly also took the matter under their serious consideration and I am told heartily join in the measure of using their endeavours to put an end to the Slave Trade; Tho' they are not in general so willing to hear of putting an end to Slavery as in this Province and the Jerseys.

The matter was debated in their Assembly; when a Law was there passed laying a duty of Twenty pounds upon every Negroe to be Imported in New York Government, but this law was not agreed to by the Governor and Council under pretence, as I hear that it would lay a difficulty on the West India People who come over for the recovery of their health with respect to their Servants, tho there was a clause in the Bill I hear allowing 18 Months in that case, However the stir which has been made as well as the alarms of danger from Surinam and Saint Vincent will I trust far open the Eyes of people to see the iniquity and danger of any farther import of Slaves that they will Petition the Assembly and not be satisfied till some effectual step be taken to prevent it. The disposition of the people is much the same in our Neighbouring Southern Province of Maryland with respect to any farther import of Slaves, as here and in New York; but they will not as yet hear any proposal tending to a general freedom. About a Year and Half past after a representation of the iniquity and danger of the Slave Trade had been laid by the Yearly Meeting of our Friends, in that Province, before their Assembly, they agreed to lay a duty on the import of Negroes, but it was too small to effect the Trade, fearing if larger to meet with opposition from the African Company. They now propose to renew their application to their Assembly. I have before me an essay of a Publication sent up from some persons of weight there who have this matter at heart, to be Published in the Maryland Gazette preparatory of an Address to the next setting of their Assembly, I have also an encouraging reply to some part of what was last fall wrote some concerned Friends in Virginia, to the same effect. As to the more Southern Provinces of Carolina and Georgia their hearts appear as yet so hardened and their Eyes to blinded thro' the great gain, they have made by the encrease and Sale of their Rice and Indigo and they are so sett upon a farther accumilation of wealth, by making farther Purchases of Land and Negroes, that they seem in general, to have no ears, nor sensibility to anything but what will promote their gain. I am informed, by a serious person lately returned from Charles Town in South Carolina that there is already by the Account of taxables computed to be thirteen Black to one White, and I was told that last Year they had received, or expected an increase of Ten thousand Negroes from Guinea. However we shall not omit to lay before such as we have reason to hope, may be instrumental in stirring up their Neighbours, to a thought of, at least, the necessity of preventing a farther Importation of Slaves: Indeed the danger, as expressed in our Public News Papers, some of the Southern Colonies are, immediatley in, of falling under the dominion of their Slaves, one would think if they retained only their reasonable faculties, would be sufficient to rouse them to a sense of the danger which already hangs over them and which must be encreased as they encrease the number of their Slaves.

Our Publick Prints of last Week contains the following articles Viz. "Lisbon. Nov. 17. A general discontent reigns among the Negroes and Slaves Natives of Brazil, who have already risen several times When rigorous methods have been used to bring them back to their duty, they fly to the Indians, in the interior part of the Country, where their numbers is said to be considerably increased. As the greater part of them are acquainted with the European manner of fighting and are provided with fire arms, there is reason to fear that their design is to drive us out of Brazil; and in consequence thereof, every body is providing for the safety of himself and affects."

"Amsterdam Dec. 19th. Private Letters from Surinam mentions that the fugitive and Rebellious Negroes are effectually chased from their Town, but that they are retired deeper into the Woods from whence it will be more difficult to drive them than from where they were before."

Extract of a Setler from the Hague. "The Zealand Vanderbruyton is just arrived from Surinam, and brings the disagreeable advices of that Settlement being in the utmost danger of destruction by the Indians. Negroes &c. who are assembled in great numbers, and carry devastation wherever they go. Many of the Plantations have been burnt and the Planters, with their families have been murdered. Advice has likewise been received of a rising of the Natives of Cayenne, at the Mouth of a River of the same Name, in five degrees North latitude. In short if some very early and forcible means are not used, both the Dutch and the French are likely to lose their possessions in South America."

The Case of the Caraibs or rather Negroes now in a State of War with the English on the Island of Saint Vincent, being the offspring of two Vessels with Negroes from Guinea, formerly cast away Of these tho' but a few, hemmed in, in a small Island without refuge or retreat require so many Regiments to suppress them, what must be the strength of the many thousands and Tens of thousands, who are so situate with an open back Country and assisted by the Indians and probably such bad people as might join them: But the understanding and hearts of the people were Slavery prevails and means of wealth abound, seem as tho' seared with an hot Iron.

As to the several Provinces of New England, they appear sufficiently apprised of the inconsistancy of the Slave Trade, as well with the Gospel as with their safety and Interest. The Assembly of New England have already endeavoured to put a final stop to any farther import, as also to put an end to Slavery amongst themselves; which I am persuaded they will still pursue, except the Colonies of Rhode Island, where that hardness of heart produced by the love of gain, has got strong footing, as some of their Merchants have long enriched themselves by sending their Vessels to the Coast of Guinea, for Slaves, which they purchase with Rum of their own distilling, these Slaves they Sell in the West Indies, where with the produce they purchase fresh loads of Molasses, for to be made into Rum; however I am not without hope, that the many amongst them who appear convinced of the iniquity of the traffick, may prevail with their legislature to put an end to this Trade. I understand some individuals, particularly a Lawyer in New

England, have undertook to take such Negroes, as have applied, under their protection and put their owners upon proving the legality of their right over those persons, they pretend to be their Slaves. This is a good beginning, which if steadily pursued, will open an effectual door, and most tend to make people consider the unreasonableness, as well as injustice of Slavery. I did intend to have promoted Petitions to the King and Parliament signed by particulars in all the Colonies and doubted not, as mentioned in my former Letters, the procuring great numbers of signers at least in Maryland and Virginia But upon consulting with some thoughtful people, we agreed, that such Petitions ought first to be made to the respective Assemblies, praying they may lay the expediency of preventing any farther trade for Slaves before the King and Parliament. The respective Assemblies are the Voice of the people they represent, but the people, tho' a large number, are not the representatives of the People. Petitions from the people tho' signed by great numbers have, of late years, very much lost credit; not being always truly expressive of the mind of the most thinking part of the Inhabitants, being often put forth by particulars, to answer some private design, or interest of their own, or of a party; it being very easy to persuade illeterate ignorant people, of which there are great numbers in these parts, to set their Names to Petitions, upon very slight representations, or in way of favour or affection, to the applier; without any Judgment of their own or looking into the grounds of the matter, or the designs of those who are promoting such Petitions. Thou may'st easily judge how readily this may be done, when I tell thee, I am informed, there is about thirty thousand people already settle on the west side of the Allegany Mountains, a part of the country but few years past settled by a few French and Indians, most of these an illerate people of whom it may be said of many they know not their right hand from their left, in seeing thro' the views of designing Men, not to mention the vast numbers of such people in the more interior parts of the several Provinces, These parts of the World might under proper regulations be a refuge and afford a comfortable subsistance to Thousands and tens yeat hundred of thousands of distressed people from many parts of Europe. The several New Governments now proposed to be bounded only by the Allegany Mountains on the East the River Ohio on the North and the Missisipy on the West, include a tract of Five or Six hundred Miles square generally good Land able to furnish, (as I have been told by some already settled there) its Inhabitants with everything, (except Salt) necessary to make them happy, I made and procured many Copies of a large extract of thy first letter to me, the contents and advices therein contained were so agreable, to many thinking people, that they have without my procurement been printed in this and the Neighbouring Government and are proposed to be so in Maryland and probably in Virginia. The answer to Parson Thompson I received and read with peculiar satisfaction; it is the most effectual plea I have met with in answer to those who plead the Jewish practice in support of Slavery It will be of much service to me if I should, as I expect to reprint my Book of the account of africa. I generally cut short on this head by reminding People that we are now under the gracious dispensation of the Gospel and—ought to be guided by its precepts and practices whatever might on account of the hardness of the human heart, have been allowed in former times. As suitable occasion offers I will communicate to thee what ever may appear in print in these parts on the subject of Slavery, and shall be glad if thou wilt do the same, by what will be published what you in my last I acquainted thee, with the situation of those people who are obliged to engage for a number of years, as Servants, to those who pay their passage; which from the good regulations made by Law in that case, and the general good—disposition in this and the more Northern Governments, is by no means attended with the difficulties and hardships thou apprehends, its indeed rather often a more favourable circumstance than when, after having paid their passage, they remain poor; these frequently after a time of hard labour and poor living, find themselves rather in debt, at the expiration of the time of those, who were in Service, who then having experience, and acquaintance, often make quicker advances in a good Settlement than the others. As to the Southern Colonies I believe few people, are sent there, whose passage is not paid except convicts in Maryland and Virginia. Those of better credit who happen to come there are I believe very seldom put to hard labour, they are rather employed as Clerks, Overseers or drivers of the Negroes; but its a bad School for their Morals; most of them becoming, soon, profligate and abandoned. When I received thy Letter the Scotch People therein mentioned, had most of them left this City; those remaining did not appear to be in want; Their case had been under the consideration of a number of Scotch Gentlemen, and others, who have formed themselves into a Company. called, the Saint Andrews' Society, formed for the protection and assistance of those of their Nation who may be in need of help. There is also a German Society of the same nature, which is of service to many distressed Strangers of that Nation. I shall always be glad to hear from thee, as often as thy time and occasion will allow, and will on my part not fail to inform thee, of every occurrence which may promote the cause of liberty and Justice to the poor africans and remain thy affectionate friend.

Anthony Benezet.

Anthony Benezet to John Fothergill, April 28, 1773

Gibson MSS 1/27, Friends House Library, London, Eng.

In 1765 Dr. John Fothergill, an eminent British physician and close friend of Benjamin Franklin, wrote Considerations Relative to the North American Colonies, *a tract which emphasized the necessity for closer ties between British and American citizens. In succeeding years, resentment between the two countries deepened, much to Fothergill's regret. Nonetheless, his efforts to conciliate the two sides were intensified and his correspondence with influential Americans became more extensive. Fothergill unsuccessfully promoted a peace conference in 1769 between American and British political leaders. The Quaker physician was absorbed in philanthropic projects and considered the slavery problem a grave and potentially disastrous threat. In his correspondence with Anthony Benezet,*

Fothergill emphasized the dangers of an immediate emancipation. He felt that the slaves needed preparation for the cultural and economic conditions of the free world. Fothergill favored a gradual end to slavery through a registration system, wage payments to slaves for a portion of their work, and educational training programs for slaves preparing them to enter society as freemen. Benezet, as his letter to Fothergill on April 28, 1773, indicated, agreed that an immediate emancipation was fraught with peril though he sought an immediate end to the heinous root of slavery's growth—the slave trade.

Philadia ye. 28th 4th Month 1773

Dear Friend John Fothergill Thy kind letter of the 29th 8th Mon: last I received in due time & greatfully acknowledge the kind sympathy therein expressed. I am likeminded with thee with respect to the difficulty & danger which would attend a sudden manumission of those negroes, in the southern Colonies, as well to themselves, as to the whites; wherefore, except, in particular cases, the obtaining their freedom & indeed the freedom of many even amongst us, is by no means the object to my concern; but the using the best endeavours in our power to draw the notice of the Government upon the grievous iniquity & great danger attendant on a farther prosecution of the Slave Trade is what a very & truly sympathizing heart cannot but earnestly desire & (under divine direction) promote to the utmost of their power. If this could be obtained, I trust, the sufferings of those already amongst us, by the interposition of government & even from selfish ends, in their owners, would be mittigated and in time providence would gradually work for the release of those whose age & situation would fit them for freedom: The large settlements, now in prospect, to be made in that vast extent of country, from the West side of the Allegany Mountains, to the Missisipy, on a breadth of four or five hundred miles, would afford a suitable and beneficial means of settlemt for many of them amongst the white people, which would in all probability be profitable as well to the Negroes, as the New settlers. It is clear to me that when ever a manumission of the bulk of the Negroes takes place, the thought of setting them in a body, by themslves, will be found as impossible as it would be dangerous both to black & whites: The only rational, safe & just expedient both natural and religious would, I think, be that they be mixed amongst the whites & by giving them a property amongst us, make them parties & interested in our welfare & security. But I do not desire to take up thy time, especially with matters of so remote a nature, it being indeed with reluctance I take up any of it, and would have avoided, was there any friend, with you, to whom I could have addressed myself with the same expectation that what we have in view would be so properly attended to. Our Meeting of Suffering in the Epistle they now write to Yours, having just mentioned that an Address had been presented to our Assembly, in consequence of which a Law had been passed laying a duty of twenty pounds per head on farther imports of Negroes; it was thought necessary that some friend Member of our Meeting of Sufferings should acquaint some friend amid yours, with the steps that had been taken, or were likely to be taken, so as to enable you to speak in support of that Law, if necessary; to which end I herewith send thee a copy of our said Address, also a copy of what I now write, on that head, to our Agent Benj. Franklin, in order to make him, agreable to his desire, acquainted with what pases here, on this momentous concern. I also send thee copies of two letters wrote from Virginia & South Carolina by persons of weight there, which will, I am persuaded, give thee satisfaction & some insight into the situation & dispostion of the people there. And as a good opportunity offers by one of our Town's Men, Joseph Stanbury, I have inclosed a number of Copies of a Pamphlet, wrote, at the time we presented our Petition, in order to lay the weight of the matter briefly before the Members of Assembly & other active members of Governmt, in this & the neighboring Provinces; it was wrote by a member of the Presbyterian communion, Benjamin Rush, a young Physician, a person who I understand, thou wast acquainted with when pursuing his studies three or four years past, with you, I also send a small Collection of religious Tracts, compiled chiefly for the use of inquiring people in our back Countries where such books are much wanted. It was endeavoured it should be so collected as to be plain, instructive & edyfying, without touching upon that which might be an occasion of fruitless debate, perhaps (when a relaxation from thoughts of another nature, may be necessary, it may afford thee some moments of satisfaction, particularly what relates to our Indians, mentiond in the preface. Now in a confidence in the goodness of thy heart, which by looking at the intention will construe the freedom I have taken in the best light I remain, with love; thy affectionate Friend

Anthony Benezet

Benjamin Rush to Granville Sharp, May 1, 1773

L. H. Butterfield, ed., *Letters of Benjamin Rush* (Princeton, 1951), 1:80-81.

With this letter to Granville Share on May 1, 1773, Dr. Benjamin Rush inaugurated a notable correspondence with the British abolitionist that spanned over three decades and touched on the momentous transformations in America and British societies during those years. The slavery issue brought the two men together and remained an important element in their long association. It is noteworthy that Rush, who had written his pamphlet, An Address to the Inhabitants of the British Settlements in America, *at the request of Anthony Benezet, was steered to Sharp by Benezet.*

Philadelphia, May 1st, 1773

Sir, From the amiable character which I have received of you from my worthy friend Mr. Anth. Benezet, I have taken the liberty of introducing myself to your correspondence by sending you a pamphlet entitled *An Address to the Inhabitants of the British Settlements in America.* It is a hasty production and was written amidst many interruptions from a business which admits of but little leisure for studies or pursuits of that nature—I mean the profession of physic. Few of the arguments are new, and yet I have endeavored by their conciseness, &c., to give them new force. A spirit of humanity and religion begins to awaken in several of the colonies in favor of the poor Negroes. The clergy begin to bear a public testimony against this violation of the laws of nature and Christianity. Nothing of consequence, however, can be done here till the ax is laid to the root of the African Company. Great events have been brought about by small beginnings. Anthony Benezet stood alone a few years ago in opposing Negro slavery in Philadelphia, and now three-fourths of the province as well as the city cry out against it. I sometimes please myself with the hopes of living to see it abolished or put upon another footing in America. The pamphlet will be left at the Pennsylvania Coffeehouse in Birchin Lane. Should you incline to reprint it in London, please to make such alterations in it as you think proper, still concealing the author's name from the public.

With esteem for your virtues, and in particular for your zeal in behalf of the Negro slaves in America, I am, sir, with great respect, your most obedient, humble servant,

Benjamin Rush.

William Dillwyn, *Brief Considerations on Slavery*, 1773

William Dillwyn, *Brief Considerations on Slavery and the Expediency of its Abolition with some Hints on the Means whereby it may be gradually effected. Recommended to the serious Attention of All, and especially of those entrusted with the Powers of Legislation* (Burlington, 1773), pp. 3-16.

In 1773 William Dillwyn, a Quaker and a former pupil and amanuensis of schoolmaster Anthony Benezet, anonymously published Brief Considerations on Slavery and the Expediency of its Abolition. *Temperate and carefully reasoned, the pamphlet appealed for legislation against further slave importations and for relaxation of restrictions against manumission. Dillwyn's detailed schemes anticipated later voluntary manumission laws passed in numerous states through the revolutionary and post-revolutionary period—laws that incorporated provisions for protecting society against the burden of supporting lazy or infirm freedmen. As Dillwyn suspected, most legislators were extremely apprehensive about the possibility that many freedmen would become worthless public charges and general nuisances. But as Dillwyn suggested, these objections were overcome by laws which guaranteed that former masters would be responsible for continuing maintenance of the ex-slaves after manumission. Dillwyn's 1773 pamphlet was only the beginning of his antislavery activities. In 1774 he crossed the Atlantic carrying letters written by Benezet to a number of influential Englishmen including Granville Sharp, John Wesley, and the Countess of Huntington. Dillwyn traveled extensively in England for over two years contacting leaders of British industry and commerce, meeting with prominent politicians, and making contacts across the spectrum of English society. Dillwyn, who made England his home in 1781, was later recognized as a vital part of the British antislavery campaign.*

The religious and moral Obligations we are under in a private capacity, to do our utmost to promote the true interests of mankind, encrease with our powers and opportunities of action. Hence arises the importance of that trust, which the wisdom of government has reposed in legislatures; in discharging which, having the will, they have also the power of promoting those interests in the most effectual manner. The object therefore, which I now take the liberty of recommending to their attention, has an indisputable claim to it; not only from its importance as relating to the community, but from a consideration which must give it great additional weight with every generous mind—the incapacity of those on whose behalf it is solicited, to plead their own cause. It is the case of the enslaved Africans—a case which tho' familiarized to us by custom, is yet in all its parts so replete with affecting circumstances, that perhaps it has not its parallel in the history of any period of time; and attended with the particular aggravation, of being acted under a government, remarkable above all others for the excellence of its constitution, and the equity of its laws. How it has happened that a nation, which has so eminently distinguished itself in asserting the common rights of mankind, and which has so often generously interposed its power for the relief of its oppressed neighbours, should tolerate so grievous an infringement of liberty in its own dominions, is difficult to comprehend. But my intention is not to expatiate on the inconsistency of these generous exertions of its power, with the toleration of the African slave-trade. I hope it may be attributed to the multiplicity and weight of other engagements, which have so much engrossed the attention of government, that the iniquitous nature of this traffick has not been adverted to; for certainly an acquaintance with it, could only be necessary for its suppression. But without a further investigation of the *cause*, it is more to my present purpose, to confine myself to such considerations, as being duly attended to, may assist the *cure* of this malignant disorder in the body politick. With this view, I shall briefly consider its inconsistency with the divine, as well as the social law; its impolicy and evil tendency; and then endeavour to point out the most probable means by which the evil may be remedied.

It cannot be denied that Slavery was allowed to the Israelites by the Mosaic law, under certain circumstances and restrictions; . . . But even though we may conceive Slavery to be reconcileable to the precepts given under that dispensation; yet to every unprejudiced mind, it must appear totally repugnant to the spirit and design of the gospel, the import of which was announced to the world, in a manner awfully expressive of its superior excellence, proclaiming "Glory to God in the highest; peace "on earth; and good will to men." These glorious purposes, our blessed Saviour, when personally among men, inculcated by his example and doctrines; and, to give these greater efficacy, finally sealed them with his blood. Various were the precepts he delivered, but those relating to our social duties, are all comprized in that excellent command, "Therefore whatsoever ye would that men should do to you, do ye even so to them; for this is the law and the prophets." Mat. 7. 12. St. Paul's opinion of those concerned in the practice now under consideration, appears by his enumerating them among a number of atrocious offenders for whom the law was made, viz. "Murderers of fathers; murderers of mothers; manslayers; whoremongers; them that defile themselves with mankind; menstealers," &c.

That it is also an offence against the social law, cannot be contradicted;

for this law is founded on the necessity of mutual security, and a reciprocation of benefits; and by the light of our natural reason, we cannot find a rule better adapted to promote these ends, than that I have quoted from the vii. of Matthew; to which both Christians and Pagans have joined in giving the distinguishing appellation of *the golden rule*. The celebrated Montesquieu and many others who have made the rights of mankind their particular study, assert that men universally have an inherent title to Liberty; and the author I have named, with no less strength than vivacity of reasoning, has refuted those ridiculous arguments, which interested men have been obliged to adduce, in support of a pretended opinion, that the colour or unpolished manners of the Africans, can operate against their claim to this first of temporal enjoyments.

In these northern provinces there are not very many, who are immediately concerned in the trade to Africa for Slaves; nor is the number of these oppressed people very considerable, when compared with that of many other colonies. Hence some, though admitting the injustice of the slave trade in general, may yet be unwilling to view it as a matter sufficiently important for the extraordinary interposition of a legislature; being perhaps insensibly biased by interest, the prevalence of custom, or the example of less enlightened times; thus lessening the force of those objections which calm reflection had suggested. I would submit to the consideration of such, the complicated distress these poor creatures suffer, in being forceably torn from that portion of happiness, which the allwise Creator allotted to them in their native state; to sustain for life, a bondage which, in our southern colonies and islands, is more cruel and oppressive than the most of us in the northern colonies have had an opportunity of forming any idea of. Add to this, the bloody wars occasioned by this infernal trade—the great proportion of them who die on the passage to, and in what is called the *seasoning* in America; and can we then hesitate a moment, in determining on the expediency of contributing whatever lies in our power to discourage it. It is true some of our forefathers, and some of the present generation, may have been, and yet are in the practice of buying and selling slaves. The reasons against it, but a few years ago; were not so well understood as they now are. The opportunities of information are become more frequent; and the usage of them in general among us, has been less likely to excite an inquiry into the nature of the trade, and our title to their services. The practice of ages cannot sanctify error; but the progress of reformation has, in all, been gradual. I doubt not there are now many men in England, whose integrity we should revere, but who, for want of proper information or attention to the subject, do yet admit the right of the British parliament to tax the colonies; but we are not, for that reason obliged to admit it. Having thus briefly considered the slave-trade as contradictory to the divine and social law, it is needless to urge the impropriety of any, and especially a free people being in anywise concerned in it. I shall therefore proceed to consider the particular inconveniences attending it, with respect to the community.

That the trade is attended with many inconveniences of an evil and impolitic tendency, has been lately clearly set forth by several writers. It will be sufficient for me to enumerate a few of them. Every thing that debases the mind, unfits it for society; and this is a distinguishing characteristick of Slavery, which naturally suppresses every generous expansion of the mind. Montesquieu, in his spirit of laws saith, "That nothing more assimilates a man to a beast, than living among freemen, himself a slave: such people as these are the natural enemies of society; and their number must always be dangerous." Therefore the having slaves in our families or neighbourhood, must have a pernicious effect on the principles and morals of our young people and servants. May we not fear that religion and morality; industry and publick spirit, have nearly declined in proportion as it has been encouraged?—The riches of a free state consists in the number of members, who enjoying its privileges and blessings, are thereby interested in its preservation and advancement. Every slave among us occupies the room of a free person, and not only lessens the riches of the state by diminishing the number of its friends, but adds one to that of its internal enemies; for such every one must be accounted, who can derive no hope from its prosperity, and may possibly be benefited by its ruin. While on the other hand, every servant on the expiration of a limited servitude, setting out with the animating hope of acquiring an independence in the community, and of enjoying the blessings of life, and the protection of the laws, heartily unites in promoting the prosperity of his country; and, as that hope is answered with success, becomes more and more deeply interested in its safety: the beneficial effects of this on our lands and produce, are very extensive, and too obvious to need a recital.—In the present contest between Great-Britain and her colonies, it seems particularly necessary on our parts to convince her, that our opposition to her claims is not merely from selfish motives—not only made because they happen to affect *our* particular interest; but from a disinterested generous love to liberty, founded on principle—on publick virtue, and a conviction that it is the unalienable right of man. But how can she believe this, when, so loudly complaining of her attacks on our political liberty, all the colonies tolerate, and many of them greatly encourage this violent invasion of national liberty; subjecting the Africans not only to the deprivation of all property, but even to the most abject state of perpetual personal slavery? If we suppose the divine blessing is necessary to ensure us success in asserting our rights; of how much consequence is it, that we should practise the part enjoined by the divine command, "Whatsoever ye would that men "should do to you, do ye even so to them?" If power only must determine our right, how little have we to expect? On the other hand, were we armed with conscious innocence, and supported by the justice of our cause; what have we to fear? With what confidence might we urge our claims? But as a late writer on this subject observes,

If we need the help of the negroes; so does Great-Britain need our help to pay off their national debt. If we desire to grow rich, and rest at ease by their toils and labours; so does Great-Britain desire the same at our expence. So that while we persist in this practice of enslaving the Africans, our mouths ought to be entirely shut, as to any duties and taxes which Great-Britain may see cause to lay upon us. Otherwise I see not, but that out of our own mouths, or by our own practice, we may be justly condemned.

Having given my sentiments on a trade and practice, which, to use the words of the author of *An essay in vindication of the continental colonies of America,* "Policy rejects; justice condemns; and piety dissuades;" I shall, from the same respectable author, add,

Shall Americans persist in a conduct which cannot be justified; or persevere in oppression, from which their hearts must recoil? If the barbarous Africans shall continue to enslave each other; let the daemon slavery remain among them, that their crime may include its punishment. Let not Christians, by administering to their wickedness, confess their religion to be a useless refinement, their profession vain, and themselves as inhuman as the savages they detest.

I cannot believe there are any in the christian faith, who have attentively, and dispassionately considered the subject, but will adopt the opinion, that Slavery, in any case, cannot be justified—that, as it is conducted in the African trade, it is a most cruel, tyrannical and violent invasion of the sacred rights of mankind; and highly offensive to Almighty God—that it is impolitick in its nature—that the practice of buying and selling slaves among ourselves is an evident encouragement of the trade; and that the encouragement of it, by any means, is inconsistent with our civil and religious interests. If we thus believe, it is certainly our indispensable duty in every station, publick or private, to exert ourselves for its suppression, whatever difficulties may be apprehended to attend its final accomplishment. The prejudices of custom are strong—those imbibed from interest, yet stronger. But in such a cause, we may be assured the blessing of Omnipotence will attend our endeavors, and in due time crown them with success; not within our own limits only; but our example will most probably have a happy influence on the conduct of others more remote. It lies in our power, in some measure, to atone for the wrongs our ancestors or ourselves have inadvertently imposed on these oppressed people in time past.

Is not then the first and most important step, absolutely to prohibit any future importations into these colonies. If by royal instructions, our governors are prevented the exercise of their own judgments; provincial addresses to the crown, would be likely to remove the difficulty. The sense of the people, conveyed by their representatives to the royal ear, on so interesting a subject, must prevail, with a prince whose virtues have endeared him to his people, although it should be opposed by men, comparatively few in number; whose avarice may continue to render them insensible to the common feelings of humanity, and whose God is gain. If we cannot obtain a *total* prohibition of the importation, we shall certainly be indulged in obtaining it for the colonies which petition for it. Even should we fail here, the conscious satisfaction of having done our duty, will be a reward sufficient for the labour.

With respect to the slaves already among us, the case is more difficult, and will consequently occasion a diversity of sentiments on the proper means of effecting their enlargement. The first question is, What does justice require? This being determined, the honest mind will endeavour to practise it. There are many of this character, who, in pursuing the inquiry, have inclined to an opinion, that some of these unhappy people are unfit for liberty; and that their manumission would be attended with ruin to themselves. Such a state of depravity is not impossible, and nothing so likely to occasion it, as a long continuance in the situation they have been in. I wish there may not be many instances of this kind. Where it happens to be the case, and the possessor, after carefully divesting himself of any sinister bias, can justify a detention on this motive, I shall not controvert his right to exercise his judgment. There are also many, who not being yet sufficiently acquainted with the subject, to see the iniquity of the practice, do not apprehend the necessity of releasing their slaves. As these would be inclined to oppose, and those I have before mentioned, for other reasons, may be rather averse to a general and indiscriminate manumission; we may perhaps infer the expediency of postponing that desirable work to a period more favourable to our wishes. In reformations of all kinds, where conviction precedes conversion, the effect is most permanent. But no objections occur to me, to the framing such laws, as will leave people at liberty to emancipate their slaves under certain restrictions.

As the laws stand at present in several of our northern governments, the act of manumission is clogged with difficulties that almost amount to a prohibition. An amendment is therefore necessary; and may be effected with advantage to the community. We may suppose all the laws alluded to, are intended to secure the publick from being chargeable with any expence, in case the manumised slave should by age, sickness, or other disability, become incapable of supporting himself: and a provision of this nature seems highly reasonable in certain cases. If, for instance, a slave is become aged and infirm in my service, it is unreasonable I should have it in my power, by manumission to deny him a support from my estate, to which perhaps his labour had contributed. But if, on the other hand, I have received no other benefit from his labour, than what was a proper compensation for the instruction I have given him, and the publick afterwards receives that benefit, it is then as reasonable, that the publick should be chargeable with any expence, occasioned by such disability. This seems to be the general principle on which our laws relating to *paupers* are formed; and I see no inconvenience in adopting it in the case now under consideration.

Admitting then, that if a slave is set at liberty at the age of twenty-one years, the publick afterwards receives all the benefit of his labour, it will follow that I may set him free at that age, clear of any charge or incumbrance on my estate. If I detain him longer, and then give him his liberty, the same reasoning supposes, that if the publick is afterwards liable to support him, in case of disability, I must pay the publick a certain sum of money proportionable to the time of such detention exceeding twenty-one years. No general rule can be exactly adapted to all cases. But I believe a law formed on these principles, would not only greatly tend to the relief of individuals, but remove some objections, to which I apprehend the present laws of several provinces are liable; particularly those which permit manumission on the master's entering security for the payment of a certain sum, in case the slave should be disabled from maintaining himself. Now as this depends on a distant contingency, an alteration in the circumstances of the master and his sureties, (if any are required) may effectually disable him or them from making good their engagements. Whereas in the mode I propose, the money due on every manumission which requires it, being paid to a proper officer, remains secure with the publick. And if the slave on whose account it was paid, should never want any assistance, the fund allotted for the purpose will be so much the richer; which is a considerable advantage in its favour.

Some may think it necessary that no manumission should legally operate in all circumstances, beyond a certain age. The difficulty which would generally occur in determining the age of a negro, might be removed be enabling a magistrate to convene three or five men, who, or a majority of them, after hearing such evidence as could be adduced, and judging from appearances, should declare their judgment of his or her age. These, with many other particular considerations, will doubtless be properly attended to, whenever a matter of this consequence, comes under the immediate notice of a legislature. Some difficulty may attend ascertaining with precision the sums which will be necessary to pay, at the respective ages of manumission, to secure the publick from any unjust burden. It is a matter that requires judgment, and a particular kind of calculation with which I am but little acquainted. But as it may further explain what I have suggested; I will venture a few more hints on the subject.

I understand that on emancipating a slave in Pennsylvania, the law requires security should be entered for 30l. without any regard to age, or any other circumstances; and that if the person so emancipated, should afterwards require assistance, any expence exceeding that sum, is paid by the township to which he or she may belong. Although this mode is liable to some exceptions, for reasons before given, I have never heard of any burden, arising therefrom, occasioning any uneasiness among the people of that province. Hence we may infer that the sum of 30l. has been generally found sufficient for the purpose. By the Breslau bills of mortality, it is found that the chances are equal, that a man of fifty years of age will live seventeen years. Let us consider what inconveniences might arise, if 20l. was paid on the manumission of a slave of that age, who afterwards lived seventeen years, in the first ten of which, we will suppose he could support himself by his labour; and that in the remaining seven he required assistance, the expence whereof amounted to 30l. which, as before-mentioned, experience has found to be sufficient. Now 20l. put to interest (or applied to the other uses of the fund, which is the same thing) for ten years, at six per centum per annum, amounts to 32l. which leaves a balance in favour of the public of 2l. besides the interest still arising on the decreasing principle, after the first ten years, and the benefit of his labour; which would further increase that balance. If this calculation is just, (and if it is erroneous, I think the error is in favour of the publick) it will be a publick advantage to permit manumission on these terms; and if it takes place at forty, a much less sum will answer the purpose; and so in a decreasing proportion to the age of twenty-one years, when, as had been before shewn, nothing can be justly expected. Now we find that if, on the manumission of a slave between the years of twenty-one and fifty, fourteen shillings is paid to the publick for every year his or her age exceeds twenty-one, it will bear a very near proportion to 20l. paid on a manumission at fifty, as above stated. I may be mistaken in the method I have taken to determine the sufficiency of that sum; but I am so confident that the community would feel no inconvenience from adopting it, that, had I a sufficient estate to authorize the proposal, I should not fear deriving a considerable advantage from undertaking to support all the negroes so manumitted, who required assistance, with the monies so paid; exclusive of the benefit accruing to the community from their labour, in which I should be only interested as an individual.

Thus I have stated, and proposed a method for settling the account, as it stands, on a manumission, with the publick. There are many who, cheerfully complying with these terms, would also remember that in some cases, there is another account depending between them and their slaves: and any encouragement or assistance they may suppose it their duty to give them in consideration of past services, will still lessen the risque of their ever becoming chargeable to the publick.

To conclude—the object I have proposed, has an undoubted claim to the most serious consideration of people of all ranks, and of every denomination; for justice is confessedly alike obligatory on all. If to relieve the person of a single debtor from a temporary imprisonment, has repeatedly been admitted as a sufficient call for the interposition of a legislature—what is not due to the prosecution of the means of preventing the miseries inseparably attendant on, and the cruelties and deplorable sufferings too often annexed to, a state of perpetual slavery; in which many thousands of our fellow-creatures are, and may be unjustly detained? Let us reconcile our practice to our avowed principles. Let not our professions of an inviolable attachment to liberty, of late so frequently echoed from one end of the continent to the other, be contradicted by a practice as unjust as it is impolitick. Doctor Young is very severe where he says

> The world's all title page, there's no contents.

Let our conduct shew our title to an exception. Let us therefore immediately consider, and adopt the most prudent measures for relieving those oppressed people; and of enemies make them friends and useful members of society, by confering on them such privileges as will interest them in the general welfare.

Being sensible of my deficiency, I should have been pleased, had the few hints I have presumed to obtrude on the publick, employed a pen more equal to the importance of my subject. Conscious, however, of my motive in giving them, I flatter myself they will meet from the candid, the reception which is due to a good intention. As a wellwisher to the religious and civil interests of my country, I am willing to contribute my mite towards the removal of an evil, which I believe to be dangerous to both: and if any thoughts I have meant to express, have the least tendency to effect it; I shall be indifferent whatever opinion is formed of the dress they appear in.

[Theodore Parsons and Eliphalet Pearson], *A Forensic Dispute,* 1773

A Forensic Dispute on The Legality of enslaving the Africans Held at the Public Commencement in Cambridge, New-England, July 21st, 1773. By Two Candidates for the Bachelor's Degree (Boston, 1773), pp. 3-26; 28-42; 47-48.

The appeal to concepts of natural rights by antislavery writers were countered by similar proslavery appeals. Indeed, many Enlightenment thinkers from whom revolutionary leaders drew inspiration—Locke, Hobbes, Hugo Grotius—had accepted slavery as consistent with natural order and selection, natural practices of subordination and tradition. At the Harvard commencement of 1773, two students formally debated the legality of enslaving the Africans. Both speakers appealed to natural rights. At the same time that the antislavery spokesman hailed doctrines of natural equality and liberty, the proslavery advocate embraced the natural right of authority. As justifications for both antislavery and proslavery positions were drawn from general concepts of natural rights, they questioned the natural rights of the black race. If blacks were something akin to mules or cows, their "natural" position in society was obvious. It is not surprising that the antislavery speaker described blacks as "descendants . . . from the same common parent with you and me, and between whom and us nature has made no distinction, save what arises from the stronger influence of the sun in the climate whence they originated. . . ." Conversely, the other speaker portrayed the black man as an "inhumanly savage" conglomerate of idiot and madman. This debate illustrates Withrop Jordan's point that "the status of Negroes could never again be characterized by placid and unheeding acceptance." The Harvard debate reflected a larger debate in America over the black race and its legitimate place in society.

A. . . . Whether the slavery, to which Africans are in this province, by the permission of law, subjected, be agreable to the law of nature? And since, fully persuaded of the truth of those principles, in which is founded the idea of natural equality, to the exclusion of a right in one individual of the human species to exercise any degree of authority over another without his consent, I am obliged to appear in favor of the negative of the proposition; and since, if I rightly remember, I have sometimes heard you express a very different sentiment, if you are disposed to join in the proposal, I will first attend to what may be offered on your part in support of it. And shall therefore only observe, that the strangely inconsistent conduct of mankind, respecting this matter, furnishes us with reflections upon the present state of human nature by no means the most agreable. To me, I confess, it is matter of painful astonishment, that in this enlightened age and land, where the principles of natural and civil Liberty, and consequently the natural rights of mankind are so generally understood, the case of these unhappy *Africans* should gain no more attention;—that those, who are so readily disposed to urge the principles of natural equality in defence of their own Liberties, should, with so little reluctance, continue to exert a power, by the operation of which they are so flagrantly contradicted. For what less can be said of that exercise of power, whereby such multitudes of our fellow men, descendants, my friend from the same common parent with you and me, and between whom and us nature has made no distinction, save what arises from the stronger influence of the sun in the climate whence they originated, are held to groan under the insupportable burden of the most abject slavery, without one chearing beam to refresh their desponding souls; and upon whose dreary path not even the feeblest ray of hope is permitted to dawn, and whose only prospect of deliverance is—in death. If indeed the law protects their lives, (which is all that can be said even here, and more—shame to mankind—more than can be said in some of our sister colonies) the only favor these unhappy people receive, from such protection, is a continuation of their misery; the preservation of a life, every moment of which is worse than non-existence. A favor this, no doubt, that in a very special manner demands acknowledgement!

B. Though conscious my friend, of my inability, the most advantageously to represent the arguments in favor of this proposition, especially when circumscribed within the narrow limits the present occasion will allow; yet clearly convinced of the propriety of attentively considering this question, especially at a period when persons of every denomination are so justly affected with a sense of Liberty, I readily comply; rather hoping that if any present, are in doubt respecting this matter, they will take occasion from hence, so fully to examine it, as to procure satisfaction to themselves, than expecting what shall be now offered on my part will have so desirable an effect.

I am well aware of the difficulty of his task who attempts to defend a proposition of this nature. An heart replete with benevolence and compassion will hardly admit reasoning that involves principles seemingly incompatible with the happiness of *any*. Suffer me therefore to entreat you, that every tender sentiment, that even the feelings of humanity may be suspended, while we calmly attend to the voice of reason, which is the voice of nature's alwise and benevolent Author.

That Liberty to all is sweet I freely own; but still 'tis what, in a state of society at least, all cannot equally enjoy, and what even in a *free* government can be enjoyed in the most perfect sense by none. Such is the nature of society, that it requires various degrees of authority and subordination; and while the universal rule of right, *the happiness of the whole,* allows greater degrees of Liberty to some, the same immutable law suffers it to be enjoyed only in less degrees by others. And though my friend, I can most cordially join with you in the benevolent wish, that it were possible that these Africans, who I am free with you to call my brethren, and to whom, it is confessed, the principles of our civil constitution allow but a small degree of liberty, might enjoy it equally with us; yet 'till I am convinced it might comport with the rule above mentioned, to allow them more I am in duty bound to appear an advocate for those principles.

Let it therefore be remembered, that the question to be considered is, "*Whether the slavery, to which Africans are in this Province, by the permission of law, subjected, be agreable to the law of nature?*"

It is, I presume, scarcely necessary to observe to you, that by the law of nature is intended that law which is the measure of all our moral actions, and by which their fitness and propriety, and consequently their justice or injustice, are to be determined. In other words, that law to which whatever action is in it's nature fit and proper, just and right, is agreable, and to which every action of an opposite nature is disagreable. This, then being intended by the law of nature, whether the justice of *African slavery*, if found agreable to this law, is defensible, will be needless to inquire. But it will be said, through this definition of the law of nature be admitted, we are still to be informed what those actions are, that are agreable to this law, and consequently right. I answer, whatever action in it's nature, concomitant circumstances being considered, tends to *happiness on the whole,* is agreable to this law, and every action of a contrary tendency is hereunto disagreable. And hence it will follow, that whatever practical principle of society, (which is to be considered as the action of the community) hath this tendency, is to be reputed just, and approved and adopted, and those of a contrary tendency consequently disapproved.

To demonstrate this, it will be necessary only to observe, that as nothing in nature can possibly be of the least consequence but happiness or misery, so the difference in the tendency of the practical principles of any society to the production of these, is the only thing that can possibly render some eligible, fit and proper, rather than others; and was it not for this distinction, it must forever remain a matter of perfect indifference, what practical principles were in any society adopted. But without stopping more fully to demonstrate the truth of this principle, it having been recognised as well by the generality of ethic writers, as by the wisdom of all good governments, I shall proceed to enquire, how far it will operate to the determination of the present question.

And in the first place, I shall enquire into the agreement of the law of nature with the idea of slavery *in general,* in opposition to that principle of natural equality, which is so zealously contended for by the advocate for universal Liberty.

By slavery *in general* I mean the involuntary subordination of the will of one to that of another; whereby, independent of all compact, the actions of the former are in all things to be directed by the will of the latter. Now if slavery *in general*, according to this definition, be agreable to the law of nature, the principle of natural equality must fall, and in order to determine the question in dispute, it will be necessary only to apply the general principle to the case of the *African* subordination, whereby it will be easy to discern if there is any thing in the nature of their particular case not agreable hereto.

I am therefore now to shew, that slavery as above defined, is not repugnant to the law of nature, and therefore that the principle of natural equality cannot be true.

That right of authority is to be found in some being involving subordination in others, independent of all voluntary contract on the part of the subordinate, is, as far as I know, universally acknowledged. Such is the right of the Governor of the universe to govern and direct the conduct of all finite existences, and such is the right of parents to govern and direct the conduct of their children. Now if it be found, that there is the same foundation for authority and subordination among different individuals of the human species, between whom no such relations as those above-mentioned do subsist, as there is for authority and subordination in those cases where it is acknowledged to be just, it will follow, that degrees of rightful authority in some, involving degrees of subordination in others, must be admitted among them likewise. In other words, if the *reason* and *foundation* of the *absolute* authority of the Governor of the universe over the creation, and the *limited* authority of parents over their children, be found to operate with equal strength in favor of a right of some individuals among mankind to exercise any degrees of authority over others, the exercise of such authority must be acknowledged just, i. e. agreable to the law of nature. And now to determine this question, it is necessary to inquire, in what the right of authority, in the cases abovementioned, is founded: And here the answer is obvious, in *the greatest good of the whole*. For since the Governor of the universe is possessed of power, wisdom, and goodness in perfection of degree, it is impossible but that the greatest happiness to the creation should be the result of his exercise of the most absolute sovereignty. And though this right of absolute authority in the Creator over his creatures be inseparable from the relation between Creator and creature, yet it is not founded simply in that relation, that is, in the idea of derived existence; but in the natural imperfection and dependance of the creature, and the natural perfection of the Creator, and the reason of the necessarily absolute subjection of the creature does not consist merely in his having *received existence*, but in his having received it from *such* a Being; a Being by the perfection of his nature qualified for the most perfect government, and under whose administration it is impossible but that the beforementioned immutable law of nature, the greatest happiness of the whole, should operate to effect. Agreable to this is the foundation of the natural authority of parents over their children; it by no means consisting in the notion of *derived existence*; but in the different qualifications of parents and children to execute this immutable law: For while parents so far excel their children in wisdom, and from natural affection are disposed to promote their happiness, it will follow, that more happiness will result to both, from the exercise of authority in parents, and subordination in children, than from the exercise of equal Liberty in each. And that this authority of parents over their children is derived from this source, and not from the natural relation subsisting between them, considered merely as parents and offspring, is moreover evident beyond all contradiction from this consideration, that whenever the parent is by any means disqualified, in the respects before mentioned, to direct the conduct of his child, the subordination of the child ceases.

If this, which I think none will deny, be a just representation of the foundation in *nature* of authority and subordination; in order to justify involuntary slavery *in general*, in opposition to the notion of *natural* equality, it is necessary only to inquire, whether among different individuals, between whom there is no such natural relation as that of parent and offspring, there be not the same reason, ground, and foundation in nature for the exercise of authority in some, necessarily involving subordination in others, which there is in cases where such relation actually subsists. And concerning this, no one surely can remain a moment undetermined, who reflects with the least degree of attention, upon the vast inequality observable between different individuals of the human species, in point of qualification for the proper direction of conduct. Now whether this inequality be considered as arising from difference in natural capacity, difference in the means of improvement, or in disposition properly to employ such means: in a word, whether it arises from nature or education, or any other supposeable quarter, it matters not, while this is in fact the case, while some are actually found so far to excel others both in respect of wisdom and benevolence, both in the knowledge of the principles of propriety, and a disposition to practice such principles, that the general end, happiness, would be better promoted by the exercise of authority in the former, though necessarily involving subordination in the latter, than by the enjoyment of equal Liberty in each, the exercise of such authority must be right, and never the less so, though the individuals by such an oeconomy subordinated, do not consent. It is fit that children should be subjected to the authority of their parents, whether they consent to such subjection or not; this is put beyond all possibility of doubt by the express declaration of wisdom which cannot err; not to mention the consent of all ages in their approbation of the principles of those civil societies which have warranted the exercise of such authority. Every law is applicable to all cases within the same reason; and since it cannot be denied that the reason of authority and subordination between parents and children, equally applies to the support of a distinction of the same kind among others not so related, it follows inevitably, that a distinction in the latter case is equally justifiable with one in the former; they are both supported by the same principle of natural law, and therefore must stand or fall together.

I have introduced these observations upon the foundation of the authority of the Governor of the universe over the creation, and of parents over their children, for the sake of example, rather than as necessary to support the general idea of inequality: I say as necessary, for while there is so manifestly great an inequality in the capacities and dispositions of mankind to direct their own as well as the conduct of others, to its only proper end, I think it demonstrable, that the principle of absolute equality could not be supported, even though we had no argument from fact by which it might be illustrated. And in truth, I think, before the principle of absolute equality can be maintained, it must be made to appear, that all mankind, in point of capacity and disposition to conduct properly, are equal.

It now remains only to apply these general principles to the particular case of *Africans* in this country, and see what degree of authority the people here are thereby warranted to exercise over them; and if it shall appear in fact, that they are not reduced by the law of this land to a degree of subordination beyond what the law of nature abovementioned, the happiness of both, requires, it will follow undeniably, that the law by which they are thus subjected is just.

A. Before you proceed to the application you mention, permit me to make an observation, that perhaps may render such application unnecessary. I think you have by no means supported the idea of slavery *in general*; but that your argument in favour of natural inequality, though ingeniously enough conducted, is manifestly inconclusive, and that the contrary, notwithstanding all you have alledged, may still be true. For though I acknowledge, that in every society the practical principle that in it's operation tends to the greatest happiness of the whole is right. i. e. agreable to the law of nature, and that the *absolute* authority of the Governor of the universe, and the *limited* authority of parents over their children is founded in the reason you alledge; and also admit, among different individuals, all those different degrees of qualification for the proper direction of conduct for which you contend; yet that the natural right of independence is hence excluded, and the principle of natural equality consequently overthrown is by no means acknowledged. The reason is obvious, that the principle for which you contend is in the nature of things utterly impracticable; your conclusion therefore, from premises implying a false hypothesis, cannot be admitted.

The exercise of authority, only in cases where such exercise is productive of happiness, is undoubtedly right: But such is the constitution of things with regard to man, such his nature, state, and condition, as renders it absolutely impossible that a principle, warranting the exercise of authority in any particular case, independent of the consent of the subordinate, should be correspondent to this end. And for this good reason, that it is impossible for human wisdom to distinguish the cases where the exercise of such authority would be proper, from those where it would not be so; and could this be effected, it would still be utterly impossible for any *practical principle* of society, for any human *law* to make the distinction. The same law which would warrant the exercise of authority in one case, must of necessity warrant it in another; unless it could be supposed, that some infallible judge could be present at all times, and in all places, and direct the operation of law in every particular case. And were even this possible, it might still be doubted whether the principle of natural equality would be overthrown. Such are the weaknesses and imperfections, the passions and prejudices of the best of men, and so deeply are all impressed with a sense of Liberty and independence, that it may well be questioned, whether a law, warranting authority in those cases only where it would be most proper, were such law possible, would operate more to the general happiness, than a law establishing the principle of natural equality: For tho' in that case, many would conduct less foolishly than they now do; yet the idea of servitude, and dependence upon the will of another, would be a perpetual, and not unfruitful source of misery. But whatever might be the effect of such a constitution, since that is confessedly impossible, it is evident beyond all contradiction, that the principle of natural equality is infinitely better adapted to the general end, happiness, than any other practical principle that can possibly be established. Hence I think it is manifest, notwithstanding the plausible appearance of your reasoning in theory, since it will not endure the true touchstone of practice, that slavery, which many to their cost know to be a practical thing, is far from being supported thereby.

Your notion of the ground and foundation of natural authority, in the examples you have adduced, is undoubtedly just, and consent in those cases, is by no means necessary to subordination, but, unfortunately for your conclusion, the cases are far from being applicable to the point in hand: For as in one case, perfection of wisdom and goodness excludes the possibility of error, and renders the most perfect subjection necessarily best; so the principle of affection implanted by the Author of nature in the breast of the parent, inspiring such a tender concern for the welfare of his offspring, and so strongly operative to the production of kind offices towards him, together with the natural inability of the child, through weakness or inexperience, to be his own director, may well warrant a general rule of limited subordination in the other. And when you have shewn me the man, or number of men, capable of infallibly directing the conduct of others, the exercise of authority in them, shall not want my approbation. And when you shall point out to me any classes of men, between whom there is such a comparative difference in point of ability for the proper direction of conduct, as between parents and children, and the *same* disposition in the superior towards the inferior, that the Author of nature has implanted in the hearts of parents towards their children, I will readily acknowledge the exercise of a like degree of authority justifiable by the law of nature.

But I am much at a loss to conceive how your reasoning in favor of slavery *in general,* were it ever so fully conclusive, could possibly justify us in thus forcibly subjugating the *Africans,* between whom and us nature seems to have made no such difference as that, upon which you suppose the notion of *natural inequality* to be founded: For I suppose you will hardly imagine the darkness of a man's skin incapacitates him for the direction of his conduct, and authorises his neighbours, who may have the good fortune of a complexion a shade or two lighter, to exercise authority over him. And if the important difference does not lay here, it seems not very easy to determine where it does; unless perchance, it be in the quality of their hair; and if the principle of subordination lies here, I would advise every person, whose hair is inclined to deviate from a right line, to be upon his guard. If indeed any should alledge, that they are distinguished by the flatness of their noses, I can't but think this circumstance against them, for if a man is to be led and governed by the nose, it may well be questioned, whether a nose of a different figure would not be better adapted to the purpose.

B. My friend, I am no enemy to humour, but I think it rarely serves to illustrate a logical conclusion. I confess my argument, as you have represented it, appears ridiculous enough; but if you had deferred your reply till I had made an application of the principle to the point in hand, perhaps it had saved you this needless expence of wit. I have not pretended, as a consequence from my principles, that every degree of superiority in point of discretion would warrant to any individual of a community a right to exercise authority over his neighbour: I have only contended, that the notion of *equality*, in the strict sense, had no foundation *in nature*; but as happiness is the only end of action, so superiority in wisdom, goodness, &c. is in the nature of things a proper foundation of authority. And as nature has made differences among creatures in these respects; so it is fit and proper, and agreable to nature's law, that different degrees of authority in point of direction of conduct should be exercised by them; and that in some cases, even among the human species, this difference is so important, as to render the exercise of authority justifiable, even without the consent of the governed: For this I have produced an example from fact, in the case of parents and children. All this you have implicitly allowed. I now go on to say, as a consequence from the same acknowledged principle, that whenever such a connection of things takes place, that any number of men cannot, consistently with the good of the whole, have a residence in any community but in a state of involuntary subordination, and that their residence in such community notwithstanding such subordination, be in fact best for the whole, such subordination. though involuntary, is no violation of the law of nature; but on the contrary to all intents and purposes correspondent thereto. This is a true conclusion from premises incontestible, principles universally acknowledged, and which you yourself have but now admitted. Subordination in this case comes fully within the reason of the subordination of children, rests on precisely the same foundation, and is therefore justifiable on precisely the same principles. For whether the necessity of such subordination arises from natural incapacity, or from any other quarter, it matters not, if this is in fact the case; if the interest of the whole does require it; let the causes or reasons of such requirement be what they may, such subordination is equally justifiable as in any other case whatever; not only in the case of children, but even in the case of consent; for the obligation to submission arising from consent, is founded in the general obligation to fulfil contracts; which obligation is ultimately founded in the good of society.

Now fully within this predicament lies, as I conceive, the particular case of *Africans* in this country. That it is only a state of limited subordination (I say *limited*, for it is to be remembered, that the authority of those to whom they are subordinate, is restricted by the superior authority of law, to which we are all subordinate, and which provides that they, as well as others, shall be treated according to the general principles of humanity) that these people can *consistently* enjoy a residence among us is, I suppose, acknowledged by all. And whether it is not better for them to reside here, notwithstanding such subordination, even regard being had to *their* interest only, than in their native country, no one can doubt, at least no one, who has a tolerably adequate conception of their misery, and wretchedness there. Figure to yourself my friend, you are not unacquainted with *African* history, figure to yourself the delightful situation of a natural inhabitant of *Africa*. View him necessarily destitute of every mean of improvement in social virtue, of every advantage for the cultivation of those principles of humanity, in which alone consists the dignity of the rational nature, and from which only source spring all that pleasure, that happiness of life, by which the human species is distinguished from the other parts of the animal creation. Consider his situation as a candidate for an eternal existence; view him as necessarily ignorant of every principle of that religion, through the happy influence of which alone the degenerate race of Adam can rationally form the most distant expectation of future felicity. View him moreover in a state of the most abject slavery, a slavery of the worst kind, a slavery of all others most destructive of human happiness,—an entire subjection to the tyrannizing power of lust and passion,—wholly devoted to the governing influence of those irregular propensities, which are the genuine offspring of depraved nature, when unassisted by philosophy or religion. Behold him actually clothed in all that brutal stupidity, that savage barbarity which naturally springs from such a source. Add to this, his condition of perpetual insecurity, arising from the state of hositility and war that forever rages in those inhospitable climes; and consider the treatment he is to expect, whom the fortune of war has subjected to the power of his enraged foe, whose natural cruelty is perpetually sharpened, and whose desire of revenge is continually cherised, by a sense of his own danger. . . . without it: But who I beseech you, ever thought the consent of a child, an ideot, or a madman necessary to his subordination? Every whit as immaterial is the consent of these miserable Africans, whose real character seems to be a compound of the three last mentioned. What can avail his consent, who through ignorance of the means necessary to promote his happiness, is rendered altogether incapable of choosing for himself? And as the consent of such a being could by no means involve subordination in a case where it would be otherwise improper, so the want of it can be no bar in a case where it would not. In all such cases it is undoubtedly the duty of those, whom providence has favored with the means of improvement in understanding, and the wisdom resulting from such improvement, to make use of their discretion in directing the conduct of those who want it.

I am sensible that I have already dwelt too long upon this argument; you will however in this connexion, permit me to add, that were involuntary subjection, in all cases, contrary to the law of nature, it is impossible to suppose, that the Governor of the universe, whose wisdom is infinite, and whose will is eternally and immutably coincident with, and *when revealed to us*, the *measure* of, this law, should ever have expressly tolerated it in any particular instance. I mention this in the present connexion, the rather because I suppose the authority, the Israelites, when under a government absolutely theocratical, were permitted to exercise over strangers, was founded in the same reason with the authority for which I contend, viz: that it was better for them to reside among a people, where they might have some opportunity for improvement in knowledge and virtue, though in a state of subordination, than to remain amongst the barbarous and idolatrous nations, whence they originated.

Were it necessary or expedient, it would be easy to shew, by comparison, in a great variety of instances not mentioned, the superiority of a slave in this country, in point of condition, to a natural inhabitant of *Africa*. And though it be too true, that these unhappy creatures are in many particular cases, cruelly treated, yet, while their importation is to them a redemption from a condition on the whole so much more miserable, we must, as I said before, justify the government in tolerating such importation; and with regard to the particular instances of abuse, we can only say *caveant qui sunt conscii*. . . .

A. Notwithstanding all you have so ingeniously alledged in support of this question, I am still obliged to confess myself one of those in whom your reasoning has failed to produce conviction: And must be excused in saying that the justice of slavery *generally* understood, is still, for aught I am able to discern, far from being supported.—It is true the Israelites when under a theocratical government were permitted, under certain circumstances, to exercise authority over strangers resident among them. And this is adduced as an argument, infallibly conclusive in favor of slavery. But is it certain that this conclusion is not drawn a little too hastily?

The Governor of the universe has, in a certain instance, expressly tolerated slavery, Nothing was ever by him tolerated but what was agreeable to the law of nature. Therefore,—Slavery is lawful. The man must have a very extraordinary talent who can deduce this conclusion from such premises.—It is readily granted, that thus much may be justly inferred from them, viz. that such a particular connexion of things *once* took place, as rendered slavery, under the *express permission* of the Governor of the universe, lawful. But will it follow from hence, that slavery is ever lawful *without such permission?* As well may we infer a right, by the law of nature, to put any who are unable to resist our power, under harrows and axes of iron, and in a word, make the *particular* precept in any case, given the *Israelites*, a measure, whereby to explain those *general* laws of nature, which are to regulate the conduct of *all mankind*. It is undoubtedly true, that every express declaration of the Governor of the universe is agreeable to, and justly explanatory of, the law of nature, as far as such declaration extends. And the conduct of any particular person, or people, which is agreeable to such declaration is most certainly right; but it can never be certainly inferred from hence, that a like conduct in others, not having the same warrant, is agreeable to this law: For the imperfection of human wisdom renders it forever uncertain, whether the cases are in all respects similar; and consequently, it can never be *certainly* determined, that the same conduct will, in both cases, have the same natural tendency to happiness; and hence the same conduct, that in the former case was right, *may* in the latter, be wrong. But could even this be ascertained, there would still remain an insuperable difficulty in determining the actions of one people to be right, *merely* from an express toleration of the same, or like actions in another: And this arises *solely* from the *want* of such toleration. If it be objected, that an action, in it's nature unfit, could not be tolerated; it may be answered, that the same action, *when so expressly* authorised, may be fit and proper, and in it's nature right, which *without such*, toleration, would not be so; and for this plain reason, that the same action, when by rightful authority permitted may have on the whole a tendency to happiness, which without such permission, would have an opposite tendency.

If this reasoning be just (the validity of which, I am happily too well acquainted with your knowledge of the principles of argumentation, to doubt whether you will dispute) how far the lawfulness of the practice of slavery among the Israelites, when expressly tolerated by the Governor of the universe, will justify a people in a like practice, to whom no such toleration has ever been granted, is by no means difficult to discern. And before the principle of natural equality can be overthrown, the tendency of slavery to the good of mankind, must, by arguments drawn from *the nature and consitution of things,* be made *evidently* to appear. . . .

Was it possible to consider this case as standing alone, independent of it's connexions with practices of a like kind in other places, and the more extensive influence it may consequently have upon the happiness of mankind, it is at least doubtful if it would then be right. I am ready to allow, that was it *certain* that their condition here is happier on the whole, than in their own country, your premises, in this *independent view* of the matter, would well warrant your conclusion; but even this I apprehend is far from being true. You have represented the misery and wretchedness of these people in their native land, in a light indeed, disagreeable enough. But I am still disposed from my apprehension of the dignity of the rational nature, at least to hope that your colouring is a little too strong; and that notwithstanding the unhappy state of degradation into which they are confessedly sunk, they are still some degrees above brutes. It is acknowledged that they are extremely unacquainted with the politer arts, and almost wholly ignorant of every thing belonging to science; and consequently strangers to all the pleasures of a scholar and a philosopher; they are also confessedly destitute of an acquaintance with the principles of urbanity and consequently want, in a great measure, the happiness resulting from a well regulated civil society; their condition is allowedly not greatly different from a state of nature; though it is to be remembered, that if modern writers of the best reputation are to be credited, their manners, in most parts of that extensive country, are far less savage and barbarous; their conveniences and enjoyments much more numerous, and in a word their manner of life much more agreable than has been heretofore represented. And indeed it is not to be wondered that those who have been disposed to make a gain by this iniquitous practice of enslaving their fellow men, should be careful, for their justification, to represent them as nearly upon a level with the brute creation as possible; not to mention the ridiculous attempts that have, in this view, been made to prove them actually of another species. But granting their condition to be, as in fact it is, comparatively low; that their sources of happiness, when compared with those which the members of a well-ordered civil society enjoy, are few; yet it is not to be forgotten, that their appetites and desires are in some good measure proportional. *Nemo desiderat quae ignorat.* The benevolent author of our being has accommodated our *natural* desires in a great measure to the *natural* means of gratification. And he who attentively considers the anxious and perplexing cares; the fatiguing and often fruitless labors; the cravings of *unnatural* appetites; the frequently disappointed views and expectations; and, in a word, the various and almost innumerable *new* sources of infelicity *naturally*, and many of them *inseparably* connected with what is commonly called a state of civilization, will perhaps perceive that the difference, in point of *real* happiness, between the scholar, the courtier, and the simple child of nature, is far from infinite. But allowing it to be very considerable, allowing that the privileges and advantages of a *free* member, of a *free society*, where useful sciences and the liberal arts are patronized and flourish, and where all those principles that beautify and adorn the rational nature are cultivated, are comparatively very great. . . . In their native country, though their condition be indeed contemptible enough, they have the blessing of *Liberty* to sweeten every pleasure, and give a relish to every enjoyment: But here, though their condition were in other respects much more favourable than it is, while conscious of perpetual and absolute dependance upon the will of others, this reflection, so opposite to the strong sense of Liberty implanted in the heart of every son of Adam, must necessarily mar the happiness of every gratification, effectually chill the sense of pleasure, and stop every natural source of felicity. A keen excruciating sense of liberty forever lost must still predominate, till, the spirit broken by the fatigue of incessant distress, they sink into a state of lifeless insensibility. And then for sooth we are presently disposed to tax them with natural stupidity; and make the very thing that our unnatural treatment has occasioned the ground of our justification.—It is well known, that stupidity is by no means the natural characteristic of these people; and when we consider the nature of their condition in this country, how miserably dejected, depressed and despised, instead of marking their want of apprehension, we ought rather to admire that there are any the least appearances of sensibility remaining in them.

But it is alleged, "that at home they are in a perpetual state of war, and that by the purchase of captives many lives are preserved, that would otherwise be devoted to destruction." Surprizing indeed; that here, as in the former case, the very evil that this practice has occasioned should be alledged in excuse of it! One must have a favourable opinion indeed of that cause which needs the support of such arguments!—It would wring drops of blood from an heart of adamant to relate the cruel sufferings of these unhappy people, in those countries, who, at the same time, have less advantages for christian knowledge, than the natives of California, or the inhabitants of the antarctic circle. But I forbear—The person that can imagine the practice of slavery in this country, considered in all it's consequences, connexions and tendencies, productive of the happiness of mankind, must, I think, allow, that the direct way to encrease their happiness is by every possible means to encrease their misery.

B. As you have not now disputed the truth of the principle, but joined with me in resting the argument upon a matter of fact, I shall no farther pursue the dispute, but leave that point to be determined by the judgment of others.

Samuel Hopkins and Ezra Stiles, "To the Public," August 31, 1773

Redwood Library, Newport, R.I.

In 1770 the Reverend Samuel Hopkins, New Light theologian and disciple of Jonathan Edwards, became the pastor of the First Congregational Church of Newport, Rhode Island—the city of steaming slave marts and the center of the black trade. Hopkins later impugned Newport's slave trade as the epitome of immorality and wickedness: "God would frown upon Newport . . . the judgments of Heaven would hang over its dwellings."

In 1773 Hopkins, who had once owned a house servant but was now violently repulsed by the black flesh peddling occurring near his own church, began to preach against the institution of slavery. In addition, he devised a scheme to send a number of trained Negro missionaries to Africa to spread the Gospel among the population, "to send the light . . . to these nations in Africa, who have been injured so much by the slave trade . . . to promote the most important interest, the kindom of Christ." Needing moral and financial support, Hopkins approached fellow townsman and Old Light clergyman, Ezra Stiles, who, although a theological rival, shared Hopkin's abhorrence of slavery. The ponderous Hopkins and the slight, delicate Stiles launched their project by appealing for contributions for the training of two black members of the First Congregational Church—Bristol Yamma, a slave, and John Quamine, a free black—for the mission to Guinea. They would be educated in "reading the Scripture and Systematized Divinity."

Hopkins and Stiles distributed the appeal among New England churches and fired off letters to influential figures in America and Europe. The black poet, Phillis Wheatley, wrote to Hopkins, "Methinks, Reverend sir, this is the beginning of that happy period foretold by the Prophets when all shall know the Lord from the least to the greatest . . . my heart expanded with sympathetic joy to see at distant time the thick cloud of ignorance dispersing from the face of my benighted country." The two ministers raised some funds but the project was never completed. The death of Quamine during the war, the general disruption of the Revolution itself, and the lack of sufficient funds all militated against the scheme. Although Stiles, as late as August 1788, was still discussing the possibility of sending Yamma on the mission, the minister lamented, "I am somewhat doubtful whether God's time is yet come to favour the Gentile Nations with the pure & benign Light of the Gospel."

To all who are desirous to promote the kingdom of Christ on earth, in the salvation of sinners, the following narrative and proposal are offered, to excite and solicit their charity and prayers.

Samuel Hopkins (1721-1803), Congregationalist minister and abolitionist who preached blistering anti-slavery sermons to a predominately slave-trading congregation in Newport, Rhode Island.

There are two Negro men, members of the first congregational church in Newport, on Rhode Island, named *Bristol Yamma*, and *John Quamine*, who were hopefully converted some years ago; and have from that time sustained a good character as christians, and have made good proficiency in christian knowledge. The latter is son of a rich man at Annamaboe, and was sent by his father to this place for an education among the English, and then to return home: Which the person to whom he was committed engaged to perform, for a good reward. But instead of being faithful to his trust, he sold him a slave for life. But God in his providence has put it in the power of both of them to obtain their freedom. They joined in purchasing a ticket in a lottery, which drew a prize of 300 dollars. With this, and some other helps, they have purchased their liberty. The former is, however, 50 dollars in debt, as he could not purchase his freedom under 200; which he must procure by his labour, unless relieved by the charity of others.

These persons, thus acquainted with christianity, and apparently devoted to the service of Christ, are about thirty years old: have good natural abilities; are apt, steady and judicious, and speak their native language; the language of a numerous, potent nation in Guinea, to which they both belong. They are not only *willing*, but *very desirous* to quit all worldly prospects and risque their lives, in attempting to open a door for the propagation of christianity among their poor, ignorant, perishing, heathen brethren.

The concurrence of all these things has led to set on foot a proposal to send them to Africa, to preach the gospel there, if upon trial they shall appear in any good measure qualified for this business. In order to this, they must be put to school, and taught to read and write better than they now can; and be instructed more fully in divinity, &c. And if, upon trial, they appear to make good proficiency; and shall be thought, by competent judges, to be fit for such a mission, it is not doubted that money may be procured, sufficient to carry the design into execution.

What is now wanted and asked is money to pay the debt mentioned, and to support them at school to make the trial, whether they may be fitted for the proposed mission. Whatever shall be given to this end, and put into the hands of the subscribers, they engage faithfully to improve to this purpose only, and to promote the proposed mission, according to their best discretion; and to be at all times ready to give an account of those who desire it, of all they shall receive, and the manner in which it has been expended.

As God has in his providence so far opened the way to this, by raising up these persons, and ordering the remarkable, concurring circumstances and events which have been mentioned; and there is, most probably, no other instance in America, where so many things conspire to point out the way for a mission of this kind, with such encouragement to pursue it, may it not be hoped it will have the patronage and assistance of all the pious and benevolent?

And it is humbly proposed to those who are convinced of the iniquity of the *slave trade*; and are sensible of the great inhumanity and cruelty of enslaving so many thousands of our fellow men every year, with all the dreadful and horrid attendants; and are ready to bear testimony against it in all proper ways, and do their utmost to put a stop to it: Whether they have not a good opportunity of doing this, by chearfully contributing, according to their ability, to promote the mission proposed: And whether this is not the best compensation we are able to make the poor Africans, for the injuries they are constantly receiving by this unrighteous practice, and all its attendants.

But, aside from this consideration, may it not be hoped that all who are heartily praying, "*Thy kingdom come,*" will liberally contribute to forward this attempt to send the glorious gospel of the blessed God, to the nations who now worship false gods, and dwell in the habitations of cruelty, and the land of the shadow of death: Especially, since the King of Zion has promised that whosoever parts with any thing in this world, *for the kingdom of God's sake*, shall receive manifold more in this present time; and in the world to come, life everlasting.

Ezra Stiles,
Samuel Hopkins.

Newport, Rhode-Island, August 31, 1773.

Ebenezer Baldwin and Jonathan Edwards, Jr., "Some Observations upon the Slavery of Negroes," October-December 1773

The Connecticut Journal, and the New-Haven Post-Boy, 8 Oct. 1773; 15 Oct. 1773; 17 Dec. 1773; 31 Dec. 1773.

On October 8, 1773, Connecticut ministers Ebenezer Baldwin and Jonathan Edwards, jr., began a series of essays on slavery in the New Haven Connecticut Journal. *Two months before the Boston Tea Party the two men declared, "Has it not a shrewd appearance of inconsistence, to make a loud outcry against the British parliament for making laws to oblige us to pay certain duties, which amount to but a mere trifle for each individual; when we are deeply engaged in reducing a large body of people to complete and perpetual slavery?"*

In 1770 the Reverend Samuel Cooke had delivered an antislavery sermon to an audience that included Thomas Hutchinson. From other New England pulpits there thundered similar refrains in the following years—from the pulpits of such as Levi Hart, Benjamin Colman, Samuel Hopkins, Ezra Stiles, and William Gordon. John Quincy Adams once remarked that the greatest glory of the American Revolution was that it connected the principles of civil government with those of Christianity. Throughout the period of the Revolution learned colonial ministers, citing Locke and Sydney, talked of natural rights and freedom in the same discourses in which they hailed the glory of the Lord. The Reverend John Wise of Ipswich, for example, taught that "Democracy is Christ's government in Church and in State." It is not surprising then that many individual clergymen, such as Baldwin and Edwards, steeped in the political literature and slogans of the period and attached to notions of civil and religious liberties, spoke out against the institution of slavery.

It has often been surprising to me, that while we in the American colonies, have been so jealous of our own liberties, and so cautious to guard against every encroachment upon them from our mother country; we have been so inattentive to our own conduct in enslaving the Negroes, or at least in joining in the trade, whereby they are enslaved. Has it not a shrewed appearance of inconsistence, to make a loud outcry against the British parliament for making laws to oblige us to pay certain duties, which amount to but a mere trifle for each individual; when we are deeply engaged in reducing a large body of people to complete and perpetual slavery? If it be lawful and right for us to reduce the Africans to a state of slavery, why is it not as right for Great Britain, France or Spain, not merely to exact duties of us; but to reduce us to the same state of slavery, to which we have reduced them? What arguments can be offered in favour of the one, which will not operate equally in favour of the other? It is said, that we in this new settled country, stand in great need of labourers, and that were it not for the slave trade, they would be so scarce, that it would be impossible to cultivate our lands? The same may be said of France or Spain; they stand in great need of slaves to cultivate their plantations in the West Indies and South America. Therefore they have a right to send a fleet heither; and carry off, from time to time, as many of us and our children as they need.

If we need the help of the Negroes, so does Great Britain need our help, to pay off their national debt. If we desire to grow rich and rest at ease, by their toils and labours; so does Great Britain desire the same at our expense.—So that while we persist in this practice of enslaving the Africans, our mouths ought to be shut entirely as to any duties or taxes, which Great Britain may see cause to lay upon us: otherwise I see not but that out of our own mouths, or by our own practice, we may justly be condemned.

But it will be said, that the cases are by no means parrallel. We are Christians; but the Africans are heathen; therefore it is right for us to enslave them, that we may bring them into this land of gospel light, and convert them to Christianity. In answer to this, I ask, is this the end, for which they are enslaved? If it be not, the argument is nothing to the purpose of justifying our conduct. If it be, it only shows, that *We do evil that good may come.* For where is the warrant in scripture to use such means to propagate the gospel of *peace* and *liberty*? Was this the method that Christ and his apostles took? Or have they prescribed that this method should be taken by any who should come after them? Is not the rule which they have left upon record this, that the preachers and propagators of the gospel should with meekness *instruct even these who oppose themselves* to the truth?

It is further urged, that it cannot be absolutely unlawful to reduce men to slavery, because there was an express permission given to the ancient Israelites to purchase slaves of the nations round about them.—This is granted: and this permission made it entirely lawful for *them* to purchase slaves. God who hath a right to dispose of the circumstances and lives of men, gave them this right; as he also gave them a right to invade and destroy the Canaanites, men, women and children, and to possess their land. And when we can produce any such grant, allowing us to enslave the Africans, then, and not 'til then, I conceive, it will be lawful for us to do it: as this is all that the permission given to the Israelites proves. It no more proves it lawful for us to enslave the Negroes, than that other permission to exterpate the Canaanites, proves it lawful for us, in the same manner to extripate the Africans, or any other nation.

It hath been also alledged in vindication of this practice, that the patriarchs, and particularly Abraham, *had servants born in his house and bought with his money.*—But in order that this argument prove any thing, it must be made to appear, *first*, that these servants were slaves in perpetual bondage, and had not forfeited their liberty, so as to be justly reduced to this state. Concerning Abraham we read in one place, that he had three hundred trained servants born in his own house: in another, we find him sojourning in different countries, without any such equipage, and as it seems solely with his wife. Hence it hath been thought with great probability, that these servants of Abraham were not perpetual slaves; but order of men, who in certain respects submitted to him as their patron and lord.—But,

Secondly, if it can be made out, that these servants, or any part of them, were Abraham's slaves, yet the argument will be lame, unless it can be also shown, that in enslaving them, he did right. For, however good a man he was, he had not arrived at sinless perfection, as appears by his repeatedly denying his wife.

In the former part of these observations published in the last paper, I made some strictures upon some of the arguments urged in favour of the practice of enslaving the Africans. Besides those already noticed, there is one much insisted on, which I mean particularly to consider at present: this is that which is drawn from the new-testament, and especially from the rules and precepts given by the apostles to the servants of that day, who are well known in general to have been slaves, requiring them to submit to and obey their respective masters. These are the premises. The consequence drawn from them is, that those servants were rightfully enslaved else the apostles would never have exhorted them to submission and obedience: and also, that it is lawful for us to reduce men to the same state of slavery, as they were in. . . .

It was the duty of those Christian servants to be submissive and obedient, not only as otherwise they would expose themselves to immediate ruin and death; but also as they would expose the whole Christian church, then in its infancy, to utter destruction. For if all the servants in the Roman empire had, upon their embracing christianity, refused to submit any longer to their several masters; no doubt it would have so provoked their heathen masters, as that they would have exerted the civil arm of the empire to the entire extripation of the Christian name. So that, from a regard to the common cause of christianity, as well as from a regard to their own particular safety, they were bound to submit to, and obey their masters.

Besides, the forementioned rules and exhortations of the apostles, so far as they have a general reference, must be understood to extend only, either to men who are right fully reduced to slavery, as it is granted they may be in some cases; or to those who although wrongfully reduced to this state, are, like those of the apostolic age, in such circumstances, that from regard to their own safety or the general good, they are bound patiently to submit to wrong.—Unless we understand those rules with those restrictions, we shall prove by them, that a man, who is in fact enslaved by another, let the iniquity be ever so great, have no right to use any vigorous means to regain his liberty; and that if one man be stronger, or any how more potent than his neighbour, and the former see cause to take the latter and make an absolute slave of him, and whip him every day, for not performing the task set him; the man enslaved is forbid by the precepts of the gospel, to stir hand or foot in asserting his liberty, or redressing his grievances. . . .

The truth is, that the scriptures were never designed to be a system of politics; and therefore Christ and his apostles never once touch upon one of these questions, viz. Whether the civil government, which was then established in the Roman empire were just and lawful; or whether the practice of enslaving men, which then obtained so universally, were agreeable to the law of nature and the will of God. It was their intention in many cases only to give us the general rules of justice and equity, without applying them to every example which came in their way. Their general rules are such as these, *Whatsoever ye would that men should do to you, do ye even so to them;—Render unto all their dues, tribute to whom tribute is due, &c.—Render unto Cesar the things which are Cesar's, and unto God the things which are God's*. It was an easy thing for them to have made application of these rules, and told us expressly whether tribute and obedience were due to *Cesar*, or to such a tyrannical civil magistrate as he was; and whether the masters in those days have an equitable right to the servitude of their slaves. So the divine Spirit could easily have told the true system of the heavenly-bodies, and the material universe. But for wise reasons doubtless, neither of these things are revealed in the scriptures. And as we cannot infer any thing either way from the silence of the scriptures on these two subjects; so neither can we infer from the like silence of the scriptures, that the slavery, which obtained in the apostolic age, was lawful.

Although all men are quick sighted enough with regard to their own interest, they are apt to be very dull of apprehension concerning the interest of others. And although we Americans are very jealous of our own liberties, and readily feel the force of arguments urged in vindiction of them; yet we seem by no means so sensible of the pertinency and force of the very same arguments, when urged in behalf of the poor Africans, who are incapable of pleading their own cause. On the other hand all the wits of men are exerted to invent some plausible apology for our conduct in reducing them to slavery, or some such arguments as will give it at least the appearance of right and justice. Accordingly many arguments have been invented and applied to this end, which seem to require an answer. And the practice itself appears to me so contrary to all the dictates of reason and the light of nature, so repugnant to all the feelings of humanity; that if these false arguments, by which men have in this particular perverted their reason, and blunted their natural sense of right and wrong, were obviated, they wou'd at once condemn this practice, even without any arguments offered against it.

Accordingly in the preceding part of these observations it has been the chief object of my attention to show the fallacy of some of these arguments. And there is one, which is by many deemed wholly unanswerable, to which I shall now particularly attend; I mean that wherein it is asserted that the Negroes imported from Africa are captives of war, and therefore rightfully enslaved. This argument has indeed been considered in the *Address to Americans*, and I think substantially answered. But as it is so important in the present question, and so much boasted of by those who urge it; I beg leave to make some further observations upon it.

In this argument as applied to justify the slavery of Negroes, it is taken for granted that all those Negroes, who are exported from Africa, are captives of war; which by no means *is* granted to be the fact; yea the contrary is capable of the most evident proof, as is manifest from the *Address* just now referred to, the authorities therein quoted, and many others which may be quoted. However, at present I shall allow it to be fact. It is also taken for granted, altho' it is by no means allowed, that they are all captives taken in a war which was unjust on their part; or that before their capture, they were engaged in an unrighteous war, and thereby forfeited both their lives and liberty. For if the war, in which they were engaged, was just on their part, if they were fighting only in defence of themselves, their families and their country, no man can pretend that here by they forfeited either their lives or liberty. Those therefore, who would justify the slavery of Negroes by this argument, must be able to prove that they are all captives taken in a war, which on their part was unjust. Unless this can be done, this argument is nothing to the purpose of justifying the slave trade as it is now carried on.

But allowing that this were the case; allowing that all the Negroes imported from Africa were engaged in a war which on their part was unjust; I cannot conceive that this wou'd justify the reducing them to a state of parpetual slavery. The argument stated in its full force is this: "Those who rise up against me in an unjust war and seek my life, thereby forfeit their own lives: And therefore I have a right to take away their lives if it be in my power. But if I have a right to take away their lives, surely if I please I may give them their lives, and deprive them of their liberty. If I have a right to take away their life, which is the greater good, much more have I a right to deprive 'em of their liberty, which is the less. Therefore all who are engaged in an unrighteous war, have forfeited both their lives and liberty."

Upon this argument I beg leave to make the following remarks.

It is not true that all who rise up against me without a sufficient cause, and seek my life, thereby forfeit their own lives. I shall first state the case of two individuals in a state of nature, and then of two nations at war with each other. Suppose a man who lives at the distance of an 100 miles from me, for some insufficient cause is so incensed at me, that he comes to a full determination to kill me; and for this purpose sets out on his journey and travels 60 miles towards the place of my abode. But then upon further reflection repents of his wicked intention, lays aside his resentment and returns home. Here is a man who has risen up against me and sought my life, and all this is perfectly known to me; But has this man so forfeited his life that I have a right for this conduct of his, to take it away? Or suppose he comes the whole of his journey with the purpose aforesaid, and makes an attack upon me in order to execute it, and then repents, gives me evidence of it, offers me restitution of the damage I have sustained, and security for his future good behaviour; have I now a right to take away his life? Or suppose that in consequence of the attack a combat ensues, in which I obtain the advantage, get him into my power, so that I can either take away his life, or punish him otherwise for his wicked attempt, recompense my damage and secure myself from the like future injuries; have I now a right to his life? may I with a good conscience take it away?—I am persuaded that in any of these cases the answer must be in the negative. And thus far the falsity of the above proposition, that he that rises up against me and seeks my life, forfeits his own, upon which so much is built in the present question, fully appears; and it also appears that when two individuals in a state of nature are at war, one of them has only *then* a right to kill the other, when it is necessary for his own defence and safety.

Now two nations are always, and that justly, considered with respect to each other, as two individuals in a state of nature: they have the same rights and are under the same laws. Let us suppose then one nation and all the individuals of it with one consent, yet without any just cause, make war upon another nation; and that in the issue of the war the former are entirely vanquished, so as to be absolutely in the power of the conquerors. Have these conquerors now a right to take this whole nation, subdued as they are, and put 'em to death in cool blood? They doubtless have, if there be no other way of defending and securing themselves and their own lives. But this I believe no one will adventure to assert. Yet they are by the supposition all equally guilty, having all given their consent to the war, and all in their proper places contributed to it, and engaged in promoting it. If therefore you will not allow that the whole nation may be put to the sword, the question arises at once. why then have the conquerors a right to put those few to the sword who were taken captive?

If it be said, that it may be necessary for the safety of the injured nation that some of the conquered should be put to death, tho' not the whole nation. If this be the case, why would you fix upon those who happened to be taken captive, rather than those who were subdued; when the nation in general submitted? Merely their having born arms in the field is no reason at all, for the other may be as much, yea much more criminal than they.

Thus it appears with regard to nations, as well as individuals, that it is by no means true, that those who rise up against me and seek my life, thereby forfeit their own and I have a right in all cases to take it away.

Here comes in a question, viz. What is it then which gives me a right in the field of battle, being engaged in a righteous cause, to kill as many of the enemy as I can? I answer, it is the right of self defence, and the right I have to promote the righteous cause in which I am engaged. But as soon as the battle is over, and the cause is won, and the enemy has submitted, I have no right to kill one more.

Thus it appears that the foundation upon which the forementioned argument in favour of enslaving captives of war is built, is insufficient to support the superstructure which is built upon it. The superstructure therefore must fall to the ground. Since we have no right to kill captives of war, it cannot be proved from the supposition of such a right, that we have a right to enslave them.

Indeed I grant that if we have no other way to defend and secure ourselves against an unrighteous enemy, but by reducing him to a state of slavery, we have a right so to do. And this holds equally with regard an individual or a nation, with regard to the whole or any part of a nation. For instance, suppose we are engaged in a righteous war, and having taken an hundred prisoners, have no other way to defend and secure ourselves but by making them slaves; in this case, I suppose we have a right to do it. But then I imagine such a case will very seldom, if ever happen. There are other ways enough to be sure in ordinary, to obtain such security. What we want is compensation of damage received, and security against future injuries; as soon as these can be obtained we ought to cease from any further hostilities, either towards the nation in general or individuals of it; and so ought to release the captives. Now in case we are victorious we may obtain both these things in other ways, viz. by taking a certain part of their goods or territory, by laying upon them a fine that shall be sufficient for this end, by depriving them of their arms, &c. But if we are vanquished in the war, it is vain to talk of retaining the captives in slavery to make good our damages and to secure us against a future injury; for it will not be in our power. And in case neither party is fully vanquished but both still remain capable of carrying on the war with vigour, and yet both find it for their interest to desist and come to an accommodation; then we may obtain the same advantage some other way, as wou'd accrue to us by retaining the captives we have made in slavery, as by an exchange of prisoners, by suffering 'em to be redeemed at a sufficient price, or by insisting that an equivalent be allowed us in the terms of the peace in some way or other. And if we be not able to procure this of our enemies, it is no more likely that we shall be able to obtain their consent to retain so many of their friends and brethren in captivity & slavery.

I Shall conclude this subject of the slavery of captives of war, with a quotation from the celebrated Dr. *Hutcheson*, late professor of moral philosophy in the university of *Glasgow*; see his short introduction to moral philosophy, book 3. chap. 3. where speaking of the slavery to which men for certain crimes may justly be condemned by civil authority, he adds,

"Nations in other respects not barbarous, condemned all captives in war, into this miserable condition; establishing an inhuman law even against themselves, and strongly conspiring to subject themselves and their posterity, upon many very possible contingencies, to the most miserable and ignominious treatment. Upon which subject the following maxims seem just.

1. "Whoever makes war without a just cause acquires no right by such violence, over either persons or goods taken, though he may detain them with external impunity.

2. "One who has a just cause, yet should set just bounds to his demands: nor can he demand any thing from the conquered except either under the name of *punishment*, *reperation of damage* done, or *precaution* against future injuries.

3. "None are punishable but such as either by some action or omission, contrary to their duty, have occasioned and contributed towards these injuries done to us by the war. And 'tis plain, this is seldom ever the case of the far greater part of the adult subjects of any state who are capable of a share in public affairs; not to speak of women and children, who make three fourths of every people, and ought to be deemed joint proprietors with the heads of families in their private properties. And tho' all heads of families payed tribute toward maintaining the war; this can't be deemed a crime in them, as they were under the immediate distress of their governors, who would otherwise have levied these taxes by force, and punished the refractory. Grant they had consented to the war, following some specious reasons published by their governors; their ignorance generally was invincible: nor was their consent of such importance as to cause the war, nor would their dissent have prevented it. Nor can we ever suppose any political union can transfer the guilt of one person upon another, who did not concur with him.

4. "Nay the very soldiers, all such at least as had no share of or influence in the public councils, as they enlisted upon presumption of being employed only in just causes, or persuaded by such reasons as their governors publish; they are *excusable entirely*, both on account of ignorance and necessity. To men once enlisted 'tis a capital crime to disobey orders. It must therefore be exceedingly inhuman to inflict any thing severe upon them by way of punishment, provided we can be secured against further dangers from them; and this we always may be from captives, by keeping them in our our own country and mixing them with our citizens or our colonies, without depriving them any way of their liberty. All this not only humanity will recommend, but a consideration of the uncertain accidents of war, and the inconstancy of fortune.

5. "Under pretence of repairing damages, the conqueror can demand nothing from the innocent citizens, except upon the same grounds that one demands it for damage done by another's slaves or cattle, to wit, this, that whoever contrives or procures any thing for his own utility, by which others without their fault receive hurt, is bound either to repair the damage, or deliver up the goods, or contrivance whatever it was, to the person injured. The conqueror may therefore justly demand from the conquered citizens, that they abandon their injust governors, the causes of the war; or that they oblige these governors to repair the damages; or that they repair

them themselves; and these three should be left to their choice. This holds most evidently as to these first citizens who at first constituted the government; or those who have power in the state, by whose council the war was undertaken; or who have it in their power to restrain their princes in their injust designs. As to others who are of no weight in public affairs, their plea against even compensating of damages is more favourable.

6. "But as soon as the defeated have repaired all damages, or the conqueror has obtained reperation to himself by force and military execution; and has also attained security against future injuries, such as a wise arbiter judges sufficient, he has no further demand on the innocent citizens. Now he may obtain all this in a much easier, and more merciful way, without depriving the innocent citizens of their liberty. The governors in the first place are bound to repair all damages, and the citizens only in the second place, when their governors cannot do it, or decline it.

7. "The children of slaves of any sort are all born free as we shewed above."—Here the author refers to book ii. 14. 3. where he writes as follows;—"But if one maintains and educates the child of another; there's no presumption here that it was done as a donation; 'tis more presumable that a debt is hereby constituted, to be discharged by the goods or future labours of this child, as far as the expence was truly made for the behoof of the child.—Nay further, as generally all this expence upon an indigent orphan would be lost entirely, if it died before it were capable of labour; the maintainer might perhaps, in the regour of justice, be allowed to charge something more on account of this hazard; and by this allowance men will be more encouraged to such necessary care of indigent orphans. But then this hazard continually decreases as the child advances in years, and cannot increase considerably the charge except for a few of the first years. An indigent orphan thus maintained is therefore in no worse case, than that of an indigent person who without any fault of his, is involved in a great debt, from whom the creditor may justly demand payment by his labours, while the debtor retains all the other natural rights of mankind, and whensoever either by his labours,—or the liberality of any friend, he can discharge it, he can no longer be justly detained in service. Now were an account of all the necessary charge of maintainance, and of the value of labour, justly stated, it would appear, that such an orphan sound in body and mind could always fully discharge such debt by his labours before he were thirty years of age: and consequently that this can never be a foundation for perpetual hereditary slavery; even allowing an extraordinary interest were charged upon the expences because of the hazard, as is done upon contracts of bottomry in trade. And yet this charge must appear pretty inhumane upon persons in any grievous distress: nor can any distress be conceived greater than that of an indigent child destitute of all aids from its parents."

8. "Whoever purchases a person for a slave, or detains him as such, is always bound to shew that this person was deprivtd of his liberty upon some just ground. The original proprietor of the matter in question is always at hand; since nature made every man master of himself, or his own

liberty. 'Tis plainly therefore incumbent upon the violent possessor to prove his title; and not upon the person deforced and claiming his liberty, to prove a negative, that he did not lose, or forfeit his liberty. Without a previous inquiry of this kind, no man can in this case be a fair purchaser.

9. "Nor is it justly pleaded here, that captives would be put to death if they could not be made slaves & sold as such: and that therefore they owe their lives and all to the purchasers. But sure no higher sort of title arises to the purchasers in this case, than to such as have done any other useful service of equal importance; such as, rescuing a fellow-citizen from robbers or murderers, ransoming them from pirates, curing diseases or wounds which without the aid of art would have been deadly. All such persons should have all expences refunded to them, and a generous compensation for their labours and art. But whoever alledged that they could claim the persons they thus served as their slaves?"

Granville Sharp to Anthony Benezet, January 7, 1774

Ms. copy in possession of Col. A. Lloyd-Baker, Hardwicke Court, Gloucester, Eng.

Granville Sharp indicated in this letter to Anthony Benezet that he was determined to make their "Ears tingle." *In particular, he continued to call upon Lord Dartmouth, the half-brother of Lord North, whose conciliatory attitude towards the colonies as American secretary led to his replacement in November 1775. Sharp, believing he had a sympathetic audience in Dartmouth, presented him with copies of American petitions, visited him at his home, and bombarded him with numerous letters. On January 16, 1773, he advised Dartmouth that the slave trade would endanger the very existence of His Majesty's American Dominions. The American petitions, however, got little support from Dartmouth, who declared in 1775, "We cannot allow the colonies to check or discourage, in any manner, a traffic so beneficial to the nation." But the oft-rebuffed Sharp continued his incessant propagandizing and lobbying. And, as he here mentions to Benezet, another ally was about to break into print on the subject of slavery—the Reverend John Wesley.*

London 7th Janry 1774

Dear Sir . . . I mentioned my having interceded with Lord Dartmouth in behalf of the Carribees "*early in the spring,*" whereas, on revising my papers, I find that my first letter to him on that subject was much earlier, being dated 10th Octo 1772. My want of success in that affair, shall not, however, discourage me from using my utmost endeavours (whenever I have opportunity or leisure) to expose the horrid oppression of slavery in our Colonies, and to urge the absolute necessity of speedily putting a stop to it. I have dispersed a great many Manuscript Papers relating to that subject (and particularly copies of the Virginia & Pennsylvania Petitions) among all those persons of my acquaintance, whose interest I thought of sufficient consequence to have weight in promoting a Reformation. And this has taken up so much of my small share of leisure, that my Tracts against slavery (intended for the Press) have proceeded very slowly, tho they were nearly finished, (as I thought) some time ago; and towards the end of last summer when I had most leisure, and had set about to finish my Tracts, I was undesignedly drawn off from the point, by a particular subject (the pernicious practice of *Duelling*) which occurred to me in the course of one of my tracts, viz. that relating to "the necessity of *submission to personal injuries*"; the same being intended to show the true meaning of the several texts usually cited for the Lawfullness of *Slavery among Christians*. My intention, indeed, was only to touch lightly on the subject of *Duelling* in a short note, annexed to the last mentioned Tract; but in examining the subject for that purpose, I found it so perplexed with contradictions, and false precedents, cited by the Law Writers, and I was unable to reduce the necessary remarks into the small Compass of a Note, and indeed I was gradually & imperceptibly led on, by the importance of the subject, to canvass it thoroughly, which cost me much more labour and time than I had, at first, proposed to allow it; and at length, on account of some violent Disputes and personal abuse among our Magistrates in the City, I thought it my Duty, as speedily as possible, to print the said Remarks in a separate Tract, distinct from the others against Slavery. To that the Writing, Printing & dispersing of this Tract, has been another cause of delay to the publication of my *Tracts against Slavery*, but, I *flatter myself, not without some good effect*; for as it has been well received by many Gentlemen of the Law; as well as others, it will certainly give more weight to my other Tracts, whenever they are published.

I have sent you 4 copies, of which I beg your acceptance, that you may give, or lend then, to such of your friends as you think proper; and more are at your service, and shall be sent, if you should have occasion for them. I think myself much obliged to you for your attention to me in writing so frequently & explicitly, on the subject of Slavery; so much obliged, indeed, that the Books, which I have sent you at different times, (and of which you desire in your last letter, to reimburse the Expence) are to be esteemed but a very small & unworthy return; especially as I have not had it in my power to *repay you in kind* by acknowledging and answering your sensible & interesting letters so duly as I could wish to have done.

A few days ago I called again at Lord Dartmouth's but was informed that his Lordship was not yet returned to Town for the Winter, and that he comes only on some particular Days of Business, or publick Levees; for which reason I went down to him this Morning at Blackheath, on purpose that I might send you some intelligence by the ship now ready to sail.

His Lordship informed me, that nothing further had yet been done relating to the *Virginia Petition*. This delay, I suppose, is occasioned by the opposition of persons interested in the African Trade, whose extraordinary influence on Administration astonishes me! I have given his Lordship a copy of the *Pennsylvania Petition*, and he promises to take particular notice of the Act of Assembly, which passed in consequence of it, for a Duty on Negroes, whenever the said Act is transmitted to His Majesty; for he don't recollect that he has yet seen it.

I mentioned also the favourable inclination of the people at *New York*, and *Boston* for the abolishing of Slavery; and, at the same time, I complained, severely of the Backwardness of the several Governors in promoting Petitions for that purpose, agreeable to the information with which you favoured me. I took the liberty also of exclaiming, *very freely*, against the iniquity of attending to mercenary or political reasons for tolerating the African Slave Trade, as being a notorious instance of *doing "evil that good may come,"* which is heinous in the sight of God, and that we have the greatest reason to expect some *dreadfull Judgment on the whole Kingdom* for such monstrous wickedness. I have reason to flatter myself that L. D. detests that traffick as much as I do, but is unwilling that *my having seen him* on this subject, *should be known*; and therefore you must not mention what I have wrote *concerning him*; except, indeed to Dr. Rush, or such other friends as you can well confide in. Petitions *to the King*, subscribed by a considerable number of respectible inhabitants of any, or each, of the Provinces, (showing their sense of the iniquity and danger of Slavery, *like that to the Assembly of Pennsilvania*) would have *considerable weight*, but this I mention as from myself. Perhaps you will say, that the indifferent reception of the Virginia Petition affords very little encouragement for you and your friends to procure more Petitions to the same effect; but we must consider, that the said Petition is *but one*, whereas the Evil to be remedied *is general*, and therefore requires a *more general* Testimony, from the persons concerned, in order to Ballance the Misrepresentations and unaccountable influence of the African Traders and West India Merchants. If the *Friends of Mankind*, on your side of the Water, can procure any such Petitions, *subscribed* (as recommended above) by a good number of the inhabitants of distinct provinces, Towns or Districts, I will again wait on L. Dartmouth to request his advice, concerning the proper manner of presenting them to his Majesty, as soon as I receive notice from you, that any such Petitions *are ready to be transmitted*; for it will, most probably, be right to inclose them, under cover, to *Lord Dartmouth himself*, for that purpose.

Be not discouraged; for even, at the worst, if the Petitions should not procure that attention, which we have a right to expect, they will, at least afford me an opportunity of making such severe remarks upon the opposition of those persons who endeavour to frustrate the Charitable purpose of them, as, I trust, will make their "Ears tingle."

I shall now hasten the publication of my Tract as much as I can; though I foresee, that I shall be yet a considerable time in accomplishing it; not only because of the bulk & number of the Tracts (which are against *oppression in general*, and contain the fundamental principles of law, both Natural & Revealed) but also because the time of my hurry in business now approaches, so that I shall have no more leisure, I fear, 'till the middle, or perhaps, the latter end of next summer, my best endeavours, however, shall not be wanting.

Sometime ago the Rev. Mr. Westley signified to me by letter, that he had a desire to write against the Slave Trade; in consequence of which, I furnished him with a large Bundle of Books and Papers on the subject; and a few days ago he sent me his Manuscript to peruse; which is *well drawn up*;

and he has reduced the substance of the Argument, respecting the gross iniquity of that Trade, into a very small compass: *his Evidence*, however, seems chiefly extracted from the Authors quoted in your several publications. As soon as this Tract is printed, I will send you some copies of it.

I must request you to give my affectionate Compliments to Mr. Emlin, when you see him: his kind assistance in endeavouring to procure Petitions, I dare say, will not be wanting.

I will write to Dr. Rush, by the same ship, if I can possibly find opportunity.

My thanks are due to you also for the several Tracts with which you have favoured me & particularly for that entitled "*the Plain Path of Christian Perfection*," because you have, thereby, given me an opportunity of communicating my sentiments on *that subject* & therefore, I propose to send you a separate letter thereupon, if I am not prevented by want of leisure.

I am, with great esteem, Dear Sir, Your Affectionate
Friend, & humble Servant

Granville Sharp

P.S. . . . My Brother has just informed me of a Message from your Friend Dr. Fothergill (whom he had acquainted that I was writing to you on this subject) signifying his opinion, that the Spanish Regulations (which I sent you before) should be strongly recommended, as a means of gradually removing Slavery *without inconvenience*; and that some regulations upon the same principles should be proposed for the gradual enfranchisement of *Slaves already in the Colonies*; and that the same should be recommended in the Petitions. This may certainly be a means of removing the obvious objection concerning the danger of allowing *a general freedom all at once*; and it may, perhaps, induce His Majesty to prevent opposition from the Colony Governors in Case the several Assemblies should be willing to set about repealing the unjust laws, which are the *principal Bars to the gradual wearing out of Slavery*; I mean those, which prohibit Masters from freeing their Slaves without a formal leave signed by the Governor, and those which render the Masters answerable for any damages that may afterwards be occasioned by the fault or imprudence of such manumitted Slaves; and also those wicked Laws or Customs whereby the Sherifs, Goalers and Parish Officers are permitted to take up such Negroes as they happen to find at *liberty*, (even tho' they have no claim to them) and either to advertise for a Claimant, that they may receive a Reward, or else to sell the poor Creatures again to the best Bidder, so that they have no Chance for Freedom in this World!, which practices are espressly contrary to the Laws of God!—"*Thou shalt not deliver unto his Master* the Servant *which is escaped* from his Master unto thee." "He shall dwell with thee, even among you, in that place *which he shall choose*" (that is, manifestly as a *Free Man*) "in one of thy Gates where it *liketh him best*: thou *shalt not oppress him*." Deut. 22, 16. This is certainly a Moral Law, founded in *reason, Justice & Mercy*, and which, therefore, must be *ever binding*: whereas the Colony Laws which I have just now mentioned, can never be made *binding* or obligatory, even tho' enacted by all the Kings & Assemblies in the World, because they are diametrically opposite in every point to the indispensable moral Law abovementioned; and ought therefore, to be held in abhorrence by all Men who sincerely believe in God! I have an Argument (founded on the abovementioned Text) which I drew up sometime ago, in defence of those persons who think it their Duty to *protect Slaves* that have escaped from their Masters.

I must request you to forward Petitions (*not* to the *King & Parliament* for the reasons mentioned in a former letter) but to the *King, only* as much as you can without in convenience to yourself, for I have reasons for desiring this, which I am not at Liberty to mention. There will not be time, I find, for me to write the promised letter (with my sentiments concerning the "plain Path of Christian perfection") by the present Ship, so that I must defer it 'till the next opportunity, which I am told will be in about a fortnight, as more Ships are preparing to Sail. . . .

I am your affectionate friend & servant

Granville Sharp

Mr. Anthony Benezet, Philadelphia

Phillis Wheatley to the Rev. Samson Occom, February 11, 1774

The Connecticut Journal, and the New-Haven Post-Boy, 1 April 1774.

". . . For in every Breast God has implanted a Principle, which we call Love of Freedom, it is impatient of oppression and pants for Deliverance. . . ." These are the words of Phillis Wheatley, the first Black poet to attract the attention of the American public, extracted from a letter written to the Reverend Samson Occom on February 11, 1774, and published in the April 1, 1774, issue of the Connecticut Journal and the New-Haven Post-Boy.

Benjamin Rush, one of a number of writers of this period who made statements concerning Phillis Wheatley, said in 1773 that her "singular genius and accomplishments are such as not only do honor to her sex but to human nature" and "that several of her poems had been printed and read with pleasure by the public." That same year her volume, Poems on Various Subjects, Religious and Moral, *was published in London. Many of the supporters of the abolitionist movement later cited her achievements at home and her international recognition as proof that people of color were capable of mental development. Historians and writers, however, have indicated that there was a lack of concern about the freedom of the slaves in her work. Despite her favored situation in the Wheatley family, Phillis Wheatley could not help be conscious of the dehumanizing institution of slavery. In July 1778 in an elegiac poem on the death of General David Wooster she again spoke on the issue of slavery. After praising the General and praying for victory for "Columbia" and an end to the war she said:*

But how presumptuous shall we hope to find
Divine acceptance with the Almighty mind
While yet o deed ungenerous they disgrace
And hold in bondage Afric: blameless race
Let virtue reign and then accord our prayers
Be victory ours and generous freedom theirs

Wheatley by 1773 had reached a degree of intellectual eminence known to few females of her day. As a former slave, she forcefully spoke out against the oppression of her people.

Rev'd and honor'd Sir, I have this Day received your obliging kind Epistle, and am greatly satisfied with your Reasons respecting the Negroes, and think highly reasonable what you offer in Vindication of their natural Rights: Those that invade them cannot be insensible that the divine Light is chasing away the thick Darkness which broods over the Land of Africa; and the Chaos which has reign'd so long, is converting into beautiful Order, and reveals more and more clearly, the glorious Dispensation of civil and

Phillis Wheatley, celebrated American black poetess. Frontispiece of her collection, Poems on Various Subjects, Religious and Moral, *published in London, 1773.*

religious Liberty, which are so inseparably united, that there is little or no Enjoyment of one without the other: Otherwise, perhaps, the Israelites had been less solicitous for their Freedom from Egyptian Slavery; I don't say they would have been contented without it, by no Means, for in every human Breast, God has implanted a Principle, which we call Love of Freedom; it is impatient of Oppression, and pants for Deliverence; and by the Leave of our modern Egyptians I will assert that the same Principle lives in us. God grant Deliverance in his own Way and Time, and get him honor upon all those whose Avarice impels them to countenance and help forward the Calamities of their fellow Creatures. This I desire not for their Hurt, but to convince them of the strange Absurdity of their Conduct whose Words and Actions are so diametrically opposite. How well the cry for Liberty, and the reverse Disposition for the exercise of oppressive Power over others agree,—I humbly think it does not require the Penetration of a Philosopher to determine.

Anthony Benezet to Moses Brown, May 9, 1774

Charles Roberts Autograph Letter Collection, Haverford College Library, Haverford, Pa.

In Moses Brown's earlier years he owned at least ten slaves and with his brothers acquired a small fortune in Rhode Island from the West Indian trade. In 1773, just before joining the Society of Friends, Brown freed the slaves and began to campaign actively against the slave trade, corresponding with many of the leading antislavery activists, especially Anthony Benezet. Because Newport was the great slave market of southern New England, prominent Rhode Island merchants such as Geoffrey Mallorne, William Ellery, Abraham Redwood, and James and Obadiah Brown made lucrative profits from the African slave trade. Moses Brown became a robust voice of opposition to slave interests in Rhode Island. On May 5, 1774, Anthony Benezet wrote to Brown about the progress of antislavery reform in the colonies. One week later a town meeting in Providence, stirred by Brown, adopted a resolution instructing Providence's deputies to attempt to force through the General Assembly an act to prohibit slave importation and to free all blacks born in the colony after a certain age. Although the resolution later proved too radical to be considered by the Assembly, Moses Brown had become a strident antislavery advocate to be feared by Newport's slave dealers.

Philadelphia y 9th 5th May 1774

Respected Friend Moses Brown Thine of the 8th last month afforded one much Satisfaction, as I was indeed, very desirous to hear of thy welfare. I acknowledge thy kind notice of my request in procuring the publication of the piece I sent therin my first letter as I have not the copy of what I wrote thee last I'm scarce capable of judging of the expediency of publishing, what I sent thee relating to the concerns growing in Europe and the Southern colonies, I rather think it would be better to delay such a publication as the concern has not yet effectually spread but with considerate friends & some thoughtful friends of other societies: a publication of that kind might occasion a reply of a contrary nature,

Moses Brown, Quaker merchant and slave trader during the mid-1700's, turned abolitionist during the Revolution.

founded upon truth from the vast number who still vindicate for one reason or other, vindicate the practice of Slavery tho' few will appear in defence of Slave Trade nevertheless I think it may with truth be said that the concern is still growing. Thomas Nichols (one if not the most considerable friend belonging to the yearly meeting of North Carolina) writes me that the meeting has appointed a standing committe to treat with the members of the Assembly in order to prevail upon them to petition the King against the continuation of the Slave Trade. Friends of Maryland are also Solicitous that their Assembly might consider what may be done in the case & hope to gain the attention of its members. And Edward Stabler clerk to the yearly meeting of Virginia writes as follows "Petersburg 24th 11ano 1773 I am informed that the petition from our house of Burgesses to the King has not met with the desired effect but that he has refused his assent to the act they they passed laying an additional duty upon all slaves brought into this country but I find it does not abate the zeal of some of our leading men against the traffic but I hope makes them consider it more deeply. I have been much in observing that the inhumanity of the trade & the pernicious tendency of it becomes more & more the subject of conversation amongst all ranks of people here." Robt. Pleasants a a friend of same province sends me the copy of a letter wrote to him by Patrick Henry one of the most active members of their Assembly of which I send thee a copy as also copies of letters I received from the chief justices, both of South & North Carolina the last I suppose thou art acquainted with as he came from Paris I judged that copies of these three letters would afford thee satisfaction to see and communicate to thy friends, but not to be published. I am told the Assembly of New York did pass a bill at their last session laying a considerable duty on any further importation of Negroes & other slaves, but it was refused by the Governor & Council. The Assembly of New Jersey have had several petitions presented to them to y purpose of obtaining a law to prevent any farther import & also to make the emancipation of slaves more easy. My friend Granville Sharp of London desires we may not be discouraged at the disappointment the Virginians have met with, with respect to their petition but repeatedly us to renew, (by petitions from every part where they may be obtained) to the King Council not the King and Parliament—our application requesting that an end may be put to any farther import of slaves as will on account of the iniquity of the practice as because of the corrupt—as well as dangerous tendency. I hope that if such an application is presented in it may in the end be attended with success notwithstanding the opposition we shalt meet with from the African Company & West India Merchants' interest. Indeed I am not discouraged having to hope & believe that which is as y little stone cut out of y mountain wilt strike at y feet of this great image & bring it down in God's name.

Thy intention of making short extracts from authors of various denominations who have written on this subject will I think be productive of good for the reasons thou mention; pray delay it as little as possible & please to send me a number & the price

My friend Granville Sharp writes me that he is compiling a treatise on the subject of Slavery &c. which as he has made this matter his particular study, & he has been sometime about it will be more considerable than any yet published more especially as he will enter more deeply on its inconsistency with y British Laws; he also writes me that the celebrated methodist preacher John Wesley had sent him a y manuscript of a piece he was on the point of publishing on the same subject for his When either of these come to my hand I purpose to communicate them to thee.

I am persuaded thy compliance with what thou apprehended truth required of thee will be a matter of comfort to thyself & be a considerable strength to the testimony against Slavery in your parts & I have little doubt but that thou wilt be comfortably supported & have rather to rejoice in the difficulties which will still thro' the concern that will necessarily devolve upon thee in a proper care over the poor Negroes who we have as well as with you are when left to themselves not only as children but as children set free in an . . . country. As to our friend Samuel Nottingham indeed he is rather to be pitied than blamed I have often confered with him on the subject of his or rather his wife's Negroes; the many rubs he has received on that account in these parts, even in public meetings I apprehend makes him more shy of spending as much time amongst us as he otherwise would. Samuel's great mistake was in his first setting out in his marriage, this first mistep has been a source of many difficulties & much sorrow to him, his wife is I am persuaded a well-minded woman She suffered much in her first husband's time which united her to friends & to Samuel; nevertheless I can't think if she had not been possessed of considerable wealth that he would have thought of her for a wife. She having possession of Estates in the Islands & of a number of Negroes has brought on all his difficulties & pierces him thro' with many very many sorrows. It is indeed a sorrowful but too common a case to see religious people, even such as are favoured with spiritual gifts, to take such inconsistent steps in marrying rich wives to whom they would show little regard if poor or for y sake of gain involving themselves in perplexing concerns So repugnant to that meek, suffering, & dependant state so strongly inculcated by our Blessed Saviour, to those who desired to be his immediate followers, in his sermon on the mount. Thence either a wrong prejudice take place by such an example or an offence is rather by the discerning youth already too much disposed to elude the cross & sell their birthright as for a mess of pottage. If indeed as the prophet expresses it "They who call many to righteousness shall shine as the stars" what an inexpressible damage is it to such who are called to preach the Gospel that they should by any mistaken steps they have taken in the spirit of y world to gain its honour its riches or friendship should present the extention of that good which God intended they should otherwise have been instrumental to bring about.

However poor Samuel is certainly still owned & favoured as a minister of the Gospel and desirous to do the best he can in his present situation his wife is much attached to the Negroes whom I am persuaded are well used she will scarce consent they should go free in her time; but I understand Saml. has by his will declared them not only free at his death & probably sooner if he should survive his wife, but also provided some of y best part of the estate he holds in Santa Crux for their residence & maintainance; a young Negro man who he has with he let go to work for himself intending to free him but y poor fellow was so incapable of making proper uses of his freedom that I understand Samuel was obliged to take him again under his own management.

I have frequently treated with Samuel on this interesting subject, indeed not without some degree of pain as well to myself as to him on account of the difficulty I was sensible he was under. Indeed, the few well minded people in the West Indies & Southern provinces who see the necessity & desire to do their poor Slaves that justice which reason, nature, & more especially Christianity requires of them, are brought under great difficulties, an instance of this kind I have had a particular opportunity of being well acquainted with in the case of Nathaniel Gilbert of Antiqua, his father was as I understand a Lawyer he left this son a considerable Estate with as I have heard about Three hundred Negroes, The son also followed the Law & was well esteemed in that capacity & also in so much repute in other men's respects as to be chosen speaker of the Assembly of that island. Through good Providence he has, by truth, became religious, & has since given up the practice of the Law & also resigned his seat in the Assembly finding as he writes me "that it led him into company which was hurtful to his soul. I will here give thee an account of some of his letters, as I am persuaded they will be matter of satisfaction to thee to see how Grace works & will doubtless still work even in such places where we would naturally have the less expectation on acct. of vice & iniquity ruling there with so high a hand. "Antiqua 29th Oct. 1768 I desire to embrace as any brethren all who love the Lord Jesus in sincerity or who are earnest in seeking an interest in his love of whatsoever denomination they may be—though all Christians cannot write in opinion yet surely they may write in loving one another—I can give you but a very bad account of the state of religion in this Island we have a small society whom I meet & sometimes speak to as the Lord enables me but there is for the most-part very little life amongst most of my few constant hearers the word seems to make a deeper impression on some Mulatoes & Negroes that it does upon the white people there is particularly a mulato woman whom I look upon to be a person endued with great grace. Your tract concerning slavery is very just & tis a matter which I have often thought even before I became acquainted with the truth, your arguments are forcible against purchasing slaves or being any way concerned in that trade, but how is a man to act who comes to the possession of them by inheritance? If a man should attempt to free a large number of Slaves the legislature (unless restrained by the . . . Almighty) would certainly interpose to hinder him; but if it was otherwise how are the poor creatures to subsist? How are they to maintain themselves?

Whilst I was member of the Assembly I have several times expressed my disapprobation of that act of our islands (which subjects y Negroes to death for running away from their masters) but without success & very little is I conceive to be expected in favour of Negroes from a legislature who will not repeal so wicked a law, as to the punishment of those who murder Negroes which is only a fine & imprisonment till the fine is paid though every General who comes to this Government has a particular instruction from the King, to use his utmost endeavours to get that act repealed so that the crime might remain as it is at common law by which every murderer is liable to loss of life & yet I never heard of a general that paid the least regard to that instruction.

February 1774 The Lord has long visited me with sore affliction in regard both of spiritual & temporal, but I hope deliverance from both is not far off. I have preached publicly for 15 months past—I have sometimes on Sundays I believe no less than eight hundred negroes who come to hear the word tho' it's the only day in the week allowed them for themselves they choose to bring their victuals with them & spend the whole day here some persons encourage their slaves to attend our meetings & others will not suffer them to come—I have several years past thought that the Lord had a controversy with with the west-Indies on account of their treatment of their Slaves. From the above extract thou mayest see the difficulties that well minded people who have a number of slaves in the Southern parts are reduced to, they may truly be said as was of y remnant of y Canaanites to the children of Israel as thorns in their sides. Indeed it may be also said to be much the case of those amongst us to the children of friends the proverb which was no more to be mentioned in Israel is truly renewed & verified in the care of these poor Africans.

The fathers have eaten sour grapes & have set their children's teeth on edge as I have heard two different worthy friends express it that those who had a number of Negroes & were desirous to do truly their duty by them. Were Slaves of Slaves.

I am very willing Doctor Everard's works should be deposited in the library thou mention, & I herewith send some other collections of religious tracts for the same service. Thou wilt find in the beginning of one of the smallest collections the Journal of Mary Gilbert She was daughter of the good man before mentioned thou wilt in the preface find some acct. of her father; Himself sent me the copy which I judging might be of service caused to be printed. Excuse the freedom & negligence with which I write, I have quite shook hands with formality & ceremony. I have no idea of true friendship but what is accompanied with freedom. Please to remember me kindly to Mary Olncy I would gladly write to her wishing that I could be instrumental to add the least degree of strength to her in the spiritual warfare I am poor, very poor, I wish earnestly for her & thee my dear friend that we may grow in true self denial and mortification to self and every thing, if there is any thing else that would exalt the creature. In the best love I am capable of I salute thee & her & indeed all (let their name & profession to religion be what it may) who as my friend Nathaniel Gilbert says tho' they may not have attained love the Lord Jesus in Sincerity or who are earnest in seeking an interest in his love.

I remain they affectionate

Anthony Benezet

Anthony Benezet to John Wesley, May 23, 1774

Georges Brookes, ed., *Friend Anthony Benezet* (Philadelphia, 1937), pp. 318-21.

After reading one of Anthony Benezet's pamphlets on slavery, the Reverend John Wesley was moved to write in his diary, "I read of nothing like it in the heathen world, whether ancient or modern." In 1774 the English founder of Methodism composed his own Thoughts upon Slavery, *a rambling disquisition which, borrowing freely from Benezet's own works, romantically described an idealized, virgin Africa being despoiled by the sinful rapine and violence of the slave trade. On May 23, 1774, Benezet informed Wesley that he had republished the pamphlet in Philadelphia. Wesley responded, "It is certainly our duty to do all in our power to check this growing evil and something may be done in spreading those tracts which place it in a true light. But I fear it will not be stopped till all the kingdoms of this earth become the Kingdoms of God."*

Wesley, until his death at age 80, remained a powerful English ally of abolitionists such as Thomas Clarkson and Granville Sharp. In one of his last letters he charged William Wiberforce to "Go, in the name of God and in the power of His might, till even American Slavery, the vilest that ever saw the sun, shall vanish away before it."

Philadelphia, the 23d, fifth month, (May) 1774.

Respected Friend, Having a good opportunity, by means of the bearer, my friend and old pupil, William Dilwyn, a valuable, religiously minded person, who is going on a voyage to your country; I make use of it, affectionately to salute thee. The Tract thou has lately published entitled, Thoughts on Slavery, afforded me much satisfaction. I was the more especially glad to see it, as the circumstances of the times made it necessary that something on that most weighty subject, not large, but striking and pathetic, should now be published. Wherefore I immediately agreed with the Printer to have it republished here.

The several settlements which are now begun, doubtless, will vastly increase shortly on that tract of land which extends some thousands of miles from the mouth of the river Mississippi, to the Northward of the Lake of Canada, instead of being, as I trust the Almighty may intend, a refuge, and affording a comfortable subsistence to thousands, and hundreds of thousands of distressed people, will be occupied, as is much the case of our Southern Provinces, by tyrants and slaves. For in all those places where slavery prevails, a poor industrious white man, cannot procure to himself and family a living, as his labour is rated (except he be some extraordinary workman) no higher than that of a Slave—so that he must, by credit or otherwise, become a Slave-keeper, with all its corrupt effects to himself and family, or lead a poor miserable life, or abandon the country.

I observe that in thy late publication on Slavery, in thy mention of the several Negro-Nations who occupy that part of Guinea, situated on, and between the two great rivers of Senegal and Gambia, thou givest a character of the whole nation of Fulys, who are numerous, which from the account given by Moor, &c. is only applicable to a part of that nation, who then resided amongst the Mandigos; having been driven out of their own country. This may be amended in case of a further publication; as it might give an advantage, to the advocate for the trade, to lessen the strength of what is strictly true.

A certain author, who calls himself an African-Merchant, in a Treatise upon the Trade from Great Britain to Africa, has endeavoured, though without real ground, to make me appear inconsistent in the account I give of those and other Negro-nations, in my Historical Account of Guinea. Indeed the whole of that Author's work is more calculated to show the iniquity, and dishonesty of the African Traders, even to one another, than to give any grounded answer to what has been written against the Slave-Trade.

Thou wilt probably have heard of the death of my dear friend, Nathaniel Gilbert, of Antigua. The account he gave me in his last letter, wrote two or three months past, was such as afforded me comfort, for the sake of poor Negroes on that Island. I rejoiced that Providence had raised them such a friend, and by his means such an opportunity of comfort in their affliction. But he is gone! It is the Lord, let him do what seemeth Him good. The same hand who raised and removed him, can, and in proper time, will raise more.

What he wrote at different times was as follows:

> I can give you but poor account of the progress of religion amongst us. We have a small religious Society here, consisting of about twenty whites, exclusive of my family, and of sixty-four Negroes and Mulatoes. (The word seems to make more impression on some Mulattoes and Negroes, than it does on the white people. There is particularly a Mulattoe woman whom I look upon to be a person endowed with great grace.) I have sometimes on Sundays, I believe, no less than eight hundred Negroes, who come to hear the word. They choose to bring their victuals with them, and spend the whole day here.
>
> I have for several years thought that the Lord had a controversy with the West-Indies, on account of the treatment of our Slaves. Whilst I was a member of the Assembly, I have several times expressed my disapprobation of that act of our Island, which subjects the Negroes to death, for running away from their Masters; but without success. And very little, I conceive, is to be expected in favour of Negroes from a legislature who will not repeal so wicked a law as to the punishment of those who murder Negroes; which is only a fine, and imprisonment till the fine is paid; though every General, who comes to this government has a particular instruction from the King to use his utmost endeavours to get that Act repealed: so that the crime might remain as it is at common law, by which every murderer is liable to loss of life.

I understand the Laws of Virginia, and North and South-Carolina are much to the same purpose as those in the Island; tending rather to promote a murderous disposition in the Master towards their poor Slaves; quite abhorrent of that universal brotherhood so strongly enjoined by the Gospel. These worse than Savage-laws, the Slave-holders apprehend necessary for their safety, and to keep their Slaves in awe. Now can anything more plainly shew the abhorance of the practice of Slave-Keeping, with everything that is good and sacred, than the pretended necessity of such detestable Laws? Laws, at which the darkest age would have repunged!

As a farther instance of the inhumanity with which the poor Negroes are treated, even in those Provinces, where they have a less proportion of Slaves, and have not the same plea for keeping them in awe; I will here add the substance of two advertisements, published in the public Prints of the province of Virginia and North-Carolina, viz. From the Williamsburg Gazette: "Run away Prince George, on the 10th instant, a lusty Negro, named Bob, &c. &c. (describing him) The said fellow is outlawed, and I will give ten pounds reward for his head severed from his body, and forty shillings if brought home alive." The other advertisement from one of the North Carolina News Papers is to the following effect. "Run away last November from the subscriber, Kent River, a Negro-fellow, named Zeb, aged 36 years. As he is outlawed; I will pay twenty pounds out of what the Act of Assembly allows in such cases, to any person who shall produce his head severed from his body, and five pounds, if brought home alive." John Mosely.

I would now leave off writing, particularly in so irregular a manner, and indeed time calls for it, the bearer being upon his departure; but I cannot be easy to do it, without here transcribing a paragraph of a letter I have just written to your country, viz.

That as dreadful as the slavery now carried on in our Colonies, is to the miserable subject thereof, yet greater, far greater, is its baneful influence on their possessors and their unhappy offspring; these being, thereby, from their childhood nurtured in such scenes and practice, as naturally beget in them habits of idleness, pride; cruelty, lasciviousness; with a train of other evils, which bear sway; and as age comes on, predominate to the introduction of a much worse kind of barbarism, than that which our Northern Ancestors were under, before they became acquainted with Christianity. With the poor Negroes the evil of their sufferings will end with this life, and the merciful Father of the family of mankind, will look on their deep affliction, and in his boundless mercy, requite them good for their sufferings; and may favour them with that greatest of blessings, humble and contrite hearts. But with respect to their lordly oppressor, the horrible abuse of their fellow-creatures, will extend its baneful influence even in the regions of eternity. For such is the depravity and hardness of heart and mind produced by it, that for many, very many of the subjects of it, it may be feared, Christ will have died in vain.

In the best love I am capable of, and with sincere wishes for thy welfare and prosperity in every thing that is truly good,

I remain thy affectionate Friend,

Anthony Benezet

Nathaniel Niles, *Two Discourses*, 1774

Nathaniel Niles, *Two Discourses on Liberty; Delivered at the North Church, in Newbury-Port, on Lord's-Day, June 5, 1774, and Published at the general Desire of the Hearers* (Newbury-Port, 1774), pp. 5-9; 18-20; 26-28; 36-39; 41-43; 54-60.

"Let us either wash our hands from blood," Nathaniel Niles exclaimed, "or never hope to escape the avenger." On June 5, 1774, Reverend Niles delivered two sermons at the North Church in Newburyport that reflected the intellectual struggle in the minds of many New England Calvinist ministers over such issues as the colonial disputes with Britain, their own religious tenets, and the existence of

African slavery in America. Niles was a student of Joseph Bellamy, the prominent Connecticut theologian and disciple of Jonathan Edwards. A man who in his lifetime was an inventor, a student of medicine and law, and a politician, Niles in 1774 was echoing from his own pulpit much of Bellamy's evangelistic, Great Awakening revivalism. He saw liberty as divine reward; oppression as divine punishment. "It is high time for us to reform," Niles declared. "We have had a rich inheritance and wasted it in riotous living . . . if we will risque our country for the sake of a few superfluities, posterity may curse our pride and luxury, and the present generation may find that death and carnage will terminate their folly." He encouraged the colonists to move toward a state of grace by throwing off impediments to human freedom such as African slavery, the antithesis of liberty. If such an institution remained unchecked, the colonists could expect "some unparalleled calamity." Linking the concepts of civil and spiritual liberty, Niles asserted that reform of social evils such as slavery would be a manifestation of the colonists' acceptance of spiritual liberty. As the Connecticut preacher later remarked, "The author's general design is to awaken in his countrymen, proper sentiments and emotions, respecting both civil and spiritual liberty. The former, without the latter is but a body without a soul."

Sermon I

I. Corrinth. Chap. VII. ver. 21. *Art thou called* being *a servant? Care not for it; but if thou mayest be made free, use it rather.*

At first glance, it is certain, this text refers to a state of *personal* servitude, and extends to every instance of the same kind. It is also as clear that the Apostle exhorts the servant to prefer liberty. This proves that the inspired writer himself, preferred liberty to a state of servitude; for he would not exhort another to prefer what was not preferable in his own esteem. Now, if Paul esteemed personal liberty a valuable inheritance, he certainly esteemed the liberty of a community a far richer inheritance; for if one man's enjoyment of it was a good, the enjoyment of two must be a greater good, and so on through the whole community. From the same manner of reasoning, the slavery of a community appears to be a proportionably greater evil, than the slavery of an individual. Hence, we may observe from the text, that *civil Liberty is a great good.*

This is the proposition to which I ask your . . . attention, and if it should appear in the sequel to contain an important truth, you will not esteem it below the gospel preacher's duty to explain and support it in public, especially at such a time as this, a time, at the very prospect of which, our generous fore-fathers would have wept in bitterness of soul. If civil liberty is a great good, it ought to be deemed one of the blessings of Heaven; these it is the preacher's duty to illustrate, that we may feel the obligations they bring us under—that we may enquire whether we have improved them for the glory of the giver, and that we may know how to conduct toward them for the future. Be pleased then to give your candid, close, and serious attention, while I endeavour to explain the nature of civil liberty, and prove that it is a great good.

As it is much less difficult to point out the nature of true coin in general, than to determine whether any particular piece is genuine, or how far it differs from the perfect standard: So it is much easier to point out the general nature of civil liberty, than to say what degree of it enters into any particular civil constitution. It is therefore most natural to enquire, in the first place, concerning the general nature of liberty; and indeed it is as necessary as natural. For until we determine this question we have no rule by which we may estimate the quantity of liberty in any particular constitution: But when once we have found the standard, we shall be prepared to examine our own constitution, or any other, at pleasure, and to determine what part of the constitution should be supported, and what may be given up with safety. An enquiry into the nature of liberty in general, is also needful on another account. Without it we cannot see the force of any evidence that may be brought to evince the value of liberty itself.

That the subject may be fairly elucidated, I will endeavour to remove some mistakes by which it has been obscured. In doing this, I observe, that liberty does not consist in persons thinking themselves free. The Jews could say we were never in bondage to any man though they wore the Roman yoke at the very same time. Again, though a certain constitution should be contended for and supported by a majority of voices; yet this would be no sure evidence that it is free: Because an hundred may as truly tyrannize over one, as one over an hundred; or otherwise, the majority may be in favour of licentiousness. What but a love of licentiousness or tyranny, or both, can induce the heathen nations to approve of their several systems of government? What but these, could induce Saul and the men of Israel to persecute David and his handful? What but one or both of these drew down the fury of Sodom on Lot—of the Jews on the prophets—on Jesus Christ—on his Apostles and their followers. What but these ever raised any one of the many terrible persecutions under which the peaceable disciples of Jesus Christ have fallen from time to time? In all these instances the majority have been unfriendly to liberty.

Civil liberty consists, not in any inclinations of the members of a community; but in the being and due administration of such a system of laws, as effectually tends to the greatest felicity of a state. Herein consists civil liberty, and to live under such a constitution, so administered, is to be the member of a free state; and he who is free from the censure of those laws, may fully enjoy all the pleasures of civil liberty, unless he is prevented by some defect, not in the constitution, but in himself.

If liberty consists in the being and administration of a civil constitution, different from such an one as has been mentioned, I must confess, my inference from the Apostle's exhortation is not just. For certain it is, that so far as a constitution doth not tend, in the highest degree, to the greatest felicity of the state, collectively considered; it is a comparitive evil and not a good.

Where there is no system of laws, not liberty, but anarchy, takes place. Some degree of liberty may, indeed, exist where neither the constitution nor the administration of it is perfect. But in order to perfect freedom, the law must extend to every member of the community alike, both in its requisitions and prohibitions. Every one must be required to do all he can that tends to the highest good of the state: For the whole of this is due to the state, from the individuals of which it is composed. Every thing, however trifling, that tends, even in the lowest degree, to disserve the interest of the state must also be forbidden. . . .

A good foundation for liberty is laid in such a constitution, but its whole worth lies in due administration. Perfect liberty takes place where such a constitution is fully administred: But where the administration is imperfect, liberty is likewise imperfect. In a perfectly free state, both the constitution, and the administration of it, are full of propriety, equality, and equilibrium.

These I take to be the out lines of genuine liberty, which, by a proper application, may assist us in our enquiries after the degree of liberty enjoyed by any particular state.

Indeed, the circumstances and occurrences, that attend human states are so numerous, extensive, and uncertain, that no one man, or body of men, can foresee and improve them all to the greatest advantage. Hence, it frequently happens, that we cannot ascertain the degree of liberty enjoyed by a community, by comparing the particular parts of a constitution, or the administration of it, with the abstract notion of liberty; for we see but a small part of the whole system. Our views are very partial. This is the case not only of individual subjects, but the body of government, itself, cannot, compleatly, comprehend the whole. Some degree of partial oppression is, therefore, to be expected in every human state, even, under the wisest administration. We may, however, determine, in some instances, whether liberty is unnecessarily infringed or not. When we see the body of a community plundered for the sake of indulging individuals in pride, luxury, idleness and debauchery,—when we see thousands rewarded with pensions, for having either devised, or attempted to execute some scheme for plundering a nation, and establishing despotism, we cannot be in doubt whether some horrid attack is not made on liberty.

We may reason thus in a few particular instances; but, in general, we must form our judgments by considering the various dispositions of mankind, and by noticing their various operations and effects, in various circumstances. We must turn our attention to the facts that have already taken place; and may reasonably conclude, that the same causes will always produce the same effects, unless something special prevents. One general inference from the whole will be, that liberty is much rather to be expected in a state where a majority, first, institutes, and then varies the constitution according as they apprehend circumstances require, than in any other.

Other things being equal, a majority has a more general and distinct knowledge of the circumstances, and exigencies of a state than a minority; and, of consequence, is more able to judge of what is best to be done. Add to this, that private interest is the great idol of the human mind; and, therefore, when a majority unite in any measures, it is to be supposed, they are such measures as are best calculated to secure the particular interests of the members of that majority; and, consequently, the general interests of the body are more effectually provided for, in this way, than by the security of the private interests of any minority whatever. And if the maxims adopted by the majority are general, both in their nature and extent, it is to be supposed, they will prove as salutary to the members of the minority as to those of the majority, and, consequently, to the whole body. Hence, though liberty is not necessarily, nor invariably connected with the voice of a majority; yet, it is much more likely to be found in connection with such a voice, than with that of a minority. Indeed, there is in general, no reason to expect liberty where a majority is counteracted, and, on the contrary, we may hope for some good degree of it, where a majority governs. . . .

Let us then, for once, imagine a state whose members are all of a free spirit; and then attend to the glory and pleasures of liberty. The individuals are all of one mind. They unite in the same grand pursuit, the highest good of the whole. Only suppose all the members of such a state to be acquainted with the best means of promoting their general end; and we shall see them all moving in perfect concert. The good of the body will be their first aim. And in subserviency to this, they will impartially regard the particular interests of individuals. You and I shall perfectly unite in our regard for your interest and for mine. Your interest will not be the more dear to you, nor the less so to me, because it is yours. In these circumstances, there would be no room for the emotions of any of the angry painful passions; but, on the contrary, every soft and pleasing affection of every soul, would be called forth into vigorous and harmonious exercise. Every individual would choose to move in his proper sphere, and that all others should move in theirs. This would at once constitute pure felicity, and exalted beauty. How *good* and how *pleasant* it is for brethren to dwell together in unity: Such a state of things, in the little community of a single family, must be productive of great good. But should it take place throughout a nation, each family would enjoy the same good from its own domestic circumstances, beside the far greater pleasure which would accrue to each individual from a consideration of the same happy condition of the whole.

Should it be said, that such a scheme as has been mentioned is merely chimerical and romantic; because there never has been, nor ever will be such a general state of mind on earth; I would say, the same objection is equally strong against the worth of a state of perfect holiness. Such a state has never taken place, in perfection, in this world, nor will it hereafter; but must we therefore suppose that holiness is of no worth? The reason why we do not experience all the pleasures of liberty, that have been mentioned, is, not any defect in liberty, but the perverseness of our selfish hearts, which prevents our pursuit and enjoyments of the delights of perfect liberty. Liberty still remains a blessing too great to be compared with any other earthly good. . . .

Let us therefore, vigorously pursue prudent measures in the present alarming state of things. Then, should it please the righteous disposer of all, to reduce us to the most abject slavery, we shall at least, have the consolation to think, that we are in no part chargeable with having riveted chains on our country, and the blessing of a clear conscience is incomparably better than the greatest temporal interest and worldly applause.

This has been a land of liberty. We have enjoyed that blessing in a great degree for a long time, It becomes us now to reflect on our ingratitude to the giver. When he has wrought salvation for us, on one occasion and another, how have we expressed our thankfulness? By bonfires, illuminations, revellings, gluttony and drunkenness. Would not a stranger have thought us worshipers of the whole race of the heathen deities, rather than of that God, who is a spirit, and who seeketh such to worship him, as do it in spirit and in truth?

We have boasted of our liberty, and free spirit. A free spirit is no more inclined to enslave others than ourselves. If then it should be found upon examination that we have been of a tyrannical spirit in a free country, how base must our character appear! And how many thousands of thousands have been plunged into death and slavery by our means?

When the servant had nothing to pay, and his master had frankly forgiven him all, and he had gone and cast his fellow servant into prison, there to remain till he should pay the last farthing; the master justly punished his ingratitude and severity with the like imprisonment. Hath not our conduct very nearly resembled the conduct of that servant? God gave us liberty, and we have enslaved our fellow-men. May we not fear that the law of retaliation is about to be executed on us? What can we object against it? What excuse can we make for our conduct? What reason can we urge why our oppression shall not be repaid in kind? Should the Africans see God Almighty subjecting us to all the evils we have brought on them, and should they cry to us, O daughter of America who art to be destroyed, happy shall he be that rewardeth thee as thou hast served us; happy shall he be that taketh and dasheth thy little ones against the stones; how could we object? How could we resent it? Would we enjoy liberty? Then we must grant it to others. For shame, let us either cease to enslave our fellow-men, or else let us cease to complain of those that would enslave us. Let us either wash our hands from blood, or never hope to escape the avenger.

To conclude, unless we adopt some prudent decisive measures in humble dependance on God; we have reason to fear some almost unparallelled calamity. If we do not exert ourselves: It would not be strange, should a military government be established, and popery triumph in our land. Then, perhaps those, who now want fortitude to deny themselves some of the superfluities of life, may see their husbands, and sons slain in battle, their daughters ravished, their wives ript up, their children dashed against the wall, and their pious parents put to the rack for the religion of Jesus. Now is the decisive moment. God sets before us life and death, good and evil, blessing and cursing, and bids us choose. Let us therefore choose the good and refuse the evil, that we may live and not die.

Sermon II

John Chapter VIII. Verse 36. *If therefore the son shall make you free ye shall be free indeed.*

The general nature of liberty is the same in all societies, though different circumstances give it different appearance. The same general principles that are the foundation of good government in a family are as truly so in the government of a nation. These maxims are applicable not only to earthly societies, but are equally so to the eternal kingdom of the great God. That government and that liberty which takes place in earthly communities is called domestic or civil, according to their extent. When these are spoken of as belonging to the kingdom of God, they are termed divine or spiritual. . . .

It was said in the former discourse that liberty consists in the being and due administration of such a set of laws, as tend to the highest good of the society. If this be so, it follows that liberty in a state is greater or less in exact proportion to the greater or less tendency of the constitution and its administration to the highest good of the community collectively considered. If therefore it appears, on examination, that the constitution of Christ's kingdom and the administration of that constitution have a stronger tendency to the good of that kingdom, than the constitution of any earthly kingdom, and the administration of that constitution, have to the highest good of that earthly kingdom; the proposition is illustrated and proved.

In a perfectly free state the laws forbid every crime against the community. Every action that would be in the least degree injurious to the state is forbidden. In order to this, the legislature must have a perfect view of all the various circumstances and occurrences that may take place with respect to each individual of which the state is composed, at all the various periods of its existence. Actions that seem to us too minute to be regarded, have their consequences, which are oftentimes vastly important and interesting to the state. How often has a single word spoken in anger by some great personage, lain at the bottom of a nation's overthrow? The tongue is a little member, but small as it is, it seteth the course of nature on fire. Well might the Apostle say, How great a matter a little fire kindleth! But,

It is impossible for any finite mind or number of minds, to ascertain every particular word and gesture that may be detrimental in its tendency to the state, and therefore, there cannot possibly be a system of human laws in which every political evil shall be forbidden. . . .

How strangly inconsistent are we in treating that liberty, which is of infinite worth, with neglect and contempt, when it is most freely offered us, while, at the same time we are ready to sacrifice, not only our fortunes, but our very lives and friends to purchase and defend that which at best is but imperfect, uncertain and temporal? To struggle for the latter is laudable, but to neglect the former, is infinitely criminal. Surely none but a madman would neglect millions which he might have at pleasure, and yet barter his life for an uncertain penny. In the affair of civil liberty, the most spirited efforts may prove ineffectual; but that which is spiritual will certainly be the consequence of a single genuine desire to enjoy it. What makes the inconsistency still the more glaring is, that while human nature shrinks at the thought of the partial oppression of an earthly tyrant, we quietly remain in a state of the most abject slavery to the worst of tyrants, the devil himself. To shake off the former, has cost many their lives, and put them beyond the capacity of enjoying the liberty; they have purchased at so dear a rate. When we need but detest the chains of sin to rise up to Kings and ensure liberty in its highest perfection. Our conduct proves that we prize time above eternity, the liberties of an earthly state, above the glorious liberty of the sons of God; the enjoyments of earth above those of heaven; sin above holiness; the service of Satan more than that of God,—yea, that we prefer the Devil himself, the implacable enemy of our souls to the Lord Jehovah, our gracious benefactor—one who would drag us down to eternal torments, to him who offers to save us from them, and fill our souls with everlasting, unmixed, ever-encreasing joys, and calls for nothing in return but our hearty acceptance, though it cost him the blood of his son. Should we accept the liberty of heaven, it will prepare us to relish the sweets of civil liberty in a manner wholly incompatible with a selfish spirit. We should then delight in the kindly aspect that civil liberty bears even on our enemies. But if we refuse spiritual liberty, that of the civil kind, will be no otherwise agreeable than as it tends to advance our own private interests, or to gratify our revenge. In the one case we shall enjoy it in its operations on all the members of the whole state; in the other we can enjoy no more of it, than terminates in the private good of an individual. This thought gives our conduct a still more inconsistent appearance, by shewing us that while we contend for civil liberty, we refuse the means of enjoying it to the best advantage, in its highest refinement and greatest extent. But our inconsistency will be seen in a still stronger point of light, if we consider, that without spiritual liberty, the other will finally prove worse than nothing. It is in itself a great blessing, but by abusing it, we may, and shall be rendered much more miserable at last, than if we had never possessed it. So long as we refuse to accept of the liberty of the gospel instead of using, we abuse every earthly good. Such an abuse of civil liberty, renders us extremely criminal in the sight of our judge, and will finally kindle his displeasure into an hotter flame that will more dreadfully consume us. In this way it is, that the prosperity of the food shall destroy him according to the prophecy of Solomon. Thus, by neglecting to embrace the gospel, we convert civil liberty, which is in itself, a delicious kind of food, into a slow poison which will render our death vastly more terrible than otherwise it would have been. It had been better for us not to have been born, or, to have been born slaves, and doomed with Lazarus to beg our bread at the doors of our rich oppressors, than to be found guilty at last of having abused the blessed privilege of liberty. In what point of view soever we look at our conduct in the light of this subject, we shall see new inconsistencies opening upon us. We boast of liberty, and value ourselves much on being free, when at the same time we are taken captive by satan at his pleasure. This is a much more shocking absurdity, than it would be for a man confined in a dungeon, to boast that he is at liberty, because he is not called on, in providence, to go into the field and labour. Should we hear one in a state of personal slavery vaunting, and boasting that he lives in a land of liberty, who would not laugh at his folly, and pity his weakness; and yet, he might have good reason to rejoice in seeing others free though he himself were in slavery. To dread and oppose a human tyrant, and yet bow voluntarily to satan, sinks us beneath the brutes. Another of our inconsistencies is this, notwithstanding all our pretences to the contrary, our refusal of spiritual liberty, proves us to be regardless of the liberty of the state. While we refuse the one and yet profess to pursue the other we only play the hypocrite. For who will believe a man loves money, merely because he exerts himself to obtain a penny, when at the same time he will not accept millions that are offered him gratis? In this case, it would be certain to a demonstration, that it was not affection to money, but something else, that put the person upon action. So, with respect to liberty; he who will not accept the greater when freely offered him, will not fight for the less from a sense of its value, if he exerts himself at all, it must be for some other end, and whenever he can answer this end more readily, by any other means, he will appear as he really is, quite cold to liberty: And when liberty shall be inconsistent with his private ends, he will be as fierce an opposer of it, as he is now an apparent advocate for it. No doubt many visibly espouse the cause of liberty purely for the sake of rising into popularity; and yet by this very means, sink themselves in the view of common-sense. For who is so blind as not to see that the licentious cannot be friends to liberty? No man can be a friend to liberty who is not likewise a friend to a free constitution, to the constitution of Christ's kingdom which is the most free? A cursing, or swearing, or drinking, or any other kind of vicious friend, either to liberty or government, is a monster of absurdity; such a monster as cannot exist even in the most romantic imagination.

Come then, my friends, let us embrace the glorious liberty of the sons of God. Every possible motive, whether of terror or allurement, is set before us. If we embrace this, we shall of necessity be genuine sons of liberty. We shall resolve that nothing but the wise superintendency of God shall ever make us submit to public oppression; for no man can be a christian and not a friend to civil liberty, in the the strictest sense. To be freemen of Jesus Christ will exceedingly sweeten the enjoyment of civil liberty if we can obtain it, or soften the fetters of slavery if we shall be forced to wear them. Spiritual liberty opens up a pleasant prospect even in the midnight of political slavery. The most abject slave may look forward and say, "a few moments more will usher me into a state of everlasting Freedom." On the contrary, what will it profit us to gain the whole world, crowns and scepters, if at last we loose our own souls, and are dragged at the chariot wheels of Satan. This is our time to secure freedom and glory. Another hour, may chain us down in eternal bondage.

God has given us rational minds. Let us then act a rational part. Let us act a consistent part, and not dishonour our high birth. . . .

Benjamin Colman, Essay on Slavery, July 20, 1774

The Essex Journal and Merrimack Packet. . ., July 20, 1774.

As the portentous difficulties between the American colonies and England intensified, some Calvinist ministers in New England began to see the hands of God at work. On July 20, 1774, a time in which the despised Coercive Acts had swelled talk of rebellion among the colonists, Deacon Benjamin Colman of Byfield Church, Newbury, Massachusetts, declared in the Essex Journal that the British ministry was the rod with which the Lord was punishing the colonies for their sins. "Search among ourselves," the Deacon implored, and look for "an accursed thing that is the troubler of our land." Central among those sins observed by Colman was that of slavery, "this cruel yoke of bondage, and this iniquity. . . ." If, for the Massachusetts minister, the troubles with the mother country represented an apocalypse, antislavery was a chance for a collective cleansing and redemption for the colonies. As external events in the country ran amuck, Colman and other New England ministers made antislavery a test of religious virtue. Only as the yoke of bondage was relieved from the wretched Africans, would God remove the yoke from the colonists and "set us at liberty."

Not only New England ministers saw Divine Judgment at work. Seven days after Colman's essay appeared in the public prints, Granville Sharp wrote to Benjamin Rush, "I must observe that the . . . evils which threaten the Colonies abroad, and the general misunderstanding of the British Constitution which at present prevails at home (Circumstances which presage the mutual destruction of both) may, with great probability of truth, be looked upon as a just punishment from God. . . ."

That we in New England, and this province in particular, are involved in sore trials and surrounded with perplexing difficulties at this day is evident to every observer of the times, and some of us begin to feel the galling yoke of oppression and slavery bearing hard upon us already, we say among ourselves, what have we done against our mother country, or the King, or Ministry, to provoke them to deal with us in this cruel and severe manner, we are loyal subjects to our King, we are willing to be governed by his righteous laws, we are no rebels, what means the heat of this anger: We are spreading our cause before God, I trust, through the province, in a private way, to seek redress of him, and in some places there is fasting with prayer in a more public manner, to implore the divine compassion, and that God would mercifully interpose in our behalf, and I wish there was more of a disposition to acknowledge God by a day set apart for general fasting and prayer. But, my fathers and brethren, as there is no evil or affliction in the city but the Lord has done it, the British ministry are only the rod which God makes use of to correct us by, he himself is the supreme and righteous ruler, and all things and events are under his controul, and as our righteous Lord loveth righteousness, and hateth, and has engaged to punish iniquity wherever it is found, though it be in his own dear people, as I trust the people of New England are so, for he has owned himself the God of New England in the great things he has done for our fathers in their day and for us in our time. I pray therefore we may refrain at present from any bitter reflection on the British ministry and search among ourselves and see if we cannot find an Achan, an accursed thing that is the troubler of our land, and for which God is at this day contending with us. Among the innumerable evils that abound among us, I look upon the oppression, bondage and slavery, exercised upon our poor brethren the Africans to be a God provoking, and wrath-procuring sin. I call them brethren, because God has told us in his word, that he has made of one blood all nations that dwell on the earth. They are as free by nature as we, or any other people; have a natural right to liberty and freedom as much as we, and it is only by power and tyranny that they are brought and kept under this cruel yoke of bondage, and this iniquity is established by a law in this province, and although there has been some feeble attempts made to break the yoke, and set them at liberty, yet the thing is not effected, but they are still kept under the cruel yoke of bondage. I pray let us think, whether we are not practising directly contrary to our Lord's precept delivered by his own mouth when he was here upon earth; I mean that universal rule of equity recorded by St. Matthew chapter 7. verse 12. "Therefore all things whatsoever ye would that men should do to you, do you even so to them, for this is the law and the prophets." Can any person in his right mind say that he is willing that himself, and his posterity, should be subjected to perpetual bondage and slavery, I presume he cannot answer in the affirmative. Some plead that it is the law of this and many other provinces, and so they do no worse than multitudes of others. But let us consider, that, that which is wrong in itself, could never be proved to be right, though all the provinces under heaven should make such a law. Others endeavour to vindicate the lawfulness of slavery from what was delivered by Moses to the children of Israel, Leviticus 25. 45, 46 verses, that people were allowed to buy of the heathen for bondmen and maids, and they were to be their inheritance and their children after them. To such I answer, that I take that to be but a temporary precept, which was not to continue after the gospel state was introduced, otherwise I think it must clash with the aforecited text, Matthew 7. 12. of doing by others as we should be willing they should do in the like case to us. What God allows, may be done till he forbids it, what God forbids is never to be done till he allows it. God calls the children of Israel a stiff-necked people, (as we may be stilled at this day) and possibly for the hardness of their hearts, and to encourage them to obedience, he might allow them to deal so by the heathen. As we read, Matthew 19. 8. our Saviour says concerning putting away wives. Moses because of the hardness of your hearts, suffered you to put away your wives; but from the beginning it was not so. Again, as Jesus Christ is the great King, and the only universal redeemer of God's elect. Among all nations Jews and Gentiles, he has come in person, to introduce a more refined excellent government, than ever was made known before, breaking down the partition wall between Jew and Gentile, set all nations upon a level as to his grace and favour, as he speaks by the apostle Peter, Acts 10. 35. But in every nation he that feareth God and worketh righteousness is accepted with him. I take it that many things that were allowed and commanded under the Jewish dispensation, are now unlawful to be done; for, says the Apostle Paul, Galations 5. 1. "Stand fast therefore in the liberty wherewith Christ has made us free and be not entangled again with the yoke of bondage." The Jewish services were good because God commanded them, for he is the supreme law-giver. The New Testament rules and orders are commanded because they are good in themselves, and tend to the good of the whole body,—God of his distinguishing goodness having reserved some better things for us. And shall we, my fathers and brethren, or can we lift up our faces with confidence before God, by solemn prayer, that he would remove the yoke of bondage from us, and set us at liberty from the burdens that lay upon us, while we keep a tenfold heavier yoke on the necks of our brethren the negroes. I confess I blush, when I hear of a proposal for a provincial fast, (although I am as desirous of it as others) when I read the 58th chapter of Isaiah, where the people are represented as keeping days of fasting and prayer, and yet obtained no gracious answers from God. "Wherefore have we fasted, say they, and thou seest not, wherefore have we afflicted our soul and thou takest no knowledge." Verse 6 "Is not this the fast that I have chosen to loose the bands of wickedness, to undo the heavy burdens, and to let the oppressed go free, and that ye break every yoke." I humbly ask, is not God in his righteous providence, (righteous I say respecting himself, although the act is most unrighteous in respect to men and instruments) holding up a glass before us, that we may see our face as to what we have done and are doing. May it not be retorted upon us as in Romans 2. 21. "Thou therefore which teachest another, teachest thou not thyself, &c." "thou that sayest men should not oppress their fellow creatures, dost thou oppress, &c." May not God say to us, as to his professing people of old, "Ye shall not fast as you do this day to make your voice to be heard on high," are not the exercises of righteousness, justice and charity, essential articles to constitute an acceptable fast, for we are not personally good, unless we are relatively good, if we are ever so importunate in prayer, if we humble ourselves to the dust, in our confessions and petitions for relief under our burdens, so long as we hold fast any of our sins, whether it be unrighteousness, oppressions, or whatever God contends with us about, we have no reason to expect relief, the Psalmist under inspiration says, "If I regard iniquity in my heart, the Lord will not hear me." I do not say that our grievances will not be redressed until we break the yoke of bondage from the negroes necks, but I must need say I do not expect it. But that we all as one, may be enabled to search out, and put away every thing from amongst us, whereby God is dishonoured and offended, to break every yoke of oppression, so that he might cause light to rise in obscurity, is I trust the prayer of every friend to New-England. *Amen.*

John Allen, *The Watchman's Alarm to Lord N———H*, 1774

John Allen, *The Watchman's Alarm to Lord N———H; or, The British Parliamentary Boston Port-Bill unwraped. Being an Oration on the Meridian of Liberty; Not to inflame but to cheer the Mind: or as an Apple of Gold in the Pictures of Silver for the mourning Captives in America. With some Observations on the Liberties of the Africans* (Salem, 1774), pp. 5-11; 16-22; 25-30; 32.

In 1773, an inflammatory pamphlet published by Baptist minister and agitator, John Allen, assaulted the British ministry, and raised the cry, "With life and spirit set up your standard! Engrave the motto!—May it be thus: Liberty, Life, or Death." A year later, the irrepressible pamphleteer, with the Boston Port bill as his target, wrote "Watchman's Alarm to Lord N———H," another strident production which carried as its frontispiece a cartoon depicting Lord North, with the port bill in his pocket, forcing taxed tea down the throat of a figure representing America. Allen noted that ". . . she furiously pukes up again in his face." Although Allen claimed that the pamphlet was designed "not to inflame but to cheer the Mind," his composition was a raging vilification of British colonial policy and a violent personal attack upon British officials.

Closely linked to Allen's attack on British tyranny and oppression was his assertion that the colonists, although grossly abused, were receiving something of a just reward. This pamphlet, perhaps more than any other in the period, underscored the semantic link between the political "slavery" of the colonists and the slavery of the Africans. In it Allen shifted the argument dramatically from an attack on British policy to a vigorous denunciation of "ye pretended votaries for freedom," the "trifling patriots" who were calling for liberty and freedom while participating in the business of slavery. The shift must have unnerved Allen's slave-trading and slave-dealing readership. ". . . The time is coming," he declared, "when . . . our Savior's words may come with full power and have their desired effect, namely, Whatsoever ye would that men should do unto you, do ye even so to them."

Men, Brethren, and Fathers, and ye that fear God, give audience.

The peculiar solemnities of this day are more immediately adapted, by the public consent of the churches, to paint forth the life and meredian of liberty. The distress you are in, and the danger there is of your losing your rights, call aloud to supplicate the throne of God for deliverance; to pray for a restoration of your just rights, and a final settlement of the sure enjoyment of them.

By liberty, is meant political liberty; and, according to the true etimology of the word, in *Fenning's* dictionary, it is a power of acting agreable to the laws which are made and enacted by the consent of the people, and no ways inconsistent with the natural rights of a single person, or the good of society. This is the liberty which is opposed to slavery.

Liberty of the mind is the free thought that expands, ruminates from sea to sea, and from rivers to the end of the earth, and none can controul it. The chariot of a thought, of a wish, of a desire, is like the wings of the morning, which flies to the *uttemost parts of the earth*; and is like the sun which rejoices to run its race; it is like the fountains which rise spontaneously free; it is like the emitting life of the vine to all its branches; like the flowing rivers, the fertile fields in their pleasant growth, or like the gentle zephyrs which diffuses its fragrant life through the globe. This is freedom which is above the controul of man, or beyond the suppression of any parliament or ministerial tyrant. This is that kingdom of liberty which no man can destroy, and therefore not the liberty we are this day to treat of and solemnize. That which calls upon every heart and commands every soul, is that of a civil and sacred nature, which is so much in danger.

Civil liberty is the people's inherent right to enjoy; namely, all the privileges of their laws according to their compact with their King; this right is ever inherent in the people, and cannot be given to kings, nor taken away by any parliament whatsoever; the enjoyment may, but the right cannot; its creation is natural and rises with every generation. This is the power of the people which *binds kings in fetters and nobles in irons.*

Sacred liberty is a satisfaction of soul in the choice of worship and adoration of God: This is Jehovah's law for the souls of men, and none but devils and priestly tyrants have ever aimed to invade this right.

But as your civil rights are destroyed, your capitol town besieged, your harbor blockaded, your port shut, trade, which is the sinews of life and liberty is stopped by power and force of arms, what have we not to fear respecting our divine liberty? This makes it a night of distress and sorrow, of great darkness and many fears: This makes me mourn for the affliction of *Joseph*; to mourn with them that mourn, to hang my harp with the rest of the captives and weep; yet not as those who are without hope, *for he that hath delivered doth deliver, in whom we trust he will yet deliver.*

But this night of sorrow naturally leads me to the words of the Prophet, for the present contemplation;

Watchman what of the night? Watchman what of the night?

What indeed! a very proper, a very important question at this time. The most remarkable transactions of the God of heaven for the deliverance of his people are made manifest as a key to unlock, or as a door to open the divine designs by interrogations. Thus when man had sinned and marred the beauty of his creation; when that light, life, love, adoration, and contemplation of his God had forsaken his soul, the God of heaven said unto him, Adam, *Where art thou?* Thus when a cloud of sorrows covered the camp of *Israel,* and God seemed to forsake his people, *Joshua,* whose name denotes the Lord's salvation, said, *If* Israel *turn their backs upon their enemies, what wilt thou do unto thy great name?* Thus *Elihu,* when he taught *Job* the corruption of his heart and nature, and how unbecoming it was in him in calling himself righteous, and justifying himself under his affliction before God, seeing his heart was corrupt, that it was not his thoughts, words, or actions that could acquit him before God, and therefore he says, *How shall a man be just with* God? How indeed! But this question I leave for the Priests to answer, who are very busy about it, but in general know nothing of the matter.

Another solemn question we have, which is, Who shall go to heaven? I hope you would be glad to know this, my hearers; you will find it, Ps. xxix. 3. *Who shall ascend unto the hill of the* Lord? *and who shall stand in his holy place? He that hath clean hands and a pure heart.* Is it him? Then it is plain, my friends, that it is not you nor me, for our hearts are *impure*. Who can it be? A very proper question. Were they the Prophets and Patriarchs? No! no! for they were like you and me, they had often unclean hands, and always a corrupt heart. Who can it be? That is the point. Are they our Ministers, then? O no, my friends, no, no, that is a settled point; certain, both in heaven and in earth, for the scripture says, *We have all sinned, and are verily men, subject to like passions,* and therefore not pure in heart. Who can they be? I think I will leave it for the Priests to tell you, whom I believe, if *Paul* was alive, would soon tell them they know but very little of this matter; this I know they will not let me go, because, they say, I have eat with unwashen hands: What then? Have not they or have not I washed them since? Will not that do? If it will I think I have as good a right to go to heaven as they have. May not one crowd in with them? No, no, they will not give you elbow room. Well, they need not be afraid, for I will not go with them, nor trust my soul among them. You may, if you please, brethren, for I have no dominion over your faith, but would fain be a helper of your joy.

Again, when sin and satan, when death and hell had invaded the rights of the whole creation and made it groan; when sinners were to be redeemed, God glorified, salvation finished, righteousness revealed, life, liberty, and glory to be made manifest to the sons of men; an inquiry, according to scripture ideas, seems to arise from the sacred throne, *Who is this that engageth his heart to approach unto me, saith the* Lord? Who, indeed? The answer you have from Christ's own own lips. Isa. lxiii. 5. *And I looked and there was none to help, and I wondered that there was none to uphold; therefore mine own arm brought salvation.*

Once more, when the church saw, prophetically saw, the great work finished, namely, righteousness shining like the light of the morning, salvation sealed as the finished work of the God of heaven, sin suffered for, the law fulfilled, God glorified, death, hell, and the grave triumphed over. She says, *Who is this?* Who is this indeed that has done all this? Few know among the Priests, and fewer desire to know among the people: But it is *I*, saith the Redeemer, *that speak in righteousness, mighty to save*. This shews what divine designs and grand displays of mercy are made manifest by scripture interrogations.

Which leads me to the contemplation words, or first inquiry,

Watchman what of the night? Watchman what of the night?

I will tell you as well as I can, but be patient, for I am not eloquent, and my talent is small, and I am but a poor man and little esteemed in *Israel*. I have read of a poor wise man who by his wisdom delivered the city, yet no man remembered the same poor man: But never you mind that, for there is nothing new under the sun.

What of the night? you ask. I will tell you, it is a *very good night*; I mean for honest men to be out in, the stars are clear, the sky is serene, the wind is calm: It is to be sure a *bad night* for thieves and robbers, who intend to catch our persons, steal our properties, and rob us of our rights, it is a very bad night for them. The scripture says, *If a thief comes, he comes in the night*; but he loves a dark night. But be not afraid, for the *morning cometh*;

remember from a *night* arose all the blessings of creation, the beauties of paradise, and all the happiness of the life that now is, and the hope of that which is to come. As it is written, *And darkness covered the face of the deep, and he said let there be light, and there was light*; therefore fear not the night, *though weeping may endure for a night, yet joy cometh in the morning.*

Yet sometimes by *night* I own we are to understand *deep troubles*, national distress, and personal sorrows, as was the case of *Jacob*, of *Job*, of the prophets, and the nations of *Israel* and of *Judah*; and it is worthy our attention for a moment; did I say, nay but for eternity, to observe the ponderous sorrows of Christ's soul, when he poured out his soul to death, when he made his soul an offering for sin, when his soul was troubled, when being in an agony, and his sweat was as the drops of blood, when his soul *was sore amazed*, when dying the just for the unjust, to bring us nigh unto God. All these sorrows in their ponderous weight and pressing feelings are set forth by the figure of a *dark night*; this, says Christ, *is your hour and power of darkness: And there was darkness over the whole land until the ninth hour.* Hence he says, *My head is wet with dew, and my locks with the drops of the night.*

Thus it appears that the word *night* denotes sorrows personally and nationally, and this is your case, as well as that of the united colonies, so far as they feel for and sympathize with you.

Not long since your Forefathers, who were the Patriarchs and Apostles of *America*, though distressed by the savage tribes, yet they enjoyed their political charter liberties settled by compact with their king.

Not long since the capital of *America*, the meridian harbor of the continent was open, your castle commanded, your colors flying, your commerce spreading, your importance growing, your laws ruling, peace and plenty flowing, your war-like spirit shining, your standards renowned: But alas! be astonished, O heavens at this, how has your loyalty almost proved your ruin; seeing your power, beholding your importance; jealous, jealous of a growing empire, the *British* Ministry take the rein of government, break the compact of their King, assume the right of making your laws, and usurp the authority of taxing your property, tyrannically and oppressively to the whole globe, continue to block up your harbor, cruelly cutting through the silver veins of trade, stained your streets with the bloody dews of death; they have seized your castle, besieged your town with all the majestic horrors of war! But lo! they look to a peaceful, serene people in the light of a few powerless, harmless doves, trembling upon the ground they tread; and only to unnecessary fearful minds terrible as an army with banners; this is their hour and power of darkness, but fear not, the *morning cometh*. . . .

Some say that the tea was not subject to any taxation, but an import duty. What is the difference, if it must be paid by an advance price by the people, without their consent to a duty or taxation? They say it was the destruction of private property. What difference does this make between its being private property or parliamentary property? The grand question is, whether any people under heaven have not, by the law of self preservation, a right to destroy any persons power or property who destroy their settled rights as a people? Besides, is it just or usual for one nation to tax the private properties of another nation and province, and oblige them under penalties of death to pay the tax? Is not this a breach upon the law of nations? And do not such law-breakers deserve to be punished by the loss of their property? Can mankind think it strange that the justly angry populace should destroy what their Governor would not stoop to save? Let the *East-India* Company ask pardon of the Public whom they have offended.

Colonel *Barre*, General *Conway*, Governor *Pownall*, Messieurs *Burkes, Dowdeswell*, and many, very many more who are the most honorable Members of the House of Commons, unwrapped it much in the same manner, and laid it aside as waste paper. Nay, the Peers of the land, the House of Lords, many of them united therein: Lord *Chatham* has much contemned it; Lord *Cambden* has boldly declared against it: Likewise the following Peers, in a paper, intitled, the Lord's Protest, distinguished themselves in the cause of *American* freedom, namely, *Richmond, Portland, Abingdon, King, Effingham, Rockingham, Abergavenny, Lester, Craven, Fitzwilliam, &c.* who all unwrapped and disapproved of the bill, the charge, and the demands. [May those illustrious Peers and Commoners, who have so nobly distinguished themselves in the cause of *America*, in opposition to those who were for taxing them, be gratefully remembered, and handed down to posterity. May their names be held in eternal honor, so long as one spark of the noble sensation of gratitude shall remain in the breast of an *American!*] But his Lordship said, "We will let the *Americans* know that we will sit quiet no longer under their insults, whatever may be the consequence; we must risque something or all is over." Upon which taking the opportunity of a thin house in great haste they in a hurry wrapped it up again, got a royal signet upon it, and set it *all over.*

A remark. Now my Lord all *is over*; all the bill is *over*, the ships are over, and the army is over, we hope, my Lord, it is all over: For we do not want no more, and your Lordship may take these back as soon as you please, for we have nothing for them to do. It puts me in mind of a soldier who served in the last war, who being ordered by his General, namely, S——x, to feed his horses with peas, rice, and corn, when the soldiers and many others had not bread to eat; the soldier therefore went to the Surgeon and desired him to draw all his teeth; why, said the Surgeon, do they ake? He said no, but his General had robbed him of his bread, and given it to his horses, and thereby he had nothing for his teeth to do, therefore he would not keep them. Thus it is, my Lord, we have nothing for his Majesty's ships and armed force to do, unless it be to kill Musketoes, and therefore we do not chuse to keep them.

It puts me in mind of what my brother Watchman said, (his name is *Jeremiah*) when I asked him what they did with the roll? And he said, *It came to pass when* Jehudi *had read three or four leaves, he cut it with a penknife, and burnt it in the fire that was upon the hearth until it all was consumed.* And it came to pass; that is enough, it is not needful to know how it came to pass, that the Watchman does not tell us, but if it comes to pass that is all we wish for peace sake.

But to be more close and serious; to hear the widows mourn for fear, labor fail, children crying, trade ceasing, children begging daily bread, the streets unoccupied, the sea uncloathed, the harbors undressed; to hear the noisy cannons roar, to see the blazing spear displayed, the bloody banner spread, and all this by breathren, by our own mother's sons, by flesh of our flesh and bone of our bone; for what they know not on the other side of the atlantic, nor do we on this continental shore: Something is surmised, we are wickedly represented to his Majesty, and therefore *we* must, says, his Lordship, risque *something, or all is over*. What must they set *Israel* to fight against *Judah*. There is the same mad mistaken paralleled case at large in *Joshua* xxii. However my Lord, you have risqued something indeed, namely, the crown and peace of the state; his Majesty's ships, army, and ammunition, and we judge all is over, they are come safe; we mean to use them well as brethren; and I wish the tea was paid for, if they may answer all the end they came for, and make way for union and peace, which has been whispered.

But it is yet a night season; methinks I hear you say, *Watchman what of the night*? What shall we do to night? I will tell you; first, praise God for the mercies of the day, humbly trust his promise for safety through the night, then do as regular people do, eat your supper, go to bed and sleep quietly until morning, then arise and pay your morning sacrifice of praise to God and go to your daily labor, and whatsoever thine hands findeth to do, do it with all thy might. Fear not the night, for the morning cometh, for the Lord our God is with us; fear them not, for there be more for us than they that be with them; fear them not.

Secondly, love your King, feelingly, firmly, and affectionately: But remember that allegiance and obedience is only due to a King, as his fidelity and coronation oath is fulfilled to you; it is the law not the man that ought to rule. The King is by consent of the people made their royal *Trustee*, or grand *Trust* for the preservation of their rights; if he fails here he is no longer King according to the laws of *England*; therefore pray that the Almighty may give him judgment as a royal diadem to his crown, for the peace of *Britain* and her union happiness with *America*; honor your Governor with reverences and duty in every branch of legal authority; be kind to the soldiery; be genteel to the officers; pray for Lord N. that the God of heaven may bless and we hope forgive him, as he did, *Ahitophel*, and send him to his own place as he did *Judas*. I have heard that his Lordship is a man of fine sensation, quick understanding, a great senator, and a faithful servant to the Crown. But how a person can be a man of honor, honesty, fine sensations, a faithful senator, who can propose, aim, and proceed to distress thousands of thousands of innocent people, by destroying their essential liberties and natural rights, by the arbitrary arm of *iron power*, and thereby bid defiance to the law of nature and nations, which *binds kings in fetters and nobles in irons*. The man who dares this is the greatest tyrant beneath the sun. Was his Lordship a man of fine sensations, of quick understanding, possessed of the feelings of humanity for the happiness of mankind, he would surely have felt the piercing pleas, the nervous reasonings, the cutting arguments, not only of Lord *Chatham*, Lord *Cambden*, and others, but of those (if I may express it) angelic arguments of Colonel *Barre* to his Lordship, for the peace of *Britain* and the happiness of *America*; but lo! nothing will do but the iron rod, and not the olive-branch, and therefore I think if the Almighty will forgive him, mankind can very well spare him. But if there should a single son of *Issachar* upon the earth, who is *born like a strong ass to couch between two burdens*, who can approve of this act, an act that deprives God of the grand designs of creation, man of his inherent rights, and the blessings of Providence; an act that takes away his labor, his bread, his all, his estate, his existence; an act that makes the widow mourn, the fatherless to cry for bread; an act that forbids the merchant to trade; his stores to be open, his wharves to be used; an act that sets land and water, winds and waves, blood and banners all in array against a loyal people, to make them love their King, whom they always adored. If there should be such a being upon the earth who can plead for this act, he must be happy; for surely the *Almighty has made him without a soul, and consequently he can have no sins to answer for*. What shall I say to such a one? He lives indeed, but he must die; *Dust thou art*, (that is all) *and unto dust thou must return*. Shall I say in the Prophet's language, *Hell from beneath moves to meet thee at thy coming*. No; heaven forbid! indeed there is no danger, for it is so full already of more sensible beings, that there is no room, in charity we hope for such there. Thus you see that we are more mild and charitable for those Persons who vainly call themselves Friends to Government: They say that we, yea and those honest *British* Members of Parliament who plead for the rights of injured *America* are a set of damned—&c. and ought to be damned. Now we are not for having these friends to government, as they falsely stile themselves, damned: No; but for their being saved even from the power of damning others. But I would say as *Samuel* did unto *Israel*; God *forbid that I should sin in ceasing to pray for you, for I bare you record that you have zeal for your* King and Country, *but not according to* the *knowledge* of the essential and charter rights of the *Americans*; therefore it it is that such multiply words without knowledge, &c. . . .

One more inquiry: *Watchman what of the night?* Do you think we deserve it? I know we deserve it from God, but not from man; and I acknowledge that you deserve it from God? I am glad you are so humbly sensible: But what if I say you deserve it from God, and will tell you for what; it is for your iniquitous and disgraceful practice of keeping *African* slaves, a custom so evidently contradictory to the laws of God, and in direct violation of the *charter* of this province, and the natural and unalienable rights of mankind; however any among you, *professing* christianity, although at the same time are guilty of so glaring a trespass on the laws of society and humanity, may inconsistently gloss over their detestable usage with the idle *pretence* of christianizing them, when it is well known more than one half those who are owners of these black people do not care what becomes of the souls of them, if they can reap the profits arising from the labor of their bodies, at least until they arrive at the age of fifty, a period which is far beyond the meridian of man's natural life. I only judge from their conduct towards these miserable creatures, more especially with regard to their education, and this assertion is notoriously verified in respect of those who hold slaves in the *West-Indies*, as well as in most parts of *America*, even where the christian religion is professed, they are not learned to read one word of the holy scripture, or say their catechize: Nay, some venture to say, were they to have learning, and to be instructed in the principles of religion, they would be of no service to any one: However, admitting their motives of importing these *Africans* to make christians of them, if they can, to be sincere, is it likely any man will be willing to bind himself for life, in order to obtain your chance salvation, by means of your prayers, feelings, movings of the spirit, *&c.* which perhaps most of you may account works of righteousness?

This truly benevolent and public-spirited way of freeing black men when they are old, reminds me of a story I heard of one who was held in bondage until he was near sixty years of age, when his master very generously offered him his freedom, after telling him he had been a faithful, honest slave, and thanked him for his past good services. But hear the honest reply of the aged, decripid, and untutored *African*, arrived at such a period of life as to occasion grey hairs, by age and hard labor; *I tank you, Maser, I tink you hab all de marrow, bes way you take care de bone.*

Blush ye pretended votaries for freedom! ye trifling patriots! who are making a vain parade of being the advocates for the liberties of mankind, who are thus making a mockery of your profession, by trampling on the sacred natural rights and privileges of the *Africans*; for while you are fasting, praying, non-importing, non-exporting, remonstrating, resolving, and pleading for a restoration of your charter rights, you at the same time are continuing this lawless, cruel, inhuman, and abominable practice of enslaving your fellow-creatures, which is so disgraceful to human nature; a practice which must redound to the eternal dishonor of any people much more to those who *wear* the christian name, and must surely make the heart of every feeling person shudder at the thought of being held in perpetual slavery, but shocking to relate, it is realized by millions of unhappy mortals in the world, a greater part of which I am sorry to say are dwellers in this *American* land of freedom!

But if ye fail of abolishing this vile custom of slave-making, either by a law of the province, common law, (which I am told has happily succeeded in many instances of late) or by a voluntary releasement, the oppressed sons of *Africa* may very justly retort this stubborn passage of sacred writ upon you, *Isaiah* lviii. 6. *Loose the bands of wickedness, undo the heavy burdens, let the oppressed go free, that ye break every yoke*: And may truly say with the same Prophet, *Isaiah* i. 13, 19. *Bring no more vain oblation: The calling of assemblies I cannot away with; it is iniquity even the solemn-meeting. If ye be willing and obedient ye shall eat the good of the land.*

But let me ask you, I mean those who are guilty in this respect, with what face can you look up to the Almighty, that just and righteous Being, and beg of him his aid and assistance in our political affairs, while we are oppressing our *African* brethren ten thousand times as much by keeping them in slavery for life? And what is a trifling three penny duty on tea in comparison to the inestimable blessing of liberty to one captive? But O shocking the very imagination! yet more amazing the reality! to know we have millions among us who are slaves to all generations, at least we design them as such, unless some kind arm should interpose in the behalf of these miserable people to put an end to their bondage. O how it makes me rejoice, yea it makes me leap for joy, when I mention the much honored names of those worthy patriots for liberty, those sincere friends to the rights and liberties of mankind, who, emulated with a spirit of liberty, have so nobly let public virtue triumph over sordid self-interest, and have released a number of valuable black servants who were held in bondage. May they and their children be blessed for this truly god-like act; and may their public-spirited example be followed by many, very many Gentlemen who are owners of slaves. Let it never be told in the streets of *America*, that nursery of freedom, that there is one bond-slave dwells therein.

To conclude this solemn and much discussed subject, however little regard may have been paid to it by those whose interest it may justly be supposed to be to slight every thing that shall be advanced in favor of the *Africans*. However the time is coming, I hope, when instead of these sorely distressed and much oppressed *Africans* retorting passages of scripture on you slave-makers, our Savior's words may come with full power and have their desired effect, namely, *Whatsoever ye would that men should do unto you, do ye even so to them.* Though little account may be made of them in the religious as well as political world, they ought to be the eternal rule of righteousness to mankind.

Some of you may remember what your late Governor *Pownall* said to his servant *Frank*, on his confining a number of birds in a cage: Says his Excellency, Whose birds are those in that cage? Mine, Sir, replied his servant. What did they cost? Two dollars, Sir. Says his Excellency, there are your two dollars for them, let them be free, for I will have no being that God has made, in bondage in my house. Soon after the Governor purchased a number of flying-squirrels to send to *England*, which he confined in a cage: His man *Frank* seeing them, enquired of his fellow-servants whose squirrels they were? They informed him they belonged to his Excellency; on which *Frank* immediately let them all free: And on his carrying the tidings to his Excellency, enquired of him, what the squirrels cost? The Governor was a little angry at first for his freedom in asking what they cost? but on telling him he had set them at liberty, and offering to pay for them, his Excellency was much pleased with the familiar, soft admonition in favor of liberty.

Sir, One word if you please as Watchman.

Watchman what of the night? I mean of the night of ministerial darkness of the gospel; what of the night, Watchman?

Who is he that makes this inquiry? Thou art sure a sensible soul, for I have not had such an enquiry ever since I have been upon my watch tower in *America*.

This enquiry, my hearers, will naturally lead me for a few minutes to speak of religious liberty, and you that do not love religion or sacred liberty may go out, there will no body take any notice of it but God, and you know and others will know that you do not mind him much; but I cause to speak a word in season to the enquirer, because among sensible people it is known that the Standing Ministers, in general, by their arbitrary authority in the churches and despotic power by councils have as much destroyed the charter rights of the church of Christ, as the *British* Ministry have the rights of the *American* subjects. . . .

But though your sorrows may yet continue, your harps hang upon the willows, and things may yet grow darker and darker, and your sorrows be like the swellings of *Jordan*, yet fear not, the morning cometh. *Though the fig-tree should not blossom, nor there should be no fruit on the vine; the labor of the olive fail, and the field yield no meat, and the flocks be cut from the field, and there shall be no herd in the stalls; yet wait on the* Lord *and be of good courage, the* morning cometh. Support your congress, maintain your union, strengthen your affection, relieve the poor, persevere in piety, patience, and prudence as a band of brethren united in one common cause, be fearless, be harmless, and may God Almighty bless you.

Caesar Sarter, Essay on Slavery, August 17, 1774

The Essex Journal and Merrimack Packet, August 17, 1774.

". . . On the whole," the West Indian planter Richard Nisbet had written in 1773, "it seems probable, that they are a much inferior race of men to the whites, in every respect." A year later, on August 17, 1774, the Essex Journal *published an antislavery address dedicated to writers such as Nisbet, to "those who are advocates for holding the Africans in Slavery." The author of the address was an obscure ex-slave named Caesar Sarter. Sarter wrote that those who maintained that the institution of slavery was by its nature promoting religion and fostering education among a savage heathen population, or that those such as Nisbet who claimed that blacks were generally a contented race under slavery, were "certainly in an error." As the public debate over the humanity and equality of the black race intensified, compositions such as Sarter's gave antislavery advocates potent ammunition. With groups of blacks petitioning colonial legislatures, with blacks such as Phillis Wheatley writing essays and poetry and Sarter publishing addresses under the mastheads of leading newspapers, Nisbet's contentions were under grave assault. If Americans could be convinced that "A dark complection may cover a fair and beautiful mind," as the Reverend Andrew Eliot observed in the same year, then antislavery writers would control a formidable philosophical wedge. Sarter declared, "Let me who have no less than eleven relatives suffering in bondage beseech you, good people, to attend to the request of a poor African, and consider the evil consequences, and gross heinousness of reducing to, and retaining in slavery, a free people."*

Please to give the following Address, To those who are Advocates for holding the Africans in Slavery, a place in your next, and you will oblige one, who is a well-wisher to his bretheren, who are now in that unhappy state.

As this is a time of great anxiety and distress among you, on account of the infringement, not only of your Charter rights; but of the natural rights and privileges of freeborn men; permit a poor, though freeborn African, who in his youth, was trapanned into Slavery, and who has born the galling yoke of bondage for more than twenty years; though at last, by the blessing of God, has shaken it off, to tell you, and that from experience, that as Slavery is the greatest, and consequently most to be dreaded, of all temporal calamities; so its opposite, Liberty, is the greatest temporal good with which you can be blest. The importance of which, you can evince to the world you are sensible of, by your manly and resolute struggles to preserve it. Your fore fathers as I have been often informed, left their native country, together with many dear friends, and came into this country then a howling wilderness inhabited, only, by savages, rather choosing, under the protection of their God, to risk their lives, among those merciless wretches, than submit to tyranny at home: While, therefore, this conduct gives you their exalted sense of the worth of Liberty, at the same time, it shows their utmost abhorrence of that Curse of Curses, Slavery.—Your Parliament, to their immortal honor be it mentioned, to whom We feel that gratitude, which so high a favour naturally produces, in an ingenious mind, have exerted their utmost abilities, to put a final stop, to so iniquitous a business, as the Slave Trade is: That they have not succeeded in their laudable endeavours was not their fault: But they were defeated by his late Excellancy only—Now, if you are sensible, that slavery is in itself, and in it consequentes a great evil; why will you not pity and relieve the poor, distressed, enslaved Africans?—Who, though they are entitled to the same natural rights of mankind, that you are, are, nevertheless groaning in bondage! A bondage which will only terminate with life: To them a shocking consideration indeed! Though too little, I fear, thought of by most of you, who enjoy the profits of their labour. As the importation of slaves into this Province is generally laid aside, I shall not pretend a refutation of the arguments, generally brought in support of it; but request you, to let that excellent rule given by our Savior, to do to others, as you would, that they would do to you, have its due weight with you. Though the thought be shocking—for a few minutes. Suppose that you were trepanned away.—The husband from the dear wife of his bosom—the wife from her affectionate husband—children from their fond parents—or parents from their tender and beloved offspring, whom, not an hour before, perhaps, they were fondling in their arms and in whom they were promising themselves much future happiness; Suppose, I say, that you were thus vanished from such a blissful situation, and plunged into miserable slavery, in a different quarter of the globe: Or suppose you were accompanied by your wife and children, parents and brethren, manacled by your side—harrowing thought! And that after having suffered the most amazing hardships, your fetters were knocked from your gailed limbs, only to expose you to keener anguish!—Exposed to sale, with as little respect to decency as though you were a brute! And after all this, if you were unwilling to part with all you held dear, even without the privilege of dropping a tear over your dear friends, who were clinging around you; equally dreading the cruel separation; which would probably prove an endless one, you must be plied with that conclusive argument, that cat-o'nine tails, to reduce you to what your inhuman masters would call Reason. Now, are you willing all this should befall you? If you can lay your hand on your breast, and solemnly affirm that you should; Why then go on and prosper! For your treatment of the Africans is an exact compliance with the above mentioned rule: But if on the other hand your conscience answers in the negative; Why, in the name of Heaven, will you suffer such a gross violation of that rule by which your conduct must be tried, in that day, in which you must be accountable for all your actions, to, that impartial Judge, who hears the groans of the oppressed and who will sooner or later, avenge them of their oppressors! I need not tell you, who are acquainted with the scriptures that this kind of oppression, is discountenanced by them. Many passages, to this purpose, might be adduced, but I shall at present, mention but one, Exod. chap. 20 ver. 16 "And he that stealeth a man, and selleth him, or if he be found in his hand, he shall surely be put to death."

Though we are brought from a land of ignorance, it is as certain that we are brought from a land of comparative innocence—from a land that flows, as it were, with Milk and Honey—and the greater part of us carried, where we are, not only deprived of every comfort of life: But subjected to all the tortures that a most cruel inquisitor could invent, or a capricious tyrant execute and where we are likely, from the vicious examples before us, to become ten fold more the children of satan, then we should probably, have been in our native country. Though 'tis true, that some of our wars proceed from petty discourds among ourselves, it is as true, that the greater part of them and those the most bloody, are occasioned, in consequence of the Slave trade.—Though many think we are happier here than there, and will not allow us the privilege of judging for ourselves, they are certainly in an error. Every man is the best judge of his own happiness and every heart best knows his own its own bitterness—While I feel the loss of my country and my friends, I can, by sad experience adopt that expression in Prov. 25th Chap. 20 verse. As he that taketh away a garment in cold weather, and as vinegar upon nitre, so is he that singeth songs to a heavy heart. Let me who have now no less than eleven relatives suffering in bondage beseech you, good people, to attend to the request of a poor African, and consider these evil consequences, and gross heinousness of reducing to, and retaining in slavery a free people. Would you desire the preservation of your own liberty? As the first step let the oppressed Africans be liberated; then, and not till then, may you with confidence and consistency of conduct, look to Heaven for a blessing on your endeavours to knock the shackles with which your task masters are hampering you, from your own feet. On the other hand, if you are still determined to harden your hearts, and turn a deaf ear to our complaints, and the calls of God, in your present Calamities; Only be pleased to recollect the miserable end of Pharoah, in Consequences of his refusal to set those at Liberty, whom he had unjustly reduced to cruel servitude. Remember the fate of Meriam for despising an Ethiopean woman, Numb. 12 chap. 1st and 10th. verses. I need not point out the absurdity of your exertions for liberty, while you have slaves in your houses. for one minutes reflection is, methinks, suffecient for that purpose—you who are deterred from liberating your slaves, by the consideration of the ill consequences to yourselves must remember that we were not the cause of being brought here. If the compelling use, against our wills to come here was a sin; to retain us, without our consent now we are here, is I think, equally culpable let ever so great inconvenience arising therefrom, accrue to you. Not to trespass too much on your patience; would you unite in this generous, this noble purpose of granting us liberty; Your honorable assembly, on our humble petition would, I doubt not, free you from the trouble of us by making us grants in some back part of the country. If in this attempt to serve my countrymen, I have advanced anything to the purpose. I pray it may not be the less noticed for coming from an African.

Ceasar Sarter

Newbury Port, August 12th, 1774

Levi Hart, *Liberty Described and Recommended*, 1775

Levi Hart, *Liberty described and recommended; in a Sermon Preached to the Corporation of Freemen in Farmington, At their Meeting on Tuesday, September 20, 1774, And published at their Desire* (Hartford, 1775), pp. 7-23.

The writings of the Reverend Levi Hart, student of Joseph Bellamy and theological brother of ministers such as Samuel Hopkins and Jonathan Edwards, jr., are representative of much of the evangelical fervor and revivalistic enthusiasm which surfaced in the antislavery movement among the Calvinist clergy. During his long ministry as pastor of the North parish in Preston, Connecticut, Hart traveled throughout New England, delivering numerous sermons that were subsequently published. Few of Hart's published theological addresses matched in intensity his Liberty Described and Recommended, *preached in Farmington, Connecticut, on September 20, 1774. To Hart, antislavery was a vehicle for redemption. He felt that unshackling the fetters of slavery would palliate the collective guilt wracking the American conscience. Failing to act positively against the evil of slavery, however, could bring terrible divine retribution, thunderbolts from heaven on the "head of the oppressor, red with uncommon wrath. . . ." Much as William Lloyd Garrison would in the 19th century, Hart sounded the call for a national moral reformation. ". . . Inlist under the Captain of the Lords's host," Hart pleaded; "fight under his banner, you may be sure of victory, and liberty shall be your lasting reward, for whom the son maketh* free *shall be* free indeed." *A few weeks after Hart delivered the Farmington sermon, the Connecticut assembly passed an act prohibiting slave importation.*

II. PETER ii, 19.

While they promise them Liberty, *they themselves are the servants of corruption; for of whom a man is overcome, of the same is he brought into* Bondage.

To assert and maintain the cause of Liberty, is far from being peculiar to the British colonies in North-America, at the present day; our venerable Ancestors sought and found it in this western world, and at no small expense of their treasure and blood, purchased it for, and conveyed it down to us. The most distinguished and worthy characters in Great-Britain have patronized, spoke and written, and some of them even died, in defence of the sacred rights of Liberty! Those antient, renowned States of Greece and Rome, in their most flourishing condition, received their greatest lusture from a set of pubilc spirited, patriotic men, whose hearts glowed with the love of liberty, who were her defenders and supporters, and whose names and writings are venerable to distant ages and nations of men, even long after those oncemighty empires are gone to decay, and perished through neglecting to follow the maxims of those wise men, those patrons of liberty, who pointed out the path to lasting empire and glory.

Indeed, the sacred cause of liberty ever hath been, and ever will be venerable in every part of the world where knowledge, and learning flourish, and men are suffered to think and speak for themselves. Yea, it must be added, that Heaven hath appeared in the cause of liberty, and that in the most open and decisive manner: For this, the Son of God was manifest in the flesh, that he might destroy the tyranny of sin and satan, assert and maintain the equal government of his Father, redeem the guilty slaves from their more than Egyptian bondage, and cause the oppressed to go free.

The whole plan of Redemption, which is by far the greatest and most noble of all the works of God made known to us, to which they all tend and in which they centre, is comprised in procuring, preaching and bestowing liberty to the captives, and the opening of the prison to the bound: And the gospel of our salvation is principally taken up in describing that glorious liberty which is purchased for sinners by the Son of God—the bondage from which he redeems us—the ransom which he paid for our redemption—the way to obtain and enjoy this Liberty, and in stating and urging the most cogent and endearing arguments, and motives, to persuade us to come out of our bondage, and accept of the Liberty wherewith Christ maketh his people free. It is on this account denominated *Gospel*, or *Good News*; and is to the sinner, like the jubilee trumpet to the enslaved Israelite.

But it must be remembered, that in proportion as Liberty is excellent, and to be desired on the one hand, so slavery or bondage is terrible and to be avoided on the other. These are justly esteemed the two extremes of happiness and misery in Society. It will not therefore be thought foreign to our subject, or an unsuitable attempt upon the present occasion, to enquire into the various significations of these two opposite terms, as they are used in the several kinds of society with which we are concerned, especially as they are introduced in our text as opposed to each other, and it is intimated, that the most fond assertors of liberty, may after all, be themselves in a state of the most abject slavery and bondage.

Liberty may be defined in general, *a power of action*, or a certain suitableness or prepardness for exertion, and a freedom from force, or hindrance from any external cause; *Liberty* when predicted of man as a moral agent, and accountable creature, is that suitableness or preparedness to be the subject of volitions, or exercises of will, with reference to moral objects; by the influence of motives, which we find belongeth to all men of common capacity, and who are come to the years of understanding.

This Liberty is opposed to that want of capacity, by which there is a total ignorance of all moral objects, and so, a natural incapacity of chusing with regard to them. *Again*, the term Liberty is frequently used to denote a power of *doing as we please*, or of executing our acts of choice; this refers principally to external action, or bodily motion; and is opposed to force or opposition:—thus the prisoner who is bound in fetters, and secured with bolts and bars in a prison, is not at liberty to go out, he is deprived of this kind of liberty, and is in bondage.

Again, Liberty may be considered and defined with reference to society:—Mankind in a state of nature, or considered as individuals, antecedent to the supposition of all social connections, are not the subjects of *this freedom*, but it is absolutely necessary to the well being of society.

Human society is founded originally in compact, or mutual agreement. All the larger circles of society originate from family connection or mutual compact between husband and wife; and mutual compact necessarily implieth certain rules and obligations which neither of the parties may violate with impunity.

In the early ages of the world, before vice and wickedness had corrupted and destroyed the original natural form of civil government, as a fine writer of our own nation expresseth it;—"each patriarch sat king, priest and prophet of his growing state." But when the wickedness of man was become exceeding great, and every imagination of his heart evil, *the earth was filled with violence:* by the daring efforts of wicked men to subvert the original excellent form of society, and introduce despotic rule where the lives and happiness of many, even whole kingdoms should depend on the will, and be subservient to the pleasure of *one man*. But as society evidently originates from mutual compact or agreement, so it is equally evident, that the members who compose it, unite in one common interest; each individual gives up all private interest that is not consistent with the general good, the interest of the whole body: And, considered as a member of society, he hath no other interest but that of the whole body, of which he is a member: The case is similar to that of a trading company, possessed of a common stock, into which every one hath given his proportion; the interest of this common stock is now the property of the whole body, and each individual is benefited in proportion to the good of the whole, and is a good or bad member in proportion as he uniteth to, or counteracteth the interest of the body. And thus it is in the present case: civil society is formed for the good of the whole body of which it is composed. Hence the welfare and prosperity of the society is the *common good*, and every individual is to seek and find his happiness in the welfare of the whole, and every thing to be transacted in society, is to be regulated by this standard.—In particular, all the laws and rules formed in such society must tend to promote the general welfare; this is the test by which they must be tried, and by which they must stand or fall; all regulations in the body, and all rewards and punishments to individuals, must be determined agreeable to this.—Those who seek and promote the public interest, are to be esteemed and rewarded; and those who counteract and oppose it, must be punished in proportion to the injury aimed or committed against the public welfare.

We may add, that as the good of the public is the end and design of all good laws and rules, established in a well regulated society, so they must be enacted by the public, *i. e.* by the wisest and best men in the society, appointed by the body for this purpose.—Men who best understand the public good, and have a common interest with the body, and who are above the narrow pursuits of private interest.—If Laws and rules in society are established by any man, or body of men, who have not a common interest with the whole body of the members, but the contrary, it is evident at first view, they will be exposed to act in opposition to the general good.—None therefore but the representatives of the whole body, in whom as far as possible, the interest of all ranks is contained, are proper to make laws for the regulation of society. For the same reason, those who are to execute the laws, should be appointed in such a manner, and by such authority, as in the best possible way secures their attachment to the general good: And, the members of civil community who are disobedient to *such laws* and oppose the administration of *such authority* agreeable to them, deserve punishment according to the degree of their opposition, and their opportunity to promote, or counteract the general good. The crime of every private member in opposing the interest of society, is greater than that of opposition to the interest of an individual, as much (other things being equal) as the interest of the society is greater and of more worth than that of an individual.

In this view of our subject, we may form some conception of the crime of a civil ruler, who sacrificeth the public interest committed to his trust by society, for the sake of his own private gain;—who betrayeth that sacred deposit, to gratify his narrow, sordid thirst of wealth or honour:—We may form *some conceptions* of his crime, but we want words to paint the horrors of it.—If a private man is without excuse, and is justly doomed to die as a traitor and rebel, when he deserts his country's cause, or basely betrays it, though to save his life, what epithets of lasting infamy are black enough to draw the picture of the inhuman paricide, who basks in the glare of riches and grandeur, at the expence of the public welfare: Yea, may we not depend that heaven itself will assert the cause of liberty, defend the injured innocent, and discharge its thunderbolts on the guilty head of the oppressor, red with uncommon wrath, to blast the man that owes his greatness to his country's ruin?

From this general view of society, we are led to observe, that civil liberty doth not consist in a freedom from all law and government,—but in a freedom from unjust law and tyrannical government:—In freedom, to act for the general good, without incurring the displeasure of the ruler or censure of the law:—And civil slavery or bondage consisteth in being obliged either by a bad set of laws, or bad and tyrannical rulers, to act in opposition to the good of the whole, or suffer punishment for our steady attachment to the general good.

Religious liberty is the opportunity of professing and practising *that religion* which is agreeable to our judgment and consciences, without interruption or punishment from the civil magistrate. And religious bondage or slavery, is when we may not do this without incurring the penalty of laws, and being exposed to suffer in our persons or property.—

Ecclesiastical liberty, is such a state of order and regularity in christian society, as gives every member opportunity to fill up his place in acting for the general good of that great and holy society to which the true church of Christ belongs, and of which they are a part. And *ecclesiastical slavery*, is such a state as subjects some branches of this society to the will of others, (not to the good of the whole glorious kingdom) and punisheth them with the loss of some, or all of the priviledges of ecclesiastical society, if they disobey such tyrannical will, however they may act for the good of the whole, and so, agreeable to the law of Christ.

Finally, there is another kind of liberty and bondage, which deserve particular attention in this place, only as they are especially pointed to in our text, but as being of principle concern to men, they may be denominated *spiritual liberty and bondage*.—This liberty is spoken of by our Lord, John viii. 32, 36. Ye shall know the truth, and the truth shall make you *free*,—if the Son make you *free*, ye shall be *free* indeed. And, by the Apostle, Rom. vi, 18. Being then made *free* from sin, ye became the servants of righteousness. Gallat. v. 1. stand fast in the liberty wherewith Christ hath made us *free*. 2. Cor. iii. 17. Where the spirit of the Lord is, there is *liberty*.

Spiritual liberty then, is freedom or readiness and engagedness of soul in the love and service of God and Christ, and discharge of the various branches of christian duty.

Spiritual bondage, takes place in the dominion of sin and satan in the soul, or that state of allienation from God and Christ, to which all impenitent sinners are subject.

This brief view of the various significations of the terms *liberty* and *slavery*, might be usefully improved in many inferences and remarks. I will detain you only with those which follow.

Inference first.

If civil liberty consisteth in acting freely, and without constraint, or fear of punishment, for the public good, and tyranny and slavery are the reverse of this,—it followeth, that every one who acts for the general good of society, is entitled to the approbation and assistance of the body. None can justly fall under the frowns of society, but those who prefer some private benefit to the public welfare: And every society which suffers, or even *connives at* the practice, in any of its members, of taking away the liberty or property of those who have done nothing against the public interest, connives at injustice, and is so far guilty of tyranny and oppression.

Of all the enjoyments of the present life that of liberty is the most precious and valuable, and a state of slavery the most gloomy to a generous mind—to enslave men, therefore, who have not forfeited their liberty, is a most attrocious violation of one of the first laws of nature, it is utterly inconsistant with the fundamental principle and chief bond of union by which society originally was, and all free societies ever ought to be formed. I mean that of a general union for the common good, by which every individual is secure of public approbation so long as he acts for the public welfare.

Could it be thought then that such a palpable violation of the law of nature, and of the fundamental principles of society, would be practiced by individuals & connived at, & tolerated by the public in British America! this land of liberty where the spirit of freedom glows with such ardour.—Did not obstinate incontestible facts compel me, I could never believe that British Americans would be guilty of such a crime—I mean that of *the horrible slave-trade*, carried on by numbers and tolerated by authority in this country. It is not my design to enter largely into the arguments on this subject; all who agree to the general principles already laid down, will join in pronouncing the African slave-trade *a flagrant violation of the law of nature, of the natural rights of mankind*. What have the unhappy Africans committed against the inhabitants of the British colonies and islands in the West-Indies; to authorize us to seize them, or bribe them to seize one another, and transport them a thousand leagues into a strange land, and enslave them for life? For life did I say? From generation to generation to the end of time! However the cruel bondage is somewhat lightened in these northern colonies, through the kindness and lenity of the masters—kindness and lenity, I mean as far as these terms are applicable in the present case; I say, however the cruel bondage of the poor Africans is somewhat lightened among us; if we would for a just estimate of the nature of the slave trade we must be acquainted with the method of procuring the slaves—transporting them, and their treatment in the West-Indies, to which, and the southern colonies a great part of them are transported, and where the nature of the slave trade is *consistently* displayed.

When the Guinea traders arrive on that coast if the trading natives are not already supplied with a proper number of slaves, they go into the back settlements and either by secret ambush, or open force, seize a sufficient number for their purpose; in accomplishing which great numbers, many times are slain, and whole towns laid in ashes. When taken they are driven like cattle to the slaughter, to the sea shore, and sold to our Guinea traders, often for a small quantity of that soul and body destroying liquor, *rum*, qualified however with a large proportion of water, by which the ignorant natives are imposed upon, cheated, and disappointed.—The poor slaves are bound and thrust into the filthy holds of the ships—men, women, fathers, daughters, mothers, sons, without distinction; where they obliged to *rot together* thro' a long sea passage, which happily releives numbers from more intolerable sufferings on the shore.—

When they are arrived at the West-Indies they are again *exposed* in the markets, and sold like beasts of burden to the inhuman planters, by whose cruelty many more of them perish. It is supposed that out of near an hundred thousand which are computed to be transported from Africa annually, almost one third perish on the passage and in seasoning; and those unhappy numbers whose hard lot it is to be doomed to longer slavery, wear out their wretched lives in misery which wants a name. The Egyptian bondage was a state of liberty and ease compared with the condition of these unhappy sufferers; and for a trifling offence their barbarous masters will seize and butcher them, with as little, and in many instances, perhaps less ceremony or regret than you would take away the life of one of your domestic animals. It would be an affront to your understandings to enter on a long course of reasoning to prove the injustice and cruelty of such a trade as this. Let us for once put ourselves in the place of the unhappy Negroes. Suppose a number of ships arrived from Africa at a neighbouring sea port to purchase slaves, and transport them to that distant and to us inhospitable climate and those burning sands—put the case that a prevailing party in the neighbouring towns were so lost to all sense of public welfare and to the feelings of humanity as to accept their bribes and join with them to effect the ruin of their fellow men. Let *this* be the devoted town—and even now while you are met to assert and exercise that invaluable liberty which is the distinguished glory of Englishmen, the honour and safety of Connecticut; in this distined hour while your hearts glow with the love of liberty and exult in her possession; behold this house surrounded, whole armies from the neighbouring towns rush on you, those who resist are at once overpowered by numbers and butchered, the survivors, husbands, wives, parents, children, brethren, sisters, the ardent lover and his darling fair one, all seized, bound and driven away to the neighbouring sea port, where all ranged on the shore promiscuously, in a manner that pity and modesty relent to name: you are sold for a trifling sum, and see your inhuman purchasers rejoiceing in their success. But the time is come for a last farewell, you are destined to different ships bound to different and far distant coasts, go husbands and wives, give and receive the last embrace; parents bid a lasting adieu to your tender offspring. What can you say? What do to comfort or advise them? Their case and yours admit not of consolation—go, mothers, weep out your sorrows on the necks of your beloved daughters whom you have nursed with so much care, and educated with such delicacy; now they must go to a distant clime, to attend the nod of an imperious mistress, covered with rags and filth (if covered at all) they must descend to the most servile and intolerable drudgery, and every the least symptom of uneasiness at their hard usuage, meet the frowns and suffer the merciless lash of a cruel master.—But why ruminate on this; behold the inhuman monsters tear you from your last embrace, bound in chains you are hurried to different vessels, crouded in their holds and transported away forever from the sight of all you love, to distant cruel lands, to live and die in slavery and bondage, without the smallest hope of ever enjoying the sweets of liberty, or revisiting your dear native country, with this only consolation, that your sons and daughters are suffering the same cruel bondage, and that from you a race of abject slaves will, probably, be propagated down for hundreds of years! *Such are the sweets of this beloved slave trade!* It is the same to the unhappy sufferers now, that it would be to us if it was our own case; and the reasons against it are as strong and powerful as they would be then—in short the man that can deliberately attend to this subject and not feel the emotions of pity, or indignation, or both, appears to be sunk quite below the feelings of humanity! Is it not high time for this colony to wake up and put an effectual stop to the cruel business of stealing and selling our fellow men, so far as it can be stopped by one province?

With what a very ill grace can we plead for slavery when *we* are the tyrants, when we are engaged in one united struggle for the enjoyment of liberty; what inconsistence and self-contradiction is this! Who can count us the true friends of liberty as long as we deal in, or publicly connive at slavery.—

The general assembly of a neighbouring colony have prohibited the importation of Negro slaves under a large penalty, and have enacted that such slaves shall be free as soon as they set foot on the shore within the colony. Can this Colony want motives from reason, justice, religion, or public spirit, to follow the example? When, O when shall the happy day come, that Americans shall be *consistently* engaged in the cause of liberty, and a final end be put to the cruel slavery of our fellow men? Then may we not expect that our liberties will be established on a lasting foundation and that British America and English liberty will flourish to the latest posterity!

Inference 2. If civil liberty consisteth in acting freely and without constraint or fear of punishment for the public good, and so, agreeable to the laws framed to promote and secure it, and civil bondage or slavery is the reverse of this. We learn the importance of intrusting those, and none but those, with the guardianship of our civil liberties who are themselves free, who are not under the dominion of that sordid selfishness and narrowness of soul by which they will betray their country, our dear Country for a little private profit or honor to themselves.

Men who know the worth of public liberty, and are able and willing defenders of it, be the consequences what they may to their private interest, are the only proper persons to be rulers or representatives of this free and happy colony. In such the votes of the freemen should unite, without the least regard to party, interest, or any private views, agreeable to the nature and solemnity of their oath, and as they value their inestimable liberties, and would dread to fall a helpless prey to tyranny and oppression.

Inference 3. If it is of such importance that we enjoy and secure civil liberty, which respects only a comparatively small circle of society which must disband, at the latest, with the close of fleeting time; of what moment is it to us all, that we are subjects of that spiritual liberty, which unites us to, and interests us in the good of the whole kingdom of God our Saviour, and which shall last forever!

It is a just way of reasoning in the present case, from the less to the greater, let me say then, with what astonishment and abhorrence should we look on a person who chuses slavery and bondage under the most cruel tyrant, with the certain prospect of a shameful, painful death, by the hand of the executioner, rather than all the sweets of English liberty!

But with what an unspeakable greater madness is chargable who prefers the guilty slavery of sin and satan, to the glorious, perfect liberty of the children of God! Yet how many make this fatal choice! How many too, who are at great expence and trouble in the cause of civil liberty and zealous assertors of it! What self-contradiction and inconsistence is here! Is not this to strain out a gnat and swallow a cammel? What is English liberty? What is American freedom? When compared with the glorious liberty of the sons of God? And what is slavery under the gauling yoke of oppression, to the hard bondage of sin and satan! Let the hitherto, willing slaves of sin and satan then *rouse up*, there is now an opportunity to escape from bondage; there is one come to preach deliverance to the captives, and the opening the prison to them who are bound. Jesus Christ the mighty king and Saviour, the scourge of tyrants, and destroyer of sin and satan, the assertor, the giver and supporter of original, perfect freedom; he sets open your prison doors, knocks off your chains, and calls you to come forth. Oh! What prisoner who will not leap for joy at the sound of this jubilee trumpet, accept the offered pardon, embrace the given freedom,—bid adieu to slavery and bondage, and stand fast in the liberty wherewith Christ makes his subjects free. Here the most perfect liberty may be enjoyed. The exalted king seeks and secures the public interest; to *this* all the branches of his good government and wise administration tend, and in this they centre, for *this* joy which was set before him, he came into our nature and world, and even endured the cross and dispised the shame.—All the subjects in this happy kingdom are united in the same honourable cause, to them their is neither Barbarian, Scythian, Greek, or Jew, bond or free, they are all one, in one cause, and pursue it animated by one spirit; they feel how good and pleasant it is for brethren to dwell together in unity.—In vain shall the tyrant satan vent his impotent rage against these happy *sons of liberty*: be wise in season then, bid adieu to the kingdom of darkness, the cause of tyranny and oppression, inlist under the Captain of the Lords host, fight under his banner, you may be sure of victory, and liberty shall be your lasting reward, for whom the son maketh *free* shall be *free indeed*.

Samuel Allinson to Patrick Henry, October 17, 1774

Allinson Letterbook, Special Collections, Rutgers University Library, New Brunswick, N.J.

On October 17, 1774, Samuel Allinson, as other Quaker reformers had done before him, attempted to enlist the assistance of colonial leader Patrick Henry in the antislavery cause. In his letter to Robert Pleasants 20 months before, Henry, a slaveholder, had expressed a moral abhorrence of the institution of slavery, calling it "repugnant to humanity" and "inconsistent with the Bible and destructive to Liberty." Henry lamented his "want of conformity" to the precepts of virtue. He was, he remarked, drawn by convenience and custom into a morally indefensible system from which he refused to break away. Allinson, undoubtedly apprised by compatriots such as Pleasants and Anthony Benezet of Henry's modest antislavery pronouncements, continued to put pressure on the Virginia leader. Pleasants asked, "Can we say, that a limited Slavery is injurious & disagreeable to ourselves &, by our practice declare, that absolute Slavery *is not unjust to a race of fellow Men because they are black?" Allinson's appeal had little effect. Henry's "want of conformity" continued unabated.*

10th Mo 17th 1774

To Patrick Henry—Respd Friend Altho' a stranger to thy person, I am not quite so to thy character, which emboldens me to take the freedom of addressing thee on a subject that often occurs to me as an important one: I mean the case of the poor Negroes in Slavery. A case which never called louder for a candid consideration & just conclusions, than at a time when many or all the Inhabitants of N. America are groaning under unconstitutional impositions destructive of their Liberty. How far the present troubles may be brought upon a people so highly favoured by the Almighty as these colonies have been since their first settlement, as a punishment in kind for this very thing, is not for a Mortal to determine, but the history of Mankind shows, that National injustice has drawn down Divine Vengeance upon a whole people, until the evil has been expiated. We complain of the violence done to the Constitution by which we, as Englishmen, claim many immunities; but seem to forget tht there is a more general Constitution framed & delivered to us from heaven; by which all Mankind are included & enjoined, that whatsoever we would that men should do unto us, we should do even so unto them—& we are expressly told "The Law & the prophets were for this end."

Let us consider whether a Negro is not entituled to the same essential justice with ourselves, in "one of the gifts of God to Man at his creation, when he endued him with the faculty of free Will." I hope it is unnecessary to cite authorities or add arguments to convince thee that Slavery is not warranted by the true principles of spirit of our Constitution—is contrary to Reason; & inconsistent with the decrees of the Divine Legislator:—and tho' it has been permitted by Him for purposes we know not, Let me submit to thy consideran whether, in this enlightened age, it will not be remembered to the lasting disgrace of so respectable a body of Men as the Congress, if they should spend so much time to secure their own liberties, & leave no vestiges of their regard to those of their *fellow Men*, in bondage to themselves?

Can we think that the Father of Mankind will approbate our endeavours to obtain our own rights, whilst we act inconsistent with ourselves? Or, is there not the greatest reason to believe, that, "The same measure which we mete shall be measured to us again?

Can we say, that a limited Slavery is injurious & disagreeable to ourselves, &, by our practice declare, that *absolute Slavery* is not unjust to a race of fellow Men because they are black?

Excuse me for dropping these hints, & let me beg thee to consider; that a fairer time never offered to give a vital blow to the shameful custom of Slavery in America—I shall not suggest in what manner; if the Congress turns their attention to the liberty of those who are under oppression amongst themselves (which surely they ought) they cannot lay a better foundation for their own, than by, at least, declaring their sentiments against the future infraction of the rights of others. "He that will have Equity, shall do Equity" I am pleased to observe in the resolutions of some of the Colonies, one resolve, "That they will not import or buy any more Negroes" &c. under a hope that it will not be temporary, limited to the continuance of the present troubles, least we should be like the people of old, who humbled themselves & did that which was right in the sight of Omnipotence whilst under affliction, but soon after they were relieved, turned again to folly, & committed the same wickedness.

Do not think me too serious, or that I make this matter of more importance than it is—The Judgments of the Lord are in the Earth, & I wish we may not only learn & practise righteousness in the present, but endeavour for its future continuance.

The People called Quakers have lately agreed, in their society capacity, to exclude any one of their members who shall import, buy, or sell a Negro; & to set aside from religious servises amongst themselves, all such who shall *detain* in bondage those they have, who, by the Quartery & Mo. y Meeting, to wh such Members belong, are thought *fit for freedom*, & advise their being set at liberty—I mention not this boastingly, for indeed we have nothing to boast of.

The emminent abilities thou art possess'd of are talents committed to thee for improvement & use; & is it not probable that all the good in thy power to do with them, will be required at thy hands? The present circumstance of things, furnishes an ample field both for reflection and action, & it is my earnest wish, that Wisdom may preside in your counsels & frame your conclusions; that "peace on earth & good will to Men" may be the happy issue of all our labours; & no measures inimical there to can be justified, upon the principles of Christianity or the practice of our Saviour.

For a stranger so long to detain thy attention, an apology may be thought necessary & I shall refer to the matter to make it: The manner thou wilt excuse, since the intention I hope appears to be good.

I am thy real friend

Saml Allinson

United States Continental Association, 1774

Records of the Continental and Confederation Congresses and the Constitutional Convention, Record Group 360, National Archives, Washington, D.C.

On October 17, 1774, the same day that Samuel Allinson wrote to Patrick Henry, William Bradford wrote to James Madison, "Philadelphia has become another Cairo; with this difference that the one is a city swarming with Merchants the other with politicians and Statesmen." Bradford was referring to the delegates to the First Continental Congress that had assembled in Philadelphia a month earlier. Three days after Bradford's letter, the members adopted and signed the Continental Association, a "Non-Importation, Non-consumption, and Non-exportation Agreement," a covenant of the colonies designed to inflict economic havoc on the mother country. The second article of the Association required the cessation of slave importation, a measure which, although practically devoid of moral implications, nevertheless struck at the hated nemesis of abolitionists—the slave trade.

The measure, aimed at inflicting grave wounds upon British trade, was the first federal action taken against slavery. But abolitionists were skeptical. Anthony Benezet wrote to Granville Sharp on November 18, 1774, "Great, indeed, humblingly great, are the appearance of things.... Thou wilt doubtless understand, the conclusions entered upon by a number of persons who met in this City from the different provinces amongst others, the resolution not to suffer any more Negroes to be imported; if they continue in this mind, when the difficulties we now labour under, are removed, it will be so far a matter of great satisfaction; but no mention being made of ceasing the imports to the West Indies and on the long & extensive river Mississippi, I expect but little good to be done, in this weighty concern, till a stop is put to the trade in & from England, & indeed in Europe. . ." Benezet's fears were well justified. Although the prohibition against slave importation was retained by the Congress through the war, flagrant violations occurred. Benjamin Rush wrote to Sharp in 1785 of the Carolinas, Virginia, and Maryland "where they still wickedly maintain that abomination to God & men, Slavery, & even continue to import Slaves contrary to the just resolution of Congress in 1774."

343

We, his Majesty's most loyal subjects the Delegates of the several Colonies of New Hampshire, Massachusetts-Bay, Rhode Island, Connecticut, New York, New Jersey, Pennsylvania, The Three lower counties of Newcastle, Kent and Sussex on Delaware, Maryland, Virginia, North Carolina and South Carolina deputed to represent them in a continental Congress held in the city of Philadelphia on the fifth day of September 1774. avowing our allegiance to his Majesty, our affection and regard for our fellow subjects in Great-Britain and elsewhere, affected with the deepest anxiety and most alarming apprehensions at those grievances and distresses, with which his Majesty's American subjects are oppressed, and having taken under our most serious deliberation the state of the whole continent, find, that the present unhappy situation of our affairs is occasioned by a ruinous System of colony administration adopted by the British Ministry about the year 1763 evidently calculated for inslaving these colonies and with them the British Empire. In prosecution of which system various acts of parliament have been passed for raising a Revenue in America, for depriving the American subjects in many instances of the constitutional trial by jury, exposing their lives to danger by directing a new and illegal trial beyond the seas for crimes alledged to have been committed in America: And in prosecution of the same System, several late cruel and oppressive acts have been passed respecting the town of Boston and the Massachusetts-Bay, and also an act for extending the province of Quebec so as to border the western frontiers of these colonies, establishing an arbitrary government therein and discouraging the settlement of British subjects in that wide extended country, thus by the influence of civil principles and ancient prejudices to dispose the inhabitants to act with hostility against the free protestant colonies, whenever a wicked Ministry shall chuse so to direct them. —

To obtain redress of these grievances, which threaten destruction to the lives, liberty and property of his Majesty's subjects in North-America we are of opinion, that a non-importation, non-consumption and non-exportation agreement faithfully adhered to will prove the most speedy, effectual and peaceable measure: And therefore we do for ourselves and the inhabitants of the several colonies whom we represent firmly agree and associate under the sacred ties of virtue, honour and love of our country as follows,

1. That from and after the first day of December next we will not import into British America from Great-Britain or Ireland, any Goods, wares or merchandize whatsoever or from any other place any such goods, wares or merchandize as shall have been exported from Great-Britain or Ireland; nor will we after that day import any East India Tea from any part of the World, nor any Mollasses, Syrups, paneles, Coffee or Piemento from the British Plantations or from Dominica, nor Wines from Madeira or the Western Islands nor foreign Indigo. —

2. That we will neither import nor purchase any Slave imported after the first day of December next, after which time we will wholly discontinue the Slave trade, and will neither be concerned in it ourselves, nor will we hire our vessels nor sell our commodities or manufactures to those who are concerned in it. —

3. As a non-consumption agreement strictly adhered to will be an effectual security for the observation of the non-importation we as above solemnly agree and associate, that from this day we will not purchase or use any Tea imported on account of the East India Company, or any on which a duty hath been or shall be paid; and from and after the first day of March next, we will not purchase or use any East India tea whatsoever, nor will we nor shall any person for or under us purchase or use any of those goods, wares or merchandize we have agreed not to import, which we shall know or have cause to suspect were imported after the first day of December except such as come under the rules and directions of the tenth article hereafter mentioned.

4. The earnest desire we have not to injure our fellow subjects in Great-Britain, Ireland or the West-Indies induces us to suspend a non-exportation until the tenth day of September 1775. at which time if the said acts and parts of acts of the British Parliament herein after mentioned are not repealed we will not directly or indirectly export any merchandize or commodity whatsoever to Great-Britain, Ireland or the West-Indies. ~~except~~ Rice to Europe.

5. Such as are merchants and use the British and Irish trade will give orders as soon as possible to their factors, Agents and Correspondents in Great-Britain and Ireland not to ship any goods to them on any pretence whatsoever as they cannot be received in America; And if any merchant residing in Great-Britain or Ireland shall directly or indirectly ship any goods, wares or merchandize for America in order to break the said non-importation agreement or in any manner contravene the same

same, or such unworthy conduct being well attested it ought to be made public, and on the same being so done, we will not from thence forth have any commercial connection with such merchant. —

6. That such as are owners of vessels will give positive orders to their Captains or masters not to receive on board their vessels any goods prohibited by the said non-importation agreement on pain of immediate dismission from their service. —

7. We will use our utmost endeavours to improve the breed of Sheep and increase their number to the greatest extent, and to that end we will kill them as sparingly as may be especially those of the most profitable kind nor will we export any to the West-Indies or elsewhere and those of us who are or may become overstocked with or can conveniently spare any Sheep will dispose of them to our neighbours especially to the poorer sort upon moderate terms. —

8. That we will in our several stations encourage frugality, economy and industry and promote agriculture, arts and the manufactures of this country, especially that of wool; and will discountenance and discourage ~~[illegible]~~ every species of extravagance and dissipation especially all horse racing and all kinds of gaming, cock fighting, exhibitions of plays, shews and other expensive diversions and entertainments — And on the death of any relation or friend none of us or any of our families will go into any further mourning dress than a black crape or ribbon on the arm or hat for Gentlemen, and a black ribbon & necklace for Ladies, and we will discontinue the giving of gloves and scarfs at funerals. —

9. That such as are venders of goods or merchandize will not take advantage of the scarcity of goods that may be occasioned by this association but will sell the same at the rates we have been respectively accustomed to do for twelve months last past — And if any vender of goods or merchandize shall sell any such goods on higher terms or shall in any manner or by any device whatsoever violate or depart from this ~~[illegible]~~ agreement no person ought nor will any of us deal with any such person or his or her factor, or Agent at any time there after for any commodity whatever. —

10. In case any merchant, Trader or other person shall import any goods or merchandize after the first day of December ~~and~~ and before the first day of February next the same ought forthwith at the election of the owner to be either reshipped or delivered up to the Committee of the County, or town wherein they shall be imported, to be stored at the risque of ~~[illegible]~~ until the non-importation

agreement shall cease; or be sold under the direction of the Committee aforesaid and in the last mentioned case the owner or owners of such goods shall be reimbursed out of the sale, the first cost and charges, the profit if any to be applied towards relieving and employing such poor inhabitants of the town of Boston as are immediate sufferers by the Boston Port Bill, and a particular account of all goods so returned, stored, or sold to be inserted in the public papers; And if any goods or merchandizes shall be imported after the said first day of February the same ought forthwith to be sent back again without breaking any of the packages thereof.

11. That a Committee be chosen in every County, City and Town by those who are qualified to vote for representatives in the Legislature, whose business it shall be attentively to observe the conduct of all persons touching this association and when it shall be made to appear to the satisfaction of a majority of any such Committee that any person within the limits of their appointment has violated this association that such majority do forthwith cause the truth of the case to be published in the Gazette to the end that all such foes to the rights of British America may be publickly known and universally contemned as the enemies of American liberty and thence forth we respectively will break off all dealings with him or her.

12. That the Committee of Correspondence in the respective colonies do frequently inspect the entries of their Custom-House and inform each other from time to time of the true state thereof and of every other material circumstance that may occur relative to this association.

13. That all manufactures of this country be sold at reasonable prices so that no undue advantage be taken of a future scarcity of goods.

14. And we do further agree and resolve, that we will have no trade, commerce, dealings or intercourse whatsoever, with any Colony or Province in North-America, which shall not accede to, or which shall hereafter violate this association, but will hold them as unworthy of the rights of freemen, and as inimical to the liberties of this country.

And we do solemnly bind ourselves and ~~them~~ our Constituents under the ties aforesaid to adhere to this association until such parts of the several acts of parliament passed since the ~~year 1763~~ close of the last war ~~as impose~~ as impose or continue duties on Tea, Wine, Molasses, Syrups, paneles, Coffee, Sugar, Pimento, Indigo foreign paper, glass and painters colours imported into America, and extend the powers of the admiralty courts beyond their ancient limits, deprive the American subject of trial by jury, authorise the judges certificate to indemnify the prosecutor from damages that he might otherwise be liable to from a trial by his peers, require oppressive security from a claimant of ships or goods seized, before he shall be allowed to defend his property, are repealed.— And until that part of the Act of the 12 G. 3 ch. 24 entitled "an Act for the better securing his Majesty's dock yards, magazines, ships, ammunition and stores" by which any persons charged with committing any of the offences therein described, in America, may be tried in any shire or county within the realm is repealed. And until the four acts passed in the last session of Parliament viz. that for stopping the port and blocking up the harbour of Boston — that for altering the charter and government of the Massachusetts Bay — and that which is entitled an act for the better administration of Justice &c, and that for extending the limits of Quebec &c are repealed. And we recommend it to the provincial conventions and to the committees in the respective colonies to establish such farther regulations as they may think proper for carrying into execution this association.

The foregoing association being determined upon by the Congress, was ordered to be subscribed by the several Members thereof and thereupon we have hereunto set our respective names accordingly.

In Congress, Philadelphia October 20th 1774.

Peyton Randolph President

N. Hamp. { Jno Sullivan / Nathl Folsom }

Massachusetts { Thomas Cushing / Saml Adams / John Adams / Robt Treat Paine }

Rhode Island { Step Hopkins / Sam: Ward }

Jos. Galloway

Pensylvania { John Dickinson / Chas Humphreys / Thomas Mifflin / E Biddle / John Morton / Geo Ross }

North Carolina { Will Hooper / Joseph Hewes / R. Caswell }

South Carolina { Henry Middleton / Thos Lynch / Christ Gadsden / E Rutledge / John Rutledge }

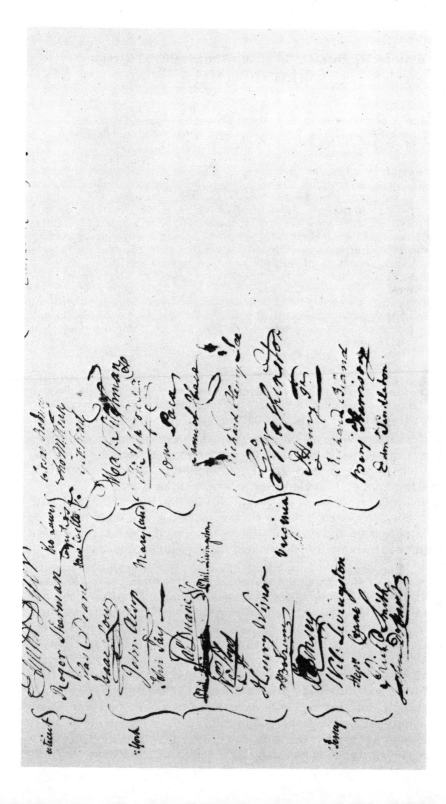

Elhanan Winchester, "Reigning Abominations" Sermon, December 30, 1774

Elhanan Winchester, *The Reigning Abominations, Especially the Slave Trade, Considered as Causes of Lamentation; Being the Substance of a Discourse Delivered in Fairfax County, Virginia, December 30, 1774. And Now Published With Several Additions* (London, 1788), pp. 3-5; 7; 17-32.

On December 30, 1774, the fiery preacher Elhanan Winchester delivered to a Fairfax, Virginia, congregation a blistering discourse on the slave trade, a jeremiad characteristic of many attacks by the Calvinist clergy upon this "reigning abomination." Winchester, an exponent of Universalism and a close friend of Benjamin Rush, reminded his listeners that throughout history great national sins had always wrought their just rewards—pestilence, famine, war, and destruction. Of all the evils "conceived in iniquity," the slave trade was the most heinous, he said, and as such, this national sin could only bring divine retribution.

Winchester's call was for redemption; his tone was urgent. As many other Calvinist ministers had done, Winchester made the vital connection between the secular problem of slavery and the religious imperatives. Only by abolishing slavery could Americans throw off their yoke of guilt and their own enslavement. Winchester's appeal had a prophetic ring: "I cannot help thinking that some revolution is at the door. . . ."

Ezek. ix. 4.

And the Lord said unto him, Go through the midst of the city, through the midst of Jerusalem, and set a mark upon the foreheads of the men that sigh and that cry for all the abominations that be done in the midst thereof.

Many and great were the iniquities committed in Jerusalem, at the time when the prophet had this vision; as you may learn from the foregoing chapter, where greater and greater abominations were successively discovered to him, by that God from whom nothing is hid.

The iniquity of Jerusalem was now full, and the city was doomed, with its inhabitants, to destruction: its sins were greater and more numerous than those of Sodom, and Samaria; the destruction of which nations was a loud warning to their more wicked sister, but was not improved to any good purpose.

The books of the co-temporary prophets, Jeremiah and Ezekiel, are mostly filled up with catalogues of crimes committed by this rebellious people, and threatenings of judgements, which were soon after executed.

There is a catalogue of sins in the xxii chapter of this prophecy, and twelve first verses, sufficient to justify the question which is asked in the 14th verse, "Can thine heart endure, or can thine hands be strong in the days that I shall deal with thee? I Jehovah have spoken it, and will do it." Terrible words indeed; and sufficient to make the heart of every sinner tremble!

But though Jerusalem was so sunk in wickedness, yet some were found therein, who were so far from committing, or even approving of these abominations, that they spent their days in sighing, and their nights in weeping, crying, and lamenting; these persons, however obscure, unknown, or despised by men, were highly approved of by God, who always regards such as are poor and contrite, and who tremble at his word. These mourners in Zion were not only known and regarded by the Lord, but were preserved in the midst of that ruin and total destruction, which overwhelmed the miserable inhabitants of that devoted city.

Before Jehovah gave command to the ministers of vengeance to smite, he sent the man, or angel, clothed with linen, who had a writer's inkhorn by his side, through the city, to mark all that were found mourning for the sins of the times; and when this was done, the others were ordered to slay without mercy or distinction, old and young, maids, little children, and women; and were ordered to begin at the sanctuary, among the antient men that were before the house, and to defile the house, and to fill the courts with the slain; but by no means to come near any of those who had the mark upon their foreheads.

In Rev. vii. we find that when the angels had power given them, to hurt the earth, and the sea, another angel ascended "from the east, having the seal of the living God; and he cried with a loud voice to the four angels, to whom it was given to hurt the earth and the sea, saying, Hurt not the earth, neither the sea, nor the trees, till we have sealed the servants of our God in their foreheads."...

Though I have been in Virginia but a few days, I have seen and heard that which greatly affects my heart, and I shall therefore take notice of some of those abominations which, I fear, greatly prevail in this country, and which threaten it with ruin and desolation, unless repentance and reformation prevent....

The most favourable construction that can be put upon the slave trade, is, that the desire of riches in general, and especially the hopes of growing suddenly rich, move men to engage therein. I say, this is the most favourable construction that can be put upon it; for I can hardly suppose, that mere wantonness, envy, cruelty, passion, revenge, or lust of power and dominion, or even ambition, can have any hand at all in this infamous traffic. And in fact, the only reason why it is not abolished, is because the interest of nations, companies, and individuals, is supposed to be connected therewith; though in the end it is more against their true interest than can be well imagined, as shall be shewn presently.

Having considered the principle from whence it originated, and to which its existence is owing, I pass to mention the horrible manner in which it is carried on. And here almost every vice that blackens and degrades human nature is employed; such as, deceiving, perfidy, decoying, stealing, lying, fomenting feuds and discords among the nations of Africa, robbery, plunder, burning, murder, cruelty of all kinds, and the most savage and unexampled barbarity.

Blush, O ye christians, to think that ye are the supporters of a commerce that employs these, and many other vices to carry it on! Could you but think seriously of the disgraceful and cruel manner in which slaves are obtained, methinks you could not attempt to justify the horrid practice. Numbers are stolen while going out on their lawful business, are never suffered to return home to take leave of their friends; but are gagged and bound, then carried on board the vessels which wait for them, never more to see their native land again, but to drag out a miserable existence in chains, hunger, thirst, cold, nakedness, hard labour, and perpetual slavery.

Think, O ye tender mothers, how would you feel, if, when ye should send your little boys or girls to fetch a pitcher, or calabash of water from the spring, you should never see them return again! if some barbarous kidnapper should watch the opportunity, and seize upon your darlings, as the eagle upon its prey! should gagg your sweet prattling babes, and force them away! how would your eyes with tears run down! how would your souls refuse to be comforted! such is the pain that many mothers feel in Africa, and God can cause it to come home to yourselves, who contribute to such an abomination as this. Think, O ye parents, how ye would feel, if when ye sent your children into the field to watch the corn, and drive the birds away, they should be thus stolen and carried off! yet this many poor Africans experience. Many poor women take their children and go down to the rivers to wash the sand, and get gold dust; while thus employed, their foes dart upon them, take their gold and their children, nor let them return to give any account to their unfortunate husbands of the disaster. The husband comes in from the little field, to eat his chearful meal with his wife and children, whom he expects to find returned with the shining ore;—but, alas! he finds them not!—he goes towards the river—he calls—but receives no answer; at last he ventures to the shore, finds the place where the partner of his little joys was employed,—but, alas! she is gone—no more to bless his longing eyes!—he returns, frantic with rage, sorrow, and despair, and curses the authors of such horrid cruelty!

Numbers are decoyed, and perfidiously carried off; and by various ways the inhuman savages that are employed in this diabolical business, make up their cargoes.

But the great engine of all is War. Those who carry on this abominable trade, endeavour to foment discord among the natives; and by money, strong drink, and various articles of superfluity (which they would be better without) set one nation against another, for no other purpose than to get all the prisoners they may take, as slaves.

Now transport yourselves in imagination to Africa, and see the two armies assembled to battle; how they meet with fury! they rush like lions and tigers to the prey; both parties fight with great obstinacy, knowing what will be the fate of the conquered; they who are taken in the field, with all the families of the conquered party, must be bound upon the spot, and delivered into the hands of strangers, who wait to receive them at a certain price, and to carry them into a foreign land, as the poor creatures think, to be eaten, but, in reality, to suffer miseries worse than death. The hopes of overcoming, and fears of being overcome, cause both parties to fight with such rage as commonly ends in the destruction of nearly half the men engaged.

But now the carnage is over; victory is declared for one party, though with great loss; perhaps two thirds of the conquered are slain upon the spot, before they will yield. Oh, the dying groans! the cries of the wounded! the shrieks of the women and children who have lost their friends in the battle, and are now to be seized on and sold!—But the scene is too shocking to describe in this assembly—let imagination conceive the rest if possible!!!

Who can describe the miseries which they experience in the passage from their country to this? Loaded with chains, confined in putrid air, exhausted with hunger, thirst, sorrow and despair, many die in the voyage; these are happy, compared with those that remain alive—you know the rest—My heart recoils at the thoughts of the shocking manner in which they are disposed of. Parents separated from their children, wives from their husbands, children from each other, &c. See, they take, if suffered, a last parting embrace—to meet no more—how affecting to those in whom humanity is not entirely extinguished!

But I must proceed to consider the baleful effects of such a shocking commerce, for a little attention may convince us that it is prejudicial to our best interests. That abundance of *idleness* is introduced through the *slave trade*, is what no sensible person can deny. They who have slaves to labor for them, rarely ever labor themselves, or bring up their children to labor: and be it remembered, that Idleness is one of the sins for which Sodom was destroyed, and is not only a great crime in itself, but lays men open to every temptation, and wholly unfits them for virtue and usefulness. Slavery not only encourages idleness among the higher class of people, but among the lower ranks also; for it is observed, that where it is allowed in any country the poorer sort of people refuse to labor for the rich, lest they should be put upon a footing with their slaves: so that the influence of this inhuman traffic extends its mischievous effects, in this respect, farther than one might imagine. When industry ceases, farewell to virtue, sobriety, and frugality.

Pride is another of the baleful effects of this trade; or whether it is not in some measure a cause, I shall not positively determine, but there is not the smallest doubt of their close connection. This is another of the sins of Sodom, and which drew down the vengeance of God upon those cities; and shall we hope to escape?

Haughtiness is another of the sins of Sodom, and is always connected with keeping slaves, as is well known to all that are acquainted with the matter.

It is to be noted, that *uncleanness* prevails in a most horrid manner where slaves are kept; for they being in a state of absolute subjection to their masters, cannot in any instance resist their will, and if they should dare to do so, they would be corrected, till they would submit to whatever their wicked pleasure might be.

But of all other effects the *slave trade* has the most immediate and direct tendency to banish all humanity and compassion from the breasts of men, and to fill them with *hardness* of *heart*, and the greatest imaginable Cruelty: The amazing barbarities exercised upon slaves by their unfeeling task masters, are truly astonishing, and will hardly be credited by people who have never seen them inflicted.

The practice of keeping slaves cannot fail of hardening the hearts of mankind, for even little children are taught, from their cradles, to consider the poor creatures as their property, and to exercise the most brutal cruelties upon them with the least pity.

In fine, the *slave trade* has introduced many vices, and brought many more to a greater height than they could otherwise have risen; and its baleful effects upon the morals of men are too evident, and it must finally (unless a speedy stop is put thereto) prove destructive to our temporal interests, as well as to our eternal welfare.

Which naturally brings me to consider the horrid fearful and dangerous consequences, with which this Capital Crime is pregnant.

I call it a *capital crime*, because God hath made it so. Exod. xxi. 16. "And he that stealeth a man, and selleth him, or if he be found in his hand, he shall surely be put to death." To this some, perhaps, may answer, "They were only forbid to steal and sell their brethren, the children of Israel, but were allowed to make slaves of the nations of the land of Canaan; therefore it is lawful to make slaves of the Africans." I grant the premises, but deny the consequence, till you can shew as good a warrant for making slaves of the Africans, as the Israelites had for destroying and enslaving the Canaanites; viz. the positive command of God: till this is done, which can never be, all such reasoning is vain and inconclusive.

God "hath made of one blood all nations of men to dwell on all the face of the earth, and hath determined the times before appointed, and the bounds of their habitation, that they should seek the Lord, if haply they might feel after him and find him." Christ hath shed his blood for all nations, and therefore why should we counteract the kind intentions of heaven, by enslaving and making them miserable, and thereby putting an effectual bar in the way of their conversion?

But were it even lawful to keep them as slaves, what just judgment is due for the barbarous and inhuman treatment they meet with from the hands of their cruel masters?

What doth holy Job tell us? O that his words might be duly considered by all that have servants!

"If I did despise the cause of my man servant, or of my maid servant, when they contended with me: what then shall I do when God riseth up? and when he visiteth, what shall I answer him? did not he that made me in the womb make him? and did not one fashion us in the womb?" Job. xxxi. 13, 14, 15.

Alas! what an account will many masters and mistresses have to give to God respecting their treatment to their slaves! they will not suffer them to contend with them at all; they do more than despise the causes of their men servants and maid servants; they will not even hear them.

Such an account as they will have to give for whipping, burning, starving them, suffering them to go naked, and to be in want of all the necessaries of life, while they themselves live in ease and affluence, procured by the labor, sweat, and blood of their slaves, will cover their faces with shame, and will make them tremble before the bar of God.

Now conscience sleeps, but how will it awake hereafter! when they shall hear words like these, "He shall have judgment without mercy, that hath shewed no mercy. Remember that thou, in thy life-time, receivedst thy good things, and likewise thy slave evil things; but now he is comforted, and thou art tormented. How much she hath glorified herself, and lived deliciously, so much torment and sorrow give her," James ii. 13. Luke xvi. 25. Rev. xviii. 7.

Alas! I would choose to be in the situation of the slaves, rather than in that of their masters; for if there is a just God, he will punish those who sin against his authority; and who is able to endure his displeasure?

But when, in addition to all these charges, which will be proved against the holders of slaves in general, and confirmed by the testimony of their own consciences, they shall be charged with refusing to instruct them in the christian religion, not even suffering them to go to a place of worship, nor allowing them to be taught to read, nor giving them time to pray, and frequently making them to work upon the Lord's day, and all this notwithstanding *that vain pretence* which they sometimes make in favour of slavery; viz. that the negroes should be brought out of their own country in order to be christianized; how will they be able to answer for themselves?

How the poor creatures groan and cry under their bitter bondage, to that God who is able to avenge them! and let their oppressors tremble at the thought that *God will bring every work into judgment*; and that eternal sorrow will be the just reward of their crimes except they repent.

Hitherto I have chiefly considered the consequences of abusing slaves, but if we have no right at all to hold them in slavery, the case is much altered, not in our favour, but against us; if the thing itself is a crime, as may be proved from our Saviour's words, "Therefore all things, whatsoever ye would that men should do to you, do ye even so unto them; for this is the law and the prophets," Matt. vii. 12. Luke vi. 31. what have not those to expect who break the law of nature, the law of God, who transgress against the instruction of the prophets, and violate the commands of Christ and his apostles?

I know some will say, that we are only to do to others as we should reasonably expect others to do to us, were we in the same circumstances, and therefore the slaves should be kept in perpetual servitude, but should be well used. But remember Christ says, "And as ye would that men should do to you, do ye to them likewise." Now the plain question is this, If you yourselves had been unlawfully captured and enslaved, without ever forfeiting your liberty by any crime, had you been sold into a foreign country, and forcibly detained in bondage; had you been certain that your master who purchased you, knew of all these circumstances when he bought you, and that he was a professor of a religion which obliged him to *do to all men as he would they should do to him*, upon pain of damnation; would you not wish that he would set you free? would you not have a right to claim your freedom as an act of justice? Acts of kindness, mercy, and generosity, are, in some sort, different from acts of justice; nothing can excuse us for a moment from being *just; generous* we may be according to our power, but justice is a debt that we must pay, or meet the disapprobation of that just Judge, who has declared, that "with what measure ye mete, it shall be measured to you again," Matt. vii. 2. Mark iv. 24. And not only so, but he uses four different expressions, to shew in what manner we are to expect it, 1. "*good measure*, 2. *pressed down*, 3. and *shaken together*, 4. and *running over*, shall men give into *your own bosom*. For with the same measure that ye mete withal, it shall be measured to you again." Luke vi. 38. If the words of Christ prove true, you that hold slaves have every thing to fear, unless you repent and reform. This abomination is sufficient to make the land desolate and waste, it is a national sin, and will bring down national punishment, unless it be repented of. If the words of Christ are true, the slaves will at length be free; and if you refuse and rebel, you will be enslaved, or devoured by the sword; and this may be depended upon. God knows how to deliver these poor oppressed creatures, and to render seven-fold to those who have so long and unjustly detained them in slavery.

Think how you would feel, at the thoughts of your posterity being slaves, to the posterity of those whom you keep now in bondage. Oh! how much blood must be shed, before such an event can take place! but remember, the blood that has been shed in Africa, this may come home, and those whom you at present oppress, may be your oppressors; and be sure, if that should be the case, they will render you ten-fold. This event may easily take place, if God pleases; the slaves are strong and numerous, notwithstanding all the miseries they suffer; they increase rapidly, and should a war break out, the consequences might be serious.

The Israelites were long enslaved in Egypt, but the time of their deliverance came at last; and now the Egyptians are in bondage themselves, and have been for ages. Take heed that this be not your case. God visits the iniquities of the fathers upon the children, unto the third and fourth generation of them that hate him. It is now the third and fourth generation since the Africans have been enslaved by the English; and perhaps the time of their deliverance is at the door. God prepare us for the things that are coming upon us!

But some say, What shall we do? the law of the province forbids us to set them free? I know it; and it is for a lamentation that it is so; but all you can do at present, is to "sigh and cry for all the abominations that are done in the midst of the land," and for this in particular; so will God set a mark upon you, and spare you in the day of indignation.

If any of you are clear from having a hand in this iniquitous trade, by all means keep so; have nothing to do with it; it is an accursed thing, for which the wrath of God will be poured out upon this nation, if the word of God be true, unless repentance and reformation prevent; for he will assuredly vindicate the cause of the oppressed, and open a door for their deliverance, even though it should be by the destruction of their oppressors.

As for you that have them in possession, and cannot set them free by the law, treat them well, and wait for the time when you may be able to give them liberty, which is the greatest blessing next to life; for I cannot help thinking that some revolution is at the door, and perhaps, is nearer and greater than we expect. In the mean time it becomes us to repent, and humble ourselves before God, and lament our own sins, and sigh and cry for all the abominations that are committed in our land; and deprecate the judgments that await our nation in general, and these colonies in particular; and let us say, "Spare thy people, O Lord, and give not thine heritage to reproach, that the heathen should rule over them: wherefore should they say among the people, Where is their God?"

Levi Hart, Thoughts on Abolition, 1775

The Connecticut Historical Society Library, Hartford, Conn.

In his 1774 sermon, Liberty Described and Recommended, *Levi Hart passionately implored Americans to enlist in the great moral and spiritual crusade of antislavery. The institution of slavery, he declared, was an evil blight on society, an affront to natural and divine law. But Hart, along with other abolitionists, recognized the practical difficulties strewn along the path to reform. In an unpublished treatise entitled* Some Thoughts on the Subject of Freeing the Negroes, *Hart discussed the objections raised against abolition, and his specific proposals to mollify those objections. His scheme provided for the indemnification of owners for the loss of private property. It called for the service of ex-slaves for a number of years in a state of indentured servitude, preparatory to their entering civil society as freedmen. These and other of Hart's provisions were later incorporated into gradual abolition laws in several states, including his own, Connecticut. Antislavery advocates were forced to combat the genuine fear among many that abolition would bring in its wake intolerable hordes of ex-slaves disrupting American society. Hart responded to this fear with an assertion with a peculiarly modern timbre—the dispossessed of society, if given property and a stake in the community, would react responsibly. ". . . The common interest which they would then have with us in the good order of ye government and preservation of private property," Hart maintained, "would be an argument of weight on the side of good behaviour in them."*

It is not my design to enter largely into the Arguments by which the slave trade is proved to be criminal & inhumane; this hath been done by abler hands: & Seems to be *now* generally conceded. If it were not, I think an appeal might be made to every man's conscience—It is a fundamental maxim, both of natural & revealed religion that we should do to others in all things, as we would that they should do to us. Every man is conscious to himself that he is not willing that others should enslave him, & can easily feel, or rather cannot avoid feeling, the consequence that if he enslave any of his fellow men he violates a fundamental maxim of natural & revealed religion. But if it is criminal to bring a fellow creature into Slavery (who hath not forfeited his liberty by any misconduct) it is also criminal to retain him in Slavery; it is in effect, a constant acting over the same crime which was committed in enslaving him at first: for if he had a right to liberty at first, his being forcibly reduced to Slavery could not deprive him of that right. This is so plainly true that an attempt to prove it would even be an

Some thoughts on the Subjects of freeing the Negro-Slaves in the Colony of Connecticutt, humbly offered to the Consideration of all friends to liberty & Justice.

c. 1775 Hart, Levi Rev. 1738-1808 of Preston

As the Subject of making & keeping Slaves, is become so interesting, I presume you will accept the following attempt in favor of the poor oppressed Africans.

It is not my design to enter largely into the arguments by which the slave trade is proved to be criminal & inhumane; this hath been done by abler hands; & seems to be now generally conceded. if it were not, I think an appeal might be made to every man's conscience — It is a fundamental maxim, both of natural & revealed religion that we should do to others in all things, as we would that they should do to us. Every man is conscious to himself that he is not willing that others should enslave him, & can easily feel, or rather cannot avoid feeling, the consequence that if he enslave any of his fellow men he violates a fundamental maxim of natural & revealed religion. But if it is criminal to bring a fellow creature into slavery (who hath not forfeited his liberty by any misconduct) it is also criminal to retain him in slavery; it is in effect, a constant acting over the same crime which was committed in enslaving him at first: for if he had a right to liberty at first, his being forcibly reduced to slavery could not deprive

First manuscript page of Levi Hart's unpublished anti-slavery pamphlet, circa 1775.

affront to the understanding of every man.—the consequence is that the Negro Slaves who have not forfeited their liberty by misconduct in this country have as good a right to their liberty as their masters & it is as direct a violation of the law of God to hold them in Servitude as it would be to reduce their masters to the Same State. It would seem then that no Just good reason can be given why the Negro Slaves should not be immediately made free, & the accursed thing put away from among us, but [several] objections have been made which however may I think, be reduced to the two following, viz. that the owners of Slaves will be injured by their being made free, unless they are some way indemnified—& that the Slaves when made free will be an insupportable burden to Society, through their imprudence, & vicious & immoral behavior. These difficulties ought to be duly considered. With respect to the first, viz. that the Slaves cannot be made free without Injury to their Masters. The true State of the case appears to be this: the Owners of the Slaves have purchased them under the patronage of Government: & the public faith is, in effect, plighted to protect & support them in the possesion of their Slaves, or indemnify them if they are taken away. This must be understood to be implied in the laws & regulations respecting Slaves in this colony & accordingly hath been so understood by the owners, as it is evident no prudent man would purchase, & pay for a Slave unless he was satisfied of the patronage of government to support his claim, any sooner than he would purchase land, or any other commodity without such Security.

It may then be considered as the common & just Sense of the owners of Negro slaves in this Colony that the faith of government is plighted to protect them in the enjoyment of their Supposed property in these Slaves as much as in the enjoyment of any other property (& therefore that no Authority on earth can deprive them of their Slaves without indemnifying them for their loss.) The most proper way therefore, in which the Slaves can be made free is for it to be done by the Act of the legislature of the colony & for the owner to be indemnified at the public cost. (This is I mean the most proper way unless when the owners are willing to manumit their Slaves without any indemnification: for every master hath a good right to give freedom to his Slave without any regard, if he think proper) yea he is bound in duty to free him in this manner, if the legislature refuse or neglect to do it, as will more fully appear before we have done I am sensible this will be objected to, by some who are not owners of Slaves as being unreasonable that they who have had no hand in the slave trade should be punished together with the guilty persons, by being obliged to bear a part of the expence of their freedom. But it will appear, when properly considered, that the whole community, & consequently the individuals, or parts of which it is made up, is concerned in the slave trade. It hath been already observed that this trade hath carried on under the patronage of the legislature but is not the legislature a representation of the whole body of the people, so that each man is in effect, present & hath his voice in the enacting the laws? else where is the mightly privilege in which the Colonists glory of being taxed only by their own consent? & what ground have we of complaint against taxation by the British parliament as less friendly to liberty than if done by our own Legislators.

If the above observations are just (and they will not be questioned?) each individual in the Colonies, as a member of the community, is as really concerned in the Slave trade as the owners of Negros & therefore as really obliged to bear his part of the expence in procuring their freedom. This is, I think . . . agreeable to reason & the law of nature. & what will be conceded by every one not blinded by interest. But it will, perhaps, be further objected, that such an indemnification to the owners of Slaves, for their freedom will bring a vast & insupportable expence upon the Colony. To this it may be answered that be the expence what it may, this is no reasonable objection in the present case. For if the Slaves have a right to their freedom & we have been guilty of robing of that invaluable Jewel hitherto it is more than time to do them Justice & the greatness of the expence attending that act of Justice only evidences the greatness of the injury done to the Negros for their liberty cannot be of greater value to their owners than to themselves. So that were it to take our whole interest, even to the last farthing to procure their freedom this could be no reasonable objection any more in the case before us than in that of a common debtor, or even a Thief or Robber who should object against paying his debts, or making restitution that it was too expensive: or that it would strip him of his whole estate to make payment.

But it may be farther observed that the expence in this case would probably be far less than is imagined, & even inconsiderable, to a generous mind.—This will be evident from the following consideration, viz.

1. Neither reason or Justice will dictate that the masters should be indemnified for their Slaves at the price which they have usually been sold, in the colonies; but only so far as their interest suffers a diminution by the freedom of their Slaves which would not be avoided by their continuing in a state of Servitude—if this be done the owners will be treated according equity & will only bear their proportion of the public expence of freeding their Slaves.—

2. All the Negro Slaves born in the colonies, & in a state of Minority must be supposed to pay for their education by a certain age: & it is equitable that they should serve their masters till they have returned an equivalent for their education—this perhaps should be somewhat later than the period of life fixed upon by authority for white children to become free, as that period was not fixed upon so much on account of the child's having returned an equivalent to the parent for his education, as that he is supposed capable at that time of life to regulate his own behaviour, & provide for himself—however, it is presumed this time of Service could not be equitably lengthened out beyond the age of 24 or 25 years for males & something less for females—but be this as it may it doth not affect the present argument.

3. None of those who either by advanced age, infirmity or any thing by which they are rendered unprofitable at present, or by which there is reason to think they will not be profitable on the whole, taking in the whole of their life yet to come; none of these I say would be any expence to the public—if they are made free their owners would be entitled to no reward as they would sustain no loss.

4. Those who are become unprofitable, by age, or any other cause, ought to be supported by their owners during the remainder of their lives—of this the owners could not complain—since they have obliged themselves by purchasing their Slaves to support them if they become unprofitable, and they have no other burden, on the

present supposition, than what they would have had, & by their own consent, if no methods were adopted for the freedom of the Slaves. I must add that it should be the care of the Selectmen of each town, or some proper persons appointed by authority for that purpose, that such aged or infirm Negroes be supported in a decent & comfortable manner.

These things being premised, the way is open to form some rational conjectures of what the expence to the public would really be in freeing the Negro Slaves agreeable to the plan already proposed.

There are in the Colony of Connecticut, according to the account published by order of the General Assembly for January 1:1774, five thousand & eighty five Negroes of which two thousand four hundred & seventy one are under twenty years of age & of the remaining 2614 those who are passed the age of 50 years will not, one with another, be esteemed of any value, suppose this to be one in ten (& it is probably more) there will remain 2353.—Of this number it may be supposed that a fifty part are born in this country, & are still in the Service of those who educated them, or of their heirs, & consequently should be made free without any indemnification to their masters. Let it be supposed that the remaining 1883 are owned by masters who purchased them at the age of 25 years & that the price was 60 pounds for males & 40 pounds for females, i.e., fifty pounds each at an average—put the case as hath already been supposed, that a tenth part, survive the age of 50 years, the remaining 1700 must be considered as dying before they are fifty years old so that the life of each one is for each year at the risque of 1 to 25, i.e., a risque to his owner of 40 shillings by the year—the service of the Slave must therefore be worth to his owner enough to support him with food & cloathing, pay the interest of his purchase & all other contingencies & produce a clear profit to his master sufficient to countervail the risque of his life wh is 40 shillings each year. & also to pay the principle or first cost by the time he arrives at the age of 50 years, this is at an average 40 shillings by the year, so that for every year which the Slave hath served his master there must be a deduction of 4 lb from his first cost. Now let 1700 the number of Slaves to be paid for by the Colony be divided by 25, the number of years in wh they are all supposed to die (of if they do not, to arrive at 40—the age when they will have paid their owners & be of no value to them) the Quotient will be 68 the number wh must be Supposed to be in each respective year of the 25 years of servitude, the price of each to diminish at the rate of 4 lb each year from the age of 25 to 37½ when those who survive will have paid. Thus 68 Slaves at 50 pounds each will amount to 3400 pounds. the price of those who are newly purchased, at the age of 24 years—& so of the rest according to the following table

No. of Slaves	Age	Price
68 --------------	25	£ 3400
68 --------------	26	3128
68 --------------	27	2856
68 --------------	28	2584
68 --------------	29	2312
68 --------------	30	2040
68 --------------	31	1768
68 --------------	32	1496
68 --------------	33	1224
68 --------------	34	952
68 --------------	35	680
68 --------------	36	408
68 --------------	37	136
68 --------------	37½	000
		£21984

The sum to be paid by the Colony to indemnify the owners, of the Slaves, for those who have lived with them to the age of 37½ years must be supposed to have paid them for their expense in purchasing them. if it be said that those whose Slaves have died between the age of 25 & 37½ ought to be indemnified for their loss, I answer if it be done it should be at the expence of those whose Slaves have over lived that time: for it is as reasonable that those last should refund the earnings of their Slaves after that time as that the others should be indemnified for the loss of theirs before its time, as appears by the preceding calculation they must be supposed to have paid their owners by that time; so that here will be no expence to the Colony. The whole list of the Colony for the year 1774 was about 1,972,072 pounds. Consequently a colony tax of 3 pence on ye pound will raise 24650—a sum more than sufficient to defray the expence by 2616 pounds. This leads to the other branch of our subject, which was to consider obviate the objections against freeing the Negroes, taken from the supposed imprudent & vicious conduct of the free Negroes & the Injury which would probably be sustained by individuals & the public through their abuse of liberty.

It is said that the Negros have not sufficient discretion to conduct their own affairs & provide for themselves, & that many of them are addicted to stealing, & other enormities *Now* & would probably be much more so if they were not under the care & government of masters who restrain them—that if they were free, they would find means to perpetrate so many horrid crimes in stealing & housebreaking if not robbing and murdering that private property would, by no means, be safe, & an irreparable injury be hereby done to the public.

To all this & everything of the like kind, it may be replied, that there is no apparent want of capacity in the Negros in general to conduct their own affairs & provide for themselves, but what is the natural consequence of the

Servile state they are in, & the treatment they receive.—Our national pride leads us to imagine them, by nature, much inferior to ourselves in intellectual powers; but this ungenerous self-applauding preference, doth not appear to be supported by fact, when proper allowance is supposed for the difference of education & condition in our favor. this difference is indeed very great, & its influence on us tolerably judged of, by those only, who have a good acquaintance with human nature & have seen the extreme difference which takes place between one person & another by education and external condition—and can judge now a state of abject Slavery breaks the spirits & benumbs the powers of the human mind.

And as to their vicious & immoral character we have need to procede with caution in censoring them as more so than ourselves lest we are found guilty of judging (unscrupulously) another man's servant & of perverting the judgment of the stranger & of the afflicted. As to their growing more vicious & disorderly, & in particular, more given to stealing by being made free the prospect is, I think, quite the contrary for then they will be members of the community, & have a common interest with others in the support of good order & preservation private property; whereas *now* they have no property to be exposed & so no interest in good order. & the preservation of it. Beside, they now feel a sense of Injury in the loss of their liberty, & view themselves as entitled to a reward from their masters for their service, & as they have no hope that their masters will do them justice, they apply the law of retalliation, & privately take & dispose of their master's interest, when they suppose they can do it with impunity.—But if the Negro were made free, these temptations to theft would be removed & the opposite motives to a virtuous behaviour set before them,—gratitude to the white people for procuring their liberty would tend strongly to unite them to our interest & preserve them from attempting to injure us, & it hath already been observed that the common interest which they would then have with us in the good order of ye government, & preservation of private property would be an argument of weight on the side of good behaviour in them. So that, for anything which appears, the consequence of freeing the Negros would not be injurious to the public, or to private property; especially as, in that case, any criminals found among them might be punished according to the laws of the land.—

But after all it will be said by some that there are many licentious persons among the Negros whose example will lead many more into vicious & destructive courses when they are at their own disposal, so that they will be very destructive members of Society, &, on the whole, the making them free will be attended with consequences more injurious than the evil designed to be avoided by it. I am sensible it would be vain to expect that every one should be convinced: the minds of men are so different & their perceptions so various. & this is a subject on which so many have been used to think in a different manner, & so many are under temptations from private interest which in many cases, insensibly blinds & influences men of character & worth, & from the influence of which, perhaps, none are perfectly free in the present life. Yet I beg liberty to submit the following scheme for obviating the difficulties, in freeing the Negro Slaves to the consideration of all serious inquirers after truth.

I. That the Slaves be made free by an act of the General Assembly of the Colony, on the terms already proposed, in the preceding part of this work.—Those under the age of 25 years, or what age soever the general assembly, in their wisdom think equitable considering the expence of their education; to continue in the service of their masters till they arrive at that age & then go out free without any reward to their masters and those who are more than fifty to continue in their masters' families, & be supported at their expence, & that it shall be the duty of the Selectmen of each town to see that they are well treated & comfortably provided for, if complaint be made to them that they are not so treated, they shall make inquiry whether complaint appear to be well founded & redress the injured in some way directed in that case by the legislature.—that those who have served 12½ years with their master, any time between the age of 25 & 50 shall go out free without any reward to their master, having rendered an equivalent to him for their price, according to the preceding calculation; and that all others between these two terms of 25 & 50 shall be redeemed by the colony in the method & on the terms above proposed, or such other as the legislature shall in their wisdom think just.

II. That by the same act of the general assembly it be provided that the Slaves continue to serve their present master (or some other person with whom they obtain liberty to live with the approbation of the Selectmen of the town) for the space of one, two, or three years, or such a given time as shall be judged meet, & that the price of their Service shall be adjusted by the Selectmen & that at the end of that time, the money due for their service shall be paid into the town treasury & properly secured for the use of the Negro in the manner hereafter specified.—and the Negro shall then be free, only with an overseer, appointed for one year to advise and instruct them in the improvement of their time & providing for themselves, & after the close of that year, the overseer shall be continued or not as the interest of the Negro appears to require.

III. That the money thus due to the Negros for their service after the passing the act for their freedom shall be a fund under the care of the Selectmen on lawful interest, for their support in case of sickness, old age, or anything by which they come to want & need assistance except in the case of those who are convicted of stealing or some other atrocious crime against the laws.

IV. That all those who are not convicted of any crime & can obtain testimonials from the Selectmen of the town where they reside of their peacable & inoffensive conduct, & who are disposed to return to Affrica, shall be transported thither, at the expence of the Colony, & shall receive the money due to them for their service specified in the two preceding articles as what belongs to them since there will be no danger of their being chargeable to the Colony after their removal thither, and what may enable them to engage in some honest calling in that country, with encouraging prospects.

V. That all such Negroes as shall be legally convicted of stealing, house breaking, immodest conduct towards, or intercourse or pretended marriage with any white person of a different sex; or any other atrocious crime specified by the act of the legislature (those only excepted for which a white person would be punished with death) shall be punished by croping, branding, or some visible mark of distinction & of their crime, & by transportation to Guinea—that the money earned by their service, specified herebefore, or so much of it as shall be found necessary, shall be laid out in their transportation, & the remainder, if any be, shall be equally distributed among those who transport themselves to Guinea for the purpose of settlement, agreable to ye preceding article.

VI. That in all other respects the Negroes continuing to reside in this Colony shall enjoy the benefit of the english laws & secure the same treatment with the white subjects.

Some such general scheme as this, I apprehend, will obviate most if not all of the difficulties objected in the way of freeing the Negroes.—The compensation proposed to be made to their masters will remove the objection of *their* being injured by the dismission of their service, & it is presumed to considerate person in the Colony who hath well weighed the matter in his thoughts will object against paying his proportion of the expence incurred in procuring their freedom.

One great, & perhaps the greatest cause of the imprudence & misconduct of free Negros, & from whence we should have the most to fear, is the sudden, very great change in their condition, from a state of absolute slavery to the same extensive freedom with englishmen. Sudden and great changes, especially from a low, to a comparatively high state, are always dangerous to the morals of persons whether white or black—provision is made to obviate this difficulty in the second article by proposing a gradual change from absolute slavery to full liberty on a plan which, it is presumed, will not be thought injurious to the Negroes by the advocates for their freedom, & which makes provision for their support in sickness or old age without burdening the Colony.

But after all, if through the power of interest & prejudice, such a considerable number should object to this plan that it could not be carried into execution, consistent with the peace and harmony of the Colony; Should this be the case it is to be lamented. However, the following proposal is made to such as object to the preceding plan, as what is calculated in some measure to answer the design & is not liable to the same objection of its bringing an expence on the Colony. It is this, viz.

That by an act of the general Assembly all the Negro Slaves in the colony under the age of fourteen shall be made free at the age of 25, or such other age as they may be supposed to have paid for the expence of their education without any reward to their masters and that all others who have served their present master 12½ years, according to the preceding calculation, or so long as shall be judged an equivalent for the purchase money to the master, shall go out free without any reward to the master—and that all other Negro Slaves in the colony shall be free on the same conditions at the close of the same number of years from the time of their being first owned by their present masters; and that no person shall be suffered, on pain of a sufficient forfiture to sell or transport or by directly or indirectly aiding or assisting in selling or transporting any Negro Slave *out* of the colony, except in the manner, & for the purposes specified in the preceding part of this work, and that no person shall sell or dispose of a Negro Slave to any person residing in this Colony for a longer term than to complete the above limited period from his being first owned by his present master. And that in all other respects the Negros shall be treated according to the method already proposed. This scheme, though not all that could be wished will, eventually, put a total stop to Slavery, & all the oppressed Negros in the Colony, will, at last, go free, & that without any expence to the Colony or injury to their masters; & therefore, cannot be objected to on that account.

Much hath been said against freeing the Negroes on account of the trouble & injury they (as it is supposed) would bring on the white people by stealing & other enormities—provision is made by the fifth article, which if properly executed must effectually deliver the Colony from that trouble & injury & be the best security for private property from suffering by them.—and this without any injustice to the Negros.—the most impartial justice will not pronounce the punishment there specified too severe.

The fourth article proposeth such encouragement to Negros of a good character to return to Affrica as would, probably, induce many of them to return thither, & cultivate the arts & manufactures of their country, not only to their own benefit, but to that of others—as that country is blessed with a rich soil, fruitful seasons, and many valuable articles of trade & commerce.

On the whole, the matter stands thus—we are bound by that great law of reason & religion which . . . us to do to others in all things as we would that they should do to us, to let the oppressed Affricans go free it appears by what hath been offered that this may be done consistently with the public safety. Why therefore shall it not be done—what reason can be given why it should be delayed—is it not an act of justice?—and is it not more than time it should take place?—If the Negro Slavery is an instance of oppression, cruel oppression, as it certainly is, it is at the extremest risque if we still hold fast the accursed thing. for He who is higher than the highest oppression sees & regardeth the oppression of the poor & the violent perverting of judgment & justice in a province & he will hear the cry & avenge the cause of the poor & needy.

The hand of heaven is stretched out against our land at this day for our sins & threatens us with the loss of our invaluable liberties by the hand of our king & the british parliament from whom we expected protection & defence.—against any who should attempt to injure us. & it is highly probably this evil is coming on us as a punishment for oppressing the injured Affricans who have as good a title to freedom as ourselves. It is gods common way to punish communities in a manner answerable to the nature of their crime hence he is praised for the punishment inflicted on the Spiritual Bablyon or crimes to his churches Rev. 16:6.

They have shd blood—& thou has given them blood to drink.—Notwithstanding the many aggravated sins of Judah & Jerusalem before the babylonish captivity—yet that dreadful evil was finally inflicted on that devoted city as a punishment for their retaining in servitude those who were their brethren & had a right to liberty, as will appear to anyone by reading the 34th chap. of Jeremiah from the 8th verse to ye end. and let me ask, are not the Negros our brethren? & have we any more right to hold them in perpetual slavery than the Jews had in the case of their brethren?—under the Mosaic dispensation, he who stole a man was to be put to death whether he sold him or retained him in his own service. See Exodus 21:16—this deserves our serious attention since it is yt great numbers, at least, of the Negro Slaves are stolen in their own country, through the influence of our guinea traders, & then sold; and it is a maxim of common sense that he who knowingly partakes with a thief in what he hath stolen, partaketh with him also in his crime. This passage especially deserves the attention of those who plead the Mosaic dispensation in support of the Affrican Slave trade.

In fine doth it not highly concern every one, in his place to exert himself in a proper manner for the liberty of the oppressed Negros? Since we are all members of the community & as such concerned in this iniquitous traffic we must each of us bear our portion of the guilt attending it till we clear our spirits by striving to put a stop to it. It is offered therefore to the serious consideration of the freemen in the several towns in this colony whether it be not their duty to instruct their representatives for the next general Assembly to exert their endeavours that an act may be passed for the freeing the Negro Slaves in this Colony in such manner, and with such conditions or limitations as the General Assembly shall in their wisdom think proper.

And if other plans prove unsuccessful & the Slaves cannot obtain justice from the General Assembly it is left with the consciences of their masters whether they are not obliged in duty to free them.—this is in their power, & if the public will not hear the voice of justice & the cries of the oppressed, this will not excuse individuals for the same crime. The masters never had any right to the Negro Slaves—It was impossible for any legislative body to give them such a right, for no such right ever existed in any such body.

Had the laws of this Colony connived at, or even patronized theft & housebreaking within the Colony & had you under the patronage of this law become possessed of large sums of money from the thief who stole it from the helpless widow or starving orphan; & did the General Assembly refuse to indemnify you for restoring to the injured their right, would you in this case refuse to restore what was thus stolen & plead in excuse that you gave the thief a valuable consideration for the money that he had stolen? though you knew it to be the property of the injured widow & not of the thief of whom you secured it? I am well assured you would not, or if you did mankind would cry out upon you as being callous not only to the dictates of conscience but to the feelings of humanity.—What must be said then if you had enjoyed the use of such stolen money till you was more than paid for the consideration by which you purchased it of the villain who stole it? The application is too easy to need a particular pointing out and the conclusion is referred to every man's conscience in the sight of God; only it is earnestly requested that the decision may be made in the view of that dread tribunal

& in the sensible awful presence of that strict & impartial judge before whom we must all appear and where both high & low, the master & his Slave must shortly stand!

Thomas Paine, Essay on Slavery, March 8, 1775

Postscript to the Pennsylvania Journal, 8 March 1775.

In November 1774 Thomas Paine, a poor corsetier from England, arrived in Philadelphia bearing a letter from Benjamin Franklin recommending him as an "ingenious worthy young man." On March 8, 1775, William Bradford's Pennsylvania Journal *carried a short essay against slavery written by Paine signed "Justice and Humanity." The tone was harsh, a bitter flailing against a malevolent established order: "That some desperate wretches should be willing to steal and enslave men by violence and murder for gain, is rather lamentable than strange: But that many civilized, nay, Christianized people should approve, and be concerned in the savage practice, is surprising." Later that year Paine began work on another essay, one which Benjamin Rush observed "burst from the press with an effect which has rarely been produced by types and paper in any age or country."*

Much of the same sense of outrage, immediacy, and torment that is woven into the short essay against slavery in 1775 appeared with striking force in Common Sense *in January 1776. Paine, from his earliest days in Philadelphia, lived near a slavemarket. He composed this antislavery piece only a few weeks after his arrival in America. It is noteworthy that the article preceding Paine's essay in the* Pennsylvania Journal *told of an aborted conspiracy among approximately 20 slaves to slaughter white slaveholders after firing their houses. Paine recognized the potential horror that awaited such slave masters. He declared, "So much innocent blood have the Managers and Supporters of this inhuman Trade to answer for. . . ."*

That some desperate wretches would be willing to steal and enslave men by violence and murder for gain, is rather lamentable than strange: But that many civilized, nay, christianized people should approve, and be concerned in the savage practice, is surprising; and still persist, though it has been so often proved contrary to the light of nature, to every principle of Justice and Humanity, and even good policy, by a succession of eminent men, and several late publications.

Our Traders in *Men (an unnatural commodity!)* must know the wickedness of that Slave-Trade, if they attend to reasoning, or the dictates of their own hearts; and such as shun and stiffle all these, willfully sacrifice Conscience, and the character of integrity to that golden idol.

The Managers of that Trade themselves, and others, testify, that many of these African nations inhabit fertile countries, are industrious farmers, enjoy plenty, & lived quietly, averse to war, before the Europeans debauched them with liquors, and bribing them against one another; & that these inoffensive people are brought into slavery, by stealing them, tempting Kings to sell subjects, which they can have no right to do, and hiring one tribe to war against another, in order to catch prisoners. By such wicked and inhuman ways the English are said to enslave towards one hundred thousand yearly; of which thirty thousands are supposed to die by barbarous treatment in the first year; besides all that are slain in the unnatural wars excited to take them. So much innocent blood have the Managers and Supporters of this inhuman Trade to answer for to the common Lord of all!

Many of these were not prisoners of war, and redeemed from savage conquerors, as some plead; and they who were such prisoners, the English, who promote the war for that very end, are the guilty authors of their being so; and if they were redeemed, as is alledged, they would owe nothing to the redeemer but what he paid for them.

They show as little Reason as Conscience who put the matter by with saying—"Men, in same cases, are lawfully made Slaves, and why may not these?" So men, in some cases, are lawfully put to death, deprived of their goods, without their consent; may any man, therefore, be treated so, without any conviction of desert? Nor is this plea mended by adding—"They are set forth to us as slaves, and we buy them without farther inquiry, let the sellers see to it."—Such men may as well join with a known band of robbers, buy their ill-got goods, and help on the trade; ignorance is no more pleadable in one case than the other; the sellers plainly own how they obtain them. But none can lawfully buy without evidence, that they are not concurring with Men-Stealers; and as the true owner has a right to reclaim his goods that were stolen, and sold; so the slave, who is proper owner of his freedom, has a right to reclaim it, however often sold.

Most shocking of all is alledging the Sacred Scripture to favour this wicked practice. One would have thought none but infidel cavillers would endeavour to make them appear contrary to the plain dictates of natural light, and Conscience, in a matter of common Justice and Humanity; which they cannot be. Such worthy men, as referred to before, judged otherways; Mr. Baxter declared, *the Slave-Traders should be called Devils, rather than Christians; and that it is an henious crime to buy them.* But some say, "the practice was permitted to the Jews." To which may be replied,

1. The example of the Jews, in many things, may not be imitated by us; they had not only orders to cut off several nations altogether, but if they were obliged to war with others, and conquered them, to cut off every male; they were suffered to use polygamy and divorces, and other things utterly unlawful to us under clearer light.

2. The plea is, in a great measure, false; they had no permission to catch, and enslave people, who never injured them.

3. Such arguments ill become us, *since the time of reformation came,* under Gospel light. All distinctions of nations, and privileges of one above others, are ceased; Christians are taught to *account all men their neighbours; and love their neighbour as themselves; and do to all men as they would be done by; to do good to all men; and Man-stealing is ranked with enormous crimes.*—Is the barbarous enslaving our inoffensive neighbours, and treating them like wild beasts subdued by force, reconcilable with all these *Divine precepts?* Is this doing to them as we would desire they should do to us? If they could carry off and enslave some thousands of us, would we think it just?—One would almost wish they could for once; it might convince more than Reason, or the Bible.

As much in vain, perhaps, will they search ancient history for examples of the modern Slave-Trade. Too many nations enslaved the prisoners they took in war: But to go to nations with whom there is no war, who have no way provoked, without farther design of conquest, purely to catch inoffensive people, like wild beasts, for slaves, is an hight of outrage against Humanity and Justice, that seems left by Heathen nations to be practised by pretended Christians. How shameful are all attempts to colour and excuse it!

As these people are not convicted of forfeiting freedom, they have still a natural, perfect right to it; and the Governments wherever they come should, in justice, set them free, and punish those who hold them in slavery.

So monstrous is the making and keeping them slaves at all, abstracted from the barbarous usage they suffer, and the many evils attending the practice; as selling husbands away from wives, children from parents, and from each other in violation of sacred and natural ties; and opening the way for adulteries, incests, and many shocking consequences for all which the guilty Masters must answer to the final Judge.

If the slavery of the parents be injust, much more is their children's; if the parents were justly slaves, yet the children are born free; this is the natural, perfect right of all mankind; they owe nothing but a just recompence to those who bring them up: And as much less is commonly spent on them than others, they have a right, in justice, to be proportionably sooner free.

Certainly one may, with as much reason and decency, plead for murder, robbery, lewdness, and barbarity, as for this practice: They are not more contrary to the natural dictates of Conscience, and feelings of Humanity; nay, they are all comprehended in it:

But the chief design of this paper is not to disprove it, which many have sufficiently done; but to intreat Americans to consider,

1. With what consistency, or decency they complain so loudly of attempts to enslave them, while they hold so many hundred thousands in slavery; and annually enslave many thousands more, without any pretence of authority, or claim upon them?

2. How just, how suitable to our crime is the punishment with which Providence threatens us? We have enslaved multitudes, and shed much innocent blood in doing it; and now are threatened with the same. And while other evils are confessed, and bewailed, why not this especially, and publicly; than which no other vice, if all others, has brought so much guilt on the land?

3. Whether, then, all ought not immediately to discontinue and renounce it, with grief and abhorrence? Should not every society bear testimony against it, and account obstinate persisters in it bad men, enemies to their country, and exclude them from fellowship; as they often do for much lesser faults?

The great Question may be—What should be done with those who are enslaved already? To turn the old and infirm free, would be injustice and cruelty; they who enjoyed the labours of their better days should keep, and treat them humanely. As to the rest, let prudent men, with the assistance of legislatures, determine what is practicable for masters, and best for them. Perhaps some could give them lands upon reasonable rent; some employing them in their labour still, might give them some reasonable allowances for it; so as all may have some property, and fruits of their labours at their own disposal, and be encouraged to industry; the family may live together, and enjoy the natural satisfaction of exercising relative affections and duties, with civil protection, and other advantages, like fellow men. Perhaps they might sometime form useful barrier settlements on the frontiers. Thus they may become interested in the public welfare, and assist in promoting it; instead of being dangerous, as now they are, should any enemy promise them a better condition.

5. The past treatment of Africans must naturally fill them with abhorrence of Christians; lead them to think our religion would make them more inhuman savages, if they embraced it; thus the gain of that trade has been pursued in opposition to the Redeemer's cause, and the happiness of men: Are we not, therefore, bound in duty to him and to them to repair these injuries, as far as possible, by taking some proper measures to instruct, not only the slaves here, but the Africans in their own countries? Primitive Christians laboured always to spread their *Divine Religion;* and this is equally our duty while there is an Heathen nation: But what singular obligations are we under to these injured people!

These are the setiments of—Justice, and Humanity.

Anthony Benezet to the Countess of Huntingdon, March 10, 1775

Archives of Selina Hastings, Countess of Huntingdon, Cheshunt College, Cambridge, Eng.

The evangelist George Whitefield wrote in a well-publicized letter of January 23, 1740, which he addressed to the Inhabitants of Maryland, Virginia, and North and South Carolina, "Your dogs are caressed and fondled at your tables; but your slaves, who are frequently styled dogs or beasts, have not an equal privilege. . . . I think God has a quarrel with you, for your cruelty to the poor Negroes." But one year later Whitefield announced that slaves would work on the plantation of "Bethesda," the Orphan House near Savannah, Georgia, which he established under the patronage of the Lady Selina, Countess of Huntingdon, for whom he served as domestic chaplain. Although continuing to hold a paternalistic concern for the protection of the physical and moral well-being of black slaves, Whitefield was convinced of the lawfulness and Biblical justification of slavery. He later remarked that God had designated certain hot climates such as Georgia for the labor of slaves who would work under the benevolent care and religious influence of Christian masters.

Anthony Benezet was a close confidant of the famous preacher. Benezet's father had worked with Whitefield in 1740 to establish a Christian school for Negroes in Nazareth, Pennsylvania, a project which was abandoned when the effort failed to attract sufficient capital. Benezet had many intimate conversations with Whitefield over the slavery issue, but was disheartened over his inability to convert the preacher to the antislavery cause. Whitefield died in 1770; slaves still worked in the fields of the Orphan House. Benezet's appeal of March 10, 1775, to the Countess to end slavery at the institution, reflected the Quaker's anguish over the "selfish views" of ministers of his time—professed moral leaders, who for reasons of "ease, reputation, honour or profit" had succumbed to the horrors of the slave system. The Countess later assured Benezet that she intended to release the slaves of Bethesda, but the Countess's assurances were drowned in the eruption of the Revolutionary War. Slaves were still held as part of the Countess's estate until after Benezet's death in 1784.

Philad.a y 10th mon 4th March 1775

Respected Friend L Huntington The kind of condescention in taking so benevolent a notice of the letter I took the freedom to write to thee concerning the deep sufferings of the oppressed People of Guinea our fellow-men & fellow heirs of the same salvation, thro Christ our Lord: and the dreadful consequent effect it has upon their Lordly oppressors & their unhappy Offspring: was greatfully received by me. I am fully united in sentiment with thee, that vain is the help of man. 'tis God alone, by his Almighty power, who can & will in his own time bring outward, as well as spiritual deliverance to his afflicted & oppressed creatures: nevertheless it has pleased God in all ages to stirr up an holy jealousy in the heart of many, to labour both by word & deed, for the deliverance of their fellow-men, from outward as well as spiritual oppression & distress: The Prophet Ezekiel reminds the people of his day, not only to attend to their call thereto, but of the judgment that will attend a neglect thereof; the principal difficulty is lest we should mistake the activity of our minds for the puttings forth of the divine hand and oh! that I may be preserved in this spot. I am sensible of the great danger which, in this respect, attends upon people of a sanguin disposition, especially such as are naturally favoured with feeling hearts; And I cannot but earnestly wish for my self as well as my brethren the welminded in every religious Denomination whose expectation is from Christ alone, however we may differ in circumstantiels in every respect, and quite clear from giving way to the subtil workings of the selfish principle, so apt imperceptibly to influence the human heart, in things that flatter our humour, & interest. Many well disposed people are ready at their first prospect of some prevailing evils, to say, with one of old, "Is thy servant a Dog that he should do this thing" and yet from a repeated sight & habit of that which flatters self, which sooths our pride & interest, we are too often gradually drawn into the practice & defence of that which we at first, like the Assyrian King, looked upon with abhorence. This I have observed to be more particularly the case with respect to the bondage of the Negroes. I have much desired that the persons persons concerned in the managem.t of the Orphan House at Georgia should be particularly guarded against giving any support to this abominable practice. I have, more than once conversed on this interesting subject with my esteemed friend George Whitefield deceas He at first clearly saw the iniquity of this horrible abuse of the human race, as manifestly appears from the letter he published on that subject, addressed to the Inhabitants of Maryland. Virginia North & South Carolina in the year 1739. after his first Journey, thr'o those Colonies, which I republished, in one of the tracts I sent thee; yet after residing in

Georgia, & being habituated to the sights & use of Slaves, his judgment became so much influenced as to paliate, &, in some measure, defend the use of Slaves, this was a matter of much concern to me, and which I repeatedly, with brotherly freedom, expressed to him. Nevertheless I esteemed & loved him, having long had oppertunity to observe his zeal for what he apprehended truth required: What particularly causes me now to remark upon his sentiments is, lest his approbation thereof should have any influence upon those who now have the management of his interest, in Georgia. some of whom, I apprehend, are like minded, if not yet more inclined to favour the use of & slavery of the Negroes than he was There is particularly in the Collection of his letters, published since his decease, one wrote, from Bristol, the 22 March 1751, which I am apprehensive may give much strength, & be a standing plea to such who catch at everything, much more, a letter wrote by a person of so much weight, to defend their favorite *Diana* by which they have their wealth. His reasonings in that letter appear to me, & indeed to every one with whom I have reasoned upon it, to be very inconclusive, rather beging the question: for tho' the spiritual advantage of the Slaves is pleaded, yet it plainly appears that the temporal advantage, resulting from their labour, is the principal motive for undertaking to defend the practice. The following is an extract of that letter viz

"Thank be to God, I think the time for favouring that Colony, (ie Georgia) seems to become. I think now is the season for us to exert our utmost for the good of the poor Ethiopians. We are told that even they are soon to stretch out their hands unto God. And who knows, but their being settled in Georgia, may be overruled for for this great end. As for the lawfulness of keeping Slaves I have no doubt, since I hear of some that were bought with Abraham's money . & some that were born in his house— And I cannot help thinking that some of those servants mentioned by the Apostles in their Epistles, were or had been slaves. It is plain that the Gibeonites were doomed to perpetual Slavery, & though liberty is a sweet thing to such as are born free, yet to those who never knew the sweets of it, slavery, perhaps, may not be so irksome. However this be, it is plain to a demonstration, that hot countries cannot be cultivated without Negroes. What a flourishing country might Georgia have been had the use of them been permitted years ago! How many white people have been destroyed for want of them; and how many thousands of pounds spent to no purpose at all? Had Mr. Henry been in America. I believe he would have seen the lawfulness & necessity of having Negroes there. And though it is true, that they are brought in a wrong way, from their own country: and it is a trade not to be approved of, yet as it will be carried on whether we will or not: I should think myself highly favoured if I could purchased a good foundation for breeding up their posterity in the nurture & admonition of the Lord"

To take example from the practise of Abraham, even, if it was applicable to the present case, which it is not, can be not president to us, in this dispensation, no more than his conduct, with respect to Agar. would license us to do the same. Many things might, as our Saviour expresse, is in the case of Jews being allowed to rut away their wives be permitted, on account of hardness of their hearts, which was quite inconsistent with the nature of the Gospel; the divine injunction to do unto others as we would be done unto It does not appear that Abraham having bought Slaves or having Slaves born in his house; Or that those servants mentioned by the Apostles were or had been Slaves: Nor the case of the Gibionites, can give the least saction to the horrible abuse of the Negroes both with respect to the method used in procuring them as well as the treatment they receive when brought to labour in our Colonies, & Island. The plea in the purchases of Slaves is a design *of making their lives comfortable & laying a foundation for breeding up their posterity in the nurture & admonition of the Lord*, yet from the whole of this letter its clear, *to a demonstration* that the main aim of his desire of purchasing Slaves was the pecuniar advantage arising therefrom, & the outward advancemt & property of the prosperity of the province. It is a very feeble argument to suppose that these worldly advantages would have influenced Mr Henry, who I suppose was a wellminded person, who saw & declared the iniquity of this practice: However we may in general retain an esteem & love for individuals, yet we must not suffer ourselves to be blinded, by its grounded pretences, founded on those selfish motives, to apt if not, thro divine help particularly guarded against to intrude in a time of weakness upon the heart, of even otherwise, valuable persons. The prophet Ezekiel Chap. 14th Verse 4 plainly declared the liability people are under, of being decieved even that the Lord will suffer them to be deceived. Were the heart does not stand in perfect singleness, in the Case of the Elders of Israel, who were then come to enquire of the Lord, probably not in the resignation to the divine will. As to the idea that hot countries cannot be cultivated without Negroes, the contrary is asserted by John Wesley, from his own experience in the Piece intituled *Thoughts on Slavery* which I herewith send as page 41. This is confirmed from the experience of the Saltzburgers in Georgia & many other in different parts of the West Indies: but even if this was not the case & it be granted that white people are unfit to perform the work, surely there are negroes enough already. viz. Eight or Nine hundred Thousands in our Colonies & Islands exceeding the whites in the proportion of 6 to or 15 to one; there is no need of encouraging the Slave-Trade by purchasing those newly imported, let such as are already in bondage be purchased to be set free, & kept as hired Servants, then will justice be done them; the trade discouraged, & the Negroes from dangerous grudging Slaves become willing minded Labourers they will then probably encrease & having an interest in the welfare of the country, will be its strength & security. It was they that our northern ancestors, after they had embraced the Christian Religion, gradually put an end to ancient Slavery or villanage: When something of this nature is adopted & not till then, we may hope effectually to extend a profitable Christian care for the Souls of these their afflicted Brethren, with a real appearance of Sincerity, & a probability of Success.

Upon the whole, as far as I know my own heart, the whole occasion of my, again, presuming to take up thy time & attention, is from no other motive, but a affectionate & sincere desire that those few welminded people, who are made sensible of the inconsistancy of this practice, with the Gospel of Christ may avoid every thing which will in any wise give countenance or strength thereto. All cannot expect to be called to the ministry of the word, even if in our time we should be favoured with that desirable effusion of the spirit which we have to hope, is not far distant; but we may all manifest our Love our Sympathy by using our best endeavours that justice may be done to these our oppressed Brethren. More especially as its to be feared that this mighty evil will remain as the blood of the oppressed Gibeonites as an Aean upon our Nations till effectual endeavours be used to remove it

I herewith send thee some copies of a late publication, on this interesting subject, being a republication of a piece lately published, by my esteemed Friend John Wesley, upon which I have made some considerable notes & additions, which have occurred since my late publication & which farther evince, the prodigious oppression & cruelty which is always more or less the constant attendant on this enormous evil; and indeed it cannot be otherwise, every thing will be of the nature of its root. "Where there is injustice in the principle there will be inhumanity in the consequence." I who take the freedom to send two copies of a translation I, not long since, made of the writings of an ancient pious Author to which are added some concurring Testimonies, to the truth. which I trust will be agreable to thee. As also, the Journal of one of our Friends (ie) John Woolman not long since deceased at York in the course of his religious visit to your country. The truly Christian resignation, simplicity & zeal which appears thro the thro the whole of his life, will, I trust, afford thee satisfaction & comfort; more especially that of his call to, & progress in the work of the ministry: so clear from selfish views, either of ease, reputation honour or profit: motives which so much influence the modern preachers of most, may I not say, too many, of every denomination. Now begging thy excuse and most favourable construction of any thing I may have improperly expressed intending *indeed*, nothing but esteem & respect to thy self, & concern for the cause of truth. I remain, in that sincerity of affection, in which I desire we may meet, in those regions of peace & love, where the wicked will cease from troubling & the weary be at rest, thy respectful Friend.

Anthony Benezet

I cannot with satisfaction omitt making a farther remark, upon my Friend George Whitefield's letter, How linient how self saving he expresses himself, in his strictures upon the Slave Trade viz. "*That they are brought in a wrong way from their own Country That it is a trade not to be approved of; but that as it will be carried on, whether* we will or not, he should think himself *highly favoured in the purchase of a good number*" Indeed we may expect this trade will continue; whilst those who have been the particular object of the notice of the Nation, as promulgators of the Gospel, reason in this manner, instead of bearing their Christian Testimony, against this outragious violation of the rights of Mankind: This worst of evils; for indeed, records of ancient times, do not afford any evil, if considered in its extent, & duration; & all its other circumstances, so complicately horrible viz. The manner by which they are procured & brought from their own country, more especially as it is done by professed Christians & overlooked by the Society for Propagsing the Gospel, the Bishops &c. The usage they generally meet with in the passage, in order to keep them from rising; proceeding often to the murder of many of them, without any check from the Law The continual lash of their hard Task Master, with few exceptions: when set to labour not not to omitt the dreadful effect this dreadful practice has upon their Lordly oppressors & their unhappy offspring, for most of whom its to be feared, Christ has shed his precious blood in vain. I would by no means. if possible to be avoided, offend the least of my fellow creatures much more such as are respectable & truth concerned for y prosperity of truth & who are; above all things, desirous to comply with the will & to have a part in the love of Christ. there, however they may differ in some circumstancial, are indeed brethren, in the fullest sense of the expression. Nevertheless, where the lives & natural as well as religious welfare of so vast a number of our Fellow Creatures is concerned, to be Silent, where we apprehend is a duty to speak our sense of that which causes us to go mourning on our way, would be criminal.

Preamble, Constitution of the Society for the Relief of Free Negroes Unlawfully Held in Bondage, 1775

William F. Poole, *Anti-Slavery Opinions before the Year 1800* (Cincinnati, 1873), pp. 43-44.

On April 14, 1775, at the Sun Tavern in Philadelphia, America's first antislavery organization, The Society for the Relief of Free Negroes Unlawfully Held in Bondage, met for the first time. Composed largely of Philadelphia Quakers, the society, as the preamble to its constitution announced, was dedicated to the assistance of "negroes and others" who had been illegally seized and forced into slavery. Although the society, which Carl Bridenbaugh has called the first "Freedman's Bureau," met only four times in 1775 and held no meetings during the course of the war, individual members continued to press for action against kidnappers and solicit support for antislavery among the larger Philadelphia community. As Tench Coxe, a supporter of the society, later remarked, "the political disturbances interrupted for a time the progress of the institution. It is well known that certain members of the Society even in the deranged situation of affairs steadily employed themselves in the propogation of their principles." When members met again in February 1784 such prominent individuals as Benjamin Rush, Robert Morris, and Anthony Benezet had endorsed their work. Many lawyers began to give free advice and assistance to the organization.

The society, reorganized as the Pennsylvania Abolition Society in 1787, was the precursor of other societies formed in the following years throughout the northern colonies. These societies devoted their efforts not only to protecting the legal rights of free Negroes, but also agitated for abolition laws, distributed antislavery propaganda, secured employment for free Negroes, and provided for their education. The development of such societies proved to be one of the most significant achievements of the early antislavery movement.

Whereas, there are in this and the neighboring states a number of negroes and others kept in a state of slavery, who, we apprehend, from different causes and circumstances, are justly entitled to their freedom by the laws and Constitution under which we live, could their particular cases be candidly and openly debated, and evidence to the best advantage for them procured; but as in their situation, they, being tied by the strong cords of oppression, are rendered incapable of asserting their freedom, and many through this inability remain unjustly in bondage through life; it therefore has appeared necessary that some aid should be extended towards such poor unhappy sufferers, wherever they may be discovered, either in this city or its neighborhood; and, as loosing the bonds of wickedness, and setting the oppressed free, is evidently a duty incumbent on all professors of Christianity, but more especially at a time when justice, liberty, and the laws of the land are the general topics among most ranks and stations of men. Therefore, being desirous, as much as in us lies, to contribute towards obtaining relief for all such as are kept thus unjustly in thralldom, we have agreed to inspect and take charge of all the particular cases which may hereafter come to our knowledge; and that our good intentions may operate the more successfully, and be of general utility to such as stand in need of our assistance, we judge it expedient to form ourselves into a regular society, by the name of "The Society for the Relief of Free Negroes unlawfully held in Bondage."

Thomas Paine, "A Serious Thought," October 18, 1775

The Pennsylvania Journal and the Weekly Advertiser, 18 October 1775.

As abolitionists applied the Revolutionary War ideology of natural rights and freedom to the cause of the black slave, some began to link antislavery with the drive for independence. On October 18, 1775, less than three months before the pamphlet, Common Sense, *appeared in print, Thomas Paine published his second antislavery piece in the* Pennsylvania Journal. *In this 350-word essay Paine foresaw the end of the tyranny of British rule in America—a rule epitomized by the "horrid cruelties" of the slave system. Six months earlier, after the Battle of Lexington, Paine had read of Lord Chatham's declaration that the Crown would lose its luster if "robbed of so principal a jewel as America." Paine retorted, "The principal jewel of the crown actually dropt out at the coronation." The final glorious separation would be a divinely inspired, just reward to the oppressive British. With independence, Americans, in gratitude for their freedom, would legislate an end to slavery. Paine had placed the responsibility for the evils of slavery principally upon the back of the British King, he of "little paltry dignity." Several months later, Thomas Jefferson did likewise in his draft of the Declaration of Independence.*

When I reflect on the horrid cruelties exercised by Britain in the East-Indies.—How thousands perished by artificial famine.—How religion, and every manly principle of honor and honesty, were sacrificed to luxury and pride.—When I read of the wretched natives being bound to the mouths of cannons, and blown away, for no other crime than because sickened with the miserable scene they refused to fight.—When I reflect on these and a thousand instances of similar barbarity, I firmly believe, that the Almighty, in compassion to mankind, will curtail the power of Britain.

And when I reflect on the ill use which she hath made of the discovery of this new world—That the little paltry dignity of earthly Kings hath been set up in preference to the great cause of the King of Kings—That instead of Christian examples to the Indians, she hath basely tampered with their passions, imposed on their ignorance, & made them the tools of treachery and murder—And when to these and many other melancholy reflections I add this sad remark, that ever since the discovery of America, she hath employed herself in the most horrid of all traffics, that of human flesh, and with a *deliberate* brutality, unknown to the most savage nations, hath yearly (without provocation and in cool blood) ravaged the hapless shores of Africa, robbing it of its unoffending inhabitants, to cultivate her stolen dominions in the west.—When I reflect on these, I hesitate not a moment to believe, that the Almighty will finally separate America from Britain—Call it Independency or what you will—if it is the cause of God and of humanity, it will go on.—And when the Almighty shall have blest us, and made us a people, *dependent only upon him*, then may our first gratitude be shewn, by an act of continental legislation, which shall put a stop to the importation of Negroes for sale, soften the hard fate of those already here, and in time procure their freedom.

HUMANUS.

Philip Freneau, "The Beauties of Santa Cruz," 1776

Philip Freneau, *The Poems of Philip Freneau written chiefly During the Late War* (Philadelphia, 1786), pp. 144-46.

Philip Freneau, poet, journalist, pamphleteer, soldier, sailor, and revolutionary, added a conspicuous voice and an important dimension—poetry—to the burgeoning antislavery vanguard. Early in the political struggles between the American colonies and Britain, Freneau had filled his songs, poems, and pamphlet satires with patriotic invective. But the poet left behind the war and the "bloody plains and iron gloom" of America in 1776 to become a secretary to an influential planter on Santa Cruz, in the West Indies. It was there that Freneau composed many of his longest and most powerful romantic poems, including "The Beauties of Santa Cruz." In that land of exotic splendor, Freneau thought he had found peace and happiness. But a further examination of the tropical grandeur, he wrote, unveiled, in its midst, the monumental example of man's inhumanity to man—slavery—in its most horrible form.

See yonder slave that slowly bends his way,
With years, and pain, and ceaseless toil opprest

Returning to America after three years, Freneau continued his political assult on the British enemy and earned the sobriquet, "The Poet of the Revolution." He also continued his assault on slavery. In the United States Magazine of February 1779, Freneau published an essay entitled "Account of the Island of Santa Cruz," in which he described the cruelty of slavery in the Indies and the shadow and terror it spread over the country. Prefaced with the lines from Julius Ceasar, "If you have tears prepare to shed them now," this essay enlightened a large number of Americans as to the brutalness of slavery. In a later poem, "To Sir Toby," Freneau itemized each barbarous act he had seen administered to slaves in Jamaica:

Philip Freneau (1752-1832), American Revolutionary War poet, whose verses often reflected the horrors of slavery.

"If there existed a hell—the case is clear
Sir Toby's slaves enjoy that portion here: . . .
Here whips excite perpetual fears,
And mingled howlings vibrate on my ears:
One with a gibbet wakes his negroe's fears,
One to the windmill nails him by the ears,
One keeps his slave in darkened dens, unfed,
One puts the wretch in pickle ere he's dead:
O'er yond' rough hills a tribe of females go,
Each with her gourd, her infant, and her hoe;
Scorched by a sun that has no mercy here,
Driven by a devil whom men call overseer—
In chains, twelve wretches to their labors haste;
Twice twelve I saw, with iron collars graced!"

70.

On yonder steepy hill, fresh harvests rise,
Where the dark tribe from Afric's sun burnt plain
Oft o'er the ocean turn their wishful eyes
To isles remote high looming o'er the main,

71.

And view soft seats of ease and fancied rest,
Their native groves new painted on the eye,
Where no proud misers their gay hours molest,
No lordly despots pass unsocial by.

72.

See, yonder slave that slowly bends this way,
With years, and pain, and ceaseless toil opprest,
Though no complaining words his woes betray,
The eye dejected proves the heart distrest.

73.

Perhaps in chains he left his native shore,
Perhaps he left a helpless offspring there,
Perhaps a wife, that he must see no more,
Perhaps a father, who his love did share.

74.

Curs'd be the ship that brought him o'er the main,
And curs'd the hands who from his country tore,
May she be stranded, ne'er to float again,
May they be shipwreck'd on some hostile shore—

75.

O gold accurst, of every ill the spring,
For thee compassion flies the darken'd mind,
Reason's plain dictates no conviction bring,
And passion only sways all human kind.

76.

O gold accurst! for thee we madly run
With murderous hearts across the briny flood,

Seek foreign climes beneath a foreign sun,
And there exult to shed a brother's blood.

77.

But thou, who own'st this sugar-bearing soil,
To whom no good the great first cause denies,
Let freeborn hands attend thy sultry toil,
And fairer harvests to thy view shall rise.

78.

The teeming earth shall mightier stores disclose
Than ever struck thy longing eyes before,
And late content shall shed a soft repose,
Repose, so long a stranger at thy door.

79.

Give me some clime, the favourite of the sky,
Where cruel slavery never sought to reign—
But shun the theme, sad muse, and tell me why
These abject trees lie scatter'd o'er the plain?

George Mason, Virginia Declaration of Rights (Draft), 1776

George Mason, Draft of the Virginia Declaration of Rights, 1776, Mason Papers, Library of Congress, Washington, D.C.

On May 15, 1776, the Virginia Revolutionary Convention named a committee "to prepare a declaration of rights, and such a plan of government as will be most likely to maintain peace and order in this colony, and secure substantial and equal liberty to the people." The architect of the declaration was a wealthy, influential planter from Fairfax County named George Mason. The owner of a large number of slaves, Mason, nevertheless, shared with many other planters the haunting fear of slavery's potentially abominable effects. Mason lamented in 1765 that the introduction of masses of discontented black slaves into Virginia could lead to the colony's decay, both in the morals and manners of the inhabitants, and conceivably in the government itself. Although Mason's draft of the declaration was not a direct assault upon slavery, the first clause gave proslavery advocates cause for concern. When Mason wrote that all men are "born equally free," Virginia conservatives were noticeably alarmed. Proclaim to the world such egalitarian nonsense, they charged, and the slave states would be ripe for insurrection and, as Robert Carter Nicholas said, "civil convulsion."

Although the final document was later amended by the committee of the whole to mollify these objections, the committee draft had a profound international effect. When the draft was reported to the convention on May 27, copies were printed "for the perusal of the members." It was this text that was republished in newspapers in America and Europe and became familiar to leading political figures. For abolitionists, the first clause was a potent weapon. A Virginia Quaker, Robert Pleasants, later wrote to Patrick Henry, "The declaration of Rights is indeed Noble, and I can but wish and hope thy great abilities & interest may be exerted towards a full & clear explanation & confirmation thereof: for without that the present struggle for liberty if attended with success, would be but partial, and instead of abolishing, might lay the foundation of greater imposition and Tirany to our posterity."

A Declaration of Rights, made by the Representatives of the good People of Virginia, assembled in full Convention; and recommended to Posterity as the Basis and Foundation of their Government.

That all Men are born equally free and independant, and have certain inherent natural Rights, of which they can not, by any Compact, deprive or divest their Posterity; among which are the Enjoyment of Life and Liberty, with the Means of acquiring and possessing Property, and pursueing and obtaining Happiness and Safety.

That Power is, by God and Nature, vested in, and consequently derived from the People; that Magistrates are their Trustees and Servants, and at all times amenable to them.

That Government is, or ought to be instituted for the common Benefit and Security of the People, Nation, or Community. Of all the various Modes and Forms of Government that is best, which is capable of producing the greatest Degree of Happiness and Safety, and is most effectually secured against the Danger of male-administration. And that whenever any Government shall be found inadequate, or contrary to these Purposes, a Majority of the Community hath an indubitable, inalienable and indefeasible Right to reform, alter or abolish it, in such Manner as shall be judged most conducive to the Public Weal.

22

That

Thomas Jefferson, Philippic on Slavery from the Declaration of Independence (Draft), 1776

Thomas Jefferson Rough Draft of the Declaration of Independence, June 1776, Library of Congress, Washington, D.C.

Thomas Jefferson's ambivalence on the subject of slavery was awesome—he was a philosopher who extolled the natural right to life and liberty and at the same time held over 250 slaves when he died; a man who many times advocated the end of the slave trade but, nevertheless, dispatched slave catchers to the North to track down runaways; a man who, as a member of the Virginia House of Burgesses, seconded a motion in support of a manumission law that was later defeated and several years later held onto most of his black property when such a law was actually adopted; a man who on many occasions expressed his moral repugnance of a system mired in "unremitting despotism" and "daily . . . tyranny" and at the same time ordered the flogging of some of the captured black escapees from the Monticello labor force. Tempered by political expedience, class allegiance, and racist ideology, Jefferson's oft-expressed libertarian antislavery beliefs remained throughout his life primarily philosophical, not grounded on any real expectation that abolition schemes would be successful or even desirable.

In the spring of 1776, however, Jefferson attempted to include a philippic against slavery in one of the most significant documents in American history—the Declaration of Independence. On June 11, 1776, the Congress appointed a committee of five to draft the Declaration—Jefferson, John Adams, Benjamin Franklin, Roger Sherman, and Robert R. Livingston. On June 28 the draft, largely the work of the Virginian, was reported to the Congress. It contained a passage indicting the British King for shackling the American colonies with the alien institution of slavery, an "assemblage of horrors" that violated the "most sacred rights of life and liberty." The philippic was, of course, excised by the Congress in deference to South Carolina and Georgia and to the interests of northern slave dealers. The draft, however, represented a strong attack against slavery, an attack that especially pleased John Adams, who later wrote, "I was delighted with its high tone, and the flights of oratory with which it abounded, especially that concerning negro slavery; which, though I knew his Southern brethren would never suffer to pass in Congress, I certainly would never oppose." But the philosophical beliefs that prompted the Virginia savant to compose the antislavery tirade did not act to restrain him two years later when, as chairman of a committee to revise and codify the Virginia statutes, he reported a bill that strengthened the state slave code. The statesman who described the slave trade as an "execrable commerce" was the same slaveholding planter who in his "Farm Book" attached such names as Guinea and Angola to the locations of slave quarters at Monticello.

+ Dr. Franklin + abolishing our most valuable laws

for taking away our charters & altering fundamentally the forms of our governments

for suspending our own legislatures & declaring themselves invested with power to legislate for us in all cases whatsoever:

he has abdicated government here, [withdrawing his governors, & declaring us out of his allegiance & protection:] [by declaring us out of his protection & waging war against us.]

he has plundered our seas, ravaged our coasts, burnt our towns & destroyed the lives of our people:

he is at this time transporting large armies of [Scotch and other] foreign mercenaries to compleat the works of death, desolation & tyranny, already begun with circumstances [scarcely paralleled in the most barbarous ages and totally] of cruelty & perfidy unworthy the head of a civilized nation:

[he has excited domestic insurrections amongst us and has] he has endeavored to bring on the inhabitants of our frontiers the merciless Indian savages, whose known rule of warfare is an undistinguished destruction of all ages, sexes, & conditions [of existence:]

[he has incited treasonable insurrections of our fellow-citizens, with the allurements of forfeiture & confiscation of our property:

he has constrained others ... on the high seas to bear arms against their country & to become the executioners of their friends & brethren, or to fall themselves by their hands.

he has waged cruel war against human nature itself, violating it's most sacred rights of life & liberty in the persons of a distant people who never offended him, captivating & carrying them into slavery in another hemi-

-sphere, or to incur miserable death in their transportation thither. this piratical warfare, the opprobrium of infidel powers, is the warfare of the Christian king of Great Britain. determined to keep open a market where MEN should be bought & sold: he has prostituted his negative for suppressing every legislative attempt to prohibit or to restrain this ~~determining to keep open a market where MEN should be bought & sold~~: execrable commerce: and that this assemblage of horrors might want no fact of distinguished die, he is now exciting those very people to rise in arms among us, and to purchase that liberty of which he has deprived them, by murdering the people upon whom he also obtruded them: thus paying off former crimes committed against the liberties of one people, with crimes which he urges them to commit against the lives of another.]

+ Dr. Franklin

in every stage of these oppressions we have petitioned for redress in the most humble terms; our repeated petitions have been answered only by repeated injuries. a prince whose character is thus marked by every act which may define a tyrant, is unfit to be the ruler of a free people who mean to be free. future ages will scarce believe that the hardiness of one man, adventured within the short compass of twelve years only, to build a foundation so broad & undisguised for tyranny [illegible], over a people fostered & fixed in principles

THE CRUSADE IN THE WAR YEARS, 1776-1783

. . . They Cannot but express their Astonishment that It has Never Bin Considered that Every Principle from which America has Acted in the Cours of their unhappy Deficultes with Great Briton Pleads Stronger than A thousand arguments in favowrs of your petioners. . . .

Prince Hall and other Black Petitioners
1777

Samuel Hopkins, A Dialogue on Slavery, 1776

Samuel Hopkins, *A Dialogue Concerning the Slavery of the Africans, Showing it to be the Duty and Interest of the American Colonies to Emancipate All the African Slaves. . .*(Norwich, 1776); reprinted in Samuel Hopkins, *Timely Articles on Slavery* (Boston, 1854), pp. 549-88.

When Samuel Hopkins, the high priest of "The New Divinity," came to Newport he brought to the pastorate of the First Congregational Church his fervent Great Awakening, Calvinist beliefs. As the Reverend Hopkins launched his militant antislavery crusade, his abolitionist creed closely reflected the New Light doctrines he had nurtured in New England pulpits for nearly 30 years—emphasis on original sin, the necessity of conversion, the abandonment of self to, as he described it, "universal, disinterested benevolence." In 1776 Hopkins wrote A Dialogue Concerning the Slavery of the Africans, *an uncompromising attack on the institution of slavery addressed to the Continental Congress incorporating the revivalistic enthusiasm so implicit in his fundamental religious beliefs. Human slavery, Hopkins declared, was a tragic violation of God's will, a "sin of a crimson dye," that cried for national repentence and conversion. Hopkins called for that "benevolence which loves one neighbor as ourselves . . . we should begin to feel towards them, in some measure, at least, as we should towards our children and neighbors." Hopkins's vision of divine reward and punishment was so acute that he attributed patriot successes during the Revolutionary struggle to God's pleasure with congressional cessation of the slave trade—"God is hereby showing us what he can do for us." The God that had fleetingly smiled on America for the legislation against the slave trade would, however, look with disfavor if the country failed to take the final step to end slavery. Only through a national reformation, a thorough purging of the "evil of our doings," could America avoid divine retribution. Hopkins's pamphlet was circulated to members of the Congress and prominent figures in all of the colonies. Later, it was reprinted by the New York Manumission Society. The voice of this Rhode Island preacher was a significant force in the American antislavery movement.*

To The Honorable Members of the Continental Congress, Representatives of the Thirteen United American Colonies

Much-honored Gentlemen: As God, the great Father of the universe, has made you the fathers of these colonies,—and in answer to the prayers of his people given you counsel, and that wisdom and integrity in the exertion of which you have been such great and extensive blessings, and obtained the approbation and applause of your constituents and the respect and veneration of the nations in whose sight you have acted in the important, noble struggle for Liberty,—we naturally look to you in behalf of more than half a million of persons in these colonies, who are under such a degree of oppression and tyranny as to be wholly deprived of all civil and personal liberty, to which they have as good a right as any of their fellow-men, and are reduced to the most abject state of bondage and slavery without any just cause.

We have particular encouragement thus to apply to you, since you have had the honor and happiness of leading these colonies to resolve to stop the slave trade, and to buy no more slaves imported from Africa. We have the satisfaction of the best assurances that you have done this not merely from political reasons, but from a conviction of the unrighteousness and cruelty of that trade, and a regard to justice and benevolence,—deeply sensible of the inconsistence of promoting the slavery of the Africans, at the same time we are asserting our own civil liberty at the risk of our fortunes and lives. This leaves in our minds no doubt of your being sensible of the equal unrighteousness and oppression, as well as inconsistence with ourselves, in holding so many hundreds of thousands of blacks in slavery, who have an equal right to freedom with ourselves, while we are maintaining this struggle for our own and our children's liberty; and a hope and confidence that the cries and tears of these oppressed will be regarded by you, and that your wisdom and the great influence you have in these colonies will be so properly and effectually exerted as to bring about a total abolition of slavery, in such a manner as shall greatly promote the happiness of those oppressed strangers and the best interest of the public.

There are many difficulties and obstacles, we are sensible, in the way of this good work; but when the propriety, importance, and necessity of it come into view, we think ourselves warranted to address you in the words spoken to Ezra on an occasion not wholly dissimilar: "Arise, for this matter belongeth unto you; we also will be with you: be of good courage and do it."

The righteous and merciful Governor of the world has given the greatest encouragement to go on, and thoroughly execute judgment, and deliver the spoiled out of the hand of the oppressor, both in his word, and in the wonderful things he has done for us since we have begun to reform this public iniquity. But, if we stop here, what will be the consequence?

It is observable that when the Swiss were engaged in their struggle for liberty, in which they so remarkably succeeded, they entered into the following public resolve: "No Swiss shall take away any thing by violence from another, neither in time of war nor peace." How reasonable and important is it that we should at this time heartily enter into, and thoroughly execute, such a resolution! And that this implies the emancipation of all our African slaves, surely none can doubt.

In this view the following Dialogue is humbly offered to your perusal, hoping that it may have your approbation and patronage.

May you judge the poor of the people, save the children of the needy, relieve the oppressed, and deliver the spoiled out of the hands of the oppressor, and be the happy instruments of procuring and establishing universal liberty to white and black, to be transmitted down to the latest posterity.

With high esteem, and the most friendly sentiments, We are, honorable gentlemen, Your very humble servants,

THE EDITORS.

Slavery of the Africans

A Dialogue

A. Sir, what do you think of the motion made by some among us to free all our African slaves? They say that our holding these blacks in slavery as we do is an open violation of the law of God, and is so great an instance of unrighteousness and cruelty that we cannot expect deliverance from present calamities, and success in our struggle for liberty in the American colonies, until we repent, and make all the restitution in our power. For my part, I think they carry things much too far on this head; and if any thing might be done for the freedom of our slaves, this is not a proper time to attend to it while we are in such a state of war and distress, and affairs of much greater importance demand all our attention, and the utmost exertion of the public.

B. Sir, I am glad you have introduced this subject, especially as you own a number of these slaves. I shall attend to it with pleasure, and offer my sentiments upon it freely, expecting you will as freely propose the objections you shall have against any thing I shall advance. And I take leave here to observe, that, if the slavery in which we hold the blacks is wrong, it is a very great and public sin, and, therefore, a sin which God is now testifying against in the calamities he has brought upon us; consequently, must be reformed before we can reasonably expect deliverance, or even sincerely ask for it. It would be worse than madness, then, to put off attention to this matter, under the notion of attending to more important affairs. This is acting like the mariner, who, when his ship is filling with water, neglects to stop the leak, or ply the pump, that he may mend his sails. There are, at the lowest computation, 800,000 slaves in British America, including the West India islands, and a greater part of these are in the colonies on the continent; and if this is, in every instance, wrong, unrighteousness, and oppression, it must be a very great and crying sin, there being nothing of the kind equal to it on the face of the earth. There are but few of these slaves, indeed, in New England, compared with the vast numbers in the islands and the southern colonies; and they are treated much better on the continent, and especially among us, than they are in the West Indies. But, if it be all wrong, and real oppression of the poor, helpless blacks, we, by refusing to break this yoke and let these injured captives go free, do practically justify and support this slavery in general, and make ourselves, in a measure at least, answerable for the whole; and we have no way to exculpate ourselves from the guilt of the whole, and bear proper testimony against this great evil, but by freeing all our slaves. Surely, then, this matter admits of no delay, but demands our first and most serious attention and speedy reformation.

A. I acknowledge the slave trade, as it has been carried on with the Africans, cannot be justified; but I am not yet convinced that it is wrong to keep those in perpetual bondage who by this trade have been transported from Africa to us, and are become our slaves. If I viewed this in the light you do, I should agree with you that it is of the highest importance that they should all be made free without delay; as we could not expect the favor of Heaven, or with any consistency ask it, so long as they are held in bondage.

B. I am glad you have attended to the affair so much as to be convinced of the unrighteousness of the slave trade. Indeed, this conviction has been so spread of late that it has reached almost all men on the continent, except some of those who are too deeply interested in it to admit the light which condemns it; and it has now but few advocates, I believe, being generally condemned and exploded. And the members of the continental congress have done themselves much honor in advising the American colonies to drop this trade entirely, and resolving not to buy another slave that shall be imported from Africa.

But I think it of importance that this trade should not only be condemned as wrong, but attentively considered in its real nature, and all its shocking attendants and circumstances, which will lead us to think of it with a detestation and horror which this scene of inhumanity, oppression, and cruelty—exceeding every thing of the kind that has ever been perpetrated by the sons of men—is suited to excite; and awaken us to a proper indignation against the authors of this violence and outrage done to their fellow-men, and to feelings of humanity and pity towards our brethren who are the miserable sufferers. Therefore, though I am not able to paint this horrid scene of barbarity and complicated iniquity to the life, or even to tell the one half which may be told in the short time allotted for this conversation, yet I will suggest a few particulars, leaving you, if you please, to consult the authors who have given a more particular description.

Most of the Africans are in a state of heathenism, and sunk down into that ignorance and barbarity into which mankind naturally fall when destitute of divine revelation. Their lands are fertile, and produce all the necessaries of life. The inhabitants are divided into many distinct nations, or clans, and, of course, are frequently entering into quarrels and open war with each other. The Europeans, English, French, and Dutch have carried on a trade with them for above one hundred years, and have taken advantage of their ignorance and barbarity to persuade them to enter into the inhuman practice of selling one another to the Europeans for the commodities which they carry to them, most of which they stand in no real need of, but might live as well or better without them, particularly spirituous liquors, which have been carried to them in great quantities by the Americans. They, by this means, have tempted and excited the poor blacks to make war upon one another in order to get captives, spreading distress, devastation, and destruction over a vast country, by which many millions have perished, and millions of others have been captivated and sold to the Europeans and Americans into a state of slavery much worse than death. And the inhabitants of the towns near the sea are taught to exert all the art and power they have to entrap and decoy one another, that they may make slaves of them, and sell them to us for rum; by which they intoxicate themselves, and become more brutish and savage than otherwise they could be, so that there are but few instances of sobriety, honesty, or even humanity, in these towns on the sea to which the Europeans have access, and they who live the farthest from these places are the least vicious, and much more civil and humane.

They stand in no need of the rum that is carried there in such quantities, by which so many thousands have been enslaved, and which has spread such infinite mischief among them; and I leave it with you to consider to what a dreadful degree the Americans have, by this abominable practice, brought the curse upon them pronounced by an inspired prophet, and how very applicable it is to this case. "Woe unto him that giveth his neighbor drink, that puttest thy bottle to him and makest him drunken also, that thou mayest look on their nakedness!" (Hab. ii. 15.) And is not this curse evidently come upon us in a dreadful degree, in such a way as to paint itself out, so that he who runs may read it? We have put the bottle to our neighbors' mouths, by carrying immense quantities of rum to them, and enticed them to drink, that we might take advantage of their weakness, and thereby gratify our lusts. By this means multitudes of them have been enslaved and carried to the West India islands, there to be kept to hard labor, and treated ten thousand times worse than dogs. In consequence of which, incredible quantities of rum, and molasses which has been distilled into rum among ourselves, have been imported, the most of which is consumed in intemperance and drunkenness, in such a dreadful degree as to exceed any thing of the kind in any part of the world; by which thousands, yea, millions, have ruined themselves, body and soul, forever. Let any one consider this, and forbear to confess, if he can, that this woe has fallen heavily upon us, and that in such a way and connection as to point out the sinful cause.

But to return. This trade has been carried on for a century and more, and for many years past above a hundred thousand have been brought off the coast in a year, so that many, many millions have been torn from their native country, their acquaintance, relations and friends, and most of them put into a state of slavery, both themselves and their children forever, if they shall have any posterity, much worse than death. When numbers of these wretched creatures are collected by the savages, they are brought into the public market to be sold, all naked as they were born. The more than savage slave merchant views them and sends his surgeon more particularly to examine them as to the soundness of their limbs, their age, &c. All that are passed as fit for sale are branded with a hot iron in some part of their body with the buyer's mark, and then confined, crowded together in some close hold, till a convenient time to put them on board a ship. When they are brought on board, all are immediately put in irons, except some of the women perhaps, and the small children, where they are so crowded together in that hot climate, that commonly a considerable number die on their passage to the West Indies, occasioned partly by their confinement, partly by the grief and vexation of their minds from the treatment they receive, and the situation in which they find themselves. And a number commonly die after they arrive at the West Indies in seasoning to the climate, so that, commonly, not above seventy in a hundred survive their transportation; by which means about thirty thousand are murdered every year by this slave trade, which amount to three millions in a century. When they are brought to the West Indies, they are again exposed to market, as if they were so many beasts, and sold to the highest bidder; where again they are separated according to the humor of the traders, without any regard to their friendships or relations, of husbands and wives, parents and children, brothers and sisters, &c., being torn from each other, without the least regard to any thing of this kind, and sent to different places, without any prospect of seeing each other again. They are then put under a taskmaster by the purchasing planter, who appoints them their work and rules over them with rigor and cruelty, following them with his cruel whip, or appointing one to do it, if possible more cruel than himself. The infirm and feeble, the females, and even those who are pregnant, or have infants to take care of, must do their task in the field equally with the rest; or if they fall behind, may be sure to feel the lash of their unmerciful driver. Their allowance of food at the same time is very coarse and scant, and must be cooked by themselves, if cooked at all, when they want to be asleep. And often they have no food but what they procure for themselves, by working on the Sabbath; for that is the only time they have to themselves. And to make any complaint or petition for relief will expose them to some severe punishment, if not a cruel death. The least real or supposable crimes in them are punished in the most cruel manner. And they have no relief, there being no appeal from their masters' sentence and will, who commonly are more like savage beasts than rational, human creatures. And to petition for liberty, though in the most humble and modest terms, is as much as their lives are worth, as few escape the most cruel death who presume to hint any thing of this kind to their masters; it being a maxim with those more than cruel tyrants, that the only way to keep them under, and prevent their thinking of the sweets of liberty, is to punish the least intimation of it in the severest manner, as the most intolerable affront and insult on their masters. Their labor is so hard, and their diet so scant and poor, and they are treated in all respects with such oppression and cruelty, that they do not increase by propagation in the islands, but constantly decrease, so that every planter must every year purchase five at least to every hundred he has on his plantation, in order to keep his number from diminishing.

But it is in vain to attempt a full description of the oppression and cruel treatment these poor creatures receive constantly at the hands of their imperious, unmerciful, worse than Egyptian taskmasters. Words cannot utter it. Volumes might be written, and not give a detail of a thousandth part of the shockingly cruel things they have suffered, and are constantly suffering. Nor can they possibly be conceived of by any one who has not been an eye witness. And how little a part does he see! They who are witnesses to any part of this horrid scene of barbarous oppression cannot but feel the truth and propriety of Solomon's words: "So I returned, and considered all the oppressions that are done under the sun; and behold, the tears of the oppressed, and they had no comforter; and on the side of the oppressors there was power, but they had no comforter. Wherefore I praised the dead which are already dead more than the living which are yet alive." (Ec. iv. 1,2.) Solomon never saw any oppression like this, unless he looked forward to this very instance in the spirit of prophecy.

A. Sir, there is one important circumstance in favor of the slave trade, or which will at least serve to counterbalance many of the evils you mention, and that is, we bring these slaves from a heathen land to places of gospel light, and so put them under special advantages to be saved.

B. I know this has been mentioned by many in favor of the slave trade; but when examined, will turn greatly against it. It can hardly be said with truth, that the West India islands are places of gospel light. But if they were, are the negroes in the least benefited by it? Have they any access to the gospel? Have they any instruction more than if they were beasts? So far from this, that their masters guard against their having any instruction to their utmost; and if any one would attempt any such thing, it would be at the risk of his life. And all the poor creatures learn of Christianity from what they see in those who call themselves Christians, only serves to prejudice them in the highest degree against the Christian religion. For they not only see the abominably wicked lives of most of those who are called Christians, but are constantly oppressed by them, and receive as cruel treatment from them as they could from the worst of beings. And as to those who are brought to the continent, in the southern colonies, and even to New England, so little pains are taken to instruct them, and there is so much to prejudice them against Christianity, that it is a very great wonder and owing to an extraordinary divine interposition, in which we may say God goes out of his common way, that any of them should think favorably of Christianity and cordially embrace it. As to the most of them, no wonder they are unteachable and get no good by the gospel, but they have imbibed the deepest prejudices against it from the treatment they receive from professed Christians; prejudices which most of them are by their circumstances restrained from expressing, while they are fixed in the strongest degree in their minds.

But if this was not the case, and all the slaves brought from Africa were put under the best advantages to become Christians, and they were in circumstances that tended to give them the most favorable idea of Christians and the religion they profess, and though all concerned in this trade, and in slavery in general, should have this wholly in view, viz., their becoming Christians, by which they should be eternally happy, yet this would not justify the slave trade, or continuing them in a state of slavery; for, to take this method to Christianize them would be a direct and gross violation of the laws of Christ. He commands us to go and preach the gospel to all nations, to carry the gospel to them, and not to go and with violence bring them from their native country without saying a word to them or to the nations from whom they are taken, about the gospel or any thing that relates to it.

If the Europeans and Americans had been as much engaged to Christianize the Africans as they have been to enslave them, and had been at half the cost and pains to introduce the gospel among them that they have to captivate and destroy them, we have all the reason in the world to conclude that extensive country, containing such a vast multitude of inhabitants, would have been full of gospel light, and the many nations there civilized and made happy, and a foundation laid for the salvation of millions of millions, and the happy instruments of it have been rewarded ten thousand fold for all their labor and expense. But now, instead of this, what has been done on that coast by those who pass among the negroes for Christians, has only served to produce and spread the greatest and most deep-rooted prejudices against the Christian religion, and bar the way to that which is above all things desirable—their coming to the knowledge of the truth, that they might be saved. So that, while by the murdering or enslaving millions of millions they have brought a curse upon themselves and on all that partake with them, they have injured in the highest degree innumerable nations, and done what they could to prevent their salvation and to fasten them down in ignorance and barbarity to the latest posterity. Who can realize all this and not feel a mixture of grief, pity, indignation, and horror, truly ineffable? And must he not be filled with zeal to do his utmost to put a speedy stop to this seven-headed monster of iniquity, with all the horrid train of evils with which it is attended?

And can any one consider all these things, and yet pretend to justify the slave trade, or the slavery of the Africans in America? Is it not impossible that a real Christian who has attended to all this should have any hand in this trade? And it requires the utmost stretch of charity to suppose that any one ever did or can buy or sell an African slave with a sincere view to make a true Christian of him.

A. All this seems to be little to the purpose, since it was granted, in the beginning of our conversation, that the slave trade, as it has been carried on, is not to be justified. But what is this to the question we proposed to consider, which is, whether it be wrong to hold the blacks we have among us in a state of slavery, or ought to set them free without delay. To this you have said little or nothing as yet.

B. All I have said upon the slave trade to show the unrighteousness, the cruelty, the murder, the opposition to Christianity and the spread of the gospel among the Africans, the destruction of whole nations and myriads of souls which are contained in this horrid practice, has been principally with a view to a more clear and satisfactory determination of the question before us, which you have now renewedly proposed, for I think the following proposition may be advanced as undeniable, viz., if the slave trade be unjustifiable and wrong, then our holding the Africans and their children in bondage is unjustifiable and wrong, and the latter is criminal in some proportion to the inexpressible baseness and criminality of the former. For,—

First. If they have been brought into a state of slavery by unrighteousness and violence, they having never forfeited their liberty or given any one a right to enslave and sell them, then purchasing them of these piratical tyrants, and holding them in the same state of bondage into which they, contrary to all right, have brought them, is continuing the exercise of the same unrighteousness and violence towards them. They have yet as much a right to their liberty as ever they had, and to demand it of him who holds them in bondage; and he denies them their right, which is of more worth to them than every thing else they can have in the world, or all the riches the unjust master does or can possess, and therefore injures them in a very high degree every hour he refuses or neglects to set them at liberty. Besides,—

Secondly. Holding these blacks in a state of slavery is a practical justification of the slave trade, and so brings the guilt of that on the head of him who so far partakes in this iniquity as to hold one of these a slave who was unrighteously made so by these sons of violence. The old adage, "the partaker is as bad as the thief," carries such a plain truth in it that every one must discern it, and it is certainly applicable to this case.

It is impossible to buy one of these blacks and detain him a slave, without partaking with him who first reduced him to this state and put it in his power thus to possess him, and practically justifying him for so doing, so as to bring upon himself the guilt of first enslaving him. It is not, therefore, possible for any of our slavekeepers to justify themselves in what they are doing, unless they can justify the slave trade. If they fail here, they bring on themselves an awful degree of the guilt of the whole.

Thirdly. By keeping these slaves, and buying and selling them, they actually encourage and promote the slave trade; and therefore, in this view, keeping slaves and continuing to buy and sell them is to bring on us the guilt of the slave trade, which is hereby supported. For so long as slaves are bought and possessed, and in demand, so long the African trade will be supported and encouraged.

A. But there is a stop put to the importation of slaves into the American colonies, as they have resolved no more shall be bought. This being the case, the keeping those we have among us in slavery is no encouragement to the slave trade.

B. I grant, if this resolution should be perpetual, and extend to the West Indies, it would discourage the slave trade so far as the Americans are concerned in it, but it would be more effectually discountenanced and condemned if slavery was wholly abolished, and it cannot be consistently done without this. For, if it be wrong to import and buy them now, it was always wrong, and, therefore, they that are already slaves among us are injured, and unjustly enslaved, and we have made them our slaves without the least right, and ought to retract it and repair the injury done to them, so far as is in our power, by setting them free and compensating them otherwise so far as we are able. There is, therefore, a palpable inconsistency in resolving to import and buy no more slaves and yet refusing to let those go out free which we have already enslaved, unless there be some insuperable impediment in the way.

The whole I have said concerning the unlawfulness of keeping the blacks in slavery, if the trade by which they are become our slaves be unlawful, may be illustrated by the following example:—

A number of robbers invaded a certain province, and took off most of their goods and effects, and carried them to a neighboring province and sold them to the inhabitants, and the robbers finding this encouragement, continued the practice for many years. At length the people of the injured province applied to their neighbors, who had their goods of the robbers, and were now in possession of them, and asked them to restore what was taken from them by violence, and to which they had a good and indisputable right, it being impossible these robbers could give a right to what they had unjustly taken from them; but the people, in whose possession the stolen goods were found, utterly refused to deliver them up to the injured people who demanded them. They told them they had indeed been greatly injured, and they must condemn the robbers as very injurious and cruel in what they had done, but as they now had these goods in their own possession, they intended to keep them, and looked on themselves under no obligation to deliver them up, though they suffered so much and would probably perish for want of them; and they intended still to buy all the robbers should bring to them.

To this the injured replied, "By partaking with these robbers in receiving the goods at their hands, you practically justify their conduct, and must share with them in their guilt. For by this means you encourage them, and are determined to go on to encourage them in this violence and rapine; and by condemning them, you equally condemn yourselves, and must remain under this condemnation till you restore the goods we demand, and resolve never to purchase any thus taken from us by violence.".

Upon this they determined to purchase no more of them, but refused to deliver up what they had already got in possession. But the oppressed told them, they did right in resolving to injure them no more in that way; but they were now very inconsistent with themselves, for if it were wrong to purchase any more, it was as wrong to withhold what they had already gotten in possession; and they had no other way to justify themselves in detaining their goods, and to be consistent, but by proceeding to take whatever those robbers should bring to them in future, and justifying themselves in so doing and the robbers in all their depredations.

A. This reasoning looks something plausible, I confess; but the Holy Scripture approves of making and keeping slaves, and this surely is sufficient to keep us in countenance.

B. I hope you will not appeal to the Holy Scripture in support of a practice which you and every one else must allow to be so inexpressibly unjust, inhuman, and cruel, as is the slave trade, and, consequently, so glaringly contrary to the whole tenor of divine revelation; and if the slave trade is such a gross violation of every divine precept, it is impossible to vindicate the slavery to which the Africans have been reduced by this trade from the Holy Scripture. Of this we have such a certainty, *a priori*, that would be a horrid reproach of divine revelation to pretend this practice can be supported by that, or even to look into it with any hope or expectation of finding any thing there in favor of it; and if there be any passages in the Bible which are capable of a construction in favor of this practice, we may be very certain it is a wrong one. In a word, if any kind of slavery can be vindicated by the Holy Scriptures, we are already sure our making and holding the negroes our slaves, as we do, cannot be vindicated by any thing we can find there, but is condemned by the whole of divine revelation. However, I am willing to hear what you can produce from Scripture in favor of any kind of slavery.

A. You know that a curse was pronounced on the posterity of Ham for his wickedness, in the following words: "A servant of servants shall he be unto his brethren." He could not be a servant unto his brethren unless they made him so, or at least held him in servitude. The curse could not take place unless they executed it, and they seem to be by God appointed to do this; therefore, while we, the children of Japheth, are making such abject slaves of the blacks, the children of Ham, we are only executing the righteous curse denounced upon them; which is so far from being wrong in us, that it would be a sin, even disobedience to the revealed will of God, to refuse to make slaves of them, and attempt to set them at liberty.

B. Do you think, my good sir, it was the duty of Pharaoh to make the Israelites serve him and the Egyptians, and to afflict them by ruling over them with rigor, and holding them in hard and cruel bondage, because God had expressly foretold this, and said it should be done? And was the Assyrian king blameless while he executed the judgments which God had threatened to inflict on his professing people? Did God's threatening them with those evils warrant this king to distress, captivate, and destroy them as he did? And will you say the Jews did right in crucifying our Lord, because by this they fulfilled the Scriptures, declaring that thus it must be? Your argument, if it is of any force, will assert and justify all this, and, therefore, I hope will be renounced by you, and by all who have the least regard for the Holy Scripture, with proper abhorrence.

But, if this argument were not so fraught with absurdity and impiety as it really is, and it were granted to be forcible with respect to all upon whom the mentioned curse was denounced, yet it would not justify our enslaving the Africans, for they are not the posterity of Canaan, who was the only son of Ham that was doomed to be a servant of servants. The other sons of Ham and their posterity are no more affected with this curse than the other sons of Noah and their posterity. Therefore, this prediction is as much of a warrant for the Africans' enslaving us, as it is for us to make slaves of them. The truth is, it gives not the least shadow of a right to any one of the children of Noah to make slaves of any of their brethren.

A. The people of Israel were allowed by God to buy and make slaves from the nations that were round about them, and the strangers that lived among them,—which could not have been the case if this was wrong and unjust,—and why have not we an equal right to do the same?

B. And why have not we an equal right to invade any nation and land, as they did the land of Canaan, and destroy them all, men, women, and children, and beasts, without saving so much as one alive? It was right for the Israelites to do this, because they had a divine permission and direction to do it, as the God of Israel had a right to destroy the seven nations of

Canaan in what way he thought best, and to direct whom he pleased to do it. And it was right for them to make bond-servants of the nations round them, they having an express permission to do it from him who has a right to dispose of all men as he pleases. God saw fit, for wise reasons, to allow the people of Israel thus to make and possess slaves; but is this any license to us to enslave any of our fellow-men, any more than their being allowed to kill the seven nations in Canaan is a warrant to us to kill any of our fellow-men whom we please and are able to destroy, and take possession of their estates? This must be answered in the negative by every one who will allow himself a moment's reflection. God gave many directions and laws to the Jews which had no respect to mankind in general; and this under consideration has all the marks of such a one. There is not any thing in it, or relating to it, from whence can be deduced the least evidence that it was designed to be a regulation for all nations through every age of the world, but every thing to the contrary. The children of Israel were then distinguished from all other nations on earth; they were God's peculiar people, and favored on many accounts above others, and had many things in their constitution and laws that were designed to keep up their separation and distinction from other nations, and to make the special favor of Heaven towards them more apparent to all who had any knowledge of them; and this law respecting bondage is suited to answer these ends. This distinction is now at an end, and all nations are put upon a level; and Christ, who has taken down the wall of separation, has taught us to look on all nations as our neighbors and brethren, without any respect of persons, and to love all men as ourselves, and to do to others as we would they should treat us; by which he has most effectually abolished this permission given to the Jews, as well as many other institutions which were peculiar to them.

Besides, that this permission was not designed for all nations and ages will be very evident if we consider what such a supposition implies; for if this be so, then all other nations had a right to make slaves of the Jews. The Egyptians had a right to buy and sell them, and keep them all in bondage forever, and the nations round about Canaan had a right to bring them into bondage, as they sometimes did, and the Babylonians and Romans had a good warrant to reduce them to a state of captivity and servitude. And the Africans have a good right to make slaves of us and our children; the inhabitants of Great Britain may lawfully make slaves of all the Americans, and transport us to England, and buy and sell us in open market as they do their cattle and horses, and perpetuate our bondage to the latest generation; and the Turks have a good right to all the Christian slaves they have among them, and to make as many more slaves of us and our children as shall be in their power, and to hold them and their children in bondage to the latest posterity. According to this, every man has a warrant to make a bondslave of his neighbor whenever it lies in his power, and no one has any right to his own freedom any longer than he can keep himself out of the power of others. For instance: if the blacks now among us should, by some remarkable providence, have the power in their hands to reduce us, they have a right to make us and our children their slaves, and we should have no reason to complain.

This would put mankind into such a state of perpetual war and confusion, and is so contrary to our loving our neighbor as ourselves, that he who has the least regard for his fellow-men, or the divine law, must reject it, and the principle from which it flows, with the greatest abhorrence. Let no Christian, then, plead this permission to the Jews, to make bondslaves of their neighbors, as a warrant to hold the slaves he has made, and, consequently, for universal slavery.

A. But what will you do with those passages in the New Testament which are in favor of slavery, and suppose Christian masters to have Christian slaves,—and the masters are so far from being directed to free them that it is supposed they may hold them in bondage,—and their mutual duties in this relation are inculcated? Paul, the apostle, is so far from being disposed to have servants made free, that he says, "Let as many servants as are under the yoke count their own masters worthy of all honor." (1 Tim. vi. 1.) And in the following words supposes that believing masters had servants, whom he exhorts to serve such masters with the more cheerfulness, out of respect to their Christian character.

B. Before I make a direct answer to this I beg leave to remind you, that, whatever other kind of slavery these passages will vindicate, they certainly will not support the slave trade, and that slavery of the negroes into which they have been brought by this trade, which is manifestly unrighteous from beginning to end; and, therefore, can be nothing to our present purpose, viz., to justify Christian masters among us in holding the blacks and their children in bondage.

I grant there are bondservants who are made so, and may be held in this state, consistent with justice, humanity, and benevolence. They are such, who have forfeited their liberty to the community of which they are members, by some particular crimes, and by debt in some instances; and are for this condemned to servitude for a longer or shorter time, and sold by the civil magistrate. And persons may put themselves into this state by their own voluntary act. There were doubtless such in the apostle's days; and if master and servant, in this case, were converted to Christianity, the servant would still be under the yoke, and the apostle's exhortation highly proper. Therefore if every master, when he embraced Christianity, was obliged to free all his servants who had not evidently forfeited their liberty, and not one who refused to do this was admitted into a Christian church, yet there might be many masters and servants in the first Christian churches; and the passages of Scripture under consideration prove no more than this, and therefore will not justify any master holding one servant in bondage against his will, so much as an hour, who has not evidently brought himself into this state by his own crimes, and been adjudged to it, after proper trial, by the civil magistrate. These Scriptures, therefore, are infinitely far from justifying the slavery under consideration; for it cannot be made to appear that one in a thousand of these slaves has done any thing to forfeit his own liberty. And if there were any such, they have never been condemned to slavery by any who are proper judges, or had any authority to act in the affair. But if this were the case of any, they certainly could not forfeit the liberty of their children, and cause them to be born slaves.

But it may be further observed, that it might be difficult in many cases at that day to determine what servants were justly in a state of bondage, and who had a right to their liberty, (which is not the case with respect to the slaves whose cause I am now pleading.) And the apostles did not think it their business to examine into every instance of slavery, and find the original ground of it, in order to determine whether the servant ought to be set free or not; and as it was taken for granted by all, or most, that the slavery which then took place was generally just, and if every one who embraced Christianity and had slaves must undergo a strict examination, and be obliged to dismiss his servants unless he could produce good evidence that they had forfeited their liberty, this, as circumstances then were, would have greatly prejudiced the world against the Christian religion and tended to retard its propagation; I say, considering all these things, the apostles might be directed not to intermeddle in this affair so far as to inquire into every instance of slavery, whether it was just or not; but to treat it as if it were so, unless there were particular, positive evidence of the contrary in any instances; only giving general rules for the direction and conduct of masters and servants, which, if applied and put into practice, would not only render this relation comfortable where it ought to subsist, but would effect the liberty of all the servants who were evidently reduced to that state unjustly, and were suited to put an end to slavery in general. Thus the apostle Paul, speaking to masters, says, "Masters, give unto your servants that which is just and equal." (Col. vi. 1.) The master who conformed to this rule must not only treat his servants with equity in all instances, but must set at liberty all who were evidently unjustly enslaved, and therefore had a right to their freedom. And if any Christian master refused to do this, he would bring upon him the censure of the church for disregarding this apostolic rule. (2 Thess. iii. 6) And the same apostle says to the servants, "If thou mayest be made free, use it rather." (1 Cor. vii. 21.) In these words it is declared that slavery is, in itself considered, undesirable, and a calamity in every instance of it, and therefore that it ought to be avoided and abolished as far as possible. And not only the servant is warranted and commanded to desire and seek to be made free, but the master is also implicitly required to set him at liberty, if there be no insuperable impediment in the way; for if the servant ought to desire and attempt to obtain his freedom, the master ought to desire it also, and assist him to obtain it if it can be effected, and will do it if he loves his servant as himself; and the church to which the servant belongs, and every member of it, ought to do all in their power to procure the freedom of every such servant; for will any one say they ought not to do their utmost in assisting their poor suffering brother to obtain his liberty, which God has commanded him to desire and seek? This apostolic command, therefore, being properly regarded, would soon put an end to most instances of slavery in the Christian church, if it did not wholly abolish it, especially at this day, when many of the impediments in the way of freeing slaves, which were in the apostles' days, are removed. And it may be left to the consciences of all slaveholders among us, whether, if it had been left to them, such a direction and command would ever have been given to any servant whatever, as is here given by the apostle; and whether, now it is given, they approve of it and practice accordingly. So far from it, that most of them, even professing Christians, hold their servants at such a distance, and treat them in such a manner, that the poor servant dare not so much as treat with his master about his freedom, and if he should say a word, is pretty sure to receive nothing but angry frowns, if not blows. And if any one undertakes to plead the cause of these oppressed poor, whose right is turned aside in the gate and they have no helper, he may expect to feel the resentment of almost every keeper of slaves who knows him. And is there one church now in this land who are ready to do what is in their power to obtain the freedom of the slaves which belong to them, or are willing calmly to consider and debate the question among themselves, whether it be right to hold the negroes in bondage? Where is the church that has done any thing of this kind? And how few churches are to be found that would not be greatly disturbed and filled with resentment if the question were seriously proposed and urged to be considered?

Let none who are conscious all this is true urge the apostle Paul's authority in favor of the slave-keeping which is practised in British America.

But to return. The apostle seems to have conducted in this case as he did in that of civil government. He considered this as a divine institution, and pointed out the end and design of it, and the duty of civil rulers and of the subject, without particularly applying it to the government Christians were then under, so as expressly to justify or condemn the particular form of government that then took place, or the conduct of those who then had the civil authority in their hands, and that for very obvious reasons, grounded on the state and circumstances of the church and of public affairs at that day. We may as well infer from this that the civil governors of that day were not unjust and tyrannical. which is most contrary to known fact, as we can that the slavery which then took place was in general just and right, from his pointing out the duties of masters and servants without mentioning and condemning any particular instances of unjust slavery.

A. You well observed that the apostles did not intermeddle with the affair of slavery so as to condemn masters for holding their slaves, or tell the servants their masters had no right to keep them in bondage, but ought to free them. I wish all were as wise and prudent now, especially ministers of the gospel; but all are not so. Many make such a clamor about holding our negroes in bondage, and some ministers have of late said so much in public about freeing our slaves, and have so inveighed against the African slave trade, and even keeping our blacks in slavery, that many of the negroes are become very uneasy, and are much more engaged to obtain their liberty than they used to be.

I think if any thing be said on this subject it should be in private; and not a word of this kind should be lisped in the hearing of our servants, much less ought ministers to say any thing about it in public, lest the blacks should all take it into their heads that they are treated hardly, and never be easy till they are set at liberty.

B. It has been observed, there were reasons peculiar to the state of things at that time, why the apostles should not be so particular on this head; which reasons do not take place now. The slavery that now takes place is in a Christian land, and without the express sanction of civil government; and it is all of the same kind and from one original, which is most notoriously unjust, and if it be unrighteous in one instance, it is so in almost every instance; and the unrighteousness of it is most apparent, and most masters have no color of claim to hold their servants in bondage; and this is become a general and crying sin, for which we are under the awful frowns of Heaven. These things, which make the case so different from the slavery which took place in the apostles' days, may be a good reason of a different conduct, and make it duty to oppose and bear testimony, both in public and more privately, against this evil practice, which is so evidently injurious to individuals, and threatens our ruin as a people.

As to making servants uneasy, and desirous of liberty, I would observe, that most of them do not want to be informed that they are greatly injured and oppressed; that they are reduced to a state of slavery without the least color of justice. They have sense and discerning enough to be sensible of this, without being told; and they think much of it almost every day, though they are obliged to keep it to themselves, having none to pity them, or so much as hear their complaints. They have a thousand times more discerning and sensibility in this case than their masters, or most others; and their aversion to slavery, and desires of liberty, are inextinguishable. Therefore, their hearing it asserted that they ought to be set at liberty gives them no new light and conviction, except it be, that he who asserts it has some discerning of what they have long known and most sensibly felt, and has courage enough to assert that in their favor which they have long felt the truth of, but dared not so much as lisp it out. But if by this means any of your servants should be more fully convinced of their right to liberty, and the injustice done them in making them slaves, will this be such a dreadful evil? Would you desire they should be held in ignorance, that you may exercise your tyranny without opposition or trouble from any quarter? As reasonably might Pharaoh be angry, and complain of Moses and Aaron for saying a word to those whom he had reduced to slavery about their cruel bondage and their obtaining their liberty.

It has always been the way of tyrants to take great pains to keep their vassals in ignorance, especially to hide from them the tyranny and oppression of which they are the subjects; and for this reason they are enemies to the liberty of the press, and are greatly provoked when their conduct is set in a true light before the public, and the unrighteousness they practise properly exposed. The complaint we are now considering seems to be of the same kind with this, and well becomes all those petty tyrants who have slaves in their possession, which they are conscious they cannot vindicate, but the unrighteousness will be detected if free inquiry and freedom of speech cannot be suppressed; and this complaint is of the same kind with the conduct of the masters of slaves in the West Indies in opposing their being taught any thing of Christianity, because they know every gleam of this light carries a discovery of the unrighteousness of the treatment they receive.

The present situation of our public affairs and our struggle for liberty, and the abundant conversation this occasions in all companies, while the poor negroes look on and hear what an aversion we have to slavery and how much liberty is prized, they often hearing it declared publicly and in private, as the voice of all, that slavery is more to be dreaded than death, and we are resolved to live free or die, etc.; this, I say, necessarily leads them to attend to their own wretched situation more than otherwise they could. They see themselves deprived of all liberty and property, and their children after them, to the latest posterity, subject to the will of those who appear to have no feeling for their misery, and are guilty of many instances of hard-heartedness and cruelty towards them, while they think themselves very kind; and therefore, to make the least complaint, would be deemed the height of arrogance and abuse; and often if they have a comparatively good master now, with constant dread they see a young one growing up, who bids fair to rule over them, or their children, with rigor.

They see the slavery the Americans dread as worse than death is lighter than a feather compared to their heavy doom, and may be called liberty and happiness when contrasted with the most abject slavery and unutterable wretchedness to which they are subjected; and in this dark and dreadful situation they look round and find no help—no pity—no hope! And when they observe all this cry and struggle for liberty for ourselves and children, and see themselves and their children wholly overlooked by us, and behold the sons of liberty oppressing and tyrannizing over many thousands of poor blacks who have as good a claim to liberty as themselves, they are shocked with the glaring inconsistence, and wonder they themselves do not see it. You must not, therefore, lay it to the few who are pleading the cause of these friendless, distressed poor, that they are more uneasy than they used to be in a sense of their wretched state and from a desire of liberty: there is a more mighty and irresistible cause than this, viz., all that passes before them in our public struggle for liberty.

And why should the ministers of the gospel hold their peace and not testify against this great and public iniquity, which we have reason to think is one great cause of the public calamities we are now under? How can they refuse to plead the cause of these oppressed poor against the cruel oppressor? They are commanded to lift up their voice, and cry aloud, and show the people their sins. Have we not reason to fear many of them have offended Heaven by their silence, through fear of the masters, who stand ready to make war against any one who attempts to deprive them of their slaves, or because they themselves have slaves which they are not willing to give up?

Might they not fully expose this iniquity, and bear a constant testimony against it, in such a manner as would have no tendency to influence our servants to behave ill in any respect, by giving them, at the same time, proper cautions and directions?

A. It is impossible to free all our negroes, especially at once and in present circumstances, without injuring them, at least many of them, and the public to a great degree. Why, then, is this urged so vehemently now? I think this proceeds from a zeal not according to knowledge.

B. If it be not a sin, an open, flagrant violation of all the rules of justice and humanity, to hold these slaves in bondage, it is indeed folly to put ourselves to any trouble and expense in order to free them. But if the contrary be true, if it be a sin of a crimson dye, which is most particularly pointed out by the public calamities which have come upon us, from which we have no reason to expect deliverance till we put away the evil of our doings, this reformation cannot be urged with too much zeal, nor attempted too soon, whatever difficulties are in the way. The more and greater these are, the more zealous and active should we be in removing them. You had need to take care, lest from selfish motives and a backwardness to give up what you unrighteously retain, you are joining with the slothful man to cry, "There is a lion in the way! a lion is in the streets!" (Pr. xxvi. 13,) while there is no insurmountable difficulty but that which lies in your own heart.

No wonder there are many and great difficulties in reforming an evil practice of this kind, which has got such deep root by length of time and is become so common. But it does not yet appear that they cannot be removed by the united wisdom and strength of the American colonies, without any injury to the slaves or disadvantage to the public. Yea, the contrary is most certain, as the slaves cannot be put into a more wretched situation, ourselves being judges, and the community cannot take a more likely step to escape ruin, and obtain the smiles and protection of Heaven. This matter ought, doubtless, to be attended to by the general assemblies, and continental and provincial congresses; and if they were as much united and engaged in devising ways and means to set at liberty these injured slaves as they are to defend themselves from tyranny, it would soon be effected. There were, without doubt, many difficulties and impediments in the way of the Jews liberating those of their brethren they had brought into bondage in the days of Jeremiah. But when they were besieged by the Chaldeans, and this their sin was laid before them, and they were threatened with desolation if they did not reform, they broke through every difficulty, and set their servants at liberty.

And how great must have been the impediments, how many the seeming unanswerable objections against reforming that gross violation of the divine command in Ezra's time, by their marrying strange wives, of which so many of the Jews were guilty, and the hand of the princes and rulers had been chief in this trespass! Yet the pious zeal of Ezra, and those who joined with him, and their wisdom and indefatigable efforts, conquered every obstacle and brought them to a thorough reformation. Would not the like zeal, wisdom, and resolution, think you, soon produce a reformation of this much greater abomination, by finding out an effectual method to put away all our slaves? Surely we have no reason to conclude it cannot be done till we see a suitable zeal and resolution among all orders of men, and answerable attempts are thoroughly made.

Let this iniquity be viewed in its true magnitude, and in the shocking light in which it has been set in this conversation; let the wretched case of the poor blacks be considered with proper pity and benevolence, together with the probably dreadful consequence to this land of retaining them in bondage, and all objections against liberating them would vanish. The mountains that are now raised up in the imagination of many would become a plain, and every difficulty surmounted.

Pharaoh and the Egyptians could not bear to think of letting the Hebrews go out free from the bondage to which they had reduced them, and it may be presumed they had as many weighty objections against it as can be thought of against freeing the slaves among us. Yet they were at length brought to drop them all, and willing to send them out free, and to be ready to part with any thing they had in order to promote it.

If many thousands of our children were slaves in Algiers, or any parts of the Turkish dominions, and there were but few families in the American colonies that had not some child or near relation in that sad state, without any hope of freedom to them or their children unless there were some very extraordinary exertion of the colonies to effect it, how would the attention of all the country be turned to it! How greatly should we be affected with it! Would it not become the chief topic of conversation? Would any cost or labor be spared, or any difficulty or hazard be too great to go through, in order to obtain their freedom? If there were no greater difficulties than there are in the case before us, yea, if they were ten times greater, would they not be soon surmounted as very inconsiderable? I know you, sir, and every one else, must answer in the affirmative without hesitation. And why are we not as much affected with the slavery of the many thousands of blacks among ourselves whose miserable state is before our eyes? And why should we not be as much engaged to relieve them? The reason is obvious. It is because they are negroes, and fit for nothing but slaves, and we have been used to look on them in a mean, contemptible light, and our education has filled us with strong prejudices against them, and led us to consider them, not as our brethren, or in any degree on a level with us, but as quite another species of animals, made only to serve us and our children, and as happy in bondage as in any other state. This has banished all attention to the injustice that is done them, and any proper sense of their misery or the exercise of benevolence towards them. If we could only divest ourselves of these strong prejudices which have insensibly fixed on our minds, and consider them as by nature and by right on a level with our brethren and children, and those of our neighbors, and that benevolence which loves our neighbor as ourselves, and is agreeable to truth and righteousness, we should begin to feel towards them, in some measure at least, as we should towards our children and neighbors in the case above supposed, and be as much engaged for their relief.

If parents have a son pressed on board a king's ship, how greatly are they affected with it! They are filled with grief and distress, and will cheerfully be at almost any cost and pains to procure his liberty; and we wonder not at it, but think their exercises and engagedness for his deliverance very just, and stand ready to condemn him who has no feeling for them and their son, and is not ready to afford all the assistance in his power in order to recover him. At the same time we behold vast numbers of blacks among us, torn from their native country and all their relations, not to serve on board a man-of-war for a few years, but to be abject, despised slaves for life, and their children after them, and yet have not the least feelings for them or desire of their freedom. These very parents, perhaps, have a number of negro slaves on whom they have not the least pity, and stand ready highly to resent it if any one espouses their cause so much as to propose they should be set at liberty. What reason for this partiality? Ought this so to be? An impartial person, who is not under the prejudices of interest, education, and custom, is shocked with it beyond all expression. The poor negroes have sense enough to see and feel it, but have no friend to speak a word for them, none to whom they may complain.

It has been observed, that if the general assemblies of these American colonies would take this matter in hand in earnest, with a concern and resolution answerable to its real importance, and the whole community were properly disposed and engaged, the freedom of the slaves among us might soon be effected without injury to the public or those who shall be set at liberty, but greatly to the advantage of both. But if this should be neglected, will it excuse individuals who have slaves in their continuing to hold them in bondage? I think not. If you, sir, had as many children in slavery at Algiers as you have African slaves in your house, would you take no pains and devise no method to obtain their liberty till the public should make some provision for the emancipation of all slaves there? If any opportunity should present to obtain their liberty, would you not greedily embrace it, though at much hazard and expense? And if their master should refuse to let them go free till there was a general emancipation of the Christian slaves in that country, would you justify him as acting a proper, humane, and benevolent part? I trow not. How then can you excuse yourself, and deliver your own soul, while you have no compassion for these black children in your house, and refuse to break the yoke, the galling yoke, from off their necks, because your neighbors will not be so just and humane to theirs?

Some masters say they will give up their slaves if all masters will do the same, but seem to think they are excused from setting theirs free so long as there is not a general manumission. What has just been observed is suited, I think, to show the insufficiency of this excuse. Besides, if you desire to have all our slaves freed, why do you not set an example by liberating your own? This might influence others to do the same, and then you might with a good grace plead the cause of these poor Africans; whereas, while you retain your own slaves your mouth is stopped, and your example serves to strengthen others, and keep them in countenance, while they practise this abominable oppression.

A. My servants have cost me a great deal of money, and it is not reasonable I should lose all that. If the public will indemnify me and pay me what my servants are worth, I am willing to free them, and none can reasonably desire to do it on any other consideration.

B. If your neighbor buys a horse, or any beast, of a thief who stole it from you, while he had no thought that it was stolen, would you not think you had a right to demand your horse of your neighbor, and pronounce him very unjust if he should refuse to deliver him to you till he had received the whole sum he had given for him? And have not your servants as great a right to themselves, to their liberty, as you have to your stolen horse? They have been stolen and sold, and you have bought them, in your own wrong, when you had much more reason to think they were stolen than he who bought your horse had to mistrust he was trading with a thief. Though your horse has passed through many hands, and been sold ten times, you think you have a right to demand and take him, in whose soever hand you find him, without refunding a farthing of what he cost him; and yet, though your negroes can prove their right to themselves, and constantly make a demand upon you to deliver them up, you refuse till they pay the full price you gave for them, because the civil law will not oblige you to do it. "Thou hypocrite!" (Luke xiii. 15.)

Had you not been amazingly inconsiderate and stupid, you would have concluded these men were stolen, and known that no man had a right to sell them, or you to buy them. And must they be forever deprived of their right, which is worth more to them than all you possess, because you have been so foolish and wicked as to buy them, and no one appears to prevent your losing by the bargain? You would do well to consider the awful denunciation by Jeremiah: "Woe unto him that buildeth his house by unrighteousness, and his chambers by wrong; that useth his neighbor's service without wages, and giveth him not for his work!" He who refuses to free his negroes, that he may save his money and lay it up for his children, and retains his slaves for them to tyrannize over, leaves them but a miserable inheritance—infinitely worse than nothing.

Besides, if indifferent persons were to judge, it would doubtless be found that many of your servants, if not all, have much more than earned what they cost you,—some of them double and treble, yea, ten times as much,—and, in this view, you ought to let them go out free, and not send them away empty, but furnish them liberally out of your store, agreeably to the divine command, they having a much better right to part of your estate than your children, and, it may be, much more likely to make a good improvement of it.

A. You speak of servants earning so much; but, for my part, I think not so much of this. Mine have never been much profit to me, and most of them do not pay for their victuals and clothes, but are constantly running in debt.

B. The master is not a proper judge in this case. How common is it for men who hire others to complain that the laborers do not earn the wages they give, and that they are continually losing by all the labor they hire. And, if it were wholly left to him who hires what wages he should give the laborer, and he was accountable to none, how soon would his hire be reduced to little or nothing. The lordly, selfish employer would soon find out that his laborers hardly earned the food he was obliged to find them. Let your uninterested, judicious neighbors judge between you and your servants in this matter, and we will give credit to their verdict. And surely you have no reason to expect we will rely on yours, as you seem not really to believe it yourself, since it looks like a contradiction to your own declaration and practice; for you have been speaking of your servants as of as much worth to you at least as their first cost, and represented it as giving up your interest if you should free them without a compensation; whereas, if what you now say be true, you will lose nothing by freeing them immediately, but rather get rid of a burden now on your hands. And if this be true, why do you not free them without delay? Your holding them in slavery is a practical contradiction to what you have now suggested.

I grant, what is evident to all the discerning who attend to it, that the introduction of such a number of slaves among us is a public detriment—an injury to the commonwealth; and, therefore, in this view, the practice ought by all means to be discouraged and abolished by our legislators. This, however, is consistent with individuals getting estates by the labor of their slaves; and that they are, in fact, in many instances very profitable to their owners, none can deny. And if this was not so, I should be very certain of obtaining what I am pleading for, even a general manumission.

A. You have repeatedly spoke of our slaves being hardly treated and abused. There may, perhaps, be some instances of this among us; but I believe they are generally treated very well, and many of them much better than they deserve. My servants, I am sure, have no reason to complain; they live as well as I do myself, and, in many respects, much better.

B. We will take it for granted, for once, that all you have said is true, and that your slaves are treated as well as they can be while they are held in a state of slavery. But will this atone for your making them your slaves, and taking from them that which is better to them than not only the best living, but all the riches on earth, and is as much to be prized as life itself—*their liberty*? As well, yea, with much more reason, may a highway robber tell a gentleman, from whom he has taken all his money, he has no reason to complain, since he had spared his life which was at his mercy, nor had wounded him or stripped him of his clothes, and go away pleased with the thought that he had treated him with great kindness and generosity.

If a ruffian should seize, ravish, and carry off a young virgin from all her relations and friends into some lonely cave in the wilderness, and when he got full possession of her there should treat her with great kindness, providing for her every necessary and comfort she could have in that situation; and when he was told of his violence and cruelty, and urged to restore her to her former liberty, he should refuse to release her, and, to justify himself, allege his kind treatment of her, that she had all the comforts of life, and lived better than himself,—would not this be so far from justifying him in the sight of the world, or being the least excuse for his barbarous treatment of her, that his offering it as such would be considered as a striking evidence of his stupidity, and that he was an unfeeling, inhuman wretch? Whether such an instance is in any measure applicable to the case before us, I leave you to judge.

But I must now ask leave to take back what was just now granted, and observe that you are not a proper judge of your treatment of your slaves, and that you may think you treat them very well, in some instances at least, if not in a constant way; they justly think themselves used very hardly, being really subjected to many hardships which you would very sensibly feel and resent if you were in their place, or should see one of your children a slave in Algiers treated so by his master. There are but few masters of slaves, I believe, who do not use them in a hard, unreasonable manner, in some instances at least, and most do so in a constant way; so that an impartial, attentive bystander will be shocked with it, while the master is wholly insensible of any wrong. They who from us have visited the West Indies, have beheld how servants are used by their masters there with a degree of horror, and pronounced them very unreasonable and barbarous; while the master, and perhaps his other domestics, have thought they were used well, being accustomed to such usage and never once reflecting that these blacks were in any sense on a level with themselves, or that they have the least right to the treatment white people may reasonably expect of one another, and being habituated to view these slaves more beneath themselves than the very beasts really are. And are we not most of us educated in these prejudices, and led to view the slaves among us in such a mean, despicable light, as not to be sensible of the abuses they suffer, when if we or our children should receive such treatment from any of our fellow-men it would appear terrible in our sight? The Turks are by education and custom taught to view the Christian slaves among them so much beneath themselves and in such an odious light, that while they are treating our brethren and children, we being judges, in the most unreasonable and cruel manner, they have not one thought that they injure them in the least degree.

Are you sure your slaves have a sufficiency of good food in season, and that they never want for comfortable clothing and bedding? Do you take great care to deal as well by them in these things as you would wish others would treat your own children were they slaves in a strange land? If your servants complain, are you ready to attend to them? Or do you in such cases frown upon them, or do something worse, so as to discourage their ever applying to you whatever they may suffer, having learned that this would only be making bad worse? Do you never fly into a passion and deal with them in great anger, deciding matters respecting them, and threatening them, and giving sentence concerning them, from which they have no appeal, and perhaps proceed to correct them, when to a calm bystander you appear more fit to be confined in Bedlam than to have the sovereign, uncontrollable dominion over your brethren as the sole lawgiver, judge, and executioner? Do not even your children domineer over your slaves? Must they not often be at the beck of an ungoverned, peevish child in the family; and if they do not run at his or her call, and are not all submission and obedience, must they not expect the frowns of their masters, if not the whip?

If none of these things, my good sir, take place in your family, have we not reason to think you almost a singular instance? How common are things of this kind, or worse, taking place between masters and their slaves? In how few instances, if in any, are slaves treated as the masters would wish to have their own children treated in like circumstances? How few are fit to be masters; to have the sovereign dominion over a number of their fellow-men, being his property, and wholly at his disposal, who must abide his sentence and orders, however unreasonable, without any possibility of relief?

A. I believe my slaves are so far from thinking themselves abused, or being in the least uneasy in a state of slavery, that they have no desire to be made free; and if their freedom were offered to them, they would refuse to accept it.

B. I must take leave to call this in question, sir; and I think you believe it in contradiction to all reason and the strongest feelings of human nature, till they have declared it themselves, having had opportunity for due deliberation, and being in circumstances to act freely, without the least constraint or fear.

There are many masters (if we believe what they say) who please themselves with this fond opinion of their goodness to their slaves, and their choice of a state of slavery in preference to freedom, without the least foundation, and while the contrary is known to be true by all who are acquainted with their slaves. If they really believe this, they by it only discover great insensibility and want of proper reflection. They have not so much as put themselves in the place of their slaves, so as properly and with due sensibility to consult what would be their own feelings on such a supposition. Have they themselves lost all desire of freedom? Are they destitute of all taste of the sweets of it, and have they no aversion to slavery for themselves and children? If they have these feelings, what reason have they to conclude their servants have not?

But it seems most of those masters do not fully believe what they so often say on this head, for they have never made the trial, nor can they be persuaded to do it. Let them offer freedom to their servants and give them opportunity to choose for themselves without being under the most distant constraint; and if they then deliberately choose to continue their slaves, the matter will be fairly decided, and they may continue to possess them with a good conscience.

Slaves are generally under such disadvantages and restraints, that however much they desire liberty they dare not so much as mention it to their masters; and if their master should order them into his presence and ask them whether they had a desire to be made free, many would not dare to declare their choice lest it should offend him, and instead of obtaining their freedom bring themselves into a more evil case than they were in before, as the children of Israel did by desiring Pharaoh to free them.

In this case such precaution ought to be taken as to give the slaves proper assurance that they may without any danger to themselves declare their choice of freedom, and that it shall be done to them according to their choice.

A. If slaves in general were made free, they would soon be in a worse state than that in which they now are. Many of them know not how to contrive for themselves so as to get a living, but must soon be maintained by their former masters or some others; and others would make themselves wretched, and become a great trouble to their neighbors and an injury to the public, by their unrestrained vices. This would doubtless be the case with most of mine were they set free, and some of them are by no means able to maintain themselves.

B. I confess this objection, at first view, seems to have some weight in it; but let us examine it, and see if it be sufficient to hold so many thousands in slavery, and their children after them, to the end of the world. Would you have all the white people, who are given to hurtful vices or are unwilling or unable to maintain themselves, made slaves, and their children after them, and be bought and sold for life like cattle in the market? Would you willingly give up your own children to this, to be slaves forever to any one who should be willing and able to purchase them, if they were as vicious or helpless as you suppose many of the blacks would be if set at liberty? I am sure you will not answer in the affirmative; and by answering in the negative, as I know you must, you will entirely remove the reason you have now offered for holding the blacks in this slavery, till you can show why the latter should be treated so very differently from the former, which I am confident you will not attempt.

A state of slavery has a mighty tendency to sink and contract the minds of men, and prevent their making improvements in useful knowledge of every kind. It sinks the mind down in darkness and despair; it takes off encouragements to activity and to make improvements, and naturally tends to lead the enslaved to abandon themselves to a stupid carelessness and to vices of all kinds. No wonder then the blacks among us are, many of them, so destitute of prudence and sagacity to act for themselves, and some are given to vice. It is rather a wonder there are so many instances of virtue, prudence, knowledge, and industry among them. And shall we, because we have reduced them to this abject, helpless, miserable state by our oppression of them, make this an argument for continuing them and their children in this wretched condition? God forbid! This ought rather to excite our pity, and arouse us to take some effectual method without delay to deliver them and their children from this most unhappy state. If your own children were in this situation, would you offer this as a good reason why they and their posterity should be made slaves forever? Were some of your children unable to provide for themselves through infirmity of body or want of mental capacity, and others of them were very vicious, would you have them sold into a state of slavery for this? or would you make slaves of them yourself? Would you not be willing to take the best care of them in your power, and give them all possible encouragement to behave well, and direct and assist them in proper methods to get a living? I know you would. And why will you not go and do likewise to your slaves? Why will you not take off the galling yoke from their necks, and restore them to that liberty to which they have as good a claim as you yourself and your children, and which has been violently taken from them and unjustly withheld by you to this day? If any of them are disposed to behave ill and make a bad use of their freedom, let them have all the motives to behave well that can be laid before them. Let them be subject to the same restraints and laws with other freemen, and have the same care taken of them by the public. And be as ready to direct and assist those who want discretion and assistance to get a living as if they were your own children, and as willing to support the helpless, infirm, and aged. And give all proper encouragement and assistance to those who have served you well, and are like to get a good living, if not put under peculiar disadvantages, as freed negroes most commonly are, by giving them reasonable wages for their labor if they still continue with you, or liberally furnishing them with what is necessary in order to their living comfortably, and being in a way to provide for themselves. This was the divine command to the people of Israel, and does it not appear at least equally reasonable in the case before us? When one of their brethren had served them the number of years that were specified, they were commanded to let him go out free; and then the following injunction is added: "And when thou sendest him out free from thee, thou shalt not let him go away empty; thou shalt furnish him liberally out of thy stock, and out of thy floor, and out of thy wine press; of that wherewith the Lord thy God hath blessed thee, thou shalt give unto him." (Deut. xv. 13, 14.)

If all who have slaves would act such a just, wise, and benevolent part towards them, and treat them in any measure as they would desire their own children and near relations should be treated, our slaves might all be set free without any detriment to themselves or the public, and their masters would be so far from losing by it that they would be abundantly rewarded for all their benevolence to these injured poor. And if our legislators would lend their helping hand, and form such laws and regulations as shall be properly suited to protect and assist those that are freed, and so as in the best manner to deter and restrain them from vicious courses, and encourage their industry and good behavior, this would be an additional security to the public against any imagined evil consequence of a general manumission of our slaves, and but a piece of justice to these poor, dependent creatures, whom we have made so by our own unrighteousness and oppression. This would encourage masters to free their slaves, and leave the objection we are now considering without the least shadow of foundation.

A. You are doubtless sensible, sir, that the legislatures in these colonies are so far from giving this encouragement to manumit our slaves, that the laws are rather a clog or hinderance to any thing of this kind, as they require the master to give security for the maintenance of his slaves if they should ever want any assistance, before he is allowed to make them free.

B. I am sorry to say there is too much truth in this. I hope our legislatures will soon attend with proper concern to this affair, and in their justice, wisdom, and goodness, enter upon measures which shall encourage and effect a general emancipation of our slaves.

But if this should not be, I think it appears, from the course of this conversation, that this will not excuse those who have slaves from setting them at liberty, even though they should be obliged to maintain them all their days. If any slaveholder can lay his hand on his breast and sincerely say, if his children were slaves at Algiers he would not desire their master to free them unless he could do it without any risk of their ever being a charge to him, then let him still hold his slaves in bondage with a quiet conscience. Otherwise I see not how he can do it.

A. If it were granted that our slaves ought to be freed, if times and the public state of the American colonies would admit, yet in our present peculiar, calamitous, distressing state, it may be very imprudent and wrong and tend to great evil to adopt this measure. Most of the slaves in populous seaport places have now little or no business to do, and are supported by their masters, while they earn little or nothing. And if they should be dismissed by their masters, they could not maintain themselves, and must suffer. And the attention and exertion of the public is so necessarily turned to the defence of ourselves, and this civil war introduces such calamity and confusion, that it cannot be expected, yea, it is quite impossible that there should be any proper care of the public, so as to make the provision and regulations which would be absolutely necessary in this case. Though I suggested this in the beginning of our conversation, yet I think you have paid little or no attention to it. I wish this might be well considered.

B. I think the facts you have now alleged as reasons against freeing our slaves at present, will, if duly considered, afford arguments for the very thing you are opposing. The slaves who are become unprofitable to their masters by the present calamitous state of our country, will be with the less reluctance set at liberty, it is hoped; and if no public provision be made for them that they may be transported to Africa, where they might probably live better than in any other country, or be removed into those places in this land where they may have profitable business and are wanted, now so many are called from their farms to defend our country; I say, if this be not done, the masters, by freeing them, would lose nothing by it, even though they continue to support them, till some way shall be open for them to help themselves. I must here again desire every owner of slaves to make their case his own, and consider, if he or his children were unjustly in a state of slavery, whether he should think such an objection against their being set at liberty of any weight. Would he not rather think it reasonable that the masters who had held them in bondage against all right and reason would consider their being, by an extraordinary providence, rendered unprofitable to them, as an admonition to break off their sins by righteousness and their iniquity by showing mercy to these poor, and that it ought to be a greater satisfaction to them thus to do justice without delay and relieve these oppressed poor, than to possess all the riches, honors, and pleasures of this world? And if these masters should disregard such an admonition and neglect this opportunity to set them at liberty, putting it off to a more convenient season, would it not be very grievous to him and overwhelm him in despair of their ever doing it? Is it not very certain that they who make this objection against freeing their slaves without delay, would not free them if the times should change and they again become profitable? If they must maintain them, can they not do it as well when they are free as while they are slaves, and ought they not to do it with much more satisfaction?

And as to the public, all necessary regulations and provision might easily and very soon be made, even in our present distressing circumstances, effectually to emancipate all our slaves, were the minds of men in general properly impressed with their misery, and they sufficiently engaged to do justice and show mercy.

This objection might be urged with much greater show of reason by the inhabitants of Jerusalem, against freeing their servants when they were not only in a state of war, but shut up, and closely besieged in that city; yet we find it was their duty to free them immediately, as the only way to escape threatened destruction; and as soon as they had done this they had respite, and would have obtained final deliverance had they not returned to their old oppression and again brought their freed servants into bondage.

This leads me to observe, that our distresses are come upon us in such a way, and the occasion of the present war is such, as in the most clear and striking manner to point out the sin of holding our blacks in slavery, and admonish us to reform, and render us shockingly inconsistent with ourselves, and amazingly guilty if we refuse. God has raised up men to attempt to deprive us of liberty, and the evil we are threatened with is slavery. This, with our vigorous attempts to avoid it, is the ground of all our distresses, and the general voice is, "We will die in the attempt, rather than submit to slavery." But are we at the same time making slaves of many thousands of our brethren, who have as good a right to liberty as ourselves, and to whom it is as sweet as it is to us, and the contrary as dreadful? Are we holding them in the most abject, miserable state of slavery, without the least compassionate feeling towards them or their posterity, utterly refusing to take off the oppressive, galling yoke? O, the shocking, the intolerable inconsistence! And this gross, barefaced inconsistence is an open, practical condemnation of holding these our brethren in slavery; and in these circumstances the crime of persisting in it becomes unspeakably greater and more provoking in God's sight, so that all the former unrighteousness and cruelty exercised in this practice is innocence compared with the awful guilt that is now contracted. And in allusion to the words of our Savior, it may with great truth and propriety be said, "If he had not thus come in his providence, and spoken unto us, (comparatively speaking,) we had not had sin in making bondslaves of our brethren; but now, we have no cloak for our sin."

And if we continue in this evil practice and refuse to let the oppressed go free, under all this light and admonition suited to convince and reform us, and while God is evidently correcting us for it as well as for other sins, have we any reason to expect deliverance from the calamities we are under? May we not rather look for slavery and destruction like that which came upon the obstinate, unreformed Jews? In this light I think it ought to be considered by us; and viewed thus, it affords a most forcible, formidable argument not to put off liberating our slaves to a more convenient time, but to arise all as one man, and do it with all our might, without delay, since delaying in this case is awfully dangerous as well as unspeakably criminal. This was hinted in the beginning of our conversation, you may remember, and I am glad of an opportunity to consider it more particularly.

A. You have repeatedly spoken of the attempt that is made to oppress and enslave the American colonies, and the calamities this has introduced, as a judgment which God has brought upon us for enslaving the Africans, and say we have no reason to expect deliverance, but still greater judgments, unless this practice be reformed. But is not this supposition inconsistent with the course of divine Providence since this war began? Have we not been strengthened and succeeded in our opposition to the measures taken against us, even beyond our most sanguine expectations; and a series of events very extraordinary and almost miraculous have taken place in our favor, and so as remarkably to disappoint our opposers and baffle them in all their plots and attempts against us? How is this consistent with the above supposition? If these calamities were brought on us for our sin in enslaving the Africans, and an expression of God's displeasure with us on that account, would he in such a signal manner appear on our side and favor, protect, and prosper us, even so that those of our enemies who are considerate and attentive have been obliged to acknowledge God was for us; I say, could this be, while we persist in that practice so offensive to him?

B. When I speak of our being under the divine judgments for this sin of enslaving the Africans, I do not mean to exclude other public crying sins found among us, such as impiety and profaneness, formality and indifference, in the service and cause of Christ and his religion, and the various ways of open opposition to it—intemperance and prodigality, and other instances of unrighteousness, etc., the fruits of a most criminal, contracted selfishness, which is the source of the high-handed oppression we are considering. But that this is a sin most particularly pointed out, and so contrary to our holy religion in every view of it, and such an open violation of all the laws of righteousness, humanity, and charity, and so contrary to our professions and exertions in the cause of liberty, that we have no reason to expect, nor can sincerely ask deliverance, so long as we continue in a disposition to hold fast this iniquity. If we should be delivered while we continue in this evil practice, and obstinately refuse thoroughly to execute judgment between a man and his neighbor, but go on to oppress the stranger, the fatherless, and the widow, we should, agreeably to the spirit of what you have just said, improve such deliverance as God said the Jews would have done had he delivered them while they refused to reform. "Will ye steal, murder, etc., and come and stand before me in this house, which is called by my name and say, We are delivered to do all these abominations?" (Jer. vii. 5-10.) Surely this is not to be expected or desired. Even the prayer for such deliverance must be an abomination to the Lord.

But your objection is worthy of a more particular answer. It has been observed, that there has been a general resolution to suppress the slave trade in these colonies, and to import no more slaves from Africa. This is a remarkable instance of our professed regard to justice, and a wise and notable step towards a reformation of this evil, and, as has been observed, a complete reformation will be the unavoidable consequence, if we will be consistent with ourselves. For no reason can be given for suppressing the slave trade which is not equally a reason for freeing all those who have been reduced to a state of slavery by that trade; and that same regard to justice, humanity, and mercy which will induce us to acquiesce in the former, will certainly oblige us to practise the latter. Have we not, therefore, reason to think that the righteous and infinitely merciful Governor of the world has been pleased to testify his well-pleasedness with that regard to righteousness and mercy which we professed and appeared to exercise in refusing to import any more slaves, and which is an implicit condemnation of all the slavery practised among us, by appearing on our side in the remarkable, extraordinary manner you have mentioned, by which wonderful interposition in our favor he has, at the same time, given us the greatest encouragement not to stop what we have begun, but to go on to a thorough reformation, and act consistently with ourselves by breaking every yoke and doing justice to all our oppressed slaves, as well as to repent of and reform all our open, public sins? So that God is hereby showing us what he can do for us, and how happy we may be under his protection, if we will amend our ways and our doings, and loudly calling us to a thorough reformation in this most kind and winning way.

But if we obstinately refuse to reform what we have implicitly declared to be wrong, and engaged to put away the holding the Africans in slavery, which is so particularly pointed out by the evil with which we are threatened, and is such a glaring contradiction to our professed aversion to slavery and struggle for civil liberty, and improve the favor God is showing us as an argument in favor of this iniquity and encouragement to persist in it, as you, sir, have just now done, have we not the greatest reason to fear yea, may we not with great certainty conclude, God will yet withdraw his kind protection from us, and punish us yet seven times more? This has been God's usual way of dealing with his professing people; and who can say it is not most reasonable and wise? He, then, acts the most friendly part to these colonies and to the masters of slaves, as well as to the slaves themselves, who does his utmost to effect a general emancipation of the Africans among us; and, in this view, I could wish the conversation we have now had on this subject, if nothing better is like to be done, were published and spread through all the colonies, and had the attentive perusal of every American.

Henry Laurens to John Laurens, August 14, 1776

Berol Collection, Butler Library, Columbia University, New York, N.Y.

South Carolina Revolutionary leader Henry Laurens, a wealthy planter and formerly a leading merchant of Charleston who had become a rich man riding the ecomonic back of the slave trade, wrote to his son, John Laurens, in August 1776, "I abhor slavery." Henry Laurens, like many Southerners who spoke against slavery during the war, blamed the British for shackling America with an institution economically disastrous and morally reprehensible. The elder Laurens wrote to a man even more passionately opposed to slavery than himself. John Laurens wrote in the same year, "I think we Americans at least in the Southern Colonies cannot contend with a good Grace for Liberty, until we shall have enfranchised our Slaves. How can we whose Jealousy has been alarm'd more at the Name of oppression sometimes than at the Reality, reconcile to our spirited Assertions of the Rights of Mankind, the galling abject Slavery of our Negroes."

In 1778, with the deep South frighteningly vulnerable to British attack, the young Colonel Laurens conceived a plan for recruiting an army of several thousand slaves in South Carolina and Georgia, the owners to be compensated at federal expense and the slaves freed after the war. Laurens's scheme was approved by the Continental Congress and endorsed by Generals Benjamin Lincoln and Nathanael Greene. Deep South legislators, however, not only saw ominous portents in opening any doors to emancipation but envisioned disgrace and humiliation in being forced to rely for defense upon the black slaves. This plan was quashed and with it John Laurens's vision of a liberated army of black Americans defending American liberty. Laurens saw the decision to thwart his aims as the "howlings of a triple-headed monster, in which prejudice, avarice and pusillanimity were united." For four years Laurens tried unsuccessfully to have the plan adopted. He was supported by his father, who in 1776 had written so personally and forthrightly to him about the institution of slavery. In June 1782 John Laurens was killed in a meaningless skirmish near the Combahee River. And with John Laurens's death, the South yielded an empassioned antislavery spokesman, a man whose promising political career could have made a difference in the antislavery movement.

Charles Town So Carolina 14 Aug 1776

. . . You know my Dear Sir, I abhor slavery. I was born in a Country where Slavery had been established by British Kings & Parliaments as well as by the Laws of that Country, Ages before my existence. I found the Christian Religion and Slavery growing under the same authority and cultivation. I nevertheless disliked it. In former days there was no combatting the prejudices of Men supported by Interest, the day I hope is approaching when from principles of gratitude as well as justice, every Man will strive to be foremost in shewing his readiness to comply with the Golden Rule; not less than £20000 Sty would all my Negroes produce if sold at public Auction tomorrow. I am not the man who enslaved them, they are indebted to English Men for that favour, nevertheless I am devising means for manumitting many of them & for cutting off the entail of Slavery—great powers oppose me, the Laws and Customs of my Country, my own & the avarice of my Country Men. What will my Children say if I deprive them of so much Estate? These are difficulties but not insuperable. I will do as much as I can in my time & leave the rest to a better hand.

I am not one of those who arrogate the peculiar care of Providence in each fortunate event, nor one of those who dare trust in Providence for defence & security of their own Liberty while they enslave & wish to continue in Slavery, thousands who are as well entitled to freedom as themselves. I perceive the work before me is great. I shall appear to many as a promoter not only of strange but of dangerous doctrines, it will therefore be necessary to proceed with caution. You are apparently deeply Interested in this affair but as I have no doubts concerning your concurrence & approbation I most sincerely wish for your advice & assistance & hope to receive both in good time. . .

Petition of Prince Hall and Other Blacks, January 13, 1777

Massachusetts Archives 212:132, Massachusetts Division of Archives, Boston, Mass., as reprinted in Massachusetts Historical Collections, Series 5, 3:436-37.

Born of an English father and mulatto mother in Barbados in 1748, Prince Hall founded the world's first lodge of black Masons. A former slave who had been freed in 1770, Hall, on January 13, 1777, with seven other blacks petitioned the Massachusetts General Court to abolish slavery and restore "the Natural Right of all men." Massachusetts's slaves had since 1773 fired off several petitions to the legislature. Indeed, Abagail Adams had informed her husband that one conspiracy of Negroes in Boston had been channeled away from possible violence by the drafting of a petition to the governor. The frenetic antislavery activity among the black population was apparent when James Swan reprinted his 1773 antislavery pamphlet "at the earnest desire of the Negroes in Boston." The early petitions to the legislature were tabled to let the question, in the General Court's language, "subside." The question, however, did not subside. The Hall petition, introduced on March 18, 1777, generated a bill in the legislature "for preventing the Practice of holding Persons in Slavery." Although the bill was referred to the Confederation Congress and in effect destroyed, Hall and his fellow black allies had, nevertheless, stirred the legislature to debate the question. Although the final resolution of the slavery issue in Massachusetts was not realized until the end of the war, it was clear in 1777 that black resistance was, as it had been in 1773-74, strong.

To the Honorable Counsel & House of [Representa]tives
for the State of Massachusitte Bay in
General Court assembled, Jan. 13, 1777.

The petition of A Great Number of Blackes detained in a State of slavery in the Bowels of a free & Christian Country Humbly shuwith that your Petitioners apprehend that they have in Common with all other men a Natural and Unaliable Right to that freedom which the Grat Parent of the Unavers hath Bestowed equalley on all menkind and which they have Never forfuted by any Compact or agreement whatever—but thay wher Unjustly Dragged by the hand of cruel Power from their Derest friends and sum of them Even torn from the Embraces of their tender Parents—from A popolous Pleasant and plentiful contry and in violation of Laws of Nature and off Nations and in defiance of all the tender feelings of humanity Brough hear Either to Be sold Like Beast of Burthen & Like them Condemnd to Slavery for Life—Among A People Profesing the mild Religion of Jesus A people Not Insensible of the Secrets of Rationable Being Nor without spirit to Resent the unjust endeavours of others to Reduce them to a state of Bondage and Subjection your honouer Need not to be informed that A Life of Slavery Like that of your petioners Deprived of Every social privilege of Every thing Requiset to Render Life Tolable is far worse then Nonexistance.

In imitation of the Lawdable Example of the Good People of these States your petiononers have Long and Patiently waited the Evnt of petition after petition By them presented to the Legislative Body of this state and cannot but with Grief Reflect that their Sucess hath ben but too similar they Cannot but express their Astonishment that It has Never Bin Consirdered that Every Principle from which Amarica has Acted in the Cours of their unhappy Deficultes with Great Briton Pleads Stronger than A thousand arguments in favowrs of your petioners they therfor humble Beseech your honours to give this petion its due weight & consideration and cause an act of the Legislatur to be past Wherby they may Be Restored to the Enjoyments of that which is the Naturel Right of all men—and their Children who wher Born in this Land of Liberty may not be heald as Slaves after they arive at the age of Twenty one years so may the Inhabitance of thes Stats No longer chargeable with the inconsistancey of acting themselves the part which thay condem and oppose in others Be prospered in their present Glorious struggle for Liberty and have those Blessing to them, &c.

Vermont Constitution, 1777

Allen Soule, ed., *Laws of Vermont* (Montpelier, 1964), pp. 5-8.

In January 1777, a general convention of delegates from towns along the Green Mountains range announced the creation of a "free and independent jurisdiction"—a new state. On April 11, 1777, Dr. Thomas Young, an influential, radical physician from Philadelphia who had with the aid of masked accomplices three years earlier helped deposit tea into the Boston Harbor, and who had an interest in the Green Mountains land, invited the people of the new state "to meet in their respective townships, and choose members for a general convention, to meet at an early day, to choose delegates for the general Congress, a committee of safety, and to form a Constitution for your state." On July 2, 1777, a convention of delegates elected by the towns adopted a constitution which named the state "Vermont." Among the several provisions of the new Vermont Constitution was a clause declaring the institution of slavery illegal, the first such specific declaration in any American state constitution. The prohibition against slavery accompanied the familiar appeals to "higher law" doctrine which had characterized other Revolutionary War documents—that "all men are born equally free and independent;" and that they have "certain natural, inherent and unalienable rights. . . ." The Vermont constitution-makers had followed these declarations to their logical conclusion. Although the state of Vermont was never the home of more than a few blacks, the

1777 antislavery provision became more than mere hyperbole—for in 1802, a Vermont court held that a slave's bill of sale, a document necessarily voided by the express provisons of the Vermont Constitution, could not even be read in evidence.

Preamble

Whereas, all government ought to be instituted and supported for the security and protection of the community as such and to enable the individuals who compose it, to enjoy their natural rights, and the other blessings which the Author of existence has bestowed upon man; and whenever those great ends of government are not obtained, the people have a right, by common consent, to change it, and take such measures as to them may appear necessary to promote their safety and happiness.

And whereas, the inhabitants of this state have, (in consideration of protection only) heretofore acknowledged allegiance to the King of Great Britain, and the said King has not only withdrawn that protection, but commenced, and still continues to carry on, with unabated vengeance, a most cruel and unjust war against them; employing therein, not only the troops of Great Britain, but foreign mercenaries, savages and slaves, for the avowed purpose of reducing them to a total and abject submission to the despotic dominion of the British parliament, with many other acts of tryanny (more fully set forth in the declaration of Congress), whereby all allegiance and fealty to the said King and his successors, are dissolved and at an end; and all power and authority derived from him, ceased in the American Colonies.

And whereas, the territory which now comprehends the State of Vermont, did antecedently, of right, belong to the government of New Hampshire; and the former Governor thereof, viz, his excellency Benning Wentworth, Esq., granted many charters of lands and corporations, within this State, to the present inhabitants and others. And whereas, the late Lieutenant Governor Colden, of New York, with others, did, in violation of the tenth command, covet those very lands; and by a false representation made to the court of Great Britain (in the year 1764, that for the convenience of trade and administration of justice, the inhabitants were desirous of being annexed to that government), obtained jurisdiction of those very identical lands, ex-parte; which ever was, and is disagreeable to the inhabitants. And whereas, the legislature of New York, ever have, and still continue to disown the good people of this State, in their landed property, which will appear in the complaints hereafter inserted, and in the 36th section of their present constitution, in which is established the grants of land made by that government.

They have refused to make re-grants of our lands to the original proprietors and occupants, unless at the exorbitant rate of 2300 dollars fees for each township; and did enhance the quitrent, three fold, and demanded an immediate delivery of the title derived before, from New Hampshire.

The judges of their supreme court have made a solemn declaration, that the charters, conveyances, &c., of the lands included in the before described premises, were utterly null and void, on which said title was founded; in consequence of which declaration, writs of possession have been by them issued, and the sheriff of the county of Albany sent, at the head of six or seven hundred men, to enforce the execution thereof.

They have passed an act, annexing a penalty thereto, of thirty pounds fine and six months imprisonment, on any person who should refuse assisting the sheriff, after being requested, for the purpose of executing writs of possession.

The Governors, Dunmore, Tryon and Colden, have made regrants of several tracts of land, included in the premises, to certain favorite land jobbers in the government of New-York, in direct violation of his Britannic majesty's express prohibition, in the year 1767.

They have issued proclamations, wherein they have offered large sums of money, for the purpose of apprehending those very persons who have dared boldly, and publicly, to appear in defence of their just rights.

They did pass twelve acts of outlawry, on the 9th day of March, A. D. 1774, impowering the respective judges of their supreme court, to award execution of death against those inhabitants in said district that they should judge to be offenders, without trial.

They have, and still continue, an unjust claim to those lands, which greatly retards emigration into, and the settlement of, this State.

They have hired foreign troops, emigrants from Scotland, at two different times, and armed them, to drive us out of possession.

They have sent the savages on our frontiers, to distress us.

They have proceeded to erect the counties of Cumberland and Gloucester, and establish courts of justice there, after they were discountenanced by the authority of Great Britain.

The free Convention of the State of New-York, at Harlem, in the year 1776, unanimously voted, "That all quit-rents formerly due to the King of Great Britain, are now due and owing to this convention, or such future government as shall be hereafter established in this State."

In the several stages of the aforesaid oppressions, we have petitioned his Britannic majesty, in the most humble manner, for redress, and have, at very great expense, received several reports in our favor; and in other instances, wherein we have petitioned the late legislative authority of New-York, those petitions have been treated with neglect.

And whereas, the local situation of this State, from New-York, at the extreme part, is upwards of four hundred and fifty miles from the seat of that government, which renders it extreme difficult to continue under the jurisdiction of said State.

Therefore, it is absolutely necessary, for the welfare and safety of the inhabitants of this State, that it should be, henceforth, a free and independent State; and that a just, permanent and proper form of government, should exist in it, derived from, and founded on, the authority of the people only, agreeable to the direction of the honorable American Congress.

We the representatives of the freemen of Vermont, in General Convention met, for the express purpose of forming such a government, confessing the goodness of the Great Governor of the Universe (who alone, knows to what degree of earthly happiness, mankind may attain, by perfecting the arts of government), in permitting the people of this State, by common consent, and without violence, deliberately to form for themselves, such just rules as they shall think best for governing their future society; and being fully convinced that it is our indispensable duty, to establish such original principles of government, as will best promote the general happiness of the people of this State, and their posterity, and provide for future improvements, without partiality for, or prejudice against, any particular class, sect, or denomination of men whatever: Do, by virtue of authority vested in us, by our constituents, ordain, declare, and establish, the following declaration of rights, and frame of government, to be the Constitution of this Commonwealth, and to remain in force therein, forever, unaltered, except in such articles, as shall, hereafter, on experience, be found to require improvement, and which shall, by the same authority of the people, fairly delegated, as this frame of government directs, be amended or improved, for the more effectual obtaining and securing the great end and design of all government, herein before mentioned.

Chapter I

A Declaration of the Rights of the Inhabitants of the State of Vermont

I. That all men are born equally free and independent, and have certain natural, inherent and unalienable rights, amongst which are the enjoying and defending life and liberty; acquiring, possessing and protecting property, and pursuing and obtaining happiness and safety. Therefore, no male person, born in this country, or brought from over sea, ought to be holden by law, to serve any person, as a servant, slave or apprentice, after he arrives to the age of twenty-one years, nor female, in like manner, after she arrives to the age of eighteen years, unless they are bound by their own consent, after they arrive at such age, or bound by law, for the payment of debts, damages, fines, costs, or the like. . . .

Jacob Green, Fast Day Sermon, April 22, 1778

Jacob Green, *A Sermon Delivered at Hanover (in New-Jersey), April 22, 1778, Being the Day of Public Fasting and Prayer Throughout the United States of America* (Chatham, 1779), pp. 3-5; 12-23.

Jacob Green, the Harvard-educated pastor of the Presbyterian Church of Hanover, New Jersey, published a pamphlet widely-circulated in early 1776 entitled "Observations on the Reconciliation of Great Britain and the Colonies" in which he discussed both the arguments for and against independency. In this pamphlet "Parson Green" appended a note on slavery, "What a shocking consideration that people who are so strenuously contending for liberty should at the same time encourage and promote slavery." On April 22, 1778, with Washington's troops still at Valley Forge, and victory over British forces a fading hope, Green delivered the "Fast Day" sermon in Hanover. "Though our contention with Great Britain is so glorious," he declared, "we have reason to be humble and mourn for the many sins and vices that prevail among us. . . . God often makes use of the worst of instruments to correct his own people, while he calls upon them to repent and reform." Green's remarks on slavery were no longer relegated, as they were in the 1776 pamphlet, to a small note. He now called slavery "the most crying sin in our land," a sin for which God was chastising the country. Many ministers including Green saw the Revolutionary War from two perspectives. Great Britain, although representing political oppression and tyranny that had to be overthrown, also represented a tool of God with which a sinful America was being punished. Green, for example, remarked, "God corrects us by Britain." The struggle of the colonies against evil British despotism was, as Green observed, "Righteous." But, the struggle was also tainted and hypocritical. Some slaveholders demanded liberty while strapping innocent blacks in bondage at the same time. Only if America collectively reformed, and threw off these violations against God's will, would the struggle with Britain end favorably. The war would, Green hoped, bring both an end to British political oppression as well as such social ills as slavery. "We should not be discouraged," he wrote, "but repent and exert ourselves in the cause of liberty, both against Britain and among ourselves."

We are called upon by our civil rulers to set apart this day for fasting and prayer. We are called upon by those who have the management or lead in our public affairs—who best know, and have the most comprehensive view of, things in these United States. We have reason to bless God that those who go foremost in affairs of state will call upon us to apply to God, yea will lead us to the throne of grace for divine aid. The proclamation points out various particulars that we ought to bear in mind this day. I might take the several things in the proclamation as subjects of discourse; and I shall pay a due regard to what is there said: but I shall mention several passages of scripture, which I think we may properly have in view this day, and which if you please you may consider as my text.

Jer. xxx. 11. *Though I make a full end of all nations whither I have scattered thee, yet will I not make a full end of thee: but I will correct thee in measure, and will not leave thee altogether unpunished.*

Isai. lviii. 6. *Is not this the fast that I have chosen; to loose the bands of wickedness, to undo the heavy burdens, and to let the oppressed go free, and that ye break every yoke?*

Rom. ii. 1, 3. *Thou art inexcusable, O man, whosoever thou art that judgest: for wherein thou judgest another thou condemnest thyself; for thou that judgest dost the same thing.—And thinkest thou this, O man, that judgest them that do such things, and dost the same, that thou shalt escape the judgment of God?*

Deut. xxx. 9. *The Lord will again rejoice over thee for good, as he rejoiced over thy fathers, if thou shalt hearken to the voice of the Lord thy God, to keep his commandments and statutes, and if thou turn unto the Lord thy God with all thy heart, and with all thy soul.*

The great and glorious God, who made and governs the world, has an intuitive view of all things in Heaven, earth and hell. He has seen from the first how our American troubles came on, and how they have proceeded. He permits the British court to oppress us, and has excited our resentment; excites us to stand for our liberties civil and religious. We have a great and wise, an holy and just, yet merciful God to apply to. When we consider our sinfulness we see our need of his infinite mercy, and implore it. When we view our contest with Britain we appeal to the justice of God with courage and confidence. By Britain we are abused, oppressed, most cruelly treated: We have been forced into this war. Liberty and other common rights of mankind we desired. These were denied. The most abject submission to unreasonable terms has been urged upon us. We cannot so meanly, so basely submit. We are contending for liberty. Our cause is just—is glorious; more glorious than to contend for a kingdom. A cause on which we may hope for a divine blessing. Though our contention with Great-Britain is so glorious, yet have we reason to be humbled and abased before God. We have reason to be humble and mourn for the many sins, the many vices that prevail among us. God has a controversy with us: How very different from that of Great-Britain! God most righteously comends and corrects us for our sins: in this case we have reason to submit, repent, and reform. Britain contends and threatens ruin; in this case we justly vindicate ourselves, and ought most vigorously to exert ourselves in a proper defence. I have always had the firmest belief that we should prevail in our contest with Britain. But I have always thought, and often told you, that God would scourge us for our sins. *What son is there whom the father chastens not?* 'Tis common for God to correct his people when working deliverance for them. Thus he often treated Israel in the days of the judges. God often makes use of the worst of instruments to correct his own people, while he calls upon them to repent and reform. God corrects us by Britain, and loudly calls upon us to repent; while the cruelty of our enemies, and the justice of our cause, is not forgot before him. While I am obliged to point out many crying sins among us, I cannot help animating you from the consideration that we are engaged in a glorious cause: We are nobly contending for the good of millions yet unborn. In this cause I would have you encouraged and emboldened, though I must lead your thoughts to some disagreeable subjects. There are sins, great and aggravated sins among us. God is angry and contending with us. We are this day called upon by our rulers to fast and pray—to confess and forsake our sins. . . .

Supporting and encouraging slavery, is one of the great and crying evils among us.—Can it be believed that a people contending for liberty should, at the same time, be promoting and supporting slavery? What foreign nation can believe that we who so loudly complain of Britain's attempts to oppress and enslave us, are, at the same time, voluntarily holding multitudes of fellow creatures in abject slavery; and that while we are abundantly declaring that we esteem liberty the greatest of all earthly blessings? I cannot but think, and must declare my sentiments, that the encouraging and supporting negro slavery is a crying sin in our land. In our contest with Britain how much has been said and published in favour of liberty? In what horrid colours has oppression and slavery been painted by us? And is it not as great a sin for us to practice it as for Britain? *Thou that sayest a man should not steal, dost thou steal?* Is not the hard yoke of slavery felt by negroes as well as by white people? Are they not fond of liberty as well as others of the human race? Is not freedom the natural unalienable right of all? What say the Congress in their declaration of independency? "We hold these truths to be self-evident, that all men are created equal, that they are endowed by their creator with certain unalienable rights, that among these are life, liberty, and the pursuit of happiness; that to secure these rights governments are instituted."—Thus the Congress. If liberty is one of the natural and unalienable rights of all men, as doubtless it is; if 'tis self-evident, *i. e.* so clear that it needs not proof, how unjust, how inhuman, for Britons, or Americans, not only to attempt, but actually to violate this right? Britain is attempting to violate it; we in America have a long time been in the actual violation of it. I have observed that sins against God directly, are, in their own nature, the greatest sins; yet there may be some particular sins against fellow creatures (which are also sins against God) especially cruelty, so circumstanced, and so aggravated, as to be the most crying sins of a particular people. Thus the transgressions of Damascus, Gaza, Tyre, Edom, Moab, and Ammon, for which God entered into judgment, and would not turn away their punishment, were cruelty to fellow creatures; because they *threshed Gilead with instruments of iron, carried away the whole captivity to deliver them to their enemies, pursued with the sword, cast off pity, ript up the women with child, and burnt the bones of kings into lime.* Amos first and second chapters. And I cannot but think our practising and patronizing negro slavery, is the most crying sin in our land. And that on this account, more than any one particular thing, God maintains his controversy with us. The reasons why I think so are two: first, because 'tis a most cruel, inhuman, unnatural sin, most directly contrary to the whole law of God comprehended in love, to love our neighbour as ourself, and do as we would be done by. The slaves have never forfeited their right to freedom; 'tis as the Congress say, a natural right, and an unalienable one. And if'tis taken away, 'tis violently taken. The Apostle Paul ranks *men stealers* (which is the sin we are guilty-of by the negro slavery) *with murderers of fathers and murderers of mothers, whore-mongers, defilers of themselves with mankind, liars, perjured persons, &c.* 1. Tim. i. 9. Secondly, because 'tis openly and avowedly doing that which we are contending against with our British enemies, and look upon so unjust and cruel in them. The whole of the present war, and all our struggles under it, and our sufferings and hardships by it, are to oppose and shun that from others, which we are tolerating and practising ourselves, and that in a greater degree than our enemies are attempting. If we were not blinded by sinful self-interest, and criminal partiality, we could not but see and feel the force of the Apostles reasoning in Rom. 2. *Thou art inexcusable, O man; for wherein thou judgest another thou condemnest thy self; for thou that judgest dost the same thing. And thinkest thou this, O man, that judgest them which do such things, and dost the same, that thou shalt escape the judgment of God. Thou that preachest a man, should not steal, dost thou steal? Thou that sayest a man, should not commit adultery, dost thou commit adultery? Thou that abhorrest idols, dost thou commit sacrilege? Thou that makest thy boast of the law, through breaking the law dishonourest thou God?* These words shew that we cannot expect to escape the judgments of heaven unless we reform and are more consistent. We are condemned out of our own mouth, and by our own practice. How often has it been said in our day that liberty is the greatest human blessing; and that 'tis oppressive and cruel to deprive us of it? How oft has it been said that slavery is more to be dreaded than death? On how many liberty poles: on how many garments and ornaments worn publicly, have been inscribed these emphatical words, *Liberty or Death!* How must these words sound in the ears of those that are held in slavery by us? How must they sound in the ears of all impartial persons? Especially how must they appear to the great governor of the world, who is no respecter of persons, but will judge all persons by the law of liberty and equity? I am persuaded these united American States must, and will groan under the afflicting hand of God, till we reform in this matter. And our case looks the darker in this respect, that 'tis an evil which the legislature might remove. Sins and vices, that creep in among people, while laws and magistrates are generally against them, are not so threatning to a state; but if the political head is sick, and the heart faint, the danger is greater. How justly might God say to us this day, as to Israel of old, *Is this the feast that I have chosen? To what purpose is the multitudes of your supplications? When you spread forth your hands I will hide my eyes from you; your hands are full of* oppression and slavery. *Put away the evil of your doings from before mine eyes, seek judgment, relieve the oppressed slave. Is not this the feast that I have chosen, to loose the bands of wickedness, to undo the heavy burdens, to let the oppressed go free*: The oppressed slaves: *And that ye break every yoke.* I doubt not but we may succeed against our British oppressors even if we should not free ourselves from the guilt of enslaving others. The cause of Britain is most unjust, and our contest with them is most righteous. But however we may be free from British oppression, I venture to say, we shall have inward convulsions, contentions, oppressions, and various calamities, so that our liberty will be uncomfortable, till we wash our hands from the guilt of negro slavery. And our neglecting to reform in this matter may protract the war to a distressing length, though we shall succeed in the end. And now how righteous is it in God to permit oppression and extortion to prevail. Is it not a punishment for our much worse oppression of the slaves.

Though the emancipation of the slaves ought to be managed by the legislatures, yet the masters of slaves need not wait for that. If those masters had a true spirit of freedom; if they abhored the very nature of slavery, they would soon free themselves from such a blot in the character of freemen. I know there are many in our land, who are sensible of this evil, and wish it remedied; but they are generally persons not so immediately guilty, not being possessed of slaves, and they are ready to say, what can we do? Let me observe, that there ought to be petitions from the friends of liberty in every county to the legislatures of the several states, humbly requesting them to take this matter under consideration. If the legislatures would come into proper measures to free the slaves in some suitable time, it would free our country from a load of guilt: I say in some suitable time, for I suppose it should not be done at once, but gradually.

I know 'tis objected, that this is not a proper time, that this cannot be entered upon in this state of war and confusion. But let me observe, that if this is one cause of God's controversy with us, and of his continuing to frown upon us, the present is the most proper time to consider and rectify this matter, that it may be a means of freeing us from our calamities. We might as well say that we cannot, in this difficult time, raise men for our army, because we are so straightened for help, and need our men at home; whereas this is the time in which it must be done. To say this is not the proper time for our legislature to consider the emancipation of our slaves, is, in my view, as absurd as for a sick man to say his stomach is so out of order that he cannot now take a disagreeable medicine, but will wait till he is better, and can take it without such difficulty. I know there are many imaginary difficulties, and many objections raised, but 'tis easy to get over them all except such as arise from self-interest, and those will not easily be got over. If we had a clear, rational view, of the worth, nature, and importance of freedom; if we had a proper view of the criminal nature of enslaving others; if we had a proper view of that tribunal, where judgment will pass without any respect to persons, by the law of loving others as our selves, we should easily get over all the difficulties that are in the case.

I would think as favourably as I can, concerning the guilty state of my country, which I most heartily wish to prosper and enjoy the divine smiles. I would excuse and extenuate, as far as possible, the unnatural sin of holding fellow creatures in perpetual bondage. I suppose the sin is less aggravated, because 'tis by many not thought to be a sin, and because 'tis so common. 'Tis like the polygamy of the ancient patriarchs. That was a common evil, and not duly considered. To marry several wives, and have a concubine or mistress beside, was an unnatural evil, as God has created an equal number of each sex. And for a person of a religious character to live in that practice now, would be scandalous, and thought to be impious; and very justly. Yet this sin in itself is by no means so great, so unnatural, so cruel, and so provoking to God, as it is to keep in perpetual bondage those who have a natural right to freedom, and have not forfeited it. Polygamy of old was a common sin and not duly considered: And slavery being so common now, and not duly weighed, may extenuate, but will not free from guilt. I have reason to hope this matter will be considered and remedied, and that God will turn to us in mercy and prosper us. We should not be discouraged, but repent and exert ourselves in the cause of liberty, both against Britain and among ourselves. I know some serious people, hearty friends to our country, are disposed to sink into discouragements when they view the many vices among us, the frowns of God upon us, and how few there are that pay any regard to the tokens of his displeasure. The abounding of vice, and insensibility under the rod of God, is certainly the darkest aspect in our public affairs. But still we may encourage ourselves in the goodness of God, and every one, as far as his influence extends, attempt a reformation, beginning with self. God is yet waiting to be gracious; he deals with us as with a people whom he designs to have and not destroy. Though he corrects, yet he shews us many favours. He remarkably appears for us, and prevents our ruin; yea, gives us advantages against our enemies. We should consider that correction is no sign of rejection. Things are yet in our favour. Though the war is protracted, and we are so long held under the rod, yet all things shall be for the best in the end. Nothing less than what we have suffered would have done for us. Nothing less would have made sufficiently deep impression on us and on posterity. Nothing less would have given us and posterity a view of the worth of the privileges we contend for. How often is it recorded by Englishmen that their ancestors have waded through rivers of blood to enjoy the privileges of freemen. Our present difficulties will be recollected with advantage to the end of time. If God is contending with us, yet he deals with us as children for whom he designs mercy: We have many tokens for good. 'Tis encouraging that our rulers regard religion, acknowlege the providence of God, and call upon us to seek him, to repent and reform. And if they are deficient in some things, yet they uprightly mean to discourage evil, and promote virtue; and whereunto they have not attained, desire that even this may be shewn unto them. I cannot but hope this day may be in some measure such a fast as God has chosen.

Some people are apt to think we have no reason to expect, and can scarce pray for an outward blessing, while so many vices abound among us. Indeed we have reason to be humbled and mourn, reason to repent and reform; but that we may not sink into discouragements consider, that God who is infinite in goodness, waits long to be gracious, and may yet try us with mercy as a means to lead us to repentance. . . . Some ask, what if we should not return to God by repentance and reformation, but that we should continue in sin, and vice continue to abound, as it has done two or three years past? I answer, that would be truly lamentable, and a very dark sign, that would much damp our hopes. God forbid it should be so. But in that case, I should expect that God would yet try us with a mixture of mercies and corrections. That we should be delivered from British tyranny, and have plenty in our land, with internal commotions, divisions, convulsions, oppressions, and other difficulties, while God gave us a space to repent and reform, which, if after all we should refuse to do, we should be ripening for heavy judgments in some future time. And how long an infinitely merciful and long suffering God may deter those judgments, we know not. I cannot but hope, yea believe, that after the war is over we shall set ourselves to reform many things that are amiss among us, slavery not excepted. I must believe this great event, this important struggle for liberty, will, in the end, be a means of putting an end to negro slavery in this land, and to many other oppressions and impositions, which a state of liberty is adapted to throw off and resist.

Our struggle for liberty is attended to through the world. All eyes are upon us; and all that are not self-interested, or grievously imposed on by misrepresentations, think our cause is just, and wish us success. Should we obtain our end, this land of liberty could not be so inconsistent, could not with any face continue and support slavery, and other oppressions contrary to a state of freedom. On the whole, my friends, we have the greatest reason to reform our lives, trust in God, and exert ourselves in our country's cause with full confidence of success.

My dear friends, I cannot leave you without a repeated earnest exhortation to repentance and reformation. Infidelity, profaneness, contempt of divine things, avarice, oppression and extortion, are provoking to God. And if God be against us, who can eventually be for us? All our exertions will be to no purpose if God does not favour us. How easily can he disappoint all our schemes and attempts? How easily can he send a sickness that will sweep away our army? How easily can he deprive us of the fruits of the earth, and cause a famine? How easily can he give some unexpected success to our enimies? How righteously might he leave us to such contentions and animosities among ourselves as would divide and destroy us? In all these ways, and many others, he has in times past disappointed the hopes of those he has chastised or destroyed. Let us then be deeply sensible how necessary 'tis that God be for us. That we be such a people as he will delight in and bless: That we be reformed, humble, and benevolent. If God be for us, we need not fear any that are, or can be against us. What a happy land will this be, if 'tis a land of true religion! It will then be a land of liberty, of peace, and plenty. We shall then live in love and peace among ourselves: And many from other nations will flock to us as the most happy people on the face of the earth. Were ever people more loudly, more kindly, and compassionately called upon to repent and turn to God!

P. S. Plan or Scheme for emancipating Slaves.

Many plans or schemes might be mentioned, but the following is proposed as most favourable to the owners of slaves, and as freeing them gradually, year after year, which in many respects might be best for them, and for the country. viz. All that shall hereafter be born, and all that are now under five years old, should be free, the males at twenty-one years old, and the females at eighteen. All above five years, and under ten years of age, to be free, the males at twenty-three years, and the females at twenty years of age. All above ten, and under 15 years old, male and female, to be free at twenty-five years old. All between fifteen and twenty years old, to be free in eight years from this time. All between twenty and twenty-five, to be free in seven years from this time. All between twenty-five and thirty, to be free in six years. All between thirty and thirty-five, to be free in five years. All between thirty-five and forty, to be free in four years. All between forty and forty-five, to be free in three years. All between forty-five and fifty, to be free in two years. All between fifty and sixty, to be free in one year. And all above sixty to serve during life, in order to be taken care of and provided for by their owners.

In this plan some would become free in one year, others in two, others in three, and so on.

The owners might from principles of equity and benevolence, free many of them in a much shorter time than is here mentioned, and no doubt many would.

Samuel Allinson-William Livingston Correspondence, July-August, 1778

Allinson Letterbook, Special Collections, Rutgers University Library, New Brunswick, N.J.

"Don Quixote of the Jerseys," a contemporary newspaper styled him. Of Whiggish inclinations, with views on social issues distinctly liberal for his generation, New Jersey governor William Livingston in 1778 placed himself squarely on the side of those reformers working for gradual abolition. When the Quaker abolitionist Samuel Allinson on July 13, 1778, challenged Livingston to become a "happy instrument" in effecting emancipation, the governor replied that he had already made his reform sentiments clear to the New Jersey Assembly. Although he reluctantly acceded to the Legislature's request that he privately withdraw an antislavery message, Livingston made it clear he would continue to work toward that end. In the 1785-86 session of the Legislature, with Livingston still in the governor's chair, New Jersey adopted a law that prohibited importing slaves and facilitated manumission. The state also established penalties for the maltreatment of slaves. It was not until 1804 that New Jersey approved a gradual abolition law, the last state to enact such a measure before the Civil War. But reformers such as Allinson, David Cooper, John Cooper and politicians such as Livingston did make a positive impact during the Revolutionary years in attacking that institution Livingston called "utterly inconsistent both with the princples of Christianty & Humanity."

7th Mo: 13th 1778

To Wm. Livingston (Governor of N.J.)

Respected Friend ... America first entered into the contest with Gt. Britain to avoid what she called *Slavery*; & to preserve & transmit to posterity her right to & possession of *Liberty*: In the doing of this, her peaceful pen, whilst she strove to accommodate the difference & avert a War, has in a united capacity in Congress declared the *absolute right of all Mankind to be free*; & yet she retains & has even since confirmed laws that hold Thousands of human beings, children of the same common Father, our brethren—possessd of our sensibilities, passions, & even heirs of Immortality; in ignoble & abject Slavery!—a slavery compard with that which was attempted upon ourselves, as superior as the Ocean to one of its rivers. And America, notwithstanding this amazing contradiction in her conduct, puts up her petitions for success on her endeavours, to Him who is "just & equal in all His ways" who "is no respecter of persons in Judgmt" but "will maintain the cause of the afflicted & the right of the poor" & she calleth her cause a righteous one. Thus the "accursed thing" remaineth in her possession, & she refuseth to put it away tho it has been often sounded in her ears: For these causes (Slavery & oppression) we read of divers Kings & their princes who have suffered utter destruction; & I fear America never can or will prosper in a right manner; or receive & enjoy true peace & its delightful fruits; until she "proclaims Liberty to the captives, & lets the oppressed go free." May not the language formerly uttered of a people, who were said to "draw near to the Almighty with their mouth "& with their lips, honour Him, but removed their hearts far from Him" be here applied to America with respect to Liberty: She claims it for herself—She Deifies it—& yet denies it to others. "The same measure that ye mete, shall be measurd to you again." Nor is there any time too busy or too difficult to enter into a serious legislative consideration of this continental evil; such a consideran will, as it is promoted with uprightness & a devoted disposin to the doing of impartial justice to the Stranger, "the poor & the oppressed," be received as a proportionate expiation of continental guilt; & it would afford me great pleasure to hear that New Jersey led the way in so noble a work, & that Govr Livingston was the happy instrument of procuring its advancement. I am not apt to speak very positive, yet I hesitate not to say, the emancipation of this people, & restoring them to liberty, will go forward & be effected in time, & will, I believe, be brot about by the immediate hand of the Almighty, if His instruments & those vested by Him with power to do it, neglect thr duty in the important task.

Thus, & by a real reformatn from other evils, wh are at least neglected, if not encouragd in Engd, America might look forward with a well grounded hope, that He, who "If a Man's ways please Him, can cause even his enemies to be at peace with him," would aid every virtuous effort, & perfect what He approved. We may talk of imploring His help—Of devoting ourselves to Worship Him—& we may set days apart for this purpose; but, until the work is really begun, & advances are made in earnest towards the mark for the prize of the high calling; & we take up the cross to Nature & cleave to Grace; in vain have we reason to expect Omnipotence will be propitious to us. The conquest of outward enemies—the overcomg of external annoyances; & obtaining what is desired and endeavoured for, in these respects; are the least matters: We may be miserable even after those are all granted; & shall, I believe, if internal virtue does not predominate. Unless pride, licentiousns, frauds & oppression, give way to humility, temperance & justice; the seeds of corruption & death will sap the foundation of real happiness.

I have wrote with freedom, but, I hope, with decency: & as I had no reflections or ill-will in my mind towards any one; so, I expect none have employed my pen. The happiness of all, upon the noble principles of *Justice & Liberty*, have been my motive & aim, &, I am, at least, conscious of having intended well. If these principles were made the poll-Star in steerg the political Bark; governmt would derive firmness, stability & respect there from.

The power of legislation, is the greatest human right delegated to man; & should be exercised with much Caution, care & Tenderness. To make laws wh, either from their inexpediency, impossibility, or severity; cannot be enforced, or wh it is not the apparent general interest to enforce; is the means of bringg Governmt into disrepute; & such had best be repealed as quick as possible upon that ground. I have so fully expressed my sentiments on this head, in my preface to the last edition of N.J. Laws, that I shall forbear saying more here than this, that I am persuaded of the efficacy of those observations, towards tha great ends of political harmony & union, if carried into practice; in lieu of measures which, tho popular, may be more inflamatory & violent, & therefore cannot endure. The former will produce a clear stream of refreshmt to the body politick, & invigorate it; the latter, like a torrent or flame, will bear down all before it, right or wrong, good or bad. It should never be forgot, that the grand design of Governmt is "for the punishmt of evil doers, & the praise of those who do well"—& the land will rejoice or moarn, as this is adhered to, or departd from.

My retired situation & insignificancy in publick life, will not, I expect, add weight to these hints; but there is a more sure criterion to judge them by, the feelings of thy own breast. I shall apologize no further than to assure thee, that I am a friend of this Governmt—a friend to the members of it, & I shall esteem it a favour ever to be thine.

Sam Allinson

Morristown 25th July 1778.

Governor Livingston (in answer)

Sir, I just now received your letter of the 13th inst. wh, I think, is so far from requiring an apology, that I not only accept it in good part, but shall always think myself under obligation to you, or any other Gentleman who shall, with equal candour & moderation, either point out my own errors, or any defect in our laws that, by my interposition, I am able to remedy: For the former, I am doubtless responsible, but as to the latter, I presume you need not be informed, that the Governor of this State is no branch of the Legislature; & I can honestly tell you, that some laws have been enacted during my administration, to which I should not have consented, had my voice been necessary to their pass.g. but being enacted by constitutional authority, I am not only bound to submit to them myself, but, by the duty of my office, to enforce them upon others: and it is the peculiar felicity of this Governt. in which, without prejudice, I think it preferable to Gt Britn. (having no jarring & contradictory interests, as those of Court & country party) that whenever the people find any law inconvenient, & petition their Representatives for its repeal, it will, of course, be abolished. . . .

Respectg the Slavery of the Negroes, I have the pleasure to be entirely of your sentiments; & I sent a Message to the Assembly the very last Sessions, to lay the foundation for their Manumission; but the house, thinkg us rather in too critical a Situation to enter on the consideration of it at that time; desired one in a private way to withdraw the Message: but I am determined, as far as my influence extends, to push the matter till it is effected: being convinced that the practice is utterly inconsistent, both with the principles of Christianity & humanity; & in Americns who have almost idolizd liberty, peculiarly odious & disgraceful.

The want of "internal virtue," & the prevalence of "pride, licentiousness, fraud & oppression" I concur with you, my friend, in heartily deplorg; & shall ever think it my duty, both as a publick mgistrate & a private Christian—as well by example as precept—to endeavour at restoring the former, & discountenancing the latter—

Together with your letter, I recd from A. Benezet a pamphlt entituled "Serious considerations on several importt subjects" accompanied with a letter from the Donor; but as the letter contains neither date nor place, I am at a loss whither to direct my acknowledgmts. for his kindness: as you know him, I shall be obliged to you, when you have opportunity, to give him my thanks for his book. The piece on Slave-keeping is excellent but the arguments agst the lawfulness of War have been answered a thousd times. May the Father of Light lead us into all truth, & overrule all the commotions of this wld to his own Glory, & the introduction of that kingdom of peace & righteousness which will endure forever.

Believe me to be, yr sincere friend

William Livingston

Mr Saml Allinson

Alexander Hamilton to John Jay, March 14, 1779

Great Britain, Berkshire, Windsor Castle, John Jay Papers, Library of Congress

On March 14, 1779, twenty-four-year-old Alexander Hamilton, aide-de-camp to General Washington, declared, in a letter to John Jay, president of the Continental Congress, that Colonel John Laurens was attempting to persuade the South Carolina legislature to raise black battalions. Hamilton thought that slaves, "for the dictates of humanity" and in the interest of the defense of the South, should be given freedom in exchange for their military service. At the time young Hamilton wrote his letter to Jay large numbers of blacks were already serving in the state and Continental armies. Slave owners were compensated by the government and the slaves were guaranteed freedom upon completion of their service. Such a policy, however, had to be forced upon reluctant American leaders. Although some blacks had served in the Continental army since the days of Lexington and Concord, Washington's order of July 9, 1775, had specifically excluded the enlistment of any "stroller, negro, or vagabond, or person suspected of being an enemy." But on November 7, 1775, Lord Dunmore, governor of Virginia, issued his electrifying proclamation that called on slaves to bear arms for the Crown. Afterwards, the slaves would be given their freedom. The governor had slashed menacingly at the deep South's Achilles' heel, stimulating visions of marauding masses of crazed Blacks taking out revenge. When hundreds of slaves donned redcoats, some wearing sashes emblazoning in black letters "Liberty to Slaves," the American military establishment quickly realized that its recruitment policy required reconsideration. By 1779 many blacks were fighting for the colonies, except for the forces from South Carolina and Georgia. One official from South Carolina reported to the Continental Congress that the militia was inadequate because many planters were forced to stay home to prevent slave insurrection and slave desertion to the enemy. The Continental Congress later recommended that South Carolina and Georgia adopt plans to raise an army of blacks. Although John Laurens made an empassioned plea to the South Carolina legislature, the effort was defeated. Washington attributed the action to "selfish passion." As for Hamilton and Jay, their antislavery views were later channeled into positive reform activity. In February 1785 they joined with others to form the New York Manumission Society.

Dear Sir, Col Laurens, who will have the honor of delivering you this letter, is on his way to South Carolina, on a project, which I think, in the present situation of affairs there, is a very good one and deserves every kind of support and encouragement. This is to raise two three or four batalions of negroes, with the assistance of the government of that state, by contributions from the owners in proportion to the number they possess. If you should think proper to enter upon the subject with him, he will give you a detail of his plan. He wishes to have it recommended by Congress to the state; and, as an inducement, that they would engage to take those batalions into Continental pay.

It appears to me, that an expedient of this kind, in the present state of Southern affairs, is the most rational, that can be adopted, and promises very important advantages. Indeed, I hardly see how a sufficient force can be collected in that quarter without it; and the enemy's operations there are growing infinitely serious and formidable. I have not the least doubt, that the negroes will make very excellent soldiers, with proper management; and I will venture to pronounce, that they cannot be put in better hands than those of Mr. Laurens. He has all the zeal, intelligence enterprise, and every other qualification requisite to succeed in such an undertaking. It is a maxim with some great military judges, that with sensible officers soldiers can hardly be too stupid; and on this principle it is thought that the Russians would make the best troops in the world, if they were under other officers than their own. The King of Prussia is among the number who maintain this doctrine and has a very emphatical saying on the occasion, which I do not exactly recollect. I mention this, because I frequently hear it objected to the scheme of embodying negroes that they are too stupid to make soldiers. This is so far from appearing to me a valid objection—that I think their want of cultivation (for their natural faculties are probably as good as ours) joined to that habit of subordination which they acquire from a life of servitude, will make them sooner become soldiers than our White inhabitants. Let officers be men of sense and sentiment, and the nearer the soldiers approach to machine perhaps the better.

I foresee that this project will have to combat much opposition from prejudice and self-interest. The contempt we have been taught to entertain for the blacks, . . . us fancy many things that are founded neither in reason nor experience; and an unwillingnes to part with property of so valuable a kind will furnish a thousand arguments to show the impracticability or pernicious tendency of a scheme which requires such a sacrifice. But it should be considered, that if we do not make use of them in this way, the enemy probably will; and that the best way to counteract the temptations they will hold out will be to offer them ourselves. An essential part of the plan is to give them their freedom with their muskets. This will secure their fidelity, animate their courage, and I believe will have a good influence upon those who remain, by opening a door to their emancipation. This circumstance, I confess, has no small weight in inducing me to wish the success of the project; for the dictates of humanity and true policy equally interest me in favour of this unfortunate class of men.

When I am on the subject of Southern affairs you will excuse the liberty I take, in saying, that I do not think measures sufficiently vigorous are persuing for our defence in that quarter. Except the few regular troops of South Carolina we seem to be relying wholly on the militia of that and the two neighbouring states. These will soon grow impatient of service and leave our affairs in a very miserable situation. No considerable force can be uniformly kept up by militia—to say nothing of many obvious and well known inconveniences, that attend this kind of troops. I would beg leave to suggest, Sir, that no time ought to be lost in making a draft of militia to serve a twelve month from the States of North and South Carolina and Virginia. But South Carolina being very weak in her population of whites may be excused from the draft on condition of furnishing the black batalions. The two others may furnish about 3,500 men and be exempted on that account from sending any succours to this army. The States to the Northward of Virginia will be fully able to give competent supplies to the army here; and it will require all the force and exertions of the three states I have mentioned to withstand the storm which has arisen and is increasing in the South.

The troops drafted must be thrown into batalions and officered in the best . . . we can. The supernumerary officers may be made use of as far as they will go.

If arms are wanted for these troops and no better way of supplying them is to be found we should endeavour to levy a contribution of arms upon the militia at large. Extraordinary exigencies demand extraordinary means. I fear this Southern business will become a very *grave* one.

With the truest respect & esteem—
I am Sir Your most Obed servant

Alex Hamilton

Want of time to copy it will apologise for sending this letter in its present state
Head Quarters
March 14th 79

The Pennsylvania Abolition Law, Introduced November 2, 1779

Records of the Pennsylvania Abolition Society, Historical Society of Pennsylvania, Philadelphia, Pa.

On March 1, 1780, the Pennsylvania Assembly, by a vote of 34 to 21, enacted the first gradual abolition law in American history. In a state whose politics had been dominated by the Quakers for generations and in which abolitionist sentiment had been generated by Quakers for almost a century, it is ironic that a measure of such significance to antislavery history was given life by the predominantly Presbyterian legislature. George Bryan, the first vice president, and later president, under the radical Pennsylvania constitution of 1776, campaigned for the act for over three years, lobbying with legislators, publishing letters in Philadelphia newspapers, attempting to allay the fears of many private individuals, particularly in back-country and southwestern Pennsylvania, who opposed abolitionist efforts. Bryan remarked that the bill "astonishes and pleases the Quakers. They looked for no such benevolent issue of our new government, exercised by Presbyterians."

Although the Society of Friends had lost political power in Pennsylvania and had only a small role in the passage of the abolition law, Anthony Benezet is said to have discussed the act with every single member of the legislature before the final vote. The majority sentiment in Pennsylvania was reflected by an anonymous letter in the Pennsylvania Gazette: *"The liberal spirit which this act breathes, the substantial justice which it dispenses, and the profound policy it suggests in almost every part, will be standing testimonies to future ages of the free principles of the people of Pennsylvania." The act declared that Negroes born after its passage would be considered as indentured servants for a period of 28 years after which they were to receive freedom. All slaves were to be registered by November 1, 1780, or be freed, and slaves were to be tried in white courts and guaranteed equal justice. The preamble to the act declared, "we conceive that it is our duty, and we rejoice that it is in our power, to extend a portion of that freedom to others, which has been extended to us, and release them from a state of thraldom, to which we ourselves were tyrannically doomed, and from which we have now every prospect of being delivered." It is conceivable that a familiar Revolutionary War figure, a passionate spokesman for the underclasses, the dispossessed, and the black slave, had a hand in writing these lines; for on November 2, 1779, the day the abolition law was introduced, Thomas Paine became clerk of the Pennsylvania Assembly.*

An Act for the gradual Abolition of Slavery.

Section I.

When we contemplate our abhorrence of that condition, to which the arms and tyranny of Great Britain were exerted to reduce us—when we look back on the variety of dangers to which we have been exposed, and how miraculously our wants in many instances have been supplied, and our deliverances wrought, when even hope and human fortitude have become unequal to the conflict—we are unavoidably led to a serious and grateful sense of the manifold blessings which we have undeservedly received from the hand of that Being, from whom every good and perfect gift cometh. Impressed with these ideas, we conceive that it is our duty, and we rejoice that it is in our power, to extend a portion of that freedom to others, which hath been extended to us; and a release from that state of thraldom, to which we ourselves were tyrannically doomed, and from which we have now every prospect of being delivered. It is not for us to enquire why, in the creation of mankind, the inhabitants of the several parts of the earth were distinguished by a difference in feature or complexion. It is sufficient to know that all are the work of an Almighty Hand. We find, in the distribution of the human species, that the most fertile as well as the most barren parts of the earth are inhabited by men of complexions different from ours, and from each other; from whence we may reasonably, as well as religiously, infer, that he who placed them in their various situations, hath extended equally his care and protection to all, and that it becometh not us to counteract his mercies. We esteem it a peculiar blessing granted to us, that we are enabled this day to add one more step to universal civilization, by removing, as much as possible, the sorrows of those who have lived in undeserved bondage and from which, by the assumed authority of the Kings of Great-Britain, no effectual, legal relief could be obtained. Weaned by a long course of experience from those narrow prejudices and partialities we had imbibed, we find our hearts enlarged with kindness and benevolence towards men of all conditions and nations; and we conceive ourselves at this particular period extraordinarily called upon, by the blessings which we have received, to manifest the sincerity of our profession, and to give a substantial proof of our gratitude.

Sect. II.

And whereas the condition of those persons who have heretofore been denominated Negro and Mulatto slaves, has been attended with circumstances which not only deprived them of the common blessings that they were by nature entitled to, but has cast them into the deepest afflictions by an unnatural separation and sale of husband and wife from each other and from their children—an injury, the greatness of which can only be conceived by supposing that we were in the same unhappy case. In justice, therefore, to persons so unhappily circumstanced, and who, having no prospect before them whereon they may rest their sorrows and their hopes, have no reasonable inducement to render their service to society, which otherwise they might; and also in grateful commemoration of our own happy deliverance from that state of unconditional submission to which we were doomed by the tyranny of Britain.

Sect. III.

Be it enacted, and it is hereby enacted, by the representatives of the freemen of the commonwealth of Pennsylvania, in general assembly met, and by the authority of the same, That all persons, as well Negroes and Mulattoes and others, who shall be born within this state from and after the passing of this act, shall not be deemed and considered as servants for life, or slaves; and that all servitude for life, or slavery of children, in consequence of the slavery of their mothers, in the case of all children born within this state, from and after the passing of this act as aforesaid, shall be, and hereby is utterly taken away, extinguished and forever abolished.

Sect. IV.

Provided always, and be it further enacted, by the authority aforesaid, That every Negro and Mulatto child born within this state after the passing of this act as aforesaid (who would, in case this act had not been made, have been born a servant for years, or life, or a slave) shall be deemed to be, and shall be, by virtue of this act, the servant of such person, or his or her assigns, who would, in such case, have been entitled to the service of such child, until such child shall attain unto the age of twenty-eight years, in the manner and on the conditions whereon servants bound by indenture for four years are or may be retained and holden; and shall be liable to like correction and punishment, and entitled to like relief in case he or she be evilly treated by his or her master or mistress, and to like freedom dues and other privileges as servants bound by indenture for four years are or may be entitled, unless the person to whom the service of any such child shall belong shall abandon his or her claim to the same; in which case the overseers of the poor of the city, township or district respectively, where such child shall be so abandoned, shall by indenture send out every child, so abandoned, as an apprentice for a time not exceeding the age herein before limited for the service of such children.

Sect. V.

And be it further enacted by the authority aforesaid, That every person, who is or shall be the owner of any Negro or Mulatto slave or servant for life, or till the age of thirty-one years, now within this state, or his lawful attorney, shall, on or before the said first day of November next, deliver or cause to be delivered in writing to the clerk of the peace of the county, or to the clerk of the court of record of the city of Philadelphia, in which he or she shall respectively inhabit, the name, and surname, and occupation or profession of such owner, and the name of the county and township, district or ward wherein he or she resideth; and also the name and names of any such slave and slaves, and servant and servants for life or till the age of thirty-one years, together with their ages and sexes severally and respectively set forth and annexed, by such person owned or statedly employed, and their being within this state, in order to ascertain and distinguish the slaves and servants for life and till the age of thirty-one years, within this state, who shall be such, on the said first day of November next, from all other persons; which particulars shall by said clerk of the sessions and clerk of the said court be entered in books to be provided for that purpose by the said clerks; and that no Negro and Mulatto, now within this state, shall from and after the said first day of November, be deemed a slave or servant for life, or till the age of thirty-one years, unless his or her name shall be entered as aforesaid on such record, except such Negro and Mulatto slaves and servants as are herein after excepted; the same clerk to be entitled to a fee of two dollars for each slave or servant so entered as aforesaid, from the treasurer of the county, to be allowed to him in his accounts.

Sect. VI.

Provided always, That any person in whom the ownership or right to the service of any Negro or Mulatto shall be vested at the passing of this act, other than such as are herein before excepted, his or her heirs, executors, administrators and assigns, and all and every of them severally shall be liable to the overseers of the poor of the city, township or district to which any such Negro or Mulatto shall become chargeable, for such necessary expence, with costs of suit thereon, as such overseers may be put to, through the neglect of the owner, master or mistress of such Negro or Mulatto; notwithstanding the name and other descriptions of such Negro or Mulatto shall not be entered and recorded as aforesaid; unless his or her master or owner shall, before such slave or servant attain his or her twenty-eighth year, execute and record in the proper county, a deed or instrument, securing to such slave or servant, his or her freedom.

Sect. VII.

And be it further enacted by the authority aforesaid, That the offences and crimes of Negroes and Mulattoes, as well slaves and servants as freemen, shall be enquired of, adjudged, corrected and punished in like manner as the offences and crimes of the other inhabitants of this state are and shall be enquired of, adjudged, corrected and punished, and not otherwise; except that a slave shall not be admitted to bear witness against a freeman.

Sect. VIII.

And be it further enacted by the authority aforesaid, That in all cases, wherein sentence of death shall be pronounced against a slave, the jury before whom he or she shall be tried, shall appraise and declare the value of such slave; and in case such sentence be executed, the court shall make an order on the state treasurer, payable to the owner for the same and for the costs of prosecution; but in case of remission or mitigation, for the costs only.

Sect. IX.

And be it further enacted by the authority aforesaid, That the reward for taking up runaway and absconding Negro and Mulatto slaves and servants, and the penalties for enticing away, dealing with, or harbouring, concealing or employing Negro and Mulatto slaves and servants, shall be the same, and shall be recovered in like manner as in the case of servants bound for four years.

Sect. X.

And be it further enacted by the authority aforesaid, That no man or woman of any nation or colony, except the Negroes or Mulattoes who shall be registered as aforesaid, shall at any time hereafter be deemed, adjudged or holden within the territories of this commonwealth as slaves or servants for life, but as free-men and free-women; except the domestic slaves attending upon delegates in Congress from the other American states, foreign ministers and consuls, and persons passing through or sojourning in this state and not becoming resident therein, and seamen employed in ships not belonging to any inhabitant of this state, nor employed in any ship owned by any such inhabitant. Provided such domestic slaves be not aliened or sold to any inhabitant, nor (except in the case of members of Congress, foreign ministers and consuls) retained in this state longer than six months.

Sect. XI.

Provided always, and be it further enacted by the authority aforesaid, That this act or any thing in it contained, shall not give any relief or shelter to any absconding or runaway Negro or Mulatto slave or servant, who has absented himself, or shall absent himself from his or her owner, master or mistress residing in any other state or country, but such owner, master or mistress shall have like right and aid to demand, claim and take away his slave or servant, as he might have had in case this act had not been made: And that all Negro and Mulatto slaves now owned and heretofore resident in this state, who have absented themselves, or been clandestinely carried away, or who may be employed abroad as seamen and have not returned or been brought back to their owners, masters or mistresses, before the passing of this act, may within five years be registered as effectually as is ordered by this act concerning those who are now within the state, on producing such slave before any two justices of the peace, and satisfying the said justices by due proof of the former residence, absconding, taking away, or absence of such slaves as aforesaid; who thereupon shall direct and order the said slave to be entered on the record as aforesaid.

Sect. XII.

And whereas attempts may be made to evade this act, by introducing into this state Negroes and Mulattoes bound by covenant, to serve for long and unreasonable terms of years, if the same be not prevented:

Sect. XIII.

Be it therefore enacted by the authority aforesaid, That no covenant of personal servitude or apprenticeship whatsoever, shall be valid or binding on a Negro or Mulatto, for a longer time than seven years, unless such servant or apprentice were, at the commencement of such servitude or apprenticeship, under the age of twenty-one years; in which case such Negro or Mulatto may be holden as a servant or apprentice respectively, according to the covenant, as the case shall be, until he or she shall attain the age of twenty-eight years, but no longer.

Sect. XIV.

And be it further enacted by the authority aforesaid, That an act of Assembly of the province of Pennsylvania, passed in the year one thousand seven hundred and five, entitled, "An act for the trial of Negroes," and another act of Assembly of the said province, passed in the year one thousand seven hundred and twenty-five, entitled, "An act for the better regulating of Negroes in this province;" and another act of Assembly of the said province, passed in the year one thousand seven hundred and sixty-one, entitled, "An act for laying a duty on Negro and Mulatto slaves imported into this province;" and also another act of Assembly of the said province, passed in the year one thousand seven hundred and seventy-three, entitled, "An act for making perpetual an act for laying a duty on Negro and Mulatto slaves imported into this province, and for laying an additional duty on said slaves," shall be, and are hereby repealed, annulled and made void.

John Bayard, Speaker.

Enacted into a Law at Philadelphia, on Wednesday, the first day of March, Anno Domini, 1780.
Thomas Paine, *Clerk of the General Assembly.*

Thomas Nicholson to *B. H.*, November 6, 1779

The Friend (March, 1844), 18:13.

Quaker antislavery leaders in the South faced much more formidable and unbending opposition than was encountered by northern reformers. The isolated Quaker society in North Carolina, limited in numbers and woefully lacking in political power, was torn between accomodating itself to religious dictates and to the predominant plantation society dependent on slave labor. With manumission in North Carolina limited to cases of meritorious service certified by county courts, Friends were restricted by law in adhering to a testimony against slavery. Slaves freed outside of the the law were fair game for seizure and reenslavement. Most Quakers kept their "servants" in a kind of quasi-slavery, keeping secretly freed blacks on their land and paying them wages. It is not surprising that the zealous antislavery advocate Thomas Nicholson of Perquimons county had acrimonious words for the man who was instrumental in alerting county officials to Nicholson's own secretly manumitted slaves. But Quakers such as Nicholson persevered. By 1781 the North Carolina Yearly Meeting, following the lead of Quaker meetings in the North, disowned slave owners.

Perquimons county, the 6th of the
Eleventh month, 1779

Friend B. H. . . . I suppose you justify yourselves under the pretended sanction of a cruel and barbarous human law, which is a violation of the present constitution, and a shame and reproach to our great pretensions to liberty and freedom. In considering the subject, the following questions and answers do very pertinently arise, viz. Can law, human law, change the nature of things? can it change darkness into light, or evil into good? By no means! Notwithstanding ten thousand laws, right is right, and wrong is wrong. As to the law under which the negroes were sold, it is evident to every wise and impartial man that fully considers it, that it hath not the strength of a spider's web in it, and is void of itself. I am fully satisfied that the courts which ordered the sales of the negroes, had no more legal power or justice on their side, to support their proceedings therein, than I have to order thyself and wife to be sold for slaves during your natural lives, and to entail cruel slavery and bondage upon your posterity to the end of time. I have been informed that as thou was once passing by my plantation, thou said that it made thy heart glad to see so many young negroes. If thy gladness arose from an expectation of a further prey to thy greedy, if not bloody hands, and if thou expects to get thy living by freebooting and the gain of oppression, it is time to turn thy view some other way. I fully believe that thou never hereafter will be able to drink any more than deadly poison in the one-fifth of the sale-money of any more of the negroes that I have manumitted, as I shall endeavour to guard them from ever falling into thy avaricious hands. As thou hast put thyself upon a level with some of the lower class to carry on thy cruel purpose, I do tell thee plainly, that although hand hath joined in hand therein, the wicked will not go unpunished. Therefore it is my advice to thee, to submit thyself to so deep a purgation, as to cause thee to vomit up again the portion of the gain of oppression, which thou hast greedily swallowed, otherwise I much question whether thou ever dies in peace of mind. That thou may happily experience this by true godly sorrow, which works repentance to salvation, never to be repented of, is the hearty prayer of thy sincere friend,

Thomas Nicholson.

Petition of New Hampshire Slaves, November 12, 1779

Issac W. Hammond, ed., "Slavery in New Hampshire," *Magazine of American History* 21 (Jan. 1889): 63-64.

The petition campaigns waged by Negroes in Massachusetts were a graphic response to contentions of some proslavery writers that slaves were a contented lot under slavery, accepting their fate and their divinely-ordained position in society. But Massachusetts Negroes were not alone in petitioning state legislatures—on November 12, 1779, 19 slaves from New Hampshire petitioned their own legislature, pleading for the "state of liberty of which we have been so long deprived." The petition was rejected by the legislature on June 9, 1780, a cryptic note in the daily journal indicating that "the House is not ripe for a determination in this matter." Not until June 26, 1857, was a law enacted in the state declaring that no person should be deprived of the right of citizenship because of color. But the legislature was far behind public opinion. The 1790 census recorded fewer than 200 slaves in New Hampshire, less than one-third the number counted in 1767 indicating a decline in the practice of slavery. Evidence of antislavery feeling was clearly expressed when a black runaway from George Washington's estate was sought in Portsmouth in 1796. The furor in the community against this search was so great that the hunt was called off.

To the Honorable, the Council and House of Representatives of said state, now sitting at Exeter in and for said state:

The petition of the subscribers, natives of Africa, now forcibly detained in slavery in said state most humbly *sheweth*, That the God of nature gave them life and freedom, upon the terms of the most perfect equality with other men; That freedom is an inherent right of the human species, not to be surrendered, but by consent, for the sake of social life; That private or public tyranny and slavery are alike detestable to minds conscious of the equal dignity of human nature; That in power and authority of individuals, derived solely from a principle of coertion, against the will of individuals, and to dispose of their persons and properties, consists the completest idea of private and political slavery; That all men being ameniable to the Deity for the ill-improvement of the blessings of His Providence, they hold themselves in duty bound strenuously to exert every faculty of their minds to obtain that blessing of freedom, which they are justly entitled to from that donation of the beneficent Creator; That through ignorance and brutish violence of their native countrymen, and by the sinister designs of others (who ought to have taught them better), and by the avarice of both, they, while but children, and incapable of self-defence, whose infancy might have prompted protection, were seized, imprisoned, and transported from their native country, where (though ignorance and unchristianity prevailed) they were born free, to a country where (though knowledge, Christianity and freedom are their boast) they are compelled and their posterity to drag on their lives in miserable servitude: Thus, often is the parent's cheek wet for the loss of a child, torn by the cruel hand of violence from her aching bosom; Thus, often and in vain is the infant's sigh for the nurturing care of its bereaved parent, and thus do the ties of nature and blood become victims to cherish the vanity and luxury of a fellow mortal. Can this be right? Forbid it gracious Heaven.

Permit again your humble slaves to lay before this honorable assembly some of those grievances which they daily experience and feel. Though fortune hath dealt out our portion with rugged hand, yet hath she smiled in the disposal of our persons to those who claim us as their property; of them we do not complain, but from what authority they assume the power to dispose of our lives, freedom and property, we would wish to know. Is it from the sacred volume of Christianity? There we believe it is not to be found; but here hath the cruel hand of slavery made us incompetent judges, hence knowledge is hid from our minds. Is it from the volumes of the laws? Of these also slaves cannot be judges, but those we are told are founded on reason and justice; it cannot be found there. Is it from the volumes of nature? No, here we can read with others, of this knowledge, slavery cannot wholly deprive us; here we know that we ought to be free agents; here we feel the dignity of human nature; here we feel the passions and desires of men, though checked by the rod of slavery; here we feel a just equality; here we know that the God of nature made us free. Is their authority assumed from custom? If so let that custom be abolished, which is not founded in nature, reason nor religion. Should the humanity and benevolence of this honorable assembly restore us that state of liberty of which we have been so long deprived, we conceive that those who are our present masters will not be sufferers by our liberation, as we have most of us spent our whole strength and the prime of our lives in their service; and as freedom inspires a noble confidence and gives the mind an emulation to vie in the noblest efforts of enterprise, and as justice and humanity are the result of your deliberations, we fondly hope that the eye of pity and the heart of justice may commiserate our situation, and put us upon the equality of freemen, and give us an opportunity of evincing to the world our love of freedom by exerting ourselves in her cause, in opposing the efforts of tyranny and oppression over the country in which we ourselves have been so long injuriously enslaved.

Therefore, Your humble slaves most devoutly pray for the sake of injured liberty, for the sake of justice, humanity and the rights of mankind, for the honor of religion and by all that is dear, that your honors would graciously interpose in our behalf, and enact such laws and regulations, as you in your wisdom think proper, whereby we may regain our liberty and be ranked in the class of free agents, and that the name of slave may not more be heard in a land gloriously contending for the sweets of freedom. And your humble slaves as in duty bound will ever pray.

Portsmouth Nov. 12, 1779.

Nero Brewster,	Pharaoh Rogers,	Romeo Rindge,
Seneca Hall,	Cate Newmarch,	Peter Warner,
Cesar Gerrish,	Pharaoh Shores,	Zebulon Gardner,
Winsor Moffatt,	Quam Sherburne,	Garrett Cotton,
Samuel Wentworth,	Kittridge Tuckerman,	Will Clarkson,
Peter Frost,	Jack Odiorne,	Prince Whipple.
Cipio Hubbard,		

Petition of Paul Cuffe and Other Blacks, February 10, 1780

Massachusetts Archives, 186: 134-36, Massachusetts Division of Archives, Boston, Mass.

Paul Cuffe, a 21-year-old free black who later achieved prominence as a master mariner, philanthropist, and African colonizer, petitioned the Massachusetts legislature in February 1780 for relief from taxation. Six others of "African extract," including Cuffe's brother John, also signed the document. The petitioners claimed that their earlier service as slaves had denied them the opportunity to accumulate property and, if forced to pay taxes, they would be reduced to a state of "beggary." They also raised the familiar cry against "taxation without representation": "We are not allowed the privilege of freeman of the State, having no vote or influence in the election of those that tax us."

Paul and John Cuffe, who had refused to pay taxes for three years, were jailed in Taunton, Massachusetts, in December 1780. Although they later fought the issue in the courts and before town meetings, the brothers were eventually forced to pay. But their effort was another example of increasing black participation in the legislative and political processes of the country and a manifestation of their desire for self-determination.

To the Honourable Council and House of Representatives in General Court Assembled for the State of the Massachusetts Bay in New England

The petition of several poor Negroes and mulattoes who are inhabitants of the Town of Dartmouth, Humbly Sheweth—

That we being chiefly of the African extract and by reason of long bondage and hard slavery we have been deprived of enjoying the profit of our labour or the advantage of inheriting estates from our parents as our neighbours the white people do having some of us not long enjoyed our own freedom and yet of late, contrary to the invariable custom and practice of the country we have been & now are taxed both in our polls and that small pittance of estate which through much hard labour and industry we have got together to sustain ourselves & families withal. We apprehend it therefore to be hard usage and will doubtless (if continued) reduce us to a state of beggary whereby we shall become a burthen to others if not timely prevented by the interposition of your justice and power & your petitioners further showeth, that we apprehend ourselves to be aggrieved, in that while we are not allowed the privilege of freemen of the State having no vote or influence in the election of those that tax us yet many of our colour (as is well known) have cheerfully entered the field of battle in the defence of the common cause and that (as we conceive) against a similar exertion of power (in regard to taxation) too well known to need a recital in this place.

Most honourable court, we humbley beseech thee would to take this into consideration and let us free from paying tax or taxes or cause us to be cleared: for we ever have been a people that was fair from all these thing ever since the days of our four fathers and therefore we take it as a heard ship that we should be so delt by now in these difficulty times for there is not to exceed more then five or six that hath a cow in this town and

Paul Cuffe, black petitioner.

therefore in our distress we send unto thee most Honourable Court for relief under the peaceableness of thee people and the mercy of God that we may be releaved for we are not alowed in vooting in the town meating in . . . to chuse an oficer and neither their was not one ever heard in the active Court of the jenerel assembley & we poor destresed miserable Black people & we have not an equal chance with white people neither by sea nor by land therefore we take it as a heard ship that poor old negeros should be rated which have been in bondage some thirty, some forty and some fifty years and now just got their liberty some by going into the service and some by going to sea and others by good fortan and also poor distressed mungrels which have no larning and no land and also no work neither where to put their head but some shelter them selves into an old rotten hut which thy dogs would not lay in—therefore we pray that these may give no offense at all by no means but that thee most Honouerable Court will take it into consideration as if it were their own case for we think it as to be a heard ship that we should be assessed and not be a . . . as we may say to eat bread therefore we humbley beg and pray thee to plead our case for us with thy people O God: that those who have the rule in their hands may be mercyfull unto the poor and needy give unto those who ask of thee and he that would borrow of thee turn thou not away empty O God be mercyfull unto the poor and give unto those who giveth ought unto the poor therefore we return unto thee again: most honouerable Court that thou wouldest consider us in these difficult times for we send in nor come unto the not with false words or neigher with lieing lips therefore we think that we may be clear from being called tories tho some few of our Colour hath rebilled and . . . how ever we think that their is more of our Collour gone into the wars according to the number of them into the respesistative towns then any other nation here and here therefore we most humbley request therefore that you would take our unhappy case into your serious consideration and in your wisdom and power grant us relief from taxation while under our present cirsumstances dispossessed and your poor petioners as in duty bound shall ever pray

Dated at Dartmouth the 10th of February 1780

John Cuffe
Adventem Child
Paul Cuffe
Samuell May

Pero Howland
Pero Russell
Pero Eggshell

John Cooper, "To the Publick," September 20, 1780

John Cooper, "To the Publick," *The New Jersey Journal*, Sept. 20, 1780.

The Pennsylvania Abolition Law of 1780 generated extensive reaction not only in Pennsylvania, but in neighboring New Jersey. Newspapers such as the New Jersey Journal *and the* Gazette *carried numerous letters and essays either extolling*

the virtues of the Pennsylvania law or attacking it as an invasion of the right to private property. On September 20, 1780, an essay written by a New Jersey antislavery writer, John Cooper, offered another side to the burgeoning debate over slavery. Cooper attacked the concept of gradual abolitionism represented by the Pennsylvania law. "And if we keep our present slaves in bondage," Cooper wrote, "and only enact laws that their posterity shall be free, we save that part of our tyranny and gain of oppression, which to us, the present generation, is of the most value." Such halfway legislation was only a sop to the demands of justice, a hypocritical gesture meant only to camouflage continuing injustice.

Cooper was echoing the antislavery cries of such Calvinist clergy members as Samuel Hopkins and Nathaniel Niles, who were demanding national repentance and regeneration through the abolition of slavery. The immediacy implicit in Cooper's appeal for national reform would not be appeased by measures designed to end the horrors of slavery in halting, sluggish steps. A nation unwilling to end legitimately the institution of slavery could only expect "a national scourge."

To the Publick

Friends and Fellow-Citizens! Whilst we are spilling our blood and exhausting our Treasure in defence of our own liberty, it would not perhaps be amiss to turn our eyes towards those of our fellow-men who are now groaning in bondage under us. We say "all men are equally entitled to liberty and the pursuit of happiness;" but are we willing to grant this liberty to all men? The sentiment no doubt is just as well as generous; and must ever be read to our praise, provided our actions correspond therewith. But if after we have made such a declaration to the world, we continue to hold our fellow creatures in slavery, our words must rise up in judgement against us, and by the breath of our own mouths we shall stand condemned.

The war has already been prolonged far beyond what we once thought the abilities of Britain would admit of; and how much longer it may please Providence to suffer it to rage, or what the final event of it may be, is to us altogether unknown. The children of Israel, we find, could not conquer their enemies whilst they, the Israelites, had "the accursed thing" amongst them. And as tyrrany is the accursed thing against which we have waged war, how can we hope to prevail against our enemies whilst we ourselves are tyrants, holding thousands of our fellow creatures in slavery under us?

The Lord did not leave it a doubt with Joshua what was the reason they could not succeed; he told him in plain terms the reason was because they had also transgressed his covenant—they had "the accursed thing" among them. And if the Lord is still the same God, deciding the controversies amongst men upon the same principles, then, although Britain may have transgressed his covenant in endeavouring to enslave us, if we are not only also, but equally in the transgression, by holding the Africans and their posterity in slavery, how can we expect he will decide in our favour, unless we recede from such transgression? Unless we abolish tyrrany, "the accursed thing," from amongst us, and do that justice to others which we ask of him for ourselves? Nay, how can we have the face even to ask of him a blessing on our endeavours, however laudable they may be, to defend ourselves against tyrrany and oppression, whilst we are thus acting the part of tyrants and oppressors? Surely we ought rather to blush at our own conduct;—to acknowledge our own transgressions, and, before we presume to solicit a blessing, endeavour, if possible, to obtain forgiveness. Can we imagine our prayers to Almighty God will meet with his approbation, or in the least degree tend to procure us relief from the hand of oppression, whilst the groans of our slaves are continually ascending mingled with them? I fear, indeed, that not only our prayers, but our publick fastings, are an abomination in his sight, and will so remain until we have washed our hands from tyranny, and the voice of a slave is not to be heard in our land.

But let me beseech us not to deceive ourselves; should we undertake to abolish tyranny, and to put an end to that other accursed thing, the gain of oppression hitherto derived from our slaves, as Saul did when he undertook to destroy Amalek. It seems, from what he said to Samuel on meeting with him soon afterwards, that he thought he had done all that was needful—that he had really fulfilled the will of the Lord. But alas! he was greatly deceived. For he had coveted, and the people had coveted, what they had no right to enjoy; and by yielding to this evil covetous spirit he drew down the vengeance of Heaven upon him, and his fairest hopes were blasted.

They could not it seems, bear to give up all—the King and the best of the things they saved. And if we keep our present slaves in bondage, and only enact laws that their posterity shall be free, we save that part of our tyranny and gain of oppression, which to us, the present generation, is of the most value—is like the King, and the best of the sheep and the oxen; and however specious or plausible the preambles of those laws or our pretentions may be, we shall plainly tread in the footsteps of Saul; and I fear our reward, like his, will be the vengeance of Heaven, and the blasting of our fairest hopes. In short, the iniquity of such a measure must be so flagrant, that, to use a trite saying, those who run may read it. It would be plainly telling our slaves, we will not do justice unto you, but our posterity shall do justice unto your posterity. And should such indeed be our language to those who are unfortunately in our power, what can we expect from the just Judge of the universe, but that he will say unto us, I will not deliver you from your tribulation, but your posterity I will deliver.

Let us, my countrymen, derive wisdom from those who have gone before us: Let the people and their rulers beware of an evil covetousness.

In our publick and most solemn declarations we say, we are resolved to die free;—that slavery is worse than death. He, therefore, who enslaves his fellow-creature must, in our esteem, be worse than he who takes his life; and yet, surprizing as it may seem, we hold thousands of our fellow-men in slavery, and slumber on under the dreadful load of guilt—Worse than murderers and yet at ease! A melancholy reflection indeed, that habit should be capable of reconciling the human mind to the greatest of all crimes—of lulling it to rest in the practice of that which ere long, must cause it to tremble before the great, the awful tribunal; where all deception will be done away, and our transgressions appear in their fullest magnitude and greatest deformity! What shall we then think of the unlawful gain, we now derive from the labour of our innocent, tho' unfortunate slaves? Myriads of whom perhaps we shall there behold smiling in the fullest fruition of peace, whilst their late lordly oppressors, conscious of their own guilt, trembling wait the awful sentence.

Let me now entreat us to pause a while, and examine our own hearts. Let us survey our ways with the impartial eye of reason and justice; and whatsoever shall appear to be out of order, that let us correct. Whilst we are making high pretentions and pompous declarations with regard to our own views and publick virtue, let us take care to act up to those pretentions and declarations; but above all things, let us candidly, in the sight of Heaven, do that justice to others which we ask for ourselves. This is the way for us to succeed in our present contest; this is the surest way that we can take to obtain Peace, Liberty and Safety.

If we are determined not to emancipate our slaves, but to hold them still in bondage, let us alter our language upon the subject of tyranny; let us no longer speak of it as a thing in its own nature detestable, because in so doing, as hath been observed, we shall condemn ourselves. But let us rather declare to the world, that tyranny is a thing we are not principled against, but that we are resolved not to be slaves, because we ourselves mean to be tyrants. Such a declaration would certainly be more candid, or at least would better correspond with the conduct I have mentioned, than those we have usually made; though perhaps it might not be quite so pleasing, for justice is so lovely, and virtue so amiable, that we all love to be deemed their votaries, however estranged we may be from their ways.

Whatever colouring slavekeeping may receive from interested individuals who wish to keep it on foot, there is something in its nature so universally odious, that we meet with but few of the slavekeepers themselves that are willing to be thought tyrants; like unchaste women, they cannot bear to be deemed what they really are; for nothing is more clear, than that he who keeps a slave is a tyrant. Without tyranny, there can be no slavery in the sense here meant. And where slavekeeping is countenanced and upheld by any state or empire, the tyranny becomes national, and the iniquity also; and in such case a national scourge may very well be looked for. If, therefore, neither the love of justice, nor the feelings of humanity are sufficient to induce us to release our slaves from bondage, let the dread of divine retribution—of national calamities—induce us to do it.

I know it is not fashionable for those who write news-paper pieces to risk their names with the pieces they publish; but I shall venture to deviate from the custom in this particular case, because however unpopular it may be, I have a desire to appear one of the testimony bearers against a practice so unjustifiable as slavekeeping is at all times and in all countries, but more especially in this at the present juncture. I have endeavoured to express my ideas in as few words as possible; and as the piece is short, so when fully and impartially considered, I hope it will prove offensive to no individual.

John Cooper.

Benjamin Colman, "Declaration and Testimony," November 7, 1780

Benjamin Colman, "Declaration and Testimony," reprinted in Joshua Coffin, ed., *A Sketch of the History of Newbury, Newburyport, and West Newbury from 1635 to 1845* (Boston, 1845), 343-46.

Intense debate over the Biblical sanctions of slavery often had serious repercussions within church congregations. Deacon Benjamin Colman, the zealous antislavery spokesman who had published several articles in New England newspapers, provoked a bitter controversy within his own church at Byfield by assailing the slaveholding practices of his pastor, Moses Parsons. On November 7, 1780, Colman wrote his "Declaration and Testimony," a vigorous assertion of his antislavery views and a justification for his attacks on Reverend Parsons. At a church meeting in March 1781, however, Colman's private crusade was thwarted; the members suspended him from fellowship and communion for his slanderous attacks until he "by repentance and confession give Christian satisfaction for the offence he has committed." Over four years later the deacon publicly admitted that his attack on Parsons, who died in December 1783, was perhaps excessively vehement and lacking in "due concern for his character." Colman was restored to his church duties, but, although his frantic antislavery testimony had been muted within his own church, he continued to speak out against the "Capital Sin of this people, for which our Land bleeds. . . ." Colman later remembered his battle within his church as divinely inspired: "And as it pleased God to open my eyes at that time to see the Abominable Wickedness of that practice, I believe Silence would have been a Crime."

The Declaration and Testimony of Benjamin Colman, together with his Complaint against the Reverend Moses Parsons, pastor of the Church in Byfield is as follows.

Viz. That God has a controversy with the people of this Land I suppose no judicious person will pretend to deny: The bloody dreaded sword of War has been drawn against us by our brethren, and has prevailed for more than five years; whereby great numbers of our brethren the inhabitants of this Land have been slain, many Towns made desolate, the Dwelling places of our people consumed by fire, the Inhabitants, many of them Slaughtered, and others driven away and reduced to extream poverty and sore distress. The widows and fatherless are multiplied amongst us and the hand of God lies heavy upon us still. The hand of God is lifted up: the War continues; our enemies are powerful and numerous: and they, flushed with their success, and expecting shortly to make a compleat conquest of America; and if God don't appear for us and stop their progress, we may rationally expect they will conquer our country. It is time for us to look about us, to search and try our ways, to consider what we have done to provoke our God, to send our unprovoked brethren, and make them his severe rod of correction to chastise us in this manner.

We have been called upon, by our Continental Congress, to humble our selves before God by fasting and prayer, to implore the mercy, and help of our God, that we may be delivered out of the hands of our cruel Oppressors.

We have observed those days set apart for prayer in the manner we have done. But as acts of Justice and Righteousness have not been Joined with our humiliations and petitions, it seems the Lord has not heard our requests for help. Isaiah 58th. 6th. 'This is the fast that I have chosen to loose the bands of Wickedness, undo the heavy burdens, and let the oppressed go free, and break every yoke.' When we keep such a fast as he has prescribed, then we may call and the Lord will answer. Then shall our light rise in Obscurity; then may we cry and he will say here I am, &c. for the Lord has promised to do so: and his Word stands firmer than heaven and earth.

I confess the Continental Congress have taken one good step towards reformation; as they have come into a resolution not to import any more slaves. But still the bands of Wickedness are not loosed: many thousands of this poor oppressed people are held down under oppression by Tyranny. And as we have come into a partial reformation, so the Lord has granted a partial deliverance: but as we have stayed our hand as to a thorough reformation, so he has stayed his hand from granting us compleat Deliverance: his Word is fulfilled, as he has said, 'with the froward he will shew himself froward and with the upright he will shew himself upright.' And can we wonder that God shuts out our prayer, and turns a deaf ear to our cries for help against our foes? Our Land is defiled with blood, we have slain many of our brethren, in taking and captivating them: and our fingers with iniquity in making merchandise of others: we have committed violence upon our brethren; and violence is still in our hands. We have turned a deaf ear to the cries of the oppressed; and this law which supports Oppression reaches through the whole of these *United States*. The Slaves in this State have petitioned for Liberty and Freedom from bondage, since our Troubles began, in the most importunate and humble manner; yet they are not set free in a general way. We have taken them, by cruel hands; rending parents from children, and children from parents; and, by violence, brought them from their own native country, (the Land that their God, and our God, had given them to possess and enjoy.) and subjected them to the most abject slavery and bondage. Magistrates, Ministers, and common people have had a hand in this Iniquitous Trade.

But in order to open people's eyes to see the horridness of this *Man-trade*, this Oppression and cruelty that has been exercised on our brethren, I beg leave to give a short sketch of the way and manner how our people come by these slaves, when they transport them from their own country.

And the account I shall give shall be from printed histories concerning the carrying on of this slave-trade and these historical accounts I have had confirmed by persons that have been eye-witnesses to these horrid transactions upon the spot. And it is as follows. When a ship of ours arrives in one of their harbours, some of the people there come on board the ship, and ask what they want? They tell them they want a cargo of slaves. They ask the master what he has to pay for them? he shews them Wine, Brandy,

Rum, Clothing, fire arms, and ammunition; as they carry all such articles as they know are most tempting to those people. And when they have agreed upon a price, by the head, or poll; they furnish out a company with arms and ammunition, to go and take a sufficient number of captives to load their ship. So they go out into their country, some twenty, some thirty, sometimes more than sixty miles; say my authors, till they come to little, defenceless towns and villages Inhabited by these poor defenceless people; and there they take as many, and of such an age as they like; others they slaughter without compassion to age or sex. The strong ones they confine with Irons: the younger ones they bind with cords; and drive them before them in droves to the Sea port; where they have a great Pound built to confine them till the Ship is ready to take them. In this situation, say my authors, some are so dismayed, at the thoughts of what they are coming to, that they refuse to eat what they feed them with; and choose to die there rather than live such a life as they expect. When their keepers perceive them refuse to eat, they sometimes take one and torture him, or her before the rest; sometimes they kill one, and cut him to pieces before their eyes; and tell the others they will do so to them, if they will not eat.

When the ship is ready they carry them on board with their boats: some try to throw themselves overboard and drown, and so forth. Those they get on board they thrust into the hold of the ship, fasten them in, and feed them with something to support their lives during the passage; there they lie, in their filth and stench, till the ship arrives at her home.

Some ships bring one hundred, some one hundred and fifty, and some near two hundred of these poor people at once. Upon taking them out, they commonly find ten, fifteen, or twenty dead in the hold, and often a number of children born on their passage, some dead, and some alive. But this is not all; there is what they call *seasoning*, to fit these wretched mortals for severe slavery, to be done to them yet; and their method is to feed them with coarse and mean food, a scant allowance, to try and prove their constitutions; in this experiment many of them die; so that the merchants that import them lay their accounts thus, viz. if six in ten live through their transportation and seasoning, they make a saving voyage. And now they sell these poor people to any one that will give them the most money for them.

Horrid manstealing! sordid gain! violent oppression and cruelty!

And has this deadful, this horrid practice been supported, or tolerated by the law of this land through the United States of America for twenty years past! and are there not many thousands of these wretched mortals, in this land, under the cruel yoke of oppression at this day! What shall we say for ourselves as a people? are not our hands defiled with blood? and our fingers with iniquity? and how can we with confidence, lift up our prayer, to that God, who is a God of knowledge, and by whom actions are weighed, for deliverance from oppression, till we have loosed the bands of wickedness, proclaimed liberty to our captives and let the oppressed go free? do not our crimes stare us in the face? and is not our God rising up out of his holy place, to retaliate our doings upon us? is he not laying righteousness to the line, and judgement to the plummet? Three, if not four, of our states are already fallen into the hands of our cruel enemies; and we have no reason to expect but that the rest will shortly fall a prey to them, if repentance and reformation don't prevent it. Had we taken these slaves captives in a just war with them, we might have had some excuse for our doings; but now we have none: for as they never molested us, our sin of oppression is aggravated; and God is now requiting blood for blood, oppression for oppression, according to his Word. Revelations 13. 10th, he that leadeth into captivity, shall go into captivity; he that killeth with the sword, must be killed with the sword.

And now, reverend sir, I entreat your candid attention to what I have to offer to you, at this time, by way of complaint; the substance of which I have offered to you as my grievous complaint for many years in private. And as these grievances increase upon my mind, and our iniquities of this kind stare us in the face, and as the Lord, by his severe corrections, seems to point directly to this our sin of unrighteousness, oppression and violence upon our brethren; I think I may be allow'd to speak my mind without giving just cause of offence, to plead the cause of the oppressed, to bear my testimony against sin, and to take God's part, in visiting this land with judgements, as at this day. And, as I have said before, I look upon this oppression as the capital sin of these states, as it has been supported by the law of the land. And although I am sensible our transgressions are multiplied, I think that *this* sin of oppression and violence, is more peculiarly pointed at than any other in the dispensations of providence. But here I would first observe, that in applying the judgements of God to a person or people, it becomes us to be modest, and cautious; as it may sometimes happen to wicked men according to the work of the righteous. But, on the other hand, it is a sore truth that God is known by the judgement he executes; and in every age he doth point out sin to the world, by some remarkable strokes, some great examples of judgements wherein men may read their sin in their punishment; as in the case of Adoni-bezek Judges 1st, 7th and Ahab 1 Kings 21, and others.

You tell us, sir, and I think very truly, that God has no unmeaning providences; that judgements tread on the heels of sin; pray, sit, what meaning do you affix to God's designs in bringing this judgement of violent oppression upon us by the hand of our brethren, if it be not to convince and humble us for the like violent oppression on our brethren? When there is so plain, so exact a resemblance, between a people's sin and God's judgements, I think it would be an argument of stupidity in us not to apply them to our selves. You tell us that unbelief is the *Damning* sin under the Gospel: I grant the truth of it: but pray, sir, What resemblance, or connection is there, between the sin of unbelief, and the Sword of violent oppression by our brethren, to take away our money, and deprive us of all our temporal enjoyments? No, Sir, the present Dispensation points us to a Sin against the Second table, viz. against our neighbour and by then: for thus stands the Controversy, they Demand our properties: we tell them we will not Yield up our rights: We will not be Slaves to them: for Liberty and property are our Just rights; we will die Sooner than we will be Slaves. Well, if liberty and property are so valuable to us, are they not as valuable to our *Neighbours?*

As to the toleration granted, by Moses, at God's direction to the Jews of old, viz. that they might buy of the heathen Captives, and keep them as their Inheritance, I have answered it before in the publick newspapers, and so need not to mention it here.

And now, Reverend Sir, I would humbly ask, have *you* had no hand in this Iniquitous, Man-stealing, or Slave-trade? have you not bought divers of these people for money; (people made of the same flesh and blood with yourself and your Children:) And kept them in Bondage? One of Which, if I Mistake not, you have Baptized, and received as a Member of the Church of Byfield; And Afterwards offered to Sell the Same Slave for a large sum of money. Pray, Sir, is this teaching the way of Righteousness? is this doing as you would be done by? is this practising the great command of our Redeemer according to that Sacred rule of equity Delivered by our Saviour's own mouth, Matthew 7: 12, Therefore all things Whatsoever ye would that men should do to you do ye even so to them: for this is the law and the prophets? have you never attended to what our Redeemer has told you, in that Same Memorable Sermon on the Mount, Matthew 5: 12, Whosoever shall break one of the least of these Commands; and shall teach men so, shall be called the least in the Kingdom of heaven? and can you say, Sir, that you have not violated that Sacred universal rule? and have you not taught others to do so, by your example? have you considered that text in Corinthians 6: 9th. know ye not that the unrighteous shall not inherit the Kingdom of God? have you been so long a preacher of the Gospel, and not learnt Righteousness? Pray, Sir, look on that text, Jeremiah 22: 13, Wo unto him that buildeth his house by Unrighteousness, and his Chambers by Wrong: that useth his Neighbour's Service without Wages, and giveth him not for his Work. Has not this been your practice, as you have kept Slaves? I beseech you, Sir, to consider who these men-stealers are Ranked with, whom We find in the first Epistle to Timothy first Chapter and ninth verse, for the law was not made for the Righteous, but for the ungodly, and for Sinners, and so forth, for murderers of fathers, and murderers of mothers, for man-slayers, for manstealers, and so forth. Here we find man-stealers Ranked amongst the most enormous crimes that Scripture gives us any account of. But, Sir, this Wicked practice of yours is not all that I Complain of: I intreat you to consider the melancholy Consequences of this your practice: for hereby, you have rendered your self incapable of discharging the duty of a faithful Watchman; for your mouth is shut; you can't reprove others, or bear publick testimony against this horrid crime, without condemning your self, and your own practice; so that others, by your neglect are hardened in their Sin, and emboldened to commit the like. I pray you sir, to consider what the Lord Saith by the Prophet Ezekiel Chapter 33, verses 2d and downward, Son of man, Speak to the Children of thy people, and say unto them, When I bring the Sword upon the land, if the people of the Land take a man of their coasts and set him for their Watchman, and so forth, and so forth, if the watchman see the Sword come, and blow not the trumpet, and the people be not warned, if the Sword come and take any person from among them, he is taken away in his iniquity, *but his blood will I require at the Watchman's hands.* O, Sir! are you not set for a Watchman in this place, and for the people of this Land? and have you ever blown the trumpet to give warning of this horrid Sin of Manstealing; this *Capital Sin* of this people, for which our Land bleeds and mourns at this day? is not the hand of God lifted up? and does he not threaten to retaliate and visit our Iniquities of this kind upon this people? And do *you* keep Silence, and not call upon this people to put away the violence that is in their hands? And do you, Sir, when you view the dispensations of providence, at this day, acquit your self as a faithful Watchman?

But if you Say you do not view this iniquitous practice in the Same light that I, and others do, I pray you to look into the fourteenth Chapter of Ezekiel, where the Lord Saith by that prophet, if any man come to enquire of the Lord having the Stumbling block of his iniquity before his face: I, the Lord will answer that man by my self. I intreat you to consider whether this Stumbling block of your iniquity has not blinded your eyes; and, if so, are you a Qualified Watchman? I confess, Sir, you cry aloud against Some Sins; If men ask or take an exorbitant price for their Corn, Meat, Butter, or Wood and so forth, you say tis this doing as you would be done by? is this loving your Neighbour as yourself? But When men buy or Sell their brethren, (for I confess I know not Which is the most criminal, the buyer, or the Seller,) and make merchandise of human flesh, here you are silent! and why, but for the reason given above, that is you are afraid to condemn your self?

And should you plead, Sir, the Law of the land, or the practice of the people, as an excuse in your favour; I answer, that neither the Law of the land, nor the commonness of the people's practice in this affair alters the nature of the Crime at all: for that which is Wrong in its own nature, can never be made right by any law or practice of men. But, to conclude at this time, tho' more might be said against this wicked practice, I intreat you to consider What the Word of God Says: but if you refuse still to hearken, I can only Say my soul shall weep in Secret places for you, and the people of this bleeding Land. I am, Reverend Sir your humble Servant,

Benjamin Colman.

Byfield in Newbury, November 7th, 1780.

Robert Pleasants to General William Phillips, May 14, 1781

Cornwallis Papers, PRO 30/11, vol. 90, ff. 10-11, G. B. Public Record Office Papers, Gifts and Deposits, Library of Congress, Washington, D.C.

When Lord Dunmore issued his proclamation on November 7, 1775, declaring that all slaves who joined the British army would receive freedom, the slaveholding populus of Virginia reacted with vehemence. Earlier, James Madison foresaw dire portents in such an action: "It is imagined our Governor has been tampering with the Slaves & that he has it in contemplation to make great Use of them in case of a civil war in this province. To say the truth, that is the only part in which this Colony is vulnerable; & if we should be subdued, we shall fall like Achilles by the hand of one that knows the secret." Madison's speculation was not idle; slaves, indeed, began to desert in large numbers after Dunmore's announcement. On November 27, 1775, Edmund Pendleton wrote to Richard Henry Lee that masses of slaves were fleeing to the King's forces. Thomas Jefferson estimated that in 1778 alone more than 30,000 Virginia slaves escaped to the British. As the black exodus continued through the war years, the lives of large numbers of white planters were significantly affected. One of these, ironically, was the abolitionist Robert Pleasants. On May 14, 1781, Pleasants, trustee of the estate of his slaveholding father and brother, wrote to British General William Phillips that several blacks from the Pleasants estate who had joined Phillips's forces in Virginia had been scheduled for manumission. Pleasants wanted assurance that the slaves would receive freedom and not reenslavement at the hands of privateers. Pleasants never received an answer for Phillips died the previous day.

Curles 5th mo. 14. 1781

General Philips From a full persuasion that Liberty is the natural right of all men, and an apprehention of duty, as Trustee of my Father and Brother John & Jonathan Pleasants Decd., respecting the rights and previledges of the Negroes which by the Law were accounted a part of their Estates, but from a consciousness of their undoubted title to freedom, did order and direct by their last Will & Testaments, that they should enjoy that enestimable previledge as they come to the age of thirty years, nearly in the following words Viz. "Believing that all mankind have an undoubted right to freedom, & commiserating the Situation of the Negroes which by the Law I am invested with the property of, and being willing & desirous that they may in a good degree partake and enjoy that enestimable Blessing, do order & direct, as the most likely means to fit them for freedom, that they be instructed to read, at least the young ones as they come of suitable age, and that each individual of them which now are or hereafter may arive to the age of thirty years may enjoy the full benefit of their labour, in a manner the most likely to answer the intention of relieving them from Bondage, and whenever the law of the Country will remit absolute freedom to them. It is my will & desire that all the slaves I am now possessed of, together with their increase, shall immediately on their coming to the age of thirty years as aforesaid become free; at least all such as will accept thereof, or that my Trustees hereafter to be named or a Majority of them may think so fitted for freedom, as that the enjoyment thereof may conduce to their happiness, which I desire they may enjoy in as full & ample a manner as if they never had been in Bondage."

Now as Sundry of these people were given to a maiden Sister of mine with these expres conditions, who is since Married to Charles Logan of the City of Philadelphia, and who jointly with her Husband hath also executed a manumition (as I am informed) for them to take place, the males at the age of twenty one & the females at Eighteen, and as divers of them are lately gone of with thy Army, with an expectation, I suppose, more fully to enjoy the liberty intended them, I conceived it to be my duty to inform thee of their peculiar circumstance, and to request if they should choose to continue where they are, that thou would give such direction concerning them, as may prevent Privatears or designing men from converting them into property; for that purpose I herewith subjoin the names of them, at least such as are grown.

I have also to represent the peculiar Situation of a Negro Man named Charles White, who was directed by my Fathers will to be free, and hath enjoy'd it for several years with as much reputation & respect in the neighbourhood as most Men in a low station, and hath acquired some property, but what makes it peculiarly hard on him is, that it is said he & his family were forced away, and it is evident he has left most of his property behind, which he need not have done had he been desirous of going away. If that should be the case I hope thou will give direction for his discharge.— There is also another case in respect to two Negroes of mine, who went away with the Army under General Arnold, in the month of January last, One a man called Carter Jack, aged between thirty & forty years, and the Other a Boy named London, about fifteen, concerning whom I wrote sometime ago to Genl Arnold, but have never been informed whether or not it got to hand; these Negroes were manumitted under hand & Seal, Jack on the 14th. 5 mo. 1777, and London, on the 21th. 7 mo following the latter to be free on the 1st. of the 12 mo 1787, who I should be glad to reclaim, as also a Horse which was taken at the same time, and from his gentle good qualities to a person of my years was very valuable, but as to the Negro Man, I don't wish his return except with his own choice. I wished to have waited on thee in person had it been convenient, but as that is not the case at present, and being desirous to give thee the earliest inteligence of the above matters, I hope thou will excuse it. Thy compliance with the above request will greatly Oblige one who is a friend to Peace, to Liberty, & to mankind in General.

Robert Pleasants

Negro Jacob a Carpenter Amy his wife & three children	5
Sukey & four .... d	5
Frank & Nelly	2
Fanny & one child	2
Jessie a Boy & Lycy a Girl	2
Charles White & Sarah his wife & their two daughters	4
Jack & London	2

Major General Philips

Mumbet Case, Court Decision, August 1781

Massachusetts Supreme Judicial Court Records, 1781-82, 96, Court File Suffolk, Vol. 1192, Case No. 159966 Clerk's Office Boston, Mass.

Elizabeth Freeman, known affectionately as "Mumbet" and "Bett," lived with her "owner," Colonel John Ashley, in Sheffield, Berkshire County, Massachusetts. In February 1781, when the brutal treatment dispensed by her ill-tempered mistress was no longer bearable, Bett left the Ashley household and refused to return. She persuaded a man named Brom, a slave mechanic, to join her in an appeal to a young Massachusetts lawyer, Theodore Sedgwick, to plead a legal suit for their freedom in the state courts. Sedgwick, later an ardent antislavery senator, once wrote of Freeman, "If there could be a practical refutation of the imagined superiority of our race to hers, the life and character of this woman would afford that refutation."

In August 1781 the case of Brom and Bett vs. John Ashley *was heard in the Inferior Court of Common Pleas, Great Barrington. Bett, an illiterate woman with extraordinary intelligence, described to the court how she had listened to the discussions of the men who had visited the Ashleys as she served table. She remembered hearing upon numerous occasions that under the new Massachusetts Constitution of 1780, all individuals were "born free and equal." She had pondered this phrase and decided that, as a person and not a beast, the constitution applied to her. Sedgwick argued before the court that slavery had never received legal sanction in Massachusetts and that the first article of the Declaration of Rights of the Constitution did, indeed, nullify the slave system. Although John Ashley insisted that the case be dropped because Brom and Bett were his legal servants, the court ordered him to pay the plaintiffs 30 shillings for damages, as well as court costs. The two had achieved freedom in a case whose precedent helped strike a death blow to slavery in Massachusetts. For many years Bett served the Sedgwicks, endearing herself to the family and the community. She died in December 1829, at the probable age of 85.*

Berkshire

At an Inferior Court of Common Pleas begun and holden at Great Barrington within & for the County of Berkshire upon the third Tuesday of August (being the twenty fifth day of the same Month) in this Year of our Lord Christ seventeen hundred & eighty one.—

Brom, a Negro Man, & Bett a Negro Woman both of Sheffield in sd County of Berkshire Plaintiffs against John Ashley of Sheffield aforesaid Esq. Defendant. In a Plea of Replevin wherein the said Brom & Bett prayed out a previous Writ of Replevin signed by the Clerk of our said Court dated the twenty eighth day of May in the Year last aforesaid, which is as follows (to wit) The Commonwealth of Massachusetts—To the Sheriff of our County of Berkshire his under Sheriff or Deputy Greeting. When we have often commanded you that justly & without delay you should cause to be replevined Brom, a Negro Man of Sheffield in our sd County Labourer, & Bett a Negro Woman of Sheffield aforesaid Spinster, whom John Ashley Esqr & John Ashley Junior both of Sheffield aforesaid have taken & being so taken detain (as it is said) unless they were taken by our special command as by the command of our Chief Justice or for Homicide or for any other just cause, whereby according to the Usage of this Commonwealth, they are not replevisable, or that you should signify to us the cause wherefore the said John Ashley and John Ashley Junr have taken & so detain the said Brom & Bett, and you having returned unto us that you have repaired unto the Houses of John Ashley & John Ashley Junr Esqs to replevy the said Brom and Bett according to the tenor of our aforesaid Writ, but the said John Ashley Esqr did not permit a delivery of ye aforesaid Brom & Bett to be made because he asserted that the said Brom and Bett were his Servants for Life, thereby claiming a right of servitude in the Persons of ye said Brom & Bett.—We unwilling that the said Brom, if he be a Freeman, and the said Bett if she be a Free woman, by such taking & claims should be deprived of the common Law, command you if the said Brom & Bett shall find you sufficient security of being before our Justice of our Inferior Court of Common Pleas, to be holdin at Great Barrington within & for our sd County of Berkshire on the third Tuesday of August next to answer the aforesaid John Ashley Esqr if they shall find you such sufficient Security; then in the meantime that you cause to be replevined the aforesaid Brom & Bett, according to the tenor of our Writs, and beside if the said Brom & Bett shall have made you secure of that complaint as aforesaid, then summon by good summoners the said John Ashley Esqr; that he be before the Justice of our said Court, on the third Tuesday of August next to answer unto the said Brom & Bett, of the taking & claim aforesaid and have there then the names of the pledges in this Writ testified by Wm Whiting Esq. at Great Barrington the twenty eighth day of May as aforesaid. The sd Brom & Bett appear (by their Attys John Reeve & Theodore Sedgwick Esqr and charges furnished vizt) And the said John Ashley comes by his Attorneys John Canfield Esqr & David Noble Gentmn) and says that the sd Brom & Bett ought not to have and maintain their suit aforesaid against him, but that the same ought to be abated & dismissed, because he says that the said Brom & Bett are & were at the time of serving the original Writ the legal Negro Servants of him the said John Ashley during their Lives, and this the sd John is ready to verify, & hereof prays the Judgment of this Court, and that the said Suit may be abated—And the said Brom & Bett (by their Attys John Reeve & Theodore Sedgwick Esqre) say that their suit aforesaid ought not to be abated, because they say that they are not, nor are either of them, nor were they or either of them, at the time of the Issuing of the original Writ the Negro Servant or Servants of him the said John Ashley during this time. & this they pray may be inquired of by ye Country. And this sd John Ashley (by his sd Attnys) likewise doth ye same—And after a full hearing of this Case the evidence therein being produced, the same Case is committed to the Jury Jonathan Holcomb Foreman and his Fellows, who being duly sworn, return this verdict that in this Case the Jury find that the said Brom & Bett are not, and were not, at the time of ye purchase of the original writ the legal Negro Servants of the sd John Ashley during life, and assess thirty shillings damages. Wherefore it is considered by the Court, and thereupon by the said Court adjudged and determined, that the sd Brom & Bett are not, nor were they at the time of ye purchase of the original Writ the legal Negro Servants of the sd John Ashley during life, and that the said Brom & Bett do recover against the said John Ashley the sum of thirty shillings lawful silver money damages, and the Costs of this Suit Taxed at five pounds fourteen Shillings & four pence like Money—And hereof ye sd Brom & Bett may have their Endevour.

The said John Ashley appeals from the Judgment of this Court to the Supreme Judicial Court to be holden at sd Great Barrington within & for the County of Berkshire aforesaid upon the first Tuesday in October next: And John Ashley Junr Esqr recognizes with sureties as the law directs, for the said John Ashley his prosecuting with effect this appeal at the said Supreme Court and eror on File.

The foregoing is a true Copy of Record

Attest Henry Wm Dwight, Clerk

Virginia Manumission Law, 1782

William Waller Hening, ed., *The Statutes at Large; Being a Collection of all the Laws of Virginia from the First Session of the Legislature in the Year 1619* (Richmond, 1823), 11:39-40

In 1782 the Virginia Assembly, repealing a prohibition against private manumission which had been in force in the state since 1723, authorized, under rigid control, private emancipations by will or other written instrument. The measure, which drew surprisingly little opposition in the Assembly and elicited little attention in the community, especially pleased Robert Pleasants and other Virginia Quakers who had been prevented in the past from freeing slaves, except for "meritorious services, to be adjudged and allowed by the Governor and council." Quakers such as Warner Mifflin and John Parrish had lobbied intensively with members of the legislature and regarded the passage of the act as a major victory for Quaker religious principles. Although the 1782 legislation resulted in a large number of private manumissions in the following years, from Robert Carter's release of 442 slaves to the freeing of numerous individual slaves, some prominent Virginians were unsure of the future implications of the legislation for their plantation society. John Randolph later wrote that although the act had been motivated by "one of the best feelings of the human heart," it failed to offer protection against the "evils" of a growing mass of free blacks. The Quaker leadership, of course, had no such reservations. When news of the legislation in Virginia reached Philadelphia, the Meeting for Sufferings announced that "the Light of Truth" had touched even Virginia, where "temporal Considerations, and long accustomed prejudices have held in obdurate blindness."

Chap. XXI

An act to authorize the manumission of slaves.

I. Whereas application hath been made to this present general assembly, that those persons who are disposed to emancipate their slaves may be empowered so to do, and the same hath been judged expedient under certain restrictions: *Be it therefore enacted*, That it shall hereafter be lawful for any person, by his or her last will and testament, or by any other instrument in writing, under his or her hand and seal, attested and proved in the county court by two witnesses, or acknowledged by the party in the court of the county where he or she resides, to emancipate and set free, his or her slaves, or any of them, who shall thereupon be entirely and fully discharged from the performance of any contract entered into during servitude, and enjoy as full freedom as if they had been particularly named and freed by this act.

II. *Provided always, and be it further enacted,* That all slaves so set free, not being in the judgment of the court, of sound mind and body, or being above the age of forty-five years, or being males under the age of twenty-one, or females under the age of eighteen years, shall respectively be supported and maintained by the person so liberating them, or by his or her estate; and upon neglect or refusal so to do, the court of the county where such neglect or refusal may be, is hereby empowered and required, upon application to them made, to order the sheriff to distrain and sell so much of the person's estate as shall be sufficient for that purpose. *Provided also,* That every person by written instrument in his life time, or if by last will and testament, the executors of every person freeing any slave, shall cause to be delivered to him or her, a copy of the instrument of emancipation, attested by the clerk of the court of the county, who shall be paid therefor, by the person emancipating, five shillings, to be collected in the manner of other clerk's fees. Every person neglecting or refusing to deliver to any slave by him or her set free, such copy, shall forfeit and pay ten pounds, to be recovered with costs in any court of record, one half thereof to the person suing for the same, and the other to the person to whom such copy ought to have been delivered. It shall be lawful for any justice of the peace to commit to the gaol of his county, any emancipated slave travelling out of the county of his or her residence without a copy of the instrument of his or her emancipation, there to remain till such copy is produced and the gaoler's fees paid.

III. *And it be further enacted,* That in case any slave so liberated shall neglect in any year to pay all taxes and levies imposed or to be imposed by law, the court of the county shall order the sheriff to hire out him or her for so long time as will raise the said taxes and levies. *Provided* sufficient distress cannot be made upon his or her estate. *Saving nevertheless* to all and every person and persons, bodies politic or corporate, and their heirs and successors, other than the person or persons claiming under those so emancipating their slaves, all such right and title as they or any of them could or might claim if this act had never been made.

Plaque located in North Scituate, Massachusetts commemorating Judge William Cushing who outlawed slavery in that state.

"I THINK THE IDEA
OF SLAVERY IS
INCONSISTENT WITH
OUR OWN CONDUCT
AND CONSTITUTION,
AND THERE CAN BE
NO SUCH THING AS
PERPETUAL SERVITUDE
OF A RATIONAL CREATURE
UNLESS HIS LIBERTY
IS FORFEITED BY
SOME CRIMINAL
CONDUCT OR GIVEN
UP BY PERSONAL
CONSENT OR
CONTRACT."
"THE RIGHTS
OF INDIVIDUALS
AND THE JUSTICE
DUE TO THEM ARE
AS DEAR AND
PRECIOUS AS
THOSE OF STATES.
INDEED THE LATTER
ARE FOUNDED UPON
THE FORMER AND
THE GREAT END
AND OBJECT OF
THEM MUST BE TO
SECURE AND SUPPORT
THE RIGHTS OF INDIVIDUALS
OR ELSE VAIN IS GOVERNMENT."
JUDGE WILLIAM CUSHING
1732 1810

Commonwealth v. *Jennison*, Chief Justice William Cushing to the Jury, 1783

Massachusetts Historical Society, *Proceedings of the Massachusetts Historical Society*, 43 (April 1874): 294

"The idea of slavery is inconsistent with our own conduct and Constitution." Thus asserted Massachusetts Chief Justice William Cushing in his charge to the jury in the 1783 case of the Commonwealth v. Jennison. *Basing his charge on the Massachusetts Constitution of 1780, Cushing stated that, with regard to slavery, "a different idea has taken place with the people of America, more favorable to the natural rights of mankind. . . ." The case resulted from a criminal action taken against Nathaniel Jennison for assault and battery after he attempted to hold a black man, Quack Walker, as a slave. In an earlier 1781 case,* Jennison v. Caldwell, *Jennison had sued John and Seth Caldwell, relatives of Walker's former owner, for profits received from Walker's labor. The lower court had ruled that Walker was a slave and Jennison was awarded damages. The parallel case,* Walker v. Jennison, *however, in which Walker sued Jennison for assault and battery, was decided in Walker's favor. The two cases were in obvious conflict. Following a two-year series of appeals and counter-appeals by both sides and by Jennison's aggressive efforts to petition both the Massachusetts legislature and the general court, the constitutional ramifications of the cases remained ambiguous. But Chief Justice Cushing's statement in the 1783 criminal trial before the Supreme Judicial Court in Worchester was a definitive affirmation of the constitutional illegality of slavery in Massachusetts. ". . . Every subject," the Chief Justice declared, "is entitled to liberty, and to have it guarded by the laws. . . ." It remains unclear whether the decision in the criminal case actually abolished slavery in the Bay State. Indeed, there is a question whether slavery ever legally existed there. The Cushing charge to the jury, however, reflected the pervasive antipathy to slavery in Massachusetts and was another of the numerous decisions against the institution in such trials as* Slew v. Whipple *(1766) and the "Mumbet" case (1781).*

Fact proved.

Justification that Quack is a slave—and to prove it 'tis said that Quack, when a child about 9 months old, with his father and mother was sold by bill of sale in 1754, about 29 years ago, to Mr. Caldwell, now deceased; that, when he died, Quack was appraised as part of the personal estate, and set off to the widow in her share of the personal estate; that Mr. Jennison, marrying her, was entitled to Quack as his property; and therefore that he had a right to bring him home when he ran away; and that the defendant only took proper measures for that purpose. And the defendant's counsel also rely on some former laws of the Province, which give countenace to slavery.

To this it is answered, if he ever was a slave, he was liberated both by his master Caldwell, and by the widow after his death, the first of whom promised and engaged he should be free at 25, the other at 21.

As to the doctrine of slavery and the right of Christians to hold Africans in perpetual servitude, and sell and treat them as we do our horses and cattle, that (it is true) has been heretofore countenanced by the Province Laws formerly, but nowhere is it expressly enacted or established. It has been a usage—a usage which took its origin from the practice of some of the European nations, and the regulations of British government respecting the then Colonies, for the benefit of trade and wealth. But whatever sentiments have formerly prevailed in this particular or slid in upon us by the example of others, a different idea has taken place with the people of America, more favorable to the natural rights of mankind, and to that natural, innate desire of Liberty, with which Heaven (without regard to color, complexion, or shape of noses) features) has inspired all the human race. And upon this ground our Constitution of Government, by which the people of this Commonwealth have solemnly bound themselves, sets out with declaring that all men are born free and equal—and that every subject is entitled to liberty, and to have it guarded by the laws, as well as life and property—and in short is totally repugnant to the idea of being born slaves. This being the case, I think the idea of slavery is inconsistent with our own conduct and Constitution; and there can be no such thing as perpetual servitude of a rational creature, unless his liberty is forfeited by some criminal conduct or given up by personal consent or contract.

David Cooper, *A Serious Address*, 1783

David Cooper, *A Serious Address to the Rulers of America on the Inconsistency of Their Conduct respecting Slavery: Forming a Contrast Between the Encroachments of England on American Liberty, and American Injustice in tolerating Slavery* (Trenton, 1783), pp. 5-24.

". . . Must not every generous foreigner feel a secret indignation rise in his breast, when he hears the language of Americans upon any of their own rights as freemen being in the least infringed, and reflects that these very people are holding thousands and tens of thousands of their innocent fellow men in the most debasing and abject slavery. . . . Yes, blush Americans!" In 1783 the New Jersey Quaker David Cooper, father-in-law of Samuel Allinson, anonymously published A Serious Address to the Rulers of America, *perhaps the most direct, incisive pamphlet assault on the hypocrisy of the Revolution, as applied to the black slaves, to appear during the period. As long as Americans continued to participate in the slave system, a system which constituted an execrable "treason" against the natural rights of man, Cooper declared, they were making a mockery of the principles of freedom and liberty upon which the Revolution and such documents as the Declaration of Independence were based. Cooper was amazed at the reluctance of the Continental Congress to enact positive antislavery legislation, and he labeled as "Mock patriots" those American leaders who had bristled under the British crown's tyranny, while continuing their own involvement in the buying and selling of slaves. As Cooper's pamphlet came off the press in Trenton, it was espied by that indefatigable antislavery propagandist, Anthony Benezet. The old Philadelphia Quaker was immediatley taken with the piece and provided copies to each member of Congress and the New Jersey Assembly. He republished the pamphlet later in the year with his own* A Short Account. *Cooper's irreverent attack suddenly gained a wide audience..*

A Sound mind in a sound body, is said to be a state of the highest human happiness individually; when these blessings are separate, a sound

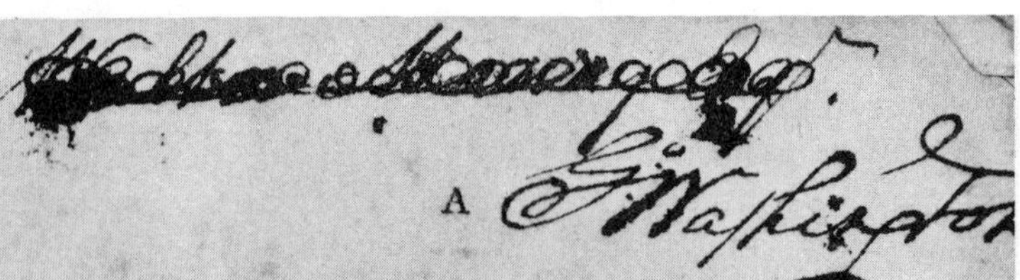

A

SERIOUS ADDRESS

TO THE

RULERS OF AMERICA,

On the Inconſiſtency of their Conduct reſpecting

SLAVERY:

FORMING A CONTRAST

Between the ENCROACHMENTS of England on American LIBERTY,

AND,

American INJUSTICE in tolerating SLAVERY.

As for me, I will aſſuredly contend for full and impartial liberty, whether my labour may be ſucceſsful or vain.

TRENTON:

Printed by ISAAC COLLINS,

M.DCC.LXXXIII.

George Washington's copy of Quaker abolitionist David Cooper's pamphlet.

mind, wise and prudent conduct, tend much to support and preserve an unsound body: On the other hand, where the body is sound, the constitution strong and healthy, if the mind is unsound, the governing principle weak and feeble, the body feels the injuries which ensue, the health and constitution often become enfeebled and sickly, and untimely death closes the scene. This reasoning holds good politically, being sometimes realized in bodies politick, and perhaps never more so than in the conduct lately exhibited to mankind by Great Britain. Her constitution was sound, strong, and firm, in a degree that drew admiration from the whole world; but, for want of a sound mind, her directing and governing powers being imprudent and unwise, to such a debilitated and sickly state is this fine constitution reduced, that, without a change of regimen, her decease may not be far remote. America is a child of this parent, who long since, with many severe pangs, struggled into birth, and is now arrived to the state of manhood, and thrown off the restraints of an unwise parent, is become master of his own will, and, like a lovely youth, hath stepped upon the stage of action. State physicians pronounce his constitution strong and sound: the eyes of the world are singularly attentive to his conduct, in order to determine with certainty on the soundness of his mind. It is the general Congress, as the head, that must give the colouring, and stamp wisdom or folly on the counsels of America. May they demonstrate to the world, that these blessings, a sound mind in a sound body, are in America politically united!

It was a claim of freedom unfettered from the arbitrary control of others, so essential to free agents, and equally the gift of our beneficent Creator to all his rational children, which put fleets and armies into motion, covered earth and seas with rapine and carnage, disturbed the repose of Europe, and exhausted the treasure of nations. Now is the time to demonstrate to Europe, to the whole world, that America was in earnest, and meant what she said, when, with peculiar energy, and unanswerable reasoning, she plead the cause of human nature, and with undaunted firmness insisted, that *all mankind* came from the hand of their Creator *equally free*. Let not the world have an opportunity to charge her conduct with a contradiction to her solemn and often repeated declarations; or to say that her sons are not real friends to freedom; that they have been actuated in this awful contest by no higher motive than selfishness and interest, like the wicked servant in the gospel, who, after his Lord had forgiven his debt, which he was utterly unable to pay, shewed the most cruel severity to a fellow servant for a trifling demand, and thereby brought on himself a punishment which his conduct justly merited. Ye rulers of America beware! Let it appear to future ages, from the records of this day, that you not only professed to be advocates for freedom, but really were inspired by the love of mankind, and wished to secure the invaluable blessing to all; that, as you disdained to submit to the unlimited control of others, you equally abhorred the crying crime of holding your fellow men, as much entitled to freedom as yourselves, the subjects of your undisputed will and pleasure.

However habit and custom may have rendered familiar the degrading and ignominious distinctions, which are made between people with a black skin and ourselves, I am not ashamed to declare myself an advocate for the rights of that highly injured and abused people; and, were I master of all the resistless persuasion of Tully and Demosthenes, could not employ it better, than in vindicating their rights as men, and forcing a blush on every American slaveholder, who has complained of the treatment we have received from Britain; which is no more to be equalled, with ours to negroes, than a barley corn is to the globe we inhabit. Must not every generous foreigner feel a secret indignation rise in his breast, when he hears the language of Americans upon any of their own rights as freemen being in the least infringed, and reflects that these very people are holding thousands and tens of thousands of their innocent fellow men in the most debasing and abject slavery, deprived of every right of freemen, except light and air? How similar to an atrocious pirate, setting in all the solemn pomp of a judge, passing sentence of death on a petty thief. Let us try the likeness by the standard of facts. The first settlers of these colonies emigrated from England, under the sanction of royal charters, held all their lands under the crown, and were protected and defended by the parent state, who claimed and exercised a control over their internal police, and at length attempted to levy taxes upon them, and, by statute, declared the colonies to be under their jurisdiction, and that they had, and ought to have, a right to make laws to bind them in all cases whatsoever. The American Congress in their declaration, July 1775, say,

"If it were *possible* for men who exercise their reason to believe that the Divine Author of our existence intended a *part* of the human race to hold an absolute property in, and an unbounded power over others, marked out by infinite goodness and wisdom, as the objects of a legal domination never rightly resistible, however severe and oppressive; the inhabitants of these colonies might at least require from the parliament of Great Britain some evidence, that this *dreadful authority* over them has been granted to that body. But a *reverence* for our *great Creator, principles of humanity,* and the dictates of *common sense,* must convince all those who reflect upon the subject, that government was instituted to promote the welfare of mankind, and ought to be administered for the attainment of that end."

Again they say,—"By this perfidy (Howe's conduct in Boston) *wives* are *separated* from their *husbands, children* from their *parents,* the aged and sick from their *relations* and *friends,* who wish to attend and *comfort* them."

"We most solemnly before God and the world declare, that exerting the utmost energy of those powers which our beneficent Creator hath graciously bestowed upon us, the arms we have been compelled by our enemies to assume, we will in defiance of every *hazard,* with unabated firmness and perseverance, employ for the preservation of our liberties, being with one mind resolved to die freemen rather than live *slaves.*"

"We exhibit to mankind the remarkable spectacle of a people attacked by *unprovoked enemies,* without any imputation, or even suspicion, of offence.—They boast of their privileges and civilization, and yet proffer no milder conditions than servitude or death."

"In our own native land, in defence of the freedom that is our birthright, and which we ever enjoyed till the late violation of it; for the protection of our property acquired solely by the honest industry of our forefathers and ourselves; against violence actually offered, we have taken up arms."

In a resolve of Congress, October 1774, they say,

"That the inhabitants of the English colonies in North-America, by the *immutable laws of nature,* are entitled to life, liberty and property; and they have never ceded to any sovereign power whatever a right to dispose of either without their consent."

Africa lies many thousand miles distant, its inhabitants as independent of us, as we are of them; we sail there, and foment wars among them, in order that we may purchase the prisoners, and encourage the stealing one another to sell them to us; we bring them to America, and consider them and their posterity for ever, our slaves, subject to our arbitrary will and pleasure; and if they imitate our example, and offer by force to assert their native freedom, they are condemned as traitors, and a hasty gibbet strikes terror on their survivors, and rivets their chains more secure.

Does not this forcible reasoning apply equally to Africans? Have we a better right to enslave them and their posterity, than Great Britain had to demand Three-pence per pound for an article of luxury we could do very well without? And Oh! America, will not a *reverence* for our *great Creator, principles* of *humanity,* nor the *dictates* of *common sense,* awaken thee to *reflect,* how far thy government falls short of impartially *promoting* the *welfare* of *mankind,* when its laws suffer, yea, justify men in murdering, torturing, and abusing their fellow men, in a manner shocking to humanity?"

How abundantly more aggravated is our conduct in these respects to Africans, in bringing them from their own country, and separating by sale these near connections, never more to see each other, or afford the least *comfort* or tender endearment of social life. But they are black, and ought to obey; we are white, and ought to rule.—Can a better reason be given for the distinction, that Howe's conduct is *perfidy* and ours innocent and blameless, and justified by our *laws*?

Thou wicked servant, out of thine own mouth shalt thou be judged.—Is a claim to take thy property without thy consent so galling, that thou wilt defy every hazard, rather than submit to it? And at the same time hold untold numbers of thy fellow men in slavery, (which robs them of every thing valuable in life) as *firmly rivetted* by *thee,* as thou art resolved to use the utmost energy of thy power, to preserve thy own freedom?

Have the Africans offered us the least *provocation* to make us their *enemies?*—Have their infants committed, or are they even *suspected* of any offence? And yet we leave them no alternative, but *servitude* or *death.*

The unenlightened Africans, in their own native land, enjoyed freedom, which was their birthright, until the more savage Christians transported them by thousands, and sold them for slaves in the wilds of America, to cultivate it for their lordly oppressors.

With equal justice may negroes say, By the *immutable laws of nature*, we are equally entitled to life, liberty and property with our lordly masters, and have never *ceded* to any power whatever, a *right* to deprive us thereof.

To the People of Great Britain.

Know then that we consider ourselves, and do insist, that we are and ought to be, as free as our fellow-subjects in Britain, and that no power on earth has a right to take our property from us without our consent.

Are the proprietors of the soil of America less lords of their property than you are of yours? &c.—Reason looks with indignation on such distinctions, and freemen can never perceive their propriety; and yet, however, chimerical and unjust such discriminations are; the Parliament assert, that they have a right to bind us in all cases without exception, whether we consent or not; that they may take and use our property when and in what manner they please; that we are pensioners on their bounty for all we possess, and can hold it no longer than they vouchsafe to permit.

If neither the *voice of justice*, the dictates of the law, the principles of the constitution, or the *suggestions* of *humanity*, can restrain your hands from shedding human blood in such an *impious* cause; we must then tell you, that we never will submit to be hewers of wood or drawers of water for any ministry or nation on earth. And in future, let *justice* and *humanity* cease to be the boast of your nation?

To the inhabitants of the colonies.

Weigh in the opposite balance, the endless miseries you and your descendants must endure, from an established arbitrary power.

Declaration of independence in Congress, 4th July, 1776.

We hold these truths to be self-evident, that *all men* are created *equal*, that they are endowed by their Creator with certain *unalienable rights*; that among these are *life, liberty*, and the *pursuit of happiness*.

Declaration of rights of Pennsylvania, July 15, 1776.

That *all men* are born *equally free* and *independent*, and have certain natural inherent and *unalienable rights*, among which are, the enjoying and defending *life* and *liberty*, acquiring, possessing and protecting *property*, and pursuing and obtaining happiness and safety.

Declaration of rights of Massachusets, Sept. 1, 1779.

All men are born *free* and *equal*, and have certain natural, essential, and *unalienable rights*; among which may be reckoned the right of enjoying and defending their *lives* and *liberties*; that of acquiring, possessing and protecting *property*; in fine, of seeking and obtaining *safety* and *happiness*.

Does this reasoning apply more forcibly in favour of a white skin than a black one? Why ought a negro to be less free than the subject of Britain, or a white face in America? Have we not all one Father? Hath not one God created us? Why do we deal treacherously every man against his brother? Mal. ii. 10.

Do Americans reprobate this doctrine when applied to themselves? And at the same time enforce it with tenfold rigor upon others, who are indeed *pensioners* on their *bounty* for all they *possess*, nor can they *hold* a single enjoyment of life longer than they *vouchsafe* to *permit*?

You who have read a description of the inhuman scenes occasioned by the slave-trade, in *obtaining, branding, transporting, selling*, and keeping in *subjection* millions of human creatures; reflect a moment, and then determine which is the most *impious cause*: and after this, if neither the *voice of justice*, nor suggestions of *humanity*, can *restrain* your *hands* from being contaminated with the practice; cease to *boast* the Christian name from him, who commanded his followers "to do unto others as they would others should do unto them."

Who would believe the same persons, whose feelings are so exquisitely sensible respecting themselves, could be so callous toward negroes, and the *miseries* which, by their *arbitrary power*, they wantonly inflict.

If these solemn *truths* uttered at such an awful crisis, are *self-evident*: unless we can shew that the African race are not *men*, words can hardly express the amazement which naturally arises on reflecting, that the very people who make these pompous declarations are slave-holders, and, by their legislative, tell us, that these blessings were only meant to be the *rights* of *white men*, not of *all men*: and would seem to verify the observation of an eminent writer; "When men talk of liberty, they mean their own liberty, and seldom suffer their thoughts on that point to stray to their neighbours."

This was the voice, the language of the supreme council of America, in vindication of their rights as men, against imposition and unjust control: Yes, it was the voice of all America, through her representatives in solemn Congress uttered. How clear, full, and conclusive! "We hold these truths to be self-evident, that all men are created equal, and endowed by their Creator with the unalienable rights of life, liberty, and the pursuit of happiness." "By the immutable laws of nature *all men* are entitled to life and liberty." We need not now turn over the libraries of Europe for authorities to prove, that blacks are born equally free with whites; it is declared and recorded as the sense of America: Cease then ye cruel task-masters, ye petty tyrants, from attempting to vindicate your having the same interest in your fellow men as in your cattle, and let blushing and confusion of face strike every American, who henceforth shall behold advertisements offering their brethren to sale, on a footing with brute beasts.

But what shall I say! Forgive it, Oh Heaven, but give ear, Oh earth! while we are execrating our parent state with all the bitterness of invective, for attempting to abridge our freedom, and invade our property; we are holding our brethren in the most servile bondage, cast out from the *benefit* of our *laws*, and subjected to the cruel treatment of the most imperious and savage tempers, without *redress*, without advocate or friend.

Our rulers have appointed days for humiliation, and offering up of prayer to our common Father to deliver us from *our* oppressors, when sighs and groans are piercing his holy ears from oppressions which we commit a thousand fold more grievous: pouring forth blood and treasure year after year in defence of our own *rights*; exerting the most assiduous attention and care to secure them by laws and sanctions, while the poor Africans are continued in chains of slavery, as creatures unworthy of notice in these high concerns, and left subject to laws disgraceful to humanity, and opposite to every precept of Christianity. One of these in effect gives fifteen pounds for the murder of a slave; that is, after a slave has absconded a certain time, twenty pounds is given to any one who shall bring his head, and but five pounds if he is brought alive. Another, which impowers certain officers to seize negroes set free, and sell them for the benefit of government: And, even during the present contest, negroes have been seized with the estates of persons who had gone over to the British, and sold by publick auction into *perpetual slavery*, and the proceeds cast into the stock for the *defence* of American *liberty*. Of the same complexion is an instance in New-Jersey: A female Quaker, about seven years since, manumitted her negroes; the times having reduced her so, as to be unable fully to discharge a debt for which she was only surety; the creditor, a great declaimer in behalf of *American freedom*, although he was offered his principal money, obtains a judgment, levies on these free negroes, who, by the assistance of some real friends of freedom, procured a *habeas corpus*, and removed their case before the justices of the supreme court. How many such mock patriots hath this day discovered, whose flinty hearts are as impervious to the tender feelings of humanity and commiseration as the nether milstone; can sport with the rights of men; wallow and riot in the plunder, which their unhallowed hands have squeezed from others! But only touch *their* immaculate interests, and what an unceasing outcry invades every ear. A love for my country, a regard for the honour of America, raises an ardent wish, that this picture may never be realized in her rulers.

It may be objected that there are many difficulties to be guarded against in setting of negroes free, and that, were they all to be freed at once, they would be in a worse condition than at present. I admit that there is some weight in these objections; but are not these difficulties of your own creating? And must the innocent continue to suffer, because we have involved ourselves in difficulties? Let us do justice as far as circumstances will admit, give such measure as we ask, if we expect Heaven to favour us with the continuance of our hard earned liberty. The work must be begun, or it can never be completed. "It is begun, and many negroes are set free." True, it is begun, but not in a manner likely to produce the desired *end*, the entire *abolition* of *slavery*. This is the business of the superintending authority, the main spring which gives motion to the whole political machine; which, were they to undertake in good earnest, I have no doubt but we should soon see a period fixed, when our land should no longer be polluted with slave-holders, nor give forth her increase to feed slaves: and indeed it hath been a matter of wonder to many, that that body, who have been so much employed in the study and defence of the *rights* of *humanity*, should suffer so many years to elapse without any effectual movement in this business. Had they, with the declaration of independence, recommended it to the different Legislatures to provide laws, declaring, that no person imported into, or born in America after that date, should be held in slavery; it would have been a step correspondent with our own *claims*, and, in time, have completed the work, nor can I see any impropriety, but what the nature of the case will justify, to have it still take place.

To shew the necessity of this matter taking its rise at the head, if any thing effectual is done, I may instance the Quakers. Some among them, it is said, always bore a testimony against slavery from its first introduction, and the uneasiness increasing, advices were given forth, cautioning their members against being concerned in importing slaves, to use those well whom they were possessed of, school their children, &c. but some of the foremost of that society having experienced the profits of their labour, no effectual stop could be put to the practice, though many became uneasy, and set their negroes free, until the difficulties attending the late French and Indian war, brought the rights of men into a more close inspection, when a rule was agreed upon, prohibiting their members from being concerned with importing, buying, or selling of slaves; and some years after a further rule was made, enjoining all those who held slaves to set them free, otherwise to be separated from religious membership.—The work was then soon accomplished, and they now say there are very few members belonging to the yearly meeting of Philadelphia who hold a slave.

When a grievance is general, it is but trifling to apply partial means; it is like attempting to destroy a great tree by nibbling at its branches. It is only the supreme power, which pervades the whole, that can take it up by the roots. The disquisitions and reasonings of the present day on the rights of men, have opened the eyes of multitudes, who clearly see, that, in advocating the rights of humanity, their slaves are equally included with themselves, and that the arguments which they advance to convict others, rebounds with redoubled force back on themselves, so that few among us are now hardy enough to justify slavery, and yet will not release their slaves; like hardened sinners, acknowledge their guilt, but discover no inclination to reform. It is true these convictions have occasioned the release of many slaves, and two or three states to make some feeble efforts looking that way; but I fear, after the sunshine of peace takes place, we have little more to expect, unless the sovereign power is exerted to finish this sin, and put an end to this crying transgression.

Let me now address that august body, who are by their brethren clothed with sovereign power, to sit at the helm, and give a direction to the important concerns of the American union. You, gentlemen, have, in behalf of America, *declared* to Europe, to the world, "That all men are born *equal*, and, by the *immutable laws* of *nature*, are *equally* entitled to liberty." We expect, mankind expects, you to demonstrate your *faith* by your *works*; the sincerity of your *words* by your *actions*, in giving the *power*, with which you are invested, its utmost *energy* in promoting *equal* and *impartial* liberty to *all* whose lots are cast within the reach of its influence; then will you be revered as the real friends of mankind, and escape the execrations which pursue human tyrants, who shew no remorse at sacrificing the ease and happiness of any number of their fellow-men to the increase and advancement of their own, are wholly regardless of others rights, if theirs are but safe and secure. We are encouraged in this expectation by the second article of your non-importation agreement in behalf of America, October 1774, *viz*. "That we will neither import nor purchase any slave imported after the first day of December next, after which time we will wholly discontinue the slave-trade, and will neither be concerned in it ourselves, nor will we hire our vessels, nor sell our commodities or manufactures to those who are concerned in it." And much would it have been for the honour of America, had it been added and confirmed by laws in each state (nor will we suffer such a stigma to remain on our land, as that it can produce slaves, therefore no child, born in any of the United States after this date, shall be held in slavery).—But the children of slaves are private property, and cannot be taken from their masters without a compensation. What! After it hath so often been echoed from America, "All men are born equally free." "No man or body of men can have a legitimate property in, or control over their fellow-men, but by their own consent expressed or implied." Shall we now disown it, in order to hold our slaves? Forbid it all honest men; it is treason against the rights of humanity, against the principles upon which the American revolution stands, and by which the present contest can only be justified; to deny it, is to justify Britain in her claims, and declare ourselves rebels. Wherefore our rulers undoubtedly ought to give these principles, these laws which themselves have declared *immutable*, a due force and efficacy. This every well-wisher to their country, either in a religious or political sense, have a right to ask and expect. But we have laws that will maintain us in the possession of our slaves: "The fundamental law of nature being the good of mankind, no human sanctions can be good, or valid against it, but are of themselves void, and ought to be resisted." Lock. Therefore none can have just cause of complaint, should so desirable an event take place, as that no person brought into, or born within any of the United States after the declaration of independence, shall be held a slave.

When I read the constitutions of the different states, they afford a mournful idea of the partiality and selfishness of man; the extraordinary care, and wise precautions they manifest to guard and secure our own rights and privileges, without the least notice of the injured Africans, or gleam of expectation afforded them, of being sharers of the golden fruitage, except in that of the Delaware state, who, to their lasting honour, while they were hedging in their own, provided against the invasion of the rights of others. By the twenty-sixth article of their constitution they resolve, that "No person hereafter imported into this state from Africa, ought to be held in slavery under any pretence whatever; and no negro, Indian or mulatto slave, ought to be brought into this state for sale from any part of the world." Had they went further, and made provision, by which slavery must at length have terminated within their jurisdiction, it would have been doing something to the purpose; and, as this is the only constitution in which posterity will see any regard paid to that abused people, I hope the same humane considerations which led them so far, will induce them to take the lead in doing their part toward putting an effectual end to this crying evil, which will ever remain a stain to the annals of America.

And you who in the several states are clothed with legislative authority, and have now an opportunity of displaying your wisdom and virtue by your laws freed from every foreign control, although this people were below notice, and their rights and interest thought unworthy of a sanction in your constitutions; let me beseech you, if you wish your country to escape the reproach and lasting infamy of denying to others what *she* hath so often, and in the most conclusive language, declared were the rights of *all*; if you wish to retain the name of Christians, of friends to human nature, and of looking up acceptably in prayer to the common Father of men, to deal with you in the same tenderness and mercy as you deal with others; that you would even now regard the rigorous oppressions of his other children, and your brethren, which they suffer under laws, which you only can abrogate. View your negro laws calculated not to protect and defend them, but to augment and heighten their calamitous situation! Cast out and rejected by the regulations formed for the defence and security of the rights and privileges, and to guard and improve the morals and virtue of the whites: Left open to the gratification of every passion and criminal commerce with one another, as though they were brutes, and not men; fornication, adultery, and all the rights of marriage union among blacks, considered beneath the notice of those rules and sanctions formed to humanize and restrain corrupt nature, or the regard of those whose duty it is to enforce them. Yes, blush Americans! Ye have laws, with severe penalties annexed, against these crimes when committed between whites; but, if committed by blacks, or by white men with black women, with the aggravated circumstances of force and violence, they pass as subjects of mirth, not within the cognizance of law, or magistrates inquiry, and lose the very name of crimes. Hence children often become familiar with these scenes of corruption and wickedness, before they are capable of distinguishing between the duties of Christianity, and the appetites of unrestrained nature. No marvel then if slave-holders are often scourged by the vices of their own offspring, which their untutored slaves have been a means of inflicting—children who, instead of being educated in the nurture and admonition of the Lord, are too often nurtured in pride, idleness, lewdness, and the indulgence of every natural appetite; that, were there no other inducement, this singly is sufficient to cause every real Christian to lift a hand against, and exert their utmost influence in, bringing their hydra mischief to a period. But when we consider the accumulated guilt, in other respects, abundantly set forth by other writers on this subject, brought on this land through the introduction of this infernal traffick, at a time when we were denied the privilege of making laws to check the mighty evil; and that near ten years have now elapsed since this restraint hath been removed, and no effectual advance yet made towards loosing the bands of wickedness, and letting the oppressed go free, or even of putting it in a train whereby it may at length come to an end; I say, it is a matter of anxious sorrow, and affords a gloomy presage to the true friends of America. Have we reason to expect, or dare we ask of him, whose *ways* are all *equal*, the continuance of his blessings to us, whilst our *ways* are so *unequal*.

I shall now conclude with the words of Congress to the people of England, a little varied to suit the present subject.

If neither the voice of *justice*, the dictates of *humanity*, the *rights* of *human nature*, and establishment of *impartial liberty now in your power*, the good of your *country*, nor the fear of an *avenging God*, can restrain your hands from this *impious practice* of holding your fellow-men in *slavery*: making traffick of, and advertising in your publick prints for sale as common merchandize, *your brethren* possessed of immortal souls equal with yourselves; then let *justice, humanity, advocates for liberty*, and the sacred name of *Christians*, cease to be the *boast* of *American rulers*.

A FARMER.

February, 1783.

Anthony Benezet to John Gough, May 29, 1783

Friends Historical Library of Swarthmore College, Swarthmore, Pa.

In early 1783 over 130 sick and infirm slaves were carefully selected from a full cargo aboard the Ship Zong and thrown alive into the sea. Ostensibly, the order to kill the weak slaves was given because of a water shortage which threatened the remaining cargo. The company which had insured the ship and its black merchandise claimed, however, that the slaves had been murdered in order to guarantee the high quality of the entire slave inventory on board. They suspected that the shipowners, realizing that ailing slaves would be worth little on the market, had schemed to saddle the insurance company with the financial loss of those tossed overboard. The company's refusal to indemnify the owners resulted in a notable trial before the Court of King's Bench in London. To Anthony Benezet and other American and English abolitionists the incident epitomized the horror and cruelty which characterized the slave trade and provided fresh ammunition with which to continue their propaganda assault. As Benezet wrote on May 29, 1783 to John Gough, a Quaker schoolmaster living in Ireland, "How much more does it become our duty, when we are assured, that so many Thousands and ten of Thousands are every year wickedly & Wantonly Murdered in the prosecution of the Guinea Trade. . . ." A few days earlier Granville Sharp had written to William Dillwyn, "There may not perhaps be ever so good an opportunity again of clear evidence to urge against that accursed branch of the African Trade & especially as those hardened Dealers alledged a necessity *to commit so horrible a cruelty, it must surely demonstrate an absolute* necessity *for the Nation to put an entire stop to Slave-dealing."*

If the publicity of the trial gave impetus to reform, the verdict itself was disappointing. Although the Somerset decision of 1772 had been interpreted by some magistrates to signal the end of slavery in England, Lord Mansfield declared in the Zong trial that for insurance purposes "the case of the slaves was the same as if horses had been thrown overboard." As David Brion Davis has pointed out, English law was flexible enough to provide for a slave's freedom while on English soil and at the same time to recognize the validity of slave property as in the Zong case. Although the Somerset decision, affirming the right of asylum for blacks while in England, had been a great symbolic victory for reformers in America and Great Britain, it offered no protection to slaves on board the Ship Zong or any other slaver.

. . . Strange Caprice of the human Mind, that thinking men can look upon the abuse of the Africans with so much indifference, I hold society with the perpetrators of such mighty evils; if we should from time to time see one Man, Woman, or Child cruelly murdered, to Answer the Humour, or the gain of individuals, & no notice taken by Government, should we not think we fell short of duty. . . . *We authorized* even only by *our Silence* such horrors, if we did not denounce the Vengeance of God *against the authors*, or *instruments of such tyranny*; how much more does it become our duty, when we are assured, that so many Thousands & ten of Thousands are every year wickedly & Wantonly Murdered in the prosecution of the Guinea Trade, which we know, & its known we know, is carried on under the sanction of Laws made by the Parliament. Laws to bring under hard Bondage a people over whom the Parliament had not the least shadow of Rights. Mention is made in the Penns Packets from the London Advertizer of March 10th of a Trial in London at Guild-hall of the 6th of March of an Action brought against some Insurers for the recovery of the Value of 132 Negroe Slaves said to be lost in the Passage from Guinea to Jamaica. It seems the Vessel made the Island of Tobago in Time but finding it in the hands of the French, they pushed on to Jamaica, when falling to the Westward, & fearing to Want Water, the Captain ordered the mate to throw Overboard 46 of the Slaves handcufft; two days after 36 more, a day or two after 40 more; the rest were Carried into Jamaica The mate who perpetrated the wicked act & who thought himself Justified, from the Captains order was the Evidence & Judgment was given in favour of the underwriters, as such a Cruel act was not judged neccessary, & the Vessell might have put into several ports, & they had 420 Gallons of Water Left. The relator who was present at the Tryal, observes, that the narration made every person Shudder, particularly himself, when he found no step was like to be taken to bring the perpetrator of such a horrid deed to Justice, he justly remarks, that when a community thus Suffers any Member to Commit such a flagrant act of Villany with impunity, it makes the Crime general & Provokes divine Wrath against the Nation. This is but one of the many instances which might be given of the Negroes lives being wickedly & cruelly played away with by the Captains & others concerned in the Trade. Where Evils of such Magnitude are neither inquired into nor redressed by those in whose power it is to put an End to the Evil, & that the Nation in general from views of gain authorize such mighty evils, what can be expected, but the divine Judgment will still attend them; & if those who are favoured with a feeling prospect of the Evils, but for fear of losing the favour of Men, or some other selfish Consideration, will not comply with the injunction "To open their Mouths for the Dumb, in the Cause of such as are appointed for Destruction" Prov. 31.8. What Can they expect, but to be partakers in the punishment. I wish thou mayst Confer with Granville Sharp upon this weighty subject. Wm. Dillwyn, who is acquainted with him, writes me, that he has lately attended most, if not all, the Bishops, who he found disposed to discourage the African Trade. Whether Friends succeed or not at present in an application to Parliament it may lay the foundation of this good Work; & they cannot but meet with the good Wishes of every sensible feeling mind. . . .

thine

Anthony Benezet

THE AFTERMATH OF THE REVOLUTION, 1783-1787

. . . [W]e have grounds to fear, that some forgetful of the days of Distress are prompted by avaricious motives to renew the iniquitous trade for Slaves to the African Coasts, contrary to every humane and righteous consideration, and in opposition to the solemn declarations often repeated in favour of universal liberty. . ."

Quaker petition to the Continental Congress, 1783

Anthony Benezet to Queen Charlotte, August 25, 1783

Friends House Library, Impey MS, London, Eng.

With the end of Revolutionary hostilities, the slave trade, a quiescent institution during the war, resumed with a vigor that profoundly disappointed abolitionists. Planters who had been deprived for seven years of the flow of black merchandise into the colonies and who had lost many slaves in the course of the war thirsted for fresh imports. In South Carolina alone several thousand new slaves were herded onto plantations after only three years of peace. Benjamin Rush wrote to Granville Sharp, "Negro slavery has revived in the Southern states. Alas! poor human nature!"

The resumption of the black trade was a bitter setback to Anthony Benezet. Weak and feeble, spending his last years as a superintendent of a black school in Philadelphia, the ancient Quaker fired off a desperate letter to the Queen of England on August 25, 1783. In it he pleaded for royal interference in the trade, that "flagrant Violation of the common Rights of Mankind." The letter was delivered with several antislavery books and tracts by the American-born painter, Benjamin West, who reported that the Queen reacted "with peculiar Marks of Condesention." One of the tracts, Benezet's own A Caution and Warning, *was neatly bound in plain white vellum with no gilding, a book which, the Queen remarked, reminded her of the simple, but elegant, Quaker dress. That was hardly the response hoped for by the somber and earnest Philadelphia abolitionist.*

To Charlotte Queen of Great Britain Impressed with a Sense of religious Duty and encouraged by the Opinion generally entertained of thy benevolent Disposition to succour the Distressed, I take the Liberty, very respectfully, to offer to thy Perusal some Tracts which I believe faithfully describe the suffering Condition of many hundred Thousands of our fellow Creatures of the african Race, great Numbers of whom, rent from every tender Connection in Life, are annually taken from their native Land to endure, in the American Islands and Plantations, a most rigorous and cruel Slavery, whereby many, very many of them, are brought to a melancholy & untimely End.

When it is considered that the Inhabitants of Britain, who are themselves so eminently Blessed in the Enjoyment of religious and civil Liberty, have long been, & yet are, very deeply concerned in this flagrant Violation of the common Rights of Mankind, and that even its national Authority is exerted, in Support of their African Slave-trade, there is much Reason to apprehend that this has been, and as long as the Evil exists, will continue to be, an Occasion of drawing down the Divine Displeasure on the Nation & its Dependencies.

May these Considerations induce thee to interpose thy kind Endeavours on Behalf of this greatly oppressed People, whose abject Situation gives them an additional Claim to the Pity & Assistance of the generous Mind, in as much as they are altogether deprived of the Means of soliciting effectual Relief for themselves, that so thou may be not only a blessed Instrument in the Hands of him, "by whom Kings reign, & Princes decree Justice," to avert the awful Judgments by which the Empire has already been so remarkably shaken, but that the Blessings of Thousands, ready to perish, may come upon thee, at a Time when the superior Advantages attendant on thy Situation in this World, will no longer be of any Avail to thy Consolation & Support.

To the Tracts on the Subject to which I have thus ventured to crave thy particular Attention, I have added some others which, at different Times, I have believed it my Duty to publish, & which I trust will afford thee some Satisfaction, their Design being for the Furtherance of that universal Peace & Good-will amongst Men, which the Gospel was intended to introduce.

I hope thou will kindly excuse the Freedom used on this Occasion by an ancient Man, whose Mind for more than forty years past, has been much separated from the common Course of the World, & long painfully exercised in the Consideration of the Miseries under which so large a Part of Mankind, equally with us the Objects of redeeming Love, are suffering the most unjust and grievous Oppression, and who sincerely desires the temporal and eternal Felicity of the Queen & her Royal Consort.

Anthony Benezet

Moses Brown to Clark and Nightingale, August 26, 1783

Moses Brown Papers, vol. 4:56, Rhode Island Historical Society, Providence, R.I.

Moses Brown, the former merchant slavemaster turned abolitionist, had many close contacts among the mercantile class of Rhode Island, a state which, as Samuel Hopkins noted, was "more deeply interested in the slave trade . . . than any other colony in New England." On August 26, 1783, Brown vented his strong antislavery opinions to Clark and Nightingale, a company about to transform one of its merchant ships into a slave ship. Brown's appeal was futile—the firm entered the trade. The undaunted Quaker continued his fervant campaign; he distributed petitions, wrote articles for Rhode Island newspapers, lobbied members of the legislature, and corresponded with Hopkins and other reformers. In February 1784 the Rhode Island Assembly passed a gradual abolition law. Although this measure which provided for the freedom of slaves born after the act was something far short of the general abolition envisioned by Moses Brown, it did make the positive assertion that the institution of slavery was incompatible with the rights of man. Much to the lament of the abolitionists, the law did not affect the slave trade itself. In the following decade, the firm of Clark and Nightingale, as well as others, was still seeking profits from the black gold of the West African coast.

Providence, 26th 8th Mo. 1783

Respected Friends, Being informed yesterday that you had in Contemplation sending a Vessel to Africa for the purpose of getting Negroes and selling them as Slaves in the West Indies; and as I have ever entertained a respectful Opinion of your humanity, as well as integrity as Merchants, and remembring how it was with me, when our Company were engaging in that Traffick, that altho' the convictions of my own Conscience were such as to be averse to the Voyage, yet in reasoning upon that Subject with those who were for pursuing it, my holding Slaves at that time so weakened my arguments, that I suffered myself, rather than break my

Connexions, to be Concern'd but as I have many times since thought, that if I had known the Sentiments of others, or had their concurring Testimonies to those Scruples, I then had, I should have been preserved from an Evil, which has given me the most uneasiness, and has left the greatest impression and stain upon my own mind of any, if not all my other Conduct in life; and it appears particularly so when I am favoured with a quiet retrospection and arraign it before the righteous judge of all men; Under these considerations I felt some engagement for your preservation from so great an evil as I have found that Trade to be, and with a view to dissuade & discourage your pursuing the Voyage, that you may avoid the unhappy reflections which I have had I am induced to Write you and desire your serious consideration on the Subject, when you feel your minds calmly disposed for pursuing such a course of life, as will preserve your Characters as Men of Humanity and feelings for the distresses & afflictions of others, which I have observed with much Satisfaction, on some occasions to be very Conspicuous.

One of your Slaves apply'd to me, some time past to afford him relief under the burden of Slavery, which he seemed sensibly affected with, and much desirous of being released from, I advised him, as he had a kind Master & lived well to return & patiently endure his situation, till way for his relief opened. I mention this to help your conception of the state of mind those must be in, under the usage of the West Indies, for if your *sensible* Domestic servants under your treatment and living, still have a part of what inspires us to love of Liberty, remaining, what anxiety must their Wretched states afford. The evils of the slave trade, have been gradually opening more & more for some years, and that Trade is now generally acknowledged to be unwarrantable upon any just Principle, you are Men of Feelings, & abilities to live without this trade, why then should you be concerned in it against your own—against the feelings of your Friends. I rest in hope, that my last has been a mistaken information, for when I delivered Clarke the Pamphlet on this subject, I understood your intention was not to trade in slaves, but in Ivory, Wax, Gold-dust. . . . If this be the case and you should give Orders to the Captn. not to suffer any Negroes on Board, it would be grateful to many of your connexions in Town, as well as your Friend.

Quaker Petition to the Continental Congress, October 4, 1783

Records of the Continental and Confederation Congresses and the Constitutional Convention, Record Group 360, National Archives, Washington, D.C.

On October 4, 1783, over 500 members of the Society of Friends signed a memorial to the Continental Congress that prayed for the end of the slave trade and reminded members of Congress of the "solemn declarations often repeated in favor of universal liberty." Two days later, Anthony Benezet, one of the signers, led a delegation of four Quakers to PrinceTown to present the petition to Congress. After conferring with the president of the Congress, Elias Boudinot, the delegation was permitted to read the petition before Congress at noon on October 8. The memorial

339

To the United States in Congress assembled

The Address of the People called Quakers—

Being through the favour of Divine Providence met as usual at this season in our annual Assembly to promote the cause of Piety and Virtue, We find with great satisfaction our well meant endeavours for the relief of an oppressed part of our fellow Men have been so far blessed, that those of them who have been held in bondage by Members of our Religious Society are generally restord to freedom, their natural and just right.

Commiserating the afflicted State into which the Inhabitants of Africa are very deeply involved by many Professors of the mild and benign doctrines of the Gospel, and affected with a sincere concern for the essential Good of our Country, We conceive it our indispensible duty to revive the lamentable grievance of that oppressed people in your view as an interesting subject evidently claiming the serious attention of those who are entrusted with the powers of Government, as Guardians of the common rights of Mankind, and advocates for liberty.

We have long beheld with sorrow the complicated evils produced by an unrighteous commerce which subjects many thousands of the human species to the deplorable State of Slavery

The Restoration of Peace and restraint to the effusion of human Blood we are persuaded excite in the minds of many of all Christian denominations gratitude and thankfu-

-ness to the all wise Controuler of human events; but we have grounds to fear, that some, forgetful of the days of Distress are prompted from avaricious motives to renew the iniquitous trade for Slaves to the African Coasts, contrary to every humane and righteous consideration; and in opposition to the solemn declarations often repeated in favour of universal liberty, thereby increasing the too general torrent of Corruption and licentiousness, and laying a foundation for future Calamities.

We therefore earnestly sollicit your Christian interposition to discourage and prevent so obvious an Evil, in such manner as under the influence of Divine Wisdom you shall see meet.

Signed in and on behalf of our Yearly Meeting held in Philadelphia for Pennsylvania, New Jersey, and Delaware, and the western parts of Maryland and Virginia dated the fourth day of the tenth Month 1783.

Isaac Zane
John Reynell
Thos. Ross
John Price Junr
Hugh Roberts
Joseph [illegible]
Isaac Pickering
William Harvey
Joshua Morris
[illegible] Haviland

Joshua Brown
George Evans
Thomas Hutson
Anthony Benezet
James Thornton
Warner Mifflin
Saml. Emlen junr
Daniel Byrnes
Geo. Dillwyn

Saml. Pemberton
Jacob Lindley
Thomas Lightfoot
Mark Reeve
William Savery Junr
John Hoskins
George Churchman
Thomas Milhous

Wm. Kersey
David Cooper
Benj. Swett
Owen Jones
Eli Yarnall
David Evans
Silas Downing
Aaron Lancaster

340

Edw Stabler
James Moon
Benjamin Swain
Samuel Coope
Allen Farquhar
Joshua Baldwin
John Cowgill
Mark Miller
John Comfort
William Smith
Jn Stapler
Francis Wilkinson
Thos Hopes Junr
Giles Knight Junr
Isaac Massey
Joshua Bunting
James Delph
William Rogers
James Smith
Christopher Hollingsworth
Joseph Bringhurst
[illegible]

Abram Griffith
John Milhous,
Thomas Matthews
Joseph Janney
Nathan Garrett
Ezra Cowgill
Joseph Townsend
Samuel Trimble
William [illegible]
Jonathan Wright
Thomas Evans
Enoch Wickersham
Jacob Swayne
William Webster
John Lynn
Isaac Coats
Richard Strode
Jonas Cattell
Joshua Hunt
Caleb Pennock
Danl Drinker
Wm Sell
[illegible]

John Hough
Joshua John
Thos Say
Benjamin Mason
James Starr
Saml Hopkins
John Tatum
Jonathan Kirkbride
Thomas Conarroe Senr
Joseph Penrock
John Parker
Richard Barnard
Thomas Redman
Jos. Heer Junr
Jacob Starr
Hugh Webster
Jacob Day
Saml Shinn
Richard Bartlett
Caleb Maris
Townsend Thomas
Wm Downing
[illegible]

Mord Moore
Griffith Minshall
Resine Weekes
Benjamin Hough
Israel Thompson
Saml Ellinson
Aaron Wills
Isaac Clarke
John Humphreys
Samuel Bunting
Philip Price
Robert Verree
Mordecai Lee
Saml Wetherill
Aaron Smith
Saml Starr
Daniel Thompson
John Collins
Jonathan Brown
Abraham Hibberd
Robert French
Abraham Worinton
Dugald Cameron
[illegible]

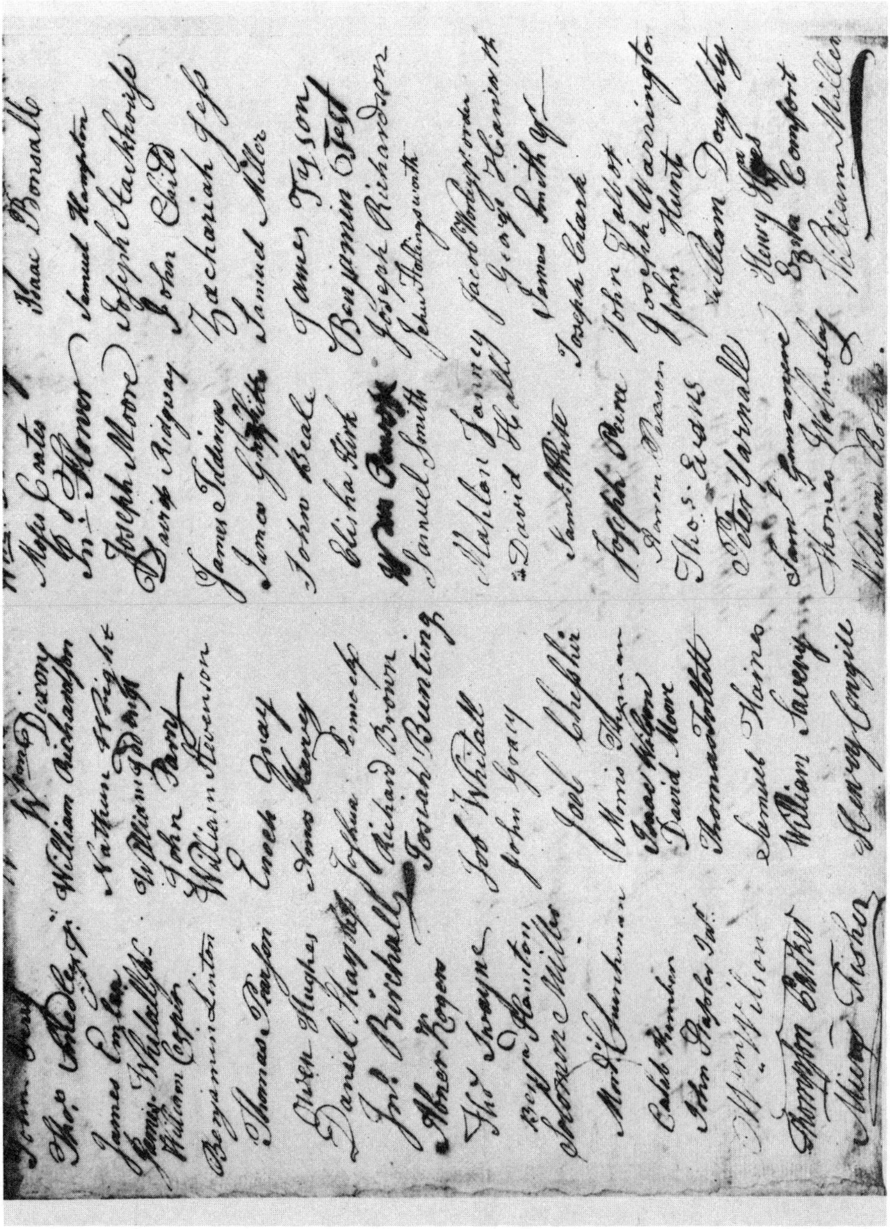

342

William Atkinson	Henry Brotherton	Joseph Burrough	Thomas Hall
Saml. Howell	James Thornton junior	Zachary Stiltredge	Moses Cadwalader
Henry Shaw	John Rively	Cornell Stevenson	Wm. Brown
Chas. Dingee	Abel James junr.	Thomas Trotter	Daniel Ballinger
Ezekiel Cleaver	Ellis Cleaver	Job Haines	Wm. Starr
Richd. Humphreys	Joseph Ball	Robert Thomas	Elijah Field
John Smith	Josh. Furman	John Franklin	Saml. Rhoads
Amos Taylor	Amos Yarnall	Nathan Lewis	Samuel Briggs
Isaac Webster	John Guest	Henry Reynolds	Thomas Parker
Edward Moore	Jacob Chesnutwood	Thomas Roger junr.	Joel Sharples
Abijah Dawes	Robert Moore	Thos. Sugar	John Robeson
Joshua Way	William Garrigues	William Ridgway	Isaac Borton
Benjamin Humphreys	Edward Garrigues	Isaac Wright	Samuel Hicks
John Carpenter	Thos. Franklin	Joseph Talbot	James Worstall
James Painter	Ebenezer Maule	Isaac Paxson	Robert White
William Cooper Junr.	Raper Hoskins	David Hilles	John Baily
Devenport Marot	Jeremiah Bernard junr.	John Todd Junr.	Bleackston Janney
Joseph Vanlaw	John Forsythe	Abah Cope	Evan Evans
William Hoopes	Jonathan Dawes	Clayton Newbold	Thomas George
Thomas Brown	Thos. Sharples	Abel Walker	Anthony Poultney
Richard Goodwin	Humd. Marshall	Geo. Bonnel	Hezekiah Bates

Cheyney Jefferis
John [illegible]
John Elliott junr.
Joseph Jenkins
Wm Jackson Junr
John Drinker
Robt Wood
Jos: Shotwell junr.
Benjamin Cathrall
Caleb Seal
Daniel Britt
Pierce Lamb
David Allen
John Evans
William Otley
John [illegible] junr
Dell Pennell
Saml [illegible]
Hugh Ely
Jacob Shoemaker junr

Jonathan Gibbs
Thomas Clifford
Gerard Blackford junr
Benjn Clarke
William Letchworth
Jonathan Worrill
Robt Lewis
Caleb Lownes
John Duncan
Evan Lewis
John Haworth
Peter Ellis
Thomas Fearnley
Edmund Hollinshead
Richard Wells
Isaac Wharton
Nathan Sharpless
Thomas Speakman
Isaac Jones
William Folwell

Joshua Lamb
Joseph Richardson junr
John Haydock
Johns Hopkins
John Morris Junr.
Thos Harrison
Samuel Taylor
John Webb
Nathan Jones
John Howell
Wm Waring
John Jackson
George Moore
Israel Roberts
George Williams
Daniel Lamb
Jacob Tomkins
William Lownes
James Jones Jur
Wm Brewer

John Maule
Oliver Paxson
Daniel Mifflin
Daniel Drawson
Jacob Parke
Wm Lippincott
Wm Atkinson
John Oldden
Ellis Yarnall
Elias Ring
William Coale
Joshua Yarnall
Jonas Potts
Nathan Williams
Philip Mayot
Daniel Trotter
Yeamans Gillingham
Charles West junr
Nathan Littler
Jesse Milhous

John Eves
Caleb Attmore
John Lofton
John Butler
Edmund Prior
James Bringhurst
Thomas Farquhar
Joseph Watt
Joseph Lukens
Saml. Clark
Thomas Fisher
Benedict Dorsey
Joseph Potts
Saml. Garrigues
Ja. Gibbons
Isaac Larkin
Joseph Brinton
John Fields
John Lewden
David Bacon

Philip Price Junr.
John Pierce
Thomas Rogers
Amos Wickett
John James
John Simpson
Henry Clifton
Aaron Oakford
Samuel Hutton
Norris Jones
Caleb Harlan
Nathan Robbins
David Cumming
Saml. Pleasants
Benj Hornor
Wm. Ellis
Jonathan Shoemaker
John Hilliar
Joseph Davies
Constantine Lord

Jesse Haines
Isaiah Kirk
Saml. Richards
John Parrish
Enoch Evans
James Cresson
John Hilton
John Pugh
George Martin
John Satterthwait
Joshua Gibbs
Thos. Hallowell
Jos. Russell
John Todd
Thomas Shoemaker
Jacob Maule
Caleb Foulke
Joshua Howell
John Morton

Ebenezer Robinson
Andw. McKee 341
Joseph Roberts
John Collins
Danl. Offley
Bartho. Mather
Isaac Jacobs
Christopher Dingee
Daniel Leeds
Joshua Sharples
Samuel Darnel
Jos. Sharpless
Wm. Jefferis
Jesse Waterman
William Clifton
Saml. Middleton
Joseph James
John Roberts
Joshua Cresson

David Bacon
Thomas Hough
John Townsend
Gideon Middleton
John Gilbert
Geo: Ashbridge
Saml. Brown
John Roberts
Robert Kirkbride
Jos: Pickering
David Hoopes
Richard Paynter
Caleb Haines
Wm. Hallowell junr.
Thos. Attmore
Phin. Buckley
James Whiteall
Jon.a Wright
Robert Rogers
Jeffrey Smedley
Lucas Gibbs
Griffith John

Rumford Dawes
Thomas Saxton
Robert Evans
Cowperthwaite Copland
William Sansom
Arthur Howell
Caleb Kirk
Isaac Thomas
Daniel Longstreth
John Forman
Daniel Dickenson
Samuel Cookson
Jimes Betts
Joseph Budd
Richard Jones
Jacob Lundy junr.
Gabriel Willson
Thos. Watson
John Horne
James Starr
John Letchworth
Edward Garnet

Charles West
Edward Bradway
Saml. Simpson
Thomas Pim
Jacob Shoemaker
Edward Jones
Harman Updegraff
Bernard Taylor
Thomas Carey
Thomas Stapler
John Peirce
John Laing
Edward Jones
Samuel Canby
Samuel Hedger
Aaron Taylor
Thomas Fisher
Thomas Bellangee
W. Linton
Vincent Lides
Richard Price
Thomas Massey Jur.

John Balderston
Philip Dennis
Ephraim Pennin
Henry Drinker
Silas Walmsley
John Ellis
William Hartshorne
Jos. Ridgway
Peter Hatton
John Scarlet
Jonath. Pickering
John Wright
Cadwalader Jones
Owen Biddle
Edward Bonsall
Moses Moon
Thomas Rogers junr.
Louis Darnel
Isaac Cadwallader
Benjamin Rice
Thomas Stokes

was subsequently referred to a committee of three. In January 1784 the committee presented the following resolution for consideration by the Congress: "Resolved, That it be recommended to the legislatures of the several states to enact such laws as to their wisdom may appear best calculated to [promote] the object of the second article in the association entered into & subscribed by the Delegates of the United State Colonies in Congress Assembled on the 20th day of October 1774." Although the resolution was designed to transfer the burden of legislation back to the states, the Congress, divided sectionally on the slavery issue, defeated the measure. Any state action against slavery had to evolve without the encouragement of the national legislature.

Rules of the Methodist Conference, December 27, 1784

Minutes of Several Conversations Between The Rev. Thomas Coke, L. D., The Rev. Francis Asbury and Others, At a Conference, Begun in Balitmore, in the State of Maryland, on The 27th of December in the Year 1784, Composing a Form of Discipline for the Ministers, Preachers and other Members of the Methodist Episcopal Church in America (Philadelphia, 1785), pp. 15-17.

"When you saw the flowing eyes, the heaving breasts, or the bleeding sides and tortured limbs of your fellow-creatures, was you a stone or a brute? Did you look upon them with the eyes of a tiger? When you squeezed the agonizing creatures down in the ship, or when you threw their poor mangled remains into the sea, had you no relenting? Did not one tear drop from your eye, one sigh escape from your breast? Do you feel no relenting now? If you do not, you must go on, till the measure of your iniquities is full. Then will the great God deal with you, as you have dealt with them, and require all their blood at your hands." (John Wesley, 1774)

For the Reverend Wesley, the institution of slavery represented an abominable sin which grievously stained those wrapped in its tentacles. For his missionary followers, Thomas Coke and Francis Asbury, Wesley's message represented a call to proselytize, to rid the world of "that execrable sum of all villanies. . . ." At the 1784 Baltimore "Christmas Conference" at which Coke and Asbury were instrumental in forming the Methodist Episcopal Church, members were directed to manumit their slaves or face excommunication. As Dr. Coke, ordained by Wesley as the first superintendent of the church in America, and Asbury, ordained a superintendent by Coke, began to spread the antislavery injunction to slave-holding congregations in Virginia, they met with bitter hostility. At one meeting they were greeted by an enraged crowd brandishing staves and clubs. On another occasion, as Coke later recalled, "a high-headed Lady" offered a mob £50 to "give that little Doctor one hundred lashes."

The open threats of violence had a pronounced effect. At a conference in Baltimore in June 1785, the minute on slavery was suspended in order "that an equal space of time be allowed all our members for consideration." Thus, the official Methodist antislavery position was tempered. Coke and Asbury, who remained strongly in favor of abolition, then tried another approach—a petition campaign was begun among a number of Virginia Methodists and aimed at the Virginia legislature. The attitudes of Virginia politicians, however, remained close to those of the majority of their constituents.

. . . Q. 42. What Methods can we take to extirpate Slavery?

A. We are deeply conscious of the Impropriety of making new Terms of Communion for a religious Society already established, excepting on the most pressing Occasion: and such we esteem the Practice of holding our Fellow-Creatures in Slavery. We view it as contrary to the Golden Law of

God on which hang all the Law and the Prophets, and the unalienable Rights of Mankind, as well as every Principle of the Revolution, to hold in the deepest Debasement, in a more abject Slavery than is perhaps to be found in any Part of the World except America, so many Souls that are all capable of the Image of God.

We therefore think it our most bounden Duty, to take immediately some effectual Method to extirpate this Abomination from among us: And for that Purpose we add the following to the Rules of our Society: viz.

1. Every Member of our Society who has Slaves in his Possession, shall within twelve Months after Notice given to him by the Assistant (which Notice the Assistants are required immediately and without any Delay to give in their respective Circuits) legally execute and record an Instrument, whereby he emancipates and sets free every Slave in his Possession who is between the Ages of Forty and Forty-five immediately, or at farthest when they arrive at the Age of Forty-five:

And every Slave who is between the Ages of Twenty-five and Forty immediately, or at farthest at the Expiration of five Years from the Date of the said Instrument:

And every Slave who is between the Ages of Twenty and Twenty-five immediately, or at farthest when they arrive at the Age of Thirty:

And every Slave under the Age of Twenty, as soon as they arrive at the Age of Twenty-five at farthest.

And every Infant born in Slavery after the abovementioned Rules are complied with, immediately on its Birth.

2. Every Assistant shall keep a Journal, in which he shall regularly minute down the Names and Ages of all the Slaves belonging to all the Masters in his respective Circuit, and also the Date of every Instrument executed and recorded for the Manumission of the Slaves, with the Name of the Court, Book and Folio, in which the said Instruments respectively shall have been recorded: Which Journal shall be handed down in each Circuit to the succeeding Assistants.

3. In Consideration that these Rules form a new Term of Communion, every Person concerned, who will not comply with them, shall have Liberty quietly to withdraw himself from our Society within the twelve Months succeeding the Notice given as aforesaid: Otherwise the Assistant shall exclude him in the Society.

4. No Person so *voluntarily withdrawn*, or so *excluded*, shall ever partake of the Supper of the Lord with the Methodists, till he complies with the above-Requisitions.

5. No Person holding Slaves shall, in future, be admitted into Society or to the Lord's Supper, till he previously complies with these Rules concerning Slavery.

N. B. These Rules are to affect the Members of our Society no farther than as they are consistent with the Laws of the States in which they reside.

And respecting our Brethren in *Virginia* that are concerned, and after due Consideration of their peculiar Circumstances, we allow them *two Years* from the Notice given, to consider the Expedience of Compliance or Non-Compliance with these Rules.

Q. 43. What shall be done with those who buy or sell Slaves, or give them away?

A. They are immediately to be expelled: unless they buy them on purpose to free them. . . .

Rules of the New York Manumission Society, 1785

Minutes of the Manumission Society of New York, New-York Historical Society, New York, N.Y., 1:3-8.

Spurred by attempts in New York of enterprising businessmen to seize free Negroes and sell them into slavery, 20 men met on January 25, 1785, at the home of a New York City innkeeper, John Simmons, to form a "Society for promoting the Manumission of Slaves; and protecting such of them as have been or may be Liberated." At that first meeting a committee of five was selected to draw up a set of rules for the infant organization. Ten days later, at a New York coffee house, the number in attendance swelled to 33, including John Jay, who was selected chairman, and Alexander Hamilton. "It is our Duty . . . both as free Citizens and Christians," declared the document adopted at the meeting, "not only to regard, with Compassion, the Injustice done to those among us, who are held as Slaves, but to endeavour, by lawful ways and means, to enable them to Share, equally with us, in that civil and religious Liberty with which an intelligent Providence has blessed these States; and to which these, our Brethren, are by nature, as much entitled as ourselves." Quaker-dominated and composed of leading merchants, bankers, and shipowners, the New York Manumission Society represented a narrow economic and social elite—a group of entrepreneurs and affluent political leaders who were active, not only in this antislavery organization, but in other philanthropic projects designed to improve the lot of the debtor and immigrant. Although not as active as its early Philadelphia counterpart, the New York society, nevertheless, engaged in wide-ranging antislavery activity well into the nineteenth century, giving legal assistance to blacks illegally held as slave merchandise, working to alleviate the more odious features of some of the state's slave laws, promoting legislation to prevent cruel treatment to slaves, establishing schools for free Negroes and overseeing their conduct to steer them from "practices of Immorality or Sinking into Habits of Idleness." The society also lobbied extensively for abolition legislation. But, it was not until 1799 that the New York legislature passed a gradual abolition law.

The benevolent Creator and Father of Men having given to them all, an equal Right to Life, Liberty and Property; no Sovereign Power, on Earth, can justly deprive them of either; but in Conformity to *impartial* Government and Laws to which they have expressly or tacitly consented—

It is our Duty therefore, both as free Citizens and Christians, not only to regard, with Compassion, the Injustice done to those, among us, who are held as Slaves, but to endeavour, by lawful ways and means, to enable them to Share, equally with us, in that civil and religious Liberty with which an indulgent Providence has blessed these States; and to which these, our Brethren, are, by nature, as much entitled as ourselves—

The Violent Attempts lately made to seize, and export for Sale, several free Negroes who were peaceably following their respective Occupations, in this City, must excite the Indignation of every Friend to Humanity, and ought to receive exemplary Punishment.

The Hope of Impunity is, too often, an invincible temptation to Transgression; and as the helpless Condition of the Persons alluded to doubtless exposed them to the outrage they experienced; so it is probable that the like Circumstances may again expose them and others to similar Violences.— Destitute of Friends and of knowledge; strugling with Poverty and; accustomed to Submission they are under great disadvantages in Asserting their Rights.—

These Considerations induce us to form ourselves into a Society to be Stiled A Society for promoting the Manumission of Slaves and protecting such of them as have been or may be Liberated.

And that the Objects of the Society may be pursued with Uniformity and Propriety, we have agreed that it shall be regulated by the following Rules.—

1st. The Society, at their next meeting shall elect, by Majority of Votes, to be taken by Ballot, a President, Vice President, Secretary and Treasurer, who shall respectively continue in Office for one Year from the Time of their Election; at the expiration of which Time and of every succeeding Year, there shall be a new Election of Officers in the same manner—

2d. The President shall have Authority to maintain Order and Decorum at the meeting of the Society; and to call a special Meeting at any Time upon the request of the standing Committee herein after mentioned——

3d. The Vice President, in the absence of the President, shall have the same Authority given to the President; and in Case the President should Die or be Displaced, the Vice President shall Officiate till a new President be Elected—

4th. The Secretary shall keep a Record of the proceedings of the Society in a Book to be provided for the purpose; and shall cause to be published, from time to time, such part of the proceedings or resolutions, as the Society may Order, or the President, with the Consent of the standing Committee between the Meetings of the Society, may think proper to direct—

5th. The Treasurer, if required by the Society, shall give Security for the faithful Discharge of the Trust reposed in him; and shall keep a regular accounts of the Monies he has received and Paid. Observing always to Pay no monies without an order signed by the President and a Majority of the Standing Committee; who are prohibited from drawing between the Slated Meetings of the Society for a larger Sum than ten Pounds unless impowered by a special Order of the Society at a previous Meeting—

6th. If any of the Officers above named should Die, Resign or be Displaced; the Society shall fill the Vacancy in the Mode prescribed by the first Rule, and if the President and Vice President or the Secretary or Treasurer be absent, at any of the Meetings, the Society may elect one to Officiate in his Room pro tempore—

7th. The Society shall meet once in every quarter, that is to say, on the second Thursday in February, on the second Thursday in May, on the second Thursday in August and on the second Thursday in November in every Year at such place as shall from time to time be agreed upon in order to receive the Reports of the standing Committee and devise the ways and means of accomplishing the Objects of this Institution.—

8th. That eight Members, with the President or Vice President be a quorum of the Society for transacting Business—

9th. Every Member on subscribing these Rules shall Pay into the Hands of the Treasurer the Sum of eight Shillings; and the Sum of four Shillings at the commencement of each quarter; and all Donations to the Society shall be made through the President who shall Pay them to the Treasurer and report the same to the Society at the next quarterly Meeting—

10th. Any Person desiring to be admitted a Member of this Society shall be proposed to the Society at a quarterly Meeting and be Ballotted for at the next quarterly Meeting and if upon counting the Ballots two thirds of the Members present shall be found to be in his favour he shall be declared a Member—

11th. The Society shall have the Power of expelling any Person whom they may deem unworthy of continuing a Member of it—

12th. A standing Committee of six Members shall be elected by Ballot at the first quarterly Meeting—four of the Committee shall be a quorum, and it shall be their Duty to carry into Execution in the recess and at the Expense of the Society, the orders given to them by the Society, and generally to pursue such measures as appear to them best calculated to attain the Ends of the Society. It shall likewise be their Duty to report their Proceedings, in writing, at the next quarterly Meeting of the Society; at which Time the two first members of the Committee, named on the Minutes shall be released from Service; and two other persons elected by Ballot to serve in their Room, and at every succeeding quarterly Meeting the same Ceremony shall be observed with respect to two other Members of the Committee in the order in which their names stand on the Minutes.

13th. The foregoing Rules shall be in force without alteration for the space of six Months from the first quarterly Meeting; after which period they shall be subject to such alteration as shall be agreed upon by a Majority of the Members of the Society at a quarterly Meeting.

Methodist-sponsored Virginia Petitions against Slavery, 1785

Frederick Co. Petition, November 8, 1785, Misc. Reel 425, Virginia State Library, Richmond, Va.

On May 26, 1785, Francis Asbury and Thomas Coke visited George Washington at Mt. Vernon in an attempt to convince the General to lend his name to a petition calling for a general emancipation of the slaves. Although Washington expressed sympathy with their motives, the two missionaries left with the document unsigned. The several antislavery petitions which Asbury and Coke circulated, particularly among Methodists, stimulated a similar, if more intense, reaction in the 1785 session of the Virginia General Assembly. James Madison reported to Washington that although several members of the Assembly supported the petitions, they were soundly rejected on November 10. In fact, the antislavery petition campaign stirred a counterattack; several proslavery petitions, railing against any proposed emancipation, were presented to the Assembly from numerous Virginia counties. In 1798 Asbury despaired that slavery might "perhaps exist in Virginia for ages."

That your Petitioners are clearly and fully persuaded that Liberty is the Birthright of Mankind, the right of every rational Creature without exception, who has not forfeited that right to the laws of his Country. That the Body of Negroes in this State have been robbed of that right without any such Forfeiture, and therefore ought in Justice to have their rights restored. That the Glorious and ever Memorable Revolution can be Justified on no other principles but what do plead with greater force for the Emancipation of our Slaves; in proportion as the Oppression excercised over them exceeds the Oppression formerly exercised by Great Britain over these States. That the Argument, "they were Prisoners of War, when they were Originally purchased" is entirely invalid, for no right of Conquest can Justly subject any Man to perpetual Slavery, much less his posterity. That the Riches & Strength of every Country consists in the number of its Inhabitants who are Interested in the support of its Government; and therefore to bind the Vast Body of Negroes to the State by the powerful ties of Interest will be the highest Policy. That the Argument drawn from the difference of Hair, Features, and Colour, are so beneath the Man of Sense, much more the Christian, that we would not insult the Honourable Assembly by enlarging upon them.—That the fear of the Enormities which the Negroes may commit, will be groundless, at least if the Emancipation be gradual, as the Activity of the Majestrates and the provision of Houses of Correction where Occasion may require, will easily Suppress the gross, flagrant, Idleness either of Whites or Blacks. But above all, that the deep Debasement of Spirit which is the necessary Consequence of Slavery, incapacitates the human mind (except in a few instances) for the Reception of the Noble and enlarged principles of the Gospel; and therefore to encourage or allow of it, we apprehend to be most opposite to that Catholic Spirit of Christianity, which desires the Establishment of the Kingdom of Christ over all the World, and produces in the Conduct every Action consonant to that Desire. That of Consequence, Justice, Mercy and Truth, every virtue that can Adorn the Man or the Christian, the Interest of Religion, the honour & real Interest of the State, and the Welfare of Mankind do unanswerably, uncontroulably plead for the Removal of this grand Abomination; And therefore that we humbly entreat the Honourable the Assembly as their Superior Wisdom may dictate to them, to pursue the most Prudential, but effectual Method for the immediate or Gradual Exterpation of Slavery. . . .

Robert Pleasants to George Washington, December 11, 1785

Copy in Robert Pleasants Letterbook, Records of Quaker meetings in Virginia, Valentine Museum, Richmond, Virginia

When Robert Pleasants attempted to enlist the services of Patrick Henry in his antislavery efforts, the Virginia abolitionist encountered a response typical of that offered by many Revolutionary leaders—a philosophical agreement with the concept of gradual abolition, but a refusal to do anything to effect it. On December 11, 1785, Pleasants tried to involve still another influential Virginian in the crusade; and again he failed. In a letter to George Washington, Pleasants rather impertinently asked the General how it would appear in the eyes of posterity for the commander of the American forces which had relieved so many from political bondage to continue to support a system mired in tyranny and oppression.

Although Washington's distaste for the excesses of slavery was genuine, he was, nevertheless, philosophically opposed to the position held by Pleasants and others who attacked the planter class and the plantation system on the slavery issue. Although the General wrote to the Marquis de Lafayette in 1786 that abolition "assuredly ought to be effected," and although he provided in his will for the release of his slaves upon the death of his wife, Washington had nothing but scorn for abolitionists, whom he saw as mischievous, impolitic zealots burdening polite society with ill-conceived demands for emancipation. Indeed, on April 12, 1786, Washington complained to Robert Morris about the work of a Quaker antislavery society in Alexandria which had brought a "vexatious" lawsuit against a slaveowner friend. ". . . If the practice of this Society. . .is not discountenanced," Washington lamented, "none of those whose misfortune it is to have slaves as attendants, will visit the City if they can possibly avoid it; because by so doing they hazard their property."

As for the letter of Robert Pleasants, there is no indication that the General even bothered to answer it.

Curles 12mo.II.1785.

Honour'd General. Seeing the Lord has done great things for thee, not only in "covering thy head in the day of Battle," but making thee instrumental in bringing about an extraordinary Revolution (a Revolution, which has given thee great Reputation among men, and calls for Reverant thankfulness to him who, Rules in the Kingdoms of men; "and declared by his Prophet, that he would not give his Glory to another, or his praise to graven Images,") a strong desire attends my mind, that thou may not in any Respect sully in thy private retreat, the honours thou hast acquired in the field. Remember the cause for which thou wert called to the command of the American Army, was the cause of liberty, and the Rights of Mankind: How Strange then must it appear to impartial thinking men, to be inform'd that many who were warm advocates for that Noble cause during the War, are now siting down in a State of ease, & dissipation, & extravigance, on the labour of Slaves, and more especially, that thou could forgo all thy sweets of domestic felicity, for a number of years, and expose thy person to the greatest fatigue & dangers in that cause, should now withhold that enestimable blessing from any who are absolutely in thy power, and after the Right of freedom is acknowledg'd to be the natural & unalianable Right of all mankind.——

I cannot suppose from the uncommon generosity of thy conduct in other respects, that this can proceed altogether from interested motives: but rather, that it is the effect of long custom, the prejudices of Education towards a Blackskin, or that some other important concerns, may have hitherto diverted thy attention from a subject so Noble & interesting, as well to thy own peace & Reputation, as the general good of that people and happiness of the community at large: But whatever may have been the cause, I sincearly wish thou may not longer delay a matter of such importance. It is a sacrifice which I fully believe the Lord is requiring of this generation, and should we not submit to it, is there not reason to fear, he will deal with us, as he did with Pharoah on a similar accasion? for as he is declared to be "no Respecter of persons," how we expect to do such Violence to that unhappy people, in this enlightened Age with impunity?—

We Read "where much is given the more will be required," and as thou hast acquered much fame in being the Successful champion of American liberty, it seems highly probable to me that thy example & influence at this time, towards a general Emansipation, would be as productive of real happiness to mankind, as thy Sword may have been; I can but wish therefore, that thou may not loose the opertunity of Crowning the great Actions of thy life, with the satisfaction of, "doing to others as thou would (in the like situation) be done by;" and finally transmit to future ages, a Character equally famous for thy Christian Virtues, as Worldly achivements; For notwithstanding thou art now receiving the tribute of praise from a grateful people, the time is coming, when all actions will be weighed in an equal ballance, and undergo an impartial examination; how inconsistant then will it appear to posterity, should it be recorded, that the great General Washington, without fee or reward, had commanded the United forces of America; and at the expence of much Blood & treasure, been instrmental in relieving those States from Tyrinny & oppression; Yet after all, had so fare continued those Evils, as to keep a number of people in Slavery, who are by Nature equally entitled to freedom as himself. O remember I besceech thee that "God will not be mocked," and is still requiring from each of us, to, "do justly, love mercy, & walk humbly before him."——

Perhaps General Washington may think it presumptious, in one who cannot boast a perticular acquaintance, to address him in this manner; but I hope when he considers the Nature of the Subject, and that I have no Selfish Views in offering these hints to his serious consideration, than what may arise from the pleasure of hearing he had done those things which belong to his present & future happiness, and the good of those over whom Providence hath placed him, he will at least excuse the freedom, & believe that I am with great Sincerity & Respect his Real friend.——

R. Pleasants

P. S. I herewith send thee a small pamphlet on the subject of Slavery said to be wrote by John Dickinson, which if thou hast not before seen I doubt not thou wilt find pleasure in the perusing.

George Washington Esq.
Mount Vernon near Alexandria

Tench Coxe to David Barclay, March 6, 1787; The Constitution of the Pennsylvania Abolition Society, April 23, 1787

Records of the Pennsylvania Abolition Society, Historical Society of Pennsylvania, Philadelphia, Pa.

On March 6, 1787, the political economist and politician Tench Coxe recounted the history of the founding of the Society for the Relief of Free Negroes, and others, unlawfully held in Bondage to David Barclay, in London. Coxe told him of the Society's rejuvenation in 1784 and of the dedicated work of men such as lawyer William Lewis to the Society's cause. On April 23 the Society adopted a Constitution drafted by Coxe, Benjamin Rush, and three others. Its mandate was now explicity emblazoned in its title, "Pennsylvania Society for Promoting the Abolition of Slavery. . . ." No longer was the Pennsylvania antislavery organization confined to a few spirited devotees. With abolitionism a vibrant political issue, the ranks of the society included such influential Pennsylvanians as Benjamin Franklin (president), Coxe and Rush (secretaries), Clement Biddle, Robert Morris, Thomas Paine, and James Pemberton. It was this reconstituted organization that made such a profound impact on the antislavery movement of the late 18th century—campaigns to assure compliance with laws protecting Blacks, encouragement of similar organizations in other states, the establishment of schools, petitions to Congress and the state legislatures, committees to supervise the morals and to secure employment for free Negroes. The spirit of the society was reflected in one of its communications directed to the London-based "Committee for abolishing the African Trade": "We look forward with pleasure to the time, when the records of modern times shall be examined with critical exactness, to know whether the souls and bodies of men were ever the objects of commerce. Whether our laws punished the stealing of a piece of plate, or a few shillings [worth] with death, and at the same time conferred upon the receiver of stolen slaves the honours of a nation. And whether it was possible for men to acknowledge the principles of human nature, and the obligations of Christianity, and yet inflict upon their fellow-creatures the oppressions and punishments which are connected with negro slavery in the West Indies and the Southern States."

Respected Friend The society for the relief of free Negroes unlawfully held in bondage have received from the hands of James Pemberton an extract of a letter from you expressing a humane desire of being informed whether Anthony Benezet's plan, or any other national mode was adopted for the relief of those people, and that if any such had been pursued you would use your endeavours to promote it. Apprehending, as we suppose, that our plan corresponded with your meaning, he was induced to lay that part of your letter before us, and we beg leave thro' him to furnish you with such documents on this interesting subject as we conceive will enable you to execute your benevolent intentions; to which we have thought it necessary to add a short account of our rise and progress.

In the early days of Pennsylvania exceptions grounded in equity and good conscience, were taken by many especially of the people called Quakers to the importation of Africans from their native country, as well as to holding in slavery any colored, people whatever. An amicable and exemplary member of that church, the late Anthony Benezet, was among many respectable characters, who discountenanced those practices and who exerted themselves among persons of all situations in life to inculcate principles that might counteract their ill effects.

In the year 1774 a family of the Indian race was brought from New Jersey to be sent for sale to Virginia or the Carolinas. The mayor of Philadelphia apprehending from Information made to him, that they had a legal claim to freedom, undertook to detain them in the city workhouse, in order that their case might undergo a strict investigation. A number of persons of various religious denominations from a serious conviction of duty & an expectation that not only this case would require their care & pecuniary assistance, but that others of a similar nature would occur, formed the present institution with the best funds they could command, for the purpose of defending the liberties of those whose want of Money, Education and Friends might subject them to a situation the more grievous from its being a violation of the laws of the land, and stiled themselves "The Society for the relief of free negroes unlawfully held in bondage."

Several cases presented themselves for their attention besides the foregoing, which proved very expensive, especially to some liberal and benevolent individuals, who generously supplied the want of funds out of their private property to a considerable amount, but the political disturbances interrupted for a time the progress of the institution. It is however well known that certain members of the society even in this deranged situation of their affairs steadily employed themselves in the propagation of their Principles. Fortunately also for the unhapply race of men whose cause they advocated, the free, sincere & earnest discussions of the natural rights of mankind which frequently took place during the war brought them more immediately into public view, & the friends of the revolution uniformly maintaining that the blessings of freedom were the rightful inheritance of the whole human species, a law for the gradual abolition of slavery was introduced into Pennsylvania to the great satisfaction of her citizens, and to the lasting honor of her Legislature.

On the return of peace attempts were made to revive the society, but not with so much success as was to be desired (tho its objects were stiled dear to many) untill the venerable patron of this plan, the late Anthony Benezet, discovered two melancholly instances of black men illegally held in bondage, who dispirited by fruitless applications to a number of individuals for their assistance in support of their rights, put an end to their miserable lives. Deeply affected by events so lamentable and shocking they made another more successful attempt to restor the institution, & it again took order in the beginning of 1784—altho the numbers were at first inconsiderable, yet the humane and just design of it has occasioned so many of all religious denominations to approve the plan, that the numbers are now much increased. There is a moderate annual contribution and several sums of money have been added to the funds by the wills of deceased persons & otherwise, yet the frequent occurrence of expensive cases has several times exhausted the stock. We have declined unnessary appeals to the Courts of Justice preferring always more amicable and frugal modes of proceeding, yet we have sometimes been under the necessity of pursuing our duty thro' the medium of the case, in which a very able counseller who from principle early espoused the cause of these people, frequently renders us his disinterested services. There are likewise several others among the Gentlemen of that profession who have stept forward in their behalf sometimes unsolicited and often without reward. Many cases have ended to perfect satisfaction, upwards of one hundred persons having been restored to their liberty since the revival of the institution—many are yet undetermined—Great attention it is conceived should be paid to the conduct and education of the blacks in order to render them useful members of society, and many benevolent & humane characters impressed with these sentiments have bequeathed legacies to a large amount for the permanent support of public schools to be open to them only whether slaves or free. Such is the state of a matter in Pennsylvania so deeply affecting the public reputation & happiness, so interesting to the friends of virture, liberty and mankind. It is highly honourable to her that, in this benevolent purpose she has given an early proof of that spirit which we trust will ever continue to actuate her citizens towards that unhappy and oppressed part of our fellow man—nor, is it less laudable on the part of her confederate sisters, that notwithstanding the forcible opposition of Interest and prejudice, many of them have already passed laws conducing to the same happy end.

In these days of liberty & light the generous and humane it is presumed, will feel a sensible pleasure in this short detail—an extensive charity of the highest dignity is presented to them. To prevent the agonizing separation of those "whom Heaven hath joined together" to preserve the helpless infant in the tender care of its affectionate parents, to secure to declining age the comforts of its rising progeny, to expand the minds and elevate by the lights of religion the souls of an unfortunate part of the human race, are among its interesting objects, tho its most immediate benefactions are the inestimable blessings of freedom. Sincerely hoping that this communication may answer the benevolent purposes of your letter.

I am in behalf of the Society, Your respectful friend

Tench Coxe

Philadelphia March 6, 1787

The Constitution of the Pennsylvania Society,
for Promoting the Abolition of Slavery,
and the Relief of Free Negroes,
Unlawfully Held in Bondage

It having pleased the Creator of the world, to make of one flesh all the children of men—it becomes them to consult and promote each other's happiness, as members of the same family, however diversified they may be, by colour, situation, religion, or different states of society. It is more especially the duty of those persons, who profess to maintain for themselves the rights of human nature, and who acknowledge the obligations of Christianity, to use such means as are in their power, to extend the blessings of freedom to every part of the human race; and in a more particular manner, to such of their fellow-creatures, as are entitled to freedom by the laws and constitutions of any of the United States, and who, notwithstanding, are detained in bondage, by fraud or violence.—From a full conviction of the truth and obligation of these principles—from a desire to diffuse them, wherever the miseries and vices of slavery exist, and in humble confidence of the favour and support of the Father of Mankind, the subscribers have associated themselves, under the title of the "Pennsylvania Society for promoting the Abolition of Slavery, and the Relief of free Negroes unlawfully held in Bondage."

For effecting these purposes, they have adopted the following constitution:

I. The officers of the society shall consist of a president, two vice-presidents, two secretaries, a treasurer, four counsellors, an electing committee of twelve, and an acting committee of six members; all of whom, except the last named committee, shall be chosen annually by ballot, on the first Second-day called Monday, in the month called January.

II. The president, and in his absence one of the vice-presidents, shall preside in all the meetings, and subscribe all the public acts of the society. The president, or in his absence, either of the vice-presidents, shall moreover have the power of calling a special meeting of the society whenever he shall judge proper. A special meeting shall likewise be called at any time, when six members of the society shall concur in requesting it.

III. The secretaries shall keep fair records of the proceedings of the society, and shall correspond with such persons and societies, as may be judged necessary to promote the views and objects of the institution.

IV. The treasurer shall keep all the monies and securities belonging to the society, and shall pay all orders signed by the president or one of the vice-presidents—which orders shall be his vouchers for his expenditures. He shall, before he enters upon his office, give a bond of not less than two hundred pounds, for the faithful discharge of the duties of it.

V. The business of the counsellors shall be to explain the laws and constitutions of the states, which relate to the emancipation of slaves, and to urge their claims to freedom, when legal, before such persons or courts as are authorised to decide upon them.

VI. The electing committee shall have the sole power of admitting new members. Two-thirds of them shall be a quorum for this purpose—and the concurrence of a majority of them by ballot, when met, shall be necessary for the admission of a member. No member shall be admitted, who has not been proposed at a general meeting of the society, nor shall an election for a member take place in less than one month after the time of his being proposed. Foreigners or persons who do not reside in this state, may be elected corresponding members of the society, without being subject to an actual payment, and shall be admitted to the meetings of the society during their residence in the state.

VII. The acting committee shall transact such business as shall occur in the recess of the society, and report the same at each quarterly meeting.— They shall have a right, with the concurrence of the president or one of the vice-presidents, to draw upon the treasurer for such sums of money as shall be necessary to carry on the business of their appointment. Four of them shall be a quorum. After their first election, two of their number shall be relieved from duty at each quarterly meeting, and two members shall be appointed to succeed them.

VIII. Every member upon his admission, shall subscribe the constitution of the society, and contribute ten shillings annually, in quarterly payments, towards defraying its contingent expences. If he neglects to pay the same for more than two years, he shall, upon due notice being given him of his delinquency, cease to be a member.

IX. The society shall meet on the first Second-day called Monday, in the months called January, April, July and October, at such place as shall be agreed to by a majority of the society.

X. No person holding a slave shall be admitted a member of this society.

XI. No law or regulation shall contradict any part of the constitution of the society, nor shall any law or alteration in the constitution be made, without being proposed at a previous meeting. All questions shall be decided, where there is a division, by a majority of votes. In those cases where the society is equally divided, the presiding officer shall have a casting vote.

The Present Officers *of the* Society.

President,
Benjamin Franklin.

Vice-Presidents,
James Pemberton,
Jonathan Penrose

Secretaries,
Benjamin Rush,
Tench Coxe.

Treasurer,
James Starr.

Counsellors,
William Lewis,
John D. Coxe,
Miers Fisher,
William Rawle.

Electing Committee,

Thomas Harrison,
Nathan Boys,
James Whiteall,

Norris Jones,
Samuel Richards,
Francis Bailey,

James Reed, Andrew Carson,
John Todd, John Warner,
Thomas Armatt, Jacob Shoemaker, jun.

Acting Committee,

Thomas Shields, William Zane,
Thomas Parker, John Warner,
John Oldden, William McElhenney.

The Northwest Ordinance, 1787

Records of the Continental and Confederation Congresses and the Constitutional Convention, Record Group 360, National Archives, Washington, D.C.

One of the most vital problems faced by the Continental Congress after the American Revolution was to provide a plan of government for the lands of the western territory. The question of the extension of slavery into this area was only part of the larger problem of providing such a plan, but it was of great significance in the history of antislavery. In March 1784 a committee chaired by Thomas Jefferson reported a scheme of government to be considered by Congress. One provision would have prohibited slavery and involuntary servitude in the territory after 1800, but upon the recommitment of the report, the antislavery clause was defeated by one vote. The deletion of the clause was a defeat for Rhode Island delegate David Howell, a member of the committee, and an indirect blow to his close friend Moses Brown and other antislavery advocates.

Further legislative maneuvers occurred as the Congress attempted to resolve the perplexing question of territorial acquisition. During these machinations a second and third attempt to ban slavery also failed as the southern states united in opposition; the northerners, fearing an alliance between the South and the West and the menacing spectre of a slave empire, were equally adamant in their stand. It was the Ordinance of 1787 that finally provided a means for the government to take a positive stand vis-a-vis antislavery in the United States. At the time of the second reading of the draft of the plan entitled "An Ordinance for the government of the Territory of the United States, Northwest of the river Ohio," Nathan Dane of Massachusetts moved that slavery be prohibited in the territory. To allay southern fears that this territory would become a haven for runaway slaves, Dane incorporated into the amendment a provision for owners to reclaim slaves escaping into the territory. The amendment was agreed to, and shortly thereafter the ordinance became law.

What broke the stalemate concerning the question of slavery and the problem of how to best govern the newly acquired land was that the so-called Northwest Ordinance applied only to the territory northwest of the Ohio River. Also, the agreement to prohibit slavery gave tacit consent to the institution's future existence in the other areas to be carved from the original territory. But the ordinance, in addition to its specific prohibition against slavery, did set an important general precedent for prohibiting slavery in proscribed areas. What began in 1784 as an attempt to prevent the expansion of slavery into the territory acquired by the new nation later became a repeating theme in national politics and governmental policies throughout the 19th century. Within two years of the settlement of one rebellion, the seeds for another had been sowed.

An ORDINANCE for the GOVERNMENT of the TERRITORY of the UNITED STATES, North-Weſt of the RIVER OHIO.

BE IT ORDAINED by the United States in Congreſs aſſembled, That the ſaid territory, for the purpoſes of temporary government, be one diſtrict; ſubject, however, to be divided into two diſtricts, as future circumſtances may, in the opinion of Congreſs, make it expedient.

Be it ordained by the authority aforeſaid, That the eſtates both of reſident and non-reſident proprietors in the ſaid territory, dying inteſtate, ſhall deſcend to, and be diſtributed among their children, and the deſcendants of a deceaſed child in equal parts; the deſcendants of a deceaſed child or grand-child, to take the ſhare of their deceaſed parent in equal parts among them: And where there ſhall be no children or deſcendants, then in equal parts to the next of kin, in equal degree; and among collaterals, the children of a deceaſed brother or ſiſter of the inteſtate, ſhall have in equal parts among them their deceaſed parents ſhare; and there ſhall in no caſe be a diſtinction between kindred of the whole and half blood; ſaving in all caſes to the widow of the inteſtate, her third part of the real eſtate for life, and one third part of the perſonal eſtate; and this law relative to deſcents and dower, ſhall remain in full force until altered by the legiſlature of the diſtrict. ——— And until the governor and judges ſhall adopt laws as herein after mentioned, eſtates in the ſaid territory may be deviſed or bequeathed by wills in writing, ſigned and ſealed by him or her, in whom the eſtate may be, (being of full age) and atteſted by three witneſſes; —— and real eſtates may be conveyed by leaſe and releaſe, or bargain and ſale, ſigned, ſealed, and delivered by the perſon being of full age, in whom the eſtate may be, and atteſted by two witneſſes, provided ſuch wills be duly proved, and ſuch conveyances be acknowledged, or the execution thereof duly proved, and be recorded within one year after proper magiſtrates, courts, and regiſters ſhall be appointed for that purpoſe; and perſonal property may be transferred by delivery, ſaving, however, to the French and Canadian inhabitants, and other ſettlers of the Kaskaskies, Saint Vincent's, and the neighbouring villages, who have heretofore profeſſed themſelves citizens of Virginia, their laws and cuſtoms now in force among them, relative to the deſcent and conveyance of property.

Be it ordained by the authority aforeſaid, That there ſhall be appointed from time to time, by Congreſs, a governor, whoſe commiſſion ſhall continue in force for the term of three years, unleſs ſooner revoked by Congreſs; he ſhall reſide in the diſtrict, and have a freehold eſtate therein, in one thouſand acres of land, while in the exerciſe of his office.

There ſhall be appointed from time to time, by Congreſs, a ſecretary, whoſe commiſſion ſhall continue in force for four years, unleſs ſooner revoked, he ſhall reſide in the diſtrict, and have a freehold eſtate therein, in five hundred acres of land, while in the exerciſe of his office; it ſhall be his duty to keep and preſerve the acts and laws paſſed by the legiſlature, and the public records of the diſtrict, and the proceedings of the governor in his executive department; and tranſmit authentic copies of ſuch acts and proceedings, every ſix months, to the ſecretary of Congreſs: There ſhall alſo be appointed a court to conſiſt of three judges, any two of whom to form a court, who ſhall have a common law juriſdiction, and reſide in the diſtrict, and have each therein a freehold eſtate in five hundred acres of land, while in the exerciſe of their offices; and their commiſſions ſhall continue in force during good behaviour.

The governor and judges, or a majority of them, ſhall adopt and publiſh in the diſtrict, ſuch laws of the original ſtates, criminal and civil, as may be neceſſary, and beſt ſuited to the circumſtances of the diſtrict, and report them to

Congreſs, from time to time, which laws ſhall be in force in the diſtrict until the organization of the general aſſembly therein, unleſs diſapproved of by Congreſs ; but afterwards the legiſlature ſhall have authority to alter them as they ſhall think fit.

The governor for the time being, ſhall be commander in chief of the militia, appoint and commiſſion all officers in the ſame, below the rank of general officers ; all general officers ſhall be appointed and commiſſioned by Congreſs.

Previous to the organization of the general aſſembly, the governor ſhall appoint ſuch magiſtrates and other civil officers, in each county or townſhip, as he ſhall find neceſſary for the preſervation of the peace and good order in the ſame : After the general aſſembly ſhall be organized, the powers and duties of magiſtrates and other civil officers ſhall be regulated and defined by the ſaid aſſembly ; but all magiſtrates and other civil officers, not herein otherwiſe directed, ſhall, during the continuance of this temporary government, be appointed by the governor.

For the prevention of crimes and injuries, the laws to be adopted or made ſhall have force in all parts of the diſtrict, and for the execution of proceſs, criminal and civil, the governor ſhall make proper diviſions thereof---and he ſhall proceed from time to time, as circumſtances may require, to lay out the parts of the diſtrict in which the Indian titles ſhall have been extinguiſhed, into counties and townſhips, ſubject, however, to ſuch alterations as may thereafter be made by the legiſlature.

So ſoon as there ſhall be five thouſand free male inhabitants, of full age, in the diſtrict, upon giving proof thereof to the governor, they ſhall receive authority, with time and place, to elect repreſentatives from their counties or townſhips, to repreſent them in the general aſſembly ; provided that for every five hundred free male inhabitants there ſhall be one repreſentative, and ſo on progreſſively with the number of free male inhabitants, ſhall the right of repreſentation increaſe, until the number of repreſentatives ſhall amount to twenty-five, after which the number and proportion of repreſentatives ſhall be regulated by the legiſlature ; provided that no perſon be eligible or qualified to act as a repreſentative, unleſs he ſhall have been a citizen of one of the United States three years and be a reſident in the diſtrict, or unleſs he ſhall have reſided in the diſtrict three years, and in either caſe ſhall likewiſe hold in his own right, in fee ſimple, two hundred acres of land within the ſame :---Provided alſo, that a freehold in fifty acres of land in the diſtrict, having been a citizen of one of the ſtates, and being reſident in the diſtrict ; or the like freehold and two years reſidence in the diſtrict ſhall be neceſſary to qualify a man as an elector of a repreſentative.

The repreſentatives thus elected, ſhall ſerve for the term of two years, and in caſe of the death of a repreſentative, or removal from office, the governor ſhall iſſue a writ to the county or townſhip for which he was a member, to elect another in his ſtead, to ſerve for the reſidue of the term.

The general aſſembly, or legiſlature, ſhall conſiſt of the governor, legiſlative council, and a houſe of repreſentatives. The legiſlative council ſhall conſiſt of five members, to continue in office five years, unleſs ſooner removed by Congreſs, any three of whom to be a quorum, and the members of the council ſhall be nominated and appointed in the following manner, to wit : As ſoon as repreſentatives ſhall be elected, the governor ſhall appoint a time and place for them to meet together, and, when met, they ſhall nominate ten perſons, reſidents in the diſtrict, and each poſſeſſed of a freehold in five hundred acres of land, and return their names to Congreſs ; five of whom Congreſs ſhall appoint and commiſſion to ſerve as aforeſaid ; and whenever a vacancy ſhall happen in the council, by death or removal from office, the houſe of repreſentatives ſhall nominate two perſons, qualified as aforeſaid, for each vacancy, and return their names to Congreſs ; one of whom Congreſs ſhall appoint and commiſſion for the reſidue of the term ; and every five years, four months at leaſt before the expiration of the time of ſervice of the members of council, the ſaid houſe ſhall nominate ten perſons, qualified as aforeſaid, and return their names to Congreſs, five of whom Congreſs ſhall appoint and commiſſion to ſerve as members of the council five years, unleſs ſooner removed. And the governor, legiſlative council, and houſe of repreſentatives, ſhall have authority to make laws in all caſes for the good government of the diſtrict, not repugnant to the principles and articles in this ordinance eſtabliſhed and declared. And all bills having paſſed by a majority in the houſe, and by a majority in the council, ſhall be referred to the governor for his aſſent; but no bill or legiſlative act whatever, ſhall be of any force without his aſſent. The governor ſhall have power to convene, prorogue and diſſolve the general aſſembly, when in his opinion it ſhall be expedient.

The governor, judges, legiſlative council, ſecretary, and ſuch other officers as Congreſs ſhall appoint in the diſtrict, ſhall take an oath or affirmation of fidelity, and of office, the governor before the preſident of Congreſs, and all other officers before the governor. As ſoon as a legiſlature ſhall be formed in the diſtrict, the council and houſe, aſſembled in one room, ſhall have authority by joint ballot to elect a delegate to Congreſs, who ſhall have a ſeat in Congreſs, with a right of debating, but not of voting, during this temporary government.

And for extending the fundamental principles of civil and religious liberty, which form the baſis whereon theſe republics, their laws and conſtitutions are erected; to fix and eſtabliſh thoſe principles as the baſis of all laws, conſtitutions and governments, which for ever hereafter ſhall be formed in the ſaid territory;---to provide alſo for the eſtabliſhment of ſtates, and permanent government therein, and for their admiſſion to a ſhare in the federal councils on an equal footing with the original ſtates, at as early periods as may be conſiſtent with the general intereſt:

It is hereby ordained and declared by the authority aforeſaid, That the following articles ſhall be conſidered as articles of compact between the original ſtates and the people and ſtates in the ſaid territory, and forever remain unalterable, unleſs by common conſent, to wit:

Article the Firſt. No perſon, demeaning himſelf in a peaceable and orderly manner, ſhall ever be moleſted on account of his mode of worſhip or religious ſentiments in the ſaid territory.

Article the Second. The inhabitants of the ſaid territory ſhall always be entitled to the benefits of the writ of habeas corpus, and of the trial by jury; of a proportionate repreſentation of the people in the legiſlature, and of judicial proceedings according to the courſe of the common law; all perſons ſhall be bailable unleſs for capital offences, where the proof ſhall be evident, or the preſumption great; all fines ſhall be moderate, and no cruel or unuſual puniſhments ſhall be inflicted; no man ſhall be deprived of his liberty or property but by the judgment of his peers, or the law of the land; and ſhould the public exigencies make it neceſſary for the common preſervation to take any perſon's property, or to demand his particular ſervices, full compenſation ſhall be made for the ſame;— and in the juſt preſervation of rights and property it is underſtood and declared, that no law ought ever to be made, or have force in the ſaid territory, that ſhall in any manner whatever interfere with, or affect private contracts or engagements, bona fide and without fraud previouſly formed.

Article the Third. Religion, morality and knowledge, being neceſſary to good government and the happineſs of mankind, ſchools and the means of education ſhall forever be encouraged. The utmoſt good faith ſhall always be obſerved towards the Indians; their lands and property ſhall never be taken from them without their conſent; and in their property, rights and liberty, they never ſhall be invaded or diſturbed, unleſs in juſt and lawful wars authoriſed by Congreſs; but laws founded in juſtice and humanity ſhall from time to time be made, for preventing wrongs being done to them, and for preſerving peace and friendſhip with them..

Article the Fourth. The ſaid territory, and the ſtates which may be formed therein, ſhall forever remain a part of this confederacy of the United States of America, ſubject to the articles of confederation, and to ſuch alterations therein as ſhall be conſtitutionally made; and to all the acts and ordinances of the United ſtates in Congreſs aſſembled, conform-

and the taxes for paying their proportion, ſhall be laid and levied by the authority and direction of the legiſlatures of the diſtrict or diſtricts or new ſtates, as in the original ſtates, within the time agreed upon by the United States in Congreſs aſſembled. The legiſlatures of thoſe diſtricts, or new ſtates, ſhall never interfere with the primary diſpoſal of the ſoil by the United States in Congreſs aſſembled, nor with any regulations Congreſs may find neceſſary for ſecuring the title in ſuch ſoil to the bona fide purchaſers. No tax ſhall be impoſed on lands the property of the United States; and in no caſe ſhall non-reſident proprietors be taxed higher than reſidents. The navigable waters leading into the Miſſiſippi and St. Lawrence, and the carrying places between the ſame ſhall be common highways, and forever free, as well to the inhabitants of the ſaid territory, as to the citizens of the United States, and thoſe of any other ſtates that may be admitted into the confederacy, without any tax, impoſt or duty therefor.

Article the Fifth. There ſhall be formed in the ſaid territory, not leſs than three nor more than five ſtates; and the boundaries of the ſtates, as ſoon as Virginia ſhall alter her act of ceſſion and conſent to the ſame, ſhall become fixed and eſtabliſhed as follows, to wit: The weſtern ſtate in the ſaid territory, ſhall be bounded by the Miſſiſſippi, the Ohio and Wabaſh rivers; a direct line drawn from the Wabaſh and Poſt Vincent's due north to the territorial line between the United States and Canada, and by the ſaid territorial line to the lake of the Woods and Miſſiſſippi. The middle ſtate ſhall be bounded by the ſaid direct line, the Wabaſh from Poſt Vincent's to the Ohio; by the Ohio, by a direct line drawn due north from the mouth of the Great Miami to the ſaid territorial line, and by the ſaid territorial line. The eaſtern ſtate ſhall be bounded by the laſt mentioned direct line, the Ohio, Pennſylvania, and the ſaid territorial line; Provided however, and it is further underſtood and declared, that the boundaries of theſe three ſtates, ſhall be ſubject ſo far to be altered, that if Congreſs ſhall hereafter find it expedient, they ſhall have authority to form one or two ſtates in that part of the ſaid territory which lies north of an eaſt and weſt line drawn through the ſoutherly bend or extreme of lake Michigan: and whenever any of the ſaid ſtates ſhall have ſixty thouſand free inhabitants therein, ſuch ſtate ſhall be admitted by its delegates into the Congreſs of the United ſtates, on an equal footing with the original ſtates in all reſpects whatever; and ſhall be at liberty to form a permanent conſtitution and ſtate government: Provided the conſtitution and government ſo to be formed, ſhall be republican, and in conformity to the principles contained in theſe articles; and ſo far as it can be conſiſtent with the general intereſt of the confederacy, ſuch admiſſion ſhall be allowed at an earlier period, and when there may be a leſs number of free inhabitants in the ſtate than ſixty thouſand.

Article the Sixth. There ſhall be neither ſlavery nor involuntary ſervitude in the ſaid territory, otherwiſe than in puniſhment of crimes whereof the party ſhall have been duly convicted: Provided always, that any perſon eſcaping into the ſame, from whom labor or ſervice is lawfully claimed in any one of the original ſtates, ſuch fugitive may be lawfully reclaimed and conveyed to the perſon claiming his or her labor or ſervice as aforeſaid.

Be it ordained by the authority aforeſaid, That the reſolutions of the 23d of April, 1784, relative to the ſubject of this ordinance, be, and the ſame are hereby repealed and declared null and void.

DONE by the UNITED STATES in CONGRESS aſſembled, the 13th day of July, in the year of our Lord 1787, and of their ſovereignty and independence the 12th.

Cha Thomson secy

An Ordinance for the government of
the Territory of the United States,
Northwest of the river Ohio.

Article the Sixth.

There shall be neither Slavery nor involuntary Servitude in the said Territory, otherwise than in punishment of crimes whereof the party shall have been duly convicted: Provided always, that any person escaping into the same, from whom labor or service is lawfully claimed in any one of the original states, such fugitive may be lawfully reclaimed and conveyed to the person claiming his or her labor or service as aforesaid. . . .

Done by the United States in Congress Assembled the 13th day of July in the year of our Lord 1787, and of their Sovereignty and Independence the twelfth.

Gouverneur Morris, Speech at Federal Convention, August 8, 1787

Max Farrand, ed., *The Records of the Federal Convention of 1787*, 4 vols. (New Haven, 1937), 2:221-23.

At the New York Constitutional Convention of 1776, the brilliant Revolutionary leader, Gouverneur Morris, had, along with John Jay, unsuccessfully fought to incorporate into the new state constitution a charge to the legislature to abolish slavery "so that in future ages every human being who breathes the air of this State shall enjoy the privileges of a free man." Ten years later Morris, a conservative member of the landed aristocracy who wrote in 1774 with "fear and trembling" of the potential havoc of social upheaval, was again a strong advocate for the abolition of slavery. The Pennsylvania delegate to the federal Constitutional Convention denounced slavery as "the curse of Heaven on the States where it prevailed." Contrasting the prosperity of the northern states with the southern "desert" of poverty and degradation, Morris, in a speech before the convention on August 8, 1787, argued against saddling the entire country with a Constitution pledged to protecting an institution which brought only blight and misery in its wake.

Morris's effort was, of course, futile. The convention yielded to pressures from southern slave spokesmen and certain northern delegates such as Oliver Ellsworth of Connecticut, who preferred not to "intermeddle." But Morris had clearly perceived the potential explosiveness of the issue which a burgeoning sectionalism would only aggravate. He later predicted that southern leaders, in order to nurture the growth of slavery, would struggle relentlessly to gain a majority in the national legislature and warned that territorial expansion would provoke an intense competition between North and South over political power. Morris agreed with James Madison that "the real difference lay, not between the small States and the large, but between the Northern and Southern States. The institution of slavery and its consequences formed the real line of discrimination."

He never would concur in upholding domestic slavery. It was a nefarious institution—It was the curse of heaven on the States where it prevailed. Compare the free regions of the Middle States, where a rich & noble cultivation marks the prosperity & happiness of the people, with the misery & poverty which overspread the barren wastes of Va. Maryd. & the other States having slaves (Travel thro' ye whole Continent & you behold the prospect continually varying with the appearance & disappearance of slavery. The moment you leave ye E. Sts. & enter N. York, the effects of the institution become visible; Passing thro' the Jerseys and entering Pa— every criterion of superior improvement witnesses the change. Proceed Southwdly, & every step you take thro' ye great regions of slaves, presents a desert increasing with ye increasing proportion of these wretched beings.)

Upon what principle is it that the slaves shall be computed in the representation? Are they men? Then make them Citizens & let them vote. Are they property? Why then is no other property included? The Houses in this City (Philada.) are worth more than all the wretched slaves which cover the rice swamps of South Carolina. The admission of slaves into the Representation when fairly explained comes to this: that the inhabitant of Georgia and S.C. who goes to the Coast of Africa, and in defiance of the most sacred laws of humanity tears away his fellow creatures from their dearest connections & dam(n)s them to the most cruel bondages, shall have more votes in a Govt. instituted for protection of the rights of mankind, than the Citizen of Pa or N. Jersey who views with a laudable horror, so nefarious a practice. He would add that Domestic slavery is the most prominent feature in the aristocratic countenance of the proposed Constitution. The vassalage of the poor has ever been the favorite offspring of Aristocracy. And What is the proposed compensation to the Northern States for a sacrifice of every principle of right, of every impulse of humanity. They are to bind themselves to march their militia for the defence of the S. States; for their defence agst those very slaves of whom they complain. They must supply vessels & seamen, in case of foreign Attack. The Legislature will have indefinite power to tax them by excises, and duties on imports: both of which will fall heavier on them than on the Southern inhabitants; for the bohea tea used by a Northern freeman, will pay more tax than the whole consumption of the miserable slave, which consists of nothing more than his physical subsistence and the rag that covers his nakedness. On the other side the Southern States are not to be restrained from importing fresh supplies of wretched Africans, at once to increase the danger of attack, and the difficulty of defence; nay they are to be encouraged to it by an assurance of having their votes in the Natl Govt increased in proportion. and are at the same time to have their exports & their slaves exempt from all contributions for the public service. Let it not be said that direct taxation is to be proportioned to representation. It is idle to suppose that the Genl Govt. can stretch its hand directly into the pockets of the people scattered over so vast a Country. They can only do it through the medium of exports imports & excises. For what then are all these sacrifices to be made? He would sooner submit himself to a tax for paying for all the Negroes in the U. States. than saddle posterity with such a Constitution.

Debate at the Constitutional Convention, August 21-22, 1787

Max Farrand, ed., *The Records of the Federal Convention of 1787*, vols. (New Haven, 1937), 2:364-65; 369-73.

On August 21, 1787, Luther Martin of Maryland, one of the few delegates to the Constitutional Convention to express moral indignation over the slavery issue, proposed a federal prohibition on slave importation. Martin's proposal ignited the most strident debate of the convention over the question. John Rutledge of South Carolina, asserting that the issue had nothing to do with religion or humanity, declared, "Interest alone is the governing principle with nations." Roger Sherman of Connecticut, although disapproving of the slave trade, hoped to drop the explosive discussion altogether, before it jeopardized the entire convention. George Mason of Virginia, whose state, unlike Georgia and South Carolina, did not thirst for large numbers of fresh Black imports, expressed concern over the unlimited importation of slaves, that species of property which produces "the most pernicious effect on manners." Mason, however, later indicated that he did favor federal protection of slave property already held. Hugh Williamson of North Carolina announced that the southern states would reject any Constitution which attempted to force a slavery prohibition upon them. Only John Dickinson of Pennsylvania seemed eager to support Martin's contention that slavery violated the principles for which the country had presumably fought the Revolution.

This nagging issue of federal intervention, which Sherman and others feared could irrevocably damage the convention, was settled by, in both Mason's and Gouverneur Morris's words, "a bargain." Throughout the convention, southern delegates had been fearful that the final Constitution would give the northern states an unfair and potentially disastrous leverage in enacting navigation and shipping laws disadvantageous to the South. Delegates from South Carolina and Georgia remained concerned, however, that the new government would, if not specifically prohibited, move to suppress slave importation. Mason later wrote, "Those two States therefore struck up a bargain with the three New England States. If they would join to admit slaves for some years, the two Southern-most States would join in changing the clause which required the 2/3 of the Legislature in any vote on navigation legislation. It was done."

The legislative maneuvering on this issue profoundly offended two very opposing sides. John C. Calhoun later lamented that the South, in sacrificing its veto over repugnant northern navigation legislation, had fallen under virtual economic bondage. Martin, voicing the antislavery position, wrote, "I think there is great reason to believe, that, if the importation of slaves is permitted until the year eighteen hundred and eight, it will not be prohibited afterwards." Martin refused to vote for the new United States Constitution.

August 21

Mr L—Martin, proposed to vary the sect: 4. art VII so as to allow a prohibition or tax on the importation of slaves. 1. As five slaves are to be counted as 3 free men in the apportionment of Representatives; such a clause wd. leave an encouragement to this trafic. 2 slaves weakened one part of the Union which the other parts were bound to protect: the privilege of importing them was therefore unreasonable—3. it was inconsistent with the principles of the revolution and dishonorable to the American character to have such a feature in the Constitution.

Mr Rutlidge did not see how the importation of slaves could be encouraged by this section. He was not apprehensive of insurrections and would readily exempt the other States from (the obligation to protect the Southern against them).—Religion &humanity had nothing to do with this question—Interest alone is the governing principle with Nations— The true question at present is whether the Southn. States shall or shall not be parties to the Union. If the Northern States consult their interest, they will not oppose the increase of Slaves which will increase the commodities of which they will become the carriers.

Mr. Elseworth was for leaving the clause as it stands. let every State import what it pleases. The morality or wisdom of slavery are considerations belonging to the States themselves— What enriches a part enriches the whole, and the States are the best judges of their particular interest. The old confederation had not meddled with this point, and he did not see any greater necessity for bringing it within the policy of the new one:

Mr. Pinkney. South Carolina can never receive the plan if it prohibits the slave trade. In every proposed extension of the powers of Congress, that State has expressly & watchfully excepted that of meddling with the importation of negroes. If the States be all left at liberty on this subject, S. Carolina may perhaps by degrees do of herself what is wished, as Virginia & Maryland have already done.

Adjourned

August 22.

Art. VII sect 4. resumed. Mr. Sherman was for leaving the clause as it stands. He disapproved of the slave trade: yet as the States were now possessed of the right to import slaves, as the public good did not require it to be taken from them & as it was expedient to have as few objections as possible to the proposed scheme of Government, he thought it best to leave the matter as we find it. He observed that the abolition of slavery seemed to be going on in the U.S. & that the good sense of the several States would probably by degrees compleat it. He urged on the Convention the necessity of despatch(ing its business.)

Col. Mason. This infernal trafic originated in the avarice of British Merchants. The British Govt. constantly checked the attempts of Virginia to put a stop to it. The present question concerns not the importing States alone but the whole Union. The evil of having slaves was experienced during the late war. Had slaves been treated as they might have been by the Enemy, they would have proved dangerous instruments in their hands. But their folly dealt by the slaves, as it did by the Tories. He mentioned the dangerous insurrections of the slaves in Greece and Sicily; and the instructions given by Cromwell to the Commissioners sent to Virginia, to arm the servants & slaves, in case other means of obtaining its submission should fail. Maryland & Virginia he said had already prohibited the importation of slaves expressly. N. Carolina had done the same in substance. All this would be in vain if S. Carolina & Georgia be at liberty to import. The Western people are already calling out for slaves for their new lands; and will fill that Country with slaves if they can be got thro' S. Carolina & Georgia. Slavery discourages arts & manufactures. The poor despise labor when performed by slaves. They prevent the immigration of Whites, who really enrich & strengthen a Country. They produce the most pernicious effect on manners. Every master of slaves is born a petty tyrant. They bring the judgment of heaven on a Country. As nations can not be rewarded or punished in the next world they must be in this. By an inevitable chain of causes & effects providence punishes national sins, by national calamities. He lamented that some of our Eastern brethren had from a lust of gain embarked in this nefarious traffic. As to the States being in possession of the Right to import, this was the case with many other rights, now to be properly given up. He held it essential in every point of view, that the Genl. Govt. should have power to prevent the increase of slavery.

Mr. Elsworth. As he had never owned a slave could not judge of the effects of slavery on character. He said however that if it was to be considered in a moral light we ought to go farther and free those already in the Country.—As slaves also multiply so fast in Virginia & Maryland that it is cheaper to raise than import them, whilst in the sickly rice swamps foreign supplies are necessary, if we go no farther than is urged, we shall be unjust towards S. Carolina & Georgia—Let us not intermeddle. As population increases; poor laborers will be so plenty as to render slaves useless. Slavery in time will not be a speck in our country. Provision is already made in Connecticut for abolishing it. And the abolition has already taken place in Massachusetts. As to the danger of insurrections from foreign influence, that will become a motive to kind treatment of the slaves.

Mr. Pinkney— If slavery be wrong, it is justified by the example of all the world. He cited the case of Greece Rome & other antient States; the sanction given by France England, Holland & other modern States. In all ages one half of mankind have been slaves. If the S. States were let alone they will probably of themselves stop importations. He wd. himself as a Citizen of S. Carolina vote for it. An attempt to take away the right as proposed will produce serious objections to the Constitution which he wished to see adopted.

General Pinkney declared it to be his firm opinion that if himself & all his colleagues were to sign the Constitution & use their personal influence, it would be of no avail towards obtaining the assent of their Constituents. S. Carolina & Georgia cannot do without slaves. As to Virginia she will gain by stopping the importations. Her slaves will rise in value, & she has more than she wants. It would be unequal to require S.C. & Georgia to confederate on such unequal terms. He said the Royal assent before the Revolution had never been refused to S. Carolina as to Virginia. He contended that the importation of slaves would be for the interest of the whole Union. The more slaves, the more produce to employ the carrying trade; The more consumption also, and the more of this, the more of revenue for the common treasury. He admitted it to be reasonable that slaves should be dutied like other imports, but should consider a rejection of the clause as an exclusion of S. Carola from the Union.

Mr. Baldwin had conceived national objects alone to be before the Convention, not such as like the present were of a local nature. Georgia was decided on this point. That State has always hitherto supposed a Genl Governmt to be the pursuit of the central States who wished to have a vortex for every thing—that her distance would preclude her from equal advantage—& that she could not prudently purchase it by yielding national powers. From this it might be understood in what light she would view an attempt to abridge one of her favorite prerogatives. If left to herself, she may probably put a stop to the evil. As one ground for this conjecture, he took notice of the sect of which he said was a respectable class of people, who carryed their ethics beyond the mere *equality of men*, extending their humanity to the claims of the whole animal creation.

Mr. Wilson observed that if S.C. & Georgia were themselves disposed to get rid of the importation of slaves in a short time as had been suggested, they would never refuse to Unite because the importation might be prohibited. As the Section now stands all articles imported are to be taxed. Slaves alone are exempt. This is in fact a bounty on that article.

Mr. Gerry thought we had nothing to do with the conduct of the States as to Slaves, but ought to be careful not to give any sanction to it.

Mr. Dickenson considered it as inadmissible on every principle of honor & safety that the importation of slaves should be authorized to the States by the Constitution. The true question was whether the national happiness would be promoted or impeded by the importation, and this question ought to be left to the National Govt. not to the States particularly interested. If Engd. & France permit slavery, slaves are at the same time excluded from both those Kingdoms. Greece and Rome were made unhappy by their slaves. He could not believe that the Southn. States would refuse to confederate on the account apprehended; especially as the power was not likely to be immediately exercised by the Genl. Government.

Mr. Williamson stated the law of N. Carolina on the subject, to wit that it did not directly prohibit the importation of slaves. It imposed a duty of £5. on each slave imported from Africa. £10. on each from elsewhere, & £50 on each from a State licensing manumission. He thought the S. States could not be members of the Union if the clause should be rejected, and that it was wrong to force any thing down, not absolutely necessary, and which any State must disagree to.

Mr. King thought the subject should be considered in a political light only. If two States will not agree to the Constitution as stated on one side, he could affirm with equal belief on the other, that great & equal opposition would be experienced from the other States. He remarked on the exemption of slaves from duty whilst every other import was subjected to it, as an inequality that could not fail to strike the commercial sagacity of the Northn. & middle States.

Mr. Langdon was strenuous for giving the power to the Genl. Govt. He cd. not with a good conscience leave it with the States who could then go on with the traffic, without being restrained by the opinions here given that they will themselves cease to import slaves.

Genl. Pinkney thought himself bound to declare candidly that he did not think S. Carolina would stop her importations of slaves in any short time, but only stop them occasionally as she now does. He moved to commit the clause that slaves might be made liable to an equal tax with other imports which he he thought right & wch. wd. remove one difficulty that had been started.

Mr. Rutlidge. If the Convention thinks that N.C; S.C. & Georgia will ever agree to the plan, unless their right to import slaves be untouched, the expectation is vain. The people of those States will never be such fools as to give up so important an interest. . . .

"Washington as a Farmer in Mt. Vernon," by G. B. Stearns, depicting the first President as a slave master.

Silhouette of 93-year-old Moses Brown—abolitionist who spanned the 18th and 19th centuries, and befriended both Anthony Benezet and William Lloyd Garrison.

Postscript

A bitter Granville Sharp remarked to Benjamin Franklin on January 10, 1788, that the detestable sections of the United States Constitution protecting the slave trade from federal prohibition and providing for a national fugitive slave law were "clearly null and void by their iniquity."[1] Samuel Hopkins despaired that the issue of slavery had been purposely taken out of the hands of the national legislature.[2] It was obvious to the antislavery leaders that the slavery issue had only been crowded into the debate at the Constitutional Convention and had not been allowed to threaten the determination of the delegates to maintain unity and forge a Constitution satisfactory to all of the states.

The Constitution itself had dealt the antislavery movement a devastating blow, and the anxieties of the reformers toward the new government proved to be well founded. With safeguards to the institution of slavery written into the Constitution, with Eli Whitney's cotton gin and the profits it held out to planters, with slave prices lucrative, slavery not only tightened its grip over the older southern states but spread in the early nineteenth century into areas such as Kentucky, Mississippi, and Alabama. The ramifications of the struggles over the extension of black bondage in the years that followed need no elaboration.

In addition to the intense desire for unity at the Constitutional Convention, most of America's political leaders remained ambivalent toward the slavery question. Much of this ambivalence stemmed from a valid concern for private property, a factor which loomed menacingly in the path of the reformers from the very beginning of the antislavery movement. With property as "natural" a right as freedom, men such as George Mason, while speaking eloquently against the extension of the slave trade and the abominable effects of the slave system, insisted on the right of slavemasters to hold onto their black possessions. Even in Philadelphia, the hub of antislavery thought, the legitimacy of slave property was strikingly evident. On May 5, 1784, four years after Pennsylvania's celebrated gradual abolition law, Philadelphia's *Freeman's Journal* printed an obituary for Anthony Benezet. Citing the Quaker's catholicism, his numerous efforts to relieve poverty and to challenge the injustice of slavery, the *Journal* effusively praised Benezet as a man "kind without reserve; courteous without deceit, and charitable without ostentation." It spoke of the abolition law, for which Benezet had labored, as "humane and righteous." In the same edition of the paper an advertisement read:

To Be SOLD
A NEGRO WENCH

> About 34 years old, who can wash, iron, cook and do every kind of houshold work in the best manner; also

a NEGRO BOY, of eight years old, who can wait on table, and is smart and active . . .

Along with the political considerations inherent in establishing union among the states and the wide acceptance of the sanctity of private property, the vital factor of race militated against national reform of slavery. Proslavery advocates and racist antislavery spokesmen such as Arthur Lee were not alone in their doubts concerning the intellectual, spiritual, and moral equality of the black race. Even Granville Sharp was haunted by uncertainty, confessing to a friend that, although he felt obliged to publicly proclaim black quality, he remained unsure.[3] If Granville Sharp was unconvinced, how could Charles Pinckney be persuaded?

Few of the Founding Fathers could square the existence of slavery in America with the precepts emblazoned in the Declaration of Independence; few tried. Most of America's political leaders shared Robert Pleasants's assessment of slavery as an "outrageous violation of the rights of Mankind; an odious degradation of human nature."[4] Most looked forward to the day when the blight would be removed, when, for a myriad of practical, economic, and moral reasons, slavery would conveniently evaporate. Jefferson, Washington, Madison and other political leaders, however, all spoke wistfully in terms of the future and refused to actively support abolition efforts. Patrick Henry declared to the Virginia State Ratifying Convention, "As much as I deplore slavery, I see that prudence forbids its abolition. I deny that the General Government ought to set them free . . ."[5]

But even with monumental obstacles to national reform, the antislavery movement of the eighteenth century had made significant progress. With the series of gradual abolition laws, judicial decisions, restrictions on slave importation and manumission laws in the northern states, slavery had become an institution "peculiar" to the South. Within a year of the conclusion of the Revolutionary War provision had been made for the abolition of slavery in all the New England states. By 1830, slaves comprised only one percent of the northern black population.[6] Had this progress not been made, had the traffic in black merchandise in all of the states been allowed to continue unabated, the nineteenth century would have been a far different American experience.

And for the black Americans, the Revolutionary period represented an awakening, both in terms of the white society's conception of the black race and in the self-esteem of the blacks themselves. In a period when the philosopher David Hume was discounting an educated Negro in Jamaica as a "parrot, who speaks a few words plainly"[7] and the Scottish jurist Lord Kames was concluding that the degeneration of Adam's progeny into the Negro race must have resulted from a separate creation,[8] antislavery reformers such as Benezet, Benjamin Rush, John Woolman, and Samuel Hopkins were speaking a far different language. Benezet wrote in 1762, "Negroes are generally sensible, humane and sociable, . . . their Capacity is as good, and as capable of improvement, as that of the White People."[9] At a time when slavery in America had become wholly identified racially with the blacks, the antislavery leaders made an incisive attack on the racial assumptions which were the philosophical foundation of the slave system. The abolitionist assault on the ideas of black race inferiority was given validity by the work of black men and women—the numerous blacks who served in the war, the many who fought for freedom in the courts, those who distinguished themselves in the arts and letters and the sciences, and those who actively worked in the antislavery movement. Antislavery leaders had legitimate evidence that their work was not a paternalistic movement in behalf of wretched beasts, but a reform effort in behalf of fellow men and women.

As the antislavery crusade moved beyond the disappointment of the Constitutional Convention, as Thomas Jefferson's visions of a "firebell in the night" took on a sober reality, as sectionalism over the slavery issue hopelessly divided the country, a new generation of reformers emerged in the new century. They were closely observed by the ancient Moses Brown, then age ninety. For him the 1830s sounded a familiar beat to different drummers—the slogans, the same appeal to the Declaration of Independence, natural rights, divine law, the same stridency on the part of some and the moderation of others, the sense of moral immediacy and outrage. And the new abolitionists invoked the spirit of the old. Reformers such as William Lloyd Garrison and Theodore Weld spoke of the work of Benezet and Woolman, distributed biographies of Granville Sharp, quoted John Wesley, and wore antislavery medallions. Garrison himself became a close friend of the aged but lucid Brown, and discussed with the Quaker on many occasions the strategy, tactics, and basic theories of the antislavery movement. And, as with the reform movement of the eighteenth century, America's antislavery leaders had European comrades and an enduring, binding slogan. On May 7, 1838, Garrison wrote to the English antislavery leader George Thompson about a friend from Philadelphia, Edward M. Davis, "he is . . . desirous to become acquainted with some of those trans-atlantic lovers of humanity, who recognize in every human being the image of God, and 'a man and a brother.' "[10]

NOTES

[1]Charles Stuart, *A Memoir of Granville Sharp* (New York, 1836), 33-34.

[2]Hopkins to Moses Brown, October 22, 1787, Moses Brown Papers, Vol. VI, 15, Rhode Island Historical Society, Providence, Rhode Island.

[3]Sharp to Jacob Bryant, October 19, 1772, Granville Sharp Letterbook, York Minster Library, Dean's Park, York, England.

[4]Pleasants to Francis Irly, November 22, 1784, Robert Pleasants Letterbook, Valentine Museum, Richmond, Virginia.

[5]Jonathan Elliot, ed. *The Debates in the Several State Conventions on the Adoption of the Federal Constitution. As Recommended in the General Convention at Philadelphia in 1787,* Vol. III (Philadelphia, 1937), 589-90.

[6]Arthur Zilversmit, *The First Emancipation: The Abolition of Slavery in the North* (Chicago, 1967), 124; William Freehling, "The Founding Fathers and Slavery," *The American Historical Review* (December, 1970), 86.

[7]*Essays Moral, Political and Literary* (London, 1898), 252.

[8]Lord Henry Home Kames, *Six Sketches on the History of Man* (Philadelphia, 1776), 44-50.

[9]*Short Account of that Part of Africa Inhabited by the Negroes . . . A* (Philadelphia), 8.

[10]Louis Ruchames, ed. *The Letters of William Lloyd Garrison, Vol. 2, A House Dividing Against Itself, 1836-1840* (Cambridge, Mass., 1972), 355.

Bibliography

As evidenced by the variety of citations to documents presented in this series, original manuscript source material relating to the early American antislavery movement is extensive—from large holdings in institutions such as the Historical Society of Pennsylvania, Haverford College Library, Connecticut State Historical Society, Massachusetts Historical Society, New Jersey Historical Society, New-York Historical Society, Rhode Island Historical Society, Rutgers University Library, Friends House Library, London, Library Company of Philadelphia, Library of Congress and the National Archives to scattered items in such institutions as the Valentine Museum, Richmond, Virginia, New York Public Library, Swarthmore College Library, and Cheshunt College, Cambridge, England, to private manuscript collections in the United States and England. Most eighteenth century pamphlets and other printed materials relating to the antislavery movement have been collected and reproduced on microcard in the Early American Imprints Project by the Readex Microprint Corporation and the American Antiquarian Society. Clifford K. Shipton and James C. Mooney, *National Index of American Imprints Through 1800, The Short-Title Evans*, 2 vols., American Antiquarian Society, Worcester, Massachusetts, 1969, acts as a bibliographic tool for this material. The following bibliography lists published materials consulted by the editors in the preparation of this volume.

Adams, A. D. *Neglected Period of Anti-Slavery in America.* Boston, 1908.

Applegarth, Albert C. *Quakers in Pennsylvania.* Baltimore, 1892.

Aptheker, Herbert. *American Negro Slave Revolts.* New York, 1943.

———, ed. *A Documentary History of the Negro People in the United States.* New York, 1951.

Armistead, Wilson. *Anthony Benezet from the Original Memoir: Revised with Additions.* London, 1859.

Axelrad, Jacob. *Philip Freneau, Champion of Democracy.* Austin, 1967.

Bailyn, Bernard. *The Ideological Origins of the American Revolution.* Cambridge, Mass., 1967.

———, ed. *Pamphlets of the American Revolution, 1750-1776.* Cambridge, Mass., 1965.

Baldwin, Alice M. *The New England Clergy and the American Revolution.* Durham, 1928.

Barclay, Robert. *An Apology for the True Christian Divinity*. New York, 1827.

Bauman, Richard. *For the Reputation of Truth: Politics, Religion, and Conflict Among the Pennsylvania Quakers, 1750-1800*. Baltimore, 1971.

Belcher, Joseph. *George Whitefield: A Biography*. New York, 1857.

Benedict, David. *A General History of the Baptist Denomination*. Boston, 1813.

Berlin, Ira. *Slaves Without Masters: The Free Negro in the Antebellum South*. New York, 1974.

Blake, W. O. *The History of Slavery and the Slave Trade*. Columbus, 1858.

Boorstin, Daniel. *The Americans: The Colonial Experience*. New York, 1958.

Boyd, Julian P., ed. *The Papers of Thomas Jefferson*. Vols. 1-12. Princeton, 1950-55.

Brackett, Jeffrey. *The Negro in Maryland*. Baltimore, 1889.

Brawley, Benjamin. *A Social History of the American Negro*. New York, 1921.

Bridenbaugh, Carl and Jessica. *Rebels and Gentlemen: Philadelphia in the Age of Franklin*. New York, 1942.

Brief Statement of the Rise and Progress of the Testimony of the Religious Society of Friends Against Slavery and the Slave Trade, A. Philadelphia, 1843.

Brookes, George. *Friend Anthony Benezet*. Philadelphia, 1937.

Buck, William J. Unpublished manuscript history of the Pennsylvania Abolition Society. Historical Society of Pennsylvania.

Butterfield, Lyman, ed. *The Adams Papers*. Series II, Family Correspondence, Vols. 1-4; Series III, General Correspondence and other Papers of the Adams Statesmen, Legal Papers of John Adams, 3 vols. Cambridge, Mass., 1963-73.

———, ed. *Letters of Benjamin Rush*, 2 vols. Princeton, 1951.

Cadbury, Henry J. "An Early Quaker Anti-Slavery Statement," *Journal of Negro History*, XXII (October, 1937), 488-93.

———. "John Hepburn and His Book Against Slavery," *Proceedings of the American Antiquarian Society*, Vol. 59, Part 1 (1949), 89-112.

———. "Negro Membership in the Society of Friends," *Journal of Negro History*, XXI (January, 1936), 151-213.

Cantor, Milton. "The Image of the Negro in Colonial Literature," *New England Quarterly*, XXXVI (December, 1963), 452-77.

Clarkson, Paul S., and Jett, R. Samuel. *Luther Martin of Maryland.* Baltimore, 1970.

Clarkson, Thomas. *The History of the Abolition of the African Slave-Trade.* 2 vols. New York, 1836.

Coffin, Joshua. *A Sketch of the History of Newbury, Newburyport, and West Newbury, from 1635 to 1845.* Boston, 1845.

Cohen, William. "Thomas Jefferson and the Problem of Slavery," *Journal of American History*, LVI (December, 1969), 503-26.

Commager, Henry S. and Morris, Richard B., eds. *The Spirit of 'Seventy-Six'.* New York, 1958.

Connolly, James C. "Slavery in colonial New Jersey and the causes operating against its extension," *Proceedings of the New Jersey Historical Society*, new series, Vol. 14 (1929), 181-202.

Corner, Betsy C., and Booth, Christopher, eds. *Chain of Friendship, Selected Letters of Dr. John Fothergill of London, 1735-1780.* Cambridge, Mass., 1971.

Corner, George W., ed. *The Autobiography of Benjamin Rush.* Princeton, 1948.

Coupland, Sir Reginold. *The British Anti-Slavery Movement.* London, 1933.

Curtin, Philip D. *The Atlantic Slave Trade,* A Census. Madison, 1969.

Cushing, John D. "The Cushing Court and the Abolition of Slavery in Massachusetts: More Notes on the Quack Walker Case," *American Journal of Legal History* (1961), 131-39.

Davis, David Brion. "The Emergence of Immediatism in British and American Antislavery Thought," *The Mississippi Valley Historical Review*, XLIX (September, 1962), 209-30.

_______. "New Sidelights on Early Antislavery Radicalism," *The William and Mary Quarterly*, 3rd Series, Vol. XXVIII, No. 4 (October, 1971), 585-94.

_______. *The Problem of Slavery in the Age of Revolution, 1770-1823.* Ithaca, 1975.

_______. *The Problem of Slavery in Western Culture.* Ithaca, 1966.

Donnan, Elizabeth, ed. *Documents Illustrative of the History of the Slave Trade to America.* Washington, D.C., 1931.

Dow, George F. *Slave Ships and Slaving.* Salem, Mass., 1927.

Drake, Thomas E. *Quakers and Slavery in America.* New Haven, 1950.

Dumond, Dwight. *Antislavery: The Crusade for Freedom in America.* Ann Arbor, 1961.

———. *A Bibliography of Antislavery in America.* Ann Arbor, 1964.

Duncan, Annie E. "Anthony Benezet," *Negro History Bulletin,* VI (January, 1943), 81, 94.

Edwards, Maldwyn. *John Wesley and the Eighteenth Century.* London, 1933.

Elkins, Stanley M. *Slavery: A Problem in American Institutional and Intellectual Life.* Chicago, 1959.

Elliot, Jonathan, ed. *The Debates in the Several State Conventions on the Adoption of the Federal Constitution As Recommended in the General Convention at Philadelphia in 1787.* 5 vols., 2nd edition. Philadelphia, 1937.

Farrand, Max, ed. *Records of the Federal Convention of 1787.* 4 vols. New Haven, 1937.

Felton, Harold W. *Mumbet, The Story of Elizabeth Freeman.* New York, 1970.

Finer, Ann, and Savage, George, eds. *The Selected Letters of Josiah Wedgwood.* New York, 1965.

Fisher, Miles M. "Friends of Humanity: A Quaker Anti-Slavery Influence," *Church History,* Vol. IV (1935), 187-202.

Fitzpatrick, John C., ed. *The Writings of George Washington from the Original Manuscript Sources, 1745-1799.* 37 vols. Washington, D.C., 1931-40.

Fladeland, Betty. *Men and Brothers: Anglo American Antislavery Cooperation.* Urbana, Illinois, 1972.

Fogel, Robert W., and Engerman, Stanley L. *Time on the Cross: The Economics of American Negro Slavery.* Boston, 1974.

Force, Peter, ed. *Tracts and Other Papers Relating Principally to the Origin, Settlement, and Progress of the Colonies in North America, from the Discovery of the Country to the Year 1776.* 5 vols. Washington, D.C., 1836-46.

Fowler, William C. "The Historical Status of the Negro in Connecticut," *Historical Magazine,* 3rd series, VIII (1874), 84.

Franklin, John Hope. *From Slavery to Freedom.* New York, 1947.

Freehling, William. "The Founding Fathers and Slavery," *American Historical Review* (December, 1970), 81-93.

Gardner, D. H. "The Emancipation of Slaves in New Jersey," *Proceedings of the New Jersey Historical Society*, new series, Vol. 9 (1924), 1-21.

Gillies, John, ed. *Memoirs of the Life of the Reverend George Whitefield*. New York, 1774.

Gipson, Lawrence Henry. *The Triumphant Empire: The Empire Beyond the Storm, 1770-1776, Vol. XIII, The British Empire Before the American Revolution*. New York, 1967.

Green, Lorenzo. *The Negro in Colonial New England, 1620-1776*. New York, 1942.

Green, V. H. H. *John Wesley*. London, 1964.

Greene, Jack P., ed. *The Reinterpretation of the American Revolution, 1763-1789*. New York, 1968.

Gummere, Amelia Mott. *Journal and Essays of John Woolman*. New York, 1922.

Hammond, Isaac W. "Slavery in New Hampshire," *Magazine of American History*, 21 (1889), 62-65.

Hartz, Louis. "Otis and Anti-Slavery Doctrine," *The New England Quarterly*, XII (1939), 745-47.

Hawke, David Freeman. *Benjamin Rush, Revolutionary Gadfly*. Indianapolis, 1971.

Heartman, Charles. *Phillis Wheatley: A Critical Attempt and a Bibliography of Her Writings*. New York, 1915.

Heimert, Alan. *Religion and the American Mind: From the Great Awakening to the Revolution*. Cambridge, Mass., 1966.

Hollander, Barnett. *Slavery in America: Its Legal History*. New York, 1963.

Houston, G. David. "John Woolman's Efforts in Behalf of Freedom," *Journal of Negro History* II (January, 1917), 126-38.

Howe, George. *History of the Presbyterian Church in South Carolina*. Columbia, 1870.

Hutchinson, William T.; Rachel, William; and Rutland, Robert; eds. *The Papers of James Madison*, vols. 1-7 (edited by Hutchinson and Rachel); vols. 8-9 (edited by Rutland and Rachel). Chicago, 1962-75.

James, Sydney V. *A People Among Peoples*. Cambridge, 1963.

Jenkins, William Sumner. *Pro-Slavery Thought in the Old South*. Chapel Hill, 1935.

Johnston, William D. "Slavery in Rhode Island, 1755-1776," *Publications of the Rhode Island Historical Society*, Vol. II (July, 1894), 113-64.

Jordan, Winthrop. *White Over Black, American Attitudes Toward the Negro, 1550-1812*. Chapel Hill, 1968.

Jorns, Auguste. *The Quakers as Pioneers in Social Work*. New York, 1931.

Kaplan, Sidney. *The Black Presence in the Era of the American Revolution, 1770-1800*. Washington, D.C., 1973.

Kirby, Ethyn Williams. *George Keith*. New York, 1942.

Klingberg, Frank J. *Anglican Humanitarianism in Colonial New York*. Philadelphia, 1940.

———. *An Appraisal of the Negro in Colonial South Carolina: A Study in Americanization*. Washington, D.C., 1941.

———, ed. *The Carolina Chronicle of Dr. Francis Le Jau*. Berkeley, Calif., 1956.

Kraus, Michael. "Eighteenth Century Humanitarianism," *The Pennsylvania Magazine of History and Biography*, LX (July, 1936), 270-86.

———. "Slavery Reform in the 18th Century—An Aspect of Trans-atlantic Cooperation," *The Pennsylvania Magazine of History and Biography*, LX (January, 1936), 53-66.

Labaree, Leonard, and Willcox, William, eds. *The Papers of Benjamin Franklin*. vols. 1-14 (edited by Labaree); vols. 15-19 (edited by Willcox). New Haven, 1959-75.

Library Company, Philadelphia. *Negro History, 1553-1903: an exhibition of books and manuscripts from the shelves of the Library Company of Philadelphia and the Historical Society of Pennsylvania*. Philadelphia, 1969.

Livermore, George. *An Historical Research Respecting the Opinions of the Founders of the Republic on Negroes as Slaves, as Citizens and as Soldiers*. Boston, 1862.

Locke, Mary S. *Anti-Slavery in America from the Introduction of the African Slaves to the Prohibition of the Slave Trade*. Boston, 1901.

Loggins, Vernon. *The Negro Author*. New York, 1931.

Lovejoy, David. "Samuel Hopkins: Religion, Slavery, and the Revolution," *New England Quarterly*, Vol. 40, no. 2 (June, 1967), 227-43.

Lynd, Staughton. *Class Conflict, Slavery, and the United States Constitution: Ten Essays*. Indianapolis, 1967.

_______ . *Intellectual origins of American Radicalism.* New York, 1968.

McColley, Robert. *Slavery and Jeffersonian Virginia.* Urbana, 1964.

McManus, Edgar J. "Antislavery Legislation in New York," *Journal of Negro History,* XLVI (1961), 207-16.

McMaster, Richard K. "Arthur Lee's Address on Slavery, An Aspect of Virginia's Struggle to End the Slave Trade, 1765-1774," *The Virginia Magazine of History and Biography,* Vol. 80, no. 2 (April, 1972), 141-53.

Marietta, Jack D. "Conscience, the Quaker Community, and the French and Indian War," *The Pennsylvania Magazine of History and Biography,* XCV (January, 1971), 3-27.

Mason, Julian D., ed. *The Poems of Phillis Wheatley.* Chapel Hill, 1966.

Mathews, Donald G. *Slavery and Methodism: A Chapter in American Morality, 1780-1845.* Princeton, 1965.

Matthews, Albert. "Notes on the Proposed Abolition of Slavery in Virginia in 1785," Colonial Society of Massachusetts, *Publications,* VI (1904), 370-80.

Meade, Robert D. *Patrick Henry: Patriot in the Making.* New York, 1957.

Mellon, Matthew T. *Early American Views on Negro Slavery.* Boston, 1934.

Merrill, Louis T. "Anthony Benezet: Antislavery Crusader and Apostle of Humanitarianism," *Negro History Bulletin,* IX (February, 1946), 99-104.

Monaghan, Frank. "Anti-Slavery Papers of John Jay," *Journal of Negro History,* XVII (October, 1932), 481-96.

Moore, George H. *Notes on the History of Slavery in Massachusetts.* New York, 1866.

Morgan, Edmund S. "Slavery and Freedom: The American Paradox," *The Journal of American History,* LIX (June, 1972), 5-29.

Moss, Simeon. "The Persistence of Slavery and Involuntary Servitude in a Free State (1685-1866)," *Journal of Negro History,* XXXV (1950), 289-314.

Needles, Edward. *An Historical Memoir of the Pennsylvania Society for Promoting the Abolition of Slavery; The Relief of Free Negroes Unlawfully Held in Bondage, and For Improving the Condition of the African Race. Compiled from the Minutes of the Society and Other Official Documents.* Philadelphia, 1848.

Notes of Debates in the Federal Convention of 1787, Reported by James Madison. Athens, Ohio, 1966.

O'Brien, William. "Did the Jennison Case Outlaw Slavery in Massachusetts?" *William and Mary Quarterly*, 3rd ser., XVII (1960), 219-41.

Pannell, Anne T. Gary. *The Political and Economic Relations of English and American Quakers (1750-1785)*. Thesis submitted for the Degree of D.Phil., St. Hugh's College, 1935. Copy at Haverford College.

Park, Edwards A., ed. *The Works of Samuel Hopkins*. 3 vols. Boston, 1852.

Parker, Percy L., ed. *The Heart of John Wesley's Journal*. New York, 1903.

Philips, Edith. *The Good Quaker in French Legend*. Philadelphia, 1932.

Phillips, Ulrich Bonnell. *American Negro Slavery*. Gloucester, Mass., 1959.

Pierre, C. E. "The Work of the Society for the Propagation of the Gospel in Foreign Parts Among the Negroes in the Colonies," *The Journal of Negro History*, I (1916), 349-60.

Poole, William F. *Anti-Slavery Opinions Before the Year 1800*. Cincinnati, 1873.

Quarles, Benjamin. *The Negro in the American Revolution*. Chapel Hill, 1961.

———. *The Negro in the Making of America*. New York, 1964.

Reilly, James F. "The Providence Abolition Society," *Rhode Island History*, Vol. 21, no. 2 (April, 1962), 33-48.

"Rev. Jacob Green of Hanover," *Proceedings of the New Jersey Historical Society*, second series, Vol. XII (1892), 191-226.

Reynolds, Reginald. *The Wisdom of John Woolman*. London, 1948.

Riddell, William R. "Pre-Revolutionary Pennsylvania and the Slave Trade," *The Pennsylvania Magazine of History and Biography*, LII (1928), 1-28.

Robinson, Donald L. *Slavery in the Structure of American Politics, 1765-1820*. New York, 1971.

Royal Commission on Historical Manuscripts, The, *Report on the archives of Cheshunt College, Cambridge and related papers*, reproduced for the Cheshunt College Foundation, Westminster and Cheshunt Colleges, 1972.

Russell, John H. *The Free Negro in Virginia, 1619-1865*. Baltimore, 1913.

Rutland, Robert A., ed. *The Papers of George Mason*. 3 vols. Chapel Hill, 1970.

Scarborough, Ruth. *The Opposition to Slavery in Georgia Prior to 1860*. Nashville, 1933.

Schatz, Walter, ed. *Directory of Afro-American Resources*. New York, 1970.

Scherer, Lester B. "A New Look at *Personal Slavery Established*," *The William and Mary Quarterly*, Third Series, Vol. XXX, No. 4 (October, 1973), 644-52.

Sinclair, Donald A. *Negro and New Jersey: a checklist of books, pamphlets, official publications, broadsides, and dissertations, 1754-1964, in the Rutgers University Library, New Brunswick, New Jersey*. New Brunswick, New Jersey, 1965.

Society of Friends, Philadelphia Yearly Meeting. *A Brief Statement of the Rise and Progress of the Religious Society of Friends, Against Slavery and the Slave Trade*. Philadelphia, 1843.

Spaid, Arthur R. M. "Slavery in Pennsylvania," *American Historical Register* (July, 1895), 1181-87.

Spector, Robert M. "The Quack Walker Cases (1781-83): Slavery, Its Abolition, and Negro Citizenship in Early Massachusetts," *The Journal of Negro History*, LII (1968), 12-32.

Steiner, Bernard C. *History of Slavery in Connecticut*. (*Johns Hopkins University Studies in Historical and Political Science*). Eleventh Series, IX-X. Baltimore, 1893.

Stuart, Charles. *A Memoir of Granville Sharp*. New York, 1836.

Sypher, Wylie. *Guinea's Captive Kings: British Anti-Slavery Literature of the XVIIIth Century*. Chapel Hill, 1942.

Syrett, Harold. *The Papers of Alexander Hamilton*. vols. 1-4. New York, 1961-62.

Tannenbaum, Frank. *Slave and Citizen*. New York, 1947.

Thompson, Mack. *Moses Brown—Reluctant Reformer*. Chapel Hill, 1962.

Thornton, John W. *The Pulpit of the American Revolution*. Boston, 1860.

Tolles, Frederick B. *Meeting House and Counting House*. Chapel Hill, 1948.

_______. *Quakers and the Atlantic Culture*. New York, 1960.

Towner, Lawrence W. "The Sewall-Saffin Dialogue on Slavery," *The William and Mary Quarterly*, Third Series, Vol. XXI, no. 1 (January, 1964), 40-52.

Turner, Edward. *The Negro in Pennsylvania*. Washington, D.C., 1911.

Tuttle, Joseph F. "Rev. Jacob Green, of Hanover, N.J., as an author, statesman, and patriot," *Proceedings of the New Jersey Historical Society*, Second Series, vol. 12 (1892-93), 189-241.

Tyerman, Luke. *The Life of the Rev. George Whitefield*. London, 1876-77.

Tyler, Moses Coit. *The Literary History of the American Revolution, 1763-1783,* Vols. 1 and 2. New York, 1897.

Tyson, George F., and Tyson, Carolyn. *Preliminary Report on Manuscript Materials in British Archives Relating to the American Revolution in the West Indian Islands.* St. Thomas, U.S. Virgin Islands, 1973.

Vaux, Roberts. *Memoirs of the Life of Anthony Benezet.* York, England, Reprinted for W. Alexander, 1817.

———. *Memoirs of the Lives of Benjamin Lay and Ralph Sandiford; Two of the Earliest of the Public Advocates of Emancipation of the Enslaved Africans.* Philadelphia, 1815.

Vibert, Faith. "The Society for the Propagation of the Gospel in Foreign Parts: Its Work for the Negroes in North America Before 1783," *The Journal of Negro History,* Vol. XVIII, no. 2 (April, 1933), 171-212.

Washburn, Emory. "Extinction of Slavery in Massachusetts," *Massachusetts Historical Collections,* 5th series, III, 438-42.

Watson, John H. "In Re Vermont Constitution of 1777, As Regards its Adoption, and its Declaration Forbidding Slavery; and the Subsequent Existence of Slavery Within the Territory of the Sovereign State," *Proceedings of the Vermont Historical Society for the Years 1919-1920* (1921), 225-56.

Wax, Donald D. "Quaker Merchants and the Slave Trade in Colonial Pennsylvania," *The Pennsylvania Magazine of History and Biography,* LXXXVI (April, 1962), 143-59.

Weeks, Stephen B. *Southern Quakers and Slavery.* Baltimore, 1896.

Wood, Peter H. *Black Majority: Negroes in Colonial South Carolina From 1670 through the Stono Rebellion.* New York, 1974.

Woods, John A. "The Correspondence of Benjamin Rush and Granville Sharp, 1773-1809," *Journal of American Studies,* I (1967), 1-38.

Woodson, Carter G. "Anthony Benezet," *Journal of Negro History* (January, 1917), 37-50.

———. *The Negro in our History.* Washington, D.C., 1922.

Works of Samuel Hopkins, D.D. with a Memoir of his Life and Character, The. 3 vols. Boston, 1852.

Wright, William C., ed. *New Jersey in the American Revolution: Political and Social Conflict, Papers Presented at the First Annual New Jersey History Symposium, December 6, 1969.* Trenton, 1970.

Zilversmit, Arthur. *The First Emancipation: The Abolition of Slavery in the North.* Chicago, 1967.

Index

C

Y

Z

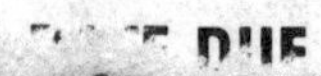